THE ROUTLEDGE HISTORY
OF WOMEN IN EUROPE
SINCE 1700

'This groundbreaking collaborative effort offers a truly European perspective on women's history. Women are not just incorporated into the mainstream narrative; their histories are used to revitalize and refashion our understanding of the European past. This is must reading for anyone wishing to comprehend the dilemmas of modernity.'
Lynn Hunt, *University of California, Los Angeles*

'This new collection provides at last a wide-ranging series of essays linked in a path-breaking conceptual framework . . . A compellingly readable and teachable collection.'
Julie Hardwick, *University of Texas at Austin*

'I welcome this book's ambition to go beyond the limits of national narratives . . . the authors demonstrate an interesting and fruitful approach.'
Gro Hagemann, *Oslo University*

'This is an ambitious and impressive book . . . the result is a volume that will prove essential reading for both students of Europe between the eighteenth and twentieth centuries and their tutors.'
Hannah Barker, *University of Manchester*

The Routledge History of Women in Europe since 1700 is a landmark publication that provides an overview of women's role and place in western Europe, spanning three centuries, from the eighteenth century to the present day. Drawing on new research and provoking valuable new insights, this comprehensive edited collection brings together renowned scholars and rising stars of the discipline to provide a ground-breaking and unique contribution to the historical study of women.

In offering a transnational history of women across western Europe, this survey provides a fundamental shift beyond traditional approaches to the subject. Women's history has tended to focus on national histories, particularly centred on France or England. However, the rise of the nation-state in Europe is a relatively recent phenomenon, coinciding with the timespan of this study, and such states do not function in isolation. Political, economic and intellectual developments of the era have not respected national boundaries and, as this collection shows, neither have women's lives or the interaction of gender and culture. Furthermore, the tendency of women's historians to focus on local or regional studies has necessitated the distillation of a vast historiography into an overarching analysis, and the chapters here integrate such findings into a coherent account that enables the revision of assumptions concerning the place of women in history, their impact on the process of history and their role in informing broader discourses such as the interaction of identity, the construction of knowledge and the relationship between micro- and macro-economies.

Structured thematically, nine specially commissioned chapters examine the key issues that span the end of the early modern era to the postmodern age. Chapters focus on women's work, sexuality, the family, education and training, religion, political participation, war and peace, popular culture and leisure, and women as producers and consumers of art. The interaction between women, ideology and female agency, the way women engaged with patriarchal and gendered structures and systems and how women carved out their identities and spaces within these informs each of these studies, which will be essential reading for students and scholars of women's and gender history.

Contributors to the volume are: Lynn Abrams, Anna Clark, Karen Hunt, Jean H. Quataert, Jane Potter, Tammy M. Proctor, Siân Reynolds, Rebecca Rogers, Deborah Simonton and Pat Starkey.

Deborah Simonton is Associate Professor of British History at the University of Southern Denmark. She has written widely on gender, work and education and her major publications include *A History of European Women's Work, 1700 to the Present* (1998) and *Gender in Scottish History* (2006).

THE ROUTLEDGE HISTORY OF WOMEN IN EUROPE SINCE 1700

Edited by
Deborah Simonton

Routledge
Taylor & Francis Group

LONDON AND NEW YORK

First published 2006
by Routledge
2 Park Square, Milton Park, Abingdon, OX14 4RN

Simultaneously published in the USA and Canada
by Routledge
711 Third Avenue, New York, NY 10017

Paperback edition published 2007

Routledge is an imprint of the Taylor & Francis Group, an informa business

Typeset in Sabon by
M Rules

British Library Cataloguing in Publication Data
A catalogue record for this book is available from the British Library

Library of Congress Cataloging in Publication Data
Routledge history of women in modern Europe/Deborah Simonton, editor.
p. cm.
Includes bibliographical references and index.
1. Women–Europe–History. 2. Women–Europe–Social conditions.
I. Simonton, Deborah, 1948–
HQ1587.R68 2006
305.4′094–dc22
2005014215
ISBN10: 0-415-30103-3 (hbk)
ISBN10: 0-415-43813-6 (pbk)
ISBN10: 0-203-96912-X (ebk)
ISBN13: 978-0-415-30103-9 (hbk)
ISBN13: 978-0-415-43813-1 (pbk)
ISBN13: 978-0-203-96912-0 (ebk)

GERALDINE SHEPHERD HEDGES (1903–86)
AND
ANNIE HARPER WILLIAMSON HASTIE (1922–2002)

CONTENTS

CONTRIBUTORS

Lynn Abrams is Professor of Gender History at the University of Glasgow. She is the author of *The Making of Modern Woman: Europe 1789–1918* (2002) and of *Myth and Materiality in a Woman's Island: Shetland 1800–2000* (2005). She also co-edited *Gender in Scottish History* (2006). She has published widely in the field of modern European women's and gender history on topics ranging from fatherhood and child welfare in Scotland to marriage, divorce and leisure in Germany.

Anna Clark is Professor of History at the University of Minnesota. She is the author of *The Struggle for the Breeches: Gender and the Making of the British Working Class* and several other publications on domestic and sexual violence, lesbian history and sexual scandal. Her most recent book is *Scandal: The Sexual Politics of the British Constitution* (2004).

Karen Hunt is Professor of History at Keele University. She has published widely on women's politics, particularly on aspects of the gendering of socialism, including *Equivocal Feminists: The Social Democratic Federation and the Woman Question, 1884–1911* (1996) and with June Hannam, *Socialist Women. Britain 1880s to 1920s* (2001).

Jane Potter is Senior Lecturer in Publishing at Oxford Brookes University. She is author of *Boys In Khaki, Girls In Print: Women's Literary Responses to The Great War, 1914–1918* (2005). Formerly a research editor at the *Oxford Dictionary of National Biography*, her research interests include wartime medical memoirs, romantic fiction and book history. She is Book Reviews Editor for the *Women's History Magazine*.

Tammy M. Proctor is Associate Professor of History at Wittenberg University in Springfield, Ohio where she teaches world, European and women's history courses. Her published work includes two books: *On Their Honour: Guides and Scouts in Interwar Britain* (2002) and *Female Intelligence: Women and Espionage in the Great War* (2003). She received her Ph.D. in European women's history in 1995 from Rutgers University and her undergraduate degrees in journalism and history from the University of Missouri.

Jean H. Quataert is Professor in History at Binghamton University, SUNY, teaching women's history, German history and the history of human rights. She has written on a range of subjects and recent publications include *The Gendering of Human Rights in the Twentieth Century* (American Historical Association series in Global and Comparative History, 2005) and *Staging Philanthropy: Patriotic Women and the National Imagination in Dynastic Germany, 1813–1916* (2001). Her *Advocating Dignity: The Human Rights System in Global Politics, 1945–2005* is in preparation (2007).

Siân Reynolds has taught at the universities of Sussex, Edinburgh and Stirling, where she is now Professor Emerita of French. She has published on French and Scottish history, as well as a number of translations. Books include *France between the Wars: Gender and Politics* (1996), *Contemporary French Cultural Studies* (co-edited with William Kidd, 2001), and *The Bibliographical Dictionary of Scottish Women* (co-edited with Elizabeth Ewan *et al.*, 2006). She is currently working on a book about Paris and Edinburgh in 1900 and translating a French crime novel.

Rebecca Rogers is Professor in the History of Education at the University René Descartes, Paris. Her publications include *Les Demoiselles de la Légion d'honneur* (1992), which dealt with the schools Napoleon established for girls in the early nineteenth century, and *From the Salon to the Schoolroom: Educating Bourgeois Women in Nineteenth-Century France* (2005). Her research interests focus on girls' education, women teachers, co-education and education in the colonies. She has published widely on such subjects in both French and English and has also written several comparative historiographical essays on gender history. She is currently working on a biography of a French woman who founded the first school for Muslim girls in Algiers in the late 1840s.

Deborah Simonton is Associate Professor of British History at the University of Southern Denmark. Her publications include *A History of European Women's Work, 1700 to the Present* (1998); she also co-edited *Gendering Scottish History: An International Approach* (1999) with Oonagh Walsh and Terry Brotherstone and *Women and Higher Education: Past Present and Future* (1996) with Mary Masson. Her research focuses on gender, childhood, education and work, especially in the eighteenth century, and she has published widely on these topics. She is writing *Women in European Culture and Society* for Routledge. She also co-edited *Gender in Scottish History* (2006).

Pat Starkey is Lecturer in the School of History and Assistant Director of the School of Combined Honours at the University of Liverpool. Her research interests are in the history of charity and voluntary organisations in the nineteenth and twentieth centuries and in women's history. Her recent publications include 'The Medical Officer of Health, the Social Worker and the Problem Family, 1943–1968: The Case of Family Service Units', *Social History of Medicine*, 11 (1998); 'The Feckless Mother: Women, Poverty and Social Workers in 1940s England', *Women's History Review*, 9 (2000), *Families and Social Workers: The Work of Family Service Units, 1940–1985* (2000) and she has co-edited with Jon Lawrence *Child Welfare and Social Action: International Perspectives* (2001).

PREFACE

European Women's History at the Crossroads

Jean H. Quataert

As a pioneer scholar of women's history, I approached this book with considerable interest and anticipation. After all, the field of European women's history today stands at the crossroads of many vibrant scholarly debates. And it also has been at the center of innovation and change in the discipline of history itself. As I expected, this collection draws on many of the innovations in 'doing' women's history developed over the past several decades. It also sets a new thematic and methodological agenda for exploring the structural and discursive worlds negotiated by different women in the societies of the European past since 1700.

Women's history, as is well known, emerged in tandem with the second wave of feminism in the West starting in the late 1960s, part of a transnational political movement deeply committed to the importance of history for social change. History mattered a great deal; it showed indeed that new social movements sustain and, in turn, are supported by research agendas that reframe the past in innovative ways, raising previously marginalized groups to new prominence. Like my own, the careers of many of the early pioneers combined feminist social advocacy outside the academy with teaching a new curricula inside and developing women's studies programs, which still serve as sites of interdisciplinary dialogues as well as places of sociability and guardians of equity.

This pioneer generation made a seemingly obvious yet, as it turns out, still profoundly challenging observation. The traditional academic field of history, which became part of the university curriculum in the early nineteenth century, had developed essentially with no regard to women's diverse lives and worlds. Its organizational and conceptual schemas as well as its working paradigms claimed to describe a universal human past while, in effect, drawing only on men's experiences in so-called public life – in state politics, diplomacy, the economy, the military, and in wartime, to mention the traditional subfields of history. Yet, women have always lived in history. What does it mean to write a history that credits women's *and* men's lives? A question as valid and radical today as it was thirty years ago. Demonstrating the partial nature of the discipline of *hi*story, early works in *her*story recovered a lost past and, in the process, began to shake up many fundamental assumptions in the wider discipline concerning matters of causality, significance, the frames for historical periods, turning points, and markers, as well as the biological basis of sex differences. The inclusion of women rewrote the parameters of class, one of the key working concepts in modern history. It drew attention to arenas beyond the points of production in factories or at construction sites that traditionally were seen to shape class consciousness, and it turned attention also to issues of reproduction and family life, neighborhood solidarities, and patterns of consumption. And the new focus on women began to critically examine the unspoken polarities that long had guided historical work: the separation of public and private spheres, of family and state, as well as of production and reproduction. The title of the book I published with Marilyn J. Boxer in 1987 put on the research agenda the important goal of *Connecting Spheres*.[1] Perhaps not surprisingly at all, the intellectual ferment generated by the challenges of women's history prepared the groundwork for the receptivity of *gender* analysis, now a vital component of recent historical scholarship and very much present in this book.

Over the years, the field of women's history has not lost its original connection to social activism, although the ties have become somewhat more attenuated. The attention of many women's historians has shifted to the broad-based feminist advocacy networks of the global women's human-rights movements just as practitioners in the field of *European* history, which also is the focus of this volume, confront the rigors of global scrutiny through tight interconnections made possible by the Internet and ease of global communications. Whether at United Nations-sponsored world conferences on women (held, for example, in Mexico City, Mexico in 1975, in Nairobi, Kenya in 1985 and in Beijing, China in 1995), specific interregional gatherings or cross-cultural symposia on global themes, feminist advocates from the West confront feminist advocates from many other regions of the globe. Each group, importantly, brings its own sense of history to these international and cross-cultural debates. History matters once again and globalization entails as much a rewriting of the historical meta-narratives as renegotiating the pace, nature, and social costs of economic integration and development.

This rewriting project points to considerable transformations in the field of European history itself. Thirty years ago, mainstream modern European historians wrote their history with little connection to the rest of the world outside of the patterns of colonial settlements and imperial domination. European intellectual, political, and economic developments in the nation-states were seen to be singular yet normative, somehow, for the rest of the world, an assumption that influenced the way non-Western scholars wrote and thought about their own specific historical pasts. This simple diffusionist model from the European center outward has come under critical scrutiny by both postcolonial scholars and European historians committed to a global dialogue. Emblematic of authors of this new literature is Dipesh Chakrabarty, whose compelling title *Provincializing Europe* also captures a new agenda.[2] Chakrabarty's objective is to turn European history away from its claims to be universally valid and normative for human development and place it as one of many studies of complex regions in interaction with other global components. In particular, for the processes of diffusion he draws critical attention to the hegemonic role of European historical thought with its notions of linear time and belief in progress. Chakrabarty makes the argument, however, by generally neglecting the complexity of European thought and by specifically excluding the role of European women's history, which, from its early inception, emerged to critique the very notion of progress inherent in the dominant European narrative. This was the main point of Joan Kelly's 1977 seminal essay 'Did Women Have A Renaissance?'[3] Increasingly, many European women's historians have been doing double duty, so to speak. They are part of a genre of feminist historiography in global dialogue, determined not to make European women's history normative and prescriptive for assessing the lives of women in other parts of the world and, thus, willing to 'provincialize' diverse European women's historic experiences in the context of global patterns. And, in the process, they see Europe as one among many areas in the world, shaped and reshaped by its continuous interaction with other regions, peoples, cultures, and religions. This is a profound change in the discipline of history, to be sure.

So, where do I place this book among the many cross-currents of contemporary intellectual debates and research? I begin with a number of observations. The authors of the chapters center their analysis on the regional clustering of western and central Europe. In this sense, they are challenging the long tradition of history-writing in both women's and European history that privileges national histories and the nation-state as *the* central analytical units. In the main, modern European history from 1700 has been written from the perspective of the distinct social, political, economic, and cultural developments of the nation-state; students, as you know, typically specialize in British history or in the history of the countries of the continent such as France or Germany or Italy; historians also write women's history through the prism of national narratives. If they engage in comparative work, say, of the political strategies of different women's movements to gain political suffrage or the transnational linkages developed to abolish state-sanctioned sex in the early twentieth century, the comparisons usually are made on the basis of presumed unified national societies. But Europe is more than the sum of its nation-states, a point brought home well by the transnational thematic focus of this book. While the authors continue to draw on discrete historiographies and empirical examples from national settings (and thus you will see references to so-called German or French or even Nordic developments as if they were homogenized and unified nations) the book is fundamentally a different narrative of the European past over the three centuries under analysis.

As a broader regional study encompassing a number of distinct countries, it repositions the components of historical developments. Thus, it argues for the importance of transnational educational projects for girls that became central to subsequent cross-national feminist reform movements for broadening women's life chances. These same projects also contained powerful discourses on proper family life and civilized behavior limiting many women's options, which were institutionalized at home and exported abroad. The book looks at leisure time as a vehicle to assess middle-class women's increasing access to public life, from all manner of political-party activities before enfranchisement to volunteer work in municipal charity and poor-relief institutions, such as orphanages, to the gender patterns of consumption expressing new identities and connections with the wider world. It demonstrates the centrality of the discourses and regulations of sexuality for the joint projects of state- and empire-building.

Furthermore, the thematic approach continues to encourage reassessment of long-standing interpretive arguments, helping break down, in particular, many different polarities at the root of much of the existing scholarship. The perspective on women's work in urban, protoindustrial and industrial settings demonstrates unmistakably the need to interconnect the levels of work and home; even the nineteenth-century bourgeois family was never merely a 'private' institution. Examinations of the impact of war on society not only destroys the tired adage that 'war is men's business'; it also shows the continuity of women's active involvement in war not only as passive victims but also as early modern camp followers providing many necessary services to soldiers from sex to the procurement of medical and material supplies to cooking and, with professional militaries in the nineteenth century, in the development of gendered medical war corps for the continental and colonial troops. The new focus critiques the assumption of women's motherly identities as inherently peaceful and men's as aggressive and warlike, bringing the construction of femininity and masculinity into wartime analysis. Importantly, it not only demonstrates the necessity of incorporating perspectives on society into the writing of warfare but also inexorably links the battlefield and homefront as one analytical field. The authors in this collection also argue for rethinking the divisions between amateur and professional and the so-called high and low culture and offer a rich tapestry of women's contributions to the cultural flourishings in Europe, from the performing arts to the writing of novels to cinema and photography, in this way continuing to rehabilitate a lost history.

True to the project of unsettling fixed boundaries, the themes push beyond Europe's borders and into colonial regimes, reinforcing a growing scholarship that draws the colonial periphery right into *the heart of empire*, to borrow again from a title of an influential work on Britain.[4] Authors in this volume, too, make similar connections. The chapters on sexuality, education, and consumption explicitly are demonstrating the parallels between, for example, reform projects to reshape working-class sexuality at home and similar patterns of regulation in British India or the deployment of notions of civilized behavior through girls' proper education into both domestic societies as well as native colonial ones. Throughout the period, European women identified with and participated in empire. Supported by colonial societies in the late nineteenth century, for example, they encouraged and directed so-called 'respectable' women's emigration to the colonies, with the effect of heightening the racial divides by establishing normative family life among the white colonial administrators and settlers. At home, many patriotic women's organizations set up theaters and bazaars to raise money for colonial troops and military expeditions; open to the broader urban public, these exhibits put on display all manner of colonial goods such as Cameroon chocolates or New Guinea cigarettes and other 'exotica' from distant lands, even including the 'natives' in the flesh: 'the small Ferida', daughter of Emin Pascha; 'Joli' brought from New Guinea by the German Anthropological Society; the 'Negro' of Dr. Ehler from Mauritius, to mention but one bazaar organized by the Berlin branch of the German Women's Association for Medical Services in the Colonies in 1903.[5] An emerging consumer culture increasingly was using patriotic messages for the sale of goods. Through these routes, patriotic and imperial cultures were becoming integrated into new consumption and leisure patterns, helping to make their messages part of the everyday exchange of goods. For the rural population, there also were mobile exhibits demonstrating the benefits of public health and sanitation and drawing implicit parallels between public hygiene and the promises of modern scientific warfare.

Of course, the connections are not only with formal empires, those areas of the globe under European colonial administration as part of a renewed imperialism of the late nineteenth century. New gender work patterns outside guild restrictions in the burgeoning textile home workshops from Lancashire to Normandy to Flanders, the Rhineland and the Saxon Oberlausitz in the seventeenth and eighteenth centuries reflected the impact of the Atlantic economy on western and central European societies. As part of a rising demand for linen and hemp, peasant villagers became protoindustrial peasant-workers engaged in manufacturing for export as part of a trade economy in slaves, coffee, tea, sugar, and indigo, as well as in light but durable textiles. Indeed, the urban baroque architecture, which still captures the imagination of so many tourists to European cities and towns, reflects the invested wealth generated by this new colonial Atlantic trade.

The focus on the multiplicity and interconnections of peoples in European society (as opposed to established national units) also works to challenge master-narratives of the European past. This is particularly true in new studies that are being done on religion, matters of faith, and the impact of religious institutions and rituals on men and women's lives in the past. Such interest brings into question the once-powerful linear assumptions behind the transition from early modern to modern societies. In particular, this transition was expressed in the evolution from so-called sacral communities of the late medieval world to the confessional states in Britain and Europe as a result of the Reformation and Catholic revival, culminating in the ongoing processes of secularization, hailed as one of the major characteristics of the 'modern' era in Europe. Importantly, religious forms, identities, and communities continue to be relevant social and political markers up until the present, coexisting and also competing with other identities, including the pulls of gender, ethnicity, and nation. By demonstrating the centrality of marginal groups to society, a different picture of religious developments also emerges, as the chapter on religion and women demonstrates. It maps out a completely distinct terrain for the discussion, no longer placing sole emphasis on the impact of Christianity on European thought and institutions. Rather, it brings into focus in the region of Europe the interactions among and between the peoples and communities of the three monotheistic religions – Christianity, Judaism, and Islam. Both Judaism and Islam are not peripheral but integral to European history, shaped by and shaping Christian identities, institutions, and ritual practices through both contact and confrontation. The history of this interaction, of course, offers dramatic challenges to the explosive contemporary debates about the clash of presumed 'alien' cultures and civilizations – as the presence of so many Muslim immigrants (from former European colonies) and former guestworkers-turned-legal-residents from Turkey living today in contemporary western and central European societies seem to raise for Christian Europe. Their numbers have grown since decolonization and the end of the formal guestworker programs in 1974. Importantly, the polarized debates are often fought most dramatically around the life choices and options for women. The attention to gender analysis and women's experiences in the chapters of this book will help you understand why women often become the symbolic centers of debates around politics and power, cultural integrity, and, more recently, the dislocating processes of economic globalization.

Each of the themes in this book, of course, cannot be separated out so neatly in the ways women and men went about their daily lives in the past. The themes are differentiated for purposes of analysis. Indeed, the authors are very much aware of the overlaps, demonstrating from different perspectives how family, labor, and leisure interact; how, in some cases, household patterns and gender work divisions structure economic development and the location of factories, and how contested notions of masculinity and femininity help shape educational and cultural systems as well as the bases of political membership and citizenship. The book, thus, has to be read as an integrated whole. All the authors, however, are committed, through various methodological routes and against different backdrops, to maintaining the focus on European *women* in the past – however diverse this category is in terms of location, religion, class, and nationality. Some see their project still in terms of filling in the gaps in our knowledge of women's multiple contributions, for example, to the production, display, and consumption of European high culture. For other authors, women's lives cannot be extracted from the gender system that is then placed as a backdrop for analysis and assessment. The commitment in this case is to women *and* gender, complementing the historical methodology in the pioneer works on women's history by recognizing the powerful gender system that shapes and is reshaped by the ways women as agents make use of their own experiences as they interact with men to impact family lives, to bring their own needs as sexual beings into work-related struggles, and to carve out space for interventions into public life as well. Only one chapter explores women's organized movements for feminist reform, representing a divergence from once-standard European women's history texts, which used feminism as the starting point for the analysis; the book maintains the ties between historical investigation and study and a present moment that is committed to greater justice and equality. The collection demonstrates unmistakably the ongoing effects of women's history and gender analysis in challenging and enriching understandings of modern European history.

Notes

1 Marilyn J. Boxer and Jean H. Quataert, eds, *Connecting Spheres: Women in the Western World, 1500 to the Present* (New York and Oxford: Oxford University Press, 1987). We subsequently prepared a second edition reflecting new interest in global interconnections: Boxer and Quataert, *Connecting Spheres: European Women in a Globalizing World, 1500 to the Present* (New York and Oxford: Oxford University Press, 2000).
2 Dipesh Chakrabarty, *Provincializing Europe: Postcolonial Thought and Historical Difference* (Princeton, NY and Oxford: Princeton University Press, 2000).
3 Originally in *Becoming Visible: Women in European History*, edited by Renate Bridenthal and Claudia Koonz and reprinted in Joan Kelly, *Women, History and Theory: The Essays of Joan Kelly* (Chicago, Ill. and London: University of Chicago Press, 1984), pp. 19–50.
4 Antoinette Burton, *At the Heart of the Empire: Indians and the Colonial Encounter in Late-Victorian Britain* (Berkeley, Calif.: University of California Press, 1998).
5 Jean H. Quataert, *Staging Philanthropy: Patriotic Women and the National Imagination in Dynastic Germany, 1813–1916* (Ann Arbor, Mich.: University of Michigan Press, 2001), pp. 239–40.

ACKNOWLEDGEMENTS

This book is built around the knowledge and experience of nine other authors. Without their understanding and grasp of the historical issues and an ability to 'think outside of the box', this project would never have come to fruition. It has been challenging to all of us, and I would like to thank my colleagues for perseverance, good humour and quick responses to my multiple queries and requests. I also appreciate the useful comments on each other's chapters and the sense of collaboration, which has informed the project throughout. I would also like to thank them for producing innovative and thought-provoking chapters. I am so glad they agreed to take this on. I am grateful to Jean H. Quataert, Lynn Abrams, Pat Starkey and Rebecca Rogers particularly for their comments on my own chapter. The families of all the contributors deserve credit and appreciation for their invaluable support throughout the time we worked on this.

I am especially thankful for the support and insight of Vicky Peters of Routledge who helped shape the project, who has taken time to read everything and who has taken the time to meet with the authors. She has been flexible, pragmatic and always supportive throughout the process. My thanks also to Liz Gooster and Philippa Grand of Routledge who ushered it into life. And to Andrew Warren, a long-time friend, for the generous 'gift' of the index, my heartfelt thanks.

The extract from *Behind the Scenes at the Museum* by Kate Atkinson published by Black Swan is used by permission of The Random House Group Limited. Two lines from T.S. Eliot's 'The Love Song of J. Alfred Prufrock' are used by permission of Faber and Faber Ltd. My appreciation goes to Wedgwood Archives, the owners Messrs Josiah Wedgwood and Sons Ltd., Barlaston, Stoke-on-Trent, and to Keele University Library where the archives are housed, and to staff of Aberdeen City Archives and Historic Collections, University of Aberdeen.

I am ever grateful to Elaine Chalus for personal and professional support and for reading sections at short notice. For various supports and help, I would like to thank Joan Fisher, of the University of Aberdeen, for her assistance with the web site, which enabled collaborative working in an innovative way. I am also grateful for their friendship. Colleagues at the University of Southern Denmark put up with me when the end was in sight – but ever so elusive. Students at Aberdeen and Southern Denmark helped me clarify ideas and to think carefully about the explanatory process. And to Karin and Christian Øllegaard, new friends in a new country, for housing, conversation and friendship, my heartfelt thanks. All authors know that they get bloody-minded when immersed in writing, and so for toleration and support, especially during a very strange

ACKNOWLEDGEMENTS

year, my ultimate appreciation goes to David Hastie. This book is dedicated to his mother and to my maternal grandmother, two women of different generations and different continents who were an example to those around them, as wives, mothers and professional women.

Deborah Simonton

1

INTRODUCTION

Writing women in(to) modern Europe

Deborah Simonton

It is precisely in the acknowledgement of its complexity and confusions that one finds both an understanding of women's history and also the basis for critical evaluation of it.[1]

Writing women into European history directly confronts a number of ideas about what constitutes Europe, how its history is written and how this history relates to the emerging meta-narratives of global or world history. European history has relevance in the face of a trend toward global or world history. It can, and should, ask what Europe's relationship is to other models of history and to the colonial and post-colonial worlds, yet, there are clear and identifiable historiographic traditions in Europe, which have shaped the paradigms within which we work. For us as historians there is still a disciplinary and historiographical frontier around Europe, even while the concept of Europe has expanded to encompass the Nordic countries and eastern Europe. How should we as European women historians respond to the challenges of changing ideas about frontiers and the concept of Europe as an entity, and to a growing awareness that England, France and Germany are not 'Europe'? One approach is to ask questions about the relationship between national boundaries – the idea of nation and nation-state – and how citizenship is constructed within a gendered narrative. Another approach is to question the position from which we write, as English-speaking historians using a European approach, in order to think more carefully about assumptions derived from English experience. And clearly we need to expand our thinking beyond the 'big three': England, France and Germany.[2]

Nevertheless, the rise of the nation-state is relatively recent and such states never have operated in isolation. As Fiona Montgomery and Christine Collette argue, 'The history of Europe is a complex one: its existence as an entity has been, and is, a matter of controversy. Its boundaries are as fluid as are those of the various states within it'.[3] In fact, for most of the period covered by this book, Germany was not a nation, and for a while it was actually two. Just as importantly, intellectual, political and economic developments have not respected national boundaries, neither has the story of women's past nor the interplay of gender and culture. Within European women's history, there has been a move to be sensitive to region and local experience, something which at once creates new boundaries while possibly breaking down old ones. To some extent, this reflects current political developments in Europe, which value regional interests and which, in parts of Europe, have created devolved power structures. By questioning the spatial paradigms within which we implicitly write, this book has helped us reflect on how new frontiers and borders produce other narratives, narratives that cross national borders and that seek respondents outside Europe. As a group of feminist historians from a number of countries, with diverse research interests both thematically and geographically, we have been in conversation about how we relate to history and how the history we write deals with the issues of geographical and methodological boundaries. We are writing women in modern Europe.

Transnational history

This book is a transnational history of women in Europe from approximately 1700. It is organised topically rather than either geographically or chronologically, and it is structured around single-voiced examinations written by scholars working across Europe and the USA. It was conceived as largely western and central European, incorporating Britain and Ireland, and treating regional variation as more significant than political boundaries. One of the greatest challenges has been to confront our own perceptions, exploring beyond our individual research areas to produce a genuinely transnational European history. The authors have striven to ensure Europe is embraced, and research on Belgium, the Netherlands, Scandinavia, the Baltic and southern Europe has been incorporated, though we would acknowledge that our own areas of familiarity have often shaped our thinking. Shared European traditions, histories and cultural developments permit an emphasis on aspects of both similarity and difference, and provide the basis for a more coherent approach, which would be difficult to sustain if widely variant cultural traditions were introduced. Some of the authors have drawn on eastern Europe, but a fully integrated history of Europe awaits both the research and an author bold enough to take it on. The state of research in women's history in eastern Europe, including European Russia, and the relative lack of information in languages the authors can read have also limited how much can be incorporated. There have been inroads on this lack of knowledge in the West about the East, such as research by Jane McDermid, Barbara Alpern Engel, Rose L. Glickman, Linda Edmondson, Beatrice Farnsworth, Lynne Viola and the recent translation of work by Natalia Pushkareva, to name a few. Work on areas outside of Russia is also beginning to trickle through.[4] Research such as this has begun to inform and influence western views of eastern European women, so that perhaps that metaphorical 'wall' is also coming down.

Moving beyond national stories is a fundamental principle of this history of women in modern Europe. Mary Nash has argued that

> A fully comprehensive view of European women's history has yet to be established. North/South, periphery/centre divides still persist in existing perceptions . . . Meta-narratives identified as being representative of European women's history, but based on a selective reading of British or French studies are still accepted as . . . a 'European discourse'.[5]

Writing 'national' women's histories has been important in reclaiming history for European women and for analysing the gendered character of nation-states.[6] Indeed, a common refrain has been concern about the lack of research on women in the national context.[7] Thus the creation of national women's history networks, many dating from the period after the founding of the International Federation for Research in Women's History (*Fédération Internationale Pour la Recherche en Histoire des Femmes*) in 1987, provide a focus and a network for promoting research and for asking questions about the future direction of European women's history.[8] These organisations point to the international and national links within European women's history and to the vibrancy of research interests in these areas.

So, if we want to move beyond what Karen Hunt calls 'the myopia of national histories' (p. 221) to unsettle the boundaries, how do we do it? The scope and scale of this book, chronologically, geographically and topically, imposes the necessity of strategies through which we can explore women's differing experiences in western Europe over the past three centuries. Differences of class, nation, locality, age, sexuality, motivation and access to power describe women's lives as much as the similarities created by gender. It is impossible to cover everything. Rebecca Rogers draws attention to how little transnational work has been done on education; Siân Reynolds would testify to how little integrative work has been done on cultural fields. Essentially we have focused on highlighting areas of common 'European' experience but have remained sensitive to important differences. We have concentrated on key developments, trends and features and have tried to draw out the shape of *European* women's history, not a series of sub-plots based on national experience. So, for example, Pat Starkey can say, in her vigorous analysis of European religious traditions, 'women have frequently experienced in remarkably similar ways the blessings and disadvantages of their faith and the institutions that seek to guard it' (p. 180). In some ways, this was probably the greatest challenge to Karen Hunt's analysis of polity and citizenship since these are necessarily tied to nation and national identity. We have also striven to ensure that no single national perspective shaped our arguments; the story is, however, illuminated with examples that come from across Europe, so French, Finnish or Italian women make an appearance. When they do so they represent their European sisters – or provide counter-examples to the main account.

Constructing the narrative

The structure of the book is central to its narrative.[9] It constructs the past from a 'non-male' non-canonical perspective on several levels: by the themes discussed, by the way the discussion is framed, by the internal agendas of chapters, by its order and organisation and by the narrative itself. The chapter themes are not typical of 'normal' histories: family, sexuality, education, work, religion, citizenship, war and peace, culture and leisure. In contrast, for example, Jeremy Black's *Eighteenth-Century Europe* certainly includes a short section on women and children (and often these are taken together, further imbedding the notion that women are mothers – though perhaps 20 per cent never are), but his other chapters are far more typical of *history*.[10] The order of the chapters in this book similarly reflects the alternative universe of the female. We begin with the family because, as Lynn Abrams writes, family is 'the very substance and texture of women's daily lives' (p. 18). Continuing with sexuality and then education, the book places aspects of female identity firmly in the centre. Chapters on work, religion, citizenship and war develop these female identities, exploring more fully how women operate outside of the personal, indeed how 'women go public' so to speak. The final two chapters, situated in leisure and culture, build on the personal and the political in addressing issues of professionalism and amateurism and the complexities of what engaging in culture meant to women. Thus, the organisation of the book and its main agenda deliberately concentrate on women's experiences and their own under-standings of their worlds. It places people as social actors 'front and centre'. This is a history written from the inside out, not a history written on a macro-level where people disappear. As Lynn Abrams argues, structural approaches to the family played down individual experience, while from demographic studies, Alison Mackinnon commented that one could easily conclude that it was regions that had babies rather than people.[11] Similarly studies of economic development project an explanatory framework that seems like inexorable forces floating free from the people who shape them.

Of course, women's lives do not fit neatly into 'themes', time or space; they are organic, fluid and certainly not of a coherent piece. Thus readers will necessarily find that the chapters and discussions overlap. This reflects the 'messiness' of women's lives but, more importantly, allows readers to make connections between aspects of women's experience. In particular, issues of ideology and its implementation through law, state policies, literature and culture form underlying themes. Gender, class and eth-nicity inform all of the chapters, as do women's relationships, whether personal or 'external'. The interaction between women, ideology and female agency, the way they engaged with patriarchal and gendered structures and systems, and how they carved out their identities and spaces within these inform much of the writing. The intercon-nectivity of the chapters is important, and was important to us as we wrote. Thus there are links between transnational education projects and feminist reform movements; discourses on sexuality inform the ways women were regarded at home and at work; discourses on family life have important implications for work patterns and the ways women shaped their religious experiences; political women figure in the examination of war and peace; while links between leisure, culture and education also translate into the ways women negotiated public and private discourses.

The book is not just about adding women; it intends to reshape the narrative. The history of women is necessarily part of a much larger story of the interaction of gender, class, ethnicity, the construction of knowledge and the complex long-term interrela-tionship between the internal world of the family and the external functioning of local, national and international economies. The past looks different when written through women's eyes. This is the point Maxine Berg and Pat Hudson make about recon-structing the industrial revolution: the pace and shape of the industrial revolution looks very different indeed when data on women's work and women's industries are included.[12] Throughout the book, we frame the discussion in a discourse that questions the construction of the dominant narrative. Thus Karen Hunt argues that politics is more than parliamentary politics and seeking governmental power. She shows that women changed the polity both in practice and in the way it was conceptualised. Tammy Proctor similarly asks us to rethink what leisure meant when women's activi-ties are factored in. She asks whether the suffrage volunteer sewing banners was working or enjoying leisure. Writing on working women, I expand the notion of work to embrace a wide range of women's activities, countering the emphasis on waged work and on visible and 'countable' work and putting the 'mill girls' into perspective. Jane Potter points to the doubly masculine perspective on war and peace; that is, 'men writing about male actors, men valorising the suffering of soldiers, and men seeking to learn lessons for future military strategy'. Thus, she demonstrates how once 'women are added to the narratives of war, the interpretation of that narrative changes irrevocably' (p. 261). So, this history argues that not only does women's history matter but, by asking different questions, visualising alternative realities, it contributes to rewriting the dominant narrative, valuing women's and men's lives.

This history of European women is situated in the feminist historiography of the past thirty years. With new approaches and methods of historical research, detailed analysis at regional and local level has illuminated social, cultural and economic change and has helped rebuild a more accurate picture of the gendered character of the past – and of writing about the past. Numerous edited collections, whether reprints from earlier publications or as specific collections addressing a common theme, have been especially valuable in addressing specific areas of research and in identifying new trends, sources and readings of women's past.[13] Surveys of European women,[14] and on topics or themes, such as family, work or feminism[15] have begun to modify and revise some of the assumptions concerning the place of women in history and the impact of women on the process of history. This volume seeks to continue that process of moving beyond 'reclamation', to provide a holistic approach to women's history, incorporating constructions of gender. Siân Reynolds has also pointed out the ways that women's history has challenged and 'de-fetishised' the archives, by asking about collection policies on the one hand and about the language and texts of the documents themselves on the other.[16] The range of sources that underpin the chapters are illustrative of the shifts in how we study women's past. For example, anthropological and linguistic approaches have changed the sorts of questions historians ask as well as shifting their sources. In education, for example, private materials, such as diaries and letters, have leavened the early emphasis on studying rulebooks and school records. A study of women and culture, both popular and high, requires an 'excursion' into interdisciplinary territory; literature opens up the realms of women and war, and the work of sexologists sheds light on some of the twilight discourses of sexuality. The tradition of continental European ethnography provides important insights into family and workplace, as does material culture, while studies of consumption shift the narratives across the chapters.

Mapping chronologies

The time span of this book – 1700 to the present – is fundamental to its rationale. It was also chosen to reflect a potentially manageable period, which would have something useful and coherent to say about women's experience. It is a period for which a 'grand narrative' for women has been created, and we need to engage with that narrative and question it. There is no particular magic about 1700. The inheritance from an earlier period has important resonance for the modern era. A number of social, economic, political and ideological shifts have their roots in the eighteenth and even the late seventeenth century, such as the revolution in science, epistemology, the Enlightenment and industrialisation. Eighteenth-century developments in commerce, ideology and politics were crucial for women as was women's contribution to them. They help explain the emergence of women as more visible actors across the three hundred years covered by this book. Using this *longue durée*, we can disentangle the dominance of narratives of industrialisation and bourgeois femininity that shape so much of our perception of the past. One of the organising principles in this history of European women was to place the bourgeois era and the domestic model into perspective. Indeed, over the longer span of time, one is inclined to agree with Pam Sharpe who sees the Victorian period as an historical aberration.[17] Thus, starting with the eighteenth century allows a more balanced exploration of the key changes of the modern period, while bringing the story to the near present allows contemporary women to make links between themselves and the past. Often it is dealt with on its own, or handled as a sociological rather than historical period. For many women's studies students, we are lucky if they study any history at all, while across history departments, student interest focuses on the 'modern' period. Thus the long span gives substance and purchase to an understanding of our own time, which is firmly attached to its moorings. At the same time, the book is not cast in a modernist, or Whig, view of history that sees a linear *progression* to the modern. We would explicitly eschew such a construction. Indeed Karen Hunt asks, 'is this the least interesting question to be asking?' (p. 220).

To be pragmatic, it is also the period we know best and thus this book comes out of years of reading, teaching and researching women's history. But it is a long period, and while Wiesner, Wunder and Hufton were able to adopt a thematic or topical approach to their accounts of the preceding three centuries, it is not realistic for the period from 1700.[18] We are operating in a more literate culture and one where a primacy on collecting, investigating and writing about life emerged as a central concern. To paraphrase Salieri, in *Amadeus*, 'We have too much history.' One of the historians' jobs is to make the past explicable, and dividing it up into palatable, understandable chunks is part of that task. Each chapter has an internal chronology, roughly mapping onto centuries, that allows the authors and, subsequently, the readers to reflect on the continuities in female experience, as well as to measure the character of changes. There is a certain pragmatism operating here. By following a parallel structure for each chapter, readers can read across periods or across topics. On the one hand, much of the secondary material that exists is organised around centuries and, on the other hand, so are many courses. Thus, using these familiar periods facilitates the way the book may be used.

A fundamental task of any historian is to decide how to 'manage' time. The way we decide about periods of time and how we label them are not neutral, but embody interpretations and are 'bound up with both historians' other tasks and their mental maps of the past'.[19] In shaping chapters, we clearly recognised that a single chronology does not map across the themes. While centuries are only spuriously coherent, they have the advantage that you know when you are talking about. But definitions of a century are also contentious and reflect different regional and cultural experience. In Britain, the 'long' eighteenth century runs from 1688 to 1815, while in France a 'short' eighteenth century from 1715 to 1789 makes sense. Also, in writing about Europe we have to recognise that language shapes how we might label the period that we study. The authors in this book have variously defined these time periods – and indeed have struggled with them in shaping their narratives. As Pat Starkey says, 'there will inevitably be some untidiness around the edges as developments spread themselves across our artificially imposed boundaries' (p. 178–9). A couple of examples show how the authors worked within the agreed framework to develop their own discussion. Anna Clark and Siân Reynolds used dominant themes to shape each of their chapters. In Clark's case, the demographic revolution of the mid-eighteenth century is therefore discussed in the nineteenth century, as contemporaries became aware of it and as it

informed debate and political action. Reynolds, however, used time and theme to structure her analysis, as she explains

> The three central chronological sections, here described as the 'long' eighteenth,
> nineteenth and twentieth centuries, will each take a particular focus: . . . [each]
> witnessed some new development of gender balance. For the first period,
> roughly 1680–1810, the centre of interest will be the *performing arts*: theatre,
> music, opera and dance. For the 'long nineteenth century' (1789–1914) the
> chosen focus is the *written word*: reading, translation and writing. Finally, the
> 'long twentieth century', from about the 1890s to 2000, will consider the *visual
> and fine arts*, including photography and cinema. In each case, there will be
> excursions forwards and back in time as appropriate. (p. 334)

One further example of how this *long durée* could be shaped was implemented by
Tammy M. Proctor who saw developments in women's leisure shaped around three
spaces that mapped onto the three centuries: community, nation and world. So, a bit
of 'untidiness' and blurring of boundaries shapes each internal narrative. Indeed, all of
us would agree that we have employed 'excursions forward and back in time as
appropriate'.

Throughout this book, we have not privileged continuity or change. The history of
women is often seen as flowing onward without clear breaks, the continuities are often
as important as the changes, and an important case has been made for framing studies in terms of the continuities in female experience.[20] Few, however, have adopted
either continuity or change as an intellectual straitjacket, and few historians have tried
to apply 'continuity' unilaterally to the period covered by this book. An exception,
however, is Bonnie Anderson and Judith Zinsser's bold if challenging abandonment of
periodisation altogether in *A History of Their Own*, where great swathes of time are
covered in thematic chapters.[21] Yet a fundamental question of historical inquiry is
'What happened?', which tautologically suggests something did happen and that something caused it to happen. Questions about change are fundamental to producing
historical understanding. We cannot privilege either continuity or change without simplifying historical explanation; we need to unravel multiple influences in a given
situation. Pam Sharpe draws attention to the potential restriction that a preoccupation
with the tension between continuity and change can create. Indeed she argues that:

> We no longer need to be hampered by overarching narratives of 'continuity'
> versus 'change'. . . . In a multi-faceted economy . . . some women's lives saw
> continuities, others changed. What must concern us now is understanding
> these individual experiences within the broad framework of the economic
> past.[22]

Continuities and connections run throughout the past 300 years, but the character of
change in women's lives is also profound. The simple fact of the dramatic shift in
women's formal political rights or the range of occupational or educational choices
serve to illustrate this. Thus, we have mapped the continuities and changes,
acknowledging that both contribute to our understanding and elucidation of women's
lives.

Gender

Most overtly, the book engages with the issues of gender. As Siân Reynolds has written, 'women's history has led to something that would never have emerged from previous (i.e. male-centred) history – the development of gender as an analytical concept, and as something with a force in history comparable to class'.[23] Thus, gender grew out of women's history, and it gives shape to the ways we think and write about women's history. It helps make sense of the process of recovering women in the past as well as focusing attention on how women became hidden. Gender informs and underpins this book, and we would agree with Natalie Zemon Davis that:

> Our goal is to discover the range in sex roles and in sexual symbolism in different societies and periods, to find out what meaning they had and how they functioned to maintain the social order or to promote change. Our goal is to explain why sex roles were sometimes tightly prescribed and sometimes fluid, sometimes markedly asymmetrical and sometimes more even.[24]

So, we ask questions about how the European past fashioned ideas about what it means to be male or female, and we look at how concepts of masculinity and femininity shaped the ways people of the past understood and constructed their society. As the authors demonstrate, gender is not an unchanging feature of the past; rather, relations between the sexes 'varied appreciably, along with political, economic or cultural changes'.[25] As the title of this book indicates, it is a history of women but, throughout, it engages with the gendered context of society. It is not a gendered history in the sense of trying to historicise masculinity and draw out issues of manliness. It is situated in the discourses of gender and gender history whilst keeping its focus on women and their engagement with the gendered world around them.

Separate spheres

The notion of the 'public' and the 'private' has informed much of women's history over the past three decades. One of the important underlying characteristics of the separate-spheres model is that it provided an explanatory framework to elaborate the decline in women's opportunities from a golden age of independence and rough and ready equality with men to a cloistered private, domesticated existence that reached its peak (or trough) in the middle of the nineteenth century. It was propped up by the belief that the development of industrial and commercial society created a separation of home and work, thus relegating women to the home and reducing their opportunities. The proportion of working women and the range of their activities and the physical and psychological spaces they occupied are clear confirmation that they were not sequestered or protected in a private place. Neither did political women stay at home, though part of the anxiety about their political activities was the result of their very visible presence in the streets. Further research, which has concentrated on individuals and groups outside of the bourgeois model, has also provided important critiques of the model and the social theories that underpinned them. The resilience of the concept, despite vigorous debates, as Lynn Abrams argues, presents challenges 'for the historian of women if she wishes to privilege this sphere as a site of female consciousness and power' (p.17). All of the authors engage with this paradigm at some level, contextualising it within their own analysis and often pointing out its porosity. Indeed, the permeability of the separate spheres has made it possible for historians to look at the ways women claimed particular spaces, whether it was the home, as Abrams suggests, or the barnyard and kitchen as a place of recognised female control on the peasant farm, or a political space and to examine the ways they negotiated 'male' spaces such as the eighteenth-century corporate town or political parties.

The narratives within

Families are central to women's lives, and in Chapter 2, Lynn Abrams suggests that family practices offer a way of thinking about women in the past that allows for women's own representation of their familial roles and identity. Families and their relationships are constantly in flux and have always meant different things and performed different functions for women at various stages of their lives. Abrams breaks the link between the family, the private sphere and women's role by demonstrating how the family has always been part of the social, embedded in the local economy and its cultural patterns. Cultural perceptions of sexuality shaped the ways women were constructed as sexual beings. Anna Clark shows that whether female sexual desire was regarded as passive or voracious, authorities always saw it as dangerous. Women have had to grapple with contradictory and negative social constructions of female desire in their own experiences. As historians try to understand female sexual experiences, debating the fluidity of identity and the competing pulls of pleasure and danger, she argues that sexuality still remains in a mysterious and alluring twilight, only half understood. Cultural constructions and enduring stereotypes shape views of upbringing and education. Rebecca Rogers shows how understanding the interaction between a society's vision of woman and the ways education enforces, modifies and challenges that vision to produce 'good girls and women' always carried a political dimension. Access to education and knowledge does indeed translate into forms of power, but the conditions of this access remain gendered, so that women's power operates in different realms, hierarchically inferior to those of men's.

Hierarchies of skill and status construct the gendered worker. In Chapter 5, I argue that ideas about who was or was not a worker affected whether women could work, what kind of work was truly accessible to them and why and where they were hired. Women were perceived as having a cluster of skills and characteristics that suited them for particular kinds of work, so their work was often defined in terms of male skill and expertise, or related to 'men in charge'. But they could be strategic and entrepreneurial, choosing within the options open to them when and where they would work and what they were prepared to do. Indeed, women have always been social actors, and Pat Starkey argues that they have also shown themselves to be resourceful and enterprising in using – and occasionally subverting – religious structures in order to further their ambitions for faith-inspired service or personal development. In Chapter 6, exploring the three main religious traditions to influence European women over the past three centuries, Christianity, Judaism and Islam, Starkey argues that women have experienced succour and support as well as denial and restriction within the religious communities into which they were born or, less often, those they had chosen. The ways that women use and rewrite the political structures are central to Karen Hunt's discussion in Chapter 7. She argues that collectively and individually women have had and continue to have an ambivalent relationship to formal politics, while perpetuation of a sexual division of politics has justified the marginalisation of most women from the exercise of real power. Yet at the level of informal politics and within civil society women have a much longer history of participation. By expanding the boundaries of politics they created a more inclusive space to change the polity and to act out citizenship. Challenging liminalities, women showed that they could be as enthralled with war as men, that they took up military activities for a range of reasons and that they could be as aggressive and violent as men. Jane Potter, in Chapter 8, also identifies society's enduring unease with women in the military and going to war. She challenges the notion of 'peace-loving ladies', but, as she illustrates, women were also integral to the peace movement, and in some ways led it, but within the movement, enduring gender constructions shaped the ways the movements operated.

Throughout the book, the authors have looked at the ways spaces were defined, and redefined, noting the complexities and shifting character of women's worlds. Thus, Tammy M. Proctor argues that women always had a complicated relationship to leisure, because they frequently engaged in facilitating the leisure of others. In Chapter 9 she looks at how women's claims to and opportunities for leisure changed and how they sought out additional spaces and times for participation in the cultural milieu. She argues that a woman's empire is no longer limited to her home, but her ability to experience life outside the home is still shaped by factors within it. The same could be said about women's interaction with 'high culture'. Siân Reynolds raises the paradox of marginalising women as creators, practitioners and even as consumers, despite their role as audience, while defining painting, reading and music as appropriate to their education. Recognising the elite character of many of the arts, the gendered contexts in which they operated and the limitations on women, she takes the practical approach of trying to fill in the gaps in a history that has, for a long time, neglected to analyse the gender of the arts. This means re-examining the canon to see how women were placed within the cultural field of their time, as performers, creators or consumers of the arts, and how they negotiated cultural spaces.

Challenging the master narrative

The interdisciplinary nature of recent research speaks to the ways in which feminist historians have questioned the categories and processes of historical writing and are in the vanguard of those reinterpreting the past. Most would now argue that the writing of women's history should also inform, nuance and contribute to the rewriting of mainstream history. History that is not written with the discoveries and theoretical approaches of women's and gender history is only a partial story. A veritable string of authors can be cited, arguing that women's history should now inform the rewriting of the canon, and more and more books are being published that try to rewrite the story of the past. This work began in earnest in the 1990s with books by Siân Reynolds on inter-war France, Maxine Berg on industrial change in England and the essays edited by Laura L. Frader and Sonya O. Rose on gender and class in Europe just to name three.[26] There are actually two motives behind this, and I may appear to be stating the obvious. On the one hand, the omission of women from the grand narratives leaves those narratives lacking, misleading and often simply wrong. The feminists of the

1970s talked about 'consciousness-raising', and this is precisely what mainstream history has needed: an awareness of the simple fact that there might be another way to look at the past, that reading the sources with 'gendered spectacles' could reveal a different 'truth'. Many standard mainstream histories were written by men about men, and not only were they, in our term, gender-blind, such an approach was not even questioned. Both the discourse and the language were male. Women's history and gender history have challenged such an approach. But we also have to follow through and not allow gendered research to sit in its own ghetto, as a sub-field of history, as a fad. As Reynolds wrote, women's history has the opportunity to rethink issues and periods from a feminist perspective, 'not so much to challenge what has so far been written as to query what has not been written',[27] using research in women's history to ask different questions and to propose alternative readings, to apply the perspectives and findings of women's history to so-called mainstream history.

On the other hand, if women's historians do not challenge and contribute to rewriting the canon, then the discoveries, approaches and alternative readings of women's history will themselves not be taken seriously. Recently a noted Scottish historian (male) indicated that women's history was passé, suggesting that we could move on and put it out of our minds. As Pat Hudson and W.R. Lee have said, 'As long as research about women's lives remains largely separate from wider issues such as these, the importance which society has attached to female activities and agency in the past (and in the present) will not change.'[28] So this is the other side of the coin: not only do we need to shape mainstream history for the sake of history, but also we need to apply our efforts for the sake of women's history. Thus in Jean H. Quataert's words, European women's history is at the crossroads.

Notes

1 Joan W. Scott, 'The Modern Period', *Past and Present*, 101 (1983), p. 141.
2 I explicitly say 'English' because many British accounts only nod to Scottish, Welsh or Irish experience.
3 Fiona Montgomery and Christine Collette, eds, *The European Women's History Reader* (London: Routledge, 2002), p. 4.
4 For example, Dorothy Atkinson, Alexandra Dallin and Gail Lapidus, eds, *Women in Russia* (Hassocks: The Harvester Press, 1978); Victoria E. Bonnell, ed. *The Russian Worker: Life and Labour under the Tsarist Regime* (Berkeley, Calif.: University of California Press, 1983); Rose L. Glickman, *Russian Factory Women: Workplace and Society, 1880–1914* (Berkeley, Calif.: University of California Press, 1984); Linda Edmondson, ed., *Women and Society in Russia and the Soviet Union* (Cambridge: Cambridge University Press, 1991); Beatrice Farnsworth and Lynne Viola, eds, *Russian Peasant Women* (Oxford: Oxford University Press, 1992); Barbara Alpern Engel, *Between the Fields and the City: Women, Work and Family in Russia, 1861–1914* (Cambridge: Cambridge University Press, 1996); Toby W. Clyman and Judith Vowles, eds, *Russia through Women's Eyes: Autobiographies from Tsarist Russia* (New Haven, Conn.: Yale University Press, 1996); Natalia Pushkareva, *Women in Russian History: From the Tenth to the Twentieth Century*, trans. by Eve Levin (New York: M.E. Sharpe, 1997); Sheila Fitzpatrick and Yuri Slezkine, eds, *In the Shadow of the Revolution: Life Stories of Russian Women, from 1917 to the Second World War* (Princeton, NY: Princeton University Press, 2000); Jane McDermid, *Revolutionary Women in Russia, 1870–1917: A Study in Collective Biography* (Manchester: Manchester University Press, 2000); *Midwives of the Revolution: Female Bolsheviks and Women Workers in 1917* (London: UCL Press, 1999); *Women and Work in Russia 1880–1930: A Study in Continuity through Change* (London: Longman, 1998); Wilma Iggers, ed., *Women of Prague: Ethnic*

Diversity and Social Change from the Eighteenth Century to the Present (Oxford: Berghahn Press, 1995); Tiina Kirss, Ene Kõresaar, Marju Lauristin, eds, *She Who Remembers Survives: Interpreting Estonian Women's Post-Soviet Life Stories* (Tartu: Tartu University Press, 2004). See also Marcelline J. Hutton *Russian and West European Women, 1860–1939: Dreams, Struggles, and Nightmares* (Lanham, Md.: Rowman & Littlefield, 2001).

5 Mary Nash, 'Rethinking Narratives in European Women's History: Motherhood, Identities and Female Agency in Twentieth-Century Spain', in Terry Brotherstone, Deborah Simonton, and Oonagh Walsh, eds, *Gendering Scottish History: An International Approach* (Glasgow: Cruithne Press, 1999), p. 113. She could have said English instead of British, given the imprecision with which 'Britain' is used.

6 See, for example, Mary Nash, *Women in the Spanish Civil War* (Denver, Col.: Arden, 1995); Diane Urquhart, *Women in Irish Politics, 1890–1940: A History Not Yet Told* (Portland: Irish Academic Press, 2000); Ute Frevert, *Women in German History from Bourgeois Emancipation to Sexual Liberation* (Oxford: Berg, 1988).

7 For example, see David F. Good, Margarete Grandner and Mary Jo Maynes, eds, *Austrian Women in the Nineteenth and Twentieth Centuries* (Oxford: Berghan Books, 1996), pp. xi-xiii; and Kirss, Kõresaar, Lauristin, eds, *She Who Remembers Survives*, pp. 13–18. See also the introduction to Eleanor Gordon and Esther Breitenbach, eds, *The World is Ill Divided: Women's Work in Scotland in the Nineteenth and early Twentieth Centuries* (Edinburgh: Edinburgh University Press, 1990). However, research over the intervening fifteen years and a major publishing project of Women's History Scotland is tackling this issue: Lynn Abrams, Eleanor Gordon, Deborah Simonton, Eileen Janes Yeo, eds, *Gender in Scottish History* (Edinburgh: Edinburgh University Press, 2006) and Elizabeth Ewan, Sue Innes, Rose Pipes, Siân Reynolds, *Biographical Dictionary of Scottish Women* (Edinburgh: Edinburgh University Press, 2006).

8 See the articles in *Bulletin d'Information* 2 (June 2003) for the Association Pour le Développement de l'Histoire des Femmes et du Genre – Mnémosyne (in France) about some of the other networks. Just a sampling includes (founding dates in parentheses): Women in Spanish, Portuguese and Latin-American Studies; Asociacón Española de Investigación Histórica sobres las Mujeres (1991); Women's History Network (UK, 1991); Women's History Scotland (1990, reorganised 1998 and renamed 2005); Women's History Association Ireland (1989); Arbeitskreis Historische Frauen- und Geschlechterforschung (1990). A mini-trend appears to be the production of dictionaries of national women, for example, in Denmark, *The Biographical Dictionary of Danish Women*, from 2000, compiled by Anna-Birte Ravn, Jytte Larsen and Marloes Schoonheim and in Scotland, Ewan, Innes, Pipes and Reynolds, eds, *The Biographical Dictionary of Scottish Women*.

9 Note that I use the term 'narrative' to indicate not a chronological tale, but 'a story, some-thing with a shape', as Siân Reynolds put it, in 'Historiography and Gender: Scottish and International Dimensions', in Brotherstone, Simonton and Walsh, eds, *Gendering Scottish History*, p. 6.

10 Jeremy Black, *Eighteenth-Century Europe, 1700–1789* (New York: St. Martin's Press, 1990, rev. edn, 1999)

11 Alison Mackinnon, 'Were Women Present at the Demographic Transition? Questions from a Feminist Historian to Historical Demographers', *Gender & History* 7 (1995), pp. 222–40.

12 Maxine Berg and Pat Hudson, 'Rehabilitating the Industrial Revolution', *Economic History Review*, 45, 1 (1992), pp. 24–50.

13 Two collections that have achieved 'classic' status are Marilyn J. Boxer and Jean H. Quataert, eds, *Connecting Spheres: Women in the Western World, 1500 to the Present*, and the new edition, *European Women in a Globalizing World, 1500 to the present* (New York: Oxford University Press, 1986 and 1999) and Renate Bridenthal, Susan Mosher Stuard, Merry E. Wiesner, eds, *Becoming Visible: Women in European History* 3rd edn (Boston, Mass.: Houghton Mifflin, 1998) – originally Renate Bridenthal and Renate Koonz. Montgomery and Collette, eds, *European Women's History Reader* and Alan Hayes and Diane Urquhart, eds, *The Irish Women's History Reader* (London: Routledge, 2001) are examples of readers that have reprinted key articles and extracts. On countries, see for example, Gisela Bock and Anne Cova (eds) *Écrire l'histoire des femmes en Europe du sud.*

XIXe-XXe siècles / [Writing Women's History in Southern Europe. 19th–20th Centuries] (Oeiras: Celta Editora, 2003); Victoria Lorée Enders and Pamela Beth Radcliff, eds, *Constructing Spanish Womanhood: Female Identity in Modern Spain* (Albany: SUNY Press, 1999); Brotherstone, Simonton and Walsh, eds, *Gendering Scottish History.* A simple check of COPAC, a union catalogue of British libraries (*http://copac.ac.uk*), shows how many edited volumes have been produced in just the past ten years alone, and the further reading at the end of each chapter in this book underlines that point.

14 Bonnie G. Smith, *Changing Lives: Women in European History since 1700* (Lexington, Mass.; D.C. Heath, 1989); Gisela Bock, *Women in European History* (Oxford: Blackwell, 2002); Lynn Abrams, *The Making of Modern Woman: Europe 1789–1918* (London: Longman, 2002); Rachel G. Fuchs and Victoria E. Thompson, *Women in Nineteenth-Century Europe* (New York: Palgrave Macmillan, 2005).

15 Deborah Simonton, *A History of European Women's Work* (London: Routledge, 1998); Karen Offen, *European Feminisms, 1700–1950: A Political History* (Stanford, Calif.: Stanford University Press, 2000); Barbara Caine and Glenda Sluga, *Gendering European History, 1780–1920* (London: Leicester University Press, 2000); Ulla Wikander, *Kvinnoarbete i Europa 1789–1950: Genus, Makt och Arbetsdelning* (Stockholm: Atlas, 1999).

16 Reynolds, 'Historiography and Gender', p. 8.

17 Pam Sharpe, ed., *Women's Work: The English Experience, 1650–1914* (London: Arnold, 1998), p. 10.

18 Merry E. Wiesner, *Women and Gender in Early Modern Europe* (Cambridge: Cambridge University Press, 1993); Heide Wunder, *He is the Sun, She is the Moon* (Cambridge, Mass.: Harvard University Press, 1998) and Olwen Hufton, *The Prospect Before Her: A History of Women in Western Europe, 1500–1800* (London: Fontana Press, 1995).

19 See Ludmilla Jordanova's discussion around the management of time and periodisation, in *History in Practice* (London: Arnold, 2000), pp. 114–40, here p. 128.

20 Judith Bennett, '"History that Stands Still": Women's Work in the European Past', *Feminist Studies,* 14 (1988) p. 278. See the debate between Bennett and Bridget Hill: 'A Study in Change: Continuity or Standing Still?' *Women's History Review,* 2, 1 (1993), pp. 5–22, and Judith Bennett, 'A Reply to Bridget Hill', *Women's History Review,* 2, 2 (1993), pp. 175–84, both republished in Sharpe, *Women's Work,* pp. 56–68 and 42–57. Judith Bennett, 'Medieval Women, Modern Women: Across the Great Divide', in D. Aers, ed. *Culture and History, 1350–1600: Essays on English Communities, Identity and Writing* (London and New York: Harvester Wheatsheaf, 1992), p. 164.

21 Bonnie S. Anderson and Judith P. Zinsser, *A History of Their Own: Women in Europe from Prehistory to the Present,* 2 vols (London: Penguin, 1988).

22 Pam Sharpe, 'Women's History and Economic History in Britain', in Pam Sharpe, ed., *Women's Work: The English Experience, 1650–1914* (London: Arnold, 1998), p. 33.

23 Siân Reynolds, 'Historiography and Gender', p. 5.

24 Natalie Zemon Davis, 'Women's History in Transition', reprinted in Joan Wallach Scott, *Feminism and History* (Oxford: Oxford University Press, 1997), p. 88.

25 Davis, 'Women's History in Transition', p. 81.

26 Siân Reynolds, *France between the Wars* (London: Routledge, 1997); Maxine Berg, *Age of Manufactures,* 2nd edn, (London: Routledge, 1994); Laura L. Frader and Sonya O. Rose, eds, *Gender and Class in Modern Europe* (Ithaca, NY: Cornell University Press, 1996).

27 Reynolds, *France between the Wars,* p. 2.

28 Pat Hudson and W.R. Lee, eds, *Women's Work and the Family Economy in Historical Perspective* (Manchester: Manchester University Press, 1990), pp. 34–5.

2

AT HOME IN THE FAMILY
Women and familial relationships

Lynn Abrams

'The family' is still often implicitly taken to be an essential and natural entity. And behind this exclusion is the unspoken assumption that the family is about women and children, about femininity and infancy.[1]

Introduction

How do we imagine the family in the past? And how do we think about women's relationship with this primary social institution? Women (and children) are so frequently associated with the family – contained within it, isolated without it, defined by it – that it has become common to talk about family in terms of the functions and roles closely associated with femininity. Hence, the family of the historical imagination is a domestic, nurturing and intimate unit, governed by women's concerns: reproduction, nurture, socialisation and the provision of sustenance. The existence of a family in the past is dependent upon the presence and work of women; a family without an adult female was not deemed worthy of the name. Certainly, by the nineteenth century, family had become intimately associated with the idea of 'home' and a woman was an essential component of home-making so that the sentiment 'A man can no more make a home than a drone can make a hive' was widely held.[2]

And yet, despite the intimate association of women's roles and functions with family, it is often implicit in discussions of women's experience rather than made explicit: 'Family is everywhere and family is nowhere to be seen'.[3] Family – as a concrete collection of individuals as well as a symbol – underpins so much of personal experience in the past from childhood to old age, but its meaning is rarely explored. The family is a set of social relationships connected by blood, property, dependency and intimacy. It is a material reality as well as an ideology and a cultural practice. As a means of basic social organisation it frames domestic and work lives, and as a symbol it influences social policy. This chapter will define family as a cultural practice, a series of interconnected rituals based upon co-residence or kin relations. It will examine how women experienced the relationships and functions implicit in family and how constructions of family – as a conduit for property inheritance for example, or as a guarantor of social stability – came to impact upon women's choices and opportunities in western Europe from 1700. This reimagining of the family as a set of relationships and rituals, which are determined by prevailing economic conditions and cultural and religious beliefs, may offer a more positive interpretation of women's association with family than has hitherto been considered.

The concept of family is so ubiquitous in modern life and in modern historiography that it is hard to imagine a time when it was not. And yet, as Sarti explains, 'family' only began to be used in western Europe to refer to a kin group living under the same roof as late as the eighteenth century. Before then, the term 'family' did not necessarily identify blood or kin relationships but relationships of dependency on the head of the household. By the eighteenth century, it seems that the French concept *famille*, referring to a married couple and their children, began to be used elsewhere, but it was not until the nineteenth century that family came to denote 'a hierarchically structured domestic community, made up of a father, a mother, children and servants [representing] a fundamental building block in society'.[4] Indeed, for comparative purposes the term 'household' is more useful as a catch-all concept that allows one to sidestep the difficulties embedded in different meanings of family over time and space. It is the rather narrow and time-specific concept of the family, analogous with the co-resident nuclear family, with which historians of the modern period in Europe are most comfortable, perhaps because it equates most closely to the concept and reality of family with which we are most familiar (although not necessarily as part of our personal experience). It is this model of family that informs the massive popularity of genealogy research in modern society, and yet we know from our own family histories that the family we live by is so rarely the family we live with. That is to say, the myths of family that inform our understandings of what family should be and how it should be experienced are often unhinged from the material reality of family life.[5] As Gillis states in his analysis of the relationship between family myth and family reality, the families we live with are 'often fragmented and impermanent [and] are much less reliable than the imagined families we live by'.[6] It is a sentiment echoed in a recent feminist study of the family in which the authors acknowledge that present debates about the family exhibit a yearning for a 'golden age of stable, loving and supportive families' which privileges the nuclear family, and yet this very narrative of family in the past 'denies the complexities of familial relationships'.[7]

An example from the author's own family history serves this point well. My great great grandfather Samuel Jay was born in rural north Essex in 1797 into a family of agricultural labourers. In 1830, Samuel married his first wife Sarah Sallows. The couple had five children together before she died in 1838. In 1839 he married for a second time to Sarah Butcher, daughter of a labourer in the same village as Samuel. Sarah appears to have died upon or after the birth of a son. In 1848 a third marriage to Amelia Howe was also short-lived for, in 1851, Samuel Jay was living with Elizabeth Butcher (sister of his second wife Sarah) listed variously as his lover and his lodger in the census, with whom he stayed for at least thirty years. The couple may have had an illegitimate daughter together, Ellen, who is recorded in the census as Samuel's daughter-in-law. Samuel Jay had at least seven children with his wives and partners. Each time a wife died he remarried to create a new family grafted onto the old, until the death of Amelia after which he seems to have rejected marriage while still forming a household with Elizabeth and the younger children from his previous marriages.[8] Samuel's family, which was continuously resident in the same village (although at different addresses) for more than eighty years, was both enduring and discontinuous. At some points it might have been described as nuclear and at other times extended. This story tells us a lot about the nature of the rural labouring family, but from the scant information available to construct this complex series of family forms we know little of the women in Samuel's life apart from the fact that they had children and died young. Indeed, they are defined solely as wives and mothers.

Women's relationship to the family is so often framed by their relationships to others: fathers, husbands, children. This approach does highlight important ways in which women's lives are defined in some way by their familial ties but also limits our understanding of women's identities and experiences over the life course. The history of the family is not the same as the history of women. As the Jay family story illustrates, families in the past no less than today were continually changing shape. The relationships within the co-residential group and beyond to kin outside the residential core were in constant flux. For women at all times and in all places this meant frequent adaptation to different sets of economic and cultural circumstances.

Historiography

In 1987 Louise A. Tilly asked whether the relationship between women's history and family history was characterised by 'fruitful collaboration or missed connection?'[9] Her quest was informed by a sense that these two vibrant fields of historical research had more to say to each other than had hitherto been the case for a combination of methodological and ideological reasons. Family history, until quite recently, tended to be dominated by demographic and structural approaches. The study of population movement and change is of course central to understandings of family forms and relationships, but until the 1970s debates about fertility changes, for instance, were carried out with little or no reference to gendered power relationships. As Alison Mackinnon has argued, demographers see fertility as 'a characteristic of populations rather than persons'.[10] Structural approaches, dominated by the spectre of late nineteenth-century ethnologist Frédéric Le Play, who almost single-handedly invented a language and a series of ideal family models (for example, the stem family, the complex household, the nuclear household), have similarly downplayed the role of women and of men as social actors informed by ideas about gender roles. The families alluded to by the historical demographers and the stucturalists are disembodied and impersonal. Women and their roles as childbearers and nurturers are implicit rather than explicit in these analyses and the tendency to treat the family as a single social and economic unit in its relationship to the rest of society resulted in the silencing of 'internal' relationships within the family as well as the disregarding of non-kin relations outwith this institution.

Arising from the structural and demographic approach to family was the theory that modernisation fundamentally altered family structures and relationships, notably that the family became more nuclear in character as opposed to kinship oriented and more centred upon affective relations as opposed to instrumental or economic relationships. The debate between those who argued for changes of this kind and those who emphasised continuity did address issues of gender, often in a controversial way. The proposition of Shorter and Stone that, before the rise of the nuclear affective family, parental and more especially maternal relations with children were characterised by instrumentalism and lack of affection or sentiment certainly placed women's role in the family in the spotlight, but the debate in general perpetuated the tendency to downplay or ignore what family meant to those who experienced it.[11] And in any case, the focus on parent–child relations was regarded by these historians as a means of advancing a more general position rather than of gaining deeper insight into the material realities of familial relations.

Women's historians, on the other hand, traditionally had little time for the family. First-wave feminists of the late nineteenth century and second-wave feminists of the 1970s both regarded the public sphere – education, paid work and citizenship – as the key to women's emancipation. Nineteenth-century feminists focused their energies on reforming women's subordinate legal position in the family in respect of property and child-custody rights. By the late twentieth century, marriage was regarded by many second-wave feminists as the keystone of women's oppression. The family as a legal and an ideological construct was regarded by historians of women as a hindrance to women's claims to participation in the economy and the polity. And the discursive construction of woman since the Enlightenment as wife and mother, domestic angel and homemaker has long been considered a constraint upon women's opportunities beyond the family and the home. The resilience of the ideology of separate spheres, of the notion of a gendered public and private, within historical writing on gender has tended to perpetuate the subordination of family to lesser importance in the disciplinary hierarchy. Notwithstanding vigorous debates amongst historians of women and gender about the value and the persistence and chronology of separate spheres as a discursive power or organising principle in social, cultural, economic and political life, the continued association of the private sphere with the domestic and the personal presents challenges for the historian of women if he or she wishes to privilege this sphere as a site of female consciousness and power.

Since the 1980s, women's historians have embraced the family in a more positive fashion, as a legitimate site of women's experience and identity. Arising from a recognition that most women's lives were structured by the ideology and the material reality of family – its demands, its structures and its relationships – historians of the labouring classes placed family centre stage and repositioned it as a complement to work. The family in these studies is imagined as a strategic unit, incorporating variable roles and relationships interacting with the outside world.[12] The family was contingent upon its position within the wider economy, and relations within the family unit as well as beyond it were influenced by ideas about appropriate gender roles, by cultural assumptions and by material circumstances. In this literature then, the family is conceived as neither necessarily oppressive nor emancipatory for women, but rather a social unit that provides the context for women's reproductive and productive experiences. Thus, for example, in the proto-industrial economy in France, the declining income to be gained from home-based handloom-weaving undertaken by men forced women into waged work to ensure the family's survival. The family economy, in these circumstances, was adaptable to the needs of the market.[13] In the industrial economy, however, familial ideology, which categorised the husband as breadwinner and wife as homemaker, impacted upon women's experiences in the workplace as they were treated as secondary or subsidiary workers, a development discussed in more detail by Deborah Simonton in Chapter 5.

Davidoff and Hall's *Family Fortunes*, a study of the English middle classes, placed the family at the heart of middle-class life and identity formation in the crucial period

1780–1850. They regarded the family as a dynamic institution within which women and men formed social bonds, exhibited gendered roles and found ways of meeting their needs. The family in this analysis does not sit apart from business; it is not synonymous with the private or the personal; rather it is implicated in the middle-class economy and the idea of family as a flexible and adaptive kinship system which 'framed middle-class provincial life'.[14] The work of Ellen Ross on women in poor working-class London families, and of Bonnie Smith on the women of the French industrial bourgeoisie, epitomises this approach.[15] For these historians, the family is the very substance and texture of women's daily lives, more so than paid work. The women in question – whether poor and struggling in London's East End, or wealthy and privileged in northern France – lived lives shaped by the material demands and the discursive construction of family. Family here incorporates a multitude of activities and experiences: marriage, childbirth, death, ritual, religion, relationships and work which, in their doing, facilitated a sense of female collective identity or at least a sense of where their common interests lay. Ultimately, some have argued that woman's familial relationships and experiences shaped her feminist consciousness in the nineteenth century, resulting in middle-class philanthropic engagement and working-class protest informed by the material conditions of everyday life.[16]

Historians of family and of women, particularly in Britain, have been less interested in the nitty-gritty day-to-day monotony of family life with which many women were accustomed. Ethnography has always been more integrated into the historical discipline outside the British Isles and, moreover, the shift to theories of gender have sidelined aspects of the past which do not appear conducive to theoretical approaches. For instance, the work of servicing the family has mostly been discussed within the context of domestic service, yet in most families this work was done by whoever was not undertaking paid work, that is, women, children and the elderly. The focus on the everyday by European historians has reoriented attention on the family as the fulcrum of private experience and as a place where individuals find meaning and assume an identity. Sarti, in her study of family and material culture in early modern Europe, demonstrates how descriptions of 'banal objects and commonplace events' may 'penetrate the experience of men and women of the past'.[17] French historian Martine Segalen has taken this further, recognising the possibilities of material culture for penetrating family relationships. For instance, Segalen points to the significance of the introduction of communal water fountains and washhouses in southern France, which resulted in changes in patterns of female sociability as women used to carrying out their laundry alone now 'found a time and a place to express their identity and sometimes their solidarity'.[18] Studies of everyday family practices in particular religious and ethnic cultures also highlight how delineated gender roles have been essential to the practice of family in the past. Within migrant Jewish communities, for instance, the task of providing the kosher eve of Sabbath meal with all its attendant ritual was invariably female.

Doing the laundry, cooking, eating and cleaning up, as well as decorating one's home, visiting kin and so on, are all part of 'doing family' as much as property inheritance, marriage, procreation and choice of living arrangements. And family life was part of everyday life, argues Gillis. Referring to European Protestants, he argues that their family life was 'transparent, unreflexive, unmediated by any representations of itself, lived on a day-to-day basis, without reference to custom or tradition'.[19] By the second half of the nineteenth century, however, family had become something that one consciously created. In Gillis's words, 'family had put itself on display'.[20] This emphasis on family practices rather than social structure is a fruitful way forwards for both historians of family and of women and gender.[21] It is an approach that potentially transcends the divisive separate-spheres dichotomy, thus positioning the family as an institution and an idea that informs all cultural experience, and it might help us to stretch ourselves across longer timespans. Family history and women's history are primarily concerned with relationships in the past – between husbands and wives, parents and children, kin and non-kin, family and community – expressed as a series of relational practices which may include care of and responsibility for others and the protection and control of family members within a complex web of kin and non-kin relations.[22] Such an approach allows one to move beyond the supposedly 'natural' association of woman with family in her role as mother, wife, care-giver, homemaker, and so on (an approach that tended to hide or silence women's role) and forces a rethinking of women's familial relationships and responsibilities over the life course and over historical time and space.

For women's historians then, the family occupies an ambiguous place in our construction of the past. For a long time, historians of women saw the family and those concepts so intimately associated with it – the home, the household, the private sphere, moral discipline – as a source of historical oppression, a place where women were confined both physically and ideologically. But more recent studies of family relationships have situated family and women's roles within it in a wider spatial and theoretical context. The family is no longer conceptualised in a rigid structural or ideological way, but rather historians are beginning to see how a focus on the practices of family might offer a way of thinking about women in the past that allows for women's own representation of their familial roles and identity.

Sources

Where is the family to be found in sources on the past and how can we know about women's relationship with the family from these sources? Historians of the family have great fortune in that the family as an idea or as an institution is ubiquitous in sources chronicling the social and cultural history of the European past. At the same time, these sources are often opaque or partial and, for the historian of women, they may result in considerable frustration by omitting them altogether or by ascribing to women so-called natural characteristics or roles.

How do people tell family stories? Traditionally, historians of the family started with parish records of births or baptisms, marriages and deaths and the population census as the most comprehensive records of family structure in past times. The method known as family reconstitution, whereby demographers attempted to reconstruct families from disparate data before the census did it for them, has been subjected to considerable criticism on the grounds that there was no attempt to deconstruct the categories used by those who recorded the data and no acknowledgement of the complex kin relations that existed within and between families. In Britain, the nineteenth-century population census may be similarly simplistic and misleading. As many historians have pointed out, the census conflated family and household and assumed that this social unit could be captured at a moment in time representing a general picture of the population in any parish, county or, indeed, the entire country. Thus the family was conceived as a hierarchical structure wherein all inhabitants of the household were related in some way to the head, normally an adult male unless there were no adult males present. Women generally appear as subordinate household members, not least if they were married. The decision in Britain in 1881 to label all married women as 'unoccupied', whether they undertook paid employment or not, is well known to historians, but this well-documented category shift must alert us to the likelihood that the categorisation of women's occupations in general is open to question or at least multiple interpretations. For instance, the label 'wife of' in the occupational category may have many different meanings depending upon the precise circumstances in that particular parish. In Glasgow's Gorbals parish, for example, wives of Jewish tailors working at home or in small workshops were frequently categorised by census enumerators as 'tailor's wife' in the late nineteenth century, but from what we know of this community it is likely that these women were working in partnership with their husbands. In the far north of Scotland, on the other hand, women were far more likely to be identified as workers in their own right on account of women's strong identity as producers. For instance, in 1881, only three adult women in the whole of Shetland were defined as 'dependant'.[23] Notwithstanding these caveats, the census can be an illuminating source, if merely for identifying the sheer diversity of household structures and the suggestion of the complex relationships that must have existed within them.

Historians of women may have criticised historical demography for its denial of women as social actors, but they have not eschewed demographic data altogether. Statistics showing average age at marriage, marriage rates, fertility rates, and so on provide a broad canvas, showing change over time and between different localities and social classes. For example, we know that western and northern Europe experienced a fertility decline from around the 1870s and that birth rates fell markedly after the Second World War after a brief post-war baby boom. What these statistics do not say is how smaller families were achieved in terms of decision-making between couples, and feminist historians have attempted to fill in the gaps, positing that shifting power relations between men and women may have influenced family size.

At the other extreme in methodological terms, oral history and written forms of personal testimony, such as autobiography and diaries, have contributed new insights into women's relationship with the family. When Elizabeth Roberts determined to research the lives of 'ordinary' working-class women in the north-west of England in the pioneering days of social history in the 1970s, she was obliged to rely on oral history for her source material. Roberts's book *A Woman's Place* and the sequel, *Women and Families* illuminated family life in the nineteenth and twentieth centuries from women's perspectives, addressing subjects such as marriage, birth control, family budgeting and neighbourhood networks.[24] Indeed, personal testimony redresses the balance of demographic data by revealing the permeability of family, the familial relationships that extended beyond households, the strategic marriage links, the networks of female kin, the importance of siblings, aunts and uncles, cousins, grandparents, indeed a whole series of familial relationships that are not constrained within a single household. The fairly common practice of children being brought up outside their birth family, often by grandmothers or sisters, owing to poverty or lack of space, emerges vividly in oral histories whereas an entry in the census would merely hint at the familial relationships at work.

Beyond these quantitative and qualitative extremes, the historian searching for women and family need not search far but may need to exercise his or her imagination a little. All kinds of legal records present narratives of particular aspects of family life, albeit mediated through legal language and the dominant discourses of the day. Divorce and separation records present an invaluable perspective on married life in those parts of Protestant Europe where civil divorce was available. In addition to detailed descriptions of a breakdown of a marriage, the reader can often discern the expectations for marriage and family life held by the spouses as well as the idealised models of conjugal life promoted by the state. So, for example, when Christian Wesel sought to divorce his wife Sophia in the Hamburg court in 1830 we gain a clear idea of his expectations of married life and specifically her responsibilities to the marriage. On the day of their marriage in May 1825, Sophia had promised to 'lighten his life with love and loyalty and by means of sincere thriftiness to preserve his earnings'. But, claimed Christian, soon after their marriage his 'modest hopes and dreams' had turned into a nightmare as it became clear that Sophia 'knew neither honesty or thrift'. By contrast, Emilie Beil stated that 'the hoped for happiness and married contentment' that she had anticipated had not materialised because her husband conducted his life outside the home and returned home every night in a drunken condition.[25]

Prenuptial marriage contracts, not uncommon amongst the propertied classes in the eighteenth and nineteenth centuries, and wills and testaments may all illuminate both ideal concepts of family and the grubby reality of family life. For instance, Kristin E. Gager's analysis of legal adoptions in early modern France utilises notary records to argue that the model of the family founded solely upon blood ties promoted by the state was rejected by couples and single women who wished to perpetuate family through inheritance, bypassing biological reproduction.[26] Lis and Soly, in their study of eighteenth-century Brabant and Flanders, exploit family requests for the incarceration in correctional institutions of unruly or disorderly members to show how families attempted to stabilise family life by removing those who threatened its fragile economic and psychic equilibrium.[27] The law intervened in most areas of family life and at all stages as a regulatory mechanism. It was brought into play at times of tension (for example at the point of marriage breakdown or to mediate in an inheritance dispute) or merely to establish the contractual relationships implicated in family life in the past.

Beyond family law, though, it is not hard to find family implicated in all kinds of official records generated by the criminal and civil courts across Europe. Religious and secular authorities responsible for distributing poor relief had much to say about familial responsibilities as well as providing detailed information on the material conditions of individuals and families requesting support. The civil courts dealt day in, day out with situations embedded in family relations: unmarried mothers petitioning the court to demand child maintenance from the fathers of their children; cases of breach of promise whereby one party – usually the woman – sought financial redress from the man she believed had promised her marriage; cases of domestic violence; and all manner of disputes concerning property. And even criminal cases reveal to the historian the everyday workings of family and kin. Criminal prosecutions for all kinds of misdemeanours, from theft to infanticide, invariably illuminate webs of familial relationships within which defendants were enmeshed. In the case of female defendants this is especially noticeable as women in past times were publicly defined by their relationship to the family: they were daughters, wives, widows and mothers.

Historians interested in the use of language and in the way it constructs the ways we conceptualise the world have made use of literary texts to unravel and indeed to challenge structural definitions of family. Naomi Tadmor's stimulating study of family and friends in eighteenth-century England is particularly concerned with how concepts of the family were used by people in the past and, from there, with re-evaluating social views about family. Using diaries, conduct books and popular novels, Tadmor demonstrates how eighteenth-century people conceived of family as a household unit that included kin but was not exclusively comprised of kin.[28] Moving forward to the twentieth century, Michael Peplar has examined the mass media and film for representations of family in post-Second World War Britain. He shows that marriage and the nuclear family dominate these representations whereas the extended family is marginal, albeit conceptualised as morally and materially supportive. From *Brief Encounter* (1945) to *Saturday Night and Sunday Morning* (1960) suggestions of alternative scenarios to marriage and the nuclear family are ultimately rejected.[29]

The universality of the family in Western culture means that it is recorded everywhere, as an abstract concept, as an ideal, or as a material set of economic and intimate relationships. The task for the historian of women is to remain critical of dominant concepts of family and to look for ways in which women themselves talked about and practised family.

The following three sections discuss three different conceptions of family, family life and the place of women within it. The first section on the eighteenth century conceptualises the family as a fluid unit, often contiguous with the household. In this period, broadly speaking, family was not exclusively defined by relations of blood or consanguinity; rather it was conceived more as a godly household and economic unit. The second section, on the nineteenth century, is concerned with the new model of familial domesticity. Less an economic unit, the family gradually became increasingly private and self-contained and practised what has been termed 'self-conscious familialism'.[30] The twentieth-century family discussed in the third section is a hybrid thing, more flexible than its Victorian predecessor, less of an economic unit than the early modern household and probably more open to public gaze and interference while at the same time becoming the prime locus for intimacy. Of course, these chronological boundaries are falsely imposed and conceal long-term continuities across the period as well as moments of profound change and differences between and within European states and social classes. The position and experience of women in relation to the family will be explored within these three frameworks: the eighteenth-century flexible family, the nineteenth-century self-conscious family, and the twentieth-century hybrid family.

The flexible family, 1700–1800

Samuel Johnson in 1755 defined the family as 'those who live in the same house'.[31] The eighteenth-century European family was, in many ways, indistinguishable from the household, not necessarily in terms of its size or structure, but rather in the conceptual sense of belonging. Before the nineteenth century, the family was not analogous to the home. It was not necessarily a self-contained unit consisting of blood kin, or at least it was not conceptualised in this way. As John Gillis states, 'most people lived for much of their lives according to the rhythms and the spaces of families other than their own by birth or marriage'.[32] For this reason, historians of the early modern period have tended to conflate family with household, which in turn implies 'a domestic unit with decision-making autonomy about production and consumption'.[33] Of course, in some instances the household consisted of little more than a stem family consisting of a married couple and their children engaged in household production. In others though, the household was a fluid entity consisting of a variety of kin such as widowed mothers, siblings and stepchildren, and non-kin such as servants, lodgers, wet nurses, tutors and apprentices, while at the same time family members might be short- or long-term residents in other households. However, family could also denote consanguinity, degrees of relatedness by blood and kin ties, but these family members might not live under the same roof. According to Flandrin, 'in former times, the word "family" . . . referred to a set of kinsfolk who did not live together, while it also designated an assemblage of co-residents who were not necessarily linked by ties of blood and marriage'.[34]

The disassociation of family from blood kin and its association with a more heterogeneous household has appealed to historians of women for whom the modern idea of the nuclear, conjugal or male-breadwinner family has been too bound up with women's role in reproduction. The early modern household, on the other hand, appears to offer women a variety of roles encompassing production, reproduction, consumption and nurture. Unlike the nineteenth-century family, which has become synonymous with the ideology of separate spheres thereby marginalising females from tasks ascribed economic value, the household, with its complexity of functions, its apparent permeability between work and family life with no apparent gender hierarchy, may appear to offer women a space freer of the constraints associated with the bourgeois model of the home.

At first sight though, the early modern household was a patriarchal institution whereby power was invested in the male head of the household. In both agrarian and urban communities, legal and moral authority rested with the head. Male heads derived this authority from their ownership and right to inheritance of land and property, but also from traditional notions of authority disseminated by the church and moralists who attempted to conceptualise the potentially unruly household as a disciplined unit in need of guidance. Patriarchal authority was not uniform in nature across Europe but could incorporate the male head's right to dispose of family property, the right to supervise family labour, the right to represent the family and, within the family, possession and custodial rights in respect of a wife and children.[35] These privileges were dependent upon the head's reciprocal responsibilities to the household and his ability to conform to the role of good father and husband.

However, this ideology of the patriarchal household has recently been called into question by those who have researched the workings of the household as a domestic economy incorporating production and consumption and to which all members of the co-resident group contribute and interact. Complex households containing a variety of kin and non-kin engaged in varied and conflicting interactions. As Julie Hardwick points out, for middling households in early modern Nantes, 'to perceive household relations only as simplistic patriarchal oppression is to ignore the greater complexity that day-to-day demands and negotiations created'.[36] Lines of authority often bypassed the head of the household as wives, servants, lodgers and children formed alliances and engaged in conflict in the course of day-to-day household management. In this scenario, women were variously positioned as subordinates and as authority figures, depending upon their social relationships with one another. For instance, the supervision of domestic servants was usually a woman's responsibility placing the wife of the head of household in a position of authority over other women, yet solidarities amongst women also developed across these lines of authority. Similarities in age and life course, as well as day-to-day personal (and often intimate) contact, may have facilitated bonds between women of different social classes. In middling households the 'hierarchy of household chores' was not always strictly drawn, with wives carrying out some tasks such as taking care of the linen and sewing alongside servants. Female networks that crossed lines of authority contributed to the good and orderly running of the household and sound *ménagement* or *Haushaltung* (a concept of household economy that incorporated financial probity, respectability and hard work). Women thus assumed important roles within the household and, as Hardwick points out for France, although this entailed considerable responsibility, it also offered them opportunities for acquiring power.[37]

At the same time, male heads of households could forfeit their authority if they were judged to have neglected to manage the household diligently. Men who drank excessively, who were lazy, who were wasteful with money, could find themselves publicly remonstrated for their lack of competence in household management. A case from agrarian southern Germany illustrates this well. In 1743, Dorothea Thumm submitted a complaint to the Neckarhausen church court about her son-in-law David Falter who she accused of not being 'as diligent as he should be'. He had neglected his *Haushaltung* by hiring others to carry out his farm work and by 'loafing around'. He complained that his mother-in-law Dorothea scolded him, calling him a 'bad manager, gambler, and drunkard'. She merely wished that he would be a more competent manager of the household.[38] The point here is that the concept of the household and more especially its efficient management implied mutual obligation of the sexes wherein each member of the household had duties and responsibilities (rather than rights and power). A husband who failed to fulfil his duties could be stripped of his authority, his 'right to manage'. By the end of the eighteenth century, wives, in alliance with the authorities, could remove a husband's right to manage by subjecting his property to inventory or even a forced sale if he was judged to be in danger of indebtedness and hence putting his entire household at risk.[39] Such cases contrast starkly with disputes heard in the nineteenth century when household management became almost exclusively associated with women.

In order to examine the position of women within the family in this period, we must do so on two levels: the economic and the personal or, in other words, their relationships to the productive unit (the household) and the reproductive unit (marriage and family). The marital alliance was the economic and emotional basis of the household and, for the majority of European women who did marry, it was in theory a guarantor of status in society. It was also potentially a source of emotional sustenance and, for a few, a springboard for achieving their own goals.

The marital relationship was the keystone of the early modern family economy. Only those who married had the opportunity to found their own household, and many European states made economic viability a condition before permission to marry was granted. The financial and material contribution of both spouses was essential. Sons of peasants brought land and maybe a farm inheritance, artisans brought their tools and their skills. Men of the middling classes brought property. In southern Europe, daughters of peasants and artisans traditionally entered marriage with a dowry consisting of some cash and material goods – maybe furniture, linen, a spindle, a loom. In Sicily, a trousseau of embroidered whitewear was the conventional dowry of a peasant girl. In Greece, the dowry might include a house or land as well as a trousseau.[40] Elsewhere in the western Mediterranean the *dot* was more common, meaning property or goods bequeathed to the man and the woman and often interpreted as a more egalitarian way of transferring property from one generation to the next. In theory then, both spouses started marriage on a roughly equal footing.

On this basis, and despite the plethora of laws that objectively assigned the wife to a subordinate position within marriage, women expected to be treated with respect by their husbands if they fulfilled their side of the marriage bargain. On the other hand, a husband who reneged on his side of the unspoken contract could anticipate his wife's opprobrium. The understanding of the complementary nature of the household economy was often central to marital disputes in the eighteenth and early nineteenth century. In the German states, for instance, where marital disputes were aired before the church courts and, if sufficiently serious might proceed to the civil courts for a legal separation or divorce, it is clear that mutuality between the spouses was highly valued by wives when the household economy was based upon a rough equality. Disputes that took place in the context of the egalitarian household economy concerned men's unacceptable behaviour that threatened to destabilise the family economic unit. Drinking, laziness and violent behaviour were deemed a danger to the *Haushalt* (household economy). As Sabean notes, these marital conflicts were not 'hierarchical dramas' about who ruled the house, but rather women were asserting their authority within the discourse of marital reciprocity.[41] A husband who neglected his business and his family had no moral right to expect his wife to treat him with any respect.

Marriage for the peasant, artisan and middle classes in eighteenth-century Europe was also an economic relationship that required the contribution of both spouses. Prescriptive household literature, although envisaging quite distinct male and female spheres of economic production and a gender hierarchy, nevertheless regarded male–female relations as interdependent. One seventeenth-century German household-economy text exemplified this attitude which made little distinction between the public and the private sphere. Accepting that the husband and wife would have different qualities, nevertheless both had to cooperate in separate management of their respective realms: men in the fields, women in the house, the dairy, the garden.[42] The 'ideal was harmony within hierarchy' and this kind of arrangement was not merely a prescriptive fantasy. In eighteenth-century France, one observer reported how

> in the lowest ranks, in the country and in the cities, men and women together cultivate the earth, raise animals, manufacture cloth and clothing. Together they use their strength and their talents to nourish and serve children, old people, the infirm, the lazy and the weak . . . No distinction is made between them about who is the boss; both are.[43]

Historians of the industrialised economy have become accustomed to the notion of differential value assigned to male and female labour.[44] Yet, within the household or family economy, women's productive work – agricultural or proto-industrial – and reproductive work was clearly valued by other members of that household and by the community. The fact that a sexual division of labour prevailed was not necessarily an indicator of inequality. The Languedoc proverb, 'A dauntless woman in the house is worth more than farm and livestock' sums up the belief that woman was valued as a producer.[45] Her work in running the house combined myriad tasks: cooking, cleaning, caring for children, lodgers and apprentices, looking after livestock and tending the kitchen garden. In addition she would participate in agricultural tasks such as hoeing, singling and the harvest, and she would undertake domestic manufacture in the form of knitting, sewing and the production of farm goods for sale and for home consumption. Wives of landless labourers hired themselves out to other households as well as working in rural industry, straw-plaiting, spinning, sewing, knitting and lacemaking. In families of the middling classes, women supervised servants, looked after other household members such as boarders, supervised apprentices, spun linen cloth for their own use and may even have worked on smallholdings as did the wives of Nantes's notaries, where they supervised the grape harvest, helped to gather in vegetables and sold the produce.[46]

This bucolic image of the self-sufficient, mutually supportive family within which women had a valued place should not be overstated however. Shifts in economic structures could play havoc with family relationships. By the beginning of the nineteenth century, coinciding with economic changes that reordered economic relations between husband and wife, the nature of marital conflict altered. As the family economy became unviable, it was superseded by an economic system that valued women's production of goods and services for cash. In these conditions, a renegotiation of reciprocities is evident whereby women's adaptability to new market relationships encouraged them to assert their authority within the marriage relationship. In Württemberg in southern Germany women became more involved in the production of cash crops and raw materials for the textile industry. In Göttingen wives of artisans began to earn money wages in domestic service. Elsewhere in Europe, such as in soft-fruit-producing areas of Scotland and olive- and grape-producing regions of Italy, the nature of male and female roles changed substantially and the household economy was no longer a suitable economic unit. Woman's role remained pivotal, but perhaps not equal. The consequence was a shifting balance of power in the family as women insisted on maintaining some control over their earnings and criticised their husbands' tendency to squander resources.[47]

Proto-industrialisation, whereby whole villages of families could be employed in their own homes producing consumer goods for capitalist merchants, had a profound impact upon the dynamics of family life. The traditional and practical separation of spheres disappeared as working the land receded and the whole family – men, women and children – were engaged in production as a team, 'transforming the sexual geography of daily life'.[48] In these circumstances, it is suggested that the traditional sexual division of labour began to break down and the distribution of tasks became more flexible. Some historians have argued that women's greater access to the means of production and their engagement in the market meant they accrued greater power.[49] Yet it appears that as independent family businesses were absorbed into a putting-out network run by the merchants, husbands maintained their authority within the home by becoming representatives of their families in their dealings with the merchants, and women took prime responsibility for childcare and housekeeping in addition to being proletarians in their own homes.[50] It was this family production unit that was transferred to the early industrial system.

The family economy in the transition to industrial capitalism was infused with gender inequalities. In the Loire region of France, where domestic handloom-weaving survived in the face of mechanisation longer than elsewhere, men's pride at maintaining their skill was retained at the expense of the proletarianisation of their wives and daughters who were forced to find waged work to supplement their menfolk's meagre and declining piece rates.[51] Thus women were employed as sweated outworkers in their own homes producing lingerie and shoes for the new luxury consumer market. Women bore the costs of the weavers' survival. In the Italian silk-producing area of Como, where agriculture continued to exist side by side with industrial production, it was the women who became proletarianised, exploited by factory owners and their own husbands.[52] The family economy then, was a system that could subordinate women at the same time as placing a value on their labour.

As gender relations within the rural labouring family were being reshaped in the late eighteenth century by the forces of market capitalism, amongst the middling classes, family relationships within and furth of the family core were being strengthened, and women's role was bolstered in the process. Women became key figures in the mobilisation of kin, which in turn provided the emotional and material ballast for the making and sustaining of family in this social milieu. These practical kin relationships were mobilised in instances of matchmaking and marriage, at baptisms, in the care of the elderly and infirm, and in financial arrangements.[53] In these households and kinship networks women were the active family makers, the 'generators of kin alliances'.[54] Women fostered female relationships centred upon female maternity rituals. Confinement and childbirth have been interpreted as a time and a space of empowerment for women, and they had their own rituals to welcome newborns at a time when baptisms tended to be occasions of male sociability. Women were also active networkers in relation to marriage alliances, often playing a key role in the choice of a suitable spouse. Once a woman was engaged to be wed, the kin community of women would work to help her accumulate her trousseau of linens. This fostering of female networks may well have provided the basis for emotional support and material aid amongst communities of women. Women formed small informal credit networks at a time when men controlled the legal borrowing and lending of money. And in cases of spousal cruelty a ready-made network of kin roundabout could be invaluable, something that applied to women of the working classes too.[55]

Amongst the middling classes then, women's role was becoming more embedded in the domestic life of the family, presaging developments in the nineteenth century that saw a much closer relationship of women and home. By contrast, woman's role in the working-class family was becoming more production driven, potentially giving her greater access to networks and relationships beyond the family, but in reality tying her into a patriarchal household system that incorporated the female double burden of homemaking and wage-earning.

So far we have been focusing on the place of married women in the family, but in early modern Europe up to 25 per cent of women never married, and the vast majority of those who did were widowed. What place was there for these women in the flexible family and what was their role? The flexible boundaries of the early modern household meant that unmarried and widowed women could find a place for themselves, either incorporated into the household of kin or, if finances were tight, of an unrelated family. However, as one eighteenth-century commentator on the condition of women astutely remarked of the spinster, 'Should her destination be to remain an inhabitant in her father's house, cheerfulness, good temper, and an obliging resignation of her will to that of others was her duty.'[56] A woman who was not attached by marriage to the household head was to sublimate her needs to those of the household and above all, she had to be useful.

Olwen Hufton has noted that

> All women lived in societies in which marriage and motherhood were regarded as the norm, spinsterhood and infertility as a blight, and in which the notion of the family economy, of the family as a composite unit permitting the sustenance of the whole, was axiomatic.[57]

She suggests that women who lived outside the family inhabited a kind of 'twilight existence'. Similarly, Miriam Slater argues that spinsterhood condemned a woman to 'a lifetime of peripheral existence . . . a functionless role played out at the margins of other people's lives without even that minimal raison d'être – the possibility of bearing children'.[58] There is some truth in both of these statements. Marriage was the only sure route to a sustainable independent household for women, but at the same time, the demographic and economic pressures on most households – frequent illness and indisposition, high mortality, recurrent childbirth and the need for more labour – meant that the accommodation of single women was often functional rather than a burden. Spinsters fulfilled a wide variety of functions in the family: as carers of the elderly, the infirm, widowed fathers and children, as housekeepers and nurses, as companions and governesses and as workers, material contributors to the household income. An extra pair of hands made all the difference. In the Shetland Islands, for example, where women were left to run the crofts in the absence of men at the fishing in the summer months, a spinster sister or widowed aunt was a common addition to the household. Indeed, a woman who did not have extra help around the house would have struggled to manage her productive and reproductive roles. Hosiery production, croft work and domestic and childcare chores were not compatible. 'Dey wida needed till a been wirkin braaly anxious at it an probably maybe been anidder woman ida hoose fur I couldna see a hoose wi wan wife ida hoose doin dat, alang wi aa da rest o her wark' (They would have needed to have been working really hard at it and probably maybe [there would have been] another woman in the house for I couldn't see a house with one wife in the house doing that along with all the rest of her work) commented one resident of the islands.[59] More common was the employment of single women as domestic servants in rural households. Those who did not become betrothed might remain as 'servants-in-husbandry' as this was a more secure prospect than trying to make a living alone. In the towns, the service sector was so large in the eighteenth century – in London it has been estimated that up to one thirteenth of the entire population was in service – that it acted as life-cycle transition for young women who could be safely incorporated into another's household, and it offered older unmarried women a place within a household economy, albeit increasingly physically separated – in living quarters situated in distant parts of the house they served – from the family who employed them.[60]

However, in England and Scotland a remarkable number of elderly spinsters and widows did manage to make an independent living with access to a small amount of land – often waste land – and maybe some livestock. Such women had become of no use to their families, regarded as too infirm or elderly to contribute meaningfully to the household economy. Plenty were the 'widows and single women of the poorer classes who lived alone in some tiny cottage away from the village, built perhaps surreptitiously on a bit of waste and hidden among fern and furze and bramble'.[61] Those who were not incorporated into the family of blood kin or into an unrelated family and who could not survive alone only had one alternative: institutional care outwith the family, an option more common in urban areas such as Amsterdam where, by the middle of the nineteenth century, almost one half of the never-married elderly lived in homes for the destitute.[62]

In the middling classes, the options for unmarried women were somewhat more constrained. Absorption into another family was possible but in a more limited sense. Some spinsters were sent to live with female siblings, especially if there were young children to care for, or they became companions to elderly relatives. The governess has become the ubiquitous image of the middle-class spinster in service, but it was not until the nineteenth century that opportunities expanded in this line of work as the more affluent middle classes began to employ governesses for their daughters.[63] Some unmarried women did find a role within a family business but they were rarely able to escape the discipline of family altogether. In the case of Hester Pinney, whose life is so nicely reconstructed by Pamela Sharpe, her success as an autonomous tradeswoman in the early modern lace trade of the English West Country and London did not bring the benefit of independence from patriarchal authority. As Sharpe points out, 'it is an anachronistic idea . . . to think that economic means could free a woman from the bonds of a potentially suffocating web of connections who were both relatives and business associates'.[64]

The early modern family, in Gillis's words, 'enabled individuals to form familial relations with strangers and to feel at home away from home'.[65] Within this flexible concept of family, women could move from one household to another assuming a variety of roles: daughter, servant, wife, mother, worker and carer, often simultaneously. In this scenario, family was not intimately associated with women's roles. 'Doing family' was not uniquely women's work. Women slipped between roles according to economic need. However, by the end of the eighteenth century, women's relationship to the family was changing in most regions of western Europe. As the early modern household economy gave way, gradually, to the modern domestic family, woman's role altered. It became more circumscribed, the value of her familial or domestic labour changed, and the work of sustaining family life became uniquely female.

The self-conscious family, 1800–1900

The nineteenth-century bourgeois family model has come to occupy a central place in the modern imagination. As Gillis observes, 'Today our mental maps are filled with homeplaces and our mental clocks set to family times that did not even exist before the nineteenth century.'[66] In terms of its structure, its functions and its ways of exhibiting a particular mode of family life, the concept of family that was developed amongst the nineteenth-century European bourgeoisie has come to dominate to such a degree that alternative forms have hitherto received only marginal attention. According to Segalen, in nineteenth-century Europe the bourgeoisie 'shared an ideology which unified them over and above their material distinctions, by placing at the centre of their values a family model which played a considerable social role . . . both within domestic groups and kinship networks'.[67] This new familial idea – and it must be stressed that this was only an idea – encompassed form and function. The single-family model centred upon the conjugal unit came to be seen as the norm, and any alternative forms such as single parenthood or cohabitation were regarded as unacceptable deviations. Moreover, family became analogous to home; the family identified those members of a related kin group who lived under the same roof. It excluded other members of the household such as boarders and servants.

This is not to say that households became any less complex or that the notion of what constituted family became more exclusive. Bourgeois households might typically contain a married couple with their several children plus additional relatives – perhaps an unmarried sister or a widowed parent – and multifarious boarders and domestic servants. So while nuclear family size declined markedly from mid-century onwards, the extended family household was ubiquitous. And kin who lived outwith the conjugal household were still regarded as family, albeit in a wider sense of consanguinity. But, amongst this social class, the meaning of family changed. It was indicative of private space and time, distinct from work in terms of spatial and temporal delineation. Hence the function of the family altered. It was no longer a multitasking unit, which incorporated production, reproduction and consumption. Rather, family became at its core an intimate place, sheltered from the outside world, a sentiment expressed by the English writer John Ruskin in his paean on 'home':

> it is a place of Peace; the shelter, not only from all injury, but from all terror, doubt and division . . . so far as the anxieties of the outer life penetrate into it . . . and the hostile society of the outer world is allowed either by husband or wife to cross the threshold, it ceases to be a home.[68]

The family thus imagined was an emotional unit geared to the sustenance of intimate relationships between husbands and wives and parents and children.

At the heart of this domestic familial ideal was the wife and mother. It has become axiomatic to state that family and home became synonymous with woman and femininity in nineteenth-century Europe. In contrast with the eighteenth century, when a household was defined by its patriarchal head, in the nineteenth century a family was not worthy of the name without a woman at its core. Conversely, a woman who lived outwith a family was pitied as lacking the opportunity to fulfil her true womanly role. A woman's source of personal fulfilment was located within the bosom of her family. The sublimation of a woman's identity in the mutual roles of wife, mother and domestic manager (and her disassociation from productive work) was an intrinsic part of this new familial ideal.

The family domain is often described as synonymous with the concept of the private sphere, as contrasted with the public sphere of work, commerce and politics. The association of these separate spheres with different gender roles was commonplace in the nineteenth century. It is now widely accepted that religious discourses – evangelical in England, Catholic in France, Lutheran in Scandinavia – effectively shaped notions of the female role as primarily domestic, but the discourse on the 'angel in the house' was remarkably pervasive and widespread. The words of one French aristocrat and restorationist – 'Women belong to the family and not to political society, and nature created them for domestic cares and not for public functions'[69] – were a concrete articulation of the ideology of separate spheres that was repeated and reaffirmed across Protestant and Catholic Europe.

In practical terms, what did this mean for women of the bourgeoisie? Did the ideology of domesticity infer women's containment within the family or did it enhance the value of the roles of domestic manager and mother? Bonnie Smith's examination of the lives of the wives of industrialists in northern France suggests both are true. On the one hand these women embraced domesticity. They created homes that were an expression of female culture centred upon family and religion. They fashioned a world in which 'feminine' values were dominant, entirely separate from the world of business: 'the bourgeois woman lived in an atmosphere and acted according to precepts entirely at odds with the industrial, market, egalitarian, and democratic world – the world, that is, of her husband'.[70] These women's lives appear to mirror almost perfectly the religious and moral injunctions imparted to them by their mothers, their teachers and the church.

Elsewhere though, women of the middle classes were creating a family life that could not be contained within the concept of the private sphere. Although there appears to be little doubt that married women of this class did withdraw from the formal world of work in line with the identification of them as dependants, they certainly maintained an interest in and influence over the business activity of their husbands and wider kin. English women contributed financial resources to family businesses, they maintained and furthered networks of family and kin as a means of sustaining the family enterprise, and some participated actively in the businesses of their menfolk.[71] In France, family businesses often combined the names of both husband and wife – the Mequillet-Noblet cotton company was typical, uniting Parisian bankers with channel-coast cotton merchants – recognising the role of marriage in harnessing the wealth and the vigour of the spouses.[72] In Glasgow, married women may have been classified in the census as 'dependants' but many played an active role in their husbands' professions and businesses, especially when they conducted their work from the family home as was often the case with ministers, doctors and lawyers.[73] Nevertheless, a married woman was not expected to have an independent economic role; however much she contributed financially or culturally to the family enterprise, she was still primarily defined and judged on her domestic role, and for some women this amounted to an almost intolerable strain. The wives of German civil servants – amongst the lower echelons of the middle classes – in their struggles to conform to the respectable lifestyle of the bourgeoisie resorted to elaborate deceptions (amongst one another) such as hiring a dinner service and extra servants for a dinner party in order to give the impression of the comfortable bourgeois lifestyle.[74] This was family on display.

Domestic family life now demanded as much of women as the complex and busy household had a century earlier. The newly fashioned home of the urban middle classes became a female space; it was women's responsibility to transform a house into a home and the home into a haven from the busy, ugly world of commerce. The middle-class dwelling place was increasingly located in the new residential areas of cities and in the suburbs such as Glasgow's West End, Hamburg's Harvestehude and London's Clapham Common and was, for the commercial classes, separated from the workplace. This segregation was mirrored in the interior of the home where family and work spaces were clearly separate. Domestic, private family rooms were distanced from the kitchen (site of much labour conducted out of view by female domestic servants) as well as bedrooms and bathrooms. Nevertheless, the home was still a workplace for women. Much labour was required to create the fussy, heavy interiors favoured by nineteenth-century middle-class families. Drawing rooms and parlours were stuffed with furniture, textiles, ornaments and adornments of every kind, antimacassars, embroidered screens and footstools, mats, tray covers, and so on, many of them made by the women of the house. Homemaking and housekeeping merged in these house-holds. The contentment of the family rested upon the skills of the woman of the house in maintaining a tight ship, or an efficient army to paraphrase the language of the doyenne of British housekeeping, Mrs Isabella Beeton. In her *Book of Household Management* published in 1861, she urged the mistress of the house to compare her-self with the 'commander of an army' and to lead by example for 'Her spirit will be seen through the whole establishment; and just in proportion as she performs her duties intelligently and thoroughly, so will her domestics follow in her path'.[75] In the larger middle-class houses, the mistress of the house needed to acquire a range of skills more suited to running a small business than a family home. She hired, fired and super-vised the servants, planned menus, oversaw the accounts, shopped, ran errands, and prepared country homes for long holiday visits. In smaller households with fewer ser-vants she would take on some of the housework personally, but always keeping in mind that she should endeavour to cultivate the appearance of gentility.

The emphasis on appearance alerts us to the permeable nature of the private domes-tic sphere in the middle-class milieu. The family and its home were on display – to the servants, to visitors, to business colleagues. Amongst working-class families this per-meability is often taken for granted by contemporary observers of social conditions in the urban environment and by historians. Families living in crowded housing and in poverty were, it is assumed, in and out of each other's dwellings, with women in par-ticular reliant upon reciprocal networks beyond the immediate family. Yet, there was hardly less pressure in these communities to conform to cultural norms and the pres-sure was, more often than not, exerted by women. The moral compulsion to keep one's front step whitened, or to maintain a clean communal stair in tenements was little dif-ferent from middle-class women's need to entertain using the best china and linen. In the case of working-class women though, external agencies as well as members of their own community passed judgement on their housekeeping skills. And, health visitors, inspectors of the poor, child-savers and a host of philanthropists carried with them middle-class notions of family domesticity. Female philanthropists, bolstered by their own faith in the maternal role in the home, believed they had a duty to the 'great social household'. In England, the housing reformer Octavia Hill deliberately used female sanitary visitors, exploiting working-class women's acceptance of discourses on clean-liness and hygiene. Jewish female philanthropists made it their job to ensure new migrants' homes were reaching acceptable domestic standards in order to avoid criti-cisms by non-Jews regarding low standards of housewifery and domestic management amongst the immigrant community.

Homemaking was hard work and yet this labour – housework, household manage-ment, childcare and the creation of the domestic interior – was defined as unproductive and therefore not valued, at least by others. However, many women did find satisfac-tion in their family role and sought to receive recognition for it when given the opportunity. In the divorce courts of Germany, women commonly cited their housekeeping and homemaking skills in evidence against their husbands, indicating that not only did women themselves recognise the value of this work in the home, but also that society in general acknowledged a woman's worth in the domestic domain. In 1871, when accused by her husband of being an extravagant spendthrift, Henriette Dethgens countered that she

> has never shown an addiction to expenditure or a particular addiction to amusements . . . she has lived happily with the plaintiff for many years, has born him many children and has become prematurely old through her fulfilment of her duties as wife, mother and housewife . . . The plaintiff has increasingly rejected her and shows this rejection by treating her unkindly . . .[76]

The notion of the orderly household still had purchase in the nineteenth century, but now it was the woman of the house who was responsible, judged on her ability to conform to the new standards of domesticity.

The nineteenth-century family was not just woman-centred, it was mother-centred. A family without a mother could hardly be deemed a family at all. Lone fathers who sought to bring up their children following the death of a spouse were pitied. It was assumed that a man would not be able to cope and that children were deemed to require 'mothering', a skill men could not acquire. In the words of a female director of a Scottish children's home, 'a widower is perfectly helpless with children. He cannot mother the bairns and be the breadwinner too; while he tries to do a *father's part*, the children miss their *mother*.'[77] Equally, a woman's identity within her family was strongly determined by her mothering role, as evidenced by this memorial to Sarah Heath from Norfolk who died at the age of thirty-five in 1810:

> Thus in the prime of life died much lamented a good Wife and an affectionate Mother whose happiness whilst on earth may truly be said to have chiefly centred in an excessive love for her Children and in the practice of those duties which will cause her loss to be deeply regretted and her Memory long revered.[78]

The mother–child relationship was at the heart of the new model of familial domesticity. Children came to fulfil an emotional and sentimental role within the family, as opposed to a financial role, and this required intensive parental and especially maternal involvement with children.

The good wife was also required to be the good mother. The good mother was an elaboration on the figure of the 'natural mother' popularised by Jean-Jacques Rousseau in his 1762 novel *Émile*. The natural mother was she who trusted her maternal instincts and who bonded with her children physically (through breast-feeding) and emotionally by spending time with them. By the early nineteenth century, pedagogues and feminists had begun to expand the concept of good mothering beyond the natural. Motherhood became a public role, a duty, a responsibility, something to be taught to girls, as Rebecca Rogers demonstrates in Chapter 4. 'Truly, the saying that "Your child will become whatever you are"', wrote the German schoolteacher Betty Gleim, 'is of such immeasurable importance, that, if she really feels it and lives by it, every mother ought to tremble before the responsibility that she takes on as a teacher and educator of the coming generation'.[79] Mothers were assuming the roles formerly ascribed to fathers: the moral education of girls and boys and even training in manliness. To what extent did mothers embrace this role? It would be wrong to generalise. Some women immersed themselves in their children's upbringing, noting all their foibles and personal details and sharing concerns and delights with their husbands. Others took a hands-off approach, spending little time with their children, especially if they employed an army of nursery-maids and nannies. Dominant ideas of motherhood were interpreted and practised in different ways, depending upon material circumstance and personal predilection but none could escape the importance accorded to motherhood in constructions of female identity.

Working-class women perhaps had less room for multiple or alternative interpretations of the maternal role. As Guttormsson has noted, 'children's work at an early age and their freedom of movement in the neighbourhood involved a degree of independence which was incompatible with middle-class conceptions of childhood'.[80] In addition, the propensity of working-class families to move house frequently, the inadequacy of housing in most urban centres and the need for many women to undertake waged work either outside or within the home militated against the middle-class notion of the family as a constant haven where family members might secure the bonds of affection. In London, frequent demolition of housing and the transitory nature of employment in the city necessitated frequent flits, much to the despair of those concerned with social stability and welfare such as this London doctor who described the poor in 1902 as 'extremely migratory in their habits . . . Comparatively few of the working classes settle down and let their own affections and those of their children take root.'[81] And in all European cities women were obliged to work from home; the identification of women as primarily domestic and only secondary workers pushed the employment of married women in particular into their own homes or small workshops. The textile trade's predilection for using outworkers or homeworkers on piece rates appeared to permit the coexistence of capitalist production and the new familial ideology, since it was argued that women with children could work when it suited them, fitting wage-earning around childcare and domestic responsibilities. But of course homework competed with familial space and time; homes became workshops, full of manufacturing accoutrements, and children were used as additional labour. Family life, as it was imagined by the middle classes, and home production were incompatible. The ideology of separate spheres, which defined the man of the house as the breadwinner and the woman as homemaker, could not fit the material circumstances of most working-class families. Nevertheless, as a hegemonic discourse it indirectly influenced the ways in which working-class families lived their lives. The churches, the state, employers and philanthropic organisations promoted the middle-class family model as the ideal way of structuring working-class lives. At the level of spatial organisation within the home, the practice amongst the British working classes of maintaining a pristine parlour – a 'shrine to respectability and domesticity' – for Sundays and entertaining, appears incomprehensible in the context of overcrowded dwellings and was seen by contemporaries as folly but, as Seccombe points out, the parlour was 'the inspiration of working-class homemakers, forging an inner sanctum against the din, dust and drudgery of daily life'.[82] More generally, employers and many male trade unionists conveniently utilised this ideology to subordinate women's labour. A French working-man's newspaper summed up this view: 'Everyone understands that her place is elsewhere than in the political arena; her place is at the domestic hearth. Public functions belong to the man; private functions belong to the woman.'[83] In Britain, the Chartists struggled with the tension between their belief in egalitarianism and in domesticity in regions where women formed a large proportion of the work-force. As Clark concludes, 'Chartists claimed the privileges of domesticity for their wives and demanded entry into the public sphere for working men.'[84] The language of the 'family wage' became an aspiration for many in the working classes who struggled to conform to the new familial model and who were judged if they deviated from it. It was not until the end of the century that some working-class families did achieve the model of familial domesticity that bourgeois Europeans had been propagating since the beginning of the century.

In the nineteenth century the new idea of family became powerful. It became associated with the home and with a series of well-defined gender roles – wife and mother, husband and father – which embodied the new model of familial domesticity. Family became a private thing, bounded by relationships between kin and by the material and physical structures of domesticity. One of the consequences of this development was what has been described as 'self-conscious familialism': the practice of doing family.[85] And because women were at the heart of family life they also became the instigators of the new family rituals which affirmed the value of family life to its members and to onlookers. Family was put on display, most obviously on the ritualised life-cycle occasions such as weddings, baptisms and funerals which, in previous eras, had not been necessarily or exclusively family events. And such occasions were increasingly feminised. Weddings became woman-centred, marking a woman's most important rite of passage and they became occasions for feminine display and female networking. And while the middle classes felt that a funeral was not an appropriate place for a woman – she was deemed too sensitive and unable to control her emotions in public – women did embody the grief at the loss of a family member by wearing black mourning clothes. Women then, represented their families at such times.

The withdrawal of the family into the private space of the home was accompanied by a self-conscious acting out of family on certain ritualised occasions: Christmas, birthdays, holidays and, increasingly, Sundays became family time in the nineteenth century, replacing the traditional rituals of the agricultural year. But for women, family time necessitated work. The effort involved in decamping a large family to a summer villa drove some middle-class women to distraction and, once ensconced on the coast or in the mountains, they rarely had a chance to rest for it was commonplace to host streams of visitors. The new family ritual of Christmas involved women in a similar frenzy of activity: as Gillis remarks, 'Christmas was made by rather than for them.' Not only did they decorate the house, purchase the presents, organise the meal, and so on, but on this day 'women were supposed to satisfy the imaginings of others, to be more wifely and more motherly on this day than on any other', in contrast with men whose role was less circumscribed on this day than on any other.[86] If Christmas was family ritual par excellence in Protestant and Catholic Europe, Sunday was Christmas in miniature, a weekly ritual which ironically required the labour of wives, mothers and female servants in order to create a family day. Evening church services in England and Wales attracted a higher proportion of women who could not attend in the daytime on account of the demands of preparing Sunday lunch. And in Jewish families, it was women's work to ensure the family welcomed in the Sabbath on Friday evening. The traditional chicken dinner on Friday night required a lot more than just cooking; 'creating a religious atmosphere was very hard work.'[87] Women cleaned the house thoroughly while their menfolk were at the synagogue, creating a semblance of the good Jewish family home. According to one Glaswegian Jew,

> during the week the house might be a chaotic place from which he was happy to retreat, but come the Sabbath and festivals, there was a transformation. Even a man who lived in a hovel – as most Jews once did – would return from the Synagogue to find a palace – the table laden, the rooms gleaming, his wife and daughters in their best clothes.[88]

Family time for women entailed working for the family in contrast with men for whom family was equated with leisure and repose.

The contraction of the concept and practice of family in the nineteenth century and its association with sentiment, left less space for those individuals – unmarried women and widows – who did not have a formal place within a domestic family unit. The early modern household had been a flexible space, literally and conceptually. The unmarried, the unattached and the widowed could be incorporated into household units as useful additions. Urban industrial Europe was less accommodating to those who existed outside a familial unit. Nineteenth-century European bourgeois society was family-centred in the way it imagined and projected itself and, increasingly, this model came to be practised within urban working-class communities too. Where did single and widowed women fit in a society in which marriage, motherhood and domesticity was held up as the ideal state and in which women were constructed as dependants? In the past, historians assumed that the rise of the private or domestic family of the nineteenth century marginalised these women, at least the poor among them. More recently, the place of the spinster has been rehabilitated by those who urge us to interpret spinsterhood as a choice for some or even an opportunity to reject the chains of domesticity as a form of resistance to the institution of marriage and motherhood. The independent businesswoman, the sprightly feminist spinster and the woman living in a female partnership have rejuvenated the negative image of the spinster and demonstrated that there were positive alternatives to the potential claustrophobia of the familial ideal.[89]

The idea of family may have changed, but its size and ability to absorb kin did not alter markedly. It is misleading to conflate the domestic familial idea with the reality of middle-class urban households in this period. Certainly the size of the nuclear family was decreasing during the nineteenth century amongst all sections of the middle class. In Glasgow for example, in 1851 the average size of the nuclear family was just 4.2 persons, yet average household size at this time was 8.1 including servants (5.2 excluding servants).[90] It seems that these households still contained a variety of co-resident kin and in this sample up to 80 per cent were female with almost one half consisting of sisters and sisters-in-law. Furthermore, not all of these co-resident women were dependent upon male heads of household. Indeed, many were living with siblings. Thus, the unmarried women of middle-class Glasgow were not necessarily existing at the margins of other people's families. Up to 50 per cent of households in some streets were headed by females, most of them widows. And many of these were independent women, supporting male and female dependants rather than being supported themselves.[91]

Nevertheless, the family model predicated upon the male breadwinner norm did impact on the choices of unmarried women and, to a lesser extent widows, especially amongst the working classes. In the absence of an inheritance, widows in this category were thrust into a state of dependence. In the northern English industrial town of Preston, 75 per cent of widowed women of all ages lived with their children, for the death of a spouse was a blow sufficient to thrust a woman into destitution. Childless widows were more likely to move in with relatives, not only because of the pressures on space but also on account of the resources she might bring to a household. A widow with no dependants herself would be able to contribute to the household pot.[92] A similar situation prevailed in the Caux region of northern France where the decline of cottage spinning and the consequent contraction in work opportunities for women meant that unmarried or widowed females were unable to support themselves. In 1851 27 per cent of widows lived with their children whereas fifty years earlier the figure had been 20 per cent.[93]

The ultimate threat to the new model family, at least in discursive terms, was the unmarried mother. The 'fallen woman' stood in stark opposition to the chaste domestic angel of the ideal family, contained by marriage and economically dependent. However, single parenthood was rarely a lifestyle choice. Most mothers of illegitimate children had aspired to family life. The majority of single mothers were in their early twenties when they became pregnant, similar to the average age of first marriage, suggesting that they believed they were in a serious relationship, one that would lead to marriage. What had changed in the nineteenth-century urban environment was an easing of the moral and social pressures on men to marry their pregnant girlfriends. Moreover, the shift in employment options for young women, with domestic service and factory work incompatible with childcare, and changes in residential patterns owing to labour mobility that often left young women far from home and their kin networks, meant that lone mothers were uniquely vulnerable. And, as Anna Clark shows in Chapter 3, mothers of illegitimate children possessed few rights. One tragic case from late nineteenth-century Edinburgh vividly illustrates the plight of the single mother. In 1887 a young, unmarried domestic servant called Catherine Gunn, who was originally from the far north-east of Scotland, gave birth to twin boys. She immediately hired a woman at 4 shillings a week to take care of the boys 'for I was in service at the time and could not do so myself'. After eleven months Catherine Gunn was no longer able to keep up these payments and she decided to have the children informally adopted. In response to an advertisement in the newspaper, two women were paid 2 pounds to take each of the boys separately. Shortly afterwards she discovered one of her sons had been murdered by his 'adoptive mother'.[94]

Catherine Gunn's plight was symptomatic of nineteenth-century attitudes towards the family. As a domestic servant she propped up the ideal middle-class domestic family, but as a single mother with two infants she was not able to form her own familial unit. Indeed, had she attempted to obtain poor relief it is likely the twins would have been removed from her and fostered with strangers. The family model engendered by the European middle classes was more self-contained than its predecessor and more rigidly conceptualised as a conjugal unit.

The hybrid family 1900–2000

If the modern family as we imagine it was conceived in the nineteenth century, it achieved maturity in the first half of the twentieth century. In the decades before the Second World War the European family seemed immutable, the conjugal ideal was firmly established and, under fascist and conservative governments alike, it was supported and promoted. After the Second World War, however, the structure of the family changed markedly, so that what individuals recognised as family began to include multiple and various formations of kin and non-kin. The decline of the male breadwinner family since its heyday in the 1950s, and the rise of multiple family forms, including single-parent families, single-person households, cohabiting couples whether they be heterosexual or homosexual, step-families and so on, may be partially explained by changes in women's opportunities and experiences, notably their increased participation in the labour market and their decreased propensity to marry and have children. However, for most of the century, the state continued to recognise and legitimise family in its nineteenth-century middle-class guise: the nuclear family with the conjugal relationship at its core, albeit through policies which addressed specific issues such as declining birth rates, rising divorce rates and perceived deterioration in standards of mothering. Women have been essential figures in both these conceptions of the family in the twentieth century. In the eyes of European states, women were still identified primarily as wives and mothers to differing degrees, and thus dependants, when in fact this century witnessed a significant growth in women's wage-earning and a decline in fertility. In material terms then, women in the twentieth century were as much producers as reproducers, but this is not reflected in the construction of the female familial role by the state, particularly in the construction of welfare systems after the Second World War. In the twentieth century official conceptions of the family were increasingly out of step with the complicated realities of family life.

It is generally agreed that the twentieth century saw profound transformations in family life. These changes were demographic, structural and material. To begin with, European co-resident families became smaller over the course of the twentieth century. Between 1901 and 1991 household size declined. From an average of around 4.5 persons at the beginning of the century, European families contained on average between 2 and 3 persons at the end. Behind this change are a number of key demographic shifts: a decline in fertility rates, high age at marriage, rising divorce rates and a relatively high proportion of women remaining single. However, the entire period between the First World War and the 1990s should not be seen as a single entity. Broadly speaking, the period 1900–45 saw a continuation of developments that had started the previous century, that is, a continuing decline in mortality and fertility rates. The period between the end of the Second World War and the 1960s was characterised by a temporary resurgence in the popularity of marriage and a baby boom. From the 1960s onwards Europe experienced a second demographic transition characterised by a shift to continuous low fertility and a move from 'uniform to pluralistic families and households'.[95] In France, for instance, between 1968 and 1989 the proportion of single-person households rose from 20 per cent to almost 27 per cent and the proportion of married couples declined from 68 per cent to 58 per cent.[96] These shifts are consequent upon a change in the function of the family whereby it is not the well-being of the family that is important but the well-being and self-fulfilment of individuals.[97]

Women's reproductive and productive behaviour is central to this transition. At the start of the twentieth century the mean number of children per woman in western Europe ranged from a high of 5.3 in Greece to a low of 2.5 in France. In the 1990s only Ireland and Sweden exceeded 2.[98] The birth rate was already declining amongst the middle classes by the start of the century, but many working-class women were desperate to limit family size on the grounds of their own health as well as economic well-being as the survey by the Women's Co-operative Guild in England so graphically demonstrated.[99] As Diana Gittins argues in respect of England, the decline in the birth rate amongst the working classes was affected by women's choices and experiences, both before and after marriage. The opening up of new job opportunities for single women in the first decades of the century and the decline of domestic service offered women greater economic and social independence. These women were more knowledgeable about sexuality and birth control and, once married, they embraced the model of the companionate marriage which emphasised complementary roles and a degree of joint decision-making including any regarding family limitation.[100]

Having embraced the smaller family, women were unwilling to alter their behaviour in response to government inducements to have more children. When the fascist governments of Italy and Germany attempted to promote fertility and maternity by means of rather crude fiscal incentives coupled with honorific awards to mothers, they failed to reverse the fertility decline. In Italy the birth rate continued to fall throughout the Fascist era and the resort to abortion in the absence of other forms of birth control underlined women's determination to maintain their autonomy in this realm.[101] Similarly, in Franco's Spain, pro-natalist policies failed because 'motherhood and parenthood were far from being attractive to most families and were seen as an economic liability.'[102] Indeed, even in France and Britain after the Second World War where the birth rate did increase, there is little evidence that this was a direct response to state cajolements and bribes. General de Gaulle's call for French women to have 12 million healthy babies for the regeneration of the French nation, and in Britain William Beveridge's conviction that 'in the next 30 years housewives as mothers have vital work to do in ensuring the adequate continuance of the British race and of the British ideal in the world' accompanied by tax benefits and family allowances were unlikely to have been a major factor in the short-lived post-war baby boom.[103] The smaller family was now the norm – large families were disparaged – and few were willing to trade relative economic comfort (achieved on the back of women's paid work) and the ability to do one's best for one's children for a larger family and state recognition.

If women were making positive choices about marriage age and family size, one might assume that family life in the twentieth century was more woman-friendly than it had been in the past in the sense that it was supportive and enabling rather than a constraint on women's opportunities and well-being. Certainly women's economic participation rates have risen across Europe since the 1960s as family size has declined, and indeed there is a correlation between the number of children a woman has and her likelihood of working outside the home. In the European Union in 1992, 68 per cent of mothers with one child undertook paid work whereas only 45 per cent of those with three children did so.[104] However, throughout the twentieth century woman's family role remained largely unchanged and this affected women's labour force participation over the life course. Until the 1980s women's participation in paid work was determined by her childcare responsibilities. Yet, as Janssens points out, women's position in society appeared to have changed more dramatically than their position within the family. Higher labour-force participation was counter-balanced by women's continued responsibility for the organisation of family life, and this in turn influenced women's choice of work, preferring part-time employment (which is often lower paid) to full-time jobs. Hence, 'the gender inequalities in family roles are thus interconnected with inequalities in the wider society and the labour market.'[105]

In material terms, most families since the Second World War had more space, more time and more disposable income with which to conduct family life than in any previous era. The combination of improvements in housing, especially for the working classes, a reduction in working hours facilitating an increase in leisure time, and the increased availability of consumer goods and the income with which to purchase them had a profound impact on the conduct of late twentieth-century family life. Until the First World War only the middle classes had been able to pursue the new domestic family lifestyle centred upon the home. Suburbanisation, whereby residential patterns shifted to the edges of cities, was a middle-class preserve until the inter-war years and the fêted garden suburbs with their cottage-style housing were limited to the more affluent, but the design of interior and exterior space in these model towns had more far-reaching influence. The separation of cooking and eating or living areas was a departure from traditional working-class arrangements. But, by the 1920s and 1930s changing patterns of working-class housing facilitated this amongst the more affluent members of the urban working classes. The development of local-authority housing, situated some distance from places of work and planned as lower-density living space with much greater opportunity for family privacy, permitted those who had moved from overcrowded housing to experience something of the family life pioneered by the middle classes, focused upon consumption rather than production. In Germany the new Weimar constitution placed housing at the top of its priorities and entrusted municipal authorities to conduct improvements. The result was garden suburbs modelled after the English experiment, with terraced and semi-detached houses with gardens to promote healthy living.

Housing improvements were not divorced from social and gender relations. The new houses were designed to accommodate a working man, a domestic wife and their children – the conjugal family based on the male breadwinner ideal. The internal spatial organisation was predicated on the assumption that the woman of the house would be homemaker rather than wage earner. Thus, in German modernist-inspired homes the kitchen took pride of place, designed to maximise domestic efficiency and minimise drudgery, 'intended to elevate woman's domestic role to that of a competent professional in charge of her specialised workplace'.[106] Fears concerning the disruption of gender relations in the post-war economy of western Europe were transmitted onto discourses about the home and family. In Germany, for instance, women were exhorted to find satisfaction in the domestic sphere rather than in the new leisure industries. The churches, conservatives and even some feminists promoted housewifery and maternalism as antidotes to pleasure-seeking. Comments upon the leisure activities of the wife of an unemployed man in 1930 exemplify this new social discourse:

The wife is particular about her appearance, but she is pleasure-seeking and her agreeable conduct is insincere. When her pleasure-seeking does not come into conflict with her duties as a mother she cares for her children in an orderly way. Several times a week she goes to the cinema in the evening or to a dance and during this time she locks the children up.[107]

Indeed housework and childcare in the bosom of the family was promoted as the ideal form of leisure for married women and newly married women often did not expect to continue participating in leisure pursuits they had formerly enjoyed, such as visiting the cinema. Instead family-based pastimes such as knitting and handicrafts, reading and games with the children were more dominant, activities deemed compatible with work as Tammy M. Proctor explains in Chapter 9.[108] But even housework came under scrutiny.[109] Efficiency and productivity was the watchword. Housewives were urged to embrace efficiency in the home by avoiding time-wasting and by utilising the new domestic appliances. The kitchen in one of the Frankfurt housing developments was specifically designed to facilitate efficiency with the rational positioning of appliances and work surfaces. Even shopping was scrutinised by some, with women criticised for popping out several times in a day. However, few could aspire to these ideals. In inter-war Germany the provision of modern, functional housing was inadequate and only the better-off could afford domestic appliances. Moreover, despite feminist arguments that women's embrace of efficiency in the home would give them more time for self-development, in fact it more likely entrenched the sexual division of labour within the home. Images of contented family life with couples and their children spending more leisure time together were only possible if the woman's burden was lessened.

Woman's place in the family remained in the kitchen. This was her workplace. The disappearance of servants from middle-class homes necessitated that the woman of the house take over all household-management tasks, but still this work had to be separated from other parts of the house as it had been in the Victorian residences inhabited by the servant-employing classes in the nineteenth century. In the 1940s the British Medical Association condemned working families from eating their meals in the kitchen, remarking: 'The kitchen is the housewife's workplace and preparation room.'[110] Cooking and eating in the same space encouraged family disintegration, muddling family time with the work of producing and clearing up after a meal. And even as late as the 1960s, in spite of employment changes that saw more women than ever before working outside the home, a British woman's magazine proclaimed to its readers:

The kitchen has become the most important room in the house. This is the room which, more than any other, you like to keep shining and bright. A woman's place? Yes. For it is the heart and the meaning of home. The place where, day after day, you make with your hands precious gifts of love.[111]

No one had any doubts about the material improvements brought about by the move to the suburbs, but many have argued that women suffered psychologically as a result of their physical isolation and their entrapment within the hegemonic familial ideal. The notion of female 'suburban neurosis' was popularised in the USA by feminist writer Betty Friedan in *The Feminine Mystique* (1963), but similarly in western Europe the image of the isolated, vacuous and often depressed housewife is ubiquitous in media representations of family life. The French film-maker Jacques Tati's film *Mon oncle* (1954) was a satirical comment on post-war suburban life, in which the house-wife was portrayed endlessly attempting to create the perfect home not least for the benefit of her neighbours; a modern version of the nineteenth-century wives of German civil servants whose dinner parties were the ultimate artifice. Celia Johnson's portrayal of the frustrated middle-class suburban wife and mother on the verge of a love affair in the British film *Brief Encounter* (1945) was a trenchant comment on the emptiness of the post-war familial ideal and on the desire of some women to escape its constraints through exploring their sexuality.

Those working-class families that were fortunate to move into the new inter-war housing began to create a lifestyle that mirrored the domestic model pioneered by the nineteenth-century middle classes. Family and home in this context converged. Some have argued the change was most visible for men who began to invest more time and effort in their family life at home. The distance of these estates from places of work and men's physical separation from work-based leisure spaces such as the pub encouraged them to engage more in family and home-based activities such as gardening and home improvement.[112] However, there were limits in the extent to which men associated themselves with family life. There were still strict divisions between male and female housework and men often drew the line at undertaking visible or public activities they perceived would undermine their masculine identity; pushing the baby's pram is the task most often mentioned in this regard. The family was still – male housework notwithstanding – a female domain.

The greatest changes in the material conditions in family life happened after the Second World War. The large-scale destruction of housing in wartime necessitated mas-sive rebuilding programmes and a chance to further fashion family life. In Britain the construction of council housing estates in the 1950s, and then in the 1960s the encour-agement of privately financed housing and similar initiatives in social housing elsewhere, resulted in the movement of people from inner-city residential areas to new suburbs, dormitory towns and, eventually, New Towns. Many of the new dwellings were medium- and high-rise apartment buildings encapsulated in the French architect Le Corbusier's massive Marseilles housing complex. But far from safeguarding family privacy and promoting a sense of community, these housing solutions had just the opposite effect. Studies of British housing estates showed that initial responses from residents were positive, largely because of the vastly improved housing conditions and facilities. But in the longer term high-density housing proved detrimental to the kind of family life the residents aspired to, particularly in respect of the needs of children. The child-centred twentieth-century family was poorly accommodated here. The single-family home with a garden was still the most desirable model for all social classes.

The conjugal family model consisting of a married couple and their children con-tinued to inform social policy – including housing policy – well into the 1960s. Throughout the 1940s and 1950s the family continued to be represented by an ideal type consisting of husband, wife and children exhibiting a degree of togetherness through privatised leisure activities based on the home. While improvements in domes-tic facilities were slow to reach the working classes – outside toilets and the absence of water-heating technology were still ubiquitous in many working-class communities –

the appearance of home entertainment in the form of radios and televisions is said to have engendered family solidarity and communication. In Britain the television broadcast of the coronation of Queen Elizabeth in 1952 is widely recalled as one of the first family-viewing events, humorously portrayed in Kate Atkinson's novel of British family life *Behind the Scenes at the Museum*. Here, Ruby Lennox describes the family gathered in her parent's living room, above the shop in York:

> Our own Coronation guest list is not so long as the Queen's. For a start we have no Commonwealth friends to invite, although Auntie Eliza is reputed to be friendly with a couple from Jamaica – one of the many taboo subjects drawn up on a separate list by George (Auntie Eliza is George's sister-in-law, married to his brother Bill). We are also, amongst other things, forbidden to talk about Auntie Mabel's operation, Uncle Tom's hand and Adrian's weediness. Uncle Tom isn't our uncle, he's Bunty's and Auntie Bab's uncle, and has been invited here today because he has nowhere else to go – Auntie Mabel is in hospital having her unmentionable operation. (Uncle Tom's hand is a wooden replica of the one that was blown off long ago). Adrian is our cousin – Uncle Clifford and Auntie Gladys' only son . . . Lucy-Vida is our cousin, Auntie Eliza and Uncle Bill's daughter (Bunty would much rather she didn't have to invite this side of the family). Auntie Babs has also brought her husband, Uncle Sidney, with her, a mild cheerful man who we hardly ever see. The Coronation audience are constantly dividing and re-dividing into different parties and factions the most common of which is that age-old favourite – men and women. Everyone is related in some way (unfortunately) to each other except for Dandy the Dog and Mrs Havis, Nell's next-door neighbour who has no family (imagine!) of her own.[113]

By the late 1960s there was one television set for every five people in western Europe, 47 million sets in total.[114] And, in Britain at least, the image of the family watching the television was reflected back in the representation of family on the television in all kinds of programmes from sitcoms to quizzes, so that 'marriage and the nuclear family emerge perhaps battered but fundamentally unchallenged.'[115]

Yet, since the Second World War the western European family has been getting smaller on average and more simple. The most important trends contributing to this were the rise in the divorce rate, especially since the 1960s, the decline of marriage and the popularity of cohabitation, the rise in the number of one-parent families and the increase in single-person households. In France, for instance, these accounted for 27 per cent of all households in 1989; in Sweden 33 per cent of households contained only one person in 1980.[116] Many of these single-person households consist of the elderly, but younger unmarried and divorced men and women have contributed to this trend. The implications for women of this reshaping of the family are not clear-cut.

Since the 1960s, changes in the structure and size of the family have reflected women's positive choices about their lives. The decline in marriage and fertility rates, the rise in the number of women remaining childless and the increase in lone-female households suggests that women – at least those amongst the more affluent and educated classes – took advantage of improvements in education and employment prospects to gain more autonomy for themselves outwith the family. The proportion of women working outside the home rose from 49 per cent in France in 1968 to 60 per cent in 1994. In Sweden the rates are even higher at 58 per cent in the 1960s to 76 per cent in the 1990s.[117] However, it was only in the past three decades of the twentieth century that unmarried women were able to cast off the sole identification with family that had cast such a shadow over their predecessors. Until then, as Katherine Holden has argued, 'the powerful links between marriage and biological motherhood, which left the nuclear family as the sole legitimate forum for intimacy, made it harder for women publicly to acknowledge relationships which lay outside', it might be added with either women or men.[118]

On the other hand, some of the structural changes in the family have not necessarily been to women's advantage. The decline of the male-breadwinner family since the 1950s has not resulted in the rise of the so-called symmetrical family: that in which roles and responsibilities were equally shared by both sexes. Women's greater participation in paid work has not been accompanied by any significant reduction in her familial responsibilities. Indeed, even in the former East Germany, where there was massive female labour-force participation – 91 per cent in 1989 – there was no concomitant shift in the gendered division of labour within the family.[119] Feminist sociologists have long drawn attention to how women are unable to trade their educational and professional qualifications for equal advantage in the labour market because 'conjugal and family life hamper women's professional interests . . . the sex-determined difference in the management of professional careers is a corollary of the persistence of the sex-determined division of domestic and child-rearing tasks'.[120] At the end of the twentieth century women still undertook the bulk of domestic household tasks. In Norway, for instance, women spent an average of thirty hours per week on household tasks compared with men's eighteen. And as European populations become increasingly elderly it is women who take most responsibility for caring for the elderly and infirm. If they do not carry out these tasks themselves, they employ other women to do it for them. The only way many professional women manage to reconcile work and family life is by paying another woman to undertake household tasks, an ironic reversion to the nineteenth-century bourgeois family model. Men, it has been argued, 'refuse to play the egalitarian game', in part because they still identified themselves as income-earners or producers whereas women have always assumed multiple roles within the family.

Since the 1960s western European countries have witnessed the increasing separation of marriage or cohabititation and parenthood. By the 1990s in Britain 17.5 per cent of all households with dependant children were classified as lone mothers.[121] The majority of these women had not, at least initially, made a positive choice of single parenthood: two-thirds were divorced, separated or widowed. Yet in Britain there has been a reluctance by the state to acknowledge these women and their children as self-contained family units, evidenced by attempts to force absent fathers to support their children financially. And lone mothers have seen their role continually debated in terms of whether they should be working outside the home or staying at home to care for the children, in the context of a discourse on the family that implicitly regarded the two-parent conjugal family with the male breadwinner at its core as the ideal. The overwhelming evidence, of course, is that this model increasingly had little purchase at the end of the twentieth century.

The twentieth-century family was a hybrid – caught between the conservative impulses of the first half of the century and the adaptations and alternative family forms of the post-Second World War era. It would be too simple to map women's experiences onto these two phases, regarding the first as a period of constraint for women as their identification with the family and the familiar roles of housewife and mother were heightened and the second as a time of liberation as women increasingly broke free of the family as the prime locus of identification in their lives. The reduction in fertility rates has been accompanied by an intensified focus on parenting and the child-centred family at the same time as women's participation in the labour market has risen. Yet family work continues to occupy more space and time in women's lives than it does in men's and, as Gillis astutely remarks, she remains 'the symbolic centre of the frantic household'.[122]

Conclusions

Across these three centuries the family has been a constant in women's lives, providing a material and a discursive framework for women's experiences. But it should be clear from the preceding discussion that the meaning and the material reality of family changed markedly over the period indicating that far from constituting something natural and thus unchanging, the family is an historically contingent institution and concept. Accordingly then, there is nothing natural about women's relationship with the family in the past. Women's role within the family is determined by specific economic and cultural conditions. The 'common-sense' notion of the family is now beginning to disappear as historians utilise the findings of demographers, scholars of kinship and of gender, which demonstrate the variety of family forms in past times as well as the mutability of categories and definitions. More recently, the shift towards understanding the family in terms of rituals and everyday practices instead of structures has opened up a new way of thinking about the family and women's place within it.

This chapter has imposed some rather artificial frameworks on the history of the family in order to simplify and hopefully clarify our understanding of the relationship between women and family life. One of the aims of this chapter was to break the link between the family, the private sphere and women's role by demonstrating how the family has always been part of the social, embedded in the local economy and its cultural patterns. The early modern flexible family with its permeable walls and its sense of inclusivity appears to have offered women a range of roles; women were not uniquely associated with the family merely on account of their role in reproduction and their tendency to attend to the domestic sphere. While it is undoubtedly the case that the family as an economic unit offered women the greatest security, the web of familial relationships within and between households may have acted as a conduit for women to engage legitimately in a range of productive and affective relationships.

A second objective of this overview was to address the problem constituted by the nineteenth-century middle-class family model. Historians of the modern period have been guilty in the past of assigning a normative function to the private, domestic, conjugal family, in part because it is this model that endured from the early nineteenth century until the 1960s and that still has considerable purchase today at the start of the twenty-first century. The ubiquity of this image of family has constrained the ways in which historians of women have interpreted women's role in this period. The dominant belief that the family was the crucible of woman's natural role, a space where she might reveal and revel in her femininity, informed interpretations of the family that regarded it as a constraint on her opportunities. And of course there is a deal of evidence to support this view. However, one should be beware of transposing an ideal model onto material reality, and it is clear that nineteenth-century families – even amongst the middle classes – were a good deal more permeable than the ideal would suggest. The self-conscious family could only be such if it was on display.

The domestic conjugal family may have been long lived but, viewed over the *longue durée*, it appears transient and temporary. The late twentieth-century multiplication of family forms has forced a re-evaluation of the apparently normative conjugal unit although it has been pointed out that the range of differently organised families in evidence today is still defined as 'other' in relation to the conjugal 'norm', and continued debates about women's familial roles indicate that women are still primarily identified by their relation to the family, notwithstanding their productive roles. It seems there will be no return to the early modern household model, such is the cultural power of the nuclear family in modern times.

The family has always meant different things and performed different functions for women at different stages of their lives. It has provided protection and nurture, economic security and emotional support and sometimes constraints and abuse. For many women though, family has provided a space within which they could perform roles and take on responsibilities valued by women themselves.

Guide to further reading

The history of the European family has spawned a vast and sprawling literature. This guide is an introduction to some of the more recent work and especially those studies that incorporate or foreground women's experience or that take gender as a prime category of analysis.

A number of recent survey texts have pulled together some of the most prominent European historians of the family and provide a good introduction to the key issues and approaches.

Burguière, André, Christiane Klapisch-Zuber, Martine Segalen and Françoise Zonabend, eds, *A History of the Family, 2 vols,* Vol. I: *Distant Worlds, Ancient Worlds*; Vol. II: *The Impact of Modernity*. London: Polity, 1996.

Kertzer, David I. and Marzio Barbagli, eds, *The History of the European Family*, 3 vols. Vol. I: *Family Life in Early Modern Times*; Vol. II: *Family Life in the Long Nineteenth Century*; Vol. III: *Family Life in the Twentieth Century*. London: Yale University Press, 2001–3.

Beyond these collections, the following represent some of the more influential and stimulating studies.

Anderson, Michael, *Approaches to the History of the Western Family 1500–1914.* Cambridge: Cambridge University Press, 1995. Concise survey of some of the main approaches taken by historians of the European family.

Bennett, Judith M. and Amy M. Froide, eds, *Singlewomen in the European Past 1250–1800.* Philadelphia, Pa.: University of Pennsylvania Press, 1999. A useful collection of case studies focusing upon the experience of widows and spinsters in medieval and early modern Europe.

Bock, Gisela and Pat Thane, eds, *Maternity and Gender Policies: Women and the Rise of the European Welfare States 1880s-1950s.* London: Routledge, 1991. Collection analysing the relationship between feminism, welfare policies and the family in northern and western Europe.

Davidoff, Leonore, Megan Doolittle, Janet Fink and Kathleen Holden, *The Family Story: Blood, Contract and Intimacy, 1830–1960*. London: Longman, 1999. A new approach to family history in England which places a series of familial and contractual relationships in the home, the household and the kin group at the heart of the analysis.

Davidoff, Leonore and Catherine Hall, *Family Fortunes: Men and Women of the English Middle Class 1780–1850*. London: Routledge, 1987. Classic study of middle-class formation with the family and gender roles at its heart.

Evans, Richard J. and W. R. Lee, eds, *The German Family*. London: Routledge, 1981. Collection of case studies illuminating the construction and experience of family in modern Germany.

Flandrin, Jean-Louis, *Families in Former Times: Kinship, Household and Sexuality*. Cambridge: Cambridge University Press, 1979. Traditional study of the variety of familial relationships in a European context.

Gillis, John, *A World of Their Own Making: A History of Myth and Ritual in Family Life*. Oxford: Oxford University Press, 1997. Stimulating history of family life in Europe and North America which argues that the myths of family and family life bear little relation to how family was lived in the past.

Gordon, Eleanor and Gwyneth Nair, *Public Lives: Women, Family and Society in Victorian Britain*. London: Yale University Press, 2003. Study of women, gender relations and the family amongst the Glasgow middle classes.

Hardwick, Julie, *The Practice of Patriarchy: Gender and the Politics of Household Authority in Early Modern France*. Pennsylvania, Pa.: Pennsylvania State University Press, 1998. Study of the early modern French household focusing upon gendered networks and strategies and how these translated into power relationships.

Hufton, Olwen, 'Women without Men: Widows and Spinsters in Britain and France in the Eighteenth Century', *Journal of Family History* 9 (1984), pp. 355–76. Comparative analysis of the situation of unmarried women in early modern society.

Kertzer, David I., *Family Life in Central Italy, 1880–1910: Sharecropping, Wage Labour and Coresidence*. New Brunswick, NJ: Rutgers University Press, 1984. A study of demography and kinship focused upon families and households in Bologna.

Kertzer, David I. and Richard P. Saller, eds, *The Family in Italy: From Antiquity to the Present*. London: Yale University Press, 1991. Wide range of articles adopting historical and anthropological perspectives on the Italian family, from inheritance and child-rearing to marriage and household formation.

Liu, Tessie, *The Weaver's Knot: The Contradictions of Class Struggle and Family Solidarity in Western France, 1750–1914*. Ithaca, NY: Cornell University Press, 1994. The story of the household economy in a French handloom-weaving district illustrating the differential impact of industrialisation on men and women in the family.

Roberts, Elizabeth, *A Woman's Place: An Oral History of Working-Class Women, 1890–1940*. Oxford: Blackwell, 1985. Classic early study of the roles of working-class women in north-west England.

Roberts, Elizabeth, *Women and Families: An Oral History, 1940–1970*. Oxford: Blackwell, 1995. Sequel to *A Woman's Place*, returns to the same communities and analyses shifts in the relationship between women, the family and the community in the post-war period.

Peplar, Michael, *Family Matters: A History of Ideas about Family since 1945*. London: Longman, 2002. A book which focuses on debates about the family in Britain as they were exercised through a range of agencies and media including the state, film, television and personal testimony.

Ross, Ellen, *Love and Toil: Motherhood in Outcast London, 1870–1918*. Oxford: Oxford University Press, 1993. A study of working-class motherhood focusing upon the family and women's roles as wives, mothers, managers and workers.

Sabean, David, *Property, Production and Family in Neckarhausen, 1700–1870*. Cambridge:

Cambridge University Press, 1990. A close historical-anthropological study of household relations in southern Germany at a time of economic and social change.

Sabean, David, *Kinship in Neckarhausen, 1700–1870*. Cambridge: Cambridge University Press, 1998. Follow up to *Property, Production and Family in Neckarhausen, 1700–1870* focusing upon kinship.

Sarti, Raffàella, *Europe at Home: Family and Material Culture, 1500–1800*. London: Yale University Press, 2002. Wide-ranging and detailed picture of how European families lived at home, dealing with material goods, diet, clothing, property, customs and family life.

Seccombe, Wally, *A Millennium of Family Change: Feudalism to Capitalism in Northwestern Europe*. London: Verso, 1992. Ambitious work of historical sociology which analyses the adaptation of the family to the changing economy from pre-industrial times, through proto-industrialisation to the industrial revolution.

Seccombe, Wally, *Weathering the Storm: Working-Class Families from the Industrial Revolution to the Fertility Decline*. London: Verso, 1993. Argues the traditional or nuclear family was a creation of the industrial revolution.

Segalen, Martine, *Love and Power in the Peasant Family: Rural France in the Nineteenth Century*. Oxford: Blackwell, 1983. A work of historical anthropology using a range of sources from proverbs to material culture to illuminate the gendered nature of familial relations in rural France.

Shorter, Edward, *The Making of the Modern Family*. London: Basic Books, 1976. Influential and much-criticised analysis of the impact of modernisation on the family.

Smith, Bonnie, *Ladies of the Leisure Class: The Bourgeoisie of Northern France in the Nineteenth Century*. Princeton, NJ: Princeton University Press, 1981. A study of the ways in which bourgeois women created a form of domesticity which met their own needs centred on the home and family.

Tadmor, Naomi, *Family and Friends in Eighteenth Century England: Household, Kinship and Patronage*. Cambridge: Cambridge University Press, 2001. A new way of thinking about family and kin based on literary sources.

Tilly, Louise A. and Joan W. Scott, *Women, Work and Family*. London: Routledge, 1987, originally 1979. Early classic analysis of the relationship between work and family and the impact on women's lives in a Europe undergoing economic transformation.

Tilly, Louise A., 'Women's History and Family History: Fruitful Collaboration or Missed Connection', *Journal of Family History* 12 (1987), pp. 303–15. A useful discussion of the relationship between the two fields of family and women's history.

Willson, Perry, ed., *Gender, Family and Sexuality: The Private Sphere in Italy, 1860–1945*. Basingstoke: Palgrave Macmillan, 2004. A collection of articles which provides much needed analysis of the relationship between gender and the family in modern Italy.

Notes

1 Leonore Davidoff, Megan Doolittle, Janet Fink and Katherine Holden, *The Family Story: Blood, Contract and Intimacy, 1830–1960* (London: Longman, 1999), p. 5.
2 Frances Power Cobbe, 'The Duties of Women' (1881) quoted in John Gillis, *A World of Their Own Making: A History of Myth and Ritual in Family Life* (Oxford: Oxford University Press, 1997), p. 123.
3 Davidoff et al., *The Family Story*, p. 7.
4 Raffàella Sarti, *Europe at Home: Family and Material Culture, 1500–1800* (London and New Haven, Conn.: Yale University Press, 2002), p. 36.
5 See John Byng-Hall interviewed by Paul Thompson, 'The Power of Family Myths' in Raphael Samuel and Paul Thompson, eds, *The Myths We Live By* (London: Routledge, 1990), pp. 216–24.
6 Gillis, *A World of Their Own Making*, p. xv.

7 Davidoff et al., *The Family Story*, pp. 3–4.
8 I am grateful to my second cousin once removed, Edward Jay, for this episode in my family history.
9 Louise A. Tilly, 'Women's History and Family History: Fruitful Collaboration or Missed Connection', *Journal of Family History* 12 (1987), pp. 303–15.
10 Alison Mackinnon, 'Were Women Present at the Demographic Transition? Questions from a Feminist Historian to Historical Demographers', *Gender & History* 7 (1995), pp. 222–40.
11 See Edward Shorter, *The Making of the Modern Family* (London: Basic Books, 1976); Lawrence Stone, *The Family, Sex and Marriage in England 1500–1800* (Harmondsworth: Penguin, 1977).
12 For example, see Louise A. Tilly and Joan W. Scott, *Women, Work and Family* (London: Routledge, 1987).
13 Tessie Liu, 'What Price a Weaver's Dignity? Gender Inequality and the Survival of Home-Based Production in Industrial France', in Laura L. Frader and Sonya O. Rose, eds, *Gender and Class in Modern Europe* (Ithaca, NY: Cornell University Press, 1986), pp. 57–76.
14 Leonore Davidoff and Catherine Hall, *Family Fortunes: Men and Women of the English Middle Class, 1780–1850* (London: Routledge, 1987), here p. 321.
15 Ellen Ross, *Love and Toil: Motherhood in Outcast London, 1870–1918* (Oxford: Oxford University Press, 1993); Bonnie Smith, *Ladies of the Leisure Class: The Bourgeoisie of Northern France in the Nineteenth Century* (Princeton, NJ: Princeton University Press, 1981).
16 See Temma Kaplan, 'Female Consciousness and Collective Action: The Case of Barcelona 1910–18', *Signs*, 7 (1982), pp. 545–66.
17 Sarti, *Europe at Home*, p. 2.
18 Martine Segalen, 'Material Conditions of Family Life', in David I. Kertzer and Marzo Barbagli, eds, *Family Life in the Long Nineteenth Century 1789–1913* (London and New Haven, Conn.: Yale University Press, 2002), p. 6.
19 Gillis, *A World of Their Own Making*, pp. 63–4.
20 ibid., p. 72.
21 See D. H. J. Morgan, *Family Connections: An Introduction to Family Studies* (Cambridge: Polity Press, 1996).
22 Janet Fink, 'Questions of Care', in Janet Fink, ed., *Care: Personal Lives and Social Policy* (Bristol: The Policy Press, 2004).
23 United Kingdom, *Census, 1881* (Zetland).
24 Elizabeth Roberts, *A Woman's Place: An Oral History of Working-Class Women 1890–1940* (Oxford: Blackwell, 1984); *Women and Families: An Oral History, 1940–1970* (Oxford: Blackwell, 1995).
25 Staatsarchiv Hamburg, Niedergericht 489: Wehsel, 24 September 1830; Präturen 211–6, II B 171: Beil 1879. See Lynn Abrams, 'Companionship and Conflict: The Negotiation of Marriage Relations in Nineteenth-Century Germany', in Lynn Abrams and Elizabeth Harvey, eds, *Gender Relations in German History* (London: UCL Press, 1996), pp. 101–20.
26 Kristin E. Gager, *Blood Ties and Fictive Ties: Adoption and Family Life in Early Modern France* (Princeton, NJ: Princeton University Press, 1996).
27 Catherina Lis and Hugo Soly, *Disordered Lives: Eighteenth Century Families and their Unruly Relatives* (Oxford: Polity, 1996).
28 Naomi Tadmor, *Family and Friends in Eighteenth-Century England: Household, Kinship, Patronage* (Cambridge: Cambridge University Press, 2001).
29 Michael Peplar, *Family Matters: A History of Ideas about Family since 1945* (London: Longman, 2002), pp. 68–99.
30 Mary-Jo Maynes, 'Class Cultures and Images of Proper Family Life', in Kertzer and Barbagli, eds, *Family Life in the Long Nineteenth Century*, p. 194.
31 Johnson quoted in Tadmor, *Family and Friends*, p. 19.
32 Gillis, *A World of Their Own Making*, p. 13.
33 J. I. Guyer, 'Household and Community in African Studies', *African Studies Review* 24 (1981), pp. 87–137, here p. 89.

34 Jean-Louis Flandrin, *Families in Former Times: Kinship, Household and Sexuality* (Cambridge: Cambridge University Press, 1979), p. 4.
35 Wally Seccombe, *A Millennium of Family Change: Feudalism to Capitalism in Northwestern Europe* (London: Verso, 1992), p. 30.
36 Julie Hardwick, *The Practice of Patriarchy: Gender and the Politics of Household Authority in Early Modern France* (Pennsylvania, Pa.: Pennsylvania State University Press, 1998), p. 87.
37 op. cit., pp. 93–4.
38 David Sabean, *Property, Production and Family in Neckarhausen, 1700–1870* (Cambridge: Cambridge University Press, 1990), p. 111.
39 op. cit., p. 114.
40 Caroline B. Brettell, 'Property, Kinship and Gender: A Mediterranean Perspective', in David I. Kertzer and Richard P. Saller, eds, *The Family in Italy: From Antiquity to the Present* (London and New Haven, Conn.: Yale University Press, 1991), pp. 340–53, here pp. 341–9.
41 Sabean, *Property and Production*, pp. 163–82.
42 Marion W. Gray, *Productive Men, Reproductive Women: The Agrarian Household and the Emergence of Separate Spheres during the Enlightenment* (Oxford: Berghahn, 2000), pp. 59–79.
43 Quoted in Tilly and Scott, *Women, Work and Family*, p. 53.
44 See Chapter 5 of this volume for a more extensive examination of the sexual division of labour.
45 Martine Segalen, *Love and Power in the Peasant Family: Rural France in the Nineteenth Century* (Oxford: Blackwell 1983), p. 108.
46 Hardwick, *Practice of Patriarchy*, pp. 94–100.
47 Sabean, *Property, Production and Family*, pp. 166–74; Sylvia Möhle, *Ehekonflikte und sozialer Wandel: Göttingen 1740–1840* (Frankfurt: Campus, 1997), pp. 115–18.
48 Seccombe, *Millennium of Family Change*, p. 207.
49 See Jean H. Quataert, 'Teamwork in Saxon Homeweaving Families in the Nineteenth Century', in Ruth-Ellen Boetcher Joeres and Mary Jo Maynes, eds, *German Women in the Eighteenth and Nineteenth Centuries* (Bloomington, Ind.: Indiana University Press, 1986).
50 See for example, Sonya O. Rose, *Limited Livelihoods: Gender and Class in Nineteenth-Century England* (London: Routledge, 1992).
51 Tessie Liu, *The Weaver's Knot: The Contradictions of Class Struggle and Family Solidarity in Western France, 1750–1914* (Ithaca, NY: Cornell University Press, 1994).
52 Anna Cento Bull, 'The Lombard Silk-Spinners in the Nineteenth Century: An Industrial Workforce in a Rural Setting', in Zygmunt G. Baranski and Shirley W. Vinall, eds, *Women and Italy: Essays on Gender, Culture and History* (Basingstoke: Macmillan, 1991), pp. 11–42.
53 Pierre Bourdieu, *Outline of a Theory of Practice* (Cambridge: Cambridge University Press, 1977), pp. 33–43.
54 Hardwick, *Practice of Patriarchy*, p. 176.
55 For examples of this in practice see Roderick Phillips, 'Gender Solidarities in Late Eighteenth Century Urban France: The Example of Rouen', *Histoire Sociale – Social History*, 13 (1980), pp. 325–37; Lynn Abrams, 'Martyrs or Matriarchs? Working-Class Women's Experience of Marriage in Germany before the First World War', *Women's History Review* 1 (1992), pp. 357–76.
56 Priscilla Wakefield (1798) in Bridget Hill, *Women Alone: Spinsters in England 1660–1850* (New Haven, Conn. and London: Yale University Press, 2001), p. 67.
57 Olwen Hufton, 'Women without Men: Widows and Spinsters in Britain and France in the Eighteenth Century', *Journal of Family History* 9 (1984), pp. 355–76, here p. 355.
58 Slater quoted in Pamela Sharpe, 'Dealing with Love: The Ambiguous Independence of the Single Woman in Early Modern England', *Gender & History* 11 (1999), pp. 209–32, here p. 210.
59 Shetland Archives, 3/2/19/2: Joan Williamson.
60 Tim Meldrum, *Domestic Service and Gender 1660–1750: Life and Work in the London Household* (London: Longman, 2000), pp. 14–15.

61 G. E. Fussell and K. R. Fussell, *The English Countrywoman* (1953) in Hill, *Women Alone*, p. 19.
62 M. Stavenuiter, 'Last Years of Life: Changes in the Living and Working Arrangements of Elderly People in Amsterdam in the Second Half of the Nineteenth Century', *Continuity and Change* 11 (1996), pp. 217–24.
63 Hill, *Women Alone*, pp. 54–66.
64 Sharpe, 'Dealing with Love', p. 226.
65 Gillis, *A World of Their Own Making*, p. 10.
66 op. cit., p. xviii.
67 Martine Segalen, 'The Family in the Industrial Revolution', in André Burguière, Christiane Klapisch-Zuber, Martine Segalen and Françoise Zonabend, eds, *A History of the Family*. Vol. II: *The Impact of Modernity* (Oxford: Polity, 1996), p. 393.
68 John Ruskin, quoted in Gillis, *A World of Their Own Making*, p. 116.
69 Vicomte de Bonald, 'De l'éducation des femmes' (1802) in Susan Groag Bell and Karen M. Offen, eds, *Women, the Family and Freedom: The Debate in Documents*, Vol. I: *1750–1880* (Stanford, Calif., Stanford University Press, 1983), p. 89.
70 Smith, *Ladies of the Leisure Class*, p. 10.
71 Davidoff and Hall, *Family Fortunes*, pp. 279–89.
72 Segalen, 'The Family in the Industrial Revolution', pp. 394–5.
73 Eleanor Gordon and Gwyneth Nair, *Public Lives: Women, Family and Society in Victorian Britain* (London and New Haven, Conn.: Yale University Press, 2003), pp. 156–61.
74 Sibylle Meyer, 'The Tiresome Work of Conspicuous Leisure: On the Domestic Duties of the Wives of Civil Servants in the German Empire (1871–1918), in Marilyn Boxer and Jean Quataert, eds, *Connecting Spheres*, 2nd edn (Oxford: Oxford University Press, 2000), pp. 185–93.
75 Isabella Beeton, *Book of Household Management* (London, 1861).
76 Staatsarchiv Hamburg, N 3000: Dethgens, 15.12.1871.
77 Stirling Archive Services, PD 41/1/1: Whinwell Children's Home Annual Report, 1907. Emphasis in original.
78 Memorial, Ranworth Church, Norfolk.
79 Quoted in Ann Taylor Allan, *Feminism and Motherhood in Germany 1800–1914* (New Brunswick, NJ: Rutgers University Press, 1991), p. 17
80 Loftur Guttormsson, 'Parent–Child Relations', in Kertzer and Barbagli, eds, *Family Life in the Long Nineteenth Century*, p. 270.
81 Sir James Crichton Browne (1902) quoted in Anna Davin, *Growing Up Poor: Home, School and Street in London 1870–1914* (London: Rivers Oram Press, 1996), p. 32.
82 Wally Seccombe, *Weathering the Storm: Working-Class Families from the Industrial Revolution to the Fertility Decline* (London: Verso, 1993), p. 146.
83 *L'Atelier* (1844) in Bell and Offen, eds, *Women, the Family and Freedom*, pp. 230–1.
84 Anna Clark, *The Struggle for the Breeches: Gender and the Making of the British Working Class* (London: Rivers Oram Press, 1995), p. 247.
85 Maynes, 'Class Cultures', p.195.
86 Gillis, *A World of Their Own Making*, p. 104.
87 Linda Fleming, 'Jewish Women in Glasgow *c.* 1880–1950: Gender, Ethnicity and the Immigrant Experience', PhD thesis, Glasgow University, 2005, p. 178.
88 Chaim Bermant, *The Walled Garden: The Saga of Jewish Life and Tradition* (New York: Macmillan, 1975) pp. 141–2.
89 Although as Clark makes clear in Chapter 4 of this volume, lesbian partnerships existed in a twilight zone at this time, hardly an accepted alternative to heterosexual marriage.
90 Gordon and Nair, *Public Lives*, pp. 38–40.
91 op. cit., pp. 169–70.
92 Michael Anderson, *Family Structure in Nineteenth Century Lancashire* (Cambridge: Cambridge University Press, 1971), p. 144.
93 Gay L. Gullickson, *Spinners and Weavers of Auffay: Rural Industry and the Sexual Division of Labour in a French Village, 1750–1850* (Cambridge: Cambridge University Press, 1986), pp. 174–5.

94 National Archives of Scotland, AD 14/89/146: Precognitions in case of Jessie King, 6 November 1888.

95 Quoted in Theo Engelen, 'Transition Prolonged: Demographic Aspects of the European Family', in David I. Kertzer and Marzio Barbagli, eds, *Family Life in the Twentieth Century* (London and New Haven, Conn.: Yale University Press, 2003), p. 306.

96 Martine Segalen and Françoise Zonabend, 'Families in France', in Burguière, et al., *History of the Family*, p. 504.

97 Quoted in Engelen, 'Transition Prolonged', p. 306.

98 Barbagli and Kertzer, 'Introduction' in Kertzer and Barbagli, eds, *Family Life in the Twentieth Century*, p. xxii.

99 Margaret Llewelyn Davies, *Maternity: Letters from Working Women* (orig. 1915, London: Virago, 1978).

100 Diana Gittins, *Fair Sex, Family Size and Structure, 1900–39* (London: Hutchinson, 1982), pp. 182–3.

101 Chiara Saraceno, 'Redefining Maternity and Paternity: Gender, Pronatalism and Social Policies in Fascist Italy', in Gisela Bock and Pat Thane, eds, *Maternity and Gender Policies: Women and the Rise of the European Welfare States, 1880s-1950s* pp. 196–212; Perry Willson, 'Flowers for the Doctor: Pronatalism and Abortion in Fascist Milan', *Modern Italy*, 2 (1996), pp. 44–62.

102 Mary Nash, 'Pronatalism and Motherhood in Franco's Spain', in Bock and Thane, eds, *Maternity and Gender Policies*, p. 175.

103 Karen Offen, 'Body Politics: Women, Work and the Politics of Motherhood in France, 1920–1950', in Bock and Thane, eds, *Maternity and Gender Policies* , pp. 138–59; *Report on Social Insurance and Allied Services (Beveridge Report)*, Cmd 6404, (HMSO, 1942).

104 François de Singly and Vincenzo Cicchelli, 'Contemporary Families: Social Reproduction and Personal Fulfillment', in Kertzer and Barbagli, eds, *Family Life in the Twentieth Century*, p. 323.

105 Angélique Janssens, 'Economic Transformation, Women's Work, and Family Life', in Kertzer and Barbagli, eds, *Family Life in the Twentieth Century*, p. 109.

106 Denise Lawrence-Zuniga, 'Material Conditions of Family Life', in Kertzer and Barbagli, eds, *Family Life in the Twentieth Century*, p. 19.

107 Alice Salomon and Marie Baum, eds, *Das Familienleben in der Gegenwart: 182 Familienmonographen* (Berlin: Deutschen Akademie für soziale und pädagogische Frauenarbeit, 1930), p. 346.

108 Claire Langhamer, *Women's Leisure in England 1920–60* (Manchester: Manchester University Press, 2000), pp. 174–80.

109 'More Free Time for the Woman' (1927) in Mary Nolan, 'Housework Made Easy: The Taylorised Housewife in Weimar Germany's Rationalised Economy', *Feminist Studies*, 16 (1999), p. 571.

110 Quoted in Davidoff et al., *The Family Story*, pp. 202–3.

111 Quoted in Gillis, *A World of Their Own Making*, p. 129.

112 See Joanna Bourke, *Working-Class Cultures in Britain, 1890–1960* (London: Routledge, 1994), pp. 81–97.

113 Kate Atkinson, *Behind the Scenes at the Museum* (London: Black Swan, 1995), pp. 79–80. Used by permission of the Random House Group Limited.

114 Lawrence-Zuniga, 'Material Conditions of Family Life', p. 29.

115 Peplar, *Family Matters*, p. 98.

116 Segalen and Zonabend, 'Families in France', p. 504; Engelen, 'A Transition Prolonged', p. 303.

117 de Singly and Cicchelli, 'Contemporary Families', p. 323.

118 Davidoff et al. *The Family Story*, p. 242.

119 Christine von Oertzen and Almut Rietzschel, 'Comparing the Post-War Germanies: Breadwinner Ideology and Women's Employment in the Divided Nation', in Angélique Janssens, ed., *The Rise and Decline of the Male Breadwinner Family* (Cambridge: Cambridge University Press, 1997), p. 175.

120 de Singly and Cicchelli, 'Contemporary families', p. 323.

121 Jane Lewis and Kathleen Kiernan, 'The Boundaries between Marriage, Nonmarriage and Parenthood: Changes in Behaviour in Postwar Britain', *Journal of Family History*, 21 (1996), p. 380.

122 Gillis, *A World of Their Own Making*, p. 236.

3

FEMALE SEXUALITY

Anna Clark

Introduction

Female sexuality is one of the most difficult subjects in women's history, because female sexual desire has been both invisible and all too visible. Instances of transgressive female sexuality, such as the prostitute, the lesbian, or the unmarried mother, often attract much public attention, as moralists fear they will undermine the social order. Yet these images have more to do with fantasies and anxieties than they do with women's experiences. It is harder to gain access to women's accounts of their own desires or experiences, since sexual issues are so often clouded by shame and secrecy.

Female sexual pleasure has always been highly shaped by social forces. We know that women have long tried to control their fertility through abstinence and abortion, but relatively reliable birth control only appeared in the late nineteenth century and it took a century of struggle for it to become widely available. The structure of the economy has shaped the age at which men and women could marry, due to inheritance patterns and waged work. Above all, attitudes towards and experiences of female sexual desire varied tremendously by class and race.

But people do not simply respond to economic structures in determining their sexual practices, of course. Cultural forms shaped how women understood their sexual desires, such as popular songs, education, religious and family attitudes. Changing attitudes towards female sexuality also derived from wider intellectual and political concerns. Changing mores concerning female sexuality shaped how doctors interpreted new knowledge about sexual pleasure and fertility. Even through the twentieth century, psychiatrists and doctors continued to debate the consequences of female anatomy for women's pleasure.

Authorities often feared that female sexual desires would become uncontrollable, endangering the sanctity of marriage and the social order in general. They experimented with different kinds of laws, institutions and regulations to manage women perceived as promiscuous. Controlling female sexuality also helped define the boundaries of race during the imperial era. Since sexual desire has often been seen as an uncontrollable emotion, it becomes a metaphor for various kinds of social and political disorder. Generalised anxiety about social change often focused on the figure of the immoral woman. But women's movements also made female sexual autonomy a centrepiece of their struggles, protesting against sexual exploitation, although questions of prostitution and abortion also divided feminists.

As this chapter will demonstrate, the modern era, from the eighteenth century onwards, represented a significant shift in experiences of and attitudes towards female sexuality. The first section concerns the eighteenth century. The long-held attitudes that female sexual desire was voracious and female sexual pleasure necessary for conception were challenged by new medical developments. A new image of the unmarried mother as a victim of male lust began to compete with the older image of the disorderly woman as the new institutions failed to control illegitimacy and prostitution. Sexuality became a political issue in the controversies that led up to the French Revolution, as libertinism and sentiment contended in philosophical debates. By the early nineteenth century, another revolution became more apparent: the demographic revolution. Beginning in the mid-eighteenth century, fertility, both illegitimate and legitimate, began to explode, but contemporary awareness of this problem only began around 1800. Working-class and middle-class women experienced sexuality in very different ways, for sexual morality differed dramatically by class. Even the experience of women who desired other women varied by class, for we have evidence of working-class crossdressers and female husbands and traces of erotic desire among Victorian middle-class women's passionate friendships. But it was prostitution, not lesbianism, that excited the concerns of nineteenth-century governments, who instituted a new system of registration and regulation in an effort to control venereal disease. In response, sections of the women's movement demanded the abolition of the regulation system, beginning an explosion of political concern about sexuality which spread to cover birth control and the sexual exploitation of children as well. The last section begins in the 1890s, when sex radicals and sexologists also began to pioneer new ways of thinking about sex. After the First World War, sexual freedom became emblematic of modernity, of the new culture of consumption, but this freedom also alarmed many people, especially as the birth rate dropped dramatically. Nationalist movements made natalism a central political concern, and totalitarian governments, such as Stalin's Soviet Union and Nazi Germany, clamped down on birth control and abortion for racist eugenic reasons. After the Second World War, continuing government control over sexuality was challenged by new liberation movements, such as feminism, the gay and lesbian movement and the New Left.

Historiography and theory

Sexual desire is not a natural, biological drive, unchanging through history; rather, the diverse emotions which constitute sexual desire are stimulated, created and constructed by social formations. Sociologists writing about 'sexual scripts' bolstered this insight by suggesting that people learn how to be heterosexual through the social messages of education and popular culture. Feminist psychoanalytic theory, adopting the insights of Freud while rejecting his misogynist and biologistic elements, promised to explore fantasy, desire and the unconscious. However, psychoanalytic theory is very difficult to apply historically because the formation of sexual attachments, and adult desires and fantasies, varied so much in different time periods.

It was feminists who pioneered the idea of the social construction of sexuality as the women's liberation movement tried to deconstruct the conventions of female desire. Feminists began to stress women's vulnerability to sexual exploitation, writing about rape and seduction. Activists against pornography such as Sheila Jeffreys sought precedents among the social-purity campaigners of the late nineteenth century, who warned of the dangers of untrammelled male desire.[1] By the early 1980s, other feminist historians such as Judith Walkowitz began to fear that the stress on sexual danger drowned out the voices of nineteenth-century women who asserted women's right to sexual pleasure.[2] In her survey of English feminist debates about sex in the late nineteenth century, Lucy Bland pointed out that both pleasure and danger must be considered.[3]

Historians have also debated the chronology of changes in attitudes towards female sexuality. For instance, in the pre-modern period, it was popularly thought that female genitals were just like those of males, but turned inside out. This was the central argument of one of the most influential books on sexuality in the past fifteen years, *Making Sex*. In this book, Thomas W. Laqueur argues that this idea derived from the ancient Greek scientist Galen. In diagrams, Galenic tracts compared the testicles to the ovaries, and the vagina to the penis, as if it were inverted. As a result, the masculine and feminine sex drives were seen as comparable in strength. Furthermore, the female orgasm was seen as necessary for conception.[4] However, several historians have argued that Laqueur ignores the long existence of competing ideas of female sexual organs as different from those of men. Aristotle's idea that female orgasm was not necessary for conception remained influential in many circles. He believed that the sperm contained a homunculus, or germ of the human being, so that the mother merely incubated the foetus.[5] Nonetheless, it is clear that the transition between the eighteenth century and the nineteenth century represented a turning point in attitudes towards female sexuality. If women's sexual pleasure was not necessary for conception, female desire would be downplayed. Nancy Cott suggested that 'passionlessness' could be quite useful to women, enabling them to assert moral superiority and rationality; by claiming sexlessness, they also had an excuse to say 'no' to their husbands and avoid unwanted pregnancies.[6]

Victorians had long been thought of as embodying sexual repression. However, some historians believed this was a myth that they needed to refute. Peter Gay, for instance, argued that behind her prudish exterior the Victorian woman really enjoyed sex, but he concentrated on a few middle-class women and men.[7] On a more sophisticated theoretical note, Michel Foucault pointed out that the myth of Victorian sexual repression depended on an understanding of sexuality as a force of nature, which could be repressed or bottled up but which would bubble up under this pressure into prostitution or be sublimated into neurosis. In contrast, he insisted that the Victorian era did not witness a repression of sex but a proliferation of discourses about sexuality.[8]

Foucault focused on medical and psychiatric discourses that constructed sexuality as a form of knowledge and as an identity. Foucault's argument that sexual discourses must be understood as a form of socially constructed knowledge has been very fruitful. Historians of the body found that during the scientific revolution, anatomists did not simply 'discover' facts about sexual organs and reproduction; rather, even their empirical investigations and depictions of the body were utterly shaped by their culturally specific understandings of gender difference. Psychoanalytic theory, for instance, could be seen as just another discourse shaped by the cultural maelstrom of late nineteenth-century Vienna. However, when analysing discourses, historians must ask who read them and what impact they had. The writings of doctors and sexologists that constituted the Foucauldian discourse were not available to the general public, especially women and working-class people, and popular sexual writings in England tended to advocate sexual restraint rather than pleasure. Feminists have also criticised Foucault for ignoring gender in his theories.

Hera Cook has recently asserted that, in England at least, late Victorian people *were* sexually repressed. In mid-Victorian England, middle-class men could indulge their sexual desires with prostitutes, but middle-class women were warned to constrain their desires. By the end of the century, however, this repression spread to men: as she writes, 'there appears to have been considerable female and some male ignorance of physical sexual activity along with diminishing mutual sexual pleasure.'[9] If the idea of the social construction of sexuality is to be taken seriously, sexual repression is a possibility. Cook's idea of sexual repression differs from the old Freudian notion that if sex desire is not expressed, it will be sublimated and will ooze out in a more neurotic form. Instead, she demonstrates how social constraints, family upbringing, the censorship of sexual information, the lack of good birth-control methods and the advocacy of sexual self-control all constructed a negative attitude towards sexuality.

But Foucault was also interested in 'governmentality': how institutional discourses studied, managed and regulated populations by creating identities such as the prostitute. Although Foucault briefly mentioned the 'hysterical woman' and the Malthusian couple as two of the four key figures in discourses of sexuality, he did not explore the way in which gender relations shaped these discourses. In part, this was because he rejected the idea of any overarching structure of domination, such as male power; instead, he regarded discourses of sexuality as dispersed among multiple nodes of power – not only the state, but also institutions of civil society, such as philanthropy. Judith Walkowitz more successfully applied a gender analysis to this theory in her study of the regulation of prostitution in nineteenth-century England. Only the female prostitute became the subject of discourses and regulation; male soldiers, their customers, escaped the disciplinary apparatus. Foucault's theory of multiple nodes of power, therefore, needs to account for the persistence of the double standard and modes of regulating sexuality that affected women much more harshly than men.

Foucault was also interested in the way discourses constructed modern identities. Before the late nineteenth century, he claimed, authorities punished sinful or criminal sexual acts, but they did not regard the people who committed them as distinct personality types. The new sexological discourses invented the modern sexual identities of heterosexual or homosexual, regarding sexual desires as revealing the innermost truth about our beings. Foucault therefore made a great conceptual leap forwards by differentiating between sexual acts and sexual identities. He profoundly changed the history of homosexuality. Rather than searching for gay or lesbian people in the past, historians began to insist that gay or lesbian identities did not exist before the modern period; instead, acts and desires were much more fluid. Working independently, lesbian historians such as Lillian Faderman came to similar conclusions, arguing that in the eighteenth and nineteenth century, women engaged in passionate romantic friendships without suspicion, only coming under attack when sexologists promulgated the lesbian stereotype.[10]

Other historians have suggested that the distinction between acts and identities cannot be mapped onto a pre-modern–modern divide. Sexual identities did exist before the modern period, such as the effeminate sodomite or the prostitute; these people were not just seen as committing certain sexual acts, rather, their sexual behaviour created a social identity. However, identity in the pre-modern period was not the same as our modern notion of an innermost essence, but more likely to be defined by social relationships. Judith Butler's theory of gender performativity also enabled theorists and historians to undercut the stability of heterosexual identity. The gender identity of 'woman' is not natural, she argued, but a performance that must be repeated over and over and that can never be perfected. Furthermore, normative identities incorporate the deviant. Butler suggests that while heterosexual women renounce their attraction to other women, they identify with them: 'the 'straight woman *becomes* the woman she "never" loved.'[11]

Yet we still need concepts to understand those sexual practices and desires which did not constitute identities, but which could not be reduced to acts, which were not seen as normative yet were not utterly deviant. For instance, many women sold sex part-time without defining themselves as prostitutes; for them, commercial sex was a 'twilight moment' which may have been shameful but which did not change their work identities as needlewomen or milliners. Similarly, we need to understand discourses that were not openly articulated, that may have been only half-understood or euphemistic. For instance, abortionists advertised in nineteenth-century newspapers that they could bring on blocked menstrual periods; women whispered to neighbours what this meant. These could be termed 'twilight discourses', shadowy and secret.[12]

Sources

Peering through the murky twilight can also serve as a metaphor for the difficulties historians face in tracing past sexual attitudes and experiences. Sexuality poses great problems of evidence for the historian, for sex tends to take place in the twilight, and historians must peer through the dim light of the past to discern people's experiences, feelings and attitudes. Heterosexual sex is the easiest to trace when it produces babies, for the birth rate can be traced through parish registers and censuses, which indicate legitimate and illegitimate fertility rates. Demographic information is very valuable in uncovering past sexual behaviour, because it surveys a large number of lower-class people whose lives went unrecorded by diaries and letters; it can also refute common stereotypes. However, demographic statistics cannot explain the reasons for such behaviour. Demographers attempted to correlate changes in sexual behaviour with other measurable phenomena, such as urbanisation or industrialisation. Although hardship clearly had an effect on illegitimacy rates, demographers often found that cultural factors could outweigh economic structures. Case records from foundling hospitals and penitentiaries where prostitutes were incarcerated provide more information about individual women's lives, but the institutional context of these sources must always be taken into account by asking how professional discourses shaped responses. Court records about rape also hint at the prevalence of sexual violence, although most assaults were never reported. Since lesbianism was not illegal in most countries, however, we cannot take advantage of the rich court records about sodomy available to historians of male homosexuality. Changing laws about sexual practices often reflect wider political concerns about social order and racial boundaries, as in Nazi Germany or European colonies.

To get at people's feelings of sexual desire is much more difficult. Some letters and diaries exist, but most people did not write about sex in such ways, and we do not know how typical those who did were. By the nineteenth century, doctors and sexologists began to survey sexual attitudes, sometimes using a statistical and some-times a case-study approach. Historians influenced by Foucault have often seen these case studies as shaped by the discourses of sexologists, who persuaded people to adopt new sexual identities, but more recently, other historians have argued that sexologists responded to letters and interviews with their subjects as they developed their theories. Social attitudes about female sexuality are much easier to explore, since desire was such a central theme in literature, medicine, morality and politics, but historians always have to remember that these sources present discourses about sexuality, rather than describing experiences.

The eighteenth century: challenges to control

Sexual attitudes of the eighteenth century are difficult to grasp, because sexual moral-ity was so controversial and debated; no consensus could be reached. Popular attitudes towards sex contrasted with those of the authorities, who tried in vain to stem a grow-ing tide of extramarital sex. Older ideas about female desire persisted and in fact were popularised while new medical knowledge challenged them. Sexual libertinism con-tributed to a revolutionary ferment, but a backlash lurked on the horizon.

Both Catholic and Protestant churches had tried to impose, or reimpose, a strict sexual morality in the seventeenth century. The counter-reformation Catholic church portrayed women as sexual temptresses, with their low-cut gowns and sparkling orna-ments. It imposed strict controls over marriage and viewed sexual desire as the ultimate sin. The Protestant churches tended to denigrate celibacy and celebrate the bonds of matrimony, including marital sexual desire, but congregations imposed tight discipline over their members' extramarital behaviour. Institutional reformatories confined women accused of prostitution, or other sexual delinquencies. Originating with the counter-reformation, nuns usually ran these institutions and aimed to reform prosti-tutes through a strict regime of privation, regimentation, prayer and work. These reformatories also disciplined wayward women, not just prostitutes. Especially in France, parents or husbands could send recalcitrant daughters and adulterous wives to these reformatories. For instance, the official state institution, *La Salpêtrière*, founded in 1658, had wards for 'debauched' girls and wives and for prostitutes, as well as for girls of good family who had strayed from the proper path. In England, the first Magdalen Hospital was established in London in 1758, motivated by philanthropic and evangelical sentiments that sinners could be reclaimed for a religious path. Like the French institutions, it required the women to wear plain grey dresses and to walk with 'downcast eyes'. The Magdalen Hospital also received girls of genteel birth who had been seduced or had given birth outside of marriage. While these institutions aimed to return prostitutes to a virtuous life of labour and even marriage, thus recognising that unchastity was not a permanent stigma, they trained prostitutes in those very over-crowded, low-paid trades that forced women to sell sex to make ends meet – laundry, service and needlework. Thirty-seven to 40 per cent of the women in the Magdalen Hospital and the similar London Lock Asylum failed to reform and left the asylum, sometimes returning to prostitution. By the mid-eighteenth century, as the cities of London and Paris grew exponentially, it became obvious that prostitution would expand far beyond the capacities of these institutions to contain it. In London, Societies for the Suppression of Vice periodically demanded that constables sweep the streets and arrest prostitutes, but prostitution itself remained legal. In Paris, the police concentrated on spying on and harassing prostitutes through arrests or extortion. In eighteenth-century Copenhagen, the authorities tried to crack down on prostitution as part of an effort to force all women (and men) into labour, regarding the cafés where prostitutes worked as dangerous nests of crime.[13] Nowhere could prostitution be suppressed successfully.

Authorities also attempted to control unmarried mothers. In France, church and state united with propertied patriarchs to ensure that well-born young women did not run off with unsuitable husbands or fall pregnant before marriage. Rape laws focused on the fear that men would abduct heiresses, and the courts treated sexual violence as a crime against husbands and fathers, rather than against the women themselves. Midwives had to turn in unmarried pregnant women to the authorities and force them to reveal the name of the father, who could be charged with the child's maintenance. In Lutheran Strasbourg, unmarried mothers could be imprisoned. In England and Scotland, unwed mothers faced humiliating public punishments, such as standing in front of the church in sackcloth and ashes. But by the mid-eighteenth century, some of these sanctions began to erode. By 1741, Swedish pregnant girls no longer had to experience the humiliation of public purification, as ministers would take their repentance in the privacy of their studies. For instance, in 1765 Frederick the Great abolished all shaming punishments for unmarried mothers, seeing them as victims of seduction.[14] The causes of illegitimacy are discussed in depth later in this chapter.

Both legitimate and illegitimate fertility increased dramatically from 1750 to 1850 in many parts of Europe. Historians generally agree that the population grew because more people were marrying, and more people were having sex outside of marriage; death rates declined, but not dramatically enough to explain population growth. By the late eighteenth century, a significant sector of the British population began to marry in their early twenties instead of their late twenties. As a result, the woman of 1791 could bear two or even three more children than her great grandmother. In contrast, the average age of marriage rose in France, Tuscany and parts of Germany.[15] Premarital sex was very common among peasants and artisans. Young couples often engaged in night-courting, caressing each other as they cuddled, fully-clothed, in the evening. If they were betrothed, they often believed they could go ahead and have sex; as a result, many brides were pregnant upon marriage.

The religious insistence on the sinfulness of desire contrasted with the prevalent popular attitude that female sexual pleasure was vigorous and necessary. The first edition of the popular sex-advice book *Aristotle's Masterpiece*, which had nothing to do with Aristotle, appeared in 1684, and many more versions and additions were published over the next two centuries. On the continent, the counterpart to *Aristotle's Masterpiece* was Nicolas de Venette's *Tableau de l'amour conjugale*, a more medical work, quickly translated into Dutch, German, English and, by 1826, Spanish. These works presented the purpose of marriage as procreation and presented sexual pleasure, for both men and women, as a means to that end. They generally refuted Aristotle's idea that women did not contribute seed to conception, which would have meant that female sexual pleasure was unnecessary; as Jane Sharp, a midwife, noted, that was the ridiculous idea of an 'idle coxcomb'. But these texts debated whether Galen was correct to assert that male and female genitals were homologous. *Aristotle's Masterpiece* tended to follow the Galenic model of the homology between penis and vagina, while de Venette rejected it. But both recounted similarities in function between the penis and the clitoris, acknowledging that without stimulating the latter, 'the fair sex neither desire mutual embraces, nor have pleasure in them, nor conceive by them'. These advice books urged men to confide in their wives and to caress them in order to incite their desires and ensure conception. The popular idea that women could not conceive without orgasm also had negative consequences for rape victims who became pregnant, since their accusations of assault were never believed. Heterosexual intercourse was believed to be essential for a woman's health. If a girl was not married early enough, the pamphlet warned, 'green sickness' could result from celibacy. De Venette regarded male and female desire as equally strong, but tended to see women as 'insatiable', who would attack their husbands in 'amorous battle'. According to a very old stereotype, men were seen as more rational and able to control their sexuality. However, Jane Sharp defended women, arguing, 'we women have no more cause to be angry, or be ashamed of what Nature hath given us than men have, we cannot be without ours no more than they can want theirs.'[16]

These popular medical books also envisioned the possibility that women might desire other women. Jane Sharp's midwifery book and some treatises on hermaphrodites speculated that women who had enlarged clitorises were a sort of hermaphrodite who might exert their lust on other women. De Venette described such women as 'tribades', but regarded them as curiosities of nature instead of sinners. Lesbianism, therefore, was not a recognised identity but an anomaly, seen only hazily, as in the twilight.

The intellectual challenges of the Enlightenment also changed attitudes towards sexuality. Medical ideas about female desire began to change over the course of the eighteenth century, as Thomas Laqueur points out. Physiologists rejected the old idea that male and female sexual organs were homologous. Turning to empirical examination of bodies rather than relying on the old authorities, they began to doubt that women had to experience sexual pleasure to conceive. For instance, in 1770, a doctor inseminated a dog with a syringe, proving 'orgasm was not necessary for conception', at least in canines. But cultural assumptions influenced these medical texts more than experiments did. Although medical texts had always regarded male and female bodies as different, new authorities began to argue that sex determined female physiology in every way, from the genitals to the skeleton to the brain. Many doctors believed that the female sexual organs controlled women's minds. They debated whether inflamed ovaries caused sexual hysteria, or whether excessive sexual desire, or even reading erotic literature, could enlarge the ovaries.[17]

While medical men had begun to ignore the importance of female pleasure, the materialist philosophers celebrated it. The new materialist philosophy of the Enlightenment critiqued the old metaphysical and religious view of society. *Philosophes* saw a 'new universe composed solely of atomized, animate bodies in motion, mechanisms driven by the laws of pleasure'.[18] Materialist philosophical ideas could also be found in pornography. Since censors prohibited both radical philosophy and pornography, publishers in the underground book trade sometimes combined the two. Historians have debated whether this philosophical pornography empowered female desire or exploited women. The author of *Thérèse philosophe* (1748) presented sex as completely natural, impelled by the body's reasons; its characters criticised meaningless religious and legal constraints on sex. Thérèse expressed her own sexual desires and vowed never to marry or have children. By explicitly describing *coitus interruptus* (withdrawal), the novel explained how she could enjoy sex without fear. Pornographic texts sometimes portrayed women initiating each other into sex. In one, Ottavia tells Tullia, 'thy garden is setting mine on fire'. However, lesbian sexual desire was usually seen as a sideline to the main heterosexual event. And as we have seen, it was not particularly innovative to portray female sexual desire as active, given the traditional link between female insatiability and irrationality. The philosopher Diderot, for instance, believed that women's lusts were naturally violent. Artificial mores, such as religion and social propriety, encouraged female irrationality and distorted women's natural desires. In his novel *La Religieuse*, greedy parents confined their daughter Suzanne in a convent. She became the prey of a wickedly lustful mother superior who seduced her, indulging her lesbian desires freely because Suzanne was so innocent she did not understand these caresses. However, when these works were translated into English, either the translator cut out the most explicit sex scenes between women, or the books were suppressed by censorship. Nonetheless, arcane allusions to female–female eroticism surfaced in erudite yet libidinous poems written for a very elite English market.[19]

The sexual cynicism apparent in this pornography was also reflected in aristocratic culture. Among the elite, men openly took mistresses and frequented courtesans. Great ladies might take lovers once they had provided their husbands with a male heir, but the double standard mandated much greater discretion and risk. Georgiana, Duchess of Devonshire, for instance, had to go into exile abroad when she bore a child by her lover. In France, husbands could force wives accused of adultery into a convent for two years, and even for life. A few aristocratic women engaged in lesbian relationships, but as a result, vicious rumours discredited their reputations. Anne Damer, a sculptress involved in the political circle of the Duchess of Devonshire, was also mocked for her allegedly Sapphic tastes and accused of interfering with the relationship of an actress and her lover.[20] In France, the actress Mlle Raucourt wrote a play with a cross-dressing heroine; she supposedly wore men's clothes in order to seduce women. But scandalous memoirs alleged that she belonged to Sectes des Anandrynes, tribades who renounced the company of men and preferred that of their own sex. These rumours severely damaged Raucourt's career.[21]

By the late eighteenth century, similar scandalous memoirs and pornographic tracts aimed to undermine the *ancien régime* by portraying aristocrats and royals as perverse, decadent, immoral and unfit to rule. For instance, radical pamphlets depicted Marie Antoinette as an incestuous mother and indiscriminate lover of both men and women. The alleged sexual adventures of aristocratic women, royal mistresses and queens personified the personal and political corruption that radicals perceived in the *ancien régime* and eroded the deference the common people were supposed to feel for them. Jean-Jacques Rousseau, most influentially, resented the power that the women of the salons held over culture and regarded them as artificial and decadent.

By the later eighteenth century, Rousseau pioneered a new move towards sensibility that challenged aristocratic and philosophical cynicism about sex. Rousseau advocated the authenticity of genuine feeling, the uniqueness of individual emotions: as he put it, 'I know my own heart'. In his *Confessions* (1770), he passionately depicted his inner sexual life as failing to conform to conventions, but all the more worthy of examination; for instance, he candidly admitted to masochistic desires and to abandoning his illegitimate children at the foundling hospital. In the novel *Julie, ou La Nouvelle*

Héloïse (1761) Rousseau wrote with great empathy about the struggles faced by Julie, his heroine, trapped into an arranged marriage while falling deeply in love with her handsome and intelligent tutor. Yet Rousseau realised that if sexual desires were indulged freely, society would be reduced to a state of nature. To resolve this problem, he laid the burden of controlling desires onto women. While men could explore their genuine emotions, women must be trained into social constraints. Rousseau advised women to dress to allure men with bows and ribbons and to gesture coquettishly. They should induce men's sexual advances, but then repel them to preserve their chastity, the highest female virtue. Julie, who succumbed to her sexual passions, died at the end of *La Nouvelle Héloïse*, her fate a warning to women.

Like many other women, Mary Wollstonecraft admired Rousseau's insistence on the authenticity of the soul and his political radicalism. But, whereas most female readers seem to have responded positively to the idea that women should be respected as the guardians of social virtue, Rousseau's insistence that women should be coquettish yet modest infuriated Wollstonecraft. She criticised the conventional double standard and the hypocrisy of valuing chastity as the only female virtue, but in her published writings she tended to regard sexual passion as dangerous and irrational. Yet she fell prey to sexual passion herself, bearing a child out of wedlock to her lover Gilbert Imlay and only marrying her lover William Godwin after becoming pregnant. She and Godwin, in somewhat different ways, developed an idea that true passion could become refined as a meeting of minds as well as bodies and should not be marked by the sanction of artificial institutions such as church and state.

During the French Revolution, Olympe de Gouges also asserted female sexual rights by claiming that women should be able to claim maintenance from the fathers of their illegitimate children. The French revolutionaries did make some changes advantageous to women, declaring that they would free them from the despotism of husbands and fathers and from the tyranny of arranged marriages, for instance, by allowing divorce. Working from the principle that the citizen must have the right to the 'full disposal of one's own body', they removed old references to abduction in the laws of rape and simply regarded it as a crime against a woman's person rather than against her husband or father. However, these laws changed only principle, not practice, and authorities rarely prosecuted men for rape. The Jacobins rejected feminism and sent Olympe de Gouges to the scaffold. They refused to regard seduction as a crime after the age of sixteen, given the difficulty due to 'the precocity of the sex and its excessive sensibility, to separate seduction from voluntary surrender'. In fact, the Jacobins were more concerned with protecting men's sexual freedom, in 1793 forbidding unmarried mothers from bringing paternity searches.[22]

The nineteenth century: class contrasts and political conflicts

By 1800, the backlash against sexual radicalism was in full force as the middle class defined itself in part through sexual morality. In France, the Civil Code of 1811 reversed the revolutionary legitimation of divorce and imposed extremely harsh penalties on women who violated the sexual double standard. Women could not sue the fathers of their illegitimate children. And husbands could prosecute adulterous wives – and their lovers – in the courts and have them condemned to prison for two years. If a husband caught his wife and lover in the act, *in flagrante delicto*, he could kill them and escape punishment for murder. Many such cases were brought to the courts, although more often, the husband would simply have his wife arrested and not go through the full prosecution.[23] In Britain, conservative evangelicals denigrated Mary Wollstonecraft and her supporters as prostitutes after her death in 1797. They depicted her as undermining the very foundations of marriage and, in doing so, endangering all social institutions with the threat of revolution. But they also warned that the sexual decadence of the aristocracy might bring the revolution to Britain's shores. The middle class increasingly contrasted its virtuous morality with perceived aristocratic libertinism. This contrast reached its apogee in the trial of Queen Caroline in 1820. King George IV put his wife on trial for adultery, even though he had abandoned her twenty-five years before and notoriously frolicked with his mistresses. For many, Caroline became a symbol of middle-class purity in contrast to the corrupt oppressive aristocracy. However, when evidence that she had taken a lover surfaced, middle-class public opinion turned against her. Nevertheless, many working-class people still supported her, because they thought she had every right to take a lover after being deserted by her husband.

Working-class morality was very different than that of the middle class in the early nineteenth century. As rising illegitimacy rates became more apparent, sexual morality became a marker of class status. Among working people, rates of premarital pregnancy were very high, ranging from 30 to 50 per cent in parts of rural England, Sweden, Vienna and the Netherlands.[24] Illegitimacy rates increased at about the same rate as marital fertility. At first, historians attributed lowered marriage ages and rising illegitimacy to industrialisation and urbanisation. Edward Shorter argues that by allowing young people to earn wages instead of having to wait to inherit property, they could enjoy sex before marriage and marry younger. Earning wages in factories, for instance, enabled young women to enjoy sex, reflecting liberated working-class sexual attitudes. But this argument has been refuted on several grounds. Illegitimacy rates were high among domestic servants, the most traditional female occupation, and generally lower among factory girls, who had more social support and slightly higher wages. Demographers demonstrate that illegitimacy rose in many areas long before industrialisation. Some rural areas had much higher rates of illegitimacy than urban industrial ones such as north-east Scotland, the Austrian Alps, Hungary and parts of Germany. Rural areas of Austria experienced extremely high illegitimacy, up to 27.8 per cent in 1870. Historians therefore now concentrate on proletarianisation, not industrialisation alone, as the cause of the decrease in marriage age and the rise of illegitimacy.[25]

Looking at life stories and ethnological accounts of village customs as well as statistics, Louise Tilly and Joan Scott argue that changes associated with the growth of a capitalist economy disrupted the regulation of desire long practised by communities. As Tilly and Scott point out, the birth of an illegitimate child or marriage at a young age did not signal women's liberation. Unmarried motherhood was very onerous, and low female wages forced women to marry young. Illegitimate children faced higher risk of dying as infants or children, especially in the first half of the nineteenth century, indicating that their mothers lacked family support and insufficient income. As Tilly and Scott argued, when young women moved to the cities in search of work, they followed traditional rural customs of sex after a promise of marriage. Early modern customs had allowed for non-reproductive sexual play before marriage, including elaborate courting customs such as bundling or night courtship. If a young man refused to marry a woman he courted, he would be pressured or shunned by the family and community. But with proletarianisation, hard times brought unemployment which prevented young men from fulfilling their promises or forced them to delay marriage; they could easily move to another city in search of work and never see their pregnant sweetheart again. However, isolated and far from home, pregnant women could not draw upon the social support of family or village to force their sweethearts to follow through with their promises. But illegitimacy was not always tied to social isolation. In Louvain, Belgium, many unmarried mothers worked as lace-makers and continued to live with their parents. They may have become pregnant in an effort to escape from their families' houses, only to find that hard times prevented marriage.[26]

A significant minority of women also became pregnant after being sexually coerced. In the records of the London Foundling Hospital, which took in the infants of unmarried mothers, 15 per cent of the women interviewed claimed that they had been 'seduced against their consent', 'forced', or raped. While it may be thought that these women would claim rape in order to make themselves look more respectable, foundling hospital officials were unlikely to believe a woman who said she had been raped by a stranger; their ideal candidate had been seduced after a promise of marriage. Some of these women were assaulted by their fellow servants. Despite the stereotype of the immoral factory workers, servants were more vulnerable to sexual assault than factory workers; servants could be assaulted as they worked alone in an empty house, while factory girls laboured together and could defend each other.[27] But most of these women who claimed that they had been sexually forced were victimised by men who courted them, not by strangers.

Historians debate whether sexual violence was an expression of male dominance or an aberration of individual men. Barret-Ducrocq regards sexual violence as 'the pathological behaviour of certain individuals', rather than tying it to the tensions of certain historical eras. Anne-Marie Sohn tries to tie violent and sexual behaviour much more tightly to specific moments. For instance, in the early nineteenth century, there were many cases of young unmarried male agricultural workers sexually attacking isolated women working in the fields. Later in the nineteenth century, when improving economic conditions allowed such men to marry, these rapes declined in number. She therefore sees rape as the result of sexual frustration. I have argued that sexual violence reflected a division in masculine mores in early nineteenth-century Britain. Many working-class men espoused a restrained, self-controlled, chivalrous masculinity. But others, especially among certain occupations of artisans, celebrated a libertine, even misogynous masculinity, singing songs that celebrated violent seductions and assaults on women.[28]

The question of sexual violence is also complicated by the question of language. The unmarried women who applied to the foundling hospital found it very difficult to articulate what happened to them, mentioning that they had been 'seduced by force', which seems to be a contradiction in terms for modern readers. This difficulty was caused by the fact that nineteenth-century society did not find the distinction between seduction and force to be very important. Rape was seen as an attack on the property of a husband or father. Whether or not a woman consented, she was damaged property. The French, for instance, defined seduction as 'a victory won over a woman's propriety by criminal manoeuvres and odious means'.[29]

Many unmarried mothers actually cohabited with the fathers of their children. In Paris, there was one consensual union for every four married couples, and the illegitimacy rate was 30 per cent. Historians initially argued that this represented an alternative morality, a defiance of the bourgeois order. Indeed, many working-class people seem to have regarded cohabitation and informal divorces as socially acceptable. However, other historians now see cohabitation as a symptom of poverty. In Paris, a wedding required an expensive certificate and paperwork from the couple's home village, including the written permission of parents. Many cohabiting couples would have preferred to marry. In Vienna, up to a third of working-class people could never hope to earn enough to marry and support a family. Some cohabited instead, while others, unable to even afford a room together, had to be content with brief visits in rooms rented by the hour.[30]

The experiences of middle-class women differed dramatically from working-class women in the early and middle nineteenth century. In proper French society, bourgeois women were supposed to appear very modest, with downcast eyes, and girls were not supposed to know anything about sex. In England, as Hera Cook observes, 'respectable women were expected to control their sexual feelings'.[31] Any woman who became pregnant or cohabited outside marriage risked total social ostracism. Of course, there were exceptions in bohemian life, such as the novelist George Eliot (Mary Ann Evans), but they were not accepted in bourgeois society. Middle-class women had little access to knowledge about sex, for the authorities quickly censored any works that gave medical information about sex to a popular audience.

Doctors disagreed about whether 'good' women were naturally sexless, or whether they simply controlled their desires. Dr William Acton asserted that most women were not normally troubled with sexual feelings and had intercourse only to oblige their husbands. Acton was extremely influential and his works went through many editions. Similarly, Dr Alexandre Mayer, 'a leading French authority', wrote in 1848 that women only submitted to sexual intercourse out of love for their husbands. Many other doctors believed that most women experienced sexual pleasure, even if their desire was less than that of men. Dr Auguste Debay argued in 1848 that it was important for men to satisfy their wives in bed with sensitivity and skill. However, female desire could be seen as dangerous. Isaac Baker Brown tried to popularise the idea that clitorectomies could cure the 'problem' of excessive female sexual excitement which he alleged led to unhealthy independence, hysteria and mental illness, but he was struck from the medical register because he did not get consent from husbands or fathers before performing this procedure, and because he was regarded as mentally unstable.[32]

The increasing prevalence of the idea that women did not need to experience orgasm in order to conceive also made female sexual pleasure seem less important. Most nineteenth-century versions of the popular sex manual *Aristotle's Masterpiece* no longer mentioned the clitoris. Even doctors who acknowledged the importance of the clitoris regarded women as sexually passive. Of course, women did not necessarily need explicit information from doctors to enjoy sex. One 1884 survey of infertile women found 68 per cent experienced sexual pleasure in marriage, and 79 per cent said they desired sex. But sexual pleasure was not the same as orgasm: one survey found that under 40 per cent of German women born between 1896 and 1906 ever had an orgasm. [33]

After 1850, illegitimacy declined sharply in most areas. By the end of the nineteenth century, sexual repression seems to have affected working-class as well as middle-class women. Mid-nineteenth-century German working-class activists were quite sexually puritanical.[34] By the late nineteenth century, many British working-class women were so ignorant of sex they did not know where the baby would come out, even when they were pregnant. In rural France, the Catholic church was able to increase its influence and inculcated a cult of virginity among girls. If they remained virgins, their villages celebrated them as 'rosières'.

The late nineteenth-century decline in fertility – first experienced by the middle class – may have resulted from sexual restraint rather than from sexual pleasure. Fertility declined first in northern Europe, especially in France. By 1877, 'for every 1000 married women aged fifteen to fifty, 248 babies were born in England, 275 in Prussia, and 279 in Belgium, but only 173 in France'. Fertility declined much more slowly in the southern and less developed areas of Europe, such as most of Italy, Spain and Portugal, but also Sweden and Ireland, where it did not decline at all. However, in Italy, fertility diminished notably in northern industrial areas.[35]

Historians have debated how far the fertility decline (known as the demographic transition) was due to traditional methods, such as abstinence, withdrawal and abortion, or the newer barrier methods, such as sponges and diaphragms. Rubber was vulcanised in 1843–4, but condoms remained twice the price of a loaf of bread, and they were associated with prostitution; the new diaphragms of the later nineteenth-century were illegal and available only to a few brave souls. Withdrawal and abstinence were by far the most common methods, but they resulted in much conflict between men and women. Withdrawal depended on the husband's cooperation, and abstinence meant the lack of sexual pleasure for both (although many, but not all working-class women saw sex as more of a duty than a pleasure). Many women felt frustrated at their inability to refuse their husbands. National differences may be important here. Hera Cook argues that by the end of the nineteenth century, both middle-class men and women controlled their fertility largely by sexual restraint. But Anne-Marie Sohn observes a greater sexual openness in late nineteenth-century France. The number of abortions sharply increased and women enjoyed a somewhat greater degree of sexual openness.[36]

Late nineteenth-century women commonly resorted to abortion. They took various poisonous herbal or chemical remedies to 'bring on their periods', such as ergot of rye, savin or lead, or even submitted to abortionists' mechanical methods. Abortion allowed women to control their fertility without getting the permission of their husbands, who usually did not know; it was a twilight knowledge whispered among women. Even middle-class women resorted to abortion, if they could find a cooperative doctor. According to 'exasperated' doctors, these women did not believe that abortion was a sin or a crime before the third month, or at least before the fifth, when the foetus began to move.[37] However, authorities harshly punished abortionists when they could find them.

The extent to which Victorians recognised the possibility of erotic relationships between middle-class women has also been debated. The French, of course, were much more aware of this possibility than the British. George Sand recalled that in schools, girls had to walk in threes, rather than twos and were forbidden to kiss each other. Authors such as Maupassant and Baudelaire were fascinated by lesbians, but they depicted them as fearful, perverse creatures.[38] But in Germany and Britain, awareness of lesbianism seems to have been much lower. Some years ago Lillian Faderman wrote an influential book arguing that late eighteenth- and early nineteenth-century women could experience passionate friendships with each other, exchanging kisses and embraces, sharing beds and sending each other torrid, romantic letters, all without exciting any suspicion. Faderman also argued that such women were unlikely to have had physical sexual experiences with each other, since they had no concept of lesbianism as an erotic activity.[39]

Then Helena Whitbread decoded the diaries of Anne Lister, an early nineteenth-century Yorkshire gentlewoman. Anne Lister did not use the word 'lesbian', but she definitely understood the concept. At age thirty, she wrote, 'I love and only love the fairer sex and thus, beloved by them in turn my heart revolts from any other love but theirs.'[40] In the diaries in which she recorded her passionately sexual relationships with several women, she noted orgasms with an 'x' in the margins of entries. Anne Lister did not face the overt stigma of lesbianism, protected by her wealth and class status, but neighbours remained suspicious of her masculinity and whispered about her close relationship with another woman. Other scholars have found cases of gossip and rumours spread about women thought to be sexually attracted to others, and satirical descriptions of masculine women in novels. By the 1870s, new all-female institutions such as settlement houses and boarding schools allowed intense female friendships to flourish, and enabled women to make lives with each other, without having to marry. However, for the most part, these relationships were not viewed as sexual or stigmatised as sexual until around the turn of the twentieth century. Yet as Martha Vicinus argues, even with the silences around female–female desire, women found ways of articulating their passions for each other through coded languages, for instance appropriating family and marital metaphors to describe their relationships.[41]

Because working-class women generally did not write diaries or letters, we do not have as much evidence of such passionate friendships among them. Instead, court records and newspapers give us a different picture of the possibility of erotic desire between working women. However, the awareness of erotic possibilities between women varied greatly between national cultures. Theo van der Meer found several cases of women prosecuted for having sex with other women in Amsterdam in the 1790s. While some of them lived on the margins of society as beggars or prostitutes, at least one was from a 'respectable' social station. The authorities learned of their cases when neighbours denounced certain houses where women met to caress each other. However, unlike men who had sex with other men, these women did not form a subculture, and these cases are very rare. Even in cultures influenced by Germanic law, which did condemn sex between women, only a few cases surfaced in comparison with the large numbers of men prosecuted for sodomy.[42]

In Britain, many hundreds of women passed as men in search of adventure, better pay and safety in travelling. Newspapers frequently gave short accounts of these women, and popular songs and pamphlets also celebrated their exploits. However, we cannot know how many of these women were motivated by lesbian desire. Many ballads told of young women who disguised themselves as men in order to find their male lovers who had joined the army or navy. These songs enabled women to reimagine a different path for heterosexual romance, as they experienced many adventures and proved their bravery on the way to finding their lovers. Yet tales of female soldiers also enabled female desire to be understood indirectly. In autobiographical accounts, female soldiers, such as the Russian Nadezhda Durova, claimed that young women flirted with them, forcing them to leave town quickly before they had to disappoint the young woman or reveal their true identities. A few cases of 'female husbands' emerged. While very rarely female husbands were portrayed as criminals attempting to swindle innocent women, usually they lived with another woman in a long-standing couple. The 'husband' blended into working-class culture, working as a carpenter or sawyer, or some such typical masculine occupation, drinking with his workmates and even behaving violently toward his 'wife'. The wife typically claimed to be completely unaware of her 'husband's' true sex. While historians have interpreted these women as precursors of lesbians, dressing as men because they could conceive of no other way of being sexual with and loving women, more recent interpretations would understand them as women who actively wanted to play a masculine role or even change sex.[43]

In general, the concept of lesbianism did not overtly appear in early nineteenth-century working-class British culture. Prostitutes and other denizens of the streets sometimes insulted masculine women as hermaphrodites, or 'moffrydites' but the term 'lesbian' was not used until later in the century. Of course, many women may have engaged in passionate, even sexual friendships with each other. One authority believed that among all-female work environments, such as needlework establishments, women 'excite each other's passions' and therefore become hysteric. Dr Michael Ryan, however, never found any hint of lesbianism among English prostitutes.[44] In contrast, French authorities often noted that prostitutes engaged in lesbian relationships, sharing beds, looking out for each other and quarrelling in jealous rages. In 1828, doctors also observed lesbian attachments among women in French prisons. Prostitution was one of the few occupations where women could make enough money, if they were lucky, to support themselves and live together, enabling those women who wished to fulfil erotic desires for other women.

Prostitution was a very common female occupation in the eighteenth and nineteenth centuries, given the fact that female wages were too low for survival. Many women who sold sex, occasionally or full time, could not be identified easily as prostitutes; they occupied discreet rooms and worked at other jobs. In St Petersburg, peasant women coming to look for work in the city often had to exchange sex for lodging or even to find a job. The women who appear in records of the police, lock hospitals (which treated venereal disease) or Magdalen reformatories were more likely to be full-time sex workers and followed quite a different trajectory than unmarried mothers. Most prostitutes had lost one or both parents. Orphans brought up in workhouses, foster care or orphanages were often sent out to earn their own living by age twelve, and thus became vulnerable to sexual exploitation. They began to have sex earlier than other women, at sixteen or even younger, although the number of child prostitutes was low. Working as domestic servants or needlewomen, they had no home to fall back on if they lost their jobs.[45]

During the nineteenth century, authorities tried to develop new institutions and regulations to deal with prostitution. Authorities also believed that by controlling prostitution, they could regulate the 'dangerous' classes, the working people who seemed so prone to revolutionary riots and strikes. The French pioneered the system of registered and regulated prostitution which spread across Europe from the early nineteenth century onwards. First put forth in the revolutionary era, the idea of regulation was revived in 1804, as fears of venereal disease also increased as troops moved all across Europe during the Napoleonic wars. But the system was only rigorously instituted in 1828. The system spread to Brussels and Russia in 1843–4. In Italy, the regulation of prostitution was introduced by Camillo Cavour, the politician who engineered the unification of Italy and who saw regulation as a way of modernising and civilising Italy. In central and eastern Europe, the regulation of prostitution had somewhat different roots in the old system of municipal brothels, resurrected in the early nineteenth century by the morals police who tried to confine prostitution to certain parts of towns or even, in some cases, to run their own brothels. In turn, the Prussian system influenced the Polish system of Warsaw in 1802. By 1870, the new unified German state supplanted these local regulations with its own system of regulation.

Although the British had long resisted the regulatory system, colonial authorities first introduced it in 1857 to Hong Kong, and in 1864 the state established a system of registration and forcible treatment in garrison and port towns in England, and extended it to Ireland, though not to Scotland. These Contagious Diseases Acts aimed to protect soldiers and sailors from venereal disease. Various systems of registration under the Contagious Diseases Acts were also put into place in the Straits Settlements (Singapore), the Cape Colony and India. Authorities tended to regard native women as potential prostitutes who could fulfil the sexual needs of soldiers but who also might infect them; registration and treatment of women was seen as the solution, rather than controlling men.[46]

In all these systems, the police were empowered to require all women who worked as prostitutes to register with the police and to submit to medical examinations for venereal disease. If they were found to be infected, they had to undergo treatment at a lock hospital. The police also wanted prostitutes to work in brothels rather than independently, because then they would be easier to observe, register and regulate. The police could also use these rules to harass any woman on the street, even if she did not sell sex. In Italy, any woman without a job found on the streets at night or in a dance-hall could be arrested, charged with being a clandestine prostitute and forced to submit to a medical exam or sent back to her family. In 1880s Warsaw, out of '4,000–5000 detained and examined . . . only 700–1200' were registered as prostitutes; the rest were working women, such as maidservants out on the street at night.[47] The policing and regulation of prostitution led to greater isolation and stigmatisation of prostitutes as they were cut off from their neighbours who might have accepted women who had sex occasionally for money.

The system of regulation failed to control both venereal disease and prostitution. For those women caught up in the system, registration was an onerous burden so, as a result, most women who engaged in sexual commerce evaded registration. They avoided working in the licensed brothels, which may have diminished in number as a result. By the late nineteenth century, the numbers of prostitutes also declined, perhaps as a result of increased economic opportunity for women. From the 1860s, state regulation of prostitution also came under sustained attack by the abolitionist movement, who wished to do away with the system. For many abolitionists, the system enshrined the double standard, accepting male unchastity as 'natural' but punishing women for being prostitutes. For others, state regulation violated the individual's rights to privacy and represented an expansion of state power. The movement brought together middle-class women, liberal individualists, socialists and churches and chapels.

In Britain, Josephine Butler spearheaded the Ladies National Association against the Contagious Diseases Acts. Many of its adherents were originally motivated by religious horror at state sanctioning of prostitution. But as they listened to prostitutes tell of the humiliation they faced at the hands of the authorities, the ladies began to see these women as their sisters and the cause as a matter of women's rights. These middle-class women faced violent attacks from angry men in garrison towns and opposition from members of parliament who believed ladies should not speak out on such matters. But they also found allies among working-class men angry at the class exploitation of prostitution. Eventually, the movement forced the government to repeal the Contagious Diseases Acts in England and Ireland in 1886. In 1888, the Acts were repealed in Canada, St Helena, Trinidad and Barbados, but the colonial governments of Jamaica, Gibraltar, Penang, Straits, India and Hong Kong insisted on keeping them, despite intense opposition from the woman's movement, missionaries and groups of colonised people such as the Bramo Somaj.[48]

In Germany, the movement against regulated prostitution brought together a broad coalition. Socialists believed that the system allowed soldiers to exploit working-class women and resulted from the elite militaristic domination of politics. Evangelical Protestants supported the state, but they viewed prostitution as a symptom of social disorder and immorality. Feminists regarded prostitution as the sexual exploitation of women. However, the authorities banned most meetings of the abolitionist movement, limiting its efficacy. Feminists also united with nationalists and the Left in Italy against the regulation system, arguing that newly unified Italy should abolish the system to prove its 'moral rebirth' as a nation. In 1876, the new government conceded to the movement by modifying the regulations so that only brothels, not individual prostitutes, would be registered. But, in practice, police regulation of prostitution continued. In France, the creation of the anti-clerical Third Republic led to intensified hostility against the Catholic church, which abolitionists blamed for the survival of the regulationist system. Liberals and radicals attacked the police system as corrupt and hypocritical. However, the system was only modified, not abolished, in 1904.

The 1880s and 1890s also witnessed increasing concern for child victims of sexual exploitation. In 1885, the white-slave scandal burst onto the British scene when journalist W. T. Stead alleged that he had been able to purchase a thirteen-year-old virgin for 10 pounds. In response, huge numbers of people, chiefly women and working-class men, demonstrated against what they perceived as the class and sexual exploitation of children. Stead obviously exaggerated the extent of the trade in very young girls, identifying the epicentre of the 'white-slave trade' as Belgium. A judicial enquiry confirmed that English girls were sold for 300 francs to Belgian brothels, and that the chief of the police had been complicit in the system. As a result, the regulationist system was repealed in Belgium. Historians first explained the white-slave agitation as a symptom of Victorian repression, a refusal to acknowledge childhood sexuality. But as the current feminist movement began uncovering the extent of child abuse today, historians have shifted ground somewhat. They acknowledge the genuine concern social activists felt for sexually abused children, but they also point out that late Victorian activists xenophobically projected their anxieties about child sexual abuse onto foreign exploiters.[49]

Anger at the state sanctioning of prostitution and the sexual exploitation of women also led to the movement to promote wider social purity by abolishing the double standard and advocating chastity for both men and women. Although members of the abolitionist movement had tried to protect the civil rights of prostitutes, the social-purity movement increased the regulation of female sexuality and advocated censorship of sexual representations in popular culture. In England, they supported the 1885 Criminal Law Amendment Act, which raised the age of consent from thirteen to sixteen for girls. However, it also allowed the police to remove girls from homes suspected of being brothels, or where women accused of being prostitutes lived, and to put them into reformatories or industrial schools. Social reformers regarded the child victims of sexual abuse as sexually contaminated themselves and incarcerated them in industrial homes where they could not 'corrupt' 'normal' children. In Germany, the movement to raise the age of consent did not commence until somewhat later, due to restrictions on women's political activity. In 1910, the Federation of German Women's Organisations wanted to raise the upper age limit for the age of consent from fourteen to sixteen. 'Clearly, although rape and sexual abuse were referred to only in veiled language, these measures were designed to protect underage girls from these crimes.'[50]

The exploitation of children also became an issue in the British Empire when the British Government attempted to change the age of consent for marriage in India in 1891. Historians debate whether the British Government was genuinely concerned with young girls, or whether it was trying to impose alien customs with its imperial power. Research has found that the British Government reluctantly initiated the Act under pressure not only from European missionaries and women's groups, but also from Indian social reformers and female activists. But British opponents of the Bill accepted the contention that Indian female sexuality was so intense that women needed to be married at young ages. The Government did not enforce the Bill very effectively, fearful of alienating Hindu traditionalists.[51]

The social-purity movement also strongly influenced the strand of the later suffragette movement that blamed male sexual desire for the ills of women. Most notoriously, Christabel Pankhurst claimed that 80 per cent of men were infected with venereal disease and advocated 'Votes for Women / Chastity for Men'. Less stridently, many feminists wished for marriages based on spiritual unity, not just physical passion. The sexual objectification of women seemed to stand in the way of women's emancipation. Many German feminists also focused on the dangers of sexual desire rather than the pleasures it could bring. For instance, in 1908 they opposed contraception and abortion because birth control would simply make women too vulnerable to men's sexual demands, even sexual abuse.[52]

Another strand of the European women's movement took a more positive approach to sex, joining with the sex radicals. Birth control became a major issue. For instance, Annie Besant and Charles Bradlaugh were put on trial for obscenity in 1877 for distributing birth-control tracts and were sentenced to two months in prison. Although that sentence was later lifted, Annie Besant was deprived of the custody of her child for being an 'immoral' woman. However, the publicity around the trial vastly increased the sale of their birth-control tracts and may have contributed to the fertility decline in England in certain areas. In the 1880s, the Dutch Dr Aletta Jacobs began using Dr Mensinga's pessary, or Dutch cap (similar to a diaphragm), after testing it on the women who came to her for contraceptive advice. After finding it safe and effective, she prescribed it in her medical practice but ran into fierce opposition from doctors and the Government. The Catholic church effectively suppressed birth-control information, and fertility actually increased in the Netherlands. Around the turn of the century, Stella Browne, Helene Stocker and the French feminists Nelly Roussel and Dr Madeleine Pelletier advocated birth control as the key to women's emancipation. Roussel denounced the idea that women must serve society by giving birth, no matter how they suffered. Instead, women needed to serve the state as citizens, workers and thinkers. Pelletier also championed abortions and attacked the middle class for its hypocrisy in practising birth control in private yet refusing to allow birth-control information to be publicly accessible for workers. But French birth-control advocates were followed by the police and often arrested.[53]

Sex and modernity in the long twentieth century

For many radicals from the 1890s onwards, overthrowing Victorian sexual repression seemed to be a marker of the new modern way of thinking, but until after the First World War, they remained an avant-garde fighting against a hostile culture. In Germany, Helene Stocker espoused the theory that sexual desire was a creative force for humanity. Following the philosophy of monism, she believed that body and soul could not be separated and that to repress the sexual drive therefore harmed the mind. Ellen Key, the Swedish feminist, argued that in 'exalted individuals' sexual desire evoked 'noble feelings, and love of everything which is high and beautiful in life', although she did see women's primary role as motherhood. In Britain, Edward Carpenter and Stella Browne challenged conventional principles of middle-class morality. In the pages of their publication, the *Adult and the Freewoman*, they debated the idea of 'free unions', monogamy, masturbation and heterosexuality. Younger feminists were no longer content with the older generation's rather ethereal ideal of spiritual passion and wanted to explore the concept of female sexual pleasure.[54]

These radicals often turned to the works of the sexologists to justify their cause. However, the sexologists did not influence popular culture or policy until the inter-war years. Many of their works were censored or were so expensive they had a limited circulation, and Anne-Marie Sohn has found that their ideas and terminology did not trickle down to ordinary people.[55] Nonetheless, for those in avant-garde circles the sexologists pioneered the open discussion of sex, especially female sexuality. But sexology could be problematic as well as inspiring for women.

Sexologists decisively rejected religious assumptions about sexuality and instead studied sex scientifically. By categorising anatomical variations and by insisting on the centrality of sexual selection to evolution, Darwin strongly influenced many sexologists. They were also influenced by Geddes and Thompson, two biologists who went even further than Darwin to posit males and females as fundamentally different, the former active, the latter passive. This focus on biological categorisation also paralleled contemporary efforts to categorise human anatomy by race. But feminists also used Darwinian ideas for their own ends. Some English feminists argued that women should use their sexual power to select men of a higher morality and therefore improve the human race. Helene Stocker 'welcomed' Darwinism as a refutation of the doctrine of original sin. 'If sexual desire was necessary and hereditary, then how could it be sinful?' Sexologists differentiated between the drive for procreation and what they variously categorised as the drive for pleasure or relationships.[56] As a result, they could acknowledge women's sexual desires went beyond the need for a child. They argued that female sexual satisfaction was necessary within marriage, and some even raised the possibility that women could be sexually satisfied beyond marriage. However, their ideas on female sexual desire could also be highly problematic.

The most sophisticated formulation of sexual desire came from Freud who strongly distinguished between the sexual drive and its object. He is notorious for first believing in the widespread incidence of childhood sexual abuse and then denying it. But by claiming that children fantasised about sex with their parents, Freud developed the theory of infantile sexual desire and the idea of the unconscious. He believed that children experienced a diffuse, 'polymorphously perverse' sexual desire that did not have a particular object. This desire gained an object through attachments to parents, especially to the mother. But children had to learn that these attachments were incestuous and forbidden, and therefore had to be transferred, when adult, to persons of the opposite sex. While it was fairly straightforward for a male to transfer his desire from his mother to an adult woman, the path to adult heterosexuality was much more difficult and circuitous for a woman. Freud believed that girls first experienced sexual arousal through the clitoris. However, this was a 'masculine' form of desire, improperly active. To reach maturity, a female not only had to transfer her desire from her mother to her father, and then to adult men, she also had to abandon clitoral eroticism for vaginal eroticism. In fact, he claimed to have discovered the vaginal orgasm in 1905.[57]

Most sexologists regarded sexual desire in much more biological terms, concentrating on the alleged differences between active masculinity and passive femininity. Sheila Jeffreys argues that sexologists used pseudo-scientific ideas to argue that it was 'normal' for women to want to be dominated and to experience pain during sex with men. Some sexologists failed to see marital rape as rape, instead, categorising rapists as perverted, psychopathological deviants, different from normal men. They also ratified the idea that adult women could not be raped, that they secretly wanted to be sexually assaulted. However, French sexologists criticised marital rape, at least on the wedding night; they warned husbands not to deflower their wives violently, concerned wives would fear sex during their married life.[58] It must also be recognised that sexologists acknowledged and categorised male masochism, although they saw it as a perversion, not as an extension of 'normal' desire.

While sexologists asserted the existence of female desire, many of them feared it could not be controlled. Continental thinkers such as Cesare Lombroso were more likely than their English counterparts to believe that sexual perversions were embedded in the female body. He regarded prostitutes as degenerate specimens. 'Normal' women, he believed, should be passive sexually, because if women expressed active sexual desire, they could lose control and endanger the social order. Lombroso also equated racial and sexological thinking, regarding prostitutes as atavistic throwbacks resembling 'primitive' races. French thinkers feared the 'New Women' who appeared around the fin-de-siècle, asserting their right to a public life and private pleasure. Newly discovering the 'unconscious forces working in the human mind', these sexologists believed that women lacked a 'rational, autonomous self'. Otto Weininger, an Austrian writer, similarly believed that men were more evolved and spiritual than women, while women were totally shaped by their sexual organs. Men risked being dragged down into the mire of material life if they engaged in sexual love for women. Weininger's misogynist, self-hating anti-Semitism was meant to justify the hostility many men felt for the fin-de-siècle New Woman. Yet some sex radicals and feminists found that his unflinching exploration of sexual passion explained why conventional morality was so destructive for women as well. He declared that 'the sexual impulse destroys the body and mind of the woman, and the psychical eroticism destroys her psychical existence', because men did not love women's true selves, but only projected onto them their own fantasies.[59]

Sexology's implications for lesbianism were also ambiguous. Some sexologists categorised homosexuals as gender inverts whose sexual desire could be explained by the idea that they had been born with the wrongly sexed body. Havelock Ellis and Edward Carpenter, two English sexologists, initially believed that heredity determined the inclinations of 'mannish' lesbians; they were 'inverts' who were born with masculine elements to their personality. Some sexologists initially hypothesised that lesbians were mannish women with enlarged clitorises. However, the Russian Dr Tarnovski found that the lesbians he examined exhibited 'normal' personalities and anatomy. Homosexual desires could also be seen as a variation of the 'normal' sexual drive, whether benign or perverse. Through the early 1900s the 'official' British medical profession held to the degeneracy theory: homosexuality was 'an acquired and depraved manifestation of the sexual passions'. However, other sexologists, such as Ellis, argued that homosexuality was a natural variation rather than a sickness or perversion. They often recognised the bisexuality of sexual desire, but more often, they regarded homosexuality as a separate identity or innate form of desire. Sheila Jeffreys argues that sexology stigmatised lesbians by stereotyping them as mannish and perverse. Their theories stigmatised the passionate friendships among girls and women which previously had not necessary been seen as sexual. Some sexologists accused feminists of stimulating artificial lesbian desires among women who would normally want to marry and have children. Even some feminist sex radicals believed that the repression of heterosexual desire would lead to 'substitute homosexuality'.[60] By the turn of the century, lesbianism was illegal in both Austria and Finland.

Sexology also had positive connotations for lesbians, however. In Germany, the sexologist Magnus Hirschfeld joined forces with feminist sex radical Helene Stocker to protest against unsuccessful German efforts to criminalise lesbianism. Using the case-study method, Ellis and Carpenter also found that many lesbians did not fit within the mannish stereotype and even those who did had many admirable qualities. Sexological discussions also made it possible for some lesbians to recognise and create their own identities. In Germany, several turn-of-the century novelists combined sexological theories of inversion with their own experiences to portray their erotic experiences with other women.[61]

Many sexologists were also very involved in the new field of eugenics, the pseudo-science of human breeding. While eugenics is now closely associated with its most evil consequence, the Nazi regime, until the 1930s eugenicist thinking was common not only among conservative racists but also among many socialists, liberals and even feminists. Some socialists argued that birth control would enable the working class to improve their own condition, and pointed out that poor maternal health and infant mortality endangered the 'race'. Some feminists believed that eugenics could give more power to women who could use birth control to experience sexual fulfilment and also to choose the most fit mate, and the most healthy time, to procreate. As Swedish feminist Ellen Key declared: 'Freedom for love's selection, under conditions favourable to the race; limitation of the freedom, not of love, but of procreation, when the conditions are unfavourable to the race.' These feminists also argued that the state should support unmarried mothers, out of concern that their children would die as infants or grow up to be stunted.[62] However, such feminists often conflicted with mainstream eugenicists, who believed that individual control of reproduction must be subordinate to the state.

In Germany and Britain, eugenicists feared that the 'unfit', i.e. the poor and the working class, would reproduce too much, swamping the 'fit' middle classes. They argued that middle-class women failed in their eugenic duty by having too few children and using birth control, not for eugenic reasons, but for fulfilment. They argued that women must subordinate their own needs for an education and a career to fulfil their primary purpose of motherhood. Unmarried mothers and prostitutes were defined as unfit and feeble-minded and were confined to reformatory institutions or hospitals. In Italy and France, eugenicists believed that population increase was necessary, even among the working class. French eugenicists focused their ire on women, whom they blamed for using birth control and abortion instead of having large families.

Eugenicists' racial theories about degeneration also influenced laws about concubinage in colonial settings. In the Dutch colonies, for instance, authorities had tolerated concubinage for centuries, because they believed that white men needed a sexual outlet, but did not want the presence of white women to interfere with the colonial mission. However, the resulting mixed-race population undermined theories of racial difference and superiority. Around 1900, colonial authorities began to ban concubinage and encouraged white women to settle in Indonesia and marry white men. White women were therefore given the responsibility to control the sexual drives of white men and to preserve the 'race'. Of course, tensions remained because such controls could never be effective.[63]

After the First World War, these radical ideas about sexology, eugenics, birth control and homosexuality moved from the fringes to the centre of society. The war had disrupted sexual relations and sexual ideas as women took over men's jobs and experienced a new freedom from dependency and chaperonage. Young women found soldiers alluring, and illegitimacy rates shot up after a long decline. But above all, the mass carnage of the battlefields traumatised society, increasing eugenic fears about a loss of population and the fragility of masculinity. A language of blood and nation began to replace the old religious rhetoric of sin and damnation. The French denounced birth-control advocates as complicit with Germans in destroying their population, and French novelists used the female vampire as a metaphor for the war that had sucked out men's lifeblood. In turn, the Germans personified France as a blood-drenched prostitute when French troops occupied the Ruhr after the war. Racial anxieties also intensified when the French used Senegalese troops in the war, resurrecting the myth of the black rapist – or the reality of mixed-race children.[64] After the war, the image of the 'New Woman' fascinated and horrified readers, as in the best-selling novel *La Garçonne*, published by Victor Marguerite in 1922, which portrayed a wild young woman who smoked, drank and had affairs with both men and women. Her short skirts and bobbed hair made modernity, and sexual freedom, boldly visible.

In the 1920s, it was often unclear whether lesbianism was just another sexual variation for adventurous sexual women, or a distinct sexual identity. *La Garçonne* shocked moralists because she was from the *grand bourgeois*, not a bohemian or working-class woman who could be dismissed as inherently immoral. French writers feared that, like 'La Garçonne', any woman could give into her desires and have sex with a woman. But French female poets, writers, artists and film-makers began to depict lesbian desire from their own perspective after the war, following the pre-war lead of Natalie Barney and Renée Vivien. These women, such as Germaine Dulac and Marie Laurencin, formed an avant-garde, international coterie in inter-war Paris. In Germany, working-class and middle-class women began to form a much more extensive subculture, especially in Berlin. Several lesbian magazines were published in which women could recount their experiences, justify their desires and publicise new meeting places. A network of bars sprang up, where women, some with cropped hair and masculine suits, could dance and flirt with each other. Lesbians also formed social, cultural and political clubs. However, these women often faced suspicion and hostility from neighbours and family; conservatives (and even some socialists) reacted with horror at what they perceived as sexual decadence.[65]

Until 1928, lesbianism remained 'twilight' knowledge in Britain. Many women still lived together in passionate friendships without necessarily seeing themselves as lesbians, and one psychologist even accepted these relationships as viable in an era when so many men had died in the war. An effort in 1920–1 to criminalise sexual relations between women in England failed, in part, because members of parliament did not want to publicise lesbianism, believing very few women even knew of its existence. As Laura Doan points out, the 1920s fashions of close-cropped hair, trousers and ties were as popular among heterosexual flappers as among lesbians. However, the 1920s also witnessed an increased hostility to spinsters, who came under suspicion as sex-starved creatures who might warp the minds of young people under their care. The trial of Radclyffe Hall's book The Well of Loneliness in 1928 did much more to publicise the concept of a lesbian identity. Hall drew on, but also modified, sexological discourses from Havelock Ellis and Edward Carpenter, as well as her experiences with women partners, to craft a novelistic plea for tolerance for lesbians as inborn 'inverts'. The novel sold well, but a conservative newspaper publisher, frustrated that his campaign against flappers and the extension of female suffrage had failed, demanded that it be censored. The Government forced the publishers to withdraw the book from circulation until 1949, but the trial publicised the concept of lesbianism much more widely than ever before. As a result, masculine fashions and female friendships suddenly became stigmatised. However, many lesbians also found Hall's ideas to be a great revelation and inspiration because it provided them with an identity and a rationale for their desires.[66]

Heterosexual behaviour had begun to change before the First World War, but these shifts became much more apparent in the 1920s. In pre-war France, the word 'to flirt' became widely used to describe seductive wordplay, kissing and caressing. By 1900, an estimated 20 per cent of French women had sex before marriage. In Britain, young people may have indulged in petting as they engaged in the courtship rituals of 'walking out' and the 'monkey rank'. But statistical studies of women's heterosexual experiences over the generations find a sharp break between the pre- and post-First World War generations. A survey of British women found that 19 per cent of married women born before 1904 had sex before their weddings, while 36 per cent of those born between 1904 and 1914 did. Only 8 per cent of married women born before 1904 had engaged in 'petting' before marriage, but 22 per cent of the next generation petted. A German study found that under 40 per cent of women born between 1895 and 1907 who were surveyed had had orgasms at any time in their lives, while 78 per cent of those born between 1907 and 1916 did. However, many women remained sexually unsatisfied in the inter-war years, as these changes percolated slowly through the generations. One French study from 1938 found that half of women were not sexually satisfied in marriage, while half regularly or sometimes experienced sexual satisfaction. In Vienna, Wilhelm Reich pointed out that workers' sex lives were constrained by their overcrowded housing; families often shared one room, giving no privacy for sex. Marie Stopes, the pioneering writer of marital advice, received thousands of letters from men and women frustrated at sexual ignorance, the difficulties of birth control and their lack of sexual pleasure.[67]

In response, sexologists argued that both men and women needed to be sexually satisfied to ensure marital happiness and the health of society, and their message finally became much more influential in popular culture during the 1920s and 1930s. The marriage-counselling movement shifted sexual morality away from the old Victorian emphasis on fear of sex imposed by authorities to a new idea of the individual's self-regulation of sex. This movement also promised to remake and transform heterosexuality with a new emphasis on 'companionate marriage'. This movement has been criticised as reinforcing 'compulsory heterosexuality' and downplaying clitoral orgasms, following Freud's lead. Some of Freud's followers warned wives that if they persisted in their 'immature' clitoral orgasms, they would never be able to have the proper vaginal orgasm. The psychoanalyst Marie Bonaparte even underwent surgery to move her clitoris closer to her vagina so that she could have an orgasm in the Freudian way. The idea that 'frigid' women also rejected their femininity put pressure on women to conform sexually. The sex-reform movement in the inter-war period, however, was not dominated by Freud's ideas, and the insistence on a vaginal rather than clitoral orgasm did not become widespread in sex advice until the 1940s. Most sex counsellors believed that a clitoral orgasm was better than leaving a woman unsatisfied. Sex counsellors urged husbands and wives to please each other sexually, insisting that husbands must learn how to bring their wives to orgasm. For instance, Marie Stopes spread information about female sexual pleasure to the masses in her book *Married Love* (1918). She criticised men for thinking that the male sexual drive was overwhelming and had to be satisfied. Instead, men must recognise when a woman became sexually receptive and learn to please her sexually, including how to stimulate the clitoris. Her 'romantic' style did not threaten popular audiences, because she portrayed women as 'mysterious coy nymphs always alluring and escaping'. The Dutch doctor Theodore van de Velde, whose *Ideal Marriage* was widely translated and extremely popular, taught men how to please their wives, including how to perform oral sex on women. He instructed couples that their goal should be simultaneous orgasms. Yet he also believed that female sexuality was passive and that men must retain control and skill in order to allow their wives to lose control. He disapproved of women on top in sex as a perversion of natural gender relations.[68]

Many sex reformers also believed in sexual or moral hygiene, which would modernise sex. They believed that uncontrolled sexual desire could be dangerous, but that properly managed and regulated, sexual pleasure could contribute to marital stability and social productivity. In Germany, social hygiene clinics were opened to counsel men and women for the purposes of eugenic marriage, but they were not very popular, since people preferred more practical information about sexual pleasure and birth control.

Socialists in Berlin and Vienna sometimes warned young people not to indulge too much in irresponsible activity, but instead, to sublimate their desires into healthy outdoor activities. In response, Wilhelm Reich criticised the social-democratic and communist sexual-hygiene movements for not focusing enough on sexual pleasure among working-class young men and women. The movement should not try to regulate and direct sexual activity, he argued, but to teach young people how to enjoy sexual pleasure. However, Reich and his followers did not always acknowledge the difficulties women in particular found in enjoying sexual pleasure and expressed hostility to homosexuality.[69]

The dramatic drop in family size among the working class also represented a significant change from the pre-First World War generation and helped make sexual pleasure possible, especially for women. Whereas working-class women of the pre-war generation tended to have large families, family size dropped to two or three children, and in many cases in Germany, only one child. Working-class women had relied on abstinence, withdrawal or abortion to control their fertility. The number of abortions in Germany and France had skyrocketed even before the war. After the war, governments in Britain and Germany slowly and reluctantly allowed health clinics to prescribe birth control for married couples, and chemists and mail-order suppliers also sold condoms. In Britain, Marie Stopes's popular works spread the knowledge and motivation for birth control to a popular audience.[70]

In Germany, the government forbade the advertisement, but not the sale, of contraceptives. Millions of men had used condoms during the war, and they became cheap and widely available. Doctors and chemists also invented new forms of diaphragms, IUDs (intrauterine devices) and chemical contraceptives, which were distributed in clinics set up by new birth-control leagues. These clinics preferred to give women chemical contraceptives and diaphragms, because condoms meant depending on men, and cervical caps and IUDs required a doctor. In 1926, the Social Democratic Government passed a law diminishing punishments for abortion, which was allowed in cases of 'medical necessity'. As James Woycke argues, once women had recourse to abortion, they realised that control of fertility was in their own hands so they became more receptive to the barrier means of birth control that were becoming more available.[71] Underground abortions were very widely practised especially among working-class women who found it difficult to get a doctor to sign off on the medical necessity clause.

Birth control and abortion also became an issue for socialists in revolutionary situations. Soviet Russia legalised abortion, through the first trimester, in 1920. In part, Alexandra Kollontai, a Bolshevik feminist, inspired these ideas through her insistence on female autonomy and free love. However, the Communist Government also faced a chaotic period of civil war in 1920, with millions of unmarried mothers and victims of rape and no resources to care for these children. During the 1920s, the Soviets claimed to be increasing access to contraception to enable women to make decisions about their sex lives and motherhood and to diminish the need for abortion. However, given the shortage of consumer goods, contraceptives were not the highest priority for the Soviet Government. Some Spanish anarchists, very interested in sex reform and eugenics, legalised abortion in Catalonia in the 1930s and promised to set up birth-control clinics to diminish need for abortion. During the turmoil of the Spanish Civil War and the hostility of the church and even many feminists to birth control, however, these promises could not be carried out.[72]

The inter-war period also witnessed a harsh backlash against these advances in contraception. The French legislature banned the distribution of contraceptive information, except condoms, in 1920, in a fit of hysteria about the decline of population after the war. The Government also prosecuted abortionists even more harshly. The birth rate did increase slightly in France in the 1920s, but Frenchwomen's long tradition of controlling their fertility could not be legislated away. In Italy, the rise of Fascism also led to increasing restrictions on birth control and abortion. The Italian birth-control movement had always been weak, in part because, unlike their northern European counterparts, Italian eugenicists saw large families as a proof of national, even imperial, virility. During the 1920s, Fascists warned that the birth rate was declining and must be reversed. From 1926–7, the Fascist Government of Mussolini heavily censored any birth-control information that might come into the country from foreign sources and punished abortion even more severely than before. However, these and other efforts to raise the birth rate were remarkably unsuccessful, and at least in one instance, women protested at the arrest of their local abortionist. In Soviet Russia, Alexandra Kollontai's ideas of sexual freedom increasingly came under attack as self-indulgence. In a 1925 interview, Lenin said that 'lack of restraint in one's sexual life is bourgeois'.[73] By the time Stalin took power, much more conservative ideas about sexuality held sway, as women's desires were subordinate to the needs of the state, and abortion was outlawed in 1936.

By 1933, the Nazis had destroyed the sex-reform movement in Germany. They had campaigned for years against what they perceived as communist and socialist sexual immorality, depicting sexualised women as symbolically responsible for Germany's defeat in the First World War. They blamed Jews for the sexual freedom of the Weimar years and promised to restore the traditional family, thus appealing to conservative and religious elements of public opinion. Upon seizing power, they immediately banned birth-control information and distribution, repealed the medical-necessity clause for abortion, closed down sex-advice clinics and burned Magnus Hirschfeld's Institute for Sex Research. They stigmatised abortion and sex reform as Jewish and communistic. They institutionalised 'promiscuous' women and arrested suspected abortionists and their clients. The Nazis, of course, were motivated by a eugenicist agenda, but one very different from that espoused by Weimar sex reformers. Racial hatred motivated them above all. In 1935, the Nazis forbade sex and intermarriage between Jews and Aryans. Neighbours harassed and denounced mixed couples to the police, although only men could be prosecuted for this offence. They put forth the idea that Aryan women were pure and needed to be protected, less they become corrupted and hypersexual. Jewish women, by contrast, were seen as racially promiscuous and dangerously seductive.[74]

Nazi sexual ideology, however, also differed from traditional conservative, especially religious, sexual morality. They did not intend to repress sex *per se*, but to ensure that sexual activities served the state and racial purity.[75] In 1935, they re-legalised certain forms of abortion to allow 'or force' the termination of 'unfit' pregnancies in women who were prostitutes, promiscuous, mentally disabled, foreign slave workers or German women impregnated by Jewish or foreign slave-worker men. A powerful strand of thought within Nazi discourse actually regarded 'Aryan' sex as healthy. Members of the Schutzstaffeln, the SS, blamed 'oriental Christians' for suppressing 'healthy' sexual attitudes. For these Nazis, sex did not need to be confined in marriage. As Julia Roos notes, 'Himmler resented the church's "moralistic" stance on extramarital sex, which he believed was conducive to the spread of male homosexual relations.' The Nazis reintroduced state-regulated brothels in 1933 and, eventually, established military brothels. They believed that men needed a sexual outlet, but unlike the Weimar sex reformers, they did not see sex as a vehicle for personal fulfilment. The SS also strengthened the position of single mothers, providing them with more welfare benefits in order to deter them from abortion and to encourage them to 'present the Fuhrer with a child'. They established secret *Lebensborn* homes for unmarried mothers. Fathers of illegitimate children gained more custody rights, but Hitler blocked a proposal to allow the SS to take in illegitimate children against the mother's will, and there is no evidence that these homes were used as places for the SS to 'mate' with Aryan women.[76]

The ambiguities of Nazi attitudes towards sex and women can also be seen in their policies toward lesbians. Once the Nazis had completely defeated feminism, they did not regard lesbians as much of a threat. In 1935, an effort to criminalise lesbianism was rejected because it would be too difficult to distinguish between lesbians and innocent female friends. The Nazis also believed that lesbianism could be a temporary state and that such women could be reclaimed for marriage. However, they also harassed lesbians. The lesbian subculture of bars, magazines and clubs disappeared, and lesbians had to adopt a protective camouflage of more feminine clothing and even false marriages. More visible lesbians could be sent to the concentration camps as 'asocial' when communism or other forms of dissidence brought them to the attention of authorities. However, the Nazis did not persecute lesbians as severely as they did homosexual men, thousands of whom died in the camps. Even then, the Nazis believed that some men who had sex with other men only once or twice could be reclaimed as soldiers.[77]

In the immediate post-war period, German fears of social chaos and contamination were projected onto women. In the occupied territories, the authorities forced women who worked in restaurants, bars and places of public entertainment to undergo examinations for venereal disease. But women who had been raped by invading Soviet soldiers were allowed to have abortions, a remnant of eugenic policies. Soon after, conservative West Germans tried to repudiate the Nazis by claiming that they were sexually promiscuous and immoral. Their solution was traditional families and sexual repression. The Nazis' restrictions on abortions were not lifted, and the network of sex-advice and birth-control clinics was not revived. Social scrutiny of young people's sexual activity was so strict that landladies could be accused of pimping for allowing tenants to have overnight visitors of the opposite sex.[78]

In the Soviet zones of eastern Europe, sexuality had to serve the state. In East Germany, abortion was recriminalised in 1950, despite women's protests. In the Soviet Union, the Government instructed doctors to report women who sought abortions in an effort to rebuild the population after the losses of the Second World War. But given the absence of other forms of contraception, which as small consumer goods were in short supply and not a priority for state industries, women in Russia and East Germany relied on abortion as their main form of birth control. The most dramatic example of state control over women's fertility came in Romania, where all abortion and birth control was banned and women were strictly monitored for pregnancies. However, in most areas of eastern Europe, unlike Romania, birth control was allowed and generous welfare benefits and daycare made it easier for women to work and take care of children. Yet, as Susan Gal notes, 'interwar communist discussions of sexual liberation and search for pleasure by women were replaced by a communist Puritanism that focused on reproductive sexuality; the existence of same-sex sexuality was simply denied.' Limitations on consumer goods made it more difficult for women to exert choices over birth control. Magazines did not stress sexual attractiveness and consumerism, and regarded sex as a duty for married women.[79]

In contrast, in 1950s' western Europe, the new consumerism was tied to marital adjustment. Freudianism gained greater influence, criticising women for clitoral orgasms and accusing them of penis envy or frigidity if they did not conform. Even in Sweden, where contraception was freely available, school sex-education curricula stressed chastity before marriage and warned that sex was primarily for procreation. General de Gaulle declared that French women must procreate to make France great once again. In Britain, governments feared a perceived expansion of street prostitution. In fact, the number of prostitutes was probably less than in the nineteenth century, but streetwalkers made London's streets seem seedy and dangerous. In 1959, the Street Offences Act forced many prostitutes off the streets and into 'commercial prostitution agencies and call-girl rackets'. But during the 1960s, a decline in demand and more economic opportunities for women led to a sharp drop in the number of prostitutes all over Europe. In France, 21 per cent of men born between 1922 and 1925 had their first sex with a prostitute, but only 6 per cent of men born between 1944 and 1951 were initiated by prostitutes, and today, almost no young men are. The same may have been true in Greece and Portugal where in previous generations, young men experienced their sexual initiation at a much younger age than young women of their own class. By the 1970s, young men and women had first sex at similar ages, probably with each other.[80]

Above all, the liberation movements of the 1960s challenged conventional sexual mores. In Germany, radicals inspired by Wilhelm Reich and Herbert Marcuse declared that Nazism had been caused, in part, by a bourgeois family structure which repressed natural sexual drives and therefore encouraged sado-masochistic impulses. They declared that Nazi influence could only be purged by overthrowing post-war restrictions on sex and experimenting with free sex and non-monogamy. Klaus Theweleit's historical volumes on *Male Fantasies* came out of this milieu. He hypothesised that German veterans after the First World War were engulfed by fears of fluid, threatening female sexuality, so in response, they yearned for hard masculine authority.[81]

The feminist movement was reborn in the tumult of the 1960s. As early as 1965, students began to agitate against regulations forbidding men to visit female students in their dorms, and, during 1968, the slogan 'make love not war' pervaded the student revolution. In part the student movement inspired women to demand their own liberation, but feminists also reacted with frustration against masculine claims for sexual freedom that ended up oppressing women. In France, restrictions on sex eroded as the women's movement established family-planning clinics and women rejected the pro-natalist message. By 1967, the Government gave in and legalised contraception. By the early 1970s, abortion began to be legalised all across Europe, in France in 1975, and in Italy in 1978, both cases demonstrating the erosion of the Catholic church's control over sexuality. Britain and West Germany, however, required social or medical reasons for abortions. By 1972, East Germans legalised abortions for much the same reasons as western governments: pressure from women who wanted to control their fertility.[82] The pill finally provided relatively safe and extremely effective contraception, as governments gradually made it available to single women.

During the 1970s and early 1980s, sections of the feminist movement also began to link pornography and sexual violence as oppressive to women. Feminists first protested against the Freudian emphasis on the vaginal orgasm. They even critiqued penetration, instead demanding clitoral orgasm.[83] Feminists also refuted the neo-Freudian idea that the rape of women and the sexual abuse of children were fantasies or individual perversions, arguing that sexual violence stemmed from structures of male domination.

The lesbian movement had its roots in both the gay-liberation movement and the feminist movement. A few lesbian clubs had sprung up in London, and the British magazine *Arena 3* started in 1963 and helped create a network of lesbians who had faced social isolation and employment discrimination.[84] By the late 1960s, lesbians could also join in the much more open and flamboyant Gay Liberation Front, but by the 1970s and 1980s lesbian separatism challenged this alliance. They proclaimed that rejecting men and having sex with women was a political act. Sheila Jeffreys' book, *The Spinster and her Enemies*, came out of this particularly historical moment, trying to trace back the lesbian heritage to the social-purity feminists of the late nineteenth century. But other feminists began to resist the message that sexual images were necessarily oppressive to women and equated the contemporary religious right with the late nineteenth-century social-purity movement. They warned that repressions on sexual expression could backfire and oppress women once again, and they also questioned the equation of celibacy with lesbian feminism, arguing that lesbianism was a sexual, not a political choice.

Between 1975 and 1989, the end of the Franco dictatorship in Spain and the end of the Cold War in eastern Europe transformed sexual cultures in similar ways. In most areas, women were able to fight back against the Catholic church's attempt to reimpose strictures on abortion. The puritanical attitudes of the Franco dictatorship and of eastern Europe Communism disappeared under the onslaught of consumer society, but also brought widespread pornography and sexualised advertising. Women in eastern Europe reacted with ambivalence. Some welcomed the new focus on sexualised femininity as pleasurable and adventurous, whereas other women, especially older women and working-class women, found these sexualised images demeaning or laughable.[85]

In western Europe, to a much greater extent than in the USA, sexual cultures have been shaped by a secular society, where cohabitation is common and same-sex partnerships legally recognised. Europeans increasingly began to believe that sex should be a matter of the private rights of the individual and that the government should not interfere. But Europe shares with the USA a media culture saturated with sexuality. While eighteenth-century people regarded female sexual desire in terms of fertility, twentieth-century people associated sex with consumption.

Conclusion

Ideas about female sexuality have changed dramatically from the eighteenth century to the late twentieth century. Even medical depictions about the female genital organs have been culturally shaped. As we have seen, popular sex manuals of the eighteenth century still believed that female orgasm was necessary for a woman to conceive and, as a result, they believed that female sexual pleasure was important, regarding male and female genitals as inverted versions of each other. By the nineteenth century, doctors depicted women's bodies as utterly different to those of men, and downplayed the importance of female desire. Freud and his followers resurrected the female sexual drive, but they insisted that only the vaginal orgasm was mature. Feminists in the 1970s had to reshape their ideas of their own bodies to claim female sexual autonomy.

Whether female sexual desire has been regarded as passive or voracious, authorities have always seen it as dangerous. Institutions to incarcerate unruly women have ranged from the late seventeenth-century La Salpêtrière to the nineteenth-century workhouses for unmarried mothers to twentieth-century homes for the feeble-minded. As Foucault pointed out, doctors and psychiatrists developed discourses that labelled homosexuals and prostitutes as deviant identities. But he failed to acknowledge that women, much more than men, risked being labelled and incarcerated (with the exception of lesbians in the nineteenth century). A man could frequent a prostitute privately and retain his public respectability, but if a woman sold sex even once or twice, middle-class moralists would denounce her as a whore. In the nineteenth century, the harassment of streetwalkers warned all women to stay off the street at night. By the twentieth century, the lesbian gained visibility as the new warning to women, as psychiatrists admonished the New Woman not to be perverse in her freedom.

Women have had to grapple with these contradictory and negative social constructions of female desire in their own experiences. Yet they have often evaded and refused these definitions. Efforts to regulate prostitutes always failed, as women who sold sex refused to register. Nineteenth-century women who loved women spoke of their desires in coded language. Early twentieth-century working women whispered the address of abortionists to each other. More openly, feminists demanded the abolition of the regulationist system and the legalisation of abortion. Yet when historians search the past to try to understand female sexual experiences, debating the fluidity of identity and the competing pulls of pleasure and danger, sexuality still remains in a mysterious and alluring twilight, only half understood.

Guide to further reading

Allen, Ann Taylor, *Feminism and Motherhood in Germany, 1800–1914*. New Brunswick, NJ: Rutgers University Press, 1991. This book surveys the debates among German feminists about abortion, unmarried mothers and prostitution.

Benabou, Erica-Marie, *La Prostitution et la police des moeurs au XVIIIeme siècle*. Paris: Perrin, 1987. Based on research in police archives, Benabou looks at the lives of eighteenth-century French prostitutes and how the police tried to regulate them.

Bland, Lucy, *Banishing the Beast: English Feminism and Sexual Morality 1885–1914*. London: Penguin, 1995. This book surveys the debates among English feminists about social purity, celibacy and birth control in the late nineteenth century and covers responses to early sexology.

Bland, Lucy and Laura Doan, eds, *Sexology in Culture: Labelling Bodies and Desires*. New York: Routledge, 1998. This is a very useful collection of essays on sexology.

Bonnet, Marie-Jo, *Les Relations Amoureuses entre Les Femmes du XVIe au XXe Siècle*. Paris: Editions Odile Jacob, 1995. A significant study of lesbians in France, concentrating on upper-class lesbians.

Clark, Anna, *Women's Silence, Men's Violence: Sexual Assault in England, 1770–1845*. London: Pandora, 1987. This book covers sexual violence in courtship, political myths of rape and ideologies of libertine masculinity.

Cook, Hera, *The Long Sexual Revolution: English Women, Sex, and Contraception 1800–1975*. Oxford: Oxford University Press, 2004. This book covers much more than birth control; Cook traces changes in sexual behaviour and attitudes for a significant challenge to most of the historiography on sexuality.

D'Cruze, Shani, *Crimes of Outrage: Sex, Violence, and Victorian Working Women*. London: UCL Press, 1998. This is a careful examination of mid- to late nineteenth-century cases of sexual assault and other types of violence against women.

Dean, Carolyn, *The Frail Social Body: Pornography, Homosexuality, and Other Fantasies in Interwar France*. Berkeley, Calif.: University of California Press, 2000. Dean shows how anxieties engendered by the First World War were projected onto women and homosexuals in cultural forms.

Doan, Laura, *Fashioning Sapphism: The Origins of Modern English Lesbian Culture*. New York: Columbia University Press, 2001. This book reinterprets the flapper style before Radclyffe Hall's trial and also the circumstances of the trial itself, demonstrating its importance for the emergence of lesbian identity.

Donoghue, Emma, *Passions between Women: British Lesbian Culture 1688–1801*. London: Scarlet Press, 1993. Donoghue challenged the idea that people could not conceive of lesbianism before the nineteenth century, revealing many eighteenth-century allusions to lesbianism.

Foucault, Michel, *The History of Sexuality: An Introduction*, trans. by Robert Hurley. New York: Vintage Books, 1990. A pioneering work that established the paradigm for the field of the history of sexuality.

Fuchs, Rachel G., *Poor and Pregnant in Nineteenth-Century Paris*. New Brunswick, NJ: Rutgers University Press, 1992. An intensive study of unmarried mothers and cohabitation, tracing changing experiences and social policies.

Gibson, Mary, *Prostitution and the State in Italy*, 2nd edn. Columbus, Ohio: Ohio State University Press, 1999. This book examines the regulationist system in Italy.

Grossmann, Atina, *Reforming Sex: The German Movement for Birth Control and Abortion Reform, 1920–1950*. New York: Columbia University Press, 1995. Grossmann demonstrates that a flourishing movement for birth control and sex reform was crushed by the Nazis.

Harsin, Jill, *Policing Prostitution in Nineteenth-Century Paris*. Paris: Princeton University Press, 1985. This book examines the regulationist system in France.

Jackson, Louise A., *Child Sexual Abuse in Victorian England*. London: Routledge, 2000. A careful study of court records and institutional records concerning child sex abuse.

Jeffreys, Sheila, *The Spinster and Her Enemies*. London: Pandora, 1985. A controversial interpretation of the social-purity movement from the point of view of lesbian feminism.

Laqueur, Thomas W., *Making Sex: Body and Gender from the Greeks to Freud*. Cambridge, Mass.: Harvard University Press, 1990. This book established a paradigm for shifts in ideas about sex and gender from the pre-modern to the modern world.

Levine, Philippa, *Prostitution, Race, and Politics: Policing Venereal Disease in the British Empire*. New York: Routledge, 2003. A comparative study of British contagious-diseases regulation in different regions of the British Empire in Asia.

McLaren, Angus, *Birth Control in Nineteenth-Century England*. New York: Holmes & Meier, 1978. A classic with much information about the practices and politics of birth control.

Oram, Alison and Annemarie Turnbull, eds, *The Lesbian History Sourcebook*. London: Routledge, 2001. An invaluable source for rare primary-source accounts of lesbianism.

Porter, Roy and Leslie Hall, *The Facts of Life: The Creation of Sexual Knowledges in Britain, 1650–1950*. New Haven, Conn.: Yale University Press, 1995. This book traces medical and popular knowledge about sex from the early modern period to the late nineteenth century and provides valuable assessment of debates.

Roberts, Mary Louise, *Civilization without Sexes: Reconstructing Gender in Postwar France, 1917–1927*. Chicago, Ill.: University of Chicago Press. This book demonstrates how the 'New Woman' became a focus for anxieties about sexual modernity in the wake of the First World War.

Schoppmann, Claudia, *Days of Masquerade: Life Stories of Lesbians during the Third Reich*, trans. Allison Brown. New York: Columbia University Press, 1998. Primary source narratives of hidden lives.

Sohn, Anne-Marie, *Du premier baiser à l'alcôve: la sexualité des français au quotidien (1850–1950)*. Paris: Aubier, 1996. This book is based on extensive archival research into letters, memoirs and court records, providing an in-depth look at changing experiences and attitudes towards courtship, marital sex, homosexuality, rape and prostitution, as well as a good narrative of dramatic changes that challenges Foucault's paradigm.

Stoler, Laura Ann, *Carnal Knowledge and Imperial Power: Race and the Intimate in Colonial Rule*. Berkeley, Calif.: University of California Press, 2002. This book established the framework for examining how interracial sex challenges the boundaries of race in imperial colonies.

Trumbach, Randolph, *Sex and the Gender Revolution*. Chicago, Ill.: University of Chicago Press, 1998. The first volume in a promised multi-part series, this book argues that violence was a pervasive part of sex in eighteenth-century London and also extensively reports on prostitution.

Vicinus, Martha, *Intimate Friends: Women who Loved Women, 1778–1928*. Chicago, Ill.: University of Chicago Press, 2004, This is a subtle dissection of the ways in which mostly elite women were able to articulate their erotic passion for each other through coded languages.

Vigarello, Georges, *A History of Rape: Sexual Violence in France from the sixteenth to the twentieth century*, trans. Jean Birrell. Cambridge: Polity, 2001. An important survey of laws and attitudes toward rape in France.

Walkowitz, Judith, *Prostitution in Victorian Society: Women, Class, and State*. Cambridge University Press: Cambridge, 1980. A path-breaking work which combines a Foucauldian analysis with careful archival research to illuminate prostitutes' experiences, government policy and the feminist response.

Notes

1 Sheila Jeffreys, *The Spinster and Her Enemies* (London: Pandora, 1985).
2 Judith Walkowitz, *City of Dreadful Delight: Narratives of Sexual Danger in Late-Victorian London* (Chicago, Ill.: Chicago University Press, 1992), p. 243. Judith Walkowitz, *Prostitution in Victorian Society: Women, Class, and State* (Cambridge: Cambridge University Press, 1980).
3 Lucy Bland, *Banishing the Beast: English Feminism and Sexual Morality 1885–1914* (London: Penguin, 1995), p. 250.
4 Thomas W. Laqueur, *Making Sex: Body and Gender from the Greeks to Freud* (Cambridge, Mass.: Harvard University Press, 1990).
5 Katherine Park and Robert Nye, 'Making Sex: Body and Gender from the Greeks to Freud (book review)', *New Republic*, 18 February, 1991, p. 53; Michael Stolberg, 'A Woman Down to Her Bones: The Anatomy of Sexual Difference in the Sixteenth and Early Seventeenth Centuries', *Isis*, 94, (2003), pp. 274–303.
6 Nancy Cott, 'Passionlessness: An Interpretation of Victorian Sexual Ideology, 1790–1850', *Signs*, 4, (1978), pp. 219–36.
7 Peter Gay, *Education of the Senses* (Oxford: Oxford University Press, 1985).
8 Michel Foucault, *The History of Sexuality: An Introduction*, trans. Robert Hurley (New York: Vintage Books, 1990).

9 Hera Cook, *The Long Sexual Revolution: English Women, Sex, and Contraception 1800–1975* (Oxford: Oxford University Press, 2004), p. 100.

10 Lillian Faderman, *Surpassing the Love of Men: Romantic Friendship and Love between Women from the Renaissance to the Present* (London: Junction Books, 1981).

11 Judith Butler, *Gender Trouble* (New York: Routledge, 1990), p. 134 and Judith Butler, *The Psychic Life of Power* (Stanford, Calif.: Stanford University Press, 1997), p. 147.

12 For further elucidation of this concept, see Anna Clark, 'Twilight Moments', *Journal of the History of Sexuality* 14, 1/2 (2005).

13 Erica-Marie Benabou, *La Prostitution et la police des moeurs au XVIIIeme siècle* (Paris: Perrin, 1987), p. 239; Randolph Trumbach, *Sex and the Gender Revolution* (Chicago, Ill.: University of Chicago Press, 1998), p. 195; Henrik Stevnsborg, 'Aims and Methods of the Official Campaign against Prostitution in Copenhagen, 1769–1780', *Scandinavian Journal of History [Sweden]*, 6, (1981), p. 212.

14 James R. Farr, *Authority and Sexuality in Early Modern Burgundy* (New York: Oxford University Press, 1995), p. 44; Kevin McQuillan, *Culture, Religion, and Demographic Behavior: Catholics and Lutherans in Alsace, 1750–1870* (Montreal: McGill-Queen's University Press, 1999), p. 81; Anders Brandstrom, 'Illegitimacy and Lone-Parenthood in XIXth Century Sweden', *Annales de Demographie Historique [France]*, 2, (1998), p. 95; Isabel V. Hull, *Sexuality, State, and Civil Society in Germany, 1700–1815* (Ithaca, NY: Cornell University Press, 1996), p. 127.

15 Massimo Livi Bacci, *The Population of Europe: A History*, trans. Cynthia De Nardi Ipsen and Carl Ipsen (Oxford: Blackwell, 2000), p. 108; John Knodel, *Demographic Behavior in the Past* (Cambridge: Cambridge University Press, 1988), p. 124.

16 Roy Porter and Leslie Hall, *The Facts of Life: The Creation of Sexual Knowledges in Britain, 1650–1950* (New Haven, Conn.: Yale University Press, 1995), p. 69; *Aristotle's Compleat Masterpiece. In Three Parts. Displaying the Secrets of Nature in the Generation of Man* (London: 1733), p. 7; *Aristotle's Masterpiece compleated, in Two Parts* (London: 1698), p. 86; Herman Roodenburg, '*Venus Minsieke Gaasthuis*: Sexual Beliefs in Eighteenth-Century Holland', in Jan Bremmer, ed., *From Sappho to de Sade: Moments in the History of Sexuality* (London: Routledge, 1989), p. 100; Nicolas de Venette, *Tableau de l'amour conjugal, ou la génération de l'Homme*, new edn (Amsterdam: n.d.), p. 151; Jane Sharp, *The Midwives Book. Or the Whole Art of Midwifry, Discovered: Directing Childbearing Women How to Behave Themselves in their Conception, Breeding, Bearing, and Nursing of Children* (London: 1671), p. 33.

17 Laqueur, *Making Sex*, pp. 63–114; Kathleen Wellman, 'Physicians and Philosophes: Physiology and Sexual Morality in the French Enlightenment', *Eighteenth-Century Studies*, 35, (2002), p. 270.

18 Margaret C. Jacob, 'The Materialist World of Pornography', in Lynn Hunt, ed., *The Invention of Pornography* (Cambridge, Mass.: Zone Books, 1993), p. 164.

19 Robert Darnton, *The Forbidden Best-Sellers of Pre-Revolutionary France* (New York: W. W. Norton, 1995), p. 292; Chorier, *Satyra sotadica* (1660) quoted in Manuela Mourao, 'The Representation of Female Desire in Early Modern Pornographic Texts, 1660–1745', *Signs*, 24, (1999), p. 580; Emma Donoghue, *Passions between Women: British Lesbian Culture 1688–1801* (London: Scarlet Press, 1993), p. 194.

20 *A Sapphick Epistle, from Jack Cavendish, to the Honorable Mrs. D-R*, (London: 1778?).

21 Jeffrey Merrick and Bryant T. Ragan, *Homosexuality in Early Modern France: A Documentary Reader* (New York: Oxford University Press, 2001), p. 204.

22 Georges Vigarello, *A History of Rape: Sexual Violence in France from the sixteenth to the twentieth century*, trans. Jean Birrell (Cambridge: Polity, 2001), pp. 88–94.

23 Patricia Mainardi, *Husbands, Wives, and Lovers: Marriage and Its Discontents in Nineteenth Century France* (New Haven, Conn.: Yale University Press, 2003), p. 17.

24 Barry Reay, 'Sexuality in Nineteenth-Century England: The Social Context of Illegitimacy in Rural Kent', *Rural History [Great Britain]*, 1, (1990), p. 221; Ann-Sofie Kalvemark, 'Illegitimacy and Marriage in Three Swedish Parishes in the Nineteenth Century', in Peter Laslett, Karla Oosterveen and Richard M. Smith, eds, *Bastardy and Its Comparative History* (Cambridge, Mass.: Harvard University Press, 1980), p. 330; Margareta R. Matovic,

'Illegitimacy and Marriage in Stockholm in the Nineteenth Century', in Laslett et al., eds, *Bastardy and Its Comparative History*, p. 336; Jan Kok, 'The Moral Nation: Illegitimacy and Bridal Pregnancy in the Netherlands from 1600 to the Present', *Economic and Social History in the Netherlands [Netherlands]*, 2, (1990), p. 10.

25 Edward Shorter, 'Female Emancipation, Birth Control, and Fertility in European History', *American Historical Review*, 78, (1973), p. 605–40; Peter Laslett, 'Introduction: Comparing Illegitimacy over Time and between Cultures', in Laslett et al., eds, *Bastardy and Its Comparative History*, p. 27; Michael Mitterauer, *The European Family: Patriarchy to Partnership from the Middle Ages to the Present*, trans. Karla Oosterveen and Manfred Horzinger (Chicago, Ill.: University of Chicago Press, 1982), p. 127; Louise A. Tilly, Joan W. Scott and Miriam Cohen, 'Women's Work and European Fertility Patterns', *Journal of Interdisciplinary History*, 6, 3, (1976), pp. 447–76.

26 Louise A. Tilly and Joan W. Scott, *Women, Work, and Family* (New York: Routledge, 1989), p. 50; Brandstrom, 'Illegitimacy and Lone-Parenthood in XIXth Century Sweden', p. 110; Jan van Bavel, 'Family Control, Bridal Pregnancy, and Illegitimacy: An Event History Analysis in Leuven, Belgium, 1846–1856', *Social Science History*, 25, (2001), pp. 449–79.

27 Anna Clark, *Women's Silence, Men's Violence: Sexual Assault in England, 1770–1845* (London: Pandora, 1987), p. 70; Shani D'Cruze found a similar percentage in affiliation cases; Shani D'Cruze, *Crimes of Outrage: Sex, Violence, and Victorian Working Women* (London: UCL Press, 1998), pp. 110–20.

28 Françoise Barret-Ducrocq, *Love in the Time of Victoria*, trans. John Howe (London: Verso, 1991), p. 46; Anne-Marie Sohn, *Du premier baiser à l'alcôve: la sexualité des français au quotidien (1850–1950)* (Paris: Aubier, 1996), p. 250; Anna Clark, *The Struggle for the Breeches: Gender and the Making of the British Working Class* (Berkeley, Calif.: University of California Press, 1995), ch. 3.

29 Clark, *Women's Silence*, p. 81; Vigarello, *A History of Rape*, pp. 50–4.

30 Rachel G. Fuchs, *Poor and Pregnant in Nineteenth-Century Paris* (New Brunswick, NJ: Rutgers University Press, 1992), p. 18; M. Frey, 'Du mariage et du concubinage dans les classes populaires a Paris (1846–1847)', *Annales: E. S. C.*, 33, (1978), p. 810; Mitterauer, *The European Family*, p. 132.

31 Sohn, *Du premier baiser*, p. 82; Cook, *Long Sexual Revolution*, p. 100.

32 Gay, *Education of the Senses*, p. 155; Porter and Hall, *Facts of Life*, p. 142.

33 Mary Lynn Stewart, *For Health and Beauty: Physical Culture for Frenchwomen, 1880s-1930s* (Baltimore, Md.: Johns Hopkins University Press, 2001), p. 113; Kirsten von Sydow, 'Female Sexuality and Historical Time: A Comparison of Sexual Biographies of German Women Born between 1895 and 1936', *Archives of Sexual Behavior*, 25, (1996), p. 479.

34 Alain Corbin, 'Backstage', in Michelle Perrot, ed., *A History of Private Life: From the Fires of Revolution to the Great War* (Cambridge, Mass.: Harvard University Press, 1990), p. 492; Mary Jo Maynes, *Taking the Hard Road: Life Course in French and German Workers Autobiographies in the Era of Industrialization* (Chapel Hill, NC: University of North Carolina Press, 1995), p. 80.

35 Joshua Cole, *The Power of Large Numbers: Population, Politics, and Gender in Nineteenth-Century France* (Ithaca, NY: Cornell University Press, 2000), p. 194; Bacci, *The Population of Europe: A History*, p. 157; Chiara Saraceno, 'Constructing Families, Shaping Women's Lives: The Making of Italian Families between Market Economies and State Interventions', in John R. Gillis, Louise A. Tilly and David Levine, eds, *The European Experience of Declining Fertility* (Oxford: Blackwell, 1992), p. 256.

36 Wally Seccombe, 'Men's "Marital Rights" and Women's "Wifely Duties": Changing Conjugal Relations in the Fertility Decline', in Gillis et al., eds, *The European Experience of Declining Fertility*, p. 68; Cook, *Long Sexual Revolution*, p. 100; Sohn, *Du premier baiser*, p. 132.

37 Angus McLaren, *Birth Control in Nineteenth-Century England* (New York: Holmes & Meier, 1978), p. 246–7.

38 Sohn, *Du premier baiser*, p. 52; Joan DeJean, *Fictions of Sappho* (Chicago, Ill.: University of Chicago Press, 1989), p. 266.

39 Faderman, *Surpassing the Love of Men*, p. 82.

40 Helena Whitbread, *I Know My Own Heart: The Diaries of Anne Lister 1791–1840* (London: Virago Press, 1988).

41 Lisa Moore, '"Something More Tender Still than Friendship": Romantic Friendship in Early-Nineteenth Century England', *Feminist Studies*, 18, (1992), p. 499; Martha Vicinus, *Independent Women: Work and Community for Single Women 1850–1920* (Chicago, Ill.: University of Chicago Press, 1985), p. 187; Martha Vicinus, *Intimate Friends: Women Who Loved Women, 1778–1928* (Chicago, Ill.: University of Chicago Press, 2004), p. 230.

42 Theo van der Meer, 'Tribades on Trial: Female Same-Sex Offenders in Late Eighteenth-Century Amsterdam', in John C. Fout, ed., *Forbidden History: The State, Society, and the Regulation of Sexuality in Modern Europe* (Chicago, Ill.: University of Chicago Press, 1991), pp. 189–210.

43 Nadezhda Durova, *The Cavalry Maiden: Journals of a Russian Officer in the Napoleonic Wars*, trans. Mary Fleming Zirin (Bloomington, Ind.: Indiana University Press, 1988), p. 114; Alison Oram and Annemarie Turnbull, eds, *The Lesbian History Sourcebook* (London: Routledge, 2001), p. 13.

44 Michael Ryan, *Prostitution in London* (London: 1839), p. 179.

45 The following paragraphs rely on these works: Jill Harsin, *Policing Prostitution in Nineteenth-Century Paris* (Paris: Princeton University Press, 1985), p. 301; Mary Gibson, *Prostitution and the State in Italy*, 2nd edn (Columbus, Ohio: Ohio State University Press, 1999), p. 110; Carine Steverlynck, 'La Traite des blanches et la prostitution enfantine en Belgique', *Paedagogica Historica [Belgium]*, 29, (1993), p. 790; Jolanta Sikorska-Kulesza and Agnieszka Kreczmar, 'Prostitution in Congress Poland', *Acta Poloniae Historica [Poland]*, 83, (2001), pp. 130–1; Barbara Alpern Engel, 'St Petersburg Prostitutes in the Late Nineteenth Century: A Personal and Social Profile', *Russian Review*, 48, (1989), pp. 24–9; Judith Walkowitz, *Prostitution in Victorian Society: Women, Class, and State* (Cambridge: Cambridge University Press, 1980), p. 16.

46 Philippa Levine, *Prostitution, Race, and Politics: Policing Venereal Disease in the British Empire* (New York: Routledge, 2003); Walkowitz, *Prostitution*, p. 50.

47 Gibson, *Prostitution in Italy*, p. 129; Sikorska-Kulesza and Kreczmar, 'Prostitution in Congress Poland', p. 124.

48 Walkowitz, *Prostitution*, p. 60; Levine, *Prostitution, Race, and Politics*, p. 94.

49 Schaepdrijver, 'Regulated Prostitution in Brussels, 1844–1877', p. 94; Steverlynck, 'La Traite des blanches et la prostitution enfantine en Belgique', p. 798; Deborah Gorham, 'The "Maiden Tribute of Modern Babylon" Re-Examined: Child Prostitution and the Idea of Childhood in Late-Victorian England', *Victorian Studies*, 21, (1978), pp. 353–79; Louise A. Jackson, *Child Sexual Abuse in Victorian England* (London: Routledge, 2000), p. 132.

50 Ann Taylor Allen, *Feminism and Motherhood in Germany, 1800–1914* (New Brunswick, NJ: Rutgers University Press, 1991), p. 225.

51 Himani Banerji, 'Age of Consent and Hegemonic Social Reform', in Clare Midgley, ed., *Gender and Imperialism* (Manchester: Manchester University Press, 1998), p. 21; British Library, India Office Library, L/PJ/6/283 1890. Judicial and Public Annual papers. Papers concerning law about restitution of conjugal rights; Tanika Sarkar, 'A Prehistory of Rights: The Age of Consent Debate in Colonial Bengal', *Feminist Studies*, 26, (2000), pp. 601–22; Mrinilini Sinha, *Colonial Masculinity: The Manly Englishman and the Effeminate Bengali in the Late Nineteenth Century* (Manchester: Manchester University Press, 1995), pp. 150–200.

52 Allen, *Feminism and Motherhood*, p. 191.

53 Michael Mason, *The Making of Victorian Sexuality* (Oxford: Oxford University Press, 1994), p. 63; Aletta Jacobs and Harriet Feinberg, eds, *Memories: My Life as an International Leader in Health, Suffrage, and Peace*, trans. Annie Wright (New York: The Feminist Press at the City University of New York, 1996), p. 50; Hettie A. Pott-Buter, *Facts and Fairy Tales about Female Labor, Family and Fertility: A Seven-Country Comparison, 1850–1990* (Amsterdam: Amsterdam University Press, 1993), p. 186; Elinor Accampo, 'The Rhetoric of Reproduction and the Reconfiguration of Womanhood in the French Birth Control Movement, 1890–1920', *Journal of Family History*, 31, (1996), pp. 357–63; Felicia Gordon, *The Integral Feminist: Madeleine Pelletier, 1874–1939: Feminism, Socialism and Medicine* (Minneapolis, Minn.: University of Minnesota Press, 1990), p. 135.

54 Ellen Key, *Love and Marriage*, trans. Arthur G. Chater (New York: Putnam, 1911), p. 39; Edward Ross Dickinson, 'Reflections on Feminism and Monism in the Kaiserreich, 1900–1913', *Central European History*, 34, (2001), p. 208; Bland, *Banishing the Beast*, p. 278.

55 Sohn, *Du premier baiser*, p. 57.

56 ibid.; Bland, *Banishing the Beast*, p. 84; Allen, *Feminism and Motherhood*, p. 87; Gert Hekma, 'A History of Sexology: Social and Historical Aspects of Sexuality', in Jan Bremmer, ed., *From Sappho to de Sade: Moments in the History of Sexuality* (New York: Routledge, 1991), p. 182.

57 Thomas W. Laqueur, 'Sexual Desire and the Market Economy during the Industrial Revolution', in Domna C. Stanton, ed., *Discourses of Sexuality from Aristotle to AIDS* (Ann Arbor, Mich.: University of Michigan Press, 1992), p. 235.

58 Sheila Jeffreys, *The Spinster and Her Enemies* (London: Pandora, 1985), pp. 130–41; Renate Hauser, 'Krafft-Ebing's Psychological Understanding of Sexual Behavior', in Roy Porter and Mikulas Teich, eds, *Sexual Knowledge, Sexual Science: A History of Attitudes to Sexuality* (Cambridge: Cambridge University Press, 1994), pp. 212–14; Vigarello, *A History of Rape*, p. 183; L. Thoinot, *Medicolegal Aspects of Moral Offenses*, trans. Arthur W. Weysse (Philadelphia, Pa.: F. A. Davis Company, 1913), p. 80; Dr L. Loewenfeld, *On Conjugal Happiness: Experiences and Reflections of a Medical Man*, trans. Ronald E. S. Krohn, 3rd edn (London: John Bale, Sons, and Danielsson, Ltd., 1913), p. 200; Stewart, *For Health and Beauty*, p. 99.

59 Cesare Lombroso and Guglielmo Ferrero, 'The Female Offender (1893)', in Lucy Bland and Laura Doan, eds, *Sexology Uncensored: The Documents of Social Science* (Chicago, Ill.: University of Chicago Press, 1998), p. 20; Mary Louise Roberts, *Disruptive Acts: The New Woman in Fin-de-Siècle France* (Chicago: University of Chicago Press, 2001), p. 78; Judy Greenway, 'It's what You Do with It that Counts: Interpretations of Otto Weininger', in Bland and Doan, eds, *Sexology in Culture*, p. 30; Otto Weininger, 'Sex and Character (1903)', in Blaikie and Doan, eds, *Sexology Uncensored*, pp. 25–7.

60 Laura Engelstein, 'Lesbian Vignettes: A Russian Triptych from the 1890s', *Signs*, 15, (1990), p. 815; Bland, *Banishing the Beast*, p. 264; Jeffreys, *The Spinster and Her Enemies*, p. 109; Key, *Love and Marriage*, p. 74; F. W. S. [Stella] Browne, *The Sexual Variety and Variability among Women* (1917) in Oram and Turnbull, eds, *Lesbian History Sourcebook*, p. 108.

61 Allen, *Feminism and Motherhood*, p. 170; Oram and Turnbull, eds, *Lesbian History Sourcebook*, pp. 101–7; Lillian Faderman and Brigitte Eriksson, *Lesbians in Germany: 1890s-1920s* (Tallahassee, Fla.: Naiad, 1990).

62 Key, *Love and Marriage*, p. 150; Dickinson, 'Reflections on Feminism and Monism in the Kaiserreich, 1900–1913', p. 200; Rachel Fuchs, 'Seduction, Paternity and the Law in Fin-de-Siècle France', *Journal of Modern History*, 72, (2000), p. 985.

63 Laura Ann Stoler, *Carnal Knowledge and Imperial Power: Race and the Intimate in Colonial Rule* (Berkeley, Calif.: University of California Press, 2002).

64 Carolyn Dean, *Sexuality and Modern Western Culture* (New York: Twayne Publishers, 1996), p. 114; Jean-Yves Le Naour, *Misères et tourments de la chair durant la grand guerre* (Paris: Aubier, 2002), p. 402; Mary Louise Roberts, *Civilization without Sexes: Reconstructing Gender in Postwar France, 1917–1927* (Chicago, Ill.: University of Chicago Press), pp. 40–62.

65 Carolyn Dean, *The Frail Social Body: Pornography, Homosexuality, and Other Fantasies in Interwar France* (Berkeley, Calif.: University of California Press, 2000), p. 196; Marie-Jo Bonnet, *Les Relations amoureuses entre les femmes du XVIe au XXe siècle* (Paris: Editions Odile Jacob, 1995), p. 316; Claudia Schoppmann, *Days of Masquerade: Life Stories of Lesbians during the Third Reich*, trans. Allison Brown (New York: Columbia University Press, 1998), pp. 4–6.

66 Laura Doan, '"Acts of Female Indecency": Sexology's Intervention in Legislating Lesbianism', in Bland and Doan, eds, *Sexology in Culture*, pp. 198–213; Laura Doan, *Fashioning Sapphism: The Origins of Modern English Lesbian Culture* (New York: Columbia University Press, 2001), p. 122; Oram and Turnbull, eds, *Lesbian History Sourcebook*, pp. 181–200.

67 Sohn, *Du premier baiser*, p. 224; Eustace Chesser, *The Sexual, Marital and Family Relationships of the Englishwoman* (London: Hutchinson's Medical Publications, 1956), p. 311; Sydow, 'Female Sexuality and Historical Time', p. 479; Laure Adler, *Secrets d'alcôve. Histoire du couple de 1830 à 1930* (Paris: 1983), p. 95.

68 Jane Lewis, 'Public Institution and Private Relationship: Marriage and Marriage Guidance, 1920–1968', *Twentieth Century British History*, Vol. I, (1990), p. 235; Hall, *Sexual Knowledge, Sexual Science*, p. 219; Cook, *Long Sexual Revolution*, p. 209; Lesley A. Hall, 'Feminist Reconfigurations of Heterosexuality in the 1920s', in Bland and Doan, eds, *Sexology in Culture*, pp. 140–3; Angus McLaren, *Twentieth-Century Sexuality: A History* (Oxford: Blackwell, 1999), pp. 50–62.

69 Atina Grossmann, *Reforming Sex: The German Movement for Birth Control and Abortion Reform, 1920–1950* (New York: Columbia University Press, 1995), p. 22; Helmut Gruber, 'Sexuality in "Red Vienna": Socialist Party Conceptions and Programs and Working-Class Life, 1920–34', *International Labor and Working-Class History*, 31, (1987), p. 41.

70 Lewis, 'Public Institution and Private Relationship', p. 238.

71 James Woycke, *Birth Control in Germany, 1871–1933* (London: Routledge, 1988), p. 105.

72 Dr A. Gens, 'The Demand for Abortion in Soviet Russia', in *Sexual Reform Congress: World League for Sexual Reform: Proceedings of the Third Congress* (London: World League for Sexual Reform, 1930); Mary Nash, 'Un/Contested Identities: Motherhood, Sex Reform, and the Modernization of Gender Identity in Early Twentieth-Century Spain', in Victoria Enders and Pamela Radcliffe, eds, *Constructing Spanish Womanhood: Female Identity in Modern Spain* (Albany, NY: SUNY Press), p. 38.

73 Roberts, *Civilization without Sexes*, p. 124; Maria Sophia Quine, *Population Politics in Twentieth-Century Europe* (London: Routledge, 1996), pp. 37–50; Eric Naiman, *Sex in Public: The Incarnation of Early Soviet Ideology* (Princeton, NJ: Princeton University Press, 1997), p. 115.

74 Patricia Szobar, 'Telling Sexual Stories in the Nazi Courts of Law: Race Defilement in Germany, 1933–1945', *Journal of the History of Sexuality*, 11, (2002), pp. 131–63.

75 Elizabeth D. Heineman, 'Sexuality and Nazism: The Doubly Unspeakable?' *Journal of the History of Sexuality*, 11, (2002), p. 32.

76 Grossmann, *Reforming Sex*, p. 122; Dagmar Herzog, 'Hubris and Hypocrisy, Incitement and Disavowal', *Journal of the History of Sexuality*, 11, (2002), pp. 9–12; Julia Roos, 'Backlash against Prostitutes' Rights: Origins and Dynamics of Nazi Prostitution Policies', *Journal of the History of Sexuality*, 11, (2002), p. 90; Georg Lilienthal, 'The Illegitimacy Question in Germany, 1900–1945: Areas of Tension in Social and Population Policy', *Continuity and Change [Great Britain]*, 5, (1990), p. 270.

77 Schoppmann, *Days of Masquerade*, pp. 5–16.

78 Grossmann, *Reforming Sex*, p. 192; Dagmar Herzog, '"Pleasure, Sex, and Politics Belong Together": Post-Holocaust Memory and the Sexual Revolution in West Germany', *Critical Inquiry*, 24, (1998), p. 414.

79 Chris Burton, 'Minzdrav, Soviet Doctors, and the Policing of Reproduction in the Late Stalinist Years', *Russian History*, 27, (2000), pp. 197–221; Susan Gal and Gail Kligman, *The Politics of Gender after Socialism* (Princeton, NJ: Princeton University Press, 2000), pp. 54–110.

80 Graham Fennell, 'Introduction', in Hans L. Zetterberg, *Sexual Life in Sweden* (New Brunswick, NJ: Transaction Publishers, 2002), p. 13; Jeffrey Weeks, *Sex, Politics and Society: The Regulation of Sexuality Since 1800*, 2nd edn (London: Longmans, 1989), p. 244; Michel Bozon, 'Reaching Adult Sexuality: First Intercourse and its Implications, From Calendar to Attitudes', in Michel Bozon and Henri Leridon, eds, *Sexuality and the Social Sciences: A French Survey on Sexual Behaviour* (Aldershot: Dartmouth, 1996), p. 152; Julien O. Teitler, 'Trends in Youth Sexual Initiation and Fertility in Developed Countries: 1960–1995', *Annals of the American Academy of Political and Social Science*, 580, (2002), p. 136.

81 Herzog, 'Pleasure, Sex, and Politics Belong Together', p. 2; Klaus Theweleit, *Male Fantasies*, trans. Stephen Conway, 2 vols (Minneapolis, Minn.: University of Minnesota Press, 1989).

82 Michael Seidman, 'The Pre-May 1968 Sexual Revolution', *Contemporary French Civilization*, 25, (2001), p. 23; Dean, *Sexuality and Modern Western Culture*, p. 67; Donna Harsch, 'Society, the State, and Abortion in East German, 1950–1972', *American Historical Review*, 102, (1997), pp. 53–84.
83 Herzog, 'Pleasure, Sex, and Politics Belong Together', p. 420.
84 Oram and Turnbull, eds, *Lesbian History Sourcebook*, p. 262.
85 Gal and Kligman, *Politics of Gender*, p. 54.

4

LEARNING TO BE GOOD GIRLS AND WOMEN

Education, training and schools

Rebecca Rogers

Introduction

In 1846 an obscure French provincial schoolteacher wrote to the administrative governing council of Algeria that

> Woman is the most powerful of all influences in Africa as in Europe, but even more so in Africa. If you convert to our civilization 100 young native girls in all classes of society and in all the races of the Regency [of Algeria], these girls will become, in the nature of things, the privileged wives of the most important men of their class; they will become our guarantee of the country's submission to our authority, as well as the irrefutable pledge of its future assimilation.[1]

She argued specifically that schooling Muslim girls was the solution to assimilating the new colonial subjects into French civilisation. This heart-felt endorsement of girls' education as a pivotal aspect of the civilising process speaks powerfully to the values attached to learning in nineteenth-century Europe. Throughout the continent educated men and women believed that progress and the spread of civilisation came through learning. More importantly, from the eighteenth century onwards, women were included in this reflection; a country's degree of civilisation increasingly depended on women's status within society, and this status in turn hinged on their access to education.

This chapter explores the emergence of such ideas about women's influence and status within European and colonial societies and argues that education was a critical element in determining women's place. The history of girls' education offers historians a way to understand enduring gender stereotypes since education is one of the primary ways that societies reproduce their values and beliefs. At the same time, by giving individuals access to reason and learning, education offers a key to understanding change. This dialectic between education as both a conservative force and a force for change helps explain how learning assigned women to certain roles, notably within the family as mothers and wives, but also opened doors for them to acquire new roles and responsibilities within the public sphere. Beginning in the seventeenth and eighteenth

93

centuries, 'enlightened' voices introduced debates about women, their status in society and their ability to reason. The argument by some that gender differences might be the product of social and cultural conditioning rather than biological determinants opened opportunities for women to claim the need for a better education. More generally, however, individuals as well as religious associations promoted the development of schools for girls as well as boys, so that women might contribute to the betterment of society, as pious wives and mothers and as skilled and obedient working women. The effect of the French Revolution and the cultural conservatism of the early years of the nineteenth century justify a chronology that considers the period from 1700 to 1830 as a whole.

By the 1830s, the needs of industrialising societies significantly changed the interest attached to the question of girls' training and learning possibilities. The debates about women's place and women's role became central as countries dealt with the enduring impact of revolutionary ideas, with the need to develop an efficient workforce and with the concern to form a docile citizenry. Increasingly, women were seen as critical within these broader processes, so that textbooks, conduct manuals and, of course, schools multiplied, offering lessons in what it meant to be a 'good' girl, wife, mother and worker. These lessons varied depending on the social class of the students, but they embraced women from all classes and even extended to women in non-European societies as nuns, missionaries and missionary wives spread the fruits of European civilisation to the imperial world. The reformed schools and the expanding educational opportunities of the latter half of the nineteenth century, combined with the emergence of a feminist movement to open doors for middle- and lower-class women, giving them access to degrees and qualifications that allowed them to enter a largely male working and professional world.

The twentieth century gradually witnessed the emergence of an integrated educational system within European countries that allowed students to progress from elementary to secondary education in schools, at the same time that middle-class women gained access to higher education, thus challenging ideas that women's minds and bodies made them unfit for certain positions and responsibilities in the working world. Despite increasing opportunities for women in the twentieth century, however, scientific developments as well as sexist and racist ideologies combined at certain historical moments and within specific countries to produce discourses about women's place in society that harked back to earlier periods. Such discourses, of course, had an impact on girls' schooling and learning possibilities. The chapter concludes with the generalisation of co-education in the 1960s and 1970s that did much to break down the existence of distinctively feminine curricula, just as the second-wave feminist movement significantly changed attitudes towards girls' education. We've come a long way, baby, but enduring gender stereotypes remain, often unconsciously reproduced within schools and educational systems that officially espouse an egalitarian social and gender ethos. The history of girls' access to learning offers a particularly fruitful vantage point to understand the interaction between a society's vision of women and the ways education enforces, modifies and challenges that vision to produce good girls and women.

Historiography and sources

The history of girls' education in Europe from 1700 until the present is relatively understudied despite the importance of education in forging gender roles. Phyllis

Stock's general book on the subject, *Better than Rubies*, was published in 1978, well before the spate of monographs on the subject, and remains the only attempt to provide an overarching narrative. As a result, no study exists that seeks to draw together the threads of the more specialised, generally nationally oriented studies that have emerged since then. General textbooks in women's history have sought at times to incorporate an analysis of education in their studies of women's changing place in society, but these rarely span three centuries, tracing continuities and change. Within the English-speaking world, the weight of Anglo-American scholarship in this field has heavily contributed to setting a certain number of agendas whose pertinence has not always been examined within other national traditions. The following discussion traces the broad frameworks within which histories of girls' education have developed while providing insights into generally lesser-known scholarship concerning continental Europe.

The early Anglo-American as well as German histories of girls' education written between the 1960s and 1980 tended to adopt a feminist perspective, emphasising how ideological and material constraints limited women's access to learning. In these narratives the actions of feminist foremothers challenged patriarchal attitudes towards women and gradually established networks of more serious schools for girls that offered the tools to envision careers beyond that of motherhood. As a result of this scholarship, portraits emerged of a variety of 'grand ladies' whose schools and writings were critical in a process of change that challenged conventional images of primarily middle-class womanhood. The focus on middle-class education was in part a product of available sources. Middle-class schools tended to generate more archival documents and the pioneering middle-class reformers – such as Emily Davies in England, the Dutch headmistress Anna Barbara Van Meerten-Schilperoort or Betty Gleim in Germany – wrote letters, petitions, reports and even diaries that allowed historians to trace the origins of their efforts, to shed insight into their network of relations and to trace their defeats as well as their successes. In many ways, this scholarship presented a 'heroic' image of female education where clear-sighted proto-feminists understood that a lack of learning contributed to women's oppression, whereas access to learning led to emancipation; schooling emerged then as an important factor in the modernisation of European societies. These early histories of girls' education established a chronology of change, where the middle decades of the nineteenth century represented a critical turning point, as the first wave of feminist organising placed education at the heart of its demands for reform. The movement from dark obscurantism to the light of wisdom and knowledge was never clear-cut and unambiguous, nor did these histories ignore how class determined access to knowledge, but the general framework was marked by the modernisation paradigm prevalent in historical scholarship at the time.

The extraordinary development of women's and then gender history in the 1980s began to complicate the historical picture, particularly through the success of a new interpretive framework which used the nineteenth-century categories of the public and private sphere to understand women's roles and status in a given society. This framework highlighted a different chronology of change, drew on a broader array of sources and nuanced existing interpretations about the characteristics and constraints of the private or domestic sphere. Once again this framework, which was mainly adopted by Anglo-American historians, tended to privilege middle-class women's experience through studies of the 'woman's culture' that emerged within all-female teaching institutions. In these interpretations girls' education for domesticity acquired new meaning and was not necessarily viewed as oppressive and reactionary. On the contrary, training for motherhood was situated within a broader cultural nexus that highlighted the new, more powerful role granted to women and mothers within British protestant evangelicalism, within the German movement around Froebel, and, to a lesser degree, within French Catholicism.[2] At the same time that historians argued for a more sympathetic reappraisal of early girls' schools, Martha Vicinus showed how the women's culture of nineteenth-century British girls' schools gave women the skills and confidence that allowed them then to move beyond feminine 'domestic' spaces into the public world.[3] Although the public–private paradigm has since been extensively criticised, within the history of girls' education it offered a way to understand how the culturally conservative messages of domestic ideology within religious, pedagogic and even early feminist writings could in fact produce a heightened concern for girls' learning thus encouraging the development of schools, the emergence of more serious curricula and a concern for better teacher-training.

The professionalisation and feminisation of the teaching corps has offered another framework to approach the history of girls' and women's access to learning. Once again, Anglo-American as well as German historians of education have been the most productive, rewriting studies of professionalisation initially conceived solely around male actors. By highlighting the ways women fought to pass the same exams as men, to form professional associations and to benefit from training, these studies have positioned women teachers and their schools more clearly with respect to emerging national systems of education and have argued for a need to see these systems in gendered terms. While these studies tended to follow a chronology that emphasised changes in the second half of the nineteenth century, the recent analysis of Christina de Bellaigue has argued for contextualising our understanding of the process of professionalisation as she calls attention to changes within the teaching profession in the early decades of the nineteenth century in England.[4] Juliani Jacobi has shown how the feminisation of the teaching profession in Germany contributed to redefining the profession and pedagogy in more feminised terms.[5]

More generally, recent scholarship has begun to revisit the binary division between professional and amateur thus rescuing for historical investigation myriad figures of female amateurism, ranging from the eighteenth and early nineteenth-century governess to the owner of dame schools or the headmistress of boarding schools. By questioning the notion of professional and by paying heed to the ways these women laid claims to authority, these studies have redirected historical attention to the years between 1780 and 1830 when schools for girls began to proliferate. These 'revisionist' approaches have drawn upon a wealth of new archives, examining sources concerning specific institutions, local communities and, at times, individual men and women. Trade books, correspondences and school advertisements have received new attention, as historians examine where girls' schools fit within a local economy.

In Catholic France and Ireland, historians of girls' education often wrote within an anti-clerical republican interpretive framework. The story of girls' access to better schooling was represented as a struggle between the republican meritocratic state and the retrograde anti-modern church. In France, this meant that serious education for girls only emerged in the 1880s following the Ferry laws, while in Ireland the

Intermediate Education (Ireland) Act of 1878 is considered to have provided the real breakthrough in girls' secondary education. Drawing upon recently opened private religious archives, historians of religious orders, including myself, have begun to challenge this interpretation while recognising that the messages transmitted within religious schools, such as those of such domestic ideologues as Hannah More in England or the German J. H. Campe, were of course culturally conservative. Still, the hierarchical organisation of religious congregations, where aspiring nuns attended novitiates and acquired both spiritual and pedagogical training, at times encouraged the emergence of more rigorous standards in girls' education, as Sarah Curtis has recently shown in her study of teaching orders in the diocese of Lyon in France.[6]

The cultural turn within social history, as well as the influence of postmodern and particularly Foucauldian approaches to history, have also left their mark on the ways historians have analysed girls' education.[7] Studies of women's culture within schools bear ample testimony to how both anthropological and linguistic approaches have changed the sorts of questions historians ask as well as their use of sources. More generally, Foucault's vision of the disciplinary nature of the modern state as well as his call to consider the relationship between power and knowledge and to understand power as operating in a diffuse fashion within all social relationships are clearly evident in many histories of girls' education. Women historians have taken seriously the call to consider schools as the sites of a broader disciplinary project, but have also increasingly heeded the ways women within schools, be they teachers or students, modified and at times resisted the dominant cultural messages within girls' schools. As a result, the early emphasis on studying rulebooks has been leavened to some extent by the use of such private documents as diaries, correspondences and memoirs that reveal how individuals circumvented norms. The interest in understanding the relationship between a disciplinary project and lived experiences is perhaps most evident in studies of teacher-training, such as that written by Anne Quartararo for France and Elizabeth Edward's recent book on English normal schools.[8]

Scholarship on twentieth-century girls' education is far less abundant than for earlier periods, although once again Anglo-American and northern European scholars have been quicker to extend their analyses toward the present. The decline of single-sex institutions partially explains that women historians have tended to focus on earlier periods, while studies of more contemporary educational politics and policies have not yet attracted widespread interest. Nonetheless, existing studies point in three directions that reflect the ways educational history has been influenced by other fields, notably sociology, anthropology, psychology and public policy. In recent years a spate of oral-history projects have sought to understand how women teachers and students experience the educational process and then make sense of it through their narratives. In part thanks to incitement from the European Union, there is also growing interest in female leadership and governance within educational institutions, as policy-makers address the fact that supposedly egalitarian educational systems have led to a widely feminised teaching body, notably in pre-school and elementary schools, whereas women principals and schools administrators are few and far between. Recently, interest in co-education, both its growth and its contemporary critics, has also stimulated a number of studies that bring gender scholarship on girls' education into the twentieth century.

In the sections that follow I will present a history of girls' and women's education that owes a great deal to Anglo-American gender scholarship. In particular, I have been inspired by the scholarship on the public and private spheres and believe that the defence of the family in the nineteenth century and the attention paid to the role of women within the family did indeed provoke improvements in girls' education. Nonetheless, countless studies have showed the interconnections between these two spheres and have warned about the dangers of studying them in isolation. I have come to view schools, then, as precisely one such bridging space between the two spheres. Women who opened and taught within schools operated within a very public world where money, status and influence all played a role, despite the messages transmitted within these institutions. Furthermore I take seriously the idea that knowledge represents a form of power, so that even the most reactionary learning experiences transmitted knowledge, be it simply the ability to read, that allowed certain women to challenge contemporary representations of femininity and thus contributed to changing women's lives. Finally, I want to acknowledge the resolutely optimistic vision of the history of girls' education that follows. Like many feminist historians, I have moved away from interpretations of women's history that view women as pawns trapped in a patriarchal society, buffeted by the masculine forces of history, be they great white dead men who held the reins of power or the more anonymous forces of industrial capital and national state-making. Certainly, women were disadvantaged compared to men in all spheres of society and in all realms of activity, except motherhood, and their range of choices was more limited. But they did have some choices, and hence agency, which allowed them to act on the historical stage, writing and reading books, opening schools, teaching girls, communicating a vision of femininity that included an access to knowledge and the ability to reason. It is thanks in great part to these women who fought for a better education for girls that we are where we are today, able to write a history of European women that makes a difference.

The limits of women's education (1700–1830)

The education of girls and women in early modern Europe varied widely according to social class and geographic location, just as it did for their male counterparts. Unquestionably, however, gender made a difference and families systematically favoured the education of their sons over that of their daughters. Amongst the rural and urban poor, who constituted the vast majority of the European population, school education generally was not an option, so that the poor at best received vocational training which rarely allowed forms of social mobility. Nonetheless, schools for the poor did multiply during the eighteenth and early nineteenth century, thanks in large part to religious associations and orders, and girls were not forgotten in this effort to bring religion to the masses. Wealthy families, on the other hand, saw other reasons to educate their daughters and this translated into forms of home education as well as the development of elite boarding schools mainly within urban areas. Access to learning was not just contingent on access to schools, however. In general, the growth of girls' education depended a great deal on contemporary attitudes about the relationship of the sexes and on women's place within society. Initiatives that favoured girls' education were always buttressed by arguments about how this education would serve to create better, more pious families. Rarely, if ever, was girls' education seen as a liberal right contributing to the development of the individual. For the entire period, then, girls' education remained limited both in its scope and its ambitions.

Eighteenth-century debates about women's place

> It is well established that men and women have the same nature and the same constitution. The proof lies in that female savages are as robust, as agile as male savages: thus the weakness of our constitution and of our organs belongs definitely to our education, and is a consequence of the condition to which we have been assigned in society.[9]

The intellectual debates of the Enlightenment period included many discussions about the relationship of the sexes where the question of education often emerged, particularly when speaking about women. Although virtually everyone accepted that fundamental differences existed between men and women, more progressive thinkers emphasised how girls' education or, more accurately, the lack of education accentuated these differences. In France many authors argued that providing a better, less frivolous education to women would contribute to regenerating French society. Among the earliest texts that denounced the state of women's education was François Poulain de la Barre's *De l'égalité des deux sexes* (*On the Equality of the Sexes*) in 1673 in which he argued essentially that the mind has no sex:

> If women studied in universities alongside men or in other universities set aside for them in particular, they could take degrees and aspire to the titles of Doctor and Master in Theology, Medicine, and [canon or civil] Law. And their natural talents, which fits them so advantageously for learning would also suit them to be successful teachers.[10]

Shortly afterwards, the Englishwoman Mary Astell published her *Serious Proposal to the Ladies* (1694) that proposed the founding of a woman's university for women who did not wish to marry. Later in the eighteenth century, Germany's first woman medical doctor Dorothea Christina Leporin wrote *Thorough Investigation of the Causes which Prevent the Female Sex from Studying* (1742) in which she stated: 'If one admits that the female sex is capable of learning then one must also admit that it has received a calling to go with it.'[11] Most treatises remained relatively unspecific about what should be done to improve women's education, although in France the Abbé de Saint Pierre in 1732 proposed a system of both boarding schools and free day schools for all girls between five and eighteen, while the pedagogue Riballier in 1785 urged the creation of public *collèges* (secondary schools) for girls watched over by the state; he argued that women's ignorance was among the primary causes of the evils in contemporary society.[12]

While men dominated the intellectual debate, women's voices were present in all European countries notably thanks to their role within an elite salon culture that thrived throughout the century and continued, along different lines, into the nineteenth century. Within French salons, women such as Mme de Geoffrin and Mme Suzanne Necker pursued their own educational agendas but also staked a claim for women's right to be listened to and to play a special role in a civilising process that placed a special emphasis on polite conversation.[13] The print revolution of the eighteenth century allowed women to gain greater prominence in public debate, notably in England and France where women writers, such as the English bluestocking, Lady Mary Wortley Montagu, championed female education and generally mixed politics. Eliza Haywood's *Female Spectator* (1744–6) was frequently re-edited in book form and was credited with bringing learning into fashion. In France, the *Journal des Dames* (1759–78) adopted an increasingly non-conformist tone as Mme de Beaumer called for a 'revolution' in female consciousness that involved stretching women's minds and range of activities; her successor Mme de Montaclos was more measured and maternalist in her writing, placing girls' education for motherhood at the centre of many articles, while acknowledging that women should be allowed to pursue careers of their choice. These elite women writers and journalists were part of a genuinely European group of intellectuals who exchanged and translated ideas across national boundaries, developing an argument for granting women greater access to the tools of reason.[14]

In the debate about women's place in society, Jean-Jacques Rousseau's writings stand out, because of their enormous influence throughout Europe and their enduring success in the nineteenth century. In his pedagogical novel, *Émile* (1762), the French philosopher proposed a model for both boys' and girls' education that emphasised a respect for the natural inclinations of the sexes who should be allowed to mature without excessive discipline and social restraints. Writing partly in response to the pernicious public influence he attributed to aristocratic salon women, he argued that women's place was within the family, while men exerted authority in public. As a result, Émile's education emphasised autonomy, independence and self-control while Sophie's education was aimed primarily at making her an agreeable and pleasing wife: 'Thus the whole education of women ought to be relative to men. To please them, to be useful to them, to make themselves loved and honoured by them, to educate them when young'. This carefully circumscribed education was a response to the figure of the salon woman with her array of female artifices; Sophie was not to have access to abstract culture and to public life in general. At the same time the Genevan philosopher admired certain aspects of 'natural' womanhood, such as their presence of mind and their sensitive observations; women's intelligence was practical and intuitive, complementing men's more scientific and speculative reasoning. It followed from this vision of male/female capabilities that girls' education needed to be carefully contained and directed toward women's social role within the family. But within the family, Rousseau granted women unusual authority:

> Woman's empire is an empire of sweetness, dexterity and good-nature . . . She must reign in her house as a minister in his State, and ensure she is given orders to do what she desires. In this respect the best households are those where women have the most authority; but when she fails to recognise the voice of authority, and when she seeks to usurp her rights and command herself, disorder ensues that can only introduce misery, scandal and dishonour.[15]

Rousseau's vision of women reigning within their household garnered increasing support throughout Europe in the nineteenth century, but also encountered 'feminist' opposition among both men and women who highlighted its limitations. Undoubtedly, the best known of these 'feminist' retorts is Mary Wollstonecraft's *Vindication of the Rights of Woman* (1792) that eloquently argued for the need to provide women with a decent education and even advocated co-education:

> If marriage be the cement of society, mankind should all be educated after the same model, or the intercourse of the sexes will never deserve the name of fellowship, nor will women ever fulfil the peculiar duties of their sex, till they become enlightened citizens, till they become free by being enable to earn their own subsistence, independent of men.[16]

During the French Revolution the concern to remake the social and political body spawned a great many debates about the relationship between the sexes and the education appropriate for the new man and woman. Revolutionaries were divided, however, about the biological basis for gender differences. While some educational proposals were very conservative, emphasising women's 'natural' limitations, others revealed frankly feminist opinions. Most prominently, the philosopher Condorcet insisted in 1791 that 'Education should be identical between men and women'; since men and women had the same rights, women should have the some opportunities as men to acquire reason.[17] The German Theodor Gottlieb von Hippel defended similar ideas a year later in his stirring plea for extending French citizenship to women and for granting them opportunities in the public sphere:

> It would have been preferable to have offered the honours of citizenship to the other sex and avoided ridicule in such a serious matter . . . Still less should women be forbidden from taking part in the inner administration and economy of the state.[18]

The egalitarian message of these more radical treatises was, however, a distinct minority among a chorus of voices who believed girls' education needed to be improved, but that this education should respect the natural differences between men and women.

Schools for the poor: the influence of religious initiatives

The concern to improve girls' education in the eighteenth century existed at the level of learned discourse, but it also translated into pedagogical practice within cities and rural communities. While the provision of schooling for the poor was patchy and often mediocre in quality, scholarship has revealed, nonetheless, a far more diverse range of institutions than has generally been acknowledged. Private rather than state initiatives fuelled the development of girls' schools prior to the last half of the nineteenth century, with the exception of the German states where communities were required to maintain schools by the late eighteenth century. Throughout Europe, schools and training for poor girls reflected commonly shared assumptions: to begin with, schooling was generally not intended to promote social mobility, but rather to allow girls to internalise basically middle-class values of sobriety, modesty, diligence, and thrift. Second, schooling was expected to transmit a certain number of tools for functioning as a woman within society, notably reading and needlework. Finally, whether lessons involved moral behaviour or sewing, religious values permeated the experience of learning for both peasant and working-class girls.

In reaction to the Protestant Reformation, the Catholic Church responded through the creation of female religious orders dedicated to providing schooling for the young.[19] A wide range of such orders emerged in the early modern period in England, France and Italy, many of which focused particular attention on the poor. These orders included the Ursulines, the Sisters of Charity (founded in 1633 by Louise de Marcillac and Saint Vincent de Paul), the Ladies of Saint-Maur or the Sisters of Saint-Charles. The structure of these orders allowed them to spread throughout Catholic areas, frequently offering a range of services: free schools for the poor, boarding schools for the wealthy, as well as health care for the impoverished. In cities, the cathedral also operated fee-paying schools: in Paris prior to the Revolution, schools existed for one-third of the female school-age population, undoubtedly a high in eighteenth-century Europe.[20] Schools for the poor spread throughout cities and rural areas offering primarily lessons in reading, religion and needlework. In France, where these orders were the most numerous, reading was conducted primarily in French not Latin, but everywhere religion formed the cornerstone of girls' education. Writing in 1716 to a mother superior concerning the opening of a girls' school, a French priest noted 'I do not mention catechism and Christian subjects because, these as you know, must take priority over everything else.'[21]

In England, Scotland and Wales, charity schools for boys and girls began to spread almost a century after France, thanks to the efforts of the Society for the Propagation of Christian Knowledge (founded in 1699); by the mid-eighteenth century, Quakers and Unitarians were also active in setting up both fee-paying and free schools. The curriculum proposed for girls was rudimentary and emphasised the inculcation of religious values as well as the acquiring of domestic skills. Character formation played a central role in this education, which recent scholarship suggests lasted an average of some three and a half years. Writing in 1805, Catherine Cappe argued: 'cultivation of social and pious affections, gentleness of temper and resignation to the will of God [were] as important to the female character in the lowest as well as the highest forms of life'.[22] Unlike in France, however, English charity schools also were expected to help a girl find a trade, notably in domestic service. By 1733 it is estimated there were some 20,000 students in charity schools throughout the country. Alongside these schools, girls also had access to village and dame schools as well as Sunday schools which all sought to rescue the lower classes 'from pressure of extreme want, the risk of ill-usage, and the wretchedness of vice'.[23] Middle-class suspicion concerning the moral character of working-class families undoubtedly contributed to the development of schools where girls were removed, albeit temporarily, from their family's bad influence. Where schools existed for lower-class girls in other European countries, the same patterns can be found: girls received lessons first and foremost in religion, followed closely by practical training in needlework.

Elementary education was undoubtedly most developed within the German states thanks to the combined influence of Enlightenment ideals, Pietism and official ordinances. By the 1770s and 1780s both Protestant and Catholic areas had incorporated compulsory education for both boys and girls into their rapidly expanding bureaucracies. The acceptance of co-education within Protestant areas, in particular, expanded the school offerings available for girls. The content of education within

German schools resembled popular programmes elsewhere, although by 1800 German schools tended to offer a somewhat greater variety of subjects that included singing and in some areas 'arts and sciences'.

Literacy rates for women highlight the contrasts that existed within Europe and point to the educational advance of countries in northern Europe. Throughout Europe, women's literacy rates were far lower than those of men, reflecting the unequal provision of schooling for boys and girls. The highest literacy rates are found in Germany where at the end of the century 95 per cent of men could sign their name and 68 per cent of women. In England female literacy in 1800 is estimated at around 45 per cent, with male literacy at around 61 per cent; in France female literacy in 1786–90 is estimated at 27 per cent (male literacy at 47 per cent), with wide discrepancies between northern and southern France. Mediterranean countries lagged far behind: in Greece, for example, male literacy in 1831 was only at 9 per cent, and women were almost universally illiterate.[24] Literacy rates are only a crude measure of educational levels, and they vary tremendously according to region, social class and gender; at the end of the eighteenth century these rates were probably the highest in Calvinist Geneva where cultural support for girls' education was exceptionally strong. Throughout Europe, however, support for poor girls' schooling always came second to that for their brothers, and this scarcely changed when one turns to examine attitudes toward middle- and upper-class girls' education.

Learned ladies and elite institutions

Traditionally, historians of education have depicted eighteenth- and early nineteenth-century girls' schools in very negative terms. While poor girls learned primarily how to pray and sew, daughters of the elite are portrayed acquiring mainly frivolous accomplishments. Early modern women schoolteachers have been described as incompetent and unqualified amateurs, whose concerns were more financial than educational, while in Catholic countries, historians have often presented religious teachers as agents of ideological control. Recent studies by Carol Gold, Susan Skedd, myself and others, however, have begun to nuance such judgements through analyses that look more closely at the teachers who opened schools and the curricula proposed. The result is the discovery of a complex variety of institutions and, above all, the realisation that managing girls' schools provided many middle-class women with working experience, either alone or with family members, an experience that has not been sufficiently acknowledged in histories of women's work. As with poor girls' schooling, the interest in improving girls' education that existed in Enlightenment circles also translated into initiatives for the wealthy, despite the fact that their home environment offered fewer dangers. While the middle and upper classes generally provided lessons to their daughters within their homes, they frequently turned to schools to finish their daughters' education.

In Europe, most middle-class institutions for girls were small privately run structures where, for a fee, girls were given lessons in a relatively wide range of subjects: literature, history, geography, some natural sciences, foreign languages (but generally not Latin and Greek), religion as well as the indispensable female accomplishments, such as sewing, embroidery, painting and music. Prior to state involvement, these institutions were run by individual proprietors, often family members, by religious orders, particularly in Catholic countries, by trustees, and even at times by parents, such as at the Dottreskolen academy for girls in Copenhagen, and their longevity depended a great deal on individual ingenuity and economic resources. Many of these schools offered a mediocre education at best, but there are examples in many European countries of institutions or women educators who took advantage of contemporary debates about the need to improve girls' education and opened schools that offered a rigorous curriculum, divided into classes of ability. The professed goal of these schools was generally to produce good wives and mothers, but by the early nineteenth century there is evidence that some women headmistresses held more ambitious views and created schools that increasingly prepared their pupils for lives beyond the home.

Within Catholic countries convent schools provided the basic model for elite girls' education. The same orders that opened free schools for the poor generally ran boarding schools as well for the wealthy, and a certain number increasingly gained a reputation for specialising in the education of an elite. The Ursulines and the Congrégation de Notre-Dame, for example, were considered among the more learned religious orders; they organised their pupils into classes of ability and taught a range of subject matters that would allow their students not only to be efficient housewives, but also to be conversant within polite society. In 1800 the Society of the Sacred Heart was founded in France and quickly established a reputation for its upper-class boarding schools that opened throughout Europe and in the colonies.

In Britain a wide range of schools existed for the middle and upper classes although few welcomed as many students as the average Catholic convent school. The curriculum within these schools varied as well, but the better institutions offered at times an adventurous curriculum. An advertisement for Mrs Florian's boarding school in Leytonshire ran thus:

> The elements of Geometry and Trigonometry are also taught as far is requisite for a perfect intelligence of the principles of Astronomy, of the geographical knowledge of our globe and of Natural Philosophy, which are illustrated by experiments and machines. The young ladies enter at the same time on a complete course of universal history and geography, ancient and modern (according for Mr. Florian's Chronological Views). Each epoch of history is illustrated by a geographical map, made by the pupil's themselves.[25]

While most schools focused on the elegant accomplishments, two in Oxfordshire in the 1760s and 1770s offered more housewifely lessons in pickling, preserving and pastry-making as well as general English, French and needlework.[26] By the late eighteenth century, a rising market for pedagogical treatises allowed women such as Hannah More and Mary Wollstonecraft, who also both ran schools, to advertise their teaching methods and to contribute to the support for more developed girls' instruction.

This same concern for providing more serious education is also evident in the northern European countries where both lay and religious women opened schools and developed pedagogical blueprints. In turn-of-the-century Copenhagen, a range of private academies provided education to girls whose families came not only from the Danish court but also from the more humble artisanal trades. The most progressive of these schools was the Dottreskolen academy (founded in 1791), which aimed to offer girls a more scientific education with men teaching most of the more academic classes. Clearly, the concern here was to train girls who could help their husbands in commercial business. Finally, the Dutch headmistress Anna Barbara Van Meerten-Schilperoort (1778–1853) established a school in Gouda that served as a model for other institutions.

In Germany, more serious girls' schools also developed during this period. Betty Gleim, for example, opened a school in Bremen in 1806, believing that only a new system of education would reform society. In addition to advocating serious academic education, she also encouraged professional training for women, modelled on a school for female teachers that the Swiss pedagogue Pestalozzi had founded at Yverdon. Her treatise *Erziehung und Untericht des weiblichen Geschlechts* (1810) (*Education and Cultivation of the Female Sex*) emphasised that the ideal of *Bildung* should apply to boys and girls; this text went on to become an important document for German-speaking feminists who used it to argue for vocational opportunities for unmarried women. Amalia Holst was another woman proprietor of a small school near Hamburg, whose writings emphasised women's need for a more academic education. She began her 1802 treatise, *Uber die Bestimmung des Weibes zur Höhern Geistesbildung* (*On the Capacity of Women for Higher Education*) with the question 'Are we only here for the sake of men?' and went on to argue that intellectual self-development and maternal duty were not conflicting goals. In Berlin the Luisenstiftung (1811) offered general education for middle-class girls and enjoyed a high reputation.

Although schools for wealthy girls appeared in all European countries, two French institutions stand out for their cultural ambition and their influence in the eighteenth and early nineteenth century: the French school for noblewomen at Saint-Cyr and the schools for the Legion of Honour. Madame de Maintenon founded the school at Saint-Cyr in 1686 to educate 250 girls from impoverished noble families. Following the precepts of Fénelon's major educational treatise, *De l'éducation des filles* (1686), she proposed a curriculum that offered women sufficient knowledge to be able to run noble households, including history, literature, Latin, music, painting and, of course, religion. Above all, however, her institution was explicitly intended to form girls who would provoke reform within their noble families, thanks to the Christian education they had received. Pupils were divided into four classes distinguished by the colour of their belts, and the curriculum was theoretically progressive.[27] Although the reputation of the school declined over the eighteenth century, it nonetheless fostered many imitations, such as the Smolny Institute for noble girls in Saint Petersburg, Russia. The latter was founded in 1764 by Catherine the Great and remained in existence until 1917. In Austria the state supported advanced education for the daughters of officers and civil servants in two institutions that date back to the end of the eighteenth century: the Offizierstöchter-Erziehungs-Institut (1775) and the Zivil-Mädchen-Pensionat (1786) that prepared girls for careers as governesses; in 1805 in Augsburg Germany the Anna Barbara von Stetten Institute provided dowries for the students who came from the middle and lower classes.

The schools of the Legion of Honour followed in the footsteps of Saint-Cyr. Napoleon I created the schools in the early 1800s in order to provide a serious education for the daughters of his military officers and civil servants. These boarding schools provided free education to some 500 students whose social background ranged from the daughters of generals to the orphans of foot soldiers. The Emperor saw these institutions as a means of cementing support for his regime but also regenerating post-revolutionary society: 'I will not restrict myself to raising a small number of girls . . . I will educate four to five hundred girls or none at all, and I will reform society.'[28] Ostensibly the schools' pedagogical objectives were limited, reflecting Napoleon's distrust of learned women:

> What will be taught to the *demoiselles* who will be brought up at Ecouen? We must begin with religion in all its rigor; in this matter do not admit any modification. In a public institution for demoiselles, religion is a serious matter; whatever else may be said about it, it is the surest guarantee for mothers and for husbands. Make believers of them, not reasoners. The weakness of women's brains, the flightiness of their ideas, their destination in the social order, the necessity for inspiring them with a constant and perpetual resignation and a mild and indulgent charity, all that cannot be obtained except by means of religion, a charitable and mild religion.[29]

But the woman he hired to run the first school at Ecouen, Jeanne Campan, had very different ideas and these ultimately won out within the classroom, just as her pedagogical writings spread far beyond the borders of France. Her students studied literature, ancient, sacred and French history, geography and geometry, a smattering of natural sciences (especially botany), in addition to more feminine lessons in sewing, hygiene and cooking. This plan of study differed from the better *ancien régime* convent schools in the time allotted for literature, geometry and the sciences. Campan's private writings reveal, moreover, that she envisioned her school in Ecouen as a 'university of women' and she had ambitious plans to position it at the centre of a vast network of girls' schools in France. Although these plans did not come to fruition, many students of the Legion of Honour went on to active careers, rather than devoting themselves to home life.

Naturally, institutions such as that of Mme Campan were unusual in the first half of the nineteenth century, but they existed, attracted students, provoked discussion and spawned imitations elsewhere in Europe, such as the boarding school of St Annunziata for elite Italian girls in Florence in 1825. The educational reformers of the second half of the century tended to downplay the significance of such predecessors whose legacy, nonetheless, is obvious in the development of later 'reformed' schools. In effect, we as historians have often been guilty of reading our feminist foremother's narratives too uncritically. In their concern to position their initiatives as new and ground-breaking they often neglected evidence that girls' education was not universally mediocre. The seeds for rethinking the purpose of girls' education were undoubtedly planted in the early modern period but they would only flower over the course of the nineteenth century.

Educating for motherhood (1830–1918)

The most dramatic and widespread changes in European girls' education occurred after 1830 in the wake of other social, economic and political changes. Industrialisation and the growth of a tertiary sector in the economy generated a need for more workers with different skills than those required to run a family farm or to darn wool. Urbanisation changed the face of European cities, providing new opportunities for women schoolteachers to open schools that addressed more varied needs than the early charity schools or the elite boarding school. The democratisation of European societies produced a rhetoric about the need to form citizens, the mothers of future citizens and then women citizens themselves; this rhetoric then was accompanied by an expansion of educational systems that led to the provision of more schools for girls. Finally, the forces of imperialism encouraged European countries to pursue their civilising mission beyond the home soil into the 'uncivilised world'; for women this meant setting up schools for girls throughout Africa, the Middle East and Asia. As more women acquired access to learning, their range of opportunities also increased and yet the available vocational choices for active women in this period before the First World War remained quite limited. The new industrial jobs tended to restrict women to those tasks that resembled traditionally feminine occupations, those that required manual dexterity, relatively little physical force and repetitive movement. In the final quarter of the century, the service sector mainly welcomed women as office workers and sales clerks. Access to more schooling and, at times, qualifying degrees rarely opened doors into anything more than teaching and caring jobs. As a result, for the years under consideration here, girls' education expanded, but it remained very focused on producing 'good' girls and women, whose place was first and foremost within the family. The relative success of this education for motherhood can be traced to a wide variety of factors, and its most vocal champions can be found in a burgeoning 'domestic' literature often inflected with religious overtones.

Domestic ideology in nineteenth-century Europe

> Man must be formed for the country's institutions; woman must be
> formed for man, as he has evolved. Our natural state and dignity are
> as wives and mothers.
>
> (Mme de Rémusat, 1824)

The expression 'domestic ideology' is used to describe the set of ideas that emphasised women's 'special' qualities – their sensitivity, their emotionalism, their maternal instincts – all those attributes that meant their 'natural' place was in the family. But domestic ideology did more than just position women within the home, it also proclaimed the importance of the home and family within society, thus enhancing the role of women and opening a wedge in a potentially repressive ideology if carried to its extreme. Domestic ideology generally went hand in hand with a certain set of religious values that emphasised woman's necessary subordination, but also her purer and more religious nature, which Coventry Patmore captured in his four-volume verse narrative *Angel in the House* (1854–62). While this ideology probably achieved its greatest eloquence and impact in Great Britain, variants can be found throughout Europe, in part thanks to the translation of pedagogical, literary and religious texts, as well as the circulation of people and ideas. Encouraging women to think about themselves in relationship to the family is often seen as a primarily middle-class phenomenon since lower-class women all had to work. Still, there is ample evidence that the messages of domestic ideology were also directed towards working-class women, be it in schools, in churches or in encounters with charitable or philanthropic ladies. For women, the messages of this ideology were conservative, and they emerged in societies that sought to respond to the upheavals caused by political and economic transformations: the twin effects of revolutionary ideals and industrialisation. Reconstituting a stronger, more moral family appealed to many across ideological lines. And yet, by granting women authority within the family, the champions of domesticity often developed a discourse that unwittingly encouraged women to think about and move beyond the private sphere. Specifically, they all called for more serious girls' education so that women might better fulfil their roles within the family. Once girls tasted the fruits of learning this carried a certain number of them to call for roles outside the family as well, thus challenging the premises of this domestic ideology.

Male and female authors trumpeted the virtues of domestic life throughout Europe, spreading this ideal in moral tales, poems, etiquette manuals, pedagogical treatises, schoolbooks and even gardening manuals, such as John Loudon's *The Suburban Gardener* (1838). In England, Sarah Ellis was the best-known ideologue of domesticity who, in *Women of England: Their Social Duties, and Domestic Habits* (1839), emphasised women's responsibility to regenerate society from within. Similar messages were repeated in the writings of the French history professor Louis Aimé-Martin or the Swiss pedagogue Adrienne Necker de Saussure. Aimé-Martin's *De l'éducation des mères de famille, ou de la civilisation du genre humain par les femmes* (*The Education of Mothers; or, the Civilization of Mankind by Women*) (1834) went through nine editions in the following thirty years and was quickly translated into English. Like many such writers, he positioned women within the family, but argued for their influence throughout society:

> The influence of women is extended over the whole of our lives; a mistress, a wife, a mother – three magic words which comprise the sum of human felicity . . . On the maternal bosom the mind of nations reposes; their manners, prejudices, and virtues – in a word the civilisation of the human race all depend upon maternal influence.[30]

Necker de Saussure's influential pedagogical treatise developed similar reasoning and offered a plan of study for girls from infancy to old age that included intellectual study but also physical exercise and womanly talents, such as drawing and singing, to develop a girl's soul and to train her eyes and ears. More overtly religious than many of her contemporaries, she was suspicious of the dangers of the world: 'society . . . is all that seduces, all that intoxicates, all that draws thoughts away from God and duties'. As a result, she positioned women in private life but believed that the public and private spheres were inextricably intertwined:

> Concerns of general interest occupy men; they defend the entire family, the city, the nation, society. On the contrary, women are responsible for individual interests or those that fall within a more restricted circle . . . Poor or rich, married or free, women have influence on private life, the happiness of families depends largely on them. We speak about private life in opposition with *political* life and public functions for we have no intention to restrict

women's actions to their household. On the contrary we believe they are destined to produce good widely, but their influence is always along similar lines. They speak to individual souls, their advice concerns the individual and the relations he entertains with those around him. As a result there is constant action and reaction between public and private life and it is this interaction which allows civilisations to progress along two lines. For while outside movement constantly brings new wisdom into families, these families can offer an example of the most perfect organization, the least subject to vices of all sorts. In this fashion a more perfectly understood domestic administration would spread its purifying influence through a thousand different channels into society.[31]

In addition to individual authors whose texts were frequently reprinted, magazines flourished as well, directed to both mothers and their daughters. In England, mothers could consult *The Magazine for Domestic Economy* (1835), in France, *La Mère institutrice (The Mother Educator)* (1834–45) while in the Netherlands Barbara van Meerten published many pedagogical texts. These works all emphasised women's special role within the family, while also at times expressing more overtly feminist arguments, often centred on the need to provide women with more serious education in the event that they should need to work. In Germany, this more feminist tone was evident in the Leipzig journalist and author Louise Otto's journal, the *Frauen-Zeitung (Woman's Newspaper)* which appeared between 1849 and 1852. The revolutionary context of 1848 stimulated, of course, a wide-ranging criticism of women's position in society. Women needed 'intellectual elevation', the newspaper argued, to teach mothers their 'most exalted duties and to counteract the prejudices that bind us . . . the family must become strong . . . for the reform of the entire nation depends on the reform of the family'.[32]

This expression of what historians have termed maternalist feminism would develop strongly in the second half of the century and undoubtedly represented an important strand in European women's efforts to improve girls' education and women's lot in society. Alongside such pronouncements, however, other voices also used domestic ideology to limit women's range of activities and to naturalise their position within the home. Be it the misogynist statement by the French socialist Proudhon that woman's place was either as a housewife or a harlot, or the Pope's elevation of the status of the Virgin Mary in his encyclical letter *Urbi primum* (1849), many mid-nineteenth century men and women believed that women's natural frailty, combined with their maternal instincts, necessarily limited their range of actions. Domestic ideology cut both ways.

Schooling for the lower classes: the civilising mission at home

Although only middle-class women would have had the time, the money and the cultural ability to read the magazines and treatises discussed previously, the tenets of domestic ideology influenced the provision of schooling for the lower classes. In part this is because middle-class men and women were active in efforts to bring lower-class girls into schoolrooms, so they might acquire the rudiments of education, but also learn how to be better wives and mothers. In many respects, the concern to educate both boys and girls was part of a far broader civilising process that involved inculcating values and behaviour involving self-restraint, respect for hierarchy, the importance of hard work and thrift and, for girls, modesty, piety and gentleness. These values were integrated into elementary systems that increasingly became both compulsory and free, thus affecting most children between the ages of six and thirteen.

The motley variety of early modern charity schools, Sunday schools and religious free schools continued to exist in the nineteenth century, but the general trend was for private initiatives to give way to public elementary schools that were incorporated into national systems of education. While boys' schools were generally the initial focus of state legislation, little by little girls were included in the systematisation of provisions for schooling that took place, be it through their inclusion in mixed-sex schools or through the creation of girls' schools. The German states were precocious in this movement; as early as 1794 the Prussian *Allgemeines Landrecht* (General Code) decreed 'The instruction in school must be continued until the child is known to possess the knowledge necessary to every rational being', and by the latter half of the century all German states decreed compulsory schooling for both sexes from age six or seven to fourteen. Such compulsory schooling also existed in Protestant Denmark as early as 1814. The strength of the voluntary system in England meant that the state did relatively little to establish uniformity; compulsory school attendance only emerged in 1880, but there were efforts to improve the quality of schooling through funding and payment by results.[33] In France, the Falloux law of 1850 required communes of 800 inhabitants to open elementary schools for girls seventeen years after the Guizot law (1833) first created a public elementary system for boys; schooling only became compulsory, free and secular with the Ferry laws of the early 1880s. Similarly, in Italy, elementary education became compulsory in 1877, but the law was not enforced, particularly in the south. Still, by 1907, 93 per cent of all school-age children attended schools. In Spain, primary schools for girls remained primarily vocational and a majority of girls did not attend school.

The spread of education for lower-class girls probably did not dramatically change the content of schooling received in charity or religious schools, but it did mean that states increasingly insisted that both boys and girls should know the rudiments; religion and needlework was no longer sufficient for being a good housewife and female worker. For girls who attended private, frequently religious, schools, the curriculum gradually expanded over the course of the century to include lessons in history, geography and often a smattering of natural sciences, particularly biology, which was considered useful for future mothers. The messages of this education remained socially conservative and often practical in its orientation. In England, the spread of schooling for lower-class girls tended to reinforce gendered differences in the curriculum, notably through the expansion of domestic subjects. Domestic economy was made a compulsory subject for girls in 1878 and grants were created in 1882 for the teaching of cookery and in 1890 for laundry work. Cary Grant, a teacher in a London elementary school, complained about the monotony of practising thimble drills or knitting pin drills for an hour at a time. The intent of such schooling, however, was to provide practical skills as well as character-training as Margaret Rankin made clear in her textbook on the art and practice of laundry work:

> There is nothing more likely to aid in the development of character in children
> than the thorough inculcation of this science of cleanliness . . . While guiding

the pupils into methodical ways of working, . . . [the teacher will] influence the character of the pupils by the formation of habits such as punctuality, cleanliness, tidiness, carefulness and order.[34]

In France, the republican elementary system that emerged in the 1880s was ostensibly less gender differentiated: boys and girls attended separate schools but they learned essentially the same subjects, aside from the presence of military training for boys and needlework for girls. A study of elementary-school textbooks has shown, however, that gendered messages persisted within the stories and moral tales that pupils read within the classroom. While boys were encouraged to develop a certain amount of independence and to think of themselves in relation to the world and work, girls were directed towards the home and marriage where they practised the feminine virtues of patience and resignation. Eliminating religion from the curriculum did little towards eliminating a vision of womanhood modelled along the image of Mary.

Improvements in lower-class girls' schooling remained strongly tied to geographic location well into the twentieth century. Female literacy and access to schools remained abysmally low in Mediterranean countries: in 1878 in Portugal a mere 10 per cent of women were literate while overall literacy in Spain was only at 47 per cent in 1900, and one can assume women's literacy was far lower. Despite the tsarist state's encouragement of elementary schools for all classes, religions and sexes (statute of 1864), the first reliable census in Russia in 1897 revealed that only 13.1 per cent of Russian women were literate (although this percentage jumped to 33 per cent in cities).[35] Interestingly, high literacy rates did not always correlate with the early establishment of compulsory primary education, as the following list indicates: Prussia (1812), Denmark (1814), Norway (1827), Greece (1834), Sweden (1842), Switzerland (1848), Scotland (1873), England and Wales (1880), France (1882). While the northern European countries did indeed enjoy high male and female literacy rates, the same is not true of Greece. Moreover, the tardy dates of compulsory schooling in Great Britain and France did not prevent private schools from contributing to relatively high literacy rates by the time elementary schooling became compulsory.

The expansion of schooling opportunities for lower-class girls occurred in part thanks to state intervention, but also through the development of private initiatives, particularly the growth of female religious orders. In France in 1865 historians estimate that 56 per cent of all girls were schooled by religious teachers. French orders were particularly active within an educational diaspora that sent nuns to open schools throughout Europe, the New World and the colonies. Although this movement began in the early modern period as nuns settled in New France, it accelerated steadily over the course of the nineteenth century, reaching a peak at the turn of the century as French religious orders were banned from teaching in 1904. Within Europe, orders such as the Sisters of Charity, the Ursulines or the Good Shepherd opened both convent and free schools for Irish, English and German Catholic girls. A strong missionary impulse pushed Catholic nuns to open schools in foreign lands, so that the transmission of religious values was often uppermost in the schools they established. Still, like their counterparts who remained at home, religious lessons were combined with lessons in the rudiments in order to form good God-fearing wives and mothers.

Bringing civilisation to 'native' girls

Belief in the civilising process permeated relationships between the classes, and also European nations' relationship with colonised societies. As a result, it is intriguing to highlight the similarity between domestic efforts to educate lower-class women and their translation onto colonial soils. Female missionary orders, laywomen as well as missionary wives were present from the outset in the colonies, developing their vision of the civilising process for imperial subjects. Not surprisingly, the women who participated in the imperial project focused their attention on other women and tended to judge the level of 'civilisation' of the colonised society on the basis of women's status. Raising the status of native women involved thinking about their education and seeking to introduce change. While many of these women were sensitive to the cultural differences they encountered, they nonetheless believed strongly in the superiority of European culture and sought through their 'civilising projects' to improve women's roles within families, which they assumed formed the cornerstones of the societies they were colonising. In this fashion, religious and lay women exported aspects of the domestic ideology that so strongly marked girls' education in Europe by seeking to transform African, Asian or Near-Eastern girls into good domestic wives and mothers. However, attitudes of cultural and racial superiority often blinded teachers to the needs and desires of the populations they encountered, thereby limiting the influence they had hoped to exert.

The British, French and Dutch were the most active in setting up schools for native girls throughout the colonial world. The women who ran these schools generally had the support of colonial authorities, although not necessarily official funds. The French Ministry of War did, however, finance women's schools: in 1839 Minister Duperre indicated that the Congrégation de Saint-Joseph de Cluny had been chosen to establish schools throughout the French colonies 'in order to effect the social transformation of the slave populations in the colonies'[36]. The nuns of this order set up girls' schools in Senegal as early as 1826, while the first boys' school was only started in 1841; by 1900 they were present throughout the world running schools in Africa, in the French Antilles and French Polynesia, in South America and Asia. Although teachers' goals varied according to the populations they encountered, early encounters reflect what appear to be strongly utopian convictions in the power of girls' education to transform native societies: 'women exert a tremendous influence on the morals of this country, so one must act through them to give this population the love of work, as well as more industrious, more active and more French habits', wrote a French colonial official as he encouraged religious missionaries to set up schools.[37] Sir Charles Wood, President of the Board of Control in India expressed a similar view in the early 1850s:

> The importance of female education in India cannot be overrated; and we have observed with pleasure the evidence which is now afforded of an increased desire on the part of many of the natives to give a good education to their daughters. By this means a far greater proportional impulse is imparted to the educational and moral tone of the people than by the education of men.[38]

The Church Missionary Society in southern India opened day schools and boarding schools for Hindu girls. In 1866 the Unitarian social reformer Mary Carpenter went to Calcutta to encourage female education; six years later she helped set up a normal school.

Although well intentioned, European women frequently misread the needs of the societies they encountered. In Indonesia, the Dutch orientalist romance with a supposedly feudal aristocratic native culture led women progressives to open schools for upper-class Javanese girls while blinding them to the needs of the poor. Concern for respecting supposed Eastern customs combined with a series of conflicting Western messages, such as, girls should both earn their own bread and fulfil their maternal destiny, so that the schools were not a success.[39] A similar failure to understand the cultural needs of the colonised female population existed in Sumatra in the early decades of the twentieth century. Here, missionaries working for the Nederlands Zendelinggenootschap (Dutch Missionary Society) sought to lead Karo women, one of several Batak peoples in the Sumatran mountain range, to emancipation through Christian morality and education. The education they proposed in religion and basic literacy was intended to free women from the restrictions imposed on them while training them to become housewives and mothers. Even when Karo families pushed for more vocational training in nursing, the Dutch teachers continued to see their task as one of producing wives and mothers, each 'more suited for her task later in life'. Despite the progressive character of girls' education in the Netherlands, Dutch teachers only reluctantly recognised that the domestic orientation of their colonial schools was inappropriate.

> In twelve years the times have also changed in this respect. And so, because the girls themselves and their parents increasingly asked for it, we must accommodate, although it is unfortunate, the demand that this training should earn one a diploma and suit one for a well-paying job elsewhere. In this way the emphasis of this work was laid ever more on the material value and the profit rather than on ideals, and increasingly the real value of this work for our mission was lost.[40]

At times, the British were also insensitive to the needs of the local population. A demand for trained domestic servants for the local settler population led the head of the Bloemfontein Training School in 1877 to reorganise the educational programme; every other week students worked eight hours a day in the laundry room, with academic lessons in the evening. This manual reorientation of studies provoked a student rebellion, supported by their parents who were all related to the local chief of the Selaka Rolong.[41] In Algeria, Mme Allix Luce's school for Muslim girls encountered opposition not from students but from local Muslim notables who declared that 'no self-respecting Muslim would ever send his daughter or choose a wife from this school'.[42] Here, the colonial effort to effect a 'fusion of the races' through girls' education ran headlong into patriarchal attitudes that believed women belonged only in the home. In many colonised areas girls' access to learning represented a distinct challenge to local representations of the gender order. Meddlesome European women teachers were better advised to stick to home soil.

Promoting kindergartens and vocational training

Provisions for lower-class girls grew over the course of the nineteenth century and acquired an increasingly vocational orientation in western European countries. The most innovative measures for this social category undoubtedly occurred within kindergarten and pre-school education. Here the influence of child-centred pedagogical methods, notably those of the Swiss Johann Heinrich Pestalozzi and the German Friedrich Froebel inspired an international movement to provide schooling for the very young. Both men saw the mother–child relationship as critical, hence its appeal to female middle-class reformers. These women were active in the development of pre-school education, intervening in public debate from mid-century onwards. Their success in setting up schools and in getting municipal, federal and, at times, national support was in large part due to the way they couched their demands in the rhetoric of domestic ideology, portraying the growth of these schools as women's special mission.

Infant schools developed throughout Europe in the early decades of the nineteenth century. Often controlled by religious authorities or philanthropic groups of women, these schools generally welcomed both boys and girls and offered primarily a religious and disciplinary environment for large groups of infants. The growth of pre-school structures throughout Europe increasingly offered women opportunities as teachers and then as inspectors, as most European societies conceded that women's maternal responsibilities gave them special authority at this level of education. In France, for example, the first women to become mid-ranking civil servants were nursery-school inspectresses in 1837 who were responsible then for overseeing the organisation of a widespread system of *salles d'asile* (nursery schools). Pre-school education received particular attention in Germany thanks to the enthusiasm generated by Froebel's ideas. The Hochschule für das Weibliche Geschlecht (High School for the Female Sex) founded in 1850 was emblematic of such efforts; students received training in philosophy, literature, mathematics and kindergarten pedagogy, as well as practical experience in a kindergarten supervised by Froebel. Although this school closed in 1852, the concern to provide women with training in teaching continued in Germany – by 1877 there were twenty kindergarten seminars in German cities to train future kindergarten teachers. Kindergarten organisations affiliated with Louise Otto's Allgemeiner deutscher Frauenverein (German Women's Association) (1865) promoted childcare and women's special role in this care. Similar movements can be found throughout Europe: in the Netherlands by 1858 there were 395 modern infant schools with 415 female teachers running them and as of 1844 a part-time training college existed for infant-school teachers. In Italy, the Swiss Protestant Mathilde Calandrini, helped spread ideas about infant schools in Tuscany and at the same time opened a preschool for poor girls and a mutual school for girls in Pisa.[43]

Concern to develop kindergarten education developed in tandem with vocational training for women, notably in teaching. Religious organisations were often behind the creation of normal schools for girls: in England the first normal school for women was founded by the Anglican National Society in the early 1840s (Whitelands Training College), similarly a Catholic teaching congregation founded the first French normal school in 1838. Increasingly, however, the state also intervened, providing teacher training for girls throughout Europe: as early as 1832 in Prussia, 1858 in Piedmont,

1860 in Florence, 1866 in Belgium and Portugal, 1869 in the Austro-Hungarian empire, 1879 in France. The growth in normal schools for women both encouraged and accompanied a tendency throughout the Western world – the feminisation of the elementary teaching profession. For women, teaching was considered an extension of their maternal responsibilities; as a result, the decision to provide training for teaching could be justified using the rhetoric of domestic ideology. At the same time, it granted women a degree of economic independence and a foot in the working world. Schoolteachers' working lives were frequently difficult, however. The *Schoolmistress* in 1885 described the 'wretchedness' of many teachers' living arrangements in London: 'The hastily swallowed breakfast, the cold meat dinner, the lonely tea (so enjoyable when shared with friends) and the solitary evening!'[44] Letters from early twentieth-century schoolteachers in France also reveal how difficult it could be for single women to assume this new professional identity; contemporaries continued to think of women teachers as surrogate mothers, and in most European countries when they married themselves, they were required to resign from their position.

The middle decades of the century also witnessed the development in many European countries of schools that sought to train girls in skills that were not just those associated with being a good housewife. In France the Saint-Simonian Elise Lemonnier created the Société pour l'Enseignement Professionnel des Femmes (The Society for Vocational Education for Women) and offered special courses in commerce, book-keeping, commercial law and industrial drawing after three years of primary education. The Lette-Verein (Lette Association) in Berlin offered a similar programme in the late 1860s for lower-class girls, and elsewhere in Vienna, Prague and Russia, reform-oriented men and women opened schools to provide girls with vocational training. For contemporaries, however, the appearance of vocational schools for girls or the proliferation of women running kindergartens were relatively minor phenomena compared to the vociferous pronouncements of middle-class ladies demanding reforms in middle-class girls' education.

Reforming middle-class girls' education

Calls to reform girls' secondary education began in England in the late 1840s and gathered momentum in the 1850s and 1860s along with similar movements elsewhere in Europe, often spearheaded by middle-class feminists. The reform movement addressed a number of concerns: the need to provide educational opportunities for women to improve their overall status, the need to provide better education for motherhood, the need to provide job training for single women, and the concern to make girls' schools truly secondary in comparison with boys' schools. As with the kindergarten movement, middle-class school reform used and reused the vocabulary of domesticity; still, the momentum that developed around this movement for educational reform led many women to challenge more directly the premises of domestic ideology: that woman's place was in the home. As a result, the development of more serious education for middle-class girls represented an important step in women's emancipation.

In Britain, recent scholarship on Scotland has revealed the emergence of more serious schools for young ladies in the 1830s, as well as the founding in 1842 of an institution for higher education: Queen's College Glasgow.[45] In England, Queen's

College (1848) and Bedford College (1848) were an initial response to the anxiety generated by the plight of single middle-class women; they were founded to raise the educational qualifications of governesses. In the following years, British women mobilised far more broadly, campaigning to improve the quality of girls' secondary education. In England, women such as Frances Buss, Dorothea Beale and Emily Davies not only brought public attention to the need to provide girls with a more rigorous education, but they also opened 'reformed' schools, notably the North London Collegiate School, revised curricula and fought for women to gain access to exams. Davies, in particular, campaigned for women to be able to pass the prestigious Cambridge Local Examination on the same basis as boys:

> Every effort to improve the education of women which assumes that they may, without reprehensible ambition, study the same subjects as their brothers and be measured by the same standards, does something towards lifting them out of the state of listless despair of themselves into which so many fall.[46]

And she went on to note that this improved education and access to the same exams would also allow women to pursue university studies in England rather than be forced to seek advanced study in France or Switzerland.

Throughout Europe, reforms movements lobbied along similar lines. Women's professional associations were often responsible for such lobbying, such as the Association of German Women Teachers and Governesses (1869) or the Czech Minerva Association. In Greece, feminists writing for the *Ladies Newspaper* (1887–1907) fought for equal educational and professional opportunities. But at times single women made their voices heard. Josephine Bachellery in France argued, albeit unsuccessfully, in 1848 for the need to create a superior normal school for girls (it was only founded in 1881), while in Austria, Marianne Hainisch was the first person to call for a *Realgymnasium* for girls in 1870. In the following years, private secondary schools developed, but the first public school was only opened in Graz in 1885 and a standardised curriculum decreed in 1900. Other notable figures in the struggle to provide middle-class girls with a more rigorous education include the Irishwomen Margaret Byers, Anne Jellicoe and Isabelle Tod who founded institutes to provide secondary education for girls in Dublin and Belfast in the 1860s. In the Netherlands Elise van Calcar and Minette Storm-van der Chijs campaigned for women's education in the 1860s as statesmen debated an important law on education; the first girls' *Hogere Burgerscholen* (citizen's high schools) then opened their doors in 1867.

These efforts to improve the quality of girls' secondary education were commented upon within numerous venues in the second half of the century – feminist newspapers or publications, government publications and universal exhibitions – and testify to the vitality of a small but growing international feminist movement. By sharing information about other school systems, feminists and educational reformers used this knowledge to challenge national stereotypes about women's more fragile minds or constitutions through examples of countries where adolescent girls studied 'masculine' subjects with no apparent harm. After a tour of American university colleges for women, the French university professor, Célestin Hippeau wrote: 'The admirable results womens' studies have achieved [in the United States] are the most triumphant answer to the objections that emerge everywhere whenever the issue of the intellectual emancipation of women has not moved beyond mere discussion.'[47] Fellow countrywoman and the first woman to obtain the *baccalauréat* degree, Julie-Victoire Daubié agreed. Her prize-winning book *La Femme pauvre (The Poor Woman)* (1866) was particularly critical of the sorry state of French girls' education at all levels, the result, she claimed, of nuns' dominance in girls' education and the state's indifference.

By the second half of the century, most western European countries had begun to develop networks of girls' schools whose relationship to a system of boys' education was increasingly under debate. For boys and men, degrees and diplomas existed that sanctioned a certain level of studies and opened doors to professional careers. In countries where national degrees existed, such as the German *Abitur*, the French *baccalauréat* or the Austrian *Matura*, a self-consciously feminist women's movement began at mid-century to argue for women's access to such degrees. These demands concerned primarily middle-class women who increasingly sought access to careers in the service sector, notably in teaching. The reform of girls' secondary schools opened up new opportunities in secondary teaching, since in most European countries – with the notable exception of the Netherlands – secondary education remained single sex well into the twentieth century. In 1880 when the French state finally established public secondary education for girls in *collèges* and *lycées*, the promoter of the law, Camille Sée, could offer a panoramic sweep of the Western world: noting the presence of serious secondary schools for girls in Russia, where the first girls' *gymnasia* appeared in 1858; in Belgium, where Isabelle Gatti de Gamond founded a model secondary school in 1864; in Austria, where *Mädchenlyzeen* were created after 1870; even in Greece, where a private institution known as the Arsakion offered secondary education as well as teacher training. James Albisetti has argued that the German model of secular secondary girls' schools that was already widespread in the 1860s provided the impetus for many of these national developments; immediately after the French law, Italian reformers introduced the first state-run *istituti femminile* (feminine institutes).[48]

On the eve of the First World War, voices no longer openly questioned women's right to receive an education, except at the level of the university, and institutions existed to provide it. Nonetheless, access to 'male' degrees remained difficult for most women graduates. In France, the public *lycées* did not prepare their female students for the *baccalauréat* until 1924 – and at all levels of education gender stereotypes continued. Lessons at the secondary level remained firmly committed to the ideal of forming good wives and mothers even if a handful of women used this education for wider purposes. Disappearance of a specifically female curriculum would only gradually occur over the course of the twentieth century. Still, despite these limitations, the expansion of formal schooling for girls meant that women could now apply for jobs in the burgeoning service sector, as office workers, postal workers and, especially, teachers. Professional positions in law, medicine or higher education remained, nonetheless, the domain of men.

Expanding women's horizons in the twentieth century

At the close of the nineteenth century, Alice Zimmern heralded the changes of the past fifty years in England as a peaceful revolution for the education of women:

Very strange though it may sound, it was in truth a Renaissance – a survival of the past, and no new experiment. Or perhaps we should more fitly describe it as the realisation of an old dream, one that has been dreamed many times in the course of the age, but has waited till the nineteenth century for its complete fulfilment . . . The treasures of learning are no longer the property of an exclusive few, and the privileges of class and sex are breaking down simultaneously. Education for all, boys and girls, rich and poor, is the modern demand, which no party dare now refuse to consider . . . All the daughters of all the households of all civilised countries are to enter into their heritage. The much-discussed 'ladder' from the elementary school to the University is becoming a fact; and its rungs are being widened, that the girls may ascend it side by side with their brothers. *La carrière ouverte aux talents*, [a career open to talent] with no distinction of class, sex, or creed, is the demand of the nineteenth century.[49]

Speaking from her position in Girton College, Cambridge, her statement may appear overly optimistic and yet there was a grain of truth in her pronouncements. The expansion of national educational systems meant virtually all west European girls were present in elementary schools by the end of the century, although they were significantly under-represented in secondary education. But access to elementary education is only one part of a story that is not universally rosy.

The following section traces the ways women used improved education during their adolescent years to enter universities and to aspire to horizons beyond the home. Higher education only concerned a minority of women until very recently, however, and expanding opportunities for women did not progress along linear paths. The troubled inter-war years, with the triumph of conservative, authoritarian and totalitarian ideologies in many countries had an impact on the offer of schooling for girls and, above all, on its ethos. In the aftermath of the Second World War, most countries sought to promote democratic values through their educational systems. For European girls this involved two important changes. To begin with, the class distinctions between elementary and secondary education gradually disappeared as elementary school became the first step in all pupils' educational journey and secondary schools increasingly welcomed both middle- and lower-class students. Second, most school systems adopted co-education as the norm, so that by the 1970s, single-sex education had become primarily the privilege of wealthier families or families seeking a private elite upbringing for their daughters. As a result, by the end of the twentieth century, the institutional specificities of girls' education had largely disappeared.

Entering higher education

A small handful of women gained access to higher education in the final years of the nineteenth century. Swiss universities led the way in accepting women to attend courses and even to obtain university degrees. The University in Zurich was the first to allow women to enrol as regular students and in 1867 granted the Russian woman Nadejda Souslova a doctoral degree in medicine. The numbers of women enrolled in Swiss universities rose relatively quickly and by 1900 they represented 20 per cent of the student body. Interestingly, the overwhelming majority of these students (between 80 and 90 per cent) were foreign women, mostly from the Russian Empire. The pattern of access to university studies varied widely in Europe. In England and Scotland, feminist groups pushed for the creation of residential colleges within established universities. At Cambridge, women such as Annie Clough and Emily Davies were responsible for the creation of Newnham (1871) and Girton (1873) colleges; Oxford followed suit a few years later with St Margaret's Hall and Somerville, and in Scotland, the University of Glasgow established Queen Margaret College in 1883. While these single-sex colleges encouraged the presence of women within British universities, they did not eliminate debates and conflicts concerning women's access to lecture courses and university degrees. The University of London was the first British university in 1878 to admit women to its degrees. In countries, such as France, Germany and the Netherlands, where specifically female colleges did not exist, resistance to the presence of female students was also high and their numbers relatively few and far between. Still, a number of women pioneers succeeded in getting university degrees: in France in 1875 Madeleine Brès was the first French women to obtain a doctorate in medicine; in Germany the Russian Johanna Evreinova earned a law degree from the University of Leipzig in 1873. In some countries, such as France, medicine was more welcoming to women, given women's caring role, while in Scotland the impropriety of teaching anatomical classes to both sexes acted as a brake.

Countless caricatures and articles at the turn of the century testify to enduring masculine hostility to women's claims for higher education, and as the numbers of women in universities increased so too did representations of the dangers this education represented. Excessive study would bring on hysteria some claimed, others feared it would weaken women's maternal desires and many claimed that it was the first step in a dangerous reversal of sex roles. The phenomenon of the New Woman, with her claims for autonomy and independence were deeply troubling to many contemporaries. In France, for example, the prolific turn-of-the-century author Colette Yver wrote novels with evocative titles such as *Les Princesses de sciences (Princesses of Science)* or *Les Cervelines (Women Egg-Heads)* where ambitious university-educated women opted for careers rather than matrimony and motherhood, causing despair, divorce and even death. These manifestations of cultural anxiety about women in higher education should not obscure, however, the small numbers of women this actually concerned. In Great Britain, women in English and Scottish universities represented 16 per cent of the student population in 1900; this figure climbed to 24 per cent in 1920, 27 per cent in 1930, but had dipped once more to 23 per cent on the eve of the Second World War. Scottish universities were less elitist and more welcoming to women: at St Andrews, women were already 40 per cent of the student body in 1907–8. In France, Germany and Italy, women students were initially far more exceptional: a mere 7 per cent for France and Germany on the eve of the First World War, 6 per cent in Italy. The percentage of French women students climbed quickly in the inter-war period, so that in 1930 the situation was similar to that in Great Britain, where 26 per cent of the student body was female. In Italy the policies of Mussolini kept the figures from rising too quickly: women were 13 per cent of the student body in 1927–8 and still only 15 per cent in 1935, while in Germany women were still only 28 per cent of the student body in 1960–1.

Women's access to higher education in the early twentieth century is testimony to significant changes in girls' secondary training which increasingly allowed them to pass successfully university entrance exams or to obtain school-leaving certificates that opened the doors to universities. But it did not translate automatically into new attitudes towards women's roles in society. Indeed, many of the new largely middle-class women students never obtained university degrees and those who did often never actually entered a profession. For these women, higher education had become a personal goal, but not one that led them away from domestic futures. Women often had to brave familial opposition, as did the brilliant French philosopher Simone de Beauvoir when she pursued her studies and achieved a teaching degree in philosophy in 1929:

> In my family milieu, it was considered peculiar for a young girl to pursue higher education; getting work implied social decline. Obviously my father was a vigorous antifeminist . . . he considered that a woman's place was in the home and in salons.[50]

Figures of European women who used their education to become doctors or lawyers or university professors remain extremely low throughout the first half of the century. Within universities there were countless examples of couples, such as Paule and Fernand Braudel, where the wife diligently read and copied for her husband without a professional position, salary or recognition. Some university-educated women used their talents to open institutions specifically for women. The German Alice Solomon was one such figure who, despite familial opposition and the absence of the *Abitur*, nonetheless pursued a degree in political economy at the University of Berlin, earning a doctorate in 1906 and then went on to found the Soziale Frauenschule (Woman's School of Social Work), and in 1925 the Deutsche Akademie für soziale und pädagogische Frauenarbeit (Germany Academy for Women's Social and Pedagogical Work). This academy trained women to become social workers, youth professionals, and so on, fields where women's presence was far more acceptable than in the ethereal ranks of the university.

A quantitative jump in women's presence as students in the university only occurred in Europe in the 1960s and 1970s as secondary education became far more available and as universities expanded and became more democratic. In France, female students were a third of the student body in 1945, 44 per cent in 1967 and 50 per cent by 1981. In most western European countries, rough parity in male and female university enrolment was achieved in the 1980s, although gender enrolments by academic discipline reveal striking differences in orientations with obvious impact on future employment opportunities. What has changed, however, is the number of women who use their university degrees to pursue professional lives afterwards. Home and motherhood are far less exclusively the ultimate goal of a girls' educational trajectory.

Ideology and girls' education

While women's access to higher education in the twentieth century represents in a sense the ideological triumph of one strand of Enlightenment ideals, that 'the mind has no sex', other ideological currents during the century proclaimed the opposite and at times had significant impact on the type of learning available to girls and women. Within Italian Fascism and German Nazism, the obsession with virility in the creation of a 'New Man' involved creating as well a 'New Woman', who was decidedly NOT a university-educated woman aspiring for economic independence. The fashioning of the Fascist or Nazi woman in schools and youth groups offers insights as well into the way learning and knowledge acquired increasingly gendered traits in these years, traits that also emerged in Franco's Spain and in Vichy France.

In Italy, the slow development of educational structures for girls in the nineteenth century meant that after Italian unification girls entered boys' schools, thus benefiting from the same instruction. By the turn of the century, enrolments for girls in both elementary and secondary education rose at the same pace as boys. With Mussolini's rise to power, complaints about the excessive democratisation of the school system as well as the undue influence of women as teachers led to a series of major reforms that severely restricted girls' educational opportunities while highlighting the regime's misogynist orientation. Giovanni Gentile, the Sicilian philosopher turned Fascist ideologue, fashioned an elitist reform of the educational system while Minister of Public Instruction from 1922 to 1924. His bias against women can be seen in efforts to defeminise the teaching profession by excluding women from holding 'masculine' positions at the secondary *licei* (high schools) in letters, Greek, Latin, history and philosophy, and by barring them from positions as directors of various schools. He also established new finishing schools for daughters of good families, *liceo femminile*, that offered a smattering of humanities, arts and crafts. Finally, he downgraded the quality of vocational education for women. While these measures did not prevent more and more girls from attending schools, they represented a clear setback in the eyes of Italian feminists. The restrictive character of schooling opportunities for women was reinforced with the promulgation of the School Charter of 1939. Article 21 read: 'The destination and social mission of women, being distinct in fascist life, have at their foundation different and special institutions of instruction.'[51] This differential treatment of men and women was particularly flagrant within the Fascist youth groups; under the cover of the umbrella youth organisation, Opera nazionale Balilla, girls learned first aid, rhythmic exercises and charity while boys did competitive sports, military-type excursions and mock-weaponry.

Policies directed towards women within the Nazi Party and state varied over time, but they were consistent in presenting women in ancillary positions, closely related to their role within the family. Nazi education policies were strictly ideological, as Frau Dr August Rebeer-Gruber, Consultant on Girls' Education to the Ministry of Education, stated: 'The task of our schooling . . . is simple: the moulding of German girls as carriers of the National Socialist point of view.'[52] She oversaw the activities of all women teachers and vigorously fought to develop a specifically feminine and non-academic curriculum that privileged home economics, psychology, folk art, eugenics and physical education. She located Nazi women within the home and felt betrayed in the late 1930s when Nazi policies reversed themselves to encourage women to assume a double burden in the workforce and at home. Gertrud Scholtz-Klink who led the Frauenwerk (Women's Bureau) for the Nazi state was also active in an educational campaign to professionalise the role of housewife, a campaign directed more to older women than to the young. Two hundred and seventy-nine schools were established to train mothers in nutrition, interior decoration, economic management of household finance, childcare, cleaning methods and sewing. Over 1.5 million women per year enrolled in nearly 84,000 motherhood classes. For elite Nazi women, the Nazis went so far as to offer a programme that led to a master's degree in household science. For younger girls, aged fourteen to nineteen, participation in the feminine branch of the Hitler Youth, Bund Deutscher Mädel (League of German Girls), allowed adolescents to serve the Nazi cause. Despite policy changes, the Nazi period represented a distinct setback to earlier struggles to achieve equal educational opportunities for girls and boys. In higher education the number of women students at universities dropped from 20,000 in 1930 to 5,500 in 1939.

In Vichy France the concept of the 'eternal feminine' emerged as the state promulgated a vision of the family where women's rights were sharply curtailed. In education, this translated into a resurgence in Catholic rather than secular education with Catholic women's groups defending the idea that women's place was in the home. Various ideologues once more directed their hostility against educated women: in 1941 René Benjamin wrote, *Vérités et rêveries sur l'éducation (Truths and Musings on Education)* where he proclaimed that 300 women with university degrees had become prostitutes; he believed 'a girl should first and foremost be the mirror image of her mother.'[53] Within secondary education, a decree the same year specified that girls' education should include lessons in music and housewifery, which were considered appropriate for their roles, while in primary education the content of manual work was made strictly sex-specific. In 1942 all girls were required to take instruction in family housekeeping for one hour a week for seven years.

Franco's Spain represented another country where a Catholic conservative discourse about what constituted true Spanish womanhood led to increasingly inegalitarian educational measures over the course of the century. The National Catholic party that was in power from 1939 until Franco's death in 1975 made it clear that girls' education should serve patriarchal politics: girls should be trained to be devout and dutiful wives and mothers. A decree of March 1945 established the Instituto de Enseñanzas Profesionales de la Mujer (Institute for Women's Professional Training). The latter's goal was expressed thus: 'The female sex is entrusted with the task of defending traditional family values and preserving the domestic arts, essential to maintain happiness in the home.' Within the university, women's presence was discouraged. While men accomplished their military obligations in a university militia, women were enrolled in a mandatory university social-service programme where they learned the fine art of home economics and received indoctrination into their special role within the nation, notably through a separate female section of the Falange.[54]

The resurgence of a domestic-oriented ideology for women within conservative or fascist regimes in the middle decades of the century should not be confused with what emerged throughout Europe in the early nineteenth century. True, propagandists once more trumpeted the significance of women's role within the home, but this role was tied to a national political agenda far more explicitly. It is important to distinguish here between the vision of the family in these different political regimes and how girls' education was expected to serve the regime. The discourse and practices of Franco's Spain probably harked back most clearly to a nineteenth-century model where girls' education was strongly religious and housewifely in its orientation, as schoolbook learning took a definite back seat. In Vichy France and even more strongly in Fascist Italy and Nazi Germany, however, the needs of a technocratic state demanded in reality more of women's education. As a result, the seeming familiarity of the domestic message belied a very different underlying purpose. While these regimes re-established the importance of biological differences in their understandings of masculinity and femininity, they could not erase history and the very real gains women had achieved in education, gains that became virtually universal in the final years of the century.

Co-education and changing visions of gender roles

In the years following the end of the Second World War, European countries reconstructed their societies and sought to heal their wounds; in terms of education this meant reforms that sought to ensure the triumph of democratic values amongst school-age children who would all, both men and women, go on to become voting citizens. It also meant more concerted efforts to provide better and more serious education to all classes of society. In Britain, the Education Act of 1944 provided all children with a free secondary education; in France, reforms in the 1960s expanded access to general non-vocational secondary schooling; in Germany, co-educational secondary schools were initiated in the 1960s. Throughout Europe, the school-leaving age moved up from twelve or thirteen in 1900 to sixteen by the 1960s. For girls and boys, however, the most significant educational change of the post-war world was probably the introduction of co-education in elementary and secondary schools. This major pedagogical transformation signalled in many cases the end of a sex-specific curriculum, but above all accompanied the emergence of a new youth culture where gender roles came under scrutiny. For girls, the messages of a woman's movement that challenged traditional attitudes towards sexuality increasingly encouraged them to believe that in their private lives they could enjoy the same liberties as boys. At the same time, the economic revival opened opportunities for women in the workforce which also meant that schooling for women was seen as a step towards enjoying the same financial independence as men in their working lives. In reality, of course, neither educational nor cultural changes were sufficiently revolutionary to efface deeply engrained gender stereotypes. Still, co-education and the effects of the women's movement changed for many girls the educational messages received in their formative years, leading them to assume that equality of the sexes was the ostensible goal of national educational systems.

By the late 1970s, co-education had become a reality in the state sector of most European countries, although in Ireland single-sex schools remained in the state sector and to some degree in England and Wales. Single-sex education also continued to exist within some subjects such as physical education and crafts in Poland, Belgium, Greece, West Germany and England and Wales. Overall, however, the decision to mingle boys and girls in the same schoolrooms and on the same school benches had become an accepted reality, in part thanks to the actions of feminist movements, but more often thanks to economic pragmatism. It was far cheaper to build one school for both sexes in the enormous expansion of educational systems between the 1960s and 1980s than to persist in providing separate schools. The achievement of co-education represented, however, a major revolution in conceptualising girls' education, as the history of its introduction reveals.

Throughout the period under examination, co-education existed primarily in elementary schools and in rural areas where the cost of maintaining two schools made single-sex education unattainable. The emergence of a movement to promote co-education dates back to the turn of the nineteenth and twentieth centuries and it contained from the outset a utopian, egalitarian and feminist message. For the early promoters, co-education entailed far more than mixed schooling; it represented an attempt to change the relationship between the sexes to build a more harmonious society. For Englishwoman Alice Woods, the head of a co-educational school at Chiswick (1884–92), co-education was

> the education of boys and girls . . . in companionship from the age of infancy to adult life, neither sex being segregated, but taught many subjects and sharing many games in common, with freedom to enjoy their leisure in one another's company.[55]

Co-education was frequently debated in international feminist congresses and was part of the New Education movement in the inter-war period. Feminists argued that it would promote greater equality between men and women, by providing girls with the same learning opportunities as boys.

Opposition to mixed schooling reveals, however, how attitudes about masculinity and femininity continued to structure European societies' approach to girls' education well into the twentieth century. Despite the improvement in girls' education accomplished over the course of the preceding century, many people remained firmly convinced that adolescent girls and boys, in particular, should not be educated in the same way and certainly not side by side. In many ways, the rise of psychological sciences and their application to the study of adolescence contributed to the belief that male and female psychological difference was different and that their education should, as a result, differ. For Catholics, Pope Pius XI's encyclical, *Divini illius magistri* (1929) represented a powerful condemnation of the 'coeducation of the sexes', a method founded 'upon a deplorable confusion of ideas that mistakes a leveling promiscuity and equality, for the legitimate association of the sexes'.[56] Opponents feared co-education for a variety of reasons that speak tellingly to the strength of widely shared gender stereotypes in Europe. Mingling adolescent boys and girls was often described as inherently immoral and likely to provoke immoral behaviour among pupils whose budding sexuality was under only tenuous control. Some pedagogues argued that co-education, by providing girls with the same lessons that boys received, was simply inappropriate. For others, co-education encouraged the homogenisation of the sexes by making boys more feminine and girls more masculine. Defenders, it should be noted, often used the same argument but viewed it in positive terms: the rough ways of boys would be tempered through their contact with girls; girls would become more assertive and confident thanks to their acquiring male traits. Most disturbing for many critics was the fear that co-education would inspire young women to seek independent lives, thus contributing to an array of ills: divorce, falling birth rates, women professionals. The American practice of co-education at the level of high schools and universities provoked many negative comments about the effects of such an education. Maurice Caullery, a French biology professor who spent a semester in the USA in 1915–16 remarked:

> One cannot help but think that the life [girls and women] have led during their studies has encouraged them to develop a taste for luxury which in many cases poses a serious threat to family life . . . [college graduates] are not prepared

either psychologically or technically for the duties of family life and place special conditions on marriage which cause many men to flee.[57]

In essence, Caullery considered that the egalitarian nature of co-education failed to provide women with an education appropriate for their future lives. The bonds of domesticity were tenacious indeed.

Nonetheless, co-education made inroads in secondary education, with the Dutch leading the way. In 1880 a girl was admitted to a classical *gymnasium* with virtually no protest; in 1899 *Hogere Burgerschool* (citizen's high schools) accepted the principle of co-education and by 1925 only 8 per cent of all girls attending this type of school were in girls' schools. In part, this easy acceptance of co-education at the secondary level stemmed from the absence of boarding school education in the Netherlands and strong feminist support for the principle of equality between the sexes well before the turn of the century. Elsewhere in Europe, co-education progressed, but often in fits and starts. In France girls were allowed into the upper classes of classical boys' *lycées* in 1922, but the systematic development of co-education at this level only occurred after 1959. In Belgium, by 1965, 67 per cent of all secondary state schools were co-educational, but virtually no Catholic schools. Despite the progress of co-education, debates about its effects have waxed and waned throughout the century, in response to a variety of factors. Early opposition to the practice tended to be conservative and particularly prevalent amongst Catholics, although some turn-of-the-century feminists were also against co-education, notably the headmistresses of girls' schools who rightly intuited that the spread of co-educational schools would decrease the number of women principals. Interestingly, the questioning of co-education, once it had become a widespread reality in the 1980s, came mainly from feminist circles in both England and Germany. Feminists noted that despite the promise of co-education, it did not lead necessarily to equal opportunities for both sexes, and that within classrooms the effect of mixed schooling were often to the detriment of girls, as boys monopolised both linguistic space and teachers' attention. While no one has called for a return to strict sex segregation within the school system, both progressive and conservative voices since the 1980s have advocated single-sex education in certain disciplines and for certain age groups. The interest in reclaiming single-sex education for feminist purposes reached a climax at the Universal Exhibition in Hanover in 2000 where primarily German feminists organised an International Women's University that attracted women throughout the world. The university chose not to focus on women's subjects, but rather to bring women from different disciplines together to discuss issues affecting all societies from a feminist perspective. The need for such an initiative illustrates how the path towards gender equality, while necessarily including access to learning, requires far more.

Conclusion: The politics of girls' education

The past three centuries have brought girls from all social backgrounds into classrooms throughout Europe. This achievement is the result of a combination of factors that are difficult to untangle given their mutual interaction, but it is important to recognise that the debate about girls' education always carried a political dimension. Religious and secular forces combined in the eighteenth century to provide the initial impetus for providing girls with education. Nuns and Protestant reformers sought to improve overall morality and to instil Christian sentiments by targeting girls because of their status within the family. Amongst the upper classes, both men and women also championed a woman's right to knowledge often for similar reasons, although a few voices saw education as an inalienable individual right, a position that would spread over the course of the following century. No matter what the reasoning behind the defence of a girls' right to learn, schools were opened and their numbers grew, offering a wide variety of educational experiences. For the minority of girls who attended schools, the lessons they received were limited in scholarly scope, intending to fit women for their proper sphere in life. The English evangelical moralist Hannah More summed it up nicely:

> To woman, therefore, whatever be her rank, I would recommend a predominance of those more sober studies, which, not having display for their object, may make her wise without vanity, happy without witnesses, and content with panegyrists; the exercise of which will not bring celebrity, but improve usefulness. . . . She should cultivate every study which, instead of stimulating her sensibility will chastise it; which will neither create an excessive or a false refinement; which will give her definite notions . . . will lead her to think, to compare, to combine, to methodise . . . That kind of knowledge which is rather fitted for home consumption than foreign exportation, is peculiarly suited to women.[58]

In the following century these principles underlay countless conduct manuals, pedagogical treatises and educational programmes, although the actual content of this education came periodically under scrutiny. Most girls' institutions continued to school and train girls for a future different to that of boys, more centred around home and family. The development of a feminist movement after the 1850s, however, began to challenge the tenets of this home-oriented education and to voice more openly the political implications of women's education; most women reformers argued that education was the necessary first step for women's social, economic and political emancipation, but some, such as the socialist French feminist Hubertine Auclert, believed true educational equality would only come when women were electors:

> Women must vote in order to be educated. Young girls will never have serious instruction, a scientific and rational instruction until women have the right to debate budgets, to introduce a pair of scales in the budget of public instruction, and to establish the principle of equality for all children in these scales, that is to say, the same number of schools, the same quantity of science for girls as for boys.[59]

The political implications of women's education were also evident in the European effort to export models of female schooling to the colonies. Whether proposing vocational training for future domestic servants or refined education for the daughters of native elites, European women argued for the ways girls' education would further the imperial project and solidify ideological control over the families of colonised subjects.

The events of the twentieth century highlighted the ideologically charged nature of girls' education and the way it played into both authoritarian and democratic political agendas. Educated women, whether they entered the workforce or not, were a force that nation-states had to acknowledge and to reckon with in educational systems whose general tendency was for increasing inclusiveness in terms of social class and sex. The solution to gender disorders could no longer be to prevent women from learning to read, as Sylvain Maréchal facetiously suggested after the French Revolution. Instead, the Nazi and Fascist states provided girls with education, but an education that insisted on their biologically determined role. Even within democratic countries, the conviction that women's destiny was in the home has had a particularly long life, despite the insights of countless feminists, including that of Simone de Beauvoir who explained in the opening line of *The Second Sex* (1949) 'One is not born a woman, one becomes one', through culture and education. The appearance of female students in universities throughout Europe and the generalisation of co-education within elementary and secondary schools has not eradicated deeply held convictions that despite women's proven ability to study the same subjects as men, their destinies are indeed different. As a result, sociological studies of European educational systems all reveal the persistence of gender inequalities despite evidence in many countries that female pupils outperform their male companions at all levels of the elementary and secondary education. These inequalities are most evident in the curriculum orientations of girls and women, their overwhelming tendency to pursue studies in literature and the arts, leaving the sciences and technological subjects to boys and men. These 'choices' have lasting consequences within European workforces as men monopolise positions of economic and political power often thanks to their educational trajectory. Access to education and knowledge does indeed translate into forms of power, as Michel Foucault has argued, but the conditions of this access remain gendered, so that women's power operates in different realms, hierarchically inferior to those of men's. Ironically, education is precisely one of those realms where women are massively present: in 1985–6, 90 per cent of pre-school teachers in France, Greece, Sweden, Spain and England and Wales were female, and the proportion of women primary teachers ranged from 61 per cent in Spain to 79 per cent in Great Britain in 1988–9.[60] Using this power over young minds to promote truly egalitarian educational systems and societies represents then the challenge for the twenty-first century.

Guide to further reading

Albisetti, James, *Schooling German Girls and Women: Secondary and Higher Education in the Nineteenth Century*. Princeton, NJ: Princeton University Press, 1988. Offers the indispensable overview of girls' education in Germany. His conclusions are particularly useful since they offer comparative insights. See, as well, his articles: 'Female Education in German-Speaking Austria, Germany, and Switzerland, 1866–1914', in David Good, Margarete Grander and Mary Jo Maynes, eds, *Austrian Women in the Nineteenth and Twentieth Centuries: Cross-Disciplinary Perspectives*. Oxford: Berghan Books, 1996; 'The Feminization of Teaching in the Nineteenth Century: A Comparative Perspective', *History of Education*, 22, (1993), pp. 253–63; 'Catholics and Coeducation in Europe before "Divini Illius Magistri"', *Paedagogica Historica*, 35, 3, (1999), pp. 667–96.

Allen, Ann Taylor, *Feminism and Motherhood in Germany, 1800–1914*. New Brunswick, NJ: Rutgers University Press, 1991. A sensitive portrayal of how maternalism played into various reform movements in Germany, including educational reform.

Bakker, Nelleke and Mineke van Essen, 'No Matter of Principle: The Unproblematic Character of Coeducation in Girls' Secondary Schooling in the Netherlands, ca. 1870–1930', *History of Education Quarterly*, 39, (1999), pp. 454–75. Traces the emergence of co-education in the Netherlands and offers comparative perspectives with other European countries.

Chaudhuri, Nupur and Margaret Strobel, *Western Women and Imperialism: Complicity and Resistance*. Bloomington, Ind.: Indiana University Press, 1992. Includes several articles on missionaries in India and South Africa.

Clark, Linda, *Schooling the Daughters of Marianne: Textbooks and the Socialization of Girls in Modern French Primary Schools*. Albany, NY: SUNY Press, 1984. A rare study of the gendered characteristics of elementary school textbooks focused on the period when the Republicans had come to power in France after 1880.

Cullen, Mary, ed., *Girls Do Not Do Honours: Irish Women in Education in the 19th and 20th Century*. Dublin: Women's Education Bureau, 1987. A strong feminist perspective on girls' education at the secondary and university level, nuns, gender roles and the curriculum.

Dyhouse, Carol, *Girls Growing Up in Late Victorian and Edwardian England*. London: Routledge, 1981. Although published over twenty years ago, this book offers a clear analysis of the social construction of femininity in both middle-class and lower-class schooling; the author draws on a wide range of both institutional and private sources. See her more recent and engaging analysis of the first women to enter British universities *No Distinction of Sex? Women in British Universities, 1870–1939*. London: University College Press, 1995.

Essen, Mineke van, 'Strategies of Women Teachers, 1860–1920: Feminization in Dutch Elementary and Secondary Schools from a Comparative Perspective', *History of Education*, 28, 1999, pp. 413–33. Provides insight into the social history of Dutch education from one of the foremost historians of women's education.

Essen, Mineke van and Rebecca Rogers, eds, 'Les enseignantes: formations, identités, représentations (XIXe-XXe siècles)', *Histoire de l'éducation*, 98, May (2003). This special issue examines the training, identities and representations of women teachers in England and its South African colony, France, the Netherlands, Australia and Germany; it includes a lengthy comparative historiographic essay on women teachers.

Gemie, Sharif, *Women and Schooling in France, 1815–1914*. Keele: Keele University Press, 1995. A study that focuses on lay primary-school teachers and their relationship to the French state using Habermas's concept of the public. He exploits an interesting variety of sources including the diary of a young apprentice schoolteacher.

Gold, Carol, *Educating Middle Class Daughters: Private Girls Schools in Copenhagen, 1790–1820*. Copenhagen: The Royal Library Museum Tusculanum Press, 1996. Offers a detailed social history of the content of schooling as well as a portrait of the teachers.

Gorham, Deborah, *The Victorian Girl and the Feminine Ideal*. Bloomington, Ind.: Indiana University Press, 1982. A pioneering study of the Victorian construction of femininity that draws on literature, advice manuals and the private archives of middle-class women.

Harten, Elke and Hans-Christian Harten, *Femmes, culture et revolution*. Paris: Des Femmes, 1993. An unusually broad range of primary sources on gender and education in the French revolution; includes a stimulating interpretation of the documents.

Kleinau, Elke and Claudia Opitz, eds, *Geschichte der Mädchen-und Frauenbildung*. Vol. II. Frankfurt and New York: Campus Verlag, 1996. An important collection of articles that traces the organisation of girls' schooling from elementary to university education as well as ideas and debates about women's education. The two volumes cover the periods from the Middle Ages to 1990 and addresses primarily German education.

Mayeur, Françoise, *L'éducation des filles en France au XIXe siècle.* Paris: Hachette, 1979. The classic synthesis of girls' education in France; an essential introduction to the topic. She is also the author of *L'Enseignement secondaire des jeunes filles sous la Troisième République.* Paris: Presses de la Fondation Nationale des Sciences Politiques, 1977, a pioneering study of the first public high schools for girls and their teachers after 1880. She has a chapter on girls' education, which is heavily French in its focus, 'The Secular Model of Girls' Education', in Michele Perrot and Geneviève Fraisse, eds, *History of Women in the West.* Vol. IV: *Emerging Feminism from Revolution to World War*, Cambridge, Mass.: Harvard University Press, 1993, pp. 228–45.

Maynes, Mary-Jo, *Schooling in Western Europe: A Social History.* Albany, NY: SUNY Press, 1984. A useful comparative synthesis of schooling in Western Europe in the late eighteenth and nineteenth centuries.

Offen, Karen, *European Feminisms, 1700–1950: A Political History.* Stanford, Calif.: Stanford University Press, 1992. This important synthesis offers a great deal of information about attitudes toward women's learning and the role of education in feminist movements throughout Europe.

Pedersen, Joyce Senders, 'The Reform of Women's Secondary and Higher Education: Institutional Change and Social Values in Mid and Late Victorian England.' *History of Education Quarterly*, 19, spring (1979), pp. 61–99; *The Reform of Girls' Secondary and Higher Education in Victorian England: A Study of Elites and Educational Change.* London: Garland, 1987. The article and book present the classic argument for how British girls' education was reformed in the second half of the nineteenth century.

Petschauer, Peter, *The Education of Women in Eighteenth-Century Germany: New Directions from the German Female Perspective. Bending the Ivy.* Lewiston, NY: The Edwin Mellen Press, 1989. A voluminous work with a great deal of useful information.

Purvis, June, *A History of Women's Education in England.* Milton Keynes: Open University Press, 1991. A slim but suggestive synthesis for the period between 1800 and 1914; contains a useful bibliography.

Rogers, Rebecca, *From the Salon to the Schoolroom: Educating Bourgeois Girls in Nineteenth-Century France.* University Park, Pa.: Pennsylvania State University Press, 2005. *Les Demoiselles de la Légion d'honneur: les maisons d'éducation de la Légion d'honneur au XIXe siècle.* Paris: Plon, 1992. 'Boarding Schools, Women Teachers, and Domesticity: Reforming Girls' Secondary Education in the First Half of the Nineteenth Century', *French Historical Studies*, 19, 1995, pp. 153–81; 'Retrograde or Modern? Unveiling the Teaching Nun in Nineteenth-Century France', *Social History*, 23, 1998, pp.146–84. My work focuses on lay and religious teachers, schools and students in France in the nineteenth century, combining a social and cultural approach.

Ruane, Christine, *Gender, Class, and the Professionalization of Russian City Teachers, 1860–1914.* Pittsburgh, Pa.: University of Pittsburgh Press, 1994. Examines women teachers' demands for greater control over the occupation and its members, as well as efforts to establish a new self-definition.

Simonton, Deborah, 'Schooling the Poor: Gender and Class in Eighteenth-Century England', *British Journal for Eighteenth-Century Studies*, 23, Autumn (2000), pp. 183–202. A very clear and useful introduction to the subject. She has also written more extensively on working-class girls' education: 'The Education and Training of Eighteenth-Century English Girls, with Special Reference to the Working Classes', Ph.D. thesis, University of Essex, 1988.

Sonnet, Martine, 'A Daughter to Educate', in Natalie Zemon Davis and Arlette Farge, eds, *A History of Women in the West.* Vol. III: *Renaissance and Enlightenment Paradoxes.* Cambridge, Mass.: Belknap Press of the Harvard University Press, 1993, pp. 101–31. This chapter offers a useful summary of early modern girls' education primarily in France and England that is focused on girls' schools. She is the author of an excellent study of girls' education in eighteenth-century Paris: *L'Éducation des filles au temps des Lumières.* Paris: Cerf, 1987.

Stock, Phyllis, *Better than Rubies: a History of Women's Education*. New York, Putnam, 1978. Although dated, this general presentation of the topic offers useful insights into the debates about girls' education throughout Europe from the Renaissance to the twentieth century. It is far more sketchy on actual institutional developments.

Thébaud, Françoise and Michelle Zancarini-Fournel, eds, 'Coéducation et mixité', *Clio. Histoire, Femmes et Société*, 18, (2003). A special issue that offers a variety of national perspectives on the issue of co-education mostly in the twentieth century, includes a historiographic essay on the subject.

Varikas, Elena, 'Subjectivité et identité de genre: L'univers de l'éducation féminine dans la Grèce du XIXème siècle', *Genèses, Sciences Sociales et Histoire*, 6, December (1991), pp. 29–51. The author is interested in the relationship between girls' education and questions of subjective and national identity. See her 'Gender and National Identity in Fin de Siècle Greece', *Gender & History* 5 (1993), pp. 269–83.

Wilson, Maggie, ed., *Girls and Young Women in Education: A European Perspective*. Oxford: Pergamon Press, 1991. The volume includes essays on Belgium, England and Wales, France, Greece, the Republic of Ireland, Poland, Spain, Sweden and West Germany, as well as a general European overview. Particularly useful for educational statistics for the post-Second World War period.

Watts, Ruth, *Gender, Power and the Unitarians in England, 1760–1860*. Harlow: Longman, 1998. An important study of the role of Unitarians in education.

Notes

1 Archives d'Outre Mer [Aix-en-Provence, France], GGA 22S/2, letter from Mme Allix to members of the Conseil d'Administration, 31 January 1846.

2 For Britain, see Leonore Davidoff and Catherine Hall, *Family Fortunes: Men and Women of the English Middle Class, 1780–1850* (Chicago, Ill.: University of Chicago Press, 1987); for Germany, Ann Taylor Allen, *Feminism and Motherhood in Germany, 1800–1914* (New Brunswick, NJ: Rutgers University Press, 1991); for France, Marie-Françoise Lévy, *De mères en filles: l'éducation des françaises (1850–1880)* (Paris: Calmann-Lévy, 1984).

3 Martha Vicinus, *Independent Women: Work and Community for Single Women* (Chicago, Ill.: University of Chicago Press, 1984).

4 Christina de Bellaigue, 'The Development of Teaching as a Profession for Women before 1870', *The Historical Journal*, 44, (2001), pp. 963–98.

5 Juliani Jacobi, 'Modernization through Feminization?' *European Education*, 32, (2000), pp. 55–79. See the historiographic essay, Mineke van Essen and Rebecca Rogers, 'Écrire l'histoire des enseignantes: une historiographie aux contours internationaux', special issue, 'Les Enseignantes: formations, identités, représentations (XIXe-XXe siècles)', *Histoire de l'Education*, 98, May (2003), pp. 5–35.

6 Sarah Curtis, *Educating the Faithful: Religion, Schooling, and Society in Nineteenth-Century France* (DeKalb, Ill.: Northern Illinois Press, 2000).

7 Two historiographic essays on French girls' education offer insights into recent trends: Patrick Harrigan, 'Women Teachers and the Schooling of Girls in France: Recent Historiographical Trends', *French Historical Studies*, 21, (1998), pp. 593–610 and Sharif Gemie, 'Institutional History, Social History, Women's History: A Comment on Patrick Harrigan's "Women Teachers and the Schooling of Girls in France"', *French Historical Studies*, 22, (1999), pp. 613–23.

8 Anne Quartararo, *Women Teachers and Popular Education in Nineteenth-Century France: Social Values and Corporate Identity at the Normal School Institution* (Newark, Del.: University of Delaware Press, 1995); Elizabeth Edwards, *Women in Teacher Training Colleges, 1900–1960: A Culture of Femininity* (London: Routledge, 2001).

9 Letter from Louise d'Epinay to the Abbé Ferdinando Galiani, printed in Dena Goodman and Katherine Ann Jenson *The Enlightenment* (New York: Houghton Mifflin, 2004), p. 167.

10 Poulain de la Barre, *De l'égalité des deux sexes* (1673), quoted in Martine Sonnet, 'A

Daughter to Educate', in Natalie Zemon Davis and Arlette Farge, eds, *A History of Women in the West*, Vol. III, *Renaissance and Enlightenment Paradoxes* (Cambridge, Mass.: Harvard University Press, 1993), pp. 105–6.

11 Dorothea Christina Leporin, *Gründliche Ursachen, die das Weibliche Geschlecht vom Studiren abhalten, darin deren Unerheblichkeit gezeiget* (Berlin, 1742), p. 96, quoted in Peter Petschauer, *The Education of Women in Eighteenth-Century Germany: New Directions from the German Female Perspective. Bending the Ivy* (Lewiston, NY: The Edwin Mellen Press, 1989), p. 233.

12 Abbé de Saint Pierre, *Projet pour perfectionner l'éducation des filles* (1732); Riballier, *De l'éducation physique et morale des enfants des deux sexes* (1785). See Pierre Rousselot, *Histoire de l'éducation des femmes en France*, 2 vols (Paris: Didier, 1983).

13 As Tammy M. Proctor shows, pp. 310–11, these salons can also be seen as part of elite women's leisure activities.

14 See Siân Reynold's discussion of women writers and translators in this volume, pp. 353–60,.

15 Jean-Jacques Rousseau, *Émile ou de l'éducation* ([1762], Paris: Flammarion, 1966), pp. 475, 535.

16 Mary Wollstonecraft, *Vindication of the Rights of Woman* ([1792], London: Penguin, 1988), p. 283. Another lesser known Englishwoman who defended co-education was Catherine Macaulay Graham in *Letters on Education* (1790).

17 Marquis de Condorcet, *Premier mémoire sur l'instruction publique* ([1791], Paris: Editions Klincksieck, 1989), pp. 65–70.

18 Theodor Gottlieb von Hippel, *Über die bürgerliche Verbesserung der Weiber* (1792) quoted in Susan Bell and Karen Offen, *Women, the Family, and Freedom: The Debate in Documents*, Vol. I, *1750–1880* (Stanford, Calif.: Stanford University Press, 1983), p. 117.

19 See Pat Starkey's discussion of teaching orders in the eighteenth century in this volume, p. 185–6.

20 Sonnet, 'A Daughter to Educate', p. 122.

21 *Établissements desservis par les Filles de la Charité, paroisse Saint-Louis-en-Ile*, Archives Nationales [France], S 160, quoted in Sonnet, 'A Daughter to Educate', p. 125.

22 Catherine Cappe, *Observations on Charity Schools, Female Friendly Societies and Other Subjects Connected with the Views of the Ladies' Committee* (London, 1805), p. 31 quoted in Deborah Simonton, 'Schooling the Poor: Gender and Class in Eighteenth-century England', *British Journal for Eighteenth-Century Studies*, 23, Autumn (2000), p. 187.

23 Cappe, *Observations on Charity Schools*, p. 19, quoted in ibid.

24 A graph of female illiteracy rates can be found in David Vincent, *The Rise of Mass Literacy: Reading and Writing in Modern Europe* (Cambridge: Polity Press, 2000), p. 10. See also Mary-Jo Maynes, *Schooling in Western Europe: A Social History* (Albany, NY: SUNY Press, 1984), pp. 7–31. See Proctor, Chapter 9 for an analysis of how literacy rates related to new leisure opportunities for women, p. 324.

25 Quoted in Nicholas Hans, *New Trends in Education in the Eighteenth Century* (London: Routledge & Kegan Paul, 1951), pp. 204–5.

26 Susan Skedd, 'Women Teachers and the Expansion of Girls' Schooling', in Hannah Barker and Elaine Chalus, eds, *Gender in Eighteenth-Century England: Roles, Representations and Responsibilities* (London: Longman, 1997) pp. 118–19.

27 See Carolyn Lougee, '*Noblesse*, Domesticity, and Social Reform', *History of Education Quarterly*, 14, (1974), pp. 87–113.

28 Quoted in Hortense de Beauharnais, *Mémoires de la Reine Hortense* (Paris: Plon, 1927), Vol. II, pp. 121–2.

29 Napoleon I, 'Notes sur l'établissement d'Ecouen'; the document is reproduced in full in French in Rebecca Rogers, *Les Demoiselles de la Légion d'honneur: les maisons d'éducation de la Légion d'honneur au XIXe siècle* (Paris: Plon, 1992), pp. 332–5.

30 Louis Aimé-Martin, *The Education of Mothers; or, the Civilization of Mankind by Women*, trans. Edwin Lee (Philadelphia, Pa.: Lea and Blanchard, 1843), p. 47.

31 Albertine Necker de Saussure, *L'Éducation progressive, ou étude du cours de la vie* (Brussels: Meline, Cans & Co, 1840), Vol. III, p. 256 and pp. 48–50. Italics in the original.

32 Quoted in Allen, *Feminism and Motherhood*, p. 73.

33 'Payment by results' is the phrase used to describe the funding reforms of Robert Lowe, Vice-President of the Education Board in 1862 whereby school grants were tied to performance results by pupils on standard exams.

34 M. C. Rankin, *The Art and Practice of Laundry Work* (London: Blackie & Son, n.d, c.1900), quoted in June Purvis, *A History of Women's Education in England* (Milton Keynes: Open University Press, 1991), p. 27.

35 Irene Vaquinhas, 'L'Historiographie sur les femmes au Portugal: le XIXe siècle', in Gisela Bock and Anna Cova, eds, *Écrire l'histoire des femmes en Europe du Sud: XIXe-XXe siècles.* (Oeiras: Celta Editora, 2003), p. 35; for Spain and Russia, Phyllis Stock, *Better than Rubies: A History of Women's Education* (New York: Putnam, 1978), respectively, pp. 157, 130.

36 Archives de Saint-Joseph de Cluny, 'Marine', 5A, letter of 30 September 1839.

37 Governor-General of Senegal, Baron Roger on 19 August 1825, quoted in Geneviève Lecuir-Nemo, '*Femmes et vocation missionnaire: Permanence des congrégations féminines au Sénégal de 1819 à 1960: adaptation ou mutation? Impact et insertion*', Ph.D. thesis, Université Paris I, 1995, p. 157.

38 Quoted in Geraldine Forbes, *Women in Modern India. The New Cambridge History of India* (Cambridge: Cambridge University Press, 1996), p. 40.

39 Frances Gouda, 'Teaching Indonesian Girls in Java and Bali, 1900–1942: Dutch Progressives, The Infatuation with "Oriental" Refinement, and "Western" ideas about proper womanhood', *Women's History Review*, 4, (1995), pp. 25–62.

40 Van Muylwijk, Annual Report 1936, quoted in Rita Smith Kipp, 'Emancipating Each Other: Dutch Colonial Missionaries' Encounter with Karo Women in Sumatra, 1900–1942', in Julia Clancy-Smith and Frances Gouda, eds, *Domesticating the Empire: Race, Gender, and Family Life in French and Dutch Colonialism* (Charlottesville, Va. and London: University Press of Virginia, 1998), p. 227.

41 Modupe Labode, 'From Heathen Kraal to Christian Home: Anglican Mission Education and African Christian Girls, 1850–1900', in F. Bowie, D. Kirkwood and S. Ardener, eds, *Women and Missions: Past and Present. Anthropological and Historical Perceptions* (Oxford: Berg, 1993), pp. 126–44.

42 Archives d'Outre Mer, GGA, 22S2, Letter to the Director General on 8 August 1861.

43 See *Histoire de l'Éducation*, 82, May (1999), special issue edited by Jean-Noël Luc, 'L'École maternelle en Europe, XIXe-XXe siècle'.

44 *Schoolmistress*, 5 February 1885, p. 249, quoted in Dina Copelman, *London Women Teachers: Gender, Class and Feminism, 1870–1930* (London: Routledge, 1996), p. 152.

45 Lindy Moore, 'Young Ladies' Institutions: The Development of Secondary Schools for Girls in Scotland, 1833–c.1870', *History of Education*, 32, (2003), pp. 249–72; Sarah Smith, 'Retaking the Register: Women's Higher Education in Glasgow and Beyond, c.1765–1845', *Gender & History*, 12, (2000), p. 311.

46 Emily Davies, 'Special Systems of Education for Women', in *Thoughts on Some Questions Relating to Women, 1860–1906* (Cambridge: Bowes & Bowes, 1910), pp. 130–4, reprinted in Bell and Offen, *Women, the Family and Freedom*, vol. 1, p. 421.

47 Célestin Hippeau, 'L'Éducation des femmes et des affranchis en Amérique', *Revue des deux mondes*, 93, (1869), p. 452.

48 James Albisetti, *Schooling German Girls and Women: Secondary and Higher Education in the Nineteenth Century* (Princeton, NJ: Princeton University Press, 1988).

49 Alice Zimmern, *The Renaissance of Girls' Education in England: A Record of Fifty Years' Progress* (London: A.D. Innes & Company, 1898), pp. 1–2.

50 Simone de Beauvoir, *Mémoires d'une jeune fille rangée* ([1958] Paris: Folio Gallimard, 1978), pp. 243–4.

51 Quoted in Victoria de Grazia, *How Fascism Ruled Women: Italy, 1922–1945* (Berkeley, Calif.: University of California Press, 1992), p. 56.

52 Quoted in Claudia Koonz, *Mothers in the Fatherland: Women, the Family and Nazi Politics* (New York: St Martin's Press, 1987), p. 200.

53 Quoted in Francine Muel-Dreyfus, *Vichy et l'éternel féminin* (Paris: Seuil, 1996), p. 253.

54 See Auroro Morcillo Gómez, 'Shaping True Catholic Womanhood: Francoist Educational Discourse on Women', in Victoria Lorée Enders and Pamela Beth Radcliff, *Constructing Spanish*

Womanhood: Female Identity in Modern Spain (Albany, NY: SUNY Press, 1999) pp. 51–69.

55 Alice Woods, ed., *Advance in Co-Education*, 1919, quoted in Kevin Brehony, 'Early Twentieth-Century Debates', in Rosemary Dean, ed., *Co-Education Reconsidered* (Milton Keynes: Open University Press, 1984), p. 2.

56 The text of the encyclical is available at <http://www.ewtn.com/library/ENCYC/P11DIVIL. HTM,article68>.

57 Maurice Caullery, *Les Universités et la vie scientifique aux Etats-Unis* (Paris: Armand Colin, 1917), cited in Malie Montagutelli, *L'Éducation des filles aux Etats-Unis de la période coloniale à nos jours* (Paris: Ophrys-Ploton, 2003), pp. 118–19.

58 Hannah More, *Strictures on the Modern System of Female Education* (London, 1799), quoted in Bell and Offen, *Women, the Family and Freedom*, Vol. I, p. 86.

59 Hubertine Auclert, *La Citoyenne*, 10 April 1881, p. 1.

60 Maggie Wilson, 'Europe: An Overview', in M. Wilson, ed., *Girls and Women in Education: A European Perspective* (Oxford: Pergamon Press, 1991), p. 214.

5

WOMEN WORKERS

Working women

Deborah Simonton

Introduction

The world of work changed significantly over the past three centuries. A shift from a rural to an urban society, and a further shift from craft to manufacture and then to white-collar work affected what people were doing, when they did it, how they did it and who they did it with. New ideas and pressures influenced the structures and knowledge base that informed work practices and are reflective of cultural shifts in the notions of work, workplace and worker. Work means a range of things depending on when, where and about whom we are speaking. Sometimes it is a powerful term, other times an indication of drudgery. Probably the most obvious shift for women was when work at home became 'not work'. This is not only about the location of work, because self-employed persons can work at home and be 'at work'. It is partly about what the work is, who is doing it and the value placed on that work. Thus domestic roles and relationships with partners and family are central to understanding women's position in the labour market. Women's place in society is the result of a complex of ideas about what they are capable of and should do, so that their work, its types, locations and structures are gendered. Similarly, gendered division of labour is historically specific and the relationship between workers is renegotiated as the context changes. But division of labour along sexual lines is not only about dividing work according to ability; it is about power, status, position and gender.

The realms of work and home were not separate and oppositional, but sites of gendered cooperation and conflict. The home was increasingly defined in terms of the female, while the workplace was increasingly constructed as male and shaped by definitions derived from escalating waged labour. Only late in the twentieth century were these notions reworked. The significance of home and family on working woman has been to define her role in terms of status, hierarchy and tasks. They were working *women*, not women *workers*. Perception of the female is crucial to defining normative options and routes, but reality meant that women often did things that dominant paradigms did not embrace. Life cycle affected the place and kind of work that women did; young unmarried women were the most mobile, while mothers and wives were usually more tied to one location. The identity of woman as not worker derived from the married woman or mother, notionally with domestic responsibilities, whereas many working females were not married or mothers. The idea of a woman establishing her own working identity challenged social perceptions, because women were identified by marital and maternal status, not as workers. These factors meant that women were often seen as casual labourers, assistants, not as real workers, a flexible workforce, 'a reserve army of labour'. This had specific implications for wages and for how women interacted with the workplace. Eugène Buret in 1840 summed up the dilemma, 'Woman is industrially speaking, an imperfect worker. If a man doesn't add his earnings to the insufficient wage of his partner, sex alone constitutes for her the cause of misery.'[1] Contemporary views thus denied the fact of women as workers as well as their identity as workers. Within such constraints, numerous women strove to create their own meaning and sense of identity out of work.

Women often worked to a different time discipline from the regulated factory, workshop or office, working when they needed to, juggling several tasks at once. Often it was piecework and low paid, but other times they moved in and out of work depending on their needs. Not only did women take up a range of work across their lives, but much of what they did did not fit standard occupational categories, so that their work was uncharted by many statistical accounts, making them invisible workers. This is because such categories are artificial, created by statisticians for census purposes, and are usually generated by notions of what men do. Additionally the contribution of many women to commercial, farming and industrial activities remained unpaid in family enterprises or as part of an informal economy that is difficult to assess.

Nevertheless, women defined themselves as workers, increasingly so as time passed and work became more clearly crystallised as a specific entity rather than as a collection of activities. The older concept of a trade, with its masculine connotations, became replaced by words such as 'occupation', 'profession', 'job' as people identified themselves and what they did. As time discipline became more centralised, women responded by either remaining in the informal economy or by joining mainstream structures. This chapter will, therefore, explore the issues of the gendered workplace across the period from about 1700, reflecting on contextual factors such as economic and political trends that influenced the redefinitions of work and woman's place in the European labour market. It will also evaluate her agency in exploiting and accommodating the paradigms that emerged.

Historiography

Research on women's work and role inside the household and in the wider economy has now reached a volume and importance which obliges full acknowledgement of its implications for economic and social history more generally. Old questions and debates . . . need to be reassessed in the light of the vital role played by gender.[2]

In this quote, Pat Hudson and William Lee framed some of the issues that shape writing on women's work: home and work, the lack of integration between economic and social history and women's history, the significance of gender and 'old questions and debates'. Sheilagh Ogilvie recently pointed out three central problems: that we do not yet know enough about the facts of women's work, that causal explanations have been only partial and often in conflict and that, therefore, we do not know the implications of women's economic position.[3]

Pioneers writing about women's work set out to recover women's past, and the first studies, such as those by Alice Clark and Ivy Pinchbeck in England and Abensour in France stand as important contributions, often unsurpassed for detail.[4] Two generations later and signalling the way forward, Natalie Zemon Davis, Louise Tilly and Joan W. Scott, Olwen Hufton and Ute Gerhard inspired new generations of scholars.[5] Particularly important was Louise Tilly and Joan W. Scott's *Women, Work and Family*, which explicitly identified and analysed relationships between women's role expectations, raised and addressed issues of life cycle, demography and familial obligations and linked these to the meanings of work and to women's decisions about 'gainful employment'. It is hard now to remember how innovative it was.

At the heart of understanding women's work in the modern period is capitalism and the industrial revolution. Alice Clark argued that the capitalist economy destroyed family industries, forced workers onto the wage market and moved women from a strong economic position in the seventeenth century to a disadvantaged one with regard to skill, devaluing their equal contribution to the family. As important as her work remains, she also initiated the debate over whether or not the period before capitalist expansion and industrialisation was a golden age for women workers. Ivy Pinchbeck, in contrast, argued that ultimately the industrial revolution led to greater leisure in the home and relieved women from the subordination, monotony and drudgery of the domestic system, while the woman worker outside the home gained better conditions, a greater variety of openings and improved status. In her reading then, industrialisation was the harbinger of a better modern world.

Important and innovative approaches came out of proto-industrial theory that characterised two different stages in economic development: pre-industrialisation and proto-industrialisation.[6] It argued for a significant change in household division of labour and greater similarity in men's and women's work. Detailed local studies prompted by proto-industrial theory greatly expanded our understanding of the geography of European enterprise, and raised important issues about economic development, familial participation, the role of rural communities, gender relations, affections and household formation. Importantly it stimulated thinking about links between economic theory and gender studies that go beyond measuring women's participation rates and has influenced much of the research on gender and work.

But as a staged model of industrial development, it disguises the fact that such stages were not universal or uniform; they were reached at different times in different parts of Europe and often in very different ways. As this chapter argues, several patterns coexisted so, for example, the domestic system continued alongside the push to centralised manufacturing, and the two often enjoyed a symbiotic relationship. Like the so-called transition from 'family economy' through 'family wage economy' to 'family consumer economy' used by Tilly and Scott and, more recently by Bridget Hill, such approaches to transition require untangling. For example, we need to be very clear that the family economy also included people working for wages – these were not the invention of a 'family wage economy' – and that people worked outside of families in a range of organisational structures and were not always motivated by 'what is good for the family'.

Proto-industrialisation theory also tends to support a 'golden age' approach to women's work. The implication is that women were involved in a wide range of activities and that industrial capitalism, with its waged labour, family wage and specialisation, destroyed them. Yet the evidence does little to support a golden age. Olwen Hufton in 1983, noted that the '*bon vieux temps* has proved remarkably elusive'.[7] More recently, Amanda Vickery vigorously argued that we should be sceptical 'about a history which blindly insists that women's status has deteriorated from a past golden age', and that there 'was no systematic reduction in the range of employments available to labouring women' due to early modern capitalism. Such a model 'rests on the dubious assumption of a lost egalitarian Eden, which has proved elusive to empirical research'.[8] Thus, situating and understanding women's work has been a fundamental part of understanding industrial capitalism.

In parallel, economic historians revised interpretations of the process of British industrialisation, arguing it was not a revolution but a very lengthy organic process. Importantly, they also revised views about continental industrialisation, recasting European transitions in their own context and not in terms of imported British experience. But Maxine Berg and Pat Hudson argued that historians' use of aggregate quantitative indicators ignored very real transformations.[9] In restating a more 'revolutionary' view of industrialisation, they argued that the *longue durée* approach specifically overlooked the impact of women's labour and wages and therefore excluded many high-productivity industries where the greatest transformations in technical processes or organisation took place.[10] Put crudely, if you add in women's work, the industrial revolution looks very different – sharper, more rapid and more dramatic. Furthermore, the gradualist approach could have serious implications for the history of women's work by undervaluing opportunities available to women in factories. Thus when industrial change is looked at from a gendered point of view, a different picture emerges. Issues of feminisation have been important to several industries and professions, and we need to look carefully at the dynamics of those processes for what they tell us about work and the operation of gender.

A theme that runs through this chapter is the relationship of gender to skill, status and honour. I have argued that gender and skill are historically specific, defined by multifaceted issues that relate to strength, tools and technology, protection of the workplace, location and men's property in skill.[11] Important examinations of how men operated to redefine and claim the workplace, such as those by Jean H. Quataert, Merry Wiesner and Sonya O. Rose, have helped to articulate some of the cultural issues that define homework, skilled work, ownership of tools and notions of honour in the workplace.[12] Gendered workplace patterns were not the result of a simple process of masculine control or patriarchy, and the character of skill and the ways that men and women negotiated their understanding of it profoundly affected the shape of the workforce.

Importantly, historical explanations need to be situated in basic research and need to avoid overarching explanations that actually hide diversity and may remove individual agency from the equation. The past thirty years produced a virtual explosion in writing on women's work dealing with a range of issues and causal explanations. Many were local studies, focused on particular periods, countries, regions or cultures and, especially, particular towns. There were important studies of women in specific sectors and outside of textiles; we are much better informed about women in printing trades, for example. New work on textiles produced in-depth studies on women in business, particularly entrepreneurial women in fashion trades, and the growth of studies on material culture opened new areas of exploration and showed new ways of thinking about women's work which is divorced from the labour model of the 1970s. Studies of class re-emerged with a new face and shed light on women's activities within families and family workshops. We have a much more nuanced picture of work relationships and especially women's agency; research has pointed up the diversity of female experience, both geographically and chronologically, and in rural and urban settings. If patriarchy, paternalism and a sense of oppression shaped some of the earliest research, then independence, female agency and gender relations shape much of the newer work. More sophisticated explanatory frameworks have been developed, and there has been more detailed study of women's work situated in a complex of local and regional factors and reflecting the social construction of women's work within the framework of their lives.[13] Importantly, feminist historians have now taken on the project of revising the canon of labour history, integrating the research, ideas and approaches that inform the history of women's work; Maxine Berg and Pat Hudson's rewriting of the industrial revolution stands as one example. As Scott said, the complexities and confusions are often the way to arrive at a better sense of what women's work was and how it was situated.

Sources

Working women are often described as difficult subjects to find in the sources. This is a problem of both perception and recording. They often were not recorded as workers simply because they were women and not conceptualised as workers. The British censuses have been challenged on this point regularly. Certainly women's work was under-recorded for most of the life of the census. But the purpose of the census was not to record work in the first place, though that function changed as it moved into the twentieth century. Men completed census returns, male heads of household who saw female family members as dependants, not as workers. And census-takers would not have challenged this.[14] Because women were less likely to be wage-earners, and more likely to work at several jobs, or seasonal work, or move around the economy, they were also less visible workers. For example, the census lists virtually none of the fish-gutters of the Sutherland coast. Working women's low status and humble origins did not help, but working women of the middling orders were not well recorded either.

They left few records of their own and, significantly, their voices are frequently missing, especially in the period before the explosion of government inquiries or near universal literacy. For the most part, where we have testimony from the earlier part of this period is where women engaged with officialdom that recorded their situation and sometimes their words. These contacts were likeliest in cases of crime, dispute or poverty, but they reflect the unusual, not the norm, and both under-represent and mis-represent women. Yet useful and valuable research has come from them, and in the nineteenth century, formal shifts in relationships between servants and masters in Hamburg could be studied through police court cases.[15] Similarly English poor law settlement examinations have provided potted biographies, though women's voices cannot be clearly extracted. Verbatim transcripts have been used effectively, but these are few and far between and rarely allow a comparative or long-term picture to be created.[16] Sources are often from an external and male gaze, since working women were least likely to write or leave written reflections. Investigations and *enquêtes* of nineteenth-century Europe provided a specific kind of lens through which to view women workers. Some of these were governmental; others resulted from a social conscience that led individuals or groups to undertake them. While these had their own agendas, nevertheless, they produced a body of information on working women and frequently gave us their voices, even if mediated.

Diaries, letters and autobiographies exist throughout the period, weighted toward the elite, of course. More work could be done on family papers, especially letters, household records and accounts; Amanda Vickery and Bonnie Smith have shown how profitable this can be.[17] Women also wrote about women. Tract and prescriptive literature provide valuable insights to the context within which work was couched, as do magazines and journals that run throughout this period. Women were observers, actors and commentators on their world, and they were writers and publishers of newspapers and magazines. The activities of eighteenth-century publican Mrs McGhie were chronicled almost exclusively in the *Aberdeen Journal*.[18] Also, better literacy together with the emergence of women's and labour movements fostered more personal accounts from a wider socio-economic spectrum. By the twentieth century there was an explosion in information and, building on older traditions of enquiry, oral history developed as a way to capture the views and histories of people who would not normally have written it down. It allowed historians to directly interrogate the subject and ask the questions that most of us cannot ask our subjects.

The history of women's work also benefits from an economic and social history that is far more sophisticated in finding, reading and utilising sources, and in understanding the economic and household context within which people worked. A range of corporate records, trade directories, town directories and official and semi-official records are a source of statistical, economic and demographic information. Recent studies have used complex sets of sources, including oral history, company records, indentures, insurance records, tax records, parental guides, newspapers and town records. So women are not actually hard to find, but creativity and frustration are dual features of the research. Women can tell us about their work, but we have to be aware of the opportunities and pitfalls of a range of seemingly innocuous and not obviously useful records to find them, and then we have to interpret the record.

The eighteenth century

In the eighteenth century, women worked with men in a familial situation, operated their own business or trade, worked on their own to support themselves or a family of children and worked to save a dowry. Some women were employers, others were employees. Some work was waged, and some not; some was paid annually, like servants, and some was paid by piece or day rates. Women's motivations to work varied, and their values and intentions often differed from those who employed them. Work was both a class and a life-cycle issue. Elite women and some of the upper bourgeoisie probably did not engage in work that generated income. The rest of women did, either occasionally or regularly. Women ran businesses, they worked in workshops, servants engaged in farm, domestic and industrial tasks, and they took up tasks such as spinning, making small items for market, hawking and petty shopkeeping. Women taught children, did washing, prepared and sold food. Some activities were so closely related to family or domestic aspects of life that they were seen as casual by-products, and some women took up jobs directly related to their 'domestic' skills.

Women of all classes kept house. Elite women's management was largely delegated, but they still shouldered this responsibility. Further down the social scale, females of all ages cleaned, cooked and maintained the household. Girls assisted, their work mirroring and complementing their mothers'; adolescent girls not needed at home frequently became servants in other homes. Housekeeping encompassed a wide range of tasks as Krünitz's *Encyklopädie* (1788) detailed:

> supervision and work in the kitchen and cellar, the rearing of cattle, pigs and poultry, the maintenance, cleaning and production of clothing and linen, bed-making, brewing, baking, washing, sewing, spinning, weaving and other work with wool and flax, and indeed anything concerning the cleanliness of the house and the maintenance of household equipment.[19]

It was work without boundaries. Household tasks, however, were relatively minimal and merged with other responsibilities. Food was often simply prepared, relying on bread, cheese and vegetables; cooked meals comprised a single pot of stew. Housing varied radically, as did standards of cleanliness, and cleaning simply was not an important part of housekeeping. Often houses had rough walls, unflagged flooring, thatched roofs and crude furniture. Sometimes, animals shared part of the house. Niemalä farmhouse (1786), Finland, contained an entrance, dairy, main room and the inevitable sauna. Family members slept in beds, on benches, on top of the oven and on the floor; in summer, young people slept in storehouses. They cooked on an open fire in pots hanging from hooks or on tripods; smoke went out through a funnel in the roof. They ate meals at a long table, men sitting on benches near the wall, and women on movable ones.[20]

Maintaining furnishings and food was more substantial in wealthier households, usually delegated to servants. Susannah Whatman wrote private, detailed instructions to cope with regular turnover and achieve proper cleaning, explaining,

> If the under servants could be depended on for doing all their business according to the instructions that could be given them, the eye of a Housekeeper would not be necessary to keep everything going on in its proper way. But this is never to be expected, and as the mistress of a large family can neither afford the time, nor have it in her power, to see what her servants are about, she must depend on the Housekeeper to see all her orders are enforced.[21]

Her instructions for polishing, scouring, cleaning and for pulling blinds and curtains to protect furnishing fabrics demonstrate that she knew the job, often completing tasks herself. Sophie von La Roche, who provided for a large family and boarders, wrote: 'I go into my kitchen and give instructions, since I myself am versed in the art of cooking. I check up on all work in the house, write my accounts'.[22]

As more consumer goods became available, the character and quantity of domestic tasks changed, and women increasingly bought things that their mothers would have made. In Paris, earthenware displaced other utensils, including 'a little Wedgwood pot', even in homes of the poor, while stoves began to replace the open hearth.[23] Tea and coffee became important cultural markers. 'So coffee-drinking has become a habit, and one so deep-rooted that the working classes will start the day on nothing else', wrote

Louis-Sebastian Mercier in the 1780s.[24] Such criticisms are part of a larger critique of luxury, which characterised women as frivolous and wasteful. In reality, increasing consumerism was an important part of women's 'job', as Vickery has shown. Elizabeth Shackleton kept meticulous accounts, logging specifics about purchases and when commissioning others to buy items 'sent remarkably detailed orders and specified how the proxy consumer was to be repaid, and the means by which the purchases should be conveyed'.[25] It was hardly a frivolous, ephemeral activity, but a vital part of supplying the household, in the style they expected to maintain.

Women's household tasks slid over into agricultural work, traversing invisible boundaries. Most rural women contributed to their own homestead or, as young women, went in search of work as agricultural servants. It was essentially full-time, unwaged and balanced with household and market tasks such as agricultural produce or textiles. Women were often co-fermiers, sharing responsibility for the farm, signing tenancies and operating in partnership with husbands. Men and women were jointly responsible in Sweden, in many Germanic regions and in France. Women were also farmers and landowners, conducting the whole array of work with hired help, such as Welshwoman Mary Elliot who left a detailed inventory of her active farm.[26] They also took on roles usually associated with men. In Wildberg, in 1736, a widow supported a family of four on a fulling mill and land that she worked, while another nearby supported six with a grain mill and land.[27] Full-time farm servants lived in and their work echoed that of the farm wife, focusing more exclusively on farm work, such as managing small animals and carrying water. Day labourers were hired for specific tasks or seasons. A large part of their work focused on the barnyard, orchard and garden, which provided vegetables, fruit, nuts and olives for the home, but could generate cash. Similarly, care of chickens, ducks, geese, pigs or even a cow was a female responsibility that, beyond produce for home consumption, could also be turned into market goods. These activities were closely linked to 'keeping house' and, like much of women's work, boundaries between tasks and earning blurred.

The implicit value systems embedded in the unchanging seasonal rhythms of work, joint working and pragmatic 'substitutability' shaped a sense of continuities in women's farm work. Yet real changes began to take place because of new land-holding practices, rotations, crops, commercialisation and the gradual introduction of new tools with gendered notions of usage, the impact falling largely into the next century as 'improvement' spread. Innovation and increasingly commercial farming, especially in England, Scotland, the Low Countries and German states, meant changes in the character of fieldwork. In areas with enclosed fields based on grain production, women had less work except at seasonal peaks. But the introduction of turnips, sugar beet and potatoes requiring hoeing and tending six months of the year led to a regular demand for more female field labour. Improved rotations produced new work peaks, which reduced seasonal unemployment, and overall opportunities for women in agricultural work increased. Specialist dairy production also increased employment for women, who were seen as having a special identity with dairying.

Farmers increasingly used day labourers instead of permanent full-time labour. Farm service often turned into day labour and boys tended to retain these better-paid jobs, so that girls were squeezed out. At the same time, girls were turning their backs on farming for 'better' jobs as domestic or industrial servants. In Sweden, Johann Süssmilch commented in 1741, 'among rural migrants to the cities, females predominate, because they are less needed in agriculture than men, and they can easily find work as servants in the cities.'[28] Often, male workers or tenants had to supply a woman's labour at haymaking, harvest or at tasks such as weeding. In south-west Scotland, a man had to bring a woman, usually his wife, to agricultural hirings because, 'he could not be in service without marriage'.[29] In much of France, eastern Netherlands and Germanic regions, women frequently provided labour service, perhaps one to three days in a week, and in Denmark even a landless labourer had to guarantee his wife's labour for sixty to seventy days a year.

Though women were less likely to be regular fieldworkers, seasonal requirements such as haymaking and the harvest drew on a large labour force of men, women and children. The organisation of the Silesian harvest was recorded in 1790:

> The cottagers begin their harvest work at sunrise . . . Their wives begin work when the cowherd puts the herd out to pasture and work until six-thirty with the men and the maid. At that time they leave work and go home and prepare the meal, which they bring to the men and the maids in the field, and they eat with them until eleven. Thereafter they remain at work until evening, but they also take a break from two to three.[30]

The use of the term 'work' is interesting. Presumably wives milked those cows, and making the meal surely was work.

As rural space was gendered, so were tasks. On smaller holdings, boundaries were less likely to be preserved, and women undertook virtually any task, regardless of its coding as male. Gendering of tasks was blurred anyway, and different local customs existed. But by and large, fiddly work was coded as female such as tying-up hops and vines, weeding and hoeing, while work associated with masculine attributes such as strength, skill or control were seen as men's. In grape-growing areas of France and Italy, women trimmed young vines in early summer and tended olives and silkworms. They prepared the soil, planted, winnowed, hoed, weeded and dug root crops. They carried soil, loaded and spread dung and carted produce. In much of southern Europe women spent three to five hours daily watering crops by hand or carrying water to cattle and other livestock in the summer. Working with horses and larger tools, supervision and 'specialist' jobs, such as shepherd, carter and stockman were seen as male prerogatives, while specific fieldwork increasingly became identified as men's work, as did ploughing, hedging and ditching. Thus, most German women were excluded from ploughing, woodcutting and long-distance transportation of agricultural produce. Women usually were barred from mowing and seldom used the scythe anywhere in Europe; threshing was often coded as male.[31]

Though women had always worked in handicraft production, they were employed in cottage industries on an exceptionally large scale. These industries were small scale, not far removed from the homestead, if at all, and were built on the industries and skills of traditional crafts and domestic manufacture. Domestic industries did not usually require apprenticeship, so women found these easier to enter than regulated trades. Entrepreneurs needed their labour, and the large numbers of women needing an income made them attractive and affordable employees. Women's motives for taking up proto-industrial work were primarily financial: in order to support themselves and to contribute to household support. Between 50 and 90 per cent of French holdings were insufficient to support even a small family of two or three children, while in places such as the Scottish Highlands subsistence agriculture led women to take up commercial spinning. Most families in the Caux depended on money earned from women's spinning, and 67.5 per cent of women who married in Auffay spun for cash during all or part of their married life.[32] Married women and women with children were unlikely to go into service, so work that could be performed around other tasks was particularly attractive. It was work that could be fitted in and was perceived as 'casual'. The minister at Keith-Hall, Scotland, believed a woman could knit 'and do some little things about her house at the same time. Or she can work at her stocking while feeding her cows'.[33]

As in agriculture, women's so-called natural abilities and nimble fingers suited them to many of the manipulative tasks associated with cottage industries. They were the spinners of Europe, working in every thread and fabric, and in cloth centres such as Rouen, Aberdeen or Augsburg thousands of urban and rural women spun. Some spun in a family setting within which the whole unit engaged in cloth production, such as in the West Riding of Yorkshire. In Scotland, most spun for linen or woollen merchants while men farmed and fished. Their labour was so important that Aberdeen officials hired a woman to teach others to spin linen, and in the Somme, officials claimed 'It is necessary that at least one woman and girl per village learns to spin so that she can show the others'.[34] The female culture associated with spinning is illustrated by the *spinnstuben*, *écreignes* or *veillées*, described by Tammy Proctor, where women came together to spin and talk, usually in winter evenings when they could share heat and light. Women also wove, sometimes alternating with men who were seen as skilled master weavers. When demand for spinning fell off with declining textiles, as in Essex, women wove in growing numbers, often competing with men. Increasingly, parents and parish officers apprenticed girls to weaving, such as Colchester sisters Sarah and Dorothy Bardwell put to John Shenton in 1757, or Mary Kemp, just one of many put to bay and say weaving in Halstead in 1769.[35] Large numbers of female silk workers worked in labour intensive preparatory stages from emptying, washing and unravelling cocoons to classifying thread or preparing it for looms. Needlecrafts built on skills learnt as girls. So they knitted, especially where needles rather than stocking frames dominated, as in the Shetlands and Russia. They closed shoes, seamed stockings and sewed gloves. Metal wares also relied on female labour. Around Thiers, Basse Auvergne, village women fixed pins to cards; in the English Black Country, their dexterity was particularly valued in button making and japanning. Apprenticed girls were common in buckle making and locksmithing. Women worked in the potteries, usually assisting male potters. A third of the workforce at Wedgwood, women made flowers, painted, enamelled, gilded, burnished, scoured and transferred engravings onto porcelain.[36]

Cottage industries covered a number of different organisational patterns, and within these women (and men) had varying degrees of control over their own work, its pace and the way it integrated with the rest of their life. This industrial work usually added to rather than substituted for women's 'normal' work, thus increasing the intensity of their labour. Most women worked within familial or small workshop settings where they supported a man who was identified as the producer: the weaver, the cobbler, the glovemaker and the stocking-frame knitter. Thus they were identified as assistants and not primary workers, and further identified as 'homeworkers'. As such 'keeping house' could be seen as their primary task and industrial activities as subsidiary. This is less apt for the metal trades and pottery, or indeed in mining, where women's tasks were less like 'natural' female ones and where the work setting was less likely to be a home. Single women and widows might work in a family setting, but they also worked on their own, in other's homes or workshops and in clusters of women who pooled their labour.

Women were also entrepreneurial. Some worked directly for putting-out manufacturers as in the Caux, Augsburg or across Scotland. In Rouen,

> If [a spinner] has enough money to pay for three pounds of raw cotton, she buys no more. She works with this small amount, and works with care. When the cotton is spun she sells it that much more advantageously as her work is perfect. From the proceeds, she subtracts enough for her subsistence, and if her small capital has now increased, she buys a larger amount of raw material.[37]

In the Nagold valley, Württemberg, they supplied both the wool and the yarn, buying directly from the Ducal court.[38] A distinctive feature of lace making in Ireland, the English Midlands, Normandy, Picardy, Flanders and Belgium was that women controlled all stages of production, whilst in most other domestic industries women were limited to preparatory or finishing tasks dependent on male workers. *Marchandes* could make comfortable profits at the height of the trade between 1730 and 1770; village women did less well, earning as little as two *sous* per day.[39]

Female wages were restricted partly because of the expectation that women did not require the same income as a man – that they were supplementing his income – and partly because plenty of women were available for hire. Hufton estimated that a woman's earning power was between a third and a half of her husband's for a working day of fifteen to sixteen hours.[40] If a rate did not suit a woman, the merchant simply replaced her. Married women were particularly vulnerable since increasing subsistence pressures often drove them to increase their work effort simply to maintain their income, in other words, to 'exploit' their own labour. For example, following a bad harvest in 1782, Aberdeenshire hand knitters redoubled efforts to maintain family income in the face of a slump in demand and competition from stocking-frame knitters and overseas workers, all of which drove prices down.[41] This willingness and necessity to work for the rates offered contributed to holding down the level of pay for female industrial work. As 'casual, supplementary' work, it never gained recognition as a primary source of income, affecting both the level of wages and the perceptions of women's income as 'pin money'. However, even to produce enough to support herself required a strenuous effort and was not 'casual' or 'supplementary'.

Within towns, women installed themselves in a range of activities, sometimes using the corporate structure, other times in unregulated, tolerated or 'female' work. This was true in cities and towns, large and small, where women worked for others, in partnership and for themselves. But the urban scene was not uniform, shaped by local trends and varying degrees of state intervention. Entrenched and gendered divisions of labour together with political and economic structures of towns inhibited women's access to business. Yet, they commonly participated in the commercial world, their economic role and status as traders was widely recognised, and the fluidity of growing commercial towns meant an expanding range of work opened to them. It was a period of flux for corporate communities. Community and guild were intertwined, as in Aberdeen, Frankfurt am Main, Helsinki or Wildberg where merchants held office in both town and guild.[42] Guilds regulated workplaces, embedded masculinity into artisanal work and, as the protectors of skilled labour, positioned themselves in opposition to domestic industry. But new working practices and pressure from 'untrained', 'unskilled' and 'dishonourable' labour challenged the solidarity, occupational controls and standing of guildsmen. This uncertainty about status heightened their need to maintain social distinctions. At the same time, the commercial world was being cast as masculine. Defoe advised men to learn the business, speak the language of business and value his credit: '[if] a man is slandered in his character, or reputation, it is injurious; . . . but if this happens to a tradesman, he is immediately blasted and undone'.[43] Business reputation was equally important to the female trader, and her ability to navigate the commercial world required a consciousness of the terrain.

Many women brought commercial experience to marriage, and wives' skills as accountants, negotiators and saleswomen were invaluable. They were important in trading networks, sold goods, managed orders and raw materials, oversaw accounts and frequently made the workshop viable. They also placed business activities first, farming out childcare, food preparation and laundry. Men valued their contribution and defended their right to share in the workshop. Dorcas Lackinton's bookkeeping 'was a very fortunate circumstance to us both', wrote her husband, London bookseller James Lackington, 'accordingly, when I was out on business, my shop was well attended. This constant attention, and good usage, procured me many customers'.[44] A wife's constant presence, proximity to the work, powerful influence over day-to-day matters and considerable authority over workers gave her standing, despite an ambiguity in her position. Her prominence and authority rested on custom and marriage, and she was only as powerful as these intangibles allowed. She could become a target for grievances against the shop or her husband, grievances that often had a highly gendered flavour.[45]

Numerous widows continued family businesses. Often it was the simplest way to maintain the family of a former colleague, but they had few rights. They hired workers for tasks they could not perform because of lack of skills or customary restrictions. Thus some printers' widows kept bookselling but resigned printing. Others did not: 'from London to Vienna we find the widow's imprimatur on eighteenth-century books'.[46] In Paris, Mademoiselle de Silly printed Haydn's Symphony No. 38 in 1779; the Göttingen University publisher Vandenhoeck and Ruprecht owed its survival to Anna, determined widow of the founder. Agnes Campbell was the wealthiest Scottish bookseller, largest printer in Edinburgh and Printer to King and Church by 1717.[47] Of course, women managers required good knowledge of business. In 1764 Margaret Craig advertised that she would continue as a merchant, claiming the 'goodwill of customers', reassuring them that 'they may depend on being well and readily served' and she would 'carefully obey' commissions from the country.[48] She literally set out her stall as a competent businesswoman, casting her business in the same language as men to claim her place in the commercial community.

Women were the milliners, mantua makers and seamstresses of eighteenth-century towns making all sorts of goods including underwear, children's clothes and grave-cloths as well as high-class millinery demanded by European fashion. Women established themselves in these niches, also the main areas where women formed corporations. Fifty-six per cent of English apprentice mistresses were mantua makers and milliners. Lucia Reeves and Co., a large firm of Essex milliners, operated in Colchester High Street for some twenty years. It was typical of the high-status concern: conscientiously run, regularly apprenticing new girls and successful enough to employ at least two women and two apprentices.[49] Guildswomen in Paris and provincial French towns strongly supported the corporate system, which gave them concrete economic benefits and better legal rights, using the privileges and structures to protect their trade. They gained a corporate identity and a notion of female honour that derived from the female nature of their trades and the independence that it allowed them to enjoy. These women scorned the skills of women in patriarchal workshops, taking pride in their legal and professional autonomy. And yet, not all women joined corporations, often because of prohibitive costs. In Clermont-Ferrand, seamstresses proudly declared themselves free of guild control and resisted tailors' attempts to incorporate them.[50] It was a good business enterprise for an able employer, attracting women with capital and some social standing; for the less fortunate, especially employees, prospects were much less promising. Certainly women were vulnerable in such seasonal trades, subject to periods of slack employment and low wages.

Women also moved around the community taking available work. Increasingly workshops employed unskilled labour and subcontractors. Women made many cheap unregulated items, such as brushes, combs, candles, soap, needles and pins, wooden bowls and spoons, without threatening craftsmen's status. Also, domestic industries operated in towns, employing women in silk making in Coventry and London, buttonmaking in Birmingham and lace making in Antwerp, Lyon and Beaulieu.

Women frequently worked in provisioning trades and kept inns and lodgings. Innkeeping was regarded as suitable for women and they could make a good living, but they operated on the margins of respectability and had to struggle to maintain and defend their reputation, using courts when necessary. When Mrs Warrand moved to the centre of Forres (Scotland), she claimed prestige from the location, the previous possessor, the laird of Macleod and the elegance with which she fitted out the inn. She traded on 'the discretion and civility which has all along been the characteristick [sic] of her House'.[51] Again, hers is the language of business, and the reference to discretion and civility is a specific allusion to the demeanour expected of Defoe's honest and 'complete tradesman'. Women dominated the marketplace as vendors of virtually any commodity. They sold from baskets, such as Fisherrow and Newhaven fishwives who walked into Edinburgh. They were highly visible as petty traders and shopkeepers: luckenbooth keepers of Edinburgh, women of Parisian boutiques and women such as Helene Amalie Ascherfeld, who expanded her deceased husband's grocery business.[52] Maria Borgström, widow of a custom collector and mother-in-law of a wealthy Helsinki merchant, earned a living selling her beer.[53] Such trading activities were accepted as extensions of women's 'natural' responsibility for provisioning.

The independent woman was frequently the most vulnerable to economic vicissitudes, but with opportunity, ability and perseverance, she could achieve income and independence, as Pamela Sharpe demonstrated in her reconstruction of the business life of Hester Pinney.[54] Female partnerships were important to businesswomen, and letters and journals show that, for some, working independently or in partnership was worth striving for. Women with little family status, capital and recognised skills moved on and off charitable rolls. Low wages often forced them to turn to whatever was available, frequently undertaking several things at once and 'making shift'. The diffi-culties of coping alone meant that many single and widowed women did not succeed. However, networks of friends, family or colleagues could give widows an advantage over spinsters. Remarriage was another option. Much of the animosity towards female workers was directed at 'masterless' women, women who appeared to challenge the rights and privileges of the corporate community. The Merchant Company of Edinburgh, for example, complained about the female shopkeepers, since 'they have no title to the privilege of trade in this city, which is hurtfull to the trading burgesses'.[55] Indeed, anxiety about 'unbridled women' was partly due to the visibility of indepen-dent female traders, outwith the control of a male, women who did not assume the natural state.

Women's work centred on the need to support hearth and home; this was seen as natural to the world around them and largely to women themselves. It carried with it a number of implications. Importantly, it meant that if necessary, married women took up a wide range of tasks to bring in income, from sale of produce to producing goods for sale, working for others or going begging. For most women, household tasks car-ried little ideological baggage and were simply a central part of their activities. However, domestic tasks contributed to making home a recognised female space, where they were in charge, frequently controlling finances. Housing architecture with a large central and communal room built around the fireplace where the women presided was fundamental to this social construction. They were often pivotal in deci-sions about household strategies, mediating with the outside world and, through market activities, contributing to immediate household needs.

When men were away, as fishermen, agricultural workers, soldiers or carters, women moved into the vacuum. When extra hands were needed, as at haying or har-vest, women 'mucked in'. They worked side by side with husbands and substituted for them either short term, taking turns at a loom, or long term, managing an entire business. This contribution was so essential and so closely associated with women that men frequently applied to remarry quickly saying they could not manage with-out a wife. In Sweden, over half of widowers remarried, especially young men most likely to need labour, housekeeper and mother, since 'for all households to function well, ideally they had to have a full "crew"'.[56] However, if some work was inter-changeable, ideas about it were not; a wife temporarily took on *his* work. When her husband was able, she should leave it to him and get on with *her* work. A wife's role in a partnership depended on her abilities, but coding tasks as 'skilled' or as men's work could prevent women from undertaking them. The picture is one of overlap-ping gender-specific boundaries, while local and regional factors affected divisions of labour.

The notion that women functioned only within the family economy is flawed in that numerous women operated throughout the economy in a way that, while compatible with family needs, was not necessarily predicated on family work, or even a shared loca-tion of work. Yet women's activities were still perceived as additional – add-ons, by-employments and, therefore, casual. The fact that women's work was task oriented, fitted in and around her 'main' household chores, made her not only a flexible worker but also a 'casual' or supplementary worker – indeed without the identity of 'worker'. Within the household and workshop, the principles of male head of household and male control of the workshop fundamentally underpinned the premise that men's work was high-status work and that female work was supplementary and supportive. She was his assistant. This had an important impact on wages, since her earnings were seen as 'pin money', and depressed wages for women who did not contribute to a family pot.

However, women negotiated such constraints, either taking up new trades, or operating in parallel, and domestic industries provided opportunities for them. As men's independent work status was threatened and with it their personal value, they sought to protect their position. Thus it became important not only to define skill and status vis-à-vis men who were poachers, but against women. As shifting definitions of status came together with re-evaluations of femininity, women were more frequently perceived as unsuited for work, particularly skilled work. An important characteristic of skill is that it is a linguistic device to claim and maintain control and exclusivity in the workplace. Relying on masculine honour and standing, vulnerable men, especially journeymen, identified women as challenging their status. They fell back on masculinity, their patriarchal role and the guild as a 'family' organisation to bolster their economic claims.

Most men and women did not go 'out to work'. Their community and neighbourhood was their milieu and their contacts and networks were a source of strength. But women were not limited by locality. They were foremost amongst migrants, and their movement into towns populated urban spaces, bringing workers to crafts, trades, shopkeeping and service. Many towns generated a commercial, outward-looking character, and women were a fundamental part of that, as workers, consumers and entrepreneurs. Their standing and position together with financial backing and need or ambition determined how they operated in the employment nexus. Their ingenuity and ability helped them make their way, supporting themselves and, usually, dependants. In the process some became very wealthy, such as Agnes Campbell, Hester Pinney and Amalia Aschenfeld. Others were not so successful, and they relied on a makeshift economy or charity. Women workers operated across the spectrum and were not confined by ideology, personal interest or social class to a domestic space or a domesticated role.

The nineteenth century

Eighteenth-century experience had strong echoes in the nineteenth century: the life-cycle patterns of women's work, the motivations to work pinned to dowries and family support and the continued presence of women in commerce. They congregated in the same areas of work: textiles, garment-making, domestic service and agriculture. Change was gradual and, for most, virtually imperceptible. However, in three key areas their experience was different from the previous century: the growth of domesticity and domestic service, the impact of agricultural 'improvement' and the shift to centralised and mechanised manufacture. The construction of domesticity revealed tensions for women who had to work, or wanted to, while for middle-class women, the century brought both restrictions and opportunities. Shifts in location of work also influenced views of work available to women. When work moved away from the home, coupled with pressure on jobs, paid work became men's property. Lynn Abrams explored the implications of domesticity and family for women in Chapter 2, but while domesticity shaped the context, many women claimed the right to work, utilising the range of choices open to them. Others simply needed to.

Social morality and the cult of the home inevitably shaped the context within which women worked. There was direct continuity in their responsibilities for home and family, but there was a fundamental difference. A clearly formulated and articulated ideology of womanhood was disseminated on an unprecedented scale. Not working was a defining characteristic of this feminine ideal, while masculinity became more unmistakably defined by concepts of male breadwinner and family wage. Family businesses became more visibly identified with males and more firmly embedded in legal and financial practices. Employment reflected bourgeois ideas of gender by the kinds of job each sex was hired for and the pay they received. Thus domestic service was promoted as appropriate female work in an appropriate setting. The family wage ideology created a working-class version of domesticity, so that for working men, respectability came to mean that wives devoted themselves to household affairs. Yet, only the most highly skilled workers earned enough to cover family expenditure, and among peasants and outworkers in insecure and unskilled trades, there was little emulation of a bourgeois ideal.

Housekeeping continued to be a central 'job', but housework was virtually created by domesticity and fostered by the technological changes of industrialisation. As Davidoff said, 'though the activities may be timeless, the context and meaning are not'.[57] As the 'family wage' became attached to visible men's work, women's household work became devalued and invisible in a way that their multifarious activities had not been previously. Though childcare, food preparation, cleaning and clothing remained the essential core of women's domestic tasks, they changed in context, meaning, scale and duration. The period from about 1780 to 1840 was crucial, marking a transition from *Hausmutter*, working in partnership with her husband presiding over agricultural estates, to *Hausfrau* or housewife, the guardian of the private sphere.

In many respects the family home became for a wife what business became for her husband; her job was to maintain and direct a well-run household, just as he ran a firm. The ideological mission of womanhood also charged women with frugality and thrift. Many tasks became more complex, creating new meaning and expectations, so that the way a woman 'kept house' defined her and her family. Housekeeping became homemaking. Decoration and display became part of femininity, woman's identity and correct bourgeois form. Cleanliness took on heightened meaning. Of course, highly ornate furnishings and the array of decorative items compounded cleaning, as did rapidly expanding manufacturing towns with their industrial debris. The reality was that many tasks were laborious and relatively unchanged by technology. Cleaning and polishing were not touched, water and fuel needed fetching, and cooking and laundry only increased in scope and scale. Indeed technological changes at the end of the century addressed the falling number of servants and probably had little effect on housewives' work.

Domestic service became a predominant route for girls searching for a livelihood and dowry. Demand grew with urbanisation, a rise in the number of prosperous households, the diffusion of domesticity and a marked increase in young people, while demand for female agricultural labour declined. In Berlin in 1885, servants comprised 32 per cent of employed females, and in 1860s London, a third of females between fifteen and twenty-four years of age. Numbers grew rapidly, but from about 1880, a slow but distinctive decline set in; by 1900, far fewer girls and a smaller proportion of the female workers turned to service.[58]

Typically she was a countrywoman, aged between mid-teens and mid-twenties. In Hamburg in 1871, two-thirds were between sixteen and twenty-five years old. Between 1825 and 1853, 60 per cent in Versailles, over half in Bordeaux and virtually all in Marseilles came from the countryside.[59] Many intended to move permanently to town; others went to accumulate dowries. Larger English aristocratic households recruited from further away, while provincial middle classes tended to hire nearby. In 1851, 75 per cent of Colchester servants came from within a ten-mile radius – walking-distance home on a day off.[60] It was common to hire girls for a country house, then take them to town. Elise Blanc started at Chateau Prévange in the Bourbonnais and went to Paris where her 'châtelains kept an apartment'.[61] Well-established networks, relatives and villagers working in cities were important contacts for girls. In 1888, Doris Viersbeck's aunt in Hamburg helped her advertise and 'shortlist' employers, accompanied her to interview and negotiated wages.[62] Townspeople preferred country girls because of a latent mistrust of urban ones, whom they saw as independent and more difficult. Thus, women of the Nord (France) sent letters to rural relatives asking for robust, moral and biddable servants.[63]

Young women saw urban service as secure migration with advantages such as wider horizons, advancement, usually higher wages and the prospect of saving for marriage. The traditional character of domestic service, based on familiar rural service and the availability of positions, explains much of its popularity. It preserved the familial context of work. Thus rural migrants in Rome saw it as a practical solution providing lodging, employment and personal safety.[64] With accommodation, board and uniforms, they stood a chance of saving, provided that they did not become ill, pregnant or lose their place. Servants moved regularly, usually for better positions, higher wages or promotion. The first position was often a step to other work; others moved back and forth between service and other occupations. In Halstead, Essex, many female weavers left Courtauld's silk mill for short periods because of the 'pull of domestic service'.[65]

Most servants were maids-of-all-work, the *Alleinmädchen*. In 1851, 61 per cent of Rochdale (England) servants were the only one in the household; over 75 per cent in 1880s Hamburg were.[66] A minority worked in large households or on country estates, experiencing the servant's hall with its career structure, where service was a finely developed hierarchy of duties and deference. Servants, such as Doris Viersbeck, preferred the large household since they could move up the ladder with commensurate gains in wages and perks.[67] The *Alleinmädchen* was responsible for an onerous burden of cleaning, cooking and helping with laundry. She worked alongside her mistress, but dirtier and heavier tasks always fell to her, so she carried heavy loads of wood, coal and laundry, emptied and washed chamber pots and boiled menstrual rags, nappies and sheets. She was nanny, lady's maid and valet. Jeanne Bouvier looked after 'two spoiled and insolent children', with all the shopping, housework and heavy laundry.[68] Away from home, with few friends, they were vulnerable and dependent on the good will and protection of their employers. They lived in and were constantly watched and subject to summonses. Employers thought a sixteen-hour day was reasonable, since housework included so many 'natural breaks'. Time to themselves and days off were rare; employers regulated outside contacts, sometimes with 'no followers' bans. This lack of independent judgement over friendships and family contact further isolated servants. They could be dismissed without cause and replaced if they became ill or infirm. They were susceptible to the demands and 'charms' of masters and male servants. Few employers hesitated to fire a servant they suspected was pregnant or even sexually active. References were essential for any new post.

Relatively good wages were an attraction. While money wages were less than for cotton operatives, the value of room, board and perks meant servants were better compensated for most of the century. McBride estimated the value of Parisian servants' wages in 1883 at 1,300 to 1,400 francs per year, compared to female cotton spinners earning approximately 780 francs per year. Wages of specialised servants were always higher.[69] So, despite difficult conditions and hard work, service held financial promise. They were often paid annually in arrears, which could create capital to invest, loan or save. Saving was difficult, however, between the vagaries of service, the range of wages and sending money to families. They risked never receiving wages if they were fired, quit or if the family fell on hard times. Cora-Elisabeth Millet-Robinet, in *La Maison rustique des dames (The Woman's Country House)* explained:

> It is preferable to pay them each month, or at least every third month, rather than once a year as is the custom . . . When money is at one's disposal, it is easy for it to be put to different use than that for which it was set aside, and this can become cause for embarrassment.[70]

Servants sometimes were paid indirectly. Merchant Pierre Lacoste paid wages directly to a chambermaid's peasant father.[71]

Tensions were inherent in the mistress–servant bond. Subjection to employers was a prime feature, and personal service was important to the relationship. They were to obey, follow orders and subsume their thoughts and feelings. German servants associated service with respect, trust and personal devotion, while mistresses used social distance to reinforce their control:

> Mother would go down and see her cook in the morning, to give orders and that kind of thing. And thereafter, if she wanted to speak to her for any reason or other bells were rung and the cook would come up. No mistress would ever go downstairs.[72]

In large households, servants' quarters reflected nuances of status, mirroring the gender and seniority of the patriarchal household. Numerous jurisdictional quarrels arose because servants persistently breached demarcation lines and used other servants' equipment.

Women's agricultural role was little changed, and *La Maison rustique des dames* described responsibilities reminiscent of the previous century:

> [She] should have all of the servant girls on the farm under her immediate supervision. The farmyard – that is, the cowshed, the dairy, the pigsty, and the chicken coop – as well as the gardens, the orchards, and the sheep, are also her responsibility. She must be aware of all the jobs to be done on the farm in order to reinforce her husband in his supervision and to replace him in times of absence or sickness.[73]

These activities were embedded less in domesticity and more in customary and practical divisions of labour.

Despite agricultural 'improvement', farming remained labour intensive, and mechanisation developed slowly. In fact, women's activity increased. Market gardening, new crops, such as soft fruit in Clydeside and Carse of Gowrie, Scotland, and accelerating urban demand for produce created work that was seen as specifically suited to women. The prevalence of female fieldworkers varied from region to region, even from village to village: demand decreased in south-east England except at peak times, but not in Northumberland and Scotland.[74] By 1851, a strong tradition against women fieldworkers in the Caux reversed with a threefold increase in the number of female day labourers and farm servants. In the Turin hinterland, with a long tradition of female fieldwork, women made up to 70 per cent of the workforce by 1881.[75] Sporadic day labour was more economical than permanent workers, and tenants continued to bring women with them as flexible workers. Indeed, farmers thought the labour of employees' wives and daughters was their clear prerogative. Thus women were in demand, but they became closely identified with specific seasonal tasks whilst men were more readily seen as permanent labour. This accentuated gendered roles, because men and women's work was different and because women became associated with specific crops and activities – tending and gathering – whereas men strengthened their association with land and stock. Women's work was no less strenuous, but neither did it incorporate the sense of ownership, status or occupation attached to men's work.

In Sicily women joined men in fields only at harvest, as did weavers from Marlhes, Scandinavian dairywomen and Bavarian household servants. Increased use of scythes instead of sickles meant men, who supposedly were physically better suited to the heavier scythe, gradually replaced women reapers. Ironically, women were considered more skilled than men with sickles, and one reason for the slow uptake of scythes was difficulty in finding skilled men. Women's displacement depended on local custom, the size of the workforce and the need for speed and care in cutting. Gradually they lost cutters' higher wages, but less well-paid work called on women: gathering, binding and stacking. Clearly, notions of strength and skill were conflated, and the allocation of women to reaping and men to mowing was associated with the masculinisation of labour.

These changes coincided with rises in domestic servants' wages and contributed to single women leaving fields for service. In England and Wales, between 1851 and 1871, female day labourers fell by 24 per cent and farm servants by 75 per cent.[76] To provide day labour in lowland Scotland, farmers built bothies and boarded girls from Ireland and the Highlands. English, French and Belgian farmers relied on gang masters who arranged and paid workers. Often gangs walked long distances and in inclement weather might have no work or pay. In 1867, Elizabeth Dickson from Norfolk told a parliamentary commission:

> Some of the work is very hard, pulling turnips and mangolds, . . . and when turnips are being put into the ground putting muck as fast as the plough goes along . . . Drawing mangolds is the hardest; globe mangolds are fit to pull your inside out, . . . I have pulled till my hands have been swelled that you can't see the knuckles on them. I have come home so exhausted that I have sat down and cried; it would be an hour before I could pull my things off; and I have been obliged to have the table moved up to me because I could not move to it.[77]

The visibility of gangs played into bourgeois moral concerns. Other women in more isolated circumstances suffered the same hard conditions but without attracting attention. The Belgian Women's Committee *Enquête* of 1892 recorded 57,000 women in gangs still working the fields especially during planting and harvest.[78]

Dairying was unambiguously coded as women's work: 'Not only was it improper for a man to milk, it was considered shameful (Sweden)'; 'Men would not consider it their work to milk a cow (Ireland)'. Churning required skill and experience and folklore granted women natural superior milking skills. They sang ancient charms, and a naked Finnish woman 'wrapped her vest around the churn', epitomising the association of female sexuality with dairying.[79] Commercial farms relied on dairymaids, housing them and paying some of the highest female wages, compensation not only for long hours and hard labour, but also for skill and responsibility. Bavarian farmers regularly paid bonuses when animals were sold; experience caring for animals was worth money. From 1836, training enabled Danish women to gain independent positions on commercial farms, very high wages, responsibility and confidence. Unusually for Denmark, some published their methods, underlining the value of their skills.[80] Since female skill was recognised, masculinisation of dairying indicates something deeper than simple transition to technologically skilled work. Swedish dairymaids gained training between 1858 and 1883 and managed village dairies, but few won expert status. From the 1880s, Sweden created [male] 'dairy advisers', so men became managers based on 'scientific' knowledge. When sealing milk in containers broke the direct relationship between the skilled worker and the product, that is, women and milk, dairying was recoded as male, modern and expert.[81]

Women made fishing possible by tending farms, making nets, fetching bait and baiting lines. They had long marketed catches: Marshside women sold shrimps in Lancashire, Newhaven fishwives were renowned in Edinburgh and Scandinavian women were indispensable as sellers and gutters. Processing the catch was women's work: gutting and packing in brine, pickling or smoking. Scots women following the fleet to process catches enjoyed the freedom of travel and independent wages, returning home with a tidy sum. One recalled, 'it was a free and easy time, you weren't restricted – like you know, in a factory where there were bosses.'[82] Women in harbours awaited the catch, processing and packing as quickly as possible. An observer timed Wick women gutting twenty-six herring a minute.[83] During the 1830s, fishing shifted to commercial organisation, and women became waged labour. Eventually they moved into canning and packing factories, into the unseen sector, as commercialisation changed fishing's family character.

New domestic industries sprang up as older ones mechanised or centralised, mechanisation often stimulated outwork, and cheaper hand technologies frequently delayed full-scale mechanisation. Old values coexisted with and were used to adapt to structural changes, thus importing old styles of behaviour into new contexts. 'Perceptions of continuity and discontinuity . . . represent coexisting realities.'[84] Thus women continued to be the spinners of Europe. Tuscan *filatrici* were described in 1811 as women who spun 'in the hours in which they are resting from their other duties', confirming the persistent view that women's work was casual and revealing a perverse sense of what constituted rest and work.[85] As spinning centralised and mechanised, pressure shifted to weaving, and women established themselves relatively easily in this 'male' trade. In Saxony, in 1872, Auguste Eichler inherited the loom while her brother received the house, and weaver Johanne Schmidt bequeathed her loom to Christiane Luise instead of to Christiane's four brothers.[86]

As cottage industry became uneconomic, new women's jobs materialised as more goods were produced and new domestic and overseas markets developed. Courtaulds deliberately established their silk factory near Halstead, in the 1790s, to capitalise on plentiful surplus female labour.[87] However, women who lost jobs in rural industry were not the same ones who gained new jobs. A sharper division of labour emerged, since men and women often worked in distinct economic sectors and at different tasks. Men hung on to skilled 'artisanal' work, and women became more overtly 'operatives'. An individual woman might not see radical changes during her lifetime, but she, her daughter and her mother could have registered important shifts in the choices they could make.

The factory became an alternative migratory route for young females, but their income remained important for families and dowries. Jeanne Bouvier told how her mother sent her to a silk factory outside Lyon, and when she did not get a pay rise, she beat her, assuming it was her fault.[88] The image of the mill girl obscured the number of married women in factories. Childless wives in Roubaix were most common, and single and married mothers worked reduced hours whilst the youngest was under five years of age. Fewer worked as children grew up; potentially mothers and daughters traded off work. Employers were ambivalent. At Cowan's paper mill, Penicuik (Scotland), in 1865,

> With a view to prevent the neglect of children in their homes, we do not employ the mothers of young children in our works, . . . [excepting] widows or women deserted by their husbands, or having husbands unable to earn a living.[89]

In contrast, local bourgeoises in Verviers and Ghent worried that women who left lost their skills and taste for work, placing additional burdens on the family. No one expected married women at Courtaulds to give up millwork, even those whose husbands were best paid.[90] Demand for female labour could pose problems for families. A Lancashire woman explained:

> So large is the demand for female labour, that fifty women can find employment where the man fails. . . . Thus it is quite true that many women do keep their husbands; the men merely doing such jobbing work as they can pick up.[91]

Many rural families had no choice and migrated to textile towns. Sometimes they changed occupations. In Saint Chamond (France), they replaced factory silk with domestic braids.[92]

Women homeworkers are most elusive, because they moved in and out of work, because statisticians did not always consider them 'workers', and because they were 'hidden' at home. Yet women assembled garments, footwear, gloves, umbrellas and numerous other items: artificial flowers, sacks, boxes, tassels, dolls' clothes and feather decorations. Russian *kustar* work ranged from lace-making and embroidery to weaving rope sandals and reins and gluing cigarette tubes. It theoretically resolved the work and childcare conundrum, though the long and intensive hours were incongruous with childcare. Sophie Ternyck, a single shirt-maker in Lille, sewed long hours at home, while her seven-year-old son ran errands.[93] Many single women apparently preferred the relative freedom of homework to the constraints of domestic service. Homeworkers ranged across social classes including wives and daughters of labourers, tailors, artisans and merchants. Some needy 'surplus' bourgeois women turned to sewing as a 'respectable' trade. Neither married nor single women fitted a single pattern. They took available work, altering strategies and domestic responsibilities as necessary.

The development of 'ready-made', or *confection*, expanded needlework, but seamstresses challenged tailors' former superiority. Men saw the root of the problem in structural and 'skill' changes caused by ready-made, not with women as seamstresses. The distinction between home and shop was crucial in protecting male control of tailoring and, as Quataert showed, the struggle resulted in attempts to alienate the household from the market economy.[94] The shift linked 'economic deterioration and deskilling . . . with a move from male space (the shop) to female space (the household)'.[95] As the 'dishonourable' sector grew at the expense of the 'honourable' one, the number of women increased, often forcing men to accept lower wages. Outwork virtually destroyed skilled female trades such as millinery, mantua making and dressmaking. Skilled women were less able to resist, because their trade structure undercut craft solidarity. Self-employed, they worked in dispersed locations and usually without the strong collective identity that tailors used to fight *confection*. Subcontracting created a fundamental gender change in needle trades; men became owners and subcontractors. They had greater access to capital and closely identified with ownership and management; it was easier for them to take control. Thus women lost the distinction between skilled and unskilled workers and their craft status.

Factories relied on outwork, such as fine embroidery in Ayrshire and Ulster and shirt-making in Toulouse, Berlin and Derry. Derry shirt factories encouraged women to take work home, salaried agents put work out and outstations allowed women to work *in situ* or to take materials home.[96] The system made women particularly vulnerable, since employers dictated pay and completion dates, and 'unsatisfactory' work was fined. Sewing machines facilitated decentralisation, but certainly did not cause it. They sped up sewing, raised expectations of productivity and increased hours of work, stress and exhaustion. Women provided their machine and, absorbing overheads, they became an even more attractive workforce. Workshops introduced machines on a large scale after mid-century, well after dispersed homework had taken firm root, so by 1860 garment making was mechanised and centralised like other industries.[97] Breaking down the production process meant the skill content deteriorated. Ottilie Baader described how this exacerbated the boring, repetitive character of work and raised the level of alienation:

> I then bought myself my own machine [after leaving the factory] and worked at home. . . . A session lasted from 6 am to 12 am, with one hour pause for lunch. I got up at 4 am, tidied the flat and prepared the food. I had a small clock in front of me while working, and so it passed that one dozen collars took no longer than another, and nothing gave me greater pleasure than when I could spare a few minutes. . . . Sometimes I had had more than enough of it: year after year at the sewing machine, always just collars and cuffs in front of me, one dozen after another. Life had no value, I was just a work machine and had no future prospects. I saw and heard nothing of what is beautiful in the world: I was simply shut off from that.[98]

Usually in partnership with men, many women stayed in business well into the century, and Stana Nenadic estimates that women ran a fifth of British businesses.[99] Etienne Jouy commented in 1809 that everywhere in the Nord, 'one generally sees women directing businesses and exercising great authority in the *ménage*'. Pauline Motte-Brédart (1795–1871) virtually ran a cotton enterprise, while her mother, mother-in-law and sister-in-law built business fortunes. Women handled records and bookkeeping, and their understanding of business allowed men to travel, confident in the knowledge that the firm was in good hands. Some women took sales trips, such as Elizabeth Strutt from Derbyshire, whose grasp of business and knowledge of the trade testify to her importance as de facto partner. However, bourgeois ideals and the removal of homes from business environs led many women to relinquish business activities. The daughters, daughters-in-law and granddaughters of Motte-Brédart slowly moved to complete domesticity, to be praised as good, sweet, excellent wives.[100]

Wives remained essential in family shops, and producers such as butchers, bakers and shoemakers depended on wives and daughters to serve customers. In 1809, Jean Negre authorised his wife 'to direct and administer his goods and affairs, to receive and furnish receipts for any sums that may be due him for whatever reason, to pursue his debtors . . . to sell and buy' in his absence.[101] Women with capital often invested in independent enterprises. In her marriage contract to a carpenter, Marie Laplange reserved 600 francs 'with which she intends to begin a little trade in groceries, *mercerie*, or something else'.[102] Widows of artisans commonly used their portion to do the same. Wedgwood's archives are replete with orders from women shopkeepers. They retained a commercial niche in grocery and provision trades, regularly keeping inns, boarding houses and running cabarets, cafés and eating houses. Some 6 per cent of female household heads in Davidoff and Hall's sample ran inns, and every male innkeeper who made a will in Witham (Essex) and Birmingham left his business unconditionally to his wife. These were important commercial activities at the centre of several subsidiary activities. However, inns became less respectable and increasingly stratified by rank, creating a dilemma for women who owned and managed them. The arrival of railways reduced business, and livery stables became more closely associated with the 'masculine monopoly of horse culture'.[103] Women remained street sellers, providing fresh food upon which towns increasingly depended, such as Antoinette Corbières, a cheese pedlar:

> Without a shop, a stall, or even a permanent bench in the market, she made the street her place of business. Along the Grande Rue Montaubon and through the side streets . . . she hawked her wares from a tray that hung around her neck. Between customers she gossiped in doorways with her friends and flirted with the butcher's son . . . Once a week she walked twenty kilometres to the country town of Molières, where, on market day, she shared a bench with her sister who sold bread.[104]

Such women operated networks of information, helping to shape neighbourhoods.

Women's charitable activity expanded parallel to their departure from workplaces. Individuals, such as Florence Nightingale, Octavia Hill, Elizabeth Fry, Josephine Butler, Flora Tristan, Amalie Sieveking, and groups such as the Société Maternelle of Paris and the Rheinisch-Westfälischer Diakonissenverein (Rhenish-Westfalian Association of

Deaconesses) at Kaiserwerth, assisted the poor, sick, needy and vulnerable. Philanthropy was justified within contemporary moral codes and active religion played an important part. But philanthropy gave women a sense of purpose and accomplishment, where the domestic ideal seemed vacuous, selfish and unproductive. This role had to be fought for, and women took criticism for abandoning families to traipse through the dirt and debris of society. Philanthropy changed women. They gained confidence and learned skills: management, fund-raising, research, finance, communication and campaigning. They also acquired a view of the world and imagined new horizons. Taking part was not easy and required women to overcome their own fears and prejudices, while widening their social consciences. Philanthropy became more politicised, with campaigns for middle-class work, better education, better working conditions, the women's movement and suffrage. Many bourgeois women had to work, especially surplus female relatives. Being governesses and companions was deemed appropriate, as private, domestic and consistent with women's caring role. From mid-century, opportunities such as teaching, nursing and clerical work emerged offering new scope, which are taken up in the next section.

Women worked for a number of reasons, the primary one being the need for survival. Thus they took up whatever work was available, which they balanced against needs that were not purely economic. Where there were choices, they made decisions based on complex considerations including pay, location, family responsibilities and personal preferences. Thus girls often chose between domestic service, factory work and urban trades, sometimes moving between all three. Their choice could depend on their point in the life cycle, on the economic state of industry and agriculture and on the point in time. If this seems obvious, it serves as a reminder that generalities sometimes obscure the range of individual choice.

During the century after the French Revolution, when hiring workers for wages became far more the norm, attitudes to women workers were shaped by conflicting notions of womanhood and sexuality on the one hand and by the needs of capitalism and of working-class families for paid labour on the other. As female employment became more visible, more clearly 'women for hire', and clashed with emergent notions of domesticity, it became grounds for debate. In many people's eyes, 'women' were not 'workers'; the terms were mutually exclusive. This view shaped the context of women's work and contributed to perceptions of women as casual temporary employees, who could and should be treated and paid differently from men. They were seen as docile, malleable creatures, subject to a well-established patriarchal regime, subordinate to men and masters. The belief in different male and female natures coincided with a belief in different abilities, so that women were seen as nimble-fingered, dexterous, careful, meticulous and quick. The combination of cheapness, docility and 'special skills' made them desirable employees.

Construction of the family wage was central to gender stereotyping and to defining women's work as secondary. The family wage was a particular issue for skilled men, inheritors of the artisan, who constituted the first trade unions. These men believed that a family wage, by which they meant *their* wage, would reduce competition for jobs. The aim was to remove women from those areas where they did the same work or worked in the same industries as men and where they were seen to be undercutting men's wages, status and control. It was important to ensure that women's work remained less well paid and inferior to men's. Men's position would then be enhanced absolutely, but also in relation to employers. This argument is reminiscent of claims for protection of skill and status deriving from guilds and artisan crafts. On one hand, it was not about women, but about protecting male craft position and independence vis-à-vis the capitalist who wished to control labour supply. On the other hand, it clearly was about gender, because women workers were the targets. The ideal of a family wage bolstered patriarchy because it was firmly attached to the image of a breadwinning male supporting a dependent wife. So, when women worked, it should be appropriate work. First, it simply meant work that men did not want. Second, it meant work that suited the feminine frame and delicacy and was situated in an appropriate place, usually the home. Thus, gendered attitudes about work took on new life, sublimation and permeated society much more widely during the century.

The twentieth century

After 1880 there was a marked increase in the number and proportion of women officially working, that is, in ways that governments recorded: waged or salaried in socially defined workplaces. Women working in the informal economy, as family members or occasionally, tended to be overlooked. The most important change was the shift in the structure of women's work. The decline of domestic service was fairly dramatic and exacerbated by the First World War, which provided a way out for many disenchanted women. The move away from homework was less clearly marked, influenced by the collapse of textiles and increased mechanisation. Women's paid work in the countryside also diminished, but unpaid rural wives remained an important workforce. A strong undercurrent promoted women's responsibility for home, nation and race, while housework became crystallised as 'occupation housewife'. Political and feminist movements furthered not only awareness of women as workers but also generated more self-esteem in women. Improved educational opportunities opened doors for many, especially in the burgeoning white-collar sector. The wars pointed up women's abilities and contributed to developing new systems of working.

Three important changes took place in the life cycle of the workforce. First, young single women remained a major part of the workforce but started later because of workplace and educational legislation and because of opportunities for higher education.[105] Second, more single adults joined the workforce as middle-class women came to see work as appropriate. Their work was more often a matter of choice or principle than necessity. Third, married women stayed at work or returned when children were older. They quit less often on marriage – leaving work was more common when children came. Their input rose to unparalleled levels in the post-war period. The pool of single women had shrunk because of earlier marriage, the rising school-leaving age and longer periods in higher education, encouraging employers to target married women and mothers. Smaller families meant that childcare finished earlier. In Scotland, the child-rearing period dropped by ten years between 1900 and 1980. The rising divorce rate, which accelerated in the 1960s, pushed more mothers into the labour market. In 1961, 20.5 per cent of Belgian married women worked, but 48.6 per cent of divorced women did, matching the participation rate of single women, 49.2.[106] The increased activity of married women in the workplace was also promoted by the creation of formalised part-time work. While employers used part-time workers to reduce labour costs, it was a boon to women who needed flexibility. The disadvantage was that it was insecure, was not recognised as real work by officialdom, including pension schemes, and was usually poorly paid, though European directives are gradually altering this. Job-sharing was one solution, because 'real' jobs are shared.

There is little doubt that the wars brought more women into the workforce through substitution or conscription. However, women did not drop other jobs and flood to the ranks. Their 'usual' employment was hit hard. Many domestic servants turned to war work, but others were dismissed, and the fall in demand for luxuries hit millinery and dressmaking. A legacy of the first war was the introduction of new working practices, especially assembly-line work. These procedures would have met with more resistance outside of wartime and only applied to large-scale production, but employing women, virtual novices in engineering industries, created a precedent. Despite backlash, longer term it was another tiny step in women becoming 'workers'. Perhaps as important as the visibility of female war workers was the effect on women. Some went from their own close-knit communities and rural surroundings into a world of factories, joining women with different stories. A Scotswoman from the central belt reflected on how this experience gave her generation a sense of identity and broadened their horizons. Women came to appreciate their own skills, gained confidence in their abilities and acquired a sense of their right to work.

Subtle shifts took place in the meaning of housework. Standards of living and housing improved, while housework was cast as freedom from drudgery and shifted towards enhanced child welfare. During the first half of the century women often kept house amidst social and economic disruption: war, rationing, depression and poverty. The creativity that post-war shortages brought out in German women was staggering: mending clothes with human hair, washing clothes in potato peelings or ox gall.[107] Doctors, social workers, teachers, health visitors and the media socialised women to adopt the pivotal role in family care, education and economic strategies in a consumer world. In 1960, Danish women were brought up to believe that housewife and mother was the fulfilment of their lives, despite demographic changes which meant that children were not on their hands for as long.[108]

The consumer economy meant women operated as managers on a much bigger and more complex scale with advertisers targeting 'homemakers'. The availability of goods and services raised expectations and, instead of simplifying housekeeping, complicated it. Despite 'convenience' foods, meals had more courses, more variety and involved more preparation. Increases in real wages meant such purchases were increasingly feasible across society, and consumption of milk, butter, meat and luxury goods rose significantly. Women controlled domestic finances, if not all household expenditure. They kept records, dealt with shopkeepers, merchants, insurance companies and other public and private services that proliferated. They became the family's public representative. In inter-war Artois, the wife was the 'lookout', responsible for watching over the survival and well-being of the family; she was the nurse, the 'clother', the 'maintainer'.[109]

Dramatic but uneven changes altered the environment in which housework was conducted and the tools and aids employed. For example, as late as 1961, 22 per cent of Britons still did not have hot-water taps. Before 1914, consumer durables such as sewing machines, clocks, bicycles, stoves and cooking utensils became available followed by electrical appliances such as irons, toasters and vacuum cleaners. But Davidoff reminds us, 'that technical improvements in equipment such as those exemplified by the use of the small electric motor are not of the same order as funda-mental changes in the organisation or aims of housework.'[110] Appliances had dubious value in saving time. A 1960s UNESCO study concluded, 'There is little sign . . . that the gains from an abundant labour saving technology [translate] into leisure. Variations in time devoted to household obligations . . . are not spectacularly large'.[111] New appli-ances and better houses encouraged more exacting levels of comfort and hygiene, increasing the amount of work women performed, altering their expectations and increasing time maintaining new products. Rather than release women to pursue other interests, rising standards bound them more closely to the family.

Several factors promoted the decline in domestic service. Political changes, pressures for women's emancipation and middle- and working-class activism collaborated to change the climate of opinion and contributed to a more independent spirit amongst servants. Attitudinal shifts joined with rapid expansion of white-collar employment to lead large numbers of young women to take up openings in retail, offices and busi-nesses. For most, an increase in personal freedom, daily contact with other young women and greater opportunities to meet men were influential. Increased education kept girls out of service, while providing skills to improve their prospects. Such edu-cational and occupational changes cost domestic service the status it had held. Service came to be seen as personally degrading and restrictive in comparison with new oppor-tunities. As long as wages remained significantly higher than other jobs, the nuisances of service mattered less, but by 1900, they were no longer much higher. When young women had real choices they left service, not always choosing better-paid or higher-status work. Roman women took up sewing, although wages and living conditions were worse.[112] The First World War sealed the fate of domestic service. Many servants took war work with its good pay and the camaraderie of other young women. They became accustomed to having money and to deciding how to spend it and their time. One woman reporting to the London City Exchange after two and a half years in munitions said, 'I feel so pleased that the war's over that I'll take any old job that comes along', but when offered domestic service, she laughed, 'Except that!'[113]

Farm wives were least likely to be recorded as workers by censuses, but they remained the most likely to work in agriculture. As family farms became more labour intensive and as economic factors made hiring help unprofitable, wives assumed an increasing share, including men's 'traditional' fieldwork and using machinery, still ful-filling their established role. They were so central to farm upkeep that farm wives in Weimar Germany worked an average of 12 per cent more hours annually than their husbands, and 40 per cent more than hired help.[114] In the 1970s in Baden-Württemberg, one man worried: 'I like farming and my farm is profitable, but when one does not get a wife and the old ones die – that's the end.'[115] In agrarian Norway, women's farm duties increased because of higher standards of hygiene and quality of dairy products, despite there being no running water in cowsheds.[116]

A division of labour continued to operate, though boundaries varied between com-munities. Finns respected the traditional gender split between male responsibility for field and forestry and female responsibility for dairies. But with increased herd size and its centrality to household income, men might work alongside women. However, the herd remained her responsibility. Portuguese men looked after things that grew above the ground (*produtos do ar*, products of the air) and women for things that grew in or near the earth (*produtos da terra*, products of the earth). Women were 'rooted to the ground; they are also considered to be less mobile, for they are attached to a particular stretch of land, their *terra*.[117] Indeed, while men were prohibited by custom from meddling in her terrain, she helped in his as necessary. Shifts took place in precise tasks, but the broad outlines of gendered division of labour remained. The view persisted that women did jobs requiring dexterity better than men, such as pea-picking and flower-cutting, but were less able to match them in jobs needing strength and stamina. So, outside of 'female' tasks, women were constrained to the most tedious and repetitive ones and barred from specialised 'skilled' ones where men retained a monopoly.

Peasant-worker strategies became permanent approaches to keeping small farms viable. In France in 1980, two-thirds of all farm households benefited from a second income.[118] In practice, most migrations were male, reminiscent of the Portuguese woman tied to her *terra*. These could be long-term or seasonal, or they could fall into a 'commuter' pattern. In Portugal in 1979, the proportion of female farmers demonstrates the level of migration. In Couto, 74.2 per cent of self-employed farmers were female, and in Paço, 68.6 per cent were.[119] Norwegian studies in 1939 and 1949 revealed that women worked more than men on farms, whilst men often had fishing or factory work.[120] Similarly, German and Basque men worked early mornings and late evenings on farms, going to outside jobs during the day.[121] Thus a major post-war trend was feminisation of agriculture; it was most pronounced on 'part-time' farms where women took over work previously performed by men. But in some communities, women took non-farm work. Danish wives working off-farm increased from 6 per cent to 26 per cent between 1960 and 1975; 12 per cent of the latter did no farmwork. Norwegian women increased by a third the hours they worked off-farm between 1979 and 1989, and Dutch women increasingly sought paid jobs: 6 per cent in 1982 and 18 per cent in 1989.[122] Women valued such off-farm work for the money, of course, but also for social contact and positive feedback. As Irish women commented, 'it is a great feeling knowing you are doing something useful and getting paid for it', and 'you are more your own person'.[123]

Some farm women became 'countrywomen'. In southern England such women held clear gendered notions of division of labour and role specialisation, identified with a myth of rurality and, despite the difficulties of rural areas with limited services, defended their rural heritage.[124] They tended to take on tasks removed from direct production, such as bookkeeping, and lived in villages. They controlled and managed household consumption: shopping, freezing and storing became paramount activities. They turned to tourism, running *pensions* or 'bed and breakfasts'. In Hartland, Cornwall, wives on medium-sized and big farms took in visitors.[125] Similarly women took up country shops, teashops and small cafés and made and marketed 'rural crafts'. In Artois, women ran the post office, the inn and the grocery.[126] They became mediators between the community and visitors, referring them to shops, events, beaches. Women filled the social-welfare gap created by a relative lack of social-service provision in rural areas, including transport. In Fróneyri (Iceland), women's mutual support constituted stepping in during crises, helping when a woman was sick, lending items for parties or picking up shopping. A formal childcare network operated: women worked alternate shifts in the fish factory to take each other's children.[127] This was important work for women and important for their communities.

Homework expanded temporarily with demand from rising incomes, and small artisanal production, such as Parisian luxury trades, lasted well into the century.

Nevertheless, fashion changes forced a decline in these trades and garment making plummeted. In Glasgow, numbers dropped by 27.5 per cent in only ten years, 1901–11.[128] Women also rejected it, preferring clerical and shop work. Ultimately, the sector shrank but did not disappear and in the 1970s and 1980s much work was still done at home, mainly clothing, but also artificial flowers, packing Christmas crackers, stuffing toys, pasting jewellery, knitting and carding pins, needles and buttons. Electrical component assembly, inspecting and packing goods, electronic office equipment and 'teleworking' created new homework. Though many trades and regions continued to rely on rural outworkers, homeworking became primarily an urban phenomenon. New homeworkers, who worked in fields where they had trained, tended to describe themselves as self-employed. They claimed greater choice and a pricing structure that compensated for overheads, holiday and sick pay. Another change was the number of ethnic minority women reliant on homework. The legacy of a post-colonial world, large numbers seeking work frequently remained at home to avoid issues of cultural and language difference, discriminatory practices, and to meet the sheer need that many in these communities faced.[129]

The main reason for working at home remained unchanged: women worked because they needed the money and homework met their needs. French government investigations in 1905 and 1911 revealed that married homeworkers provided up to half of family income.[130] Primarily homeworkers had family responsibilities. In Parisian needle trades in 1907, half were married, 37 per cent widowed and 16 per cent single; 12 per cent of single women had children.[131] Whether or not women undertook homework depended on husbands' incomes and their reliability. In Glasgow, wives took it up when men were laid off, became ill or worked irregularly. Homeworkers also clustered in localities with concentrations of 'male' trades, such as heavy engineering, dock work and shipbuilding, where local work for women was limited.[132] Women might stay in homework when a subsistence crisis lifted, but at that point they made deliberate choices about what they were prepared to do.

Many believed that homework gave them control over their work and time. For more skilled work, bordering on freelance, it was not necessarily a myth, depending on how much women were prepared to contribute to their exploitation. However, homeworking did not support a familial idyll, since labour at home severely impinged on family life. Systems of control meant the employer, not the employee, exercised power, and division of labour left the homeworker discretion over only trivial parts of the work. Those who retained some craft, such as knitters, commented that when they did not have the satisfaction of completion by sewing up garments, 'they miss it'.[133] When employers owned the machines, they operated another level of control, while 'unsatisfactory' work was not paid for. Women homeworkers had to balance their perceptions of the benefits of such work and its location against the restrictions it placed on them. Only where financial need was not so great, where they worked at home for other reasons and where their skill or trade allowed room for manoeuvrability, was there an element of discretion.

Manufacturing shifts with new processes and 'light industries' relied heavily on a female workforce: in chemicals, electronics, food-processing, pharmaceuticals, electrical equipment, household furnishing, optics and precision engineering. But men took the lion's share of the new jobs, and openings were not rapid enough to replace traditional jobs. Primarily, industries with an established female workforce augmented their use of female labour, especially those that first adopted new production methods and assembly lines, since it was logical to expand with a proven workforce. Women became less likely to be restricted to a narrow range of work and appeared in increasing numbers across manufacturing. They were no longer marginalised in 'female' industries and were less at risk from economic fluctuations and decline in single industries. At Magneti Marelli engineering works in Milan, 'about half its workforce was female and its management methods rivalled those of many contemporary American firms'. As Willson explained,

> This was one of the first examples of a 'modern industrial workforce' in Italy, fairly stable and employed in a highly mechanised and 'scientifically organized' factory. . . . but the two factors which are most important to explain this pattern were management strategy and the large numbers of women in the labour force.[134]

New industries had a vested interest in tapping 'green labour', a workforce with little industrial heritage and one more likely to accept new conditions of employment and processes. The belief that women were calmer and steadier made them an attractive labour force. Mechanised jobs required less strength and skill and therefore commanded a lower wage, so women remained cheap labour. The concept of woman as worker and woman as woman clearly contributed to shaping their employment.

A key feature of the occupational pattern was its 'lumpiness', that is, men were far more likely to produce certain products or work in particular industries and women in others. The automobile industry stands out as retaining its male craft traditions. In Coventry and in the Renault plant in Boulogne-Billancourt, women workers were tiny proportions, as machinists sewing car trims, car cleaners or working in canteens.[135] A similar split existed in other industries. Magneti Marelli expanded radio production, increasing recruitment of women, whilst men made accumulator batteries.[136] Women did not get 'technical work', and specialist equipment and tools were kept for men, although men's higher-paid manual labour was frequently replaced with machines tended by considerably lower-paid women. Men were associated with repairing and maintaining machinery, whilst women were required to feed it, stop it and start it but not to mess with it. In Armentières, men maintaining the factory heater were paid better than women operatives.[137] Work regarded as skilled was carefully preserved for men and reinforced by segregated workplaces so that women did not appear to be threatening men's jobs or status. But in many industries, women replaced no one, since the work was new, such as working on wrapping machines in the Dutch margarine industry. In fact further technical changes meant that machines replaced women.[138]

Young women were enthusiastic about the higher wages and increased freedom that factory work represented. They found 'more life' there, a partial escape from parents and looking after younger children. They had money to spend and took pleasure in the collective experience; a young Belfast women said, 'We were happy . . . You stood all day at your work and sung them songs.'[139] In contrast are those who wished to work only until marriage, though often it was not possible. Choice, of course, is complicated. When work was necessary and factories provided the best option, choice was likely to be viewed differently than when marriage had the highest value, factory work was boring and there were few options.

The twentieth century saw the virtual creation of 'white-collar' work. Educational improvement led to a better-educated workforce, who could take on tasks requiring literacy and understanding and many wanted 'something better' than manual work. Middle-class women formed a much more substantial part of the labour force, directly challenging notions of femininity, and with the growth of feminism they became a more vociferous and significant group. Gender contributed heavily to policies of hiring women in white-collar jobs and shaped the kind of work available. Hiring women meant employers could limit the number of men they hired and still offer them a career path, keeping women in lower-paid jobs without one. A post-office official in 1870 argued that the salaries that attracted only men of an 'inferior' class were sufficient to attract ladies of a 'superior' class.[140] Much work was new, especially selling at counters, typing, telephony, nursing and social work, and many occupations were female from the outset. 'White-bloused' workers were involved in the transition of the workplace just as men, but they had fewer opportunities for higher status work. White-bloused work grew as domestic service declined, but they drew on different cohorts. Domestic servants were mainly migrating rural women, and often younger; white-bloused workers were primarily urban. It was precisely their knowledge and confidence in the urban setting that contributed to their desire for clerical work and their usefulness at it. The first female office workers, factory inspectors and professionals tended to be drawn from middle-class families of a good educational standard, usually higher than the men in the same and higher grades. The first sales assistants tended to be modestly educated and drawn from lower middle-class and working-class women.

Women had long worked in shops and quasi-professions and had handled clerical work in family firms, so they had a heritage in white-collar work. Retailing changed with the development of a wider consumer economy and with new forms of merchandising, notably, the emergence of chain stores and department stores. Tasks were different in that shop assistants maintained stock control, cashiered and sold and displayed goods. They were less likely to make-up goods or develop personal relationships with customers, but new products and a greater range of merchandise led to a need for well-informed sales staff and to in-house training. Related expansion took place in mail- and web-ordering in the late twentieth century. The Army and Navy Stores and the Bon Marché ran services before 1900, but real growth came in the twentieth century. Reliant on technology for handling orders, warehouse work remained labour intensive and exhausting, with women's pay dependent on the speed they selected goods for dispatch. Offices across the economy demanded more record-keeping and correspondence, and clerical work expanded and created new jobs. Women initially joined smaller public sector offices and businesses already associated with females. Banks, insurance companies, shipping firms and big merchant houses hired them only to a narrow range of tasks. Less than half the women in German banks were entrusted with banking and, at the Prudential, women mainly copied documents connected with new working-class insurance.[141] The largest scale employers of female clerks were European civil services. Almost uniformly women first entered telegraphy, and telephonists were virtually female from the outset, except for night work. Gradually women gained other clerical and quasi-administrative jobs. Unquestionably female clerical workers became more visible. The demand for paid work for middle-class women coupled with better access to education and feminism provided the impetus and means for women to become professionals. But clear gendered attitudes and prohibitive practices operated to keep certain areas female and to protect the old liberal professions. Nursing, teaching and social work always had a large female membership while law, medicine, pharmacy, clergy and management remained male dominated.

The First World War gave women opportunities of promotion, formerly blocked by separate promotion structures; some who had left on marriage returned for the war. Afterwards, many kept their jobs and, with the return of full male employment and continued expansion, openings multiplied. Key features after the Second World War were a rapid rise in the number of white-bloused workers, surpassing men, and the introduction of far more married women as marriage bars fell. Gradually more women reached administrative levels, though the 'glass ceiling' continued to restrict opportunities, while they slowly gained some parity with men over pay and conditions. The technological explosion altered the character of the workplace, adding new twists to what are very durable constructs about gender and technology. Patterns of career breaks and part-time work coloured the texture of the white-bloused world. A rise in married women's work marked the post-war workforce, especially women 'returners' who took career breaks. White-collar work was no longer the preserve of men, the young unmarried and 'spinsters'.

Segregation was a feature of the workplace. Within retail, men worked where training was required, where goods were expensive, or where work was rough and heavy; women predominated in light and untrained work with low pay. Of course, pay was low because they were women. Men retained strong continuity between the artisan and the new salesman. Thus they sold jewellery, women's gloves and stockings, and were butchers and fishmongers, while women sold provisions and women's clothes. Women's growing experience and good record as managers during the First World War helped them gain higher status responsible posts and, in 1930s London, female buyers outnumbered men. Nevertheless, segregation persisted. In the 1980s, men still held top jobs in management, training and stock control, and dominated departments with expensive or bulky consumables. Women, more visible on display counters, sold to women.

The desire to preserve exclusivity created structural and cultural barriers that limited access and promotion for women in professions. Suzanne Borel made a highly publicised entry to the French Diplomatic Service, but was not allowed to undertake consular duties abroad 'on account of having no political rights'. She reflected: 'Few women are better placed than I to appreciate the cunning, often combined with treachery and persistence, employed by men to place obstacles in the path of those unfortunate women who stray from the beaten track.'[142] Simply preventing women's entry was more effective than arguing they were inappropriate members, and law and medicine simply prohibited them, until statutes, regulations and attitudes changed. Thus perceptions of what it meant to be female were joined with protectiveness of traditionally male professions to restrict not only women's entry, but their movement within them.

Women proactively claimed white-collar work. Feminists saw these jobs as liberation, opportunity and independence, and there were far more applicants than jobs. Paquet-Mille's, *Nouveau guide pratique des jeunes filles dans le choix d'une profession (New Practical Guide for Girls in the Choice of a Profession)* argued: 'The French woman . . . has understood that she will attain her true social freedom only by knowledge and work.'[143] They claimed typewriting as suitable, even relying on stereotypes:

'Women as a rule are quick workers; . . . and a sedentary occupation being suitable to them, they can perfectly work well for long hours when necessary.'[144] As new work, it avoided competition with men, and promised respectable prospects for middle-class women. Strict discipline and sexually segregated employment were positive features, and typists took considerable pride in work. Jo Brouwer, a Dutch typist, exclaimed, 'I was as happy as Larry and thought it truly made an impression when, with an aristocratic air, I announced that I had now become an office gentleman [*sic*].'[145] Weimar shop assistants regarded themselves as 'a cut above' factory workers who 'did not know how to behave', while clerks and secretaries regarded themselves as above shop assistants, because their work was more worthwhile and better remunerated.[146] Women's entry was not uncontested, but it is important that women perceived clerking as a viable option, that they were not simply 'recruited' or 'introduced' but that many voices claimed white-collar work for them at a time when the workplace was undergoing radical redefinition.

Women's manufacturing work involved the production of lighter, smaller articles, often in a mechanised or automated setting, usually routine, boring and part of a fragmented work process. The fact that it was paid less than men's work is a virtual truism that had as much to do with the worker as the work. There is a clear link between the attributes of women accustomed to sewing piecework to the new assembly processes. The relationship of women to machines was not straightforward. On the one hand mechanisation supposedly allowed more women to be employed and to replace skilled, and expensive, men. On the other, women were not supposed to understand the machines and were only there to tend and operate them. Yet machinery could be used to determine both 'skill' and 'deskilling', and often provided an opportunity to regender work. Indeed, women's work cannot be disentangled from their sex, since perceptions of what women could do were inextricably tied to what employers and male workers perceived women to be. Specialisation was common in manufacturing, but also typified white-collar work, where it helped to solidify hierarchical structures, restricting promotion between levels. Tasks and ranks became more closely associated with different levels of education, and bridging the gaps became more difficult.

Natural difference between men and women formed the focus of views of women as workers across the working world. Work was contested on two levels. First, what was appropriate for women to do to retain their gentility with regard to mixing with men, and whether to work or not; and second, what abilities and character women had and what they were capable of. So, while white-collar work was 'suitable' for females, particularly middle-class women with no means of support, careful decisions were made about where they worked, such as those first working in French urban post offices. They were not placed in working-class areas nor near railway stations, which were unsuitable for 'naturally high strung' women.[147] In the dispute surrounding Norwegian women telegraphers' fight for equal pay in 1898, gender was invoked to women's disadvantage. The Director reported that women were less competent than men, particularly on complicated equipment and in technical aspects of the work, despite equal training, equal workloads and, on the whole, better marks on training courses. One anonymous female telegrapher retorted, 'The primary reason why female telegraphers manifest little interest in the technical aspects of their work is that our lords and masters, men, have since time immemorial regarded themselves as the only ones competent in this field.'[148] Within the tertiary sector women and men were separated, occupationally and physically, by practices of segregation and stratification. Pay scales and grading were designed so as to provide two quite separate gendered hierarchies, preventing women from moving into administrative and higher-grade work. Although professions and careers opened, 'the glass ceiling' tended to operate an unwritten rule preventing women from reaching the highest echelons. One of the debates throughout the period was 'equal pay for equal work', but where that was achieved, other forms of discrimination operated to prevent the equal participation of women in work. Not the least of these is that women were still not perceived first as workers. Masculinity is tied up with men's work, while women's femininity is still tied to her domestic role. It was not all promise and success, but the shift in kinds of work and new opportunities were important milestones for women.

Conclusion

Women worked across the economic spectrum, in most types of workplaces and settings and, throughout the past three centuries, have been central to the economy and to household support. In this time, there were important changes, as the economy shifted from a largely agrarian one with most workplaces dispersed and located in or near homes to one where the workplace and the home are usually quite separate. This however, is less true than we think, with the number of homeworkers, from those assembling Christmas crackers in their kitchens or knitting for the market to academics writing in bedrooms and studies or women running small businesses from home or offering bed and breakfast. The shape of work is different, since most women work in an urban economy and most work is centralised. Women's work in the countryside is less agricultural and more likely to be service based than it was in 1700, and industrial work is more likely to be in factories. New light industries largely replaced textiles. Service shifted from farm service to domestic service and then took on a whole new meaning as the white-bloused sector provided new opportunities for women.

The demographics of the workforce also changed. From a position where almost all females worked regardless of marital status and age (except for the very elite – depending on how you define work), by the end of the twentieth century, the very youngest were more likely to be in school. Married women have always worked, but their work increasingly became hidden and less recognised as work during the nineteenth century. Many continued to work however, either before and after having children, or by devising work strategies that allowed them to juggle children and work, such as taking in washing or homework. In the twentieth century, housework shifted so that it could take up as little or as much time as women wanted – except in times of stress such as during the wars, when what had to be done was done. In the second half of the century, married women became increasing likely to stay at work until children were born and to return after the youngest reached school age. Many took only statutory maternity leave and returned to work quickly. Single women worked both home and away, so to speak, though the domestic ideal affected middle-class girls significantly. This was precisely the group that pursued the goal of higher education and worthwhile jobs and careers. A mobile group, single women worked before marriage often to save for marriage, but always a significant number of women remained single, either out of choice or circumstance. In the eighteenth and nineteenth centuries, broadly speaking, these women could struggle to survive. With low pay, sometimes dependants to support and the assumptions that women would marry, they utilised a range of strategies and hard work to manage, including joining forces, forming partnerships and sharing costs. Widows fared best if they retained some capital, maybe a trade they had shared with a husband and some 'social capital'. As wages rose and as more opportunities opened, particularly for educated single women, marital status became less significant in defining the working woman.

Ideas about who was or was not a worker affected whether women could work, what kind of work was truly accessible to them and why and where they were hired. Women were perceived as having a cluster of skills and characteristics, which suited them for particular kinds of work. They were seen as amenable, quiescent and subservient; they were dexterous and patient. Thus, fiddly work that could include everything from weeding and tying up peas and hops to spinning, calico-printing and sewing were therefore appropriate women's work. Men claimed high status work, whether working with horses to managing and supervising others. Needless to say, these stereotypes relied largely on perceptions of women as women and men as men, not on actual abilities. Men's taking over mowing with scythes is a pertinent example. Supposedly women were unable to handle this heavy implement, but they were able to cart manure on their backs and to carry water to terraces and, indeed, to use other mowing tools that were equally heavy.

Women's work was thus often defined in terms of attributes associated with skill and expertise or ones that related to 'men in charge'. Men tended to believe they had a right to certain work and particularly to work that defined their standing and status, their place as men, that is, their masculinity. Women frequently appeared to acquiesce in these definitions, particularly women who were prepared to take whatever work was available and at whatever wage to ensure that they could contribute to household support or to support themselves. But this probably underestimates the decisions that women made in taking work. We know from testimony sprinkled throughout the period that many women liked working, and that they even enjoyed work that was hard. They also resented soul-destroying, body-breaking work, such as pulling mangolds. But they could be strategic and entrepreneurial, choosing, within the options open to them, when and where they would work and what they were prepared to do. Women alternated domestic service with factories; some left service for sewing; they claimed the typewriter and the work associated with it; they moved to factories with spinning, or they took up something else; they rejected domestic service for shops. They fought for education, breaking bourgeois ideas of femininity and demanded professional status. So while women were often not seen as workers, but as working women, women cast themselves as women workers.

Guide to further reading

Abensour, Léon, *La Femme et le féminisme en France avant la révolution*. Geneva: Slatkine-Maganotis, 1923; 1966. The classic history of French women of the *ancien régime* with discussion of work and guilds.

Berg, Maxine, *The Age of Manufactures: Industry, Innovation and Work in Britain, 1700–1820*. London: Routledge, 1994. Key study on eighteenth-century manufacturing that embeds women and their significance into processes of industrialisation, exploring a range of domestic industries.

Bradley, Harriet, *Men's Work, Women's Work*. Oxford: Polity Press, 1989. Good overview of men and women's work in Britain, dealing with specific areas of work.

Cammarosano, Simonetta Ortaggi, 'Labouring Women in Northern and Central Italy in the Nineteenth Century', in *Society and Politics in the Age of the Risorgimento*. Davis, John A. and Paul Ginsborg, eds, pp. 152–83. Cambridge: University of Cambridge Press, 1991. Excellent regional study.

Canning, Kathleen, *Languages of Labor and Gender: Female Factory Work in Germany, 1850–1914*. Ithaca, NY: Cornell University Press, 1996. Focuses on the changing meanings of women's work in Germany during the shift from agrarian to the industrial state, with emphasis on gender, rhetoric and imagery as well as women's self-perceptions.

de Groot, Gertjan and Marlou Schrover, eds, *Women Workers and Technological Change in Europe in the Nineteenth and Twentieth Centuries*. London: Taylor & Francis, 1995. Excellent collection with good geographic coverage, including Scandinavia and the Netherlands, focusing on the relationship between women and technology.

Duchen, Claire, *Women's Rights and Women's Lives in France, 1944–1968*. London: Routledge, 1994. Situates work in debates about women's place and women's rights in post-war France.

Engel, Barbara Alpern, *Between the Fields and the City: Women, Work and Family in Russia, 1861–1914*. Cambridge: Cambridge University Press, 1996. Examines the significance of Russian peasant women's migration from villages to factories and cities.

Farnsworth Beatrice and Lynne Viola, eds, *Russian Peasant Women*. Oxford: Oxford University Press, 1992. An important collection of articles, several directly on work, others contextualising it in the lives of peasant women before and after the revolution.

Frader, Laura L. and Sonya O. Rose, eds, *Gender and Class in Modern Europe*. Ithaca, NY and London: Cornell University Press, 1996. A superb collection of articles addressing gender and work.

Franzoi, Barbara, *At the Very Least She Pays the Rent: Women and German Industrialization, 1871–1914*. London and Westport, Conn.: Greenwood Press, 1985. Examines the relationship between female labour and production processes focusing on women at the intersection of work and family.

Glucksmann, Miriam, *Women Assemble: Women Workers and New Industries in Inter-War Britain*. London: Routledge, 1990. Detailed study of the new industries with good insights on workplace relationships and the culture of women as workers.

Gordon, Eleanor and Esther Breitenbach, eds, *The World is Ill Divided: Women's Work in Scotland in the Nineteenth and Early Twentieth Centuries*. Edinburgh: Edinburgh University Press, 1990. Path-breaking collection of articles on women's work in Scotland.

Gullickson, Gay, L., *Spinners and Weavers of Auffay*. Cambridge: Cambridge University Press, 1986. Detailed regional study of workers during the transition from domestic industry to factory work; explores negotiations between male and female roles.

Hausen, Karin, ed., *Frauen Suchen Ihre Geschichte*. Munich: Verlag C. H. Beck, 1987. Excellent collection of articles on German women; articles by Ellerkamp and Jungmann, Meyer, Schulte and Wierling relate to home and work.

Hilden, Patricia Penn, *Women, Work and Politics: Belgium 1830–1914*. Oxford: Clarendon Press, 1993. Good insights to women's work in Belgium, especially issues of the factory.

Hill, Bridget, *Women, Work and Sexual Politics in Eighteenth-Century England*. Oxford: Basil Blackwell, 1989. Detailed empirical survey that takes a life-cycle approach to women's work.

Hudson, Pat and W. R. Lee, eds, *Women's Work and the Family Economy in Historical Perspective*. Manchester: Manchester University Press, 1990. Collection of thematically linked essays in which the authors challenge a view of history that sees women as participating in social processes defined in terms of male experience.

Hufton, Olwen, *The Prospect Before Her: A History of Women in Western Europe, 1500–1800*.

London: Fontana Press, 1995. This authoritative survey gives a well-rounded view of women in Europe.

John, Angela V., ed., *Unequal Opportunities: Women's Employment in England, 1800–1918*. Oxford: Basil Blackwell, 1986. Collection of articles on a range of women's work with a helpful introduction discussing overarching issues.

McBride, Theresa, *The Domestic Revolution: The modernisation of Household Service in England and France, 1820–1920*. London: Croom Helm, 1976. Slightly ageing, this is still the classic comparative study of domestic service.

Maynes, Mary Jo, Birgitte Söland and Christina Benninghaus, eds, *Secret Gardens, Satanic Mills: Placing Girls in European History, 1750–1960*. Bloomington, Ind.: Indiana University Press, 2004. A number of articles link girls' work to their experiences of growing up, leisure and sexuality.

Mouvement Social, 1987, 140. A special issue on work, particularly useful for nineteenth- and twentieth-century France.

Ogilvie, Sheilagh, *A Bitter Living: Women, Markets and Social Capital in Early Modern Germany*. Oxford: Oxford University Press, 2003. An excellent detailed empirical study, including the eighteenth century, exploring the character of women's work and the factors that shaped it.

Pinchbeck, Ivy, *Women Workers and the Industrial Revolution 1750–1850*, 3rd edn. London: Virago, 1981. The classic study of women workers in Britain.

Quataert, Jean, H. 'The Shaping of Women's Work in Manufacturing Guilds, Households and the State in Central Europe, 1648–1870', *American Historical Review*, 90, 1985, pp. 1122–48. Important article analysing the issues of honourable and dishonourable work and the centrality of gender.

Reynolds, Siân, *France Between the Wars: Gender and Politics*. London: Routledge, 1996. Provides important insights to the interplay of work, gender and society in the inter-war period.

Rose, Sonya, O., *Limited Livelihoods: Gender and Class in Nineteenth-Century England*. Berkeley, Calif.: University of California Press, 1992. Argues that gender was a central organising principle of the nineteenth-century industrial transformation in England.

Sharpe, Pamela, ed., *Women's Work, The English Experience, 1650–1914*. London: Arnold, 1998. Incorporates key articles on Englishwomen's work, with linking commentary and integrating empirical and theoretical studies.

Simonton, Deborah. *A History of European Women's Work, 1700 to the present*. London: Routledge, 1998. A survey, it fleshes out the arguments of this chapter.

Tilly, Louise and Joan Scott, *Women, Work and Family*, 2nd edn. London: Methuen, 1987. Since publication in 1978, the classic account of women's work and its relationship to family in France and England based around three economic family formations.

Valenze, Deborah, *The First Industrial Woman*. Oxford: Oxford University Press, 1995. Important work examining underlying assumptions of gender and women's centrality to the economic development of England.

Verdon, Nicola, *Rural Women Workers: Gender, Work and Wages in the Nineteenth-Century Countryside*. London: Boydell, 2002. Accessible study that explores English rural women's economic opportunities contextualised by region, age, marital status, children and local custom.

Whelan, Bernadette, ed., *Women and Work in Ireland, 1500–1930*. Dublin: Four Courts Press, 2000. Collection of articles covering key areas of women's work in Ireland; useful overview chapter.

Willson, Perry R., *The Clockwork Factory, Women and Work in Fascist Italy*. Oxford: Clarendon Press, 1993. A detailed industry study with excellent insight into the work relationships in 'new industries' and the issues of work for twentieth-century Italian women.

Notes

1 *The Misery of the Working Classes* (1840) quoted in Joan W. Scott, 'L'ouvrière! Mot Impie, Sordide . . .': Women Workers in the Discourse of French Political Economy, 1840–1860', in Patrick Joyce, ed., *The Historical Meanings of Work* (Cambridge: Cambridge University Press, 1980), pp. 125–6.

2 Pat Hudson and W. R. Lee, eds, *Women's Work and the Family Economy in Historical Perspective* (Manchester: Manchester University Press, 1990), pp. 34–5.

3 Sheilagh Ogilvie, *A Bitter Living: Women, Markets and Social Capital in Early Modern Germany* (Oxford: Oxford University Press, 2003), pp. 1–16.

4 Alice Clark, *Working Life of Women in the Seventeenth Century* (London: Routledge, 1919); Ivy Pinchbeck, *Women Workers in the Industrial Revolution, 1750–1850* (London: Routledge, 1930); Léon Abensour, *La Femme et le féminisme en France avant la révolution* (Geneva: Slatkine-Maganotis, 1923).

5 Natalie Zemon Davis, 'Women in the Crafts in Sixteenth-Century Lyon', *Feminist Studies*, 81 (1982), pp. 47–80; 'Women's History in Transition: The European Case', *Feminist Studies*, 3 (1976), pp. 83–103; Louise Tilly and Joan W. Scott, *Women, Work and Family* (London: Holt, Rinehart & Winston, 1978); Olwen Hufton, 'Women and the Family Economy of Eighteenth Century France', *French Historical Studies*, 9 (1975), pp. 1–22; Ute Gerhard, *Verhältnisse und Verhinderungen. Frauen arbeit, Familie und Rechte der Frauen ins 19. Jahrhundert. Mit Dokumenten* (Frankfurt: Suhrkamp, 1978).

6 See L. A. Clarkson, *Proto-Industrialisation: the First Phase of Industrialisation?* (London: Macmillan, 1985) and Maxine Berg, ed., *Markets and Manufacture in Early Industrial Europe* (London: Routledge, 1991).

7 Olwen Hufton, 'Women in History: Early Modern Europe', *Past and Present*, No 101, p. 126.

8 Amanda Vickery, 'Golden Age to Separate Spheres? A Review of the Categories and Chronology of English Women's History', *Historical Journal*, 36, 2 (1993), pp. 402–5.

9 Maxine Berg and Pat Hudson, 'Rehabilitating the Industrial Revolution', *Economic History Review*, 45, 1 (1992), pp. 24–50.

10 Maxine Berg, 'What Difference Did Women's Work Make to the Industrial Revolution?' *History Workshop Journal*, 35 (1993), pp. 22–44.

11 Deborah Simonton, *A History of European Women's Work, 1700 to the Present* (London: Routledge, 1998).

12 Jean H. Quataert, 'The Shaping of Women's Work in Manufacturing Guilds, Households and the State in Central Europe, 1648–1870', *American Historical Review*, 90 (1985), pp. 1122–48; Merry Wiesner, 'Women's Work in the Changing City Economy, 1500–1650', in Marilyn Boxer and Jean H. Quataert, eds, *Connecting Spheres* (Oxford: Oxford University Press, 1987), pp. 64–74 and 'Guilds, Male Bonding and Women's Work in Early Modern Germany', *Gender & History*, 1, 2 (1989) pp. 125–37; Sonya O. Rose, *Limited Livelihoods: Gender and Class in Nineteenth-Century England* (Berkeley, Calif.: University of California Press, 1992).

13 Two excellent recent examples are Clare Haru Crowston, *Fabricating Women: The Seamstresses of Old Regime France, 1675–1791* (Durham, NC: Duke University Press, 2001) and Ogilvie, *A Bitter Living*.

14 Edward Higgs, 'Women, Occupations and Work in the Nineteenth-Century Censuses', *History Workshop Journal*, 23 (1987), pp. 59–80.

15 Katharina Schlegel, 'Mistress and Servant in Nineteenth-Century Hamburg: Employer/Employee Relationships in Domestic Service, 1880–1914', *History Workshop*, 15 (1983), pp. 60–77.

16 Peter Earle, *A City Full of People* (London: Methuen, 1994), pp. 188–9.

17 Amanda Vickery, *The Gentleman's Daughter: Women's Lives in Georgian England* (New Haven, Conn.: Yale University Press, 1998); Bonnie Smith, *Ladies of the Leisure Class: The Bourgeoises of Northern France in the Nineteenth Century* (Princeton, NY: Princeton University Press, 1981).

18 Deborah Simonton, 'Claiming their Place in the Corporate Community: Women's Identity in Eighteenth-Century Towns', *Women's History Magazine*, 42 (Autumn 2002), pp. 2–8.

19 Quoted in Ute Frevert, *Women in German History: From Bourgeois Emancipation to Sexual Liberation* (Oxford: Berg, 1988), p. 23.

20 *Seurasaari Open-Air Museum Guide* (Helsinki: National Board of Antiquities, 1996).

21 Christina Hardyment, ed., *The Housekeeping Book of Susannah Whatman, 1776–1800* (London: National Trust, 1987), p. 51.

22 Michael Maurer, ed., *'Ich bin mehr Herz als Kopf', Sophie von La Roche: Ein Lebensbild in Briefen* (Munich: CH Beck, 1983), p. 289.

23 Daniel Roche, *The People of Paris: an Essay in Popular Culture in the Eighteenth Century*, trans. Marie Evans with Gwynne Lewis (Leamington Spa: Berg, 1987) pp. 137–43.

24 Helen Simpson, ed., *The Waiting City: Paris 1782–88. Being an abridgement of Louis-Sebastian Mercier's 'Le Tableau de Paris'* (Philadelphia, Pa.: J. B. Lippincott, 1933), p. 78.

25 Vickery, *Gentleman's Daughter*, pp. 164–5.

26 Lesley Davison, 'Spinsters Were Doing it for Themselves: Independence and the Single Woman in Early Eighteenth-Century Rural Wales', in Michael Roberts and Simone Clarke, eds, *Women and Gender in Early Modern Wales* (Cardiff: University of Wales Press, 2000), pp. 193–4.

27 Sheilagh Ogilvie, *State Corporatism and Proto-Industry: The Württemberg Black Forest, 1580–1797* (Cambridge: Cambridge University Press, 1997), p. 82.

28 *Die Göttliche Ordnung in der Veränderungen des menschlichen Geschlechts*, quoted in Bengt Ankarloo, 'Agriculture and Women's Work: Directions of Change in the West, 1700–1900', *Journal of Family History* 4, (1979), p. 115.

29 Quoted in Rab Houston, 'Women in the Economy and Society of Scotland', in R. A. Houston and I. D. Whyte, eds, *Scottish Society, 1500–1800* (Cambridge: Cambridge University Press, 1989), p. 121.

30 Quoted in Heide Wunder, *He is the Sun, She is the Moon* (Cambridge, Mass.: Harvard University Press, 1998), pp. 18, 65.

31 W. R. Lee, 'Women's Work and the Family: Some Demographic Implications of Gender-Specific Rural Work Patterns in Nineteenth-Century Germany', in Hudson and Lee, eds, *Women's Work and the Family Economy*, pp. 52 and 52n.

32 Olwen Hufton, 'Women, Work and Marriage in Eighteenth-Century France', in R. B. Outhwaite, ed., *Marriage and Society: Studies in the Social History of Marriage* (London: Europa, 1981), p. 187; Gay L. Gullickson, 'The Sexual Division of Labor in Cottage Industry and Agriculture in the Pays de Caux 1750–1850', *French Historical Studies* 12 (1981), p. 187.

33 Quoted in Ian Whyte, 'Protoindustrialisation in Scotland', in Pat Hudson, ed., *Regions and Industries: A Perspective on the Industrial Revolution in Britain* (Cambridge: Cambridge University Press, 1989), p. 247.

34 Sir John Sinclair, ed., *The Statistical Account of Scotland, 1791–1799*, ed. Donald J. Witherington and Ian R. Grant (Wakefield: E. P. Publishing, 1982), pp. 315–16; Arch. Départ., Somme, quoted in Abensour, *La Femme en France*, p. 199.

35 Bays and says are types of wool cloth. G.B., Public Record Office, Board of Inland Revenue, Apprenticeship Registers, 1710–1808, Vol. 53; Essex Record Office, Chelmsford D/P 96/14, Halstead Parish Apprenticeship Indentures.

36 Keele University Library, Wedgwood Archives 46–29123; 95–17476 to 95–17510; 29111–46 to 29245–46; 133–26816.

37 Quoted in William Reddy, *The Rise of Market Culture: The Textile Trade and French Society, 1750–1900* (Cambridge: Cambridge University Press, 1984), p. 31.

38 Sheilagh Ogilvie, 'Women and Proto-Industrialisation in a Corporate Society: Württemberg Woollen Weaving, 1590–1760', in Hudson and Lee, eds, *Women's Work and the Family Economy*, pp. 84–5, 88–9.

39 Hufton 'Women and the Family Economy', pp. 14–15.

40 ibid., p. 13.

41 Whyte, 'Protoindustrialisation in Scotland', pp. 242, 247.

42 *Aberdeen Journal*, 3 October 1758; Ogilvie, *State Corporatism*, p. 311; *Helsinki 1700, Narinnka 1995* (Helsinki: Helsinki City Museum, 1995).

43 Daniel Defoe, *Complete English Tradesman* (London: Augustus M. Kelly, 1969), pp. 33, 132.

44 James Lackington, *Memoirs of the First 45 Years of the Life of John Lackington* (London: Garland Reprint, 1974), p. 326.

45 Arlette Farge, *Fragile Lives: Violence, Power and Solidarity in Eighteenth-Century Paris* (London: Polity, 1993) pp. 114–15. See Robert Darnton, *The Great Cat Massacre and other Episodes in French Cultural History* (London: Penguin, 1991).

46 Olwen Hufton, 'Women without Men: Widows and Spinsters in Britain and France in the Eighteenth Century', *Journal of Family History*, 9 (1984), pp. 364–5.

47 H. C. Robbins Landon, *Haydn: The Symphonies (36–48)* (London: Decca, 1972), p. 9; Wunder, *He is the Sun*, p. 92; Alistair J. Mann, 'Embroidery to Enterprise: The Role of Women in the Book Trade of Early Modern Scotland', in Elizabeth Ewan and Maureen Meikle, eds, *Women in Scotland, c.1100–c.1750* (East Linton: Tuckwell, 1999), pp. 142–5.

48 *Aberdeen Journal*, 11 June 1764.

49 Simonton, 'Education and Training', Appendix 5.8.

50 Crowston, *Fabricating Women*, p. 408–9.

51 *Aberdeen Journal*, 1 August 1758.

52 Luckenbooths were small, often semi-temporary, shops frequently run by women. Wunder, *He is the Sun*, p. 91.

53 *Narinnka*, p. 246.

54 Pamela Sharpe, 'Dealing with Love: The Ambiguous Independence of Single Women in Early Modern England', *Gender & History*, 11, 2 (July 1999), pp. 209–32.

55 Quoted in Elizabeth C. Sanderson, *Women and Work in Eighteenth-Century Edinburgh* (London: Macmillan, 1996), p. 39.

56 Sølvi Sogner, '". . . A Prudent Wife is from the Lord." The Married Peasant Women of the Eighteenth Century', *Scandinavian Journal of History*, 9, 2 (1984), pp. 125–6.

57 Leonore Davidoff, 'The Rationalisation of Housework', in Diana Leonard Barker and Sheila Allen, eds, *Dependence and Exploitation in Work and Marriage* (London: Longman, 1976), p. 123.

58 Dorothee Wierling, '"Ich hab meine Arbeit gemacht – was wollt sie mehr?" Dienst Mädchen im städtischen Haushalt der Jahrhundertwende', in Karin Hausen, ed., *Frauen Suchen ihre Geschichte* (Munich: Verlag C. H. Beck, 1987) p. 146; Cécile Dauphin, 'Single Women', in Geneviève Fraisse and Michelle Perrot, eds, *A History of Women in the West*, Vol. IV, *Emerging Feminism from Revolution to World War*, (Cambridge, Mass.: The Belknap Press, 1993), p. 433; P. Bairoch et al., *The Working Population and its Structure* (Brussels: Université Libre de Bruxelles, 1968).

59 Schlegel, 'Mistress and Servant', p. 75; Dauphin, 'Single Women', p. 433.

60 Leonore Davidoff and Catherine Hall, *Family Fortunes: Men and Women of the English Middle Class, 1780–1850* (London: Hutchinson, 1987), p. 389.

61 'Madame Elise Blanc' in Erna Olafson Hellerstein, Leslie Parker Hume and Karen Offen, eds, *Victorian Women: A Documentary Account of Women's Lives in Nineteenth-Century England, France and the United States* (Brighton: Harvester Press, 1981) p. 347.

62 Schlegel, 'Mistress and Servant', pp. 60–3.

63 Smith, *Ladies of the Leisure Class*, p. 76.

64 Simonetta Ortaggi Cammarosano, 'Labouring Women in Northern and Central Italy in the Nineteenth Century', in John A. Davis and Paul Ginsborg, eds, *Society and Politics in the Age of the Risorgimento* (Cambridge: Cambridge University Press, 1991), p. 175.

65 Judy Lown, *Women and Industrialization: Gender at Work in Nineteenth-Century England* (London: Polity Press, 1990), p. 60.

66 Edward Higgs, 'Domestic Service and Household Production', in Angela John, ed., *Unequal Opportunities: Women's Employment in England, 1800–1918* (Oxford: Basil Blackwell, 1986), p. 136; Schlegel, 'Mistress and Servant', p. 64.

67 Schlegel, 'Mistress and Servant', p. 61.

68 James McMillan, *Housewife or Harlot: The Place of Women in French Society, 1870–1940* (New York: St Martin's Press, 1981), pp. 70–1.

69 Theresa McBride, *The Domestic Revolution: The Modernisation of Household Service in England and France, 1820–1920* (London: Croom Helm, 1976), pp. 60–4.

70 Extract in Hellerstein et al. *Victorian Women*, p. 295.

71 Margaret Darrow, *Revolution in the House: Family, Class and Inheritance in Southern France, 1775–1825* (Princeton, NY: Princeton University Press, 1989), p. 237n.

72 Wierling, 'Ich hab meine Arbeit gemacht', pp. 147, 157, 165–6; quote in Carol Dyhouse, 'Mothers and Daughters in the Middle-Class Home, c. 1870–1914' in Jane Lewis, ed., *Labour and Love, Women's Experience of Home and Family, 1850–1940* (Oxford: Basil Blackwell, 1986), p. 32.

73 Extract in Hellerstein et al., *Victorian Women*, p. 294.

74 K. D. M. Snell, 'Agricultural Seasonal Unemployment, the Standard of Living and Women's Work in the South and East', *Economic History Review*, 34, (1981), pp. 107–437. See the critique of Snell in Pamela Sharpe, *Adapting to Capitalism: Working Women in the English Economy, 1700–1850* (Basingstoke: Macmillan, 1996), ch. 4.

75 Gay L. Gullickson, *Spinners and Weavers of Auffay* (Cambridge: Cambridge University Press, 1986), pp. 53, 114–15; Donna Gabaccia, 'In the Shadows of the Periphery: Italian Women in the Nineteenth Century', in Boxer and Quataert, eds, *Connecting Spheres*, p. 171.

76 Alan Armstrong, *Farmworkers in England and Wales: A Social and Economic History, 1770–1980* (London: BT Batsford, 1988), p. 95.

77 G.B. Parliamentary Papers, Children's Employment Commission, 1867, 6th Report, XVI, pp. 91–2.

78 Patricia Penn Hilden, *Women, Work and Politics: Belgium 1830–1914* (Oxford: Clarendon Press, 1993), pp. 156, 171. They still harvest tobacco in France and celery in England.

79 Joanna Bourke, *Husbandry to Housewifery: Economic Change and Housework in Ireland, 1890–1914* (Oxford: Clarendon Press, 1993), p. 83; quoted in Lena Sommestad, 'Gendering Work, Interpreting Gender: The Masculinization of Dairy Work in Sweden, 1850–1950', *History Workshop Journal*, 37 (1994), p. 60.

80 Regina Schulte, 'Bauernmägde in Bayern am Ende des 19. Jahrhunderts' in Hausen, ed., *Frauen Suchen Ihre Geschichte*, pp. 118–19; Bodil Hansen, 'Rural Women in Late Nineteenth-Century Denmark', *Journal of Peasant Studies* 9, 2 (1982), pp. 227–31.

81 Lena Sommestad, 'Education and De-Feminization in the Swedish Dairy Industry', *Gender & History*, 4, 1 (1992), pp. 36–7 and 'Gendering Work, Interpreting Gender', pp. 59, 62–3.

82 Quote in Harriet Bradley, *Men's Work, Women's Work* (Oxford: Polity Press, 1989), p. 99.

83 Charles Weld, *Two Months in the Highlands* (1860) in T. C. Smout and Sydney Wood, eds, *Scottish Voices, 1745–1960* (London: Fontana Press, 1990), p. 88.

84 Douglas Holmes and Jean H. Quataert, 'An Approach to Modern Labor: Worker Peasantries in Historic Saxony and the Friuli Region over Three Centuries', *Comparative Studies in Society and History*, 28, 2 (1986), pp. 200–3.

85 Cammarosano, 'Labouring Women in Northern and Central Italy', p. 161.

86 Jean H. Quataert, 'Teamwork in Saxon Homeweaving Families in the Nineteenth Century', in Ruth-Ellen B. Joeres and Mary Jo Maynes, eds, *German Women in the Eighteenth and Nineteenth Centuries: A Social and Literary History* (Bloomington, Ind.: Indiana University Press, 1986), p. 12.

87 Lown, *Women and Industrialization*, pp. 28–9.

88 Tilly and Scott, *Women, Work and Family*, p. 113.

89 Quoted in John Holley, 'The Two Family Economies of Industrialism: Factory Workers in Victorian Scotland', *Journal of Family History*, 6 (1981), p. 64.

90 Hilden, *Belgium 1830–1914*, pp. 74–5; Lown, *Women and Industrialization*, pp. 36, 81.

91 Ellen Barlee, *A Visit to Lancashire in December 1862* (London: Seely, 1863), p. 32.

92 Elinor Accampo, *Industrialization, Family Life and Class Relations: Saint Chamond, 1815–1914* (Berkeley, Calif.: University of California Press, 1989), p. 89.

93 Louise Tilly, 'Three Faces of Capitalism: Women and Work in French Cities', in J. H. Merriman, ed., *French Cities in the Nineteenth Century* (London: Hutchinson, 1982), pp. 184–5.

94 Quataert, 'The Shaping of Women's Work', pp. 1135–43.

95 Joan Scott, 'Men and Women in the Parisian Garment Trades', in Pat Thane, Geoffrey Crossick and Roderick Floud, eds, *The Power of the Past* (Cambridge: Cambridge University Press, 1984), pp. 75–6.

96 Brenda Collins, 'Sewing Outwork in Ulster', in Maxine Berg, ed., *Markets and Manufacturers in Early Industrial Europe* (London: Routledge, 1991), pp. 141–2, 148–50.

97 Quataert, 'The Shaping of Women's Work', p. 1144.

98 Ottilie Baader, 'Factory and Home Work as a Seamstress', in Andrea van Dülmen, ed., *Frauen, ein historisches Lesebuch* (Munich: Verlag C. H. Beck, 1991), pp. 161, 162.

99 Stana Nenadic, 'The Social Shaping of Business Behaviour in the Nineteenth-Century Women's Garment Trades', *Journal of Social History*, 31, 3 (1998), p. 626.

100 Smith, *Ladies of the Leisure Class*, pp. 35–8, 43–8.

101 Darrow, *Revolution in the House*, p. 169.

102 Ibid., p. 160.

103 Davidoff and Hall, *Family Fortunes*, pp. 299–301.

104 Darrow, *Revolution in the House*, p. 171.

105 See Rogers in this volume, pp. 118–20.

106 Bairoch et al., *Working Population and its Structure*, Table C3.

107 Frevert, *Women in German History*, p. 260.

108 Bente Rosenbeck, 'Boundaries of Femininity, Denmark, 1880–1980', *Scandinavian Journal of History*, 12, (1987), pp. 49–50.

109 Marie Christine Allart, 'Les Femmes du trois villages de l'Artois: travail et vécu quotidien (1919–1939)', in Marcel Gillet, ed., *Histoire des femmes du nord*, special issue of *Revue du Nord*, 63, 250 (1981), p. 718.

110 Davidoff, 'Rationalization of Housework', p. 145.

111 J. Robinson, P. Converse, A. Szalai, 'Everyday Life in Twelve Countries', in A. Szalai, ed., *The Use of Time* (UNESCO, 1972), p. 125.

112 Cammarosano, 'Constructing Families', pp. 175–6.

113 Quoted in Deirdre Beddoe, *Back to Home and Duty: Women between the Wars, 1919–1939* (London: Pandora, 1989), p. 51.

114 Renate Bridenthal, 'Beyond "Kinder, Küche, Kirche": Weimar Women at Work', *Central European History*, 6, 2 (1973), p. 152.

115 Günter Golde, *Catholics and Protestants: Agricultural Modernization in Two German Villages* (London: Academic Press, 1975), p. 117.

116 Ida Blom, '"Hun er den Raadende over Husets øokonomiske Angliggender"? Changes in Women's Work and Family Responsibilities in Norway since the 1860s', in Hudson and Lee, eds, *Women's Work and the Family Economy*, p. 166.

117 Joaode Pina-Cabral, *Sons of Adam, Daughters of Eve: The Peasant World View of the Alto Minho* (Oxford: Clarendon Press, 1986), p. 83.

118 Annie Moulin, *Peasantry and Society in France since 1789* (Cambridge: Cambridge University Press, 1981), p. 188.

119 Pina-Cabral, *Sons of Adam, Daughters of Eve*, pp. 18–19.

120 Blom, 'Changes in Women's Work and Farming Responsibilities', p. 166.

121 Golde, *Catholics and Protestants*, p. 114; Davydd J. Greenwood, *Unrewarding Wealth: The Commercialization and Collapse of Agriculture in a Spanish Basque Town* (Cambridge: Cambridge University Press, 1976), p. 51.

122 Henrik Mørkeberg, 'Working Conditions of Women Married to Selfemployed Farmers', *Sociologica Ruralis*, 18, (1978), pp. 95–8; Arild Bleksaune, Wava G. Haney, and Marit S. Hougen, 'On the Question of Feminization of Production on Part-Time Farms: Evidence from Norway', *Rural Sociology*, 58 (1993), pp. 118–19; Hans Hillebrand and Ursula Blom, 'Young Women on Dutch Family Farms', *Sociologia Ruralis*, 33 (1993), pp. 179, 181.

123 Sally Shortall, 'Power Analysis and Farm Wives: An Empirical Study of the Power Relationships Affecting Women on Irish Farms', *Sociologica Ruralis*, 32, 4 (1992), p. 439.

124 Sue Stebbing, 'Women's Roles and Rural Society', in Tony Bradley and Philip Lowe, eds, *Locality and Rurality: Economy and Society in Rural Regions* (Norwich: Geo Books, 1984), pp. 202–5.

125 Mary Bouquet, 'Women's Work in Rural South-West England', in Long, ed., *Family and Work in Rural Societies*, p. 148.

126 Allart, 'Les Femmes du trois villages de l'Artois', p. 712.

127 Marie Johnson, 'Domestic Work in Rural Iceland: An Historical Overview', in Long, ed., *Family and Work in Rural Societies*, p. 171.

128 Alice J. Albert, 'Fit Work for Women: Sweated Home-Workers in Glasgow, c. 1875–1914', in Eleanor Gordon and Esther Breitenbach, eds, *The World is Ill Divided: Women's Work in Scotland in the Nineteenth and Early Twentieth Centuries* (Edinburgh: Edinburgh University Press, 1990), pp. 162–3.

129 David Owen, *Ethnic Minority Women and the Labour Market* (Manchester: Equal Opportunities Commission, 1994), pp. 49, 157.

130 M. J. Boxer 'Protective Legislation and Home Industry: The Marginalization of Women Workers in Late Nineteenth-Century and Early Twentieth-Century France', *Journal of Social History*, 19 (1986), p. 52.

131 McMillan, *Housewife or Harlot*, pp. 66–7.

132 Albert, 'Fit Work for Women', pp. 164, 166.

133 Sheila Allen and Carol Wolkowitz, *Homeworking Myths and Realities* (London: Macmillan Education, 1987), pp. 243–9.

134 Perry R. Willson, *The Clockwork Factory: Women and Work in Fascist Italy* (Oxford: Clarendon Press, 1993), pp. 11, 129.

135 P. Fridenson, 'Les Premiers Ouvriers français de l'automobile (1890–1914)', *Sociologie du Travail*, 21 (1979), pp. 297–325; Linda Grant, 'Women in a Car Town: Coventry 1920–45', in Hudson and Lee, eds, *Women's Work and the Family Economy*, pp. 222–3.

136 Willson, *The Clockwork Factory*, p. 103.

137 Sylvie Zerner, 'De la couture aux presses: l'emploi féminin entre les deux guerres', *Mouvement Social*, 140 (1987), p. 22.

138 Gertjan DeGroot and Marlou Schrover, 'Between Men and Machines: Women Workers in New Industries, 1870–1940', *Social History*, 20, 3 (1995), p. 295.

139 Bonnie S. Anderson and Judith P. Zinsser, *A History of their Own: Women in Europe from Prehistory to the Present*, vol. II (London: Penguin, 1988), p. 259.

140 Ellen Jordan, 'The Lady Clerks at the Prudential: The Beginning of Vertical Segregation by Sex in Clerical Work in Nineteenth-Century Britain', *Gender & History*, 8, 1 (1996), p. 71.

141 Carole Elizabeth Adams, *Women Clerks in Wilhelmine Germany: Issues of Class and Gender* (Cambridge: Cambridge University Press, 1988), pp. 14–15; Jordan, 'The Lady Clerks at the Prudential', p. 66.

142 Quoted in Siân Reynolds, *France between the Wars: Gender and Politics*, (London: Routledge, 1996), p. 95.

143 Extract in Eleanor S. Riemer and John Fout, eds, *European Women: A Documentary History, 1789–1945* (New York: Schocken Books, 1980), pp. 43–4.

144 Form Letter to Businessmen, Society for Promoting the Employment of Women, c. 1877, reprinted in ibid., p. 37.

145 Francisca de Haan, *Gender and the Politics of Office Work: The Netherlands, 1860–1940* (Amsterdam: Amsterdam University Press, 1998), p. 26.

146 Quoted in Frevert, *German Women in History*, p. 181.

147 Susan Bachrach, 'La Feminisation des PTT au tournand du siècle', *Mouvement Social*, 140 (1987), pp. 72, 78. My translation.

148 Gro Hagemann, 'Feminism and the Sexual Division of Labour: Female Labour in the Norwegian Telegraph Service around the Turn of the Century', *Scandinavian Journal of History*, 10 (1985), pp. 146–7.

6

WOMEN RELIGIOUS AND RELIGIOUS WOMEN

Faith and practice in women's lives

Pat Starkey

Introduction

Callum Brown has recently argued that by withdrawing their support for institutional Christianity and cancelling what he calls their 'subscription to [its] discursive domain' women have accelerated the inexorable decline of a centuries-old religious culture and moral consensus in Britain. He claims that in recent centuries Christianity in all its many and various manifestations attracted more female adherents than male so that their demonstrable flight from the churches since the 1960s has resulted in a dramatic drop in attendance at worship as they, the erstwhile most pious and most diligent members of all denominations, appear no longer to find relevance in Christian teachings and ritual.[1]

By so forcefully inserting women into the long-standing meta-narrative of secularisation – however that may be defined, and whether, indeed, it may be defined at all – Brown has added a further dimension to an already complex web of explanations for the quantifiable falling off in traditional British religiosity. His argument that a similar pattern of religious decline may be observed throughout most of western Europe is one with which many commentators would agree, even if they are willing to concur only cautiously, if at all, with his explanation of its causes. But the religious landscape of both Britain and Continental Europe has been enriched by more than one belief system, and it may be argued that as institutional Christianity has suffered a reduction in importance, some of the territory it has abandoned has been taken over by other religions and quasi-religions. The search for the numinous may not have been forsaken to the same extent as has loyalty to ancient traditions and institutions. It may also be seen in a wide variety of guises, including, for example, the rise of so-called New-Age movements, strongest in Europe and Britain, where Christianity is weakest. A particular example of the employment of presumed supernatural agents in attempts to understand and manage life's events may be seen in France, which has witnessed both a steady decline in church attendance and the emergence of as many as 40,000 professional fortune tellers. Can that transfer of function from a traditional to an unorthodox resource be described as secularisation? And, it may also be asked, to what extent is the cult of celebrity, so prominent a feature of European contemporary life, an attempt to fill a gap in human psychological experience? To take just one example, is it accurate to describe the phenomenon characterised at the time by the *Independent* newspaper as 'recreational mourning' at the death of Diana, Princess of Wales, a 'spiritual' one, as has so often been suggested? If such phenomena as fortune-telling and personality cults increase in the face of a decline in formal cultic practice, might it not be suggested that they represent a popular reaction to an increasingly irreligious culture and express an unmet psychological, emotional or spiritual need?

The term 'secularisation', therefore, may sometimes slip off the tongue too easily without the necessary careful nuancing. But, although it evades the imposition of a generally agreed definition, it remains a convenient shorthand for the decline in traditional religious belief and observance. Combined with the rapidly changing patterns of social organisation and shifting institutional loyalties that characterise most of Europe at the beginning of the twenty-first century, it prompts a number of questions for those interested in the history of women and religion. How did we get to this point? What effect, if any, has this process had on women? And what effect have women had on the process?

Most commentators would argue that the move away from conventional religious sentiment and practice is no new phenomenon but something that has been proceeding steadily over the past three hundred years, although it has accelerated during the past fifty. Many feminists have identified religion as a critical factor, perhaps the most critical factor, in the fostering of patriarchy and in the disadvantaging of women in relation to men, and have welcomed the benefits that decreasing adherence to some belief systems has brought. And if, as Hugh McLeod has reminded us, secularisation may be used as a catch-all description of the way in which modernisation has occurred in western Europe, then its close relationship to the increasing autonomy and opportunity for women that characterises the period, particularly the second half of the twentieth century, comes as no surprise.[2] But that still leaves unanswered a fundamental question: if religion has been so detrimental to women, why is it that during the past three centuries of European history, Christianity has continued to attract so many more female adherents than male? Even as recently as the 1990s, in a period of rapid decline in conventional observance in France, when fewer than 70 per cent of the population declared themselves to be Catholic and fewer than 10 per cent were observant, it has been estimated that women accounted for 75 per cent of the active membership of the Roman Catholic church.[3] In the same period, even churches that claimed to have reversed the trend towards decline and to have recruited new members exhibited a similar membership pattern. Male leaders of the Black-led, generally charismatic, evangelical churches in Britain have admitted that the percentage of women in their congregations ranged between 65 and 95 per cent of the whole.[4]

This chapter will consider some ways in which women have experienced religious traditions, practices and institutions during the past three hundred years, noting aspects that have been impugned as disadvantageous to women as well as those features of religious observance that women have found emotionally and intellectually satisfying. It will also attempt to assess the changes that have occurred in women's commitment. Although issues specific to Christianity will form the major part of our discussion, consideration will also be given to aspects of other numerically significant religions that have played an important part in the evolution of European culture and society, particularly Judaism and Islam. We will consider these within the chronological framework adopted in this book, but there will inevitably be some untidiness around the edges as developments spread themselves across our artificially imposed boundaries. This also means that our consideration of Islam in Europe will be confined almost entirely to the twentieth century. Within each period, three main themes will form the basis of the discussion: women for whom religion informed their way of life, whether or not this was lived within community; women in their domestic situations and the expectation that their role should be confined to the home and family; and women and their relationships with religious institutions, particularly those aspects of institutional organisation that sought to restrict female participation. As well as their exclusion from participation in cultic practices, consideration will be given to their propensity to feature in religious discourse as temptresses or as beings particularly susceptible to temptation.

Historiography

Much has been written about Christianity in Europe from its origins to the present day: both politically and socially it is tightly woven into the fabric of the European past and the impact of its institutions on every aspect of life has been an integral part of historical writing. During the past thirty years or so, the growing interest in women's history has enhanced this work by adding to it scholarly examination of the experience of Christian women. Selecting just a few for mention is an invidious process and inevitably will omit important contributions to scholarship, but among recent works that give us an overview of women's past, not just of their religious past, those by Lynn Abrams, Gisela Bock and Karen Offen demonstrate clearly the influence, for good or ill, that Christianity and Christian institutions have exerted on women's lives.[5] The work of Callum Brown, already mentioned, has drawn attention to issues relating to women and Christianity, and sociologists of religion such as Steve Bruce, Malcolm Cook and Grace Davie have greatly added to our understanding of more recent developments.[6] There is also a considerable literature devoted to European Jewry, and here, too, the growth of interest in women's history and gender history has prompted interest in the activities of religious women. In addition to the work of Abrams, Bock and Offen mentioned above, that by Ellen Umansky, for example, has contributed to our knowledge of the historico-theological context of Jewish women's experience, as has that of Jonathan Webber. Subject-specific web sites and discussion lists devoted to the study of Jewish women's past also proliferate.[7] Less has been written about European Islam, although there is a growing literature – an inevitable consequence of the generally increased interest in women's past but one prompted also by moves to understand and appreciate those new Europeans whose background and traditions owe much to distant cultures. The work of the Moroccan sociologist Fatima Mernissi and the Egyptian-born Leila Ahmed, although not dealing with geographically specific issues, have made significant contributions to Western attempts to understand Islam, its history and its demands on women. Yasmin Ali, another sociologist, and Anne-Sofie Roald, a Swedish convert to Islam, have also enhanced the discussion of contemporary Muslim women living in a Western culture.[8] Much of the literature originates in the work of Muslim women who are conscious of the impact that the politics associated with their religion has had on the wider political agenda. Ahmed and Mernissi, in particular, draw on their faith's historical roots in order to make its treatment of women comprehensible to a Western readership: it may well be that their confidence that they

179

can attract sympathetic and interested readers helps to enable them to challenge some of the traditions that have puzzled and sometimes alienated Western commentators. And the recent work by Haifaa Jawaad and Tansin Benn attempts a similar task.[9]

Although the more general studies have the merit of helping us to understand the importance of religion as just one aspect of women's experience, specialists focusing on women religious, on women reformers, on women whose faith provided the impulse for philanthropic work and on women who believed their mission field to be the home have further enhanced our insight. Web sites, discussion lists, academic conferences and symposia, supported by scholars from around the world and crossing national and language barriers, are witness to the importance attached to the inclusion of women in our efforts to reconstruct and understand the religious past and the inclusion of religion in the reconstruction of women's experiences.

Comparatively little has been written about the historical roots common to all three monotheistic religions, in so far as they affect women,[10] and in many ways, writing a chapter about Christian Europe would have been an easier task than attempting to take a wider view of the continent's religious history, and could have been justified as a study of the dominant religious culture as it has affected European women during the past three hundred years. But that would have been to distort the picture and to have failed to give proper weight to the experience of significant minorities of women, particularly since the nineteenth century. The result is an unavoidably superficial study – three hundred years and at least three major religious traditions cannot be examined within the compass of one chapter – but by highlighting areas of common experience it may be possible to demonstrate that, in spite of theological variety, women have frequently experienced in remarkably similar ways the blessings and the disadvantages of their faith and the institutions that seek to guard it.

The religious landscape of Europe

If the meaning and extent of secularisation has occasioned as much disagreement as agreement among commentators, the mapping of developments within European religious traditions since the beginning of the eighteenth century – a period characterised by considerable cultural, intellectual and socio-political change, and not unconnected challenges to religious faith and allegiance – also produces a sometimes untidy outline that requires careful qualification and definition. Although purporting to witness to unchanging truth, religion does not remain unaltered after contact with challenging theories or practices, and one of the characteristics of the past three hundred years has been religious fragmentation as a consequence of resistance to new ideas: the confusions and anxieties thereby generated have been compounded at times by a reluctance to disturb the status quo and by a degree of class-based angst. For example, the Enlightenment of the eighteenth century, often credited with, or blamed for, the injection of a degree of scepticism towards religion was an elitist movement, directly affecting only small groups of intellectuals, some of whom were anxious to keep it that way, imagining that their new ideas might have unsettling effects on the existing order. The story of Voltaire's wish that his wife and servants should continue to believe in God is well known but still instructive. Although he had abandoned religious belief himself, he recognised that their faith inspired in members of his household a morality that protected him and his property, and he was anxious that it should not be upset.

But as literacy spread and the lower classes could no longer so easily be protected from material that might disrupt their belief systems, Christians of all classes had to become more open to both philosophical and scientific advance, and sometimes to allow the incorporation of once unacceptable ideas into orthodox belief and praxis. But, as Owen Chadwick has reminded us, this presented no long-lasting difficulty. Christian theology and ecclesiology has always shown itself capable of adjusting to new knowledge. 'When a theory could be shown to be well-founded [churches] hesitated and cast regretful glances backward, but accepted it because it was true and soon were again serene.'[11] Scientific observation and discovery is but one area where this has occurred. As we consider the changing relationship between women and religious institutions, specifically Jewish and Christian ones, we may also observe an occasionally reluctant but nevertheless inexorable move towards the acceptance of 'modern' attitudes to women in all areas of life, as changing ideas about women's role in society have been shown to be 'well founded' and to challenge long-held perceptions about their role within and outwith religious organisations.

Although Christianity has been the dominant European religion since late Roman times, the history of the continent and its several religions is comprehensible only within the context of the wider world. Geographically and historically Europe has been and is increasingly linked with regions far from its borders, and the religions that flourish on European soil are witness to those connections. But the plurality that has resulted has frequently been an agent of difficulty, dissension and strained loyalties. Religion has constituted the major supra-local bond everywhere in Europe, binding together co-religionists and giving to religious adherence and loyalty the ability at times to strengthen and at others to threaten politically imposed boundaries. The resultant persecutions and wars of religion, or wars with strong religious associations, have been a frequent and are still an undiminished element in European experience, as the situations in regions such as the Balkans and Northern Ireland demonstrate only too clearly.

The European past and its culture, while deeply rooted in Christian history, has also been enriched by encounters with other religions, and in spite of sporadic tensions has been coloured particularly by contributions from Judaism and Islam. European Jewish communities have a long history. They have frequently suffered the disadvantages and discriminations that attach to minorities – they have been used and abused, valued and persecuted; in some situations they have sought to maintain their ethnic and religious distinctiveness, in others they have found it politic to assimilate to the host population. In modern Europe, such social assimilation only became possible after the emancipation of the Jews and the slow and uneven process of social acceptance.[12] The break-up of 'classical Judaism' in the eighteenth century meant that many experienced a loosening of ties with the ancient world view that had been fostered by their tradition and were challenged to reconceptualise what it meant to be a Jew. It has been argued that this sometimes painful process permitted the acceptance of Enlightenment ideas of humanity and universality and eventually led to a form of religious modernity that legitimated the adoption of a critical approach to historical sources and, in consequence, permitted questions to be asked about the relationship between the individual Jew's ethno-religious identity and his or her emerging national identity.[13] The forms such questions have taken have inevitably been determined by local circumstances and have resulted in sometimes surprising alliances. In France, for example, in spite of its hostility to religion, many Jews identified with the Revolution that had brought them citizenship. In nineteenth-century Germany many Jews, even if convinced Zionists, were keen to remain loyal to the state while attempting to cling to their ethnic identity; as J. Reinhartz has shown, only a minority were even tempted to go to Palestine until events after 1933 left few other choices open to them.[14] It was within this context that it became possible for some, but not all, Jews to reconsider their religion's traditional views about many aspects of life, including the treatment of women.

Islam also has a long European history, beginning with the conquest of most of the Iberian peninsula in the eighth century and extending its influence to Sicily, southern and much of coastal Italy and France. In the process, it made a vital, though sometimes little acknowledged, contribution to the economic, cultural and intellectual life of the whole continent. Although Muslims were finally ejected from the Iberian peninsula in the fifteenth century, pockets of loyalty to the faith persisted in other regions of Europe, most notably in the east and in the Balkans, the sites of other waves of Muslim expansion.[15]

This mosaic of differing religious loyalties across the continent has been further complicated by war and colonialism and by the migration and settlement patterns that followed in their wake, particularly during the twentieth century. In spite of attracting sporadic hostility and violence, thriving Jewish populations grew up in many European cities, only to be decimated by Nazi persecution, leaving small remnant communities. The post-1948 exodus to Israel further reduced an already dwindling population, although the number of Jews in France has since increased as a result of immigration from North Africa. By contrast, Islam has become steadily more visible since the mid-twentieth century. Once-colonised Muslim peoples from North Africa have been recruited as additions to the French labour force; Britain has been glad of the services of labourers from her former colonial possessions in the Indian subcontinent and the West Indies, thereby initiating a process whereby Muslim immigrants have been joined by adherents of other religions such as Hinduism and Sikhism as well as by local variants of Christianity. Migrant workers from Turkey have contributed to the diversity of the populations of Germany, Belgium and the Netherlands. To this mix, dominated by the Abrahamic religions, have been added other traditions such as Buddhism with memberships both immigrant and convert. The Nordic countries, too, have experienced a fundamental change in ethnic composition in the second half of the twentieth century, as immigrants, many of them Muslim, have begun to establish permanent communities.[16] Although the numbers are small, some have converted to Christianity, while some native Europeans have found religious satisfaction in Islam: a similarly statistically insignificant number of conversions between Judaism and Christianity have taken place.

Refugees and people granted asylum from life-threatening situations in their own countries have also contributed to alterations to the contours of the religious landscape. Italy, although historically an exporter of labour, has found itself the destination of choice for refugees and asylum seekers from North Africa and, more recently, from the Balkans and former Yugoslavia. Wars, social unrest and famine throughout the world have produced the tragedy of large numbers of displaced persons, many of whom have tried to gain entry into wealthy European societies in order to make tolerable lives for themselves and their families. The very diverse geographical origins of refugees, when added to those of longer-established communities, have had a profound impact on the European manifestations of the major monotheistic religions so that they exhibit a wide social, linguistic and ethnic mix, demonstrating what Anne-Sofie Roald has characterised as varied 'cultural base patterns' that have coloured religious conventions with associations of national or local customs.[17] These have sometimes acquired an almost ineradicable link with particular cultic practices so that the boundaries between local custom and religious practice have become confused and blurred, in some cases labelling as religious practices that are tribal, rather than theological, in origin. To take just one example, female circumcision, often wrongly believed to be an Islamic practice but in fact associated with a number of predominantly tribal, rather than religious, populations, may assume religious significance in some immigrant communities that, in the European situation, may well be Muslim. As Yasmin Ali has commented, in such circumstances, when a justification is demanded for some practice or belief rooted in 'ethnic' tradition, there is frequently a knee-jerk appeal to Islam as a means of avoiding having to face the question.[18] This, combined with the reluctance of host populations to gainsay what may be considered sacred to religious tradition frequently results in unspoken attitudes characterised by disgust on one side and defensiveness on the other.

Changes in the religious composition of local communities have received concrete expression in the built environment. As once-Christian populations have become less committed to attendance at religious services, and as newcomers have found it necessary to express their religious identity, so churches have closed and mosques have opened. In 1970, for instance, there was only one mosque in Italy. By the mid-1990s, the country had more than sixty mosques and about 120 Islamic prayer halls. A similar pattern may be observed in northern Europe. Denmark's first mosque was built in 1969, but by the 1990s between seventy-five and 100 buildings that could be classified as mosques were to be found there.[19] The experience of Italian and Danish cities is replicated throughout western Europe.

None of the major European religions is exempt from confusion and division, and the social and theological differences that each reflects often give rise to a variety of attitudes towards women. Christian churches and denominations are notoriously schismatic. The ancient divisions into eastern (Orthodox) and western (Catholic) versions of the faith have been further complicated in western Europe by the consequences of the Protestant Reformation and the later splintering of the Protestant churches into countless denominations and sects, adding colour and theological interest but giving rise to a long history of interdenominational hostility, only partly tempered by ecumenical activity in the twentieth century. Judaism, too, presents a far from united façade and the divisions between Jews, while frequently the topic of jokes that attempt to make light of them, in reality are serious theological or procedural differences. There are, for instance, marked differences in interpretation of Jewish religious law, culture and customs between Sephardi and Ashkenazi Jews, in part reflecting their geographical origins, and between Orthodox, conservative and liberal strains of Judaism, as a consequence of the uneven process of assimilation to western European culture. And Islam is similarly fragmented. Migration has produced different 'versions' of Islam, for example, reflecting the grafting of Asian or North African custom onto the Muslim root and producing practices that give rise to a range of different lifestyles and markedly different expectations of women's roles, all of which may in certain circumstances claim religious authority. This is in marked contrast to religions such as

Hinduism and Sikhism, whose memberships tend to be rooted in narrower ethnic and linguistic traditions and are, therefore, less likely to exhibit wide variations in practice.[20]

The variety of religious belief found on European soil is such that its impact on women, whether as members of religious institutions or in their individual experience, can be described and quantified in only the most general terms. Nevertheless, although it is clear that women have frequently found their faith to be an essential and deeply rewarding part of their experience, it is possible to highlight those areas of life which all religions presume to regulate and to identify examples where female adherents have suffered what they have perceived to be adverse demands leading them, in some cases, to question the roles they have found themselves expected to adopt.

Given so colourful and varied a mosaic of faith, is it possible to assess the extent to which religious experience has been important to European women – or, for that matter, to men – in the past three centuries? What measures can be used? As Gail Malmgreen has observed, mere membership of a church (or, she might equally have added, a mosque or a synagogue) or even observance of its rites and attendance at its services does not necessarily indicate either commitment or active support, still less inner belief.[21] If that is true of the nominally observant, might it also be true of those professionally religious women whose Christian commitment exceeded mere atten-dance and who chose to join spiritual communities, such as convents or lay sororities, thus making a public statement of adherence to a Rule and, it might be supposed, to a conviction that God had called them to a particular way of life? Even in those cases, the complex interplay in women's lives between belief, social custom, class and per-sonal circumstances combine to make impossible the quantification of anything so nebulous and intensely personal as 'faith' and 'religious experience'. Moreover, such evidence as we have is limited to the experience of a few women. It is impossible to dis-cover what 'ordinary' women thought or believed, and we are driven to have to work with such estimates as have been made on the basis of those written records – for example, registers, diaries and letters – that have happened to survive. But they are, by and large, records generated by or about men and women of relative importance, or with the ability to write, and cannot possibly be representative of the major part of a population which, even in our period, lacked the skills or the resources to create for the future a picture of their present. Nor, it has to be said, was much interest in their lives evinced until twentieth-century social historians began to pay specific attention to his-tory 'from below'. In the process, they uncovered women's past and initiated a series of discoveries that have increased as a consequence of second-wave feminism since the 1970s and the urge to include women in the historical narrative. Much has been recov-ered, but even so, their illiteracy or lack of social importance has allowed most of our foremothers (and forefathers) to become quasi-anonymous figures in a landscape largely peopled by others of their kind. Although our view of the history of women's religious experience is, therefore, necessarily a cloudy one, there is little reason to doubt that the perceived certainties of religion served many of the same functions in the past as they appear to serve in the present. They have supplied personal comfort and secu-rity in an unstable and unsafe world, offered meaning and explanation for daily life and have helped women to make sense of their experience within the perspective of an alternative and eternal reality. Moreover, at a practical day-to-day level, churches of all denominations have frequently provided almost the only relief from their domestic situation that some women could enjoy without attracting criticism. They have been places where family concerns could be shared with other women and where a range of prayerful and other overtly religious activities have taken place. In addition, as Tammy Proctor has noted in her contribution to this book, churches and other places of worship also provided scope for leisure activities for women; while their menfolk had many other opportunities for social life, frequently denied to their wives and daughters, women were able without censure to use the church as a meeting place.[22]

The eighteenth century: post-reformation/s societies

Women have frequently been credited with greater religious sentiment and commitment than men, but they have always been accorded less importance in the institutional manifestations of Christianity, which have always favoured male leadership and control. But in spite of this limitation, women have frequently employed church teaching and structures in order to position themselves within the wider scope of religiously inspired activities and to achieve a degree of autonomy. For example, women belonging to the Religious Society of Friends were active in relief work aimed at ameliorating the sufferings of prisoners and the sick from the mid-seventeenth century, many of those they helped being victims of persecution by both Cromwellian and monarchist governments in England. Elsewhere in this volume, Anna Clark has drawn our attention to those nuns who created a role for themselves in managing institutions that aimed to reform prostitutes through a strict regime of privation, regimentation, prayer and work and, as will be shown, during the nineteenth century this process of creating specifically female task-oriented space increased. During the eighteenth century, such work was not limited just to combating recognised social evils. Convents and monasteries had long-established teaching functions, generally directed towards boys intended for the monastic life or girls of wealthy parents. In addition, teaching orders, such as the Ursulines, which originated in Italy, were given official papal recognition in the mid-sixteenth century for the work of educating poor girls and were firmly established by the eighteenth century. Many other, often smaller and more locally based orders also helped to address hitherto unmet needs. Relief of poverty and care for the sick provided the impulse for the foundation of some orders. At the beginning of the eighteenth century, the Sisters of Charity in France provided nuns to work in at least 200 hospitals or institutions for the poor and destitute. By the 1789 Revolution, the number had more than doubled. They, together with members of other religious orders, whose congregations by then numbered about 55,000 women, were abolished in France in 1792, as were all male orders, and revolutionary antipathy to religion was further manifested in the public disrobing and whipping of some Sisters of Charity.[23] Resistance to actions of this sort by the revolutionary powers was, to a great extent, led by women who were reputed to have held more fiercely to their vows and their faith than were men: it was women who hid priests and provided secret spaces for worship, they who occupied churches and defended holy objects, and they who gave secret Christian burials to the dead and invoked the traditional saintly help for women in childbirth.[24] It was women, too, who in the early days of Revolution led demonstrations against attempts to destroy the conventional religious symbols that ornamented cemeteries.[25] While it is possible to suggest that this might have been informed as much by primitive and proprietorial anxieties that the last resting places of loved family members were being attacked as by a sense of outrage at the desecration of sacred monuments, religious sentiment attaching to the understanding of the nature of death and memorial may well have played its part. One consequence of the active resistance by women, whether professed religious or not, led, in Gisela Bock's words, to the feminisation of Catholicism and, because of the central role played by the Virgin in their demonstrations, to its greater Marianisation. This is a process which, it has been argued, accelerated during the nineteenth century.[26]

But however dramatic or significant their activities, whether they taught children, cared for the sick or devoted themselves to prayer and contemplation within an enclosed female space, women religious were a minority. Most women would have expected to marry and anxieties about the place of women in the home, and their relationships with men, have given rise to discussion and prescription in European churches throughout Christian history and particularly since the Protestant Reformation when, as Olwen Hufton has argued, traditional teaching that emphasised the importance of filial obedience to parents was interpreted to mean obedience to all hierarchies. Within the domestic arena, both Catholics and Protestants expected women to accept a subservient role. That churchmen found it necessary to inveigh against women's attempts to live parts of their lives outside the constraints of a patriarchally ordered household suggests that some challenge was being mounted to their essentially masculine interpretation of religious tradition and, by extension, to the priestly or ministerial authority of those who claimed to know the mind of God because 'the church of their persuasion was the repository of divine truth'.[27]

Although the debate is couched in Christian terms in eighteenth-century Europe, some light may be thrown on its origins by the Muslim sociologist, Fatima Mernissi, who has argued that the ideological underpinning of notions of inferiority is not unique to Christianity. She claims that all monotheistic religions, as inheritors of a common tradition, are shot through with the conflict between the divine and the feminine.[28] The seedbed for that conflict may be found in the Genesis creation myths, central to Jewish, Christian and Muslim constructions of woman. The notion that she was made after man, from man and for man's use is fundamental. Fashioned from one of his ribs, she was a late event in the creation process and was made as a helpmeet, although there are some significant differences between Judaeo-Christianity and Islam in the ways in which this has been interpreted.[29] The Hebrew Scriptures are accepted by Christianity as an essential propaedeutic for the Christian narrative and incorporated into the canon. Thus Judaism and Christianity have both made woman instrumental in man's fall into sin – 'the woman gave me of the tree and I did eat', Adam protested, thereby shifting primary responsibility for his failure to his partner.[30] This theme is taken up by the Christian Scriptures, with Eve made responsible for the Fall and the subsequent expulsion from Paradise. God cursed Eve before he cursed Adam and made her subject to her husband. The first epistle to Timothy is unequivocal: 'Adam was not deceived, but the woman being deceived was in the transgression.' This inequality then extended to other areas, the implication being that her responsibility for tempting Adam carried with it the penalty of silence and subjection.[31] The first epistle to the Corinthians carries the refinement that man is the image and glory of God, but that woman is the glory of the man, allowing the interpretation that woman, as well as being easily led, is a creature of a lower order – she, unlike man, was not made in God's image.[32] Although Mohammed was clearly familiar with some of the Hebrew myths, their appearance in the Koran is distinctive. There Adam and Eve are represented as being jointly responsible for transgression and its consequences, allowing Islam to claim that, unlike the other monotheistic traditions, it accords woman an essential spiritual equality with man.[33] But spiritual equality is a slippery concept. Both Catholicism and post-Reformation Protestant Christianity have made similar explicit claims for this notion of parity, although, as in Islam, in the practicalities of daily life any such ideal has frequently been of little effect. That women are accorded inferior positions in their relationships with men is rationalised by an appeal to an essential equality that, nevertheless, permits the imposition of divinely designed sex-specific roles for men and women. However great the potential theoretical differences between the three religions, they share a conceptualisation of womanhood that leads to similar treatment of women both within the religious institution and in wider society for much of the period from 1700: inferior beings, weak in the face of temptation and liable to tempt men, women must be protected and controlled.[34]

Traditional, conservative exegesis of all three sets of sacred texts defined women's essential roles in relation to men – they are made for men's delight and their responsibility is to cater to men's domestic and sexual needs. This assumption of female utility and consequent inferiority is, however, mitigated by the claim that women possess an inherent dignity, a superior essence, that is denied to men. For example, both male and female Jewish commentators argued for women's spiritual equality, while denying the exercise of that equality in any but the most limited way and demanding that women be restricted both spatially and religiously. Such arguments lay considerable emphasis on the glories and responsibilities of motherhood and the privilege of serving husband and family. Gerda Lerner has plotted a progression from the eighteenth-century patriarchal glorification of motherhood, with its roots in an ancient 'marginalisation of women in the formation of religious and philosophical thought' that allowed men to appoint themselves 'as the definers of divine truth and revelation', to its culmination in the nineteenth-century glorification of women's domestic role.[35] Small wonder that the developments in the twentieth century that have mounted vigorous challenge to nineteenth-century conceptions, whether they be religious or secular, have given rise to heart-searching as well as hostility.

The glorification of domesticity to which Lerner alludes has its roots in the Hebrew scriptures. The 'woman of worth' described in Proverbs 31:27, who has traditionally exemplified the ideal for the Jewish woman, rises before dawn and works tirelessly into the night to provide for her household and to assist the needy.[36] She has also been held up for emulation by Christian women. Although adhering to the traditional position as outlined in the Hebrew Scriptures, Christians have also used examples of Jesus's encounters with women in the Gospels both to underline the distinctiveness of their religion and to argue that its founder showed them a degree of consideration and respect that was unusual in first-century Judaic Palestine. It is noteworthy, however, that such commentators have frequently been content to overlook the fact that he declined to criticise those social structures that oppressed them.[37]

Thus, supposedly fully occupied with their household tasks, women who made excursions outside the home during the eighteenth century, especially if in the quest for greater intellectual stimulation, occasioned disapproval and anxiety and, sometimes, chauvinistic comment. For example, some few Parisian women – many of them Jewish – enjoyed the experience of the salons, in which both men and women met to discuss cultural and scientific matters. This met with unqualified disapproval in some quarters. As Linda Colley has pointed out, the conservative evangelical Christian Thomas Gisborne claimed that such women were the least eligible of wives, but that their sort was, fortunately, rarely seen in Great Britain.[38] While they may have wished to distance themselves from such nationalistic stereotypes, women frequently colluded with the conventional view of the dutiful wife, which was an important element in both evangelical and Catholic teaching and which was compounded in the early part of our period by an understanding of femininity that ruled out the possibility that women might demonstrate intellectual interests or abilities.[39] For instance, in the eighteenth century, Sophia Hume argued that women should not exhibit any interest in mathematics, science or philosophy, claiming that the result of such pursuits would engender pride and a vain mind – pride and vanity being the antithesis of truly feminine qualities informed by religious teaching, which stressed humility, subservience and, increasingly, domesticity.[40]

But if excluded from those scientific and cultural activities that were coded as masculine, some women attempted to increase their active participation in religion, also coded as masculine, albeit in a specifically feminine way that avoided posing an overt challenge to their exclusion from the performance of ritual associated with their cult. For example, Judaic law has traditionally assumed the male to be the normative Jew for religious observance; men have been obliged to obey all the commandments, but women have been required only to observe the negative ones. Women have, therefore, been relieved of such positive requirements as saying daily prayers (compulsory for men), with the result that religious education has been deemed essential for boys so that they are equipped to perform that function, but, by the same token, unnecessary for girls. Nevertheless, as Lerner has shown, many Jewish women in our period led satisfying religious lives, albeit quite separate from those of their menfolk. Evidence from the seventeenth and eighteenth centuries has revealed collections of prayers to be recited by women in the course of their work in their homes. Lerner suggests that this demonstrates a close identification for women between their domestic tasks, such as bread-making, and the spiritual activities of the men in the synagogue: the home was their, essentially feminine, place of worship. Synagogue worship could be left to men because women had created for themselves an exclusively female sacred space. This was reinforced by the requirement that the preparation of the traditional Sabbath meal, with all its attendant ritual, was traditionally a female duty that accorded to women an important liturgical role, even though it was confined to the safe and private space of the household. For some, appeal to the matriarchs, such as Sarah, Rebecca and Rachel, in their function as saviours of their children, reinforced the importance of women by celebrating their power as mothers to save the people of Israel,[41] but for some Jewish women this was inadequate to their spiritual needs. A short-lived movement in eighteenth- and nineteenth-century Poland and Russia, initiated by Hannah Rachel Werbermacher, tried to emulate male religious practice by constructing a parallel organisation. They practised all the customary religious ceremonies and adopted religious dress. This radical departure from tradition had limited appeal, however, and when the movement faded the women concerned returned to the home and to conventional practice.[42]

Like their Jewish sisters, most Christian women during the eighteenth, nineteenth and for much of the twentieth centuries were expected to adopt a non-participatory position in relation to religious services. They were reminded of the injunctions attributed to St Paul, that they should be subject to their husbands, resist any temptation to teach men and remain silent at meetings of the community. But some post-Reformation sects such as the Religious Society of Friends had among their membership women who were prepared loudly to protest that these were false readings of Scripture, and in this their founder, George Fox, supported them. A notable example of this defiant attitude was Margaret Fell. In the mid-seventeenth century, while in prison on charges of refusing to swear an oath to the king – itself a daring challenge to the relationship between the church and the state – she wrote a pamphlet entitled *Women's Speaking Justified, Proved and Allowed of by the Scriptures, All Such as Speak by the Spirit and Power of the Lord Jesus and How Women Were the First that Preached the Tidings of the Resurrection of Jesus, and Were Sent by Christ's Own Command before He Ascended to the Father* (John 20:17). Hers was a voice that had few echoes during the eighteenth century, but the strains were to be taken up a hundred years later by women of faith who believed themselves called to step outside the bounds of what had been traditionally allowed to them.

Another element in traditional teaching that is gradually subject to challenge in our period is that which states that women are a constant source of temptation and distraction. Some interpretations of the Genesis myth of the Fall have focused on the possibility that the temptation was a sexual one and have pointed to this as the origin of Christianity's unease about human sexuality. But it might also be argued that this unease owes more to Christianity's Hellenistic origins than to its Jewish ones; its almost Stoic emphasis, derived from St Paul, on celibacy and mastery of the body contrasts sharply with the celebration of human sexuality that can be detected in Judaism. The dangers that sexual expression held for spiritual growth had been enunciated in the early third century by Tertullian, who argued that a man was enabled to think spiritual thoughts only if he kept away from sexual contact with women. Other influential early Christian writers such as Jerome (*c.* 340–420 CE) and his near contemporary Augustine (*c.* 354–430 CE), perpetuate the repugnance felt for activity that results in the loss of control, for however short a time. Jerome, though, allowed himself mild dissent. He conceded, grudgingly, that sexual activity within marriage has some purpose – if nothing else, it could produce virgins. But why should sexuality produce such anxiety? Is it possible that the fear engendered by a basic biological function may well have been occasioned by men's anxiety about the power of their own sexuality and their inability to resist sexual temptation rather than any active attempts at seduction by the women they encountered? However complex its origins, the unease persisted and has been evident in the ways in which churches and churchmen have always interested themselves in the control of sexuality, particularly of female sexuality. It is common to all branches of European Christianity, from sixteenth-century Protestant reformers such as Luther in Germany and John Knox in Scotland, who believed that women should be controlled and kept under the authority of men, to twentieth-century popes who sought to regulate women's dress as well as their fertility. The need to control and regulate female sexual behaviour also intersected with the impulse to reform those women thought to be behaving inappropriately and to protect society from them, while it also was subject to pressure from religious women anxious to carve a space for themselves in activities outside the home. Like their sisters in mainland Europe, Irish Catholic nuns became involved in these reforming activities and established so-called

Magdalene homes in the mid-eighteenth century, where women thought to be guilty of sexual misdemeanours were given religious teaching and taught to be hard-working and subservient.

Women's danger to men lay not only in their ability to lead them astray but also in their power to render them ritually unclean. Purity laws, particularly those related to the 'polluting' effects of menstruation, are to be found in the traditions of all monotheistic religions. Formulated in the Hebrew scriptures, where, it must be acknowledged, they run alongside regulations for dealing with the potentially polluting effects of male sexuality, they restricted physical contact with menstruating women and required them to take ritual baths in order to cleanse themselves at the end of their period, a practice that is still followed by many Orthodox women. In their essentials, notions of ritual purity have been absorbed into both Islam and Christianity. Although influential churchmen such as Pope Gregory the Great (*c.* 540–604 CE) expressed some doubt about the necessity for menstruating women to absent themselves from church, women's access to religious buildings or to particularly sacred spaces was frequently restricted in the medieval and early modern periods and beyond in order to avoid the risk of 'contamination'. Similar restrictions on female access to holy places are to be found in Islamic practice. Menstruation mythologies, often linked to quasi-religious or magical beliefs have a history that extends well into the twentieth century. Childbirth, too, was deemed to require purification, with women believed to be unclean for a longer time after the birth of a female child than after a male. The 'churching' of Christian women after childbirth, originally a ceremony designed to cleanse women after parturition, although now generally metamorphosed into a service of thanksgiving for the safe delivery of a child and explicitly distanced from earlier practices by most churches, is still associated with notions of purification in some communities.

The eighteenth century, therefore, saw both continuity and discontinuity. Although attempts were made to control women and to deny them their own space, arguably one of the least women-friendly consequences of the Protestant Reformation, moves by women to break free from some of the restraints and to create for themselves opportunities for service are also evident. The Catholic Reformation, too, provided stimulus for action. As Rosemary Raughter has shown, Catholic women throughout western Europe responded to the spirit and teachings of the Reformation by aligning themselves with parochially based activities and by joining the emerging movement of lay, devotional and charitable associations; by this means they both expressed their Christian commitment in devotion and service and, in the process, developed a new and active, specifically female, apostolate.[43]

The nineteenth century: The age of feminine religion?

The process of moving out into more public areas of activity became unstoppable as Christian women claimed what they were convinced were the responsibilities of their religious commitment, whatever their denominational allegiances. By the 1870s, Catholic women involved in orders devoted to teaching, nursing and education outnumbered the combined forces of the clergy, both secular and religious. Raughter has drawn examples of the ways in which women internalised the teachings associated with the Catholic Reformation from Ireland, but the development of activities inspired by Christian teaching, albeit with different denominational and therefore theological emphases, may be seen in the deeds of other notable Christians such as Elizabeth Fry, a member of the Society of Friends, best known for her pastoral and evangelistic work in the dangerous and unpleasant world of early nineteenth-century prisons in London. She also engaged in more 'normal' activities for well-to-do women; she set up a village school, provided food and clothing for the poor and helped to vaccinate the children of the parish against smallpox.[44] In Germany, the Protestant Amalie Sieveking established the Female Association for the Care of the Poor and the Sick in Hamburg in 1832 in order to combine spiritual and moral assistance to the poor.[45] Concern to provide for the needy or outcast, for which unequivocal dominical authority could be claimed, provided a satisfying outlet for women whose comfortable social and financial circumstances allowed them to distance themselves from their domestic tasks.[46] But although later generations might applaud their courage and initiative, some contemporaries took a more jaundiced view. Both Josephine Butler, who waged campaigns against legalised prostitution in England, India, France and Switzerland, and Elizabeth Fry were criticised for neglecting their families, demonstrating only too clearly the contemporary expectation that married women should fulfil a private, domestic role and that involvement in 'political' or public activity, however laudable, was inappropriate.

Jewish women, too, found useful activity in philanthropic and educational work of various sorts. In 1872, Henriette Goldschmidt of Leipzig opened kindergartens for lower-class children, so that their mothers could more easily take up employment; at the same time, Betsy Park set up a women's club in the Netherlands which aimed to help women to use their needlework skills as a source of income. Lina Morgernstern of Berlin founded soup kitchens, as did Helene Mercier in Holland. No less than their Christian sisters, these Jewish women understood their activities to be inspired by the precepts of their religious faith. As Bock has shown, Bertha Pappenheim, the founder in 1902 of the Women's Care Club and in 1904 of the Jewish Women's League, gave unequivocal expression to the powerful link between spirituality and service in the numbers of prayers she composed, one of which was designed to be recited by the chair before a meeting.[47]

Although Protestant Christianity and Judaism inspired their adherents, it was Catholicism, as the dominant Christian tradition in the eighteenth and nineteenth centuries, that provided the motivation for most of the religious associations that flourished in Europe. Many of these were actively involved in teaching and in hospital work as well as in care for the poor, while contemplative orders attracted those women who believed that their calling was to the work of prayer rather than activity. They were joined by Protestant sisterhoods and orders of deaconesses, which began to appear from the 1830s, one of the most influential being that at Kaiserwerth, founded in 1836 in order to train women for nursing and social work on lines that were thought to resemble those of the early Church. In addition, a range of other charitable organisations owing their origins to faith and Christian principles must also be added to the roll. Like those of their Catholic sisters in active rather than contemplative orders, they frequently worked to alleviate forms of social distress. Nineteenth-century Christian Norwegian women, although denied a role in the administration of their churches, were permitted enfranchisement in the temperance movement and proved themselves to be active participants in the fight against drunkenness. The picture in Norway was as varied as elsewhere. Some radical Christian communities were prepared to allow women to take a fairly active part in the social outreach of the church, but it has to be noted that this was not universal. In spite of evidence that they were able and willing to make a valuable contribution to pastoral and evangelistic work, they were denied full membership rights of at least one Norwegian missionary society until as late as 1974.[48] The money they contributed to such work was, of course, gratefully accepted. But although they sometimes chafed under the limitations imposed on them, middle-class Christian women throughout Europe found ways to engage in a wide range of reforming and philanthropic activities, including the establishment of homes for 'fallen' women and orphanages, while their working-class sisters might find themselves recruited as Bible women. In cities such as London, their task was to visit the homes of the poor both to evangelise and to encourage improvement in their standards of housewifery.[49]

By contrast, some elements in German Protestantism, even its female wing – the League of Protestant Women – resisted any movement towards anything that could be perceived as emancipatory for women.[50] But this was not a necessary feature of Lutheranism. Trying to ease their way into the public sphere, some Danish women utilised the nineteenth-century cult of domesticity, which confined women's activities to the home and family, in order to rationalise their missionary work on behalf of the Lutheran church. Constructing themselves as society's housewives, they employed the metaphor of the home in order to argue that, just as they would not hesitate to clear the dirt from their domestic cellars, so they had a responsibility to clear society of the 'filth' of prostitution.[51] Such activities, whether performed by Catholic or Protestant women, have received differing treatment from historians. James McMillan and Karin Lützen have pointed to them as illustrative of ways in which women have been able to devise socially useful vehicles for the expression of their Christian commitment, at the same time as achieving a public role and in the process subverting traditional restrictive teaching. In contrast, Eric Hobsbawm has suggested that we need to examine critically the readiness of the Church to modify its position in relation to women's activities of this sort and to yield reluctantly to the increasing pressure from women to escape the restraints of domesticity. He has argued that the institution's support was bought at the cost of a continued commitment to subordination and a condemnation of the competing discourse of female emancipation, which was being offered by contemporary socialism. The church won. Hobsbawm has shown that before the First World War – a period when there were 'more female religious professionals than at any time since the Middle Ages' – the women who opted for the defence of their sex through piety and Christian service enormously outnumbered those who opted for liberation by secular means.[52] If that is the case, then we have to ask why religion was the more attractive option for participant women. Could it be that the old and familiar Gospel injunctions to love and service had been so successfully internalised that they could not easily be dislodged by new dogma, whatever its potential for personal liberation?

The personal satisfaction that women could gain from putting Christian teaching into practice could sometimes run alongside more earthly ambitions and serve useful social purposes, particularly for those families that aspired to influence and status. Leonore Davidoff and Catherine Hall have cited examples of early nineteenth-century evangelical family networks in England, particularly among clergy families, where women were used both to further family alliances and to satisfy the need for Anglican clergy to be married, thus marking clearly the difference between themselves and the celibate Catholic priesthood.[53] As in late medieval and early modern aristocratic and mercantile networks, mutually convenient marriage arrangements could be an effective way to satisfy family ambition, especially at a time when clerical status was high. But ambition for a good, and even financially advantageous, match must have been only one element in the attraction of a clergy daughter to a man in holy orders looking for a wife – and in the attraction of a cleric to a marriageable young woman. He would be rewarded with a well-trained partner who would almost certainly have internalised the current expectations of a clergy wife and mother and who would be ready to play her part in the mission of the church. From the woman's point of view, even though she was denied any official role, the social status she would gain would be augmented by the possibility of a potentially satisfying, if unpaid, occupation of a parson's wife.

Women who found meaning and fulfilment within church-based activities also provided the church with a degree of validation, female religiosity balancing institutional ambition. Karen Offen has shown that in both France and Germany in the mid-nineteenth century, the notion of women's difference from men and their dissimilar but equally beneficial involvement in communal life provided grounds for valorising the contribution that women could make. The Virgin Mary, whose importance in popular spirituality increased through the nineteenth century, provided a powerful resource for women, many of whom took their personal anxieties to her and positioned her at the centre of their devotional lives. It is not surprising that her miraculous appearances in the nineteenth century were frequently witnessed by women and girls, thus reinforcing the feminine element in Catholic belief by increasing the devotion to Mary. Simultaneously these visions gave both fame and a reputation for privileged sanctity to those who claimed to have seen her. If, in Lynn Abrams's words, 'the visionaries were using the church's construction of woman as the spiritual and pious sex for their own ends' the church, too, found ways to exploit the revived devotion.[54] Pope Pius IX, fleeing from the revolution in Rome in 1859, invoked its positive power when he called for the promulgation of the dogma of the Immaculate Conception of Mary – the notion that Mary was without original sin. The essence of this dogma was that sanctifying grace was given to her before sin could take effect in her soul, with the result that holiness, innocence and justice were conferred upon her and she was free from all depraved emotions, passions and debilities. Taken to its conclusion, the topos accords to Mary a form of perfection and freedom from sin already accorded to Christ and, it may be supposed, allowed women who emulated her submissive behaviour to bathe in the reflected rays of glorified womanhood. Little is known about Mary, but the mythologies that surround her stress her willingness to yield to the divine purpose and to play her part as a mother. In spite of some of the titles that have been applied to her, titles such as 'Seat of Wisdom' or 'Mother of Good Counsel', she was primarily extolled for her holiness and used to provide a model of womanhood characterised by maternity and domesticity rather than intellectual or worldly activity. As men defected from the church, the Pope hoped that by according enhanced recognition to the Virgin he would retain women's allegiance and harness the power of Christian mothers in its service. But the price of enhanced recognition was subordination, offered on terms that stressed the vital role that women as mothers could play in a project that emphasised the importance of the home in the education of future Catholics.[55]

The nineteenth century saw many changes in women's role and participatory activity within religious institutions, largely reflective of changes in society as a whole. In so far as these affected European Judaism, there were major variations in practice between different Jewish communities. Jewish schools that admitted girls began to be established in the mid-nineteenth century. This overturning of the traditional practice of denying education to girls was the result of activity by the Alliance Israelite Universelle, which argued for a better integration of Jews through the reforming of Jewish society and culture so that it was brought more into line with modern European society. This process extended to the training of women teachers, generally at the Alliance's school establishment in Paris.[56] The move to improve the quality of secular education was mirrored in some sections of Jewish society by the impulse to include women and girls in religious education. This was a consequence of assimilation to European society and accommodation to its mores, based on the conviction that Judaism was a historical religion in constant interaction with its environment, rather than an outright challenge to established practice.[57] It was the urge to consider the implications of greater assimilation that led the Frankfurt Conference of Reform Jews to establish a committee in 1845 to investigate the religious status of women. Abraham Geiger, one of the major philosophical spokesmen of the German Reform, and an articulate advocate of Jewish women's spiritual equality with men, argued in 1846 that the traditional position regarding Jewish women could no longer be upheld. As a result, some steps were taken to improve their position, as part of a number of measures taken in the formation of Reform Judaism: for the first time, women could be included in the quorum necessary for worship, the *minyan*; the benediction recited by men to express their gratitude to God that they had not been born women was abolished; formal religious instruction for girls was introduced; and, in the Reform synagogue in Berlin, women and men were seated on same floor during worship, instead of women being confined to the balcony, often sitting behind a screen. Some parts of the service were read and sung in German, in order to allow women to participate more fully.[58]

Like their Jewish sisters, most Christian women during the eighteenth, nineteenth and for much of the twentieth centuries were expected to adopt a non-participatory position in relation to religious services. They were reminded of the injunctions attributed to St Paul, that they remained subject to their husbands, did not presume to teach men and remained silent at meetings of the community.[59] But, unlike Judaism, where women's attendance at synagogue was not considered vital to their spiritual health and was, therefore, markedly lower than that of men in the mid-nineteenth century, historians of women estimate that church membership in England showed a persistent female majority of between 60 and 70 per cent.[60] Certainly, the 1851 religious census in England revealed that churchgoing was a largely female activity, and in the 1880s Charles Booth commented that 'the female sex forms the mainstay of every religious assembly of whatever class'. A survey conducted in the early years of the twentieth century by Richard Mudie Smith claimed that nearly twice as many women as men attended Church of England services.[61] The picture in the rest of Europe was remarkably similar. A study of Saxony in 1902 commented on the proportion of female churchgoers and fifty years later, in an Andalusian rural community, religion was seen as women's business.[62] By the end of the nineteenth century in France, women's attendance at the key services of the Catholic church greatly outnumbered that of men, and in Protestant Berlin at about the same time, women formed about two-thirds of the congregations.[63] Furthermore, what Abrams has called the 'feminisation of popular religion' in the nineteenth century is so dramatic as to demand comment.[64] As she has shown, in parts of Europe, notably France, Belgium and Spain, there was a huge increase in the numbers of nuns professed during the nineteenth century.

Across the English Channel, the ideal of the religious life exerted a similar attraction. By the end of the century, there were more than ninety women's sisterhoods claiming allegiance to the Church of England as very large numbers of women took advantage of this opportunity to express their faith. Like their Catholic sisters, many of them became involved in the work of rescuing women from prostitution and established institutions for so-called 'fallen women'. The Clewer sisters ran houses of mercy in their mother house in Berkshire and also in Soho, where William Gladstone took some of the women he had rescued from the London streets. These were representative of numerous organisations, frequently run by women for the reformation of other women and informed by an urgency to impose Christian standards on society.[65] Susan Mumm has argued that this received a guarded welcome from the Anglican Church hierarchy, which preferred deaconess orders to sisterhoods as channels for women's work because deaconesses enjoyed a reputation for obedience to episcopal authority. Women, however, appeared to have preferred sisterhoods, for the same reason – membership enabled them more successfully to resist institutional control. Sisterhoods, owing obedience primarily to their mothers superior, attracted considerably greater numbers than orders of deaconesses.[66] Nearly all were actively involved in socially useful work. In addition to reforming work with 'fallen women', sisterhoods ran orphanages and schools, provided skilled nursing staff for hospitals and engaged in innovatory missionary work in the poorest parts of English cities.

The state, too, involved itself in the work of reformation of women, although this took the form of regulation and, in England, the forcible gynaecological examination and incarceration of those suspected of working as prostitutes. This excited a variety of responses from churches. The Church of England supported it, to the fury of Josephine Butler. The wife of an Anglican priest, she perceived the flawed nature of legislation designed to reduce the spread of venereal disease by targeting women but failing to curb the activities of their clients. She was given greater encouragement by the Roman Catholic hierarchy than any in her own church for her attempts to persuade parliamentarians of the need to repeal the Contagious Diseases Acts in Britain and to fight against the institution of state-regulated prostitution in Europe, particularly in France and Switzerland.[67] She would have taken some satisfaction from the knowledge that the Church of England, which distanced itself from her activities at the end of the nineteenth century, claimed her as an Anglican saint in the twentieth!

In spite of the many reservations entertained by some church authorities, even the establishment of sisterhoods and orders of deaconesses did not challenge fundamentally the received views about women's subordination in the religious arena – neither sisters nor deaconesses attempted to usurp any priestly role, for example – but the more upfront activities of women were something different. Even the feisty Catherine Booth, wife of the founder of the Salvation Army, in nineteenth-century England, entertained some doubts about whether it was proper for women to be religious leaders, although she entertained no scruples about her right to preach.[68] And in spite of its commitment to egalitarianism, the Society of Friends imposed limits on the exercise of female power. Matilda Sturge, for example, found herself excluded from the main national governing bodies of the society, which limited their membership to men. This was despite her active involvement in the society's work as an energetic member of her local monthly meeting, her work as a teacher in the Quaker First Day School in Bristol, as superintendent of the Sunday School for Girls, organiser of a mothers' meeting, Clerk of her local women's monthly meeting, assistant clerk to the national women's yearly meeting and a member of the Quaker Home Mission Committee.[69] For those who believed that they had God-given gifts that they were ready to use in the service of the institution, the denial to them of the right actively to participate found its rationale in the nineteenth-century division of life into public and private, with women's role being located firmly in the private domain, reinforced by biblical injunctions that were read as giving divine authority to female silence and inactivity. In some cases an appeal to biblical authority barely concealed a vicious misogyny. Bjørg Seland has related how Bishop Johan Christian Heuch buttressed his argument that Swedish women should be barred from participation in all public life by appealing to the Scriptures and by warning against the dissolution of family life and the disintegration of morals, which he believed would result from the entry of women. He also added a note of mockery by inviting parliamentarians to imagine their mother being allowed to speak in the national assembly:

> Imagine the venerable lady in her pitiable falsetto holding forth with all the eagerness and fanaticism that so easily seizes the woman . . . am I the only one who would have fled in terror from the Chamber, if one imagines one's mother in such a situation?

In order to reinforce the Christian imperative that woman's God-given role was to obey and serve her husband or father, appeals were made to both the sort of biblical injunctions already discussed and those given emphasis by reference to other presumed feminine characteristics, including loyalty and devotion. Accounts of women's faithfulness during Christ's passion and death allowed the construction of women as God's closest workers, as more faithful to Christ when he was on earth than were his male followers, for example, and both flattered women and legitimised their subordination. As Bjørg Seland has argued in her discussion of the nineteenth-century Norwegian church, by the use of such 'romanticising and laudatory rhetoric' men could legitimise formal discrimination.[70]

Woman's responsibility was not merely to ensure the physical well-being of her family, but also, by so doing, to demonstrate its spiritual health. Christians who contested this exclusively domestic role for women sometimes framed it within the campaign to permit greater educational opportunities and, by extension, greater employment opportunities to women. For example, practising Anglican Christians, such as Emily Davies, gave lip service to Pauline teaching about the subjection of women while also appearing to undermine it. As Laura Morgan Green has shown in her recent work on cultural conflict and Victorian literature, such pioneering women frequently spoke with a forked tongue, using an apparently orthodox vocabulary to express ideas of potentially radical import, in Davies's case in favour of the higher education of women.[71] This was not an exclusively English device to subvert inconvenient biblical injunctions. In Sweden, Sophie Leijonhufvud, while protesting an adherence to traditional doctrine as taught within Lutheranism (Luther had envisaged few other functions than childbearing and domesticity to women, whom he believed to be childish and muddleheaded), rebutted theological arguments against giving women the opportunity to pursue their education, arguing that this posed no danger to true Christian femininity.[72] In Iceland, in the 1880s, Briet Bjarnheinsdottir took a similar line.[73]

Those northern European women who campaigned for the provision of opportunities in higher education and employment for women challenged the ways in which the sacred texts had generally been used by claiming to discern their ultimate intentions. Marie Maugeret, for example, editor of monthly periodical *Le Féminisme chrétien* in Paris insisted that feminism could be reconciled with Christianity, and asserted women's right to work.[74] Nevertheless, the right of women to seek employment outside the home was a grey area, reflecting the difficulty that Christian preachers and writers experienced when they tried to delineate precisely the female role. Women were bound to care for and influence their families, but what if the financial support of the family required that the mother undertake paid employment? The tension was created between the ideal of the home-loving pious wife and mother whose husband was able to support her financially and the equally home-loving and pious woman whose conscientious fulfilment of her role demanded that she leave the home to help to support her family. Inevitably, there were different expectations for women of different classes. Only those with financial resources had the luxury of trying to reconcile their Christian duty to remain at home servicing their families with their aspirations for employment or even philanthropic activity outside the home. Poor women had no such choice, and it is significant that Christian charities working with poor women did not hesitate to find work for them, even if that necessitated putting their children into the care of strangers or into an orphanage while the mothers worked to pay for their keep.

Not all Christian women were prepared to accept teaching that restricted their opportunities outside the home. For example, in the mid-nineteenth century the editors of a Swedish periodical, *Tidskrift för hemmet*, used both Old and New Testament references to give a scriptural – some might say fundamentalist – spin to the argument that women, especially single women, should be properly prepared for employment both to mitigate the contempt in which unmarried women tended to be held and to fulfil the ungendered prophecy in Genesis that 'You shall work in the sweat of your brow'. No one should think that she or he was immune from the divine requirement to work. Moreover, Christ's parable of the talents, which condemned those who failed to make good use of the resources they had been given, was used to underline the anti-Christian nature of failing to develop God-given abilities. To counter those who protested that allowing women into higher education – and, by extension, into the workplace – would be detrimental to morality, they argued cogently that the lecture room was probably a more moral place than the ballroom and pointed out that orthodox Church members had entertained few scruples about women being educated in order to perform a social and decorative function on the dance floor.[75] Unlike Josephine Butler, who appeared to argue that there were exceptions to general rules (among which exceptions she counted herself), Sophie Leijonhufvud, the editor of *Tidskrift för hemmet*, adopted the more radical – and divisive – stance of reserving to women the right to choose and interpret for themselves those biblical passages that they considered central to women's position.[76]

Not all women were convinced by feminist readings of the holy books, however. Jenny P. d'Héricourt, a French Protestant woman, contested established views about women in the middle of the nineteenth century, by insisting that claims for the equality of the sexes based on Christian belief could not be sustained. She argued that both the Old and New Testaments proclaimed the inferiority of woman, imposing on her the

> most absolute submission to her father, to her husband, refusing her every right as daughter, spouse, mother, alienating her from the priesthood, from science, from instruction, denying her intelligence, outraging her modesty, torturing her feelings, permitting the sale and exploitation of her beauty, preventing her from inheriting or owning property.[77]

The picture she drew may have been a crude one, but many European women writers in the past three hundred years fundamentally would not want to disagree with her.

The twentieth century: A post-Christian age?

The feminisation of religion, arguably begun during the course of the eighteenth century, accelerated during the course of the nineteenth. The next hundred years were to see considerable changes in women's relationship to religion, particularly to the religious institutions to which they belonged and the styles of life promoted there, reflecting general societal changes. Moreover, the contours of the religious landscape were to alter dramatically as a result of demographic and cultural developments.

In some situations, Christian women continued to be impeded in their ambitions to be active workers by a rigid interpretation of traditional teaching about the place of women in society and the church. Nevertheless, using women in French Social Catholicism before the First World War as examples, James McMillan has been able to show how women were able to make a distinctive contribution both to their church and to society in general in spite of a potentially restrictive Christian, in this case Roman Catholic, discourse. Social Catholicism was essentially a movement of the political right; its members did not question conventional biologically determined gender roles and wholeheartedly supported a domestic ideology that stressed the role of women within the home at the same time as contributing to a new politicisation of Catholic women. It came into being in the late nineteenth century, at a time when the fortunes of the church were at a low ebb in France and aimed to aid the process of re-Christianisation by evangelising the working classes and eliminating the evils associated with industrialisation. Although they were active at every level of the movement, women were responsible for initiating a network of charitable societies – *Le Rampart des Oeuvres* (Defence of Works) – established to counter the effects of increasing alienation from the church and the alleviation of the miseries of industrial society. Some practical projects aimed to promote class reconciliation. Influenced partly by Russian populists and partly by the work of Toynbee Hall, founded in London in the 1880s, one venture led by an aristocratic Breton nun and some of her sisters aimed to work with the population in a poor area of Paris. When that failed because of lack of funds, the same group began work with children. By 1903, they had established two houses in Paris. By 1908, they were running six *missions sociales*, which provided a variety of childcare facilities and popular-education classes and served as bases for establishing contacts with working-class families. Other schemes organised by Social

Catholic women included those designed to help combat tuberculosis and others that aimed to assist women to give birth in their homes and to provide post-natal care. Social Catholic women were involved in the struggle to provide decent working-class housing and became active in the development of female Catholic trade unions. They also set up the Action Sociale de la Femme, which aimed to keep better-heeled women prominent in the movement abreast of social problems. Amongst other topics, the groups began to discuss the possibilities of new roles for women outside the home and issued bulletins about a range of subjects of interest, including suffrage and the legal incapacity of married women. By the end of the First World War, the Social Catholic Movement provided powerful support for women's suffrage.[78]

Social Catholicism, with its commitment to traditional gender roles, offered no challenge to conventional Catholicism. Within other Christian churches, however, debates about the movements towards the appointment of women to leadership roles brought to public notice the continued ambivalence about women's ability to assume the same religious responsibilities as men. Those who opposed any change to the current position appealed to the teaching of the Gospel narratives which, when combined with other New Testament material that appears unequivocally to place women in a position of subjection to men, allowed the inference that the Christian position is one that accords dignity to woman in the place allotted to her: the home. As Davidoff and Hall have shown, the economic advances, particularly in English society, that made it possible for nineteenth- and early twentieth-century middle-class women to withdraw from the workplace into the moral haven of the home powerfully reinforced the development of the notion of separate spheres of action for men and women and was endorsed by evangelical preachers.[79] Commenting on more recent developments, Gita Sahgal and Nira Yuval-Davis have noted the revival of commitment, common to all religions, to a black and white view of life and achieved by religious trends that tend to be grouped together as fundamentalism.[80] Yuval-Davis has illustrated her argument by reference to interviews with women who have made a deliberate decision to embrace Ultra-Orthodox Judaism. In spite of all its restrictions, or perhaps because of them, they have found within it a sense of identity and belonging, a framework that offers a total way of life within which they can pursue the challenge of striving for improvement if not perfection.[81] Identity, structure and challenge have been elements in other European religions that have been grasped by women who have valued the security, certainty and protection they afford. Increasingly required to understand their role to be a domestic one, women of all religious traditions have shown themselves not unwilling to trade the insecurity of the world outside the home, with all its dangers and temptations, for this protection and confidence. Cosy domesticity, authenticated by faith, has proved an attractive option for many. In more recent times this has been one of the features within fundamentalism, whatever its credal foundations, that has been attractive to some women; its clear boundaries and professions of timeless truth purporting to provide a safe and stable foundation for life. The significance attached to women's domestic functions was given practical expression in rural Greek Orthodox communities observed in the late 1970s: the women believed that their almost obsessive cleaning and food preparation, especially when visitors were expected, had symbolic, religious, importance. It was their responsibility to ensure that their family's exterior aspect reflected its inner, spiritual one.[82]

The sanctity of Christian marriage and the essential role that the wife and mother must play within the home have been powerful elements within Catholic teaching throughout the twentieth century. So successfully were they promulgated that many Catholic women who also called themselves feminists refused to critique the institution of marriage, bowing to doctrinal pronouncements from the Vatican on its sacramental character and on the evils of civil divorce. For some women, the only solution was to try to hold to contradictory views – those informed by their feminism and those held in obedience to their Catholic faith. The resulting tension frequently was resolved by abandoning one or the other. In the early twentieth century, for example, the Catalan Catholic feminist, Dolors Monserda de Macia, in *Estudi feminista* said:

> It is not in my mind to speak against or detract in the slightest way from the submission that women, by natural law, by the mandate of Jesus Christ, and by their willing acceptance on contracting matrimony have to have for men, as this submission is altogether necessary . . . or the correct running of the family and society.[83]

In spite of the very considerable changes in views about marriage and the status of women that have coloured debates throughout Europe over the past hundred years – and that have been manifested in the liberalisation of civil-divorce laws, a gradual acceptance of artificial means of contraception and the legalisation of abortion in some circumstances – official Roman Catholic teaching has continued to reinforce the traditional position. In the first half of the twentieth century Pope Pius XI's *Divini redemptoris* restated Catholic arguments on male authority in the family, while his successor, Pope Pius XII, went further and circulated no fewer than seventy-two pronouncements on women, covering issues from dress codes to women's submission in marriage and efforts to refocus their attention on home and children. In October 1945, in a broadcast from Vatican City, he outlined the political and social obligations that underlay 'woman's dignity': her unique role in the domestic sphere and her control of the education of her children.[84] It is a comparison that they may not welcome, but papal assertions in the mid-twentieth century had a lot in common with the positions espoused by those of many of the late twentieth- and early twenty-first century so-called 'fundamentalist' evangelical Christian churches.

Like Judaism and Christianity, Islam also claims that its belief system accords value to women. Like them, it has to provide justification for views that sit uneasily with modern practice. One argument suggests that in the seventh century the new faith rescued women from the disadvantageous position in which they were to be found in Arabia in pre-Islamic times, put an end to such practices as female infanticide and gave women greater economic and social security.[85] All that may well be true, but Muslim women have still understood their role to be a domestic rather than a public one although, as both Leila Ahmed and Anour Majid have recently argued, the restrictions may not have originated with Islam. In their view, the subjection experienced by many Muslim women may be traced to a corruption of the original purity of the Islamic message by contact with other traditions, so that the revolutionary egalitarianism that characterised early Islam became eclipsed by the absorption into its world of other, particularly Christian, teaching, that introduced non-Arab prejudices against women and that helped to influence the subsequent evolution of a Muslim view of woman's nature and her role.[86]

The notion that Islam or any other Eastern religion accorded dignity and value to women contrasted sharply with the belief, particularly of evangelicals in the eighteenth and nineteenth centuries, that Christianity had played a vital part in raising the status of women. This view was reinforced by the experience of women missionaries who, as Billie Melman has been able to show, contributed to Western perceptions of life in the East but were not themselves always particularly well-informed.[87] Nineteenth-century British women, imbued with ideals informed by a mixture of imperialism, religion and a desire to break free from the oppressive constraints of British life may well have found it easy to condemn what they perceived as the captivity of women in Asian and African rural situations and to have misunderstood the nature of life in the *zenana* or the harem.[88] In this they were supported by male imperialists, often known at home for their intransigent opposition to feminism. Lord Cromer, for example, a vocal opponent of women's suffrage in Britain, used his perceptions of the subordination of women in early twentieth-century Egypt as part of his platform for an attack on the 'backwardness' of Islam and the impossibility of its reform. This 'proof' of the inferiority of Islam provided the justification for Western efforts to undermine Muslim religion and society.[89] In her analysis of the work of the Baptist Zenana Mission, Laura Lauer has shown that most missionary societies were operating within this accepted imperial stereotype 'in which the oriental Other was seen as materially different from and in opposition to the English norm', a thesis that was frequently adopted by the upper classes in colonised societies whose interests lay with the colonial powers.[90]

Many women have attempted to use their holy books to give themselves a legitimate basis for enlarging their sphere of influence. Some – often aided by men – have attempted to challenge the restrictive treatment advocated by their religious leaders and justified by theology, by revisiting the sacred texts in order to question and even to subvert the traditional, frequently androcentric, exegesis. That Jewish, Christian and Muslim women should take the fight to the texts is, of course, significant. It overturns the popular perception of fundamentalism, a notion that equates fundamentalism with 'fanaticism', 'religious practices that I don't like' or, as Sahgal and Yuval-Davis have noted grimly, with the abusive labelling of Muslims as 'the barbaric Other,' and is often used carelessly to describe those, particularly religious conservatives, who may well be extreme in their views but may not be, strictly speaking, fundamentalist.[91] It may perhaps be argued that, far from being truly fundamentalist, men and women who attack any deviation from what they consider to be essential to their faith, without a careful assessment of that faith's early history, may have missed the essence of the original teaching. By returning to the essentials of their religion as revealed in their scriptures, many twentieth-century women, both Christian and Muslim, set out to demonstrate that early Christianity and early Islam offered new freedoms to women but that their religions traditions took a 'wrong' turn near the beginning of their history; it may be argued that such women have constructed themselves as neo-fundamentalists. Women's revisiting of the texts is also significant because all three monotheistic traditions place great importance on the authority of divinely revealed scriptures assumed to be authoritative for all time. They are all, to use a Muslim description, 'People of the Book'. The books differ, but all are rooted in the Hebrew Scriptures, augmented in the case of Christianity by the New Testament and in Islam by the Koran and the *Hadith*, the body of traditions relating to Mohammed.

But in order to challenge effectively a position that made them of lesser value and accorded them a narrowly prescribed role, at the same time as insisting that they remained within the bounds of orthodoxy, women frequently had to adopt an almost schizoid position. They had to nod in the direction of acknowledging the authority of the sacred text at the same time as suggesting alternative interpretations or challenging the traditional hermeneutic history. This has been especially true of Islam, where twentieth-century feminist scholarship concentrated on the chains of transmission of the *Hadith* and sought to show the impossibility of tracing some ideas back to the Prophet and his original followers, an essential element in any claim for authenticity and authority. In addition, it was necessary for scholars of all traditions to acknowledge that the process of selection of key texts in relation to any moral or religious issue may also produce a range of opinions. Whether or not the selection was made with the conscious intent to produce a particular view, the method by which it was made determines the character of the interpretation. Christians, for example, are notoriously divided about their use of Scripture. Some insist that every word is divinely inspired, but find themselves forced to explain away some Old Testament injunctions, for example the Levitical food laws, while insisting that others have continued divine sanction. Other Christians wish to understand Scripture by using intellectual tools that stress the mythological and symbolic. There are some marked differences, too, in the interpretation of Jewish religious law, culture and customs between Sephardi and Ashkenazi Jews and between conservative and liberal strains of Judaism, just as there are between Muslims of Arab extraction, Muslims from the Indian subcontinent and Muslims from European countries such as Bosnia or Turkey.

Encounters with Western custom over recent years have driven some Muslim women to challenge teaching that has been accorded the dignity of tradition. They have drawn attention to the fact that the Koran does not contain any clear or specific legislative detail directed at keeping women in their houses, away from contact with men. It has been noted, for example by writers such as Barbara Freyer Stowasser, that some of the Koranic injunctions about seclusion, when read in context, actually refer to the wives of the Prophet: guidelines intended for less exalted women merely stress modest behaviour and advise women to wrap their cloaks around them when they go out. And there is a sort of even-handedness about the instructions – if Muslim women are to cover themselves modestly, Muslim men are to respond by lowering their gaze.[92] There is little to choose between the Koranic instructions as thus interpreted and the Christian teachings that warn against excessive adornment and immodest female dress.[93] And both advocate covering the head, although, with a few exceptions, it is the Muslim custom that has excited comment and occasional hostility in the past fifty years or so.

In some situations, Islam has adapted fairly readily to the host culture. Sweden in the late twentieth century, for example, provides an illustration of such adaptation. The importance attached to the integration of the immigrant population by the Swedes appears to have wrought subtle changes in the ways that Muslim women have begun to perceive their roles. In a society that stresses the importance of equal opportunities and where the notion of a housewife is virtually non-existent, Roald reports that Muslim women, both convert and immigrant, have reacted positively to an ethos that expects them to contribute to society by taking an active part in the labour market.[94] If Roald's picture of late twentieth-century Sweden is correct, then the acceptance of local behaviour on the part of Muslim women, even though it must conflict with what have traditionally been accepted as Islamic customs, has been achieved relatively painlessly. But their ready acceptance of Swedish lifestyles may owe as much to their own origins as to the powerful messages of an advanced Scandinavian culture. Throughout Europe, those immigrants who have moved from urban situations have frequently found the process of assimilation easier to accomplish than those of their compatriots whose roots were in more rural and conservative regions. The acceptance or rejection of 'Western' patterns of behaviour may represent little more than compatibility of lifestyle based on previous experience.

The tension between the demands of their faith and the expectations of secular society in relation to women's domestic role has been mirrored in the more explicitly religious aspects of women's lives. Within Orthodox Judaism, for example, their role is sharply differentiated from men's. Women are not allowed to lead prayers, to become rabbis or judges or to hold any other religious position. Moreover, their evidence is not admissible in court and a Jewish woman cannot obtain a religious divorce unless her husband permits it.[95] On the face of it, therefore, women are both inferior to men and must be subject to their will, but, true to the notion that Judaism is aware of and responsive to its social context, it has been noted that since the rise of twentieth-century feminism, a lot of energy has been expended in rationalising this and in arguing that Jewish women's position is 'really' even more important and powerful than men's. The explanation that men have to work harder and become involved in large numbers of religious activities as a consequence of their lower spiritual status has a whiff of excessive protest about it and does not sit easily with some of the laws of ritual purity that deny women access to holy things or that submit them to rules of personal hygiene that seem, to some commentators at least, to be inspired by disgust.[96] Nevertheless, because Jewishness is inherited through the maternal line, the woman is constructed as the transmitter of the Jewish genetic inheritance, as well as being the guardian of the Jewish home, which is the foundation of the Jewish people. An honourable position, perhaps, but might it not be argued that this also places a heavy burden on the shoulders of the woman while leaving the man free of domestic responsibility? Women have frequently been debarred from formal religious functions in order to perform their domestic duties, which in some modern European communities might include wage-earning in order to free their husbands for spiritual observance. As Nira Yuval-Davis's research has shown, even when both partners worked outside the home, Orthodox Jewish women in Britain in the 1990s were still made to understand that the cooking and cleaning were their responsibility specifically in order to free their husbands to follow their religious studies – 'you encourage men to learn and you remove the petty worries in their life.'[97]

Historically, Jewish women were not permitted to lead or to take any part in public prayer and were sometimes even prevented from learning Hebrew or studying the sacred texts.[98] Rachel Siegel, an Ashkenazi Jew, remembering her childhood in Lausanne in Switzerland, described sitting with her mother in their synagogue in the 1930s, incapable of following the Hebrew prayers in the Prayer Book and quite unable to work out which page they were on or what to say or do. Her solution was to follow her mother's cues about when to stand and when to sit, 'embarrassed and ashamed at faking it' and not entirely certain that her mother could properly follow the service either. Her brothers, meanwhile, the beneficiaries of a religious education, were able to participate confidently in the service.[99] The new freedoms associated with Reform Judaism attracted only a minority and by the end of the nineteenth century the exclusion of women from religious study contrasted sharply with opportunities becoming available to women in secular society. And even within Reform Judaism and its potential for enhancing the religious experience of women, a reluctance to take the final step in acknowledging spiritual equality by ordaining women to the rabbinate remained. A rare exception, Regina Jones, who completed her rabbinical studies at the Berlin Academy in the late 1930s, was denied formal ordination but Rabbi Max Dienemann of Offenbach took the unusual step of privately granting her a Hebrew rabbinical diploma and she functioned briefly as a rabbi until she fell victim to the Nazis and died in a concentration camp in 1940.[100] Motivated by similar convictions and with the advantage of membership of a wealthy and influential family but without benefit of ordination although possessing a powerful sense of mission, an English Jew, Lily Montagu, devoted herself to the revitalisation of Judaism as living faith. She wrote an article on the 'Spiritual Possibilities of Judaism Today' in the *Jewish Quarterly Review* in 1899 and, with the assistance of Claude Montefiore, she called together a group of men and women who shared her concerns. In 1902, the Jewish Religious Union was established. In 1918, Montagu preached her first sermon at London's Liberal Jewish Synagogue. And from 1928 until her death in 1963, Montagu served as chairman and spiritual leader of the London West Central Liberal Jewish Synagogue and became the first woman to gain formal recognition as a 'lay minister'. Her activities were not confined to Britain. She was Secretary to the World Union for Progressive Judaism from 1902 and, during the 1928 World Union Conference, she preached at the Reform Synagogue in Berlin – the first Jewish woman ever to occupy a pulpit in Germany. Support for Regina Jones and for Lily Montagu was arguably the result of their personal charisma and an acknowledgment of the realities consequent on assimilation to European cultural norms rather than any new interpretation of scripture, and it represented only a partial acknowledgement of the importance of permitting women full participation. But as one of the consequences of the acceptance of modern ideas was an alteration of the role of the rabbi, forcing him to become less of a social and spiritual leader and more a teacher, and as his activities were increasingly restricted to administrative and pastoral functions, women's exclusion from the role came to some to speak entirely of social attitudes and tradition.[101] However, it was not until the 1970s, with the ordination of Julia Neuberger and Jacqueline Tabick in England, more than a hundred years after the 1846 Breslau conference had affirmed women's equality, that Reform women were accorded positions of leadership.[102] Conservative and Orthodox Jews have, however, continued to adhere to traditional practice.

In spite of some relaxations, generations of women have continued to internalise the gendered demands of their religion. In 1907, speaking to the Union of Jewish Women, Lady Desart argued that woman's sphere and her real power was in the home, thus appearing to compensate women for their lack of authority in the outside world by replacing it with an equivalent, but domestic, power base. This may have begun to assume more significance after the end of the First World War, with the demise of synagogue worship and the increased emphasis on the home as the centre of Judaism.[103] But the Second World War denied some women the opportunity to exercise such power, and even many of those spared the horrors of persecution experienced a dislocation of their domestic life and were expected to put right its results. Mrs John Sebag-Montefiore, speaking to the International Conference of Jewish Women in Paris, bemoaned the lack of Jewish communal life and unfamiliarity with Jewish worship exhibited by children who had been evacuated during the war. She placed sole responsibility for remedying this on the mother and argued that it was for her to consider how to keep the Jewish child staunchly loyal to Judaism when it had been forced to live a large part of its life in a Christian environment.[104]

During the twentieth century, opportunities for Christian women to take more public roles within their churches began to increase. However, even in dissenting churches such as the Quakers, the Unitarians and the Methodists and, at the end of the nineteenth century, the Salvation Army, reservations were still expressed about the extent to which they should be decision-makers.[105] The Church of England denied women the right to elect members to its governing body; moreover the debate about whether they should take communion after male worshippers in order to demonstrate their subordination was still alive in 1922. But the move to include women as equal members proved an irresistible – if gradual and uneven – process. The twentieth century slowly began to witness the ordination of women, but it was not until after the Second World War that the northern European state churches permitted them to take leadership posts, and not until the final years of the twentieth century that the Anglican church allowed them to become priests, but not bishops.[106] In spite of the shortage of clergy, which, it has been argued, helped to provide the stimulus for female ordination in some churches, Catholic and Orthodox churches still resist the notion of female priesthood. The Roman Catholic position, restated in an apostolic letter of Pope John Paul II in 1994, rehearsed again the arguments against change: the current position accords with God's will, which cannot be influenced by sociological and cultural forces; women have their own essential role within the church and are not deemed inferior to men.[107] He reinforced this in his 'Letter to Women' a year later.[108]

It has sometimes been argued that women have been written out of the Christian narrative and that the evidence for the active participation of women in the leadership of the early church has been conveniently ignored by later male Christian writers. Barbara Freyer Stowasser makes a similar case for the disappearance of women from public worship in Islam. She has argued that there is overwhelming evidence in the *Hadith* that in the early days of Islam women prayed in the mosques together with the men. She draws attention to the number and variety of traditions that range around the detail of women's religious observance, drawing from them the conclusion that debates on this point occupied the minds of early Muslims and eventually resulted in women's disappearance from public prayer.[109] Could the argument have gone the other way? Both Christianity and Islam had their origins in urban situations, giving rise to the suggestion that as urban living disrupts the balance of labour between the sexes that is often characteristic of rural life, women have found themselves forced into the background.[110] There are interesting questions here that need exploration, especially in relation to female migrants to Europe from essentially rural situations for whom seclusion among family and neighbours might have been a protection but that, when transferred to European housing conditions, has become an imprisonment. Twentieth-century female migrants to Europe, attempting to reproduce the conditions of their homeland, may have found the isolation of life in European cities as oppressive as any seclusion experienced by their grandmothers. Nevertheless, security and familiarity are closely connected and, as Yasmin Ali has argued, it may be that the existing order of migrant communities in sometimes hostile situations is sanctioned by the ways that things are done in an ever more mythologised version of the homeland and reinforced by reference to those teachings of Islam that appear to support the status quo.[111]

Female sexuality had lost little of its power to perturb by the twentieth century. That women had the potential – consciously or unconsciously – to lead men astray remained a constant element in religious thought, and the need to reform them was frequently, and necessarily, closely tied to the need to protect them in the minds of both individuals and religious institutions. Twentieth-century Ireland witnessed a resurgence of the notion that women were responsible for corrupting men: they were guilty 'because their immodest dress dragged men, incapable of resisting, into serious sin'.[112] As the preacher at the pilgrimage shrine of Knock at the Feast of the Assumption in 1937 told his thousands of hearers, 'If the young women of Ireland were pure and modest, there need never be any fear for the faith in Ireland.'[113] But clearly the women of Ireland were not pure and modest and were to blame for enticing men by wearing 'scanty underwear or tight-fitting abbreviated bathing costumes . . . sprawling on the beach'. Presumably these were the same women, or their friends, who were condemned by the Sisters of Mercy at the Mary Immaculate Training College in Limerick for wearing slacks, which should have been avoided because they threw the female figure into undue prominence![114] And even in the 1990s, in churches whose theological position differed markedly from that of Irish Roman Catholicism, the songs and choruses sung by Black-led churches in Britain have been shown to depict women as particularly prone to sexual sin.[115]

Southern Europe experienced similar anxieties. As Nancy Tapper has demonstrated in her study of provincial towns in Turkey, 'women are at once "sacred" because of their reproductive powers and dangerous and in need of control because of the imputed nature of their sexuality.'[116] 'Provocative' clothing is an obvious source of distraction that invites censure or control, but an interesting feature of the practical working out of anxiety about women's sexuality is the way that it has been intimately linked with women's hair. The remedy has been to require women to cover their hair, though there is some uncertainty about whether this affords protection to men by removing a source of temptation or protection for women by making them less attractive and, therefore, less liable to harassment. Some Jewish women shaved their heads on marriage and wore a wig, ostensibly in order to discourage the attentions of men other than their husbands – a custom still followed in some European Orthodox communities. Christian women were urged by St Paul to avoid adornment and elaborate hairstyles and to cover their heads while praying.[117] Some Orthodox Jewish women still wear wigs, and the wearing of hats or some sort of head-covering in church would have been commonplace in many nineteenth- and twentieth-century European churches. Women belonging to some Protestant sects still cover their heads, but it is the veil worn by many Muslim women in Europe, with its connotations as much of cultural and ethnic difference as of female subjection, that has given rise to considerable discussion both among Muslims and non-Muslims. Twentieth-century writers have examined both the Koran and the *Hadith*, together with their chains of transmission in order to uncover the early history of veiling and the cultural context that may have given rise to it. They have raised problems associated with the translation of such texts and of the cultural norms that have informed the interpretations attached to them, with the result that some claim that the Koran does not instruct them to wear veils. As in the case of the injunction to remain in their houses, some see a distinction between instructions given to the wives of the Prophet and those to the generality of Muslim women. Moreover, as Stowasser has argued, seclusion and veiling, both of which may have Persian or even Byzantine, rather than Islamic, origins have been legitimised by exegetes who have construed the vague and general Koranic provisions in a manner that makes them specific and of universal application.[118] As we have seen, women are urged to wrap their cloaks round them when they go out – but cloaks are not veils.

Women who choose to don the headscarf or *hijab* or, in some communities, the *chador* or the *burkha*, garments that envelop the whole body, are increasingly frequently seen on European streets, their dress in marked contrast to that of most other religious women; even nuns in many European communities have abandoned both head-coverings and habits. While European reaction to this practice has ranged from hostility to mystification to sympathetic tolerance, within Muslim communities, too, it has excited strong and widely differing opinions. Fatima Mernissi, for example, believes the custom to be antipathetic to women. She claims that by its practice of trying to veil it no religion has done more than Islam for the occultation of the feminine.[119] Other Muslim women have disagreed and have remarked on the shallowness of a debate that has seen the scarf simply as a sign of female oppression.[120] For those women who choose to be veiled, to whatever degree, the custom may serve a variety of functions. Both veiling and unveiling may be seen as political acts or as means of asserting Islamic identity. Localised debates, for example about whether or not Muslim girls should be allowed to wear the veil in schools, have taken place throughout Europe. But from the late 1980s, through to the early twenty-first century, two European countries in particular – Turkey and France – both secular states and sensitive about the desirability of a clear separation between religion and the state, have been in the forefront of disputes about the wearing of the scarf in public. In Turkey, where the wives of both the leader and the deputy leader of the Justice and Development Party, victorious in the general election in the autumn of 2003, wore headscarves, moves were set in train to loosen those regulations that forbade the traditional head-covering in government offices, schools and universities. Unlike Turkey, confident in its Islamic identity, France banned the wearing of any overt symbol of religious allegiance, whether a cross, the Jewish *kippa* or the Muslim *hijab* in 2003. Girls were sent home from school and women taking part in official activities were barred if they persisted in wearing their head covering.[121] It has been suggested that in the latter case this reflected French unease that a section of its population should make a public statement about a supranational loyalty. It is not without significance that signs of Jewish and Christian allegiance were included in the 2003 regulations almost as an afterthought, having been tolerated for generations. As Islam was the second largest religion in the country by the end of the twentieth century and as the ethnic composition of its membership provided a constant and often uncomfortable reminder of France's colonial past, it had the potential to wield great influence. However, the head of the official commission that reported on this issue in December 2003 argued that the law proposed by the commission aimed to put all religions on an equal footing and was designed so that all religions 'could live together in public places'.[122]

Although there are wide variations in styles of Muslim dress for women, whether it covers the body to a greater or lesser extent, it draws attention to the wearer, some of it hostile. Swedish women, for example, have complained about the discrimination that their distinctive dress has caused, in spite of Sweden's ethnic discrimination laws.[123]

British Muslim women, interviewed recently about their decision to start wearing religious dress, have made clear that this is as much a political as an entirely spiritual decision. Some wished their identity as Muslims to be made public, as an act of solidarity with Muslim women around the world. Others wished to demonstrate that, in the aftermath of the attacks on the World Trade Center in September 2001, not all Muslims were terrorists and that they took pride in their religious identity.[124]

Whether its prime function has been spiritual or social, religion has served as an identifier, a means of giving significance to the individual. This function may, during the past three centuries, have been superseded by other powerful identifiers, such as nationalism; conversely, it may also have been united with such forces.[125] The Lutheran church, for example, organised some of the resistance to Nazism in Norway, and, in Poland under Communist rule, the Roman Catholic church provided a powerful focus for nationalist sentiment by basing its administration on the old Polish territories and by providing an alternative to the political reality. That the Church's popularity has fallen considerably since the collapse of the Soviet Union and the creation of an autonomous Polish state would appear to confirm the view that it served an important political purpose that was only loosely religious.[126] Moreover, the wider European pattern of female observance but male leadership is one that has become increasingly evident, particularly in Polish cities. Tony Walter and Grace Davie have recently observed an increasing imbalance in church attendance between the sexes in Britain, and it has recently been shown that males may number as few as between 5 and 35 per cent in some Black-led churches in Britain.[127] A similar pattern is evident in south-eastern Europe where, in 1979, Lucy Rushton noted that women in Macedonia attended church more frequently than men.[128] Judaism, too, has experienced a drop in numbers of regular worshippers and an increased incidence of Jews marrying outwith their tradition, a pattern that has caused considerable anxiety to Jewish leaders.

The twentieth century saw a rapid acceleration in the loosening of those restrictions that had been imposed on Christian women, ostensibly in response to religious prescription. It also saw a dramatic acceleration in the decline of institutional Christianity and, if Callum Brown is correct, in female religiosity. Churches have closed in large numbers since 1900; fewer men were presenting themselves for ordination at the end of the twentieth century than at the beginning or even in mid-century; many fewer women were offering themselves for service within sisterhoods although most Protestant denominations began to ordain women to positions of local leadership. A similar pattern affecting observance can be seen within Judaism. However, in many parts of Europe, Islam, even if is still relatively statistically insignificant, has become increasingly visible and has provided a catalyst for debate about the role of religion in society and about relationships between the many and varied religious traditions to be found among Europeans. In all these debates, the role of women is an important element.

Conclusion

Women have experienced succour and support as well as denial and restriction within the religious communities into which they were born or, less often, those they had chosen. In spite of official rhetoric and the emphasis on restriction of opportunity and a domestic ideology that has characterised the major religious traditions in Europe in the past three hundred years, women have shown themselves to be resourceful and enterprising in using – occasionally subverting – the structures in order to further their ambitions for faith-inspired service or personal development.

Remarkable similarities exist between the three major monotheisms. But whether their allegiance is to an Abrahamic religion or to a tradition more recently arrived in Europe, faced with what purported to be God-given instructions for their behaviour, women who wished to remain within their religious tradition while adapting to social norms have had to adopt a stance that permitted them to demonstrate their orthodoxy while challenging ways in which that orthodoxy had traditionally been defined. Using the scriptures as their starting point and acknowledging their importance at the same time as revisiting the hermeneutic traditions associated with them has sometimes enabled women to question views and practices to which long usage has given an authority they may not originally have possessed. It is a tightrope from which many have fallen, and while those who have succeeded in their challenges may not have been representative of their contemporaries, they have helped in the process of defining new orthodoxies, which are gradually affecting women in the European manifestations of all three monotheistic religions. The societal and individual consequences of declining institutional influence, particularly of European Christian churches, of 'believing without belonging', and the growth of religious traditions associated with immigrant communities, together with the emergence of greater freedom to experiment, make it certain that the religious landscape of the Continent for the next three hundred years will have little in common with that from the eighteenth to the twenty-first century.

Guide to further reading

Secularisation

Brown, Callum, *The Death of Christian Britain: Understanding Secularisation, 1800–2000*. London and New York: Routledge, 2001. This is a controversial and thought-provoking analysis of triggers towards the rejection of Christian commitment in Britain. Brown highlights the significance of the 1960s in the development of a view of the world that no longer finds formal religion a useful tool for understanding and managing life's events.

Mcleod, Hugh, *Religion and the People of Western Europe*. Oxford: Oxford University Press, 1981. Mcleod's book gives a very useful overview of religious belief and practice in western Europe that helps to provide a context for any discussion of women and religion.

McLeod, Hugh and W. Ustorf, eds, *The Decline of Christendom in Western Europe*. Cambridge: Cambridge University Press, 2003. This is a collection of essays exploring the nature and multiple forms of secularisation from sociological, theological and historical perspectives. Although it is not an easy read, it helps to demonstrate the complexity of both the abandonment of religious belief and its significance.

General histories of women

None of the works listed below focuses specifically on religion, but by describing many aspects of women's lives, including religion, they help to demonstrate its place in individual women's lives and its impact on other areas of their experience and to reduce the temptation that the historian of religion might too sharply separate religious from other experience.

Abrams, Lynn, *The Making of Modern Woman: Europe 1789–1918*. London: Longman, 2002. This broad-ranging work is a valuable introduction to women's lived experience and works from the premise that significant changes in the ways that women constructed their identities took place in the period roughly dating from the French Revolution.

Bock, Gisela, *Women in European History*, trans. by Allison Brown. Oxford: Blackwell, 2002. This work illustrates the conditions that women have faced and explores their struggle for civil, political and social rights through discussion of their ideas and ideals.

Hufton, Olwen, *The Prospect before Her: A History of Women in Western Europe*. London: Harper-Collins, 1995. Volume I explores in considerable detail the history of women's lives from the sixteenth to the nineteenth century, by considering the interaction between belief and practice – between those religiously and culturally constructed ideals of womanhood and the realities of daily living. It sets the scene for later studies and enables those of us interested in later periods to understand some of the roots of the ways in which womanhood has been constructed.

Offen, Karen, *European Feminisms, 1700–1950: A Political History*. Stanford, Calif.: Stanford University Press, 2000. Offen explores the ways in which male hegemony in Continental Europe has been challenged. She sets out to read history from a feminine perspective and argues that sexual difference is at the heart of human thought and politics.

Women and religion

Beck, Wolfgang and Saul Friedländer, eds, *The Jews in European History*. Cincinnati, Ohio: Hebrew Union College Press, 1994. This collection of essays explores aspects of European Jewish experience from the Middle Ages to the second half of the twentieth century. Although the study of women is secondary to its main purpose, it provides a useful context by demonstrating the tensions experienced by Jewish people in their attempts to retain their identity while accommodating to their social context.

Holden, Pat, ed., *Women's Religious Experience*. London: Croom Helm, 1983. A series of essays that use case studies to explore women's experience of religion in a variety of social situations. The overall theme is that women may not necessarily view their experience of institutional religion as oppressive but rather that their exclusion from some of its demands may leave them free to explore and celebrate their own worth.

Malmgreen, Gail, ed., *Religion in the Lives of English Women*. London: Croom Helm, 1986. Focusing specifically on England, Malmgreen and her fellow contributors explore the extent to which women's spiritual impulses and religious vocations persisted in a more or less hostile environment as sources of strength, self-definition and accomplishment.

Mernissi, Fatima, *Women and Islam: An Historical and Theological Enquiry*. Oxford: Oxford University Press, 1991. A Muslim sociologist from Morocco, Mernissi writes about her faith and its institutional expression from a feminist and critical perspective. Her work is sometimes controversial but always stimulating.

Roald, A.S., *Women in Islam: The Western Experience*. London and New York: Routledge, 2001. From her experience as a Swedish convert to Islam, Roald explores what it means to be a Muslim woman attempting to live out her faith in an advanced European society. Her particular insights enable the non-Muslim reader to understand both the experience of living as a convert and the tensions that being part of so visible a minority may produce.

Ruether, Rosemary and Eleanor McLaughlin, eds., *Women of Spirit: Female Leadership in the Jewish and Christian Traditions*. New York: Simon & Schuster, 1979. Is it legitimate for women to exercise leadership roles within the Judaeo-Christian tradition? Ruether and McLaughlin explore some of the theological and social issues and their possible resolutions.

Notes

1 Callum Brown, *The Death of Christian Britain: Understanding Secularisation 1800–2000* (London: Routledge, 2001).

2 Hugh McLeod and W. Ustorf, *The Decline of Christendom in Western Europe, 1750–2000* (Cambridge: Cambridge University Press), p. 14.

3 Grace Davie, 'Religion and *Laïcité*', in Malcolm Cook and Grace Davie, eds, *Modern France: Society in Transition* (London: Routledge, 1991), pp. 193, 201; Sandy Tippett-Spirtou, *French Catholicism: Church, State and Society in a Changing Era* (Basingstoke: Macmillan: 2000), p. 170.

4 Elaine Foster, 'Women and the Inverted Pyramid of the Black Churches in Britain', in Gita Sahgal and Nira Yuval-Davis, eds, *Refusing Holy Orders: Women and Fundamentalism in Britain* (London: Virago, 1992), p. 49.

5 Lynn Abrams, *The Making of Modern Woman* (London: Longman, 2002); Gisela Bock, *Women in European History* (Oxford: Blackwell, 2002); Karen Offen, *European Feminisms 1700–1950: A Political History* (Stanford, Calif.: Stanford University Press, 2000).

6 Steve Bruce, *Religion in the Modern World: From Cathedrals to Cults* (Oxford: Oxford University Press, 1996); Davie, 'Religion and *Laïcité*'; Grace Davie, *Religion in Britain since 1945: Believing without Belonging* (Oxford: Blackwell, 1994).

7 Ellen Umansky, 'Women in Judaism', in Rosemary Ruether and Eleanor McLaughlin, eds, *Women of Spirit* (New York: Simon & Schuster, 1979); Jonathan Webber, 'Between Law and Custom: Women's Experience of Judaism', in Pat Holden, ed., *Women's Religious Experience. Cross-Cultural Perspectives* (London: Croom Helm, 1983); see for example, the Jewish Women's Archive, <http://www.jwa.org>, which is largely devoted to bio-graphical studies of Jewish women, or the multidisciplinary Women in Judaism at <http://www.utoronto.ca/wjudaism/journal/journal_index.html>.

8 See, for example, Fatima Mernissi, *Women and Islam: An Historical and Theological Enquiry* (Oxford: Blackwell, 1991); Fatima Mernissi, *The Veil and the Male Elite: A Feminist Interpretation of Women's Rights in Islam* (Reading, Mass.: Addison-Wesley, 1987); Fatima Mernissi, *Islam and Democracy: Fear of the Modern World* (London: Virago, 1993); Leila Ahmed, *Women and Gender in Islam. Historical Roots of a Modern Debate* (New Haven, Conn.: Yale University Press, 1992); for Yasmin Ali, see for exam-ple, 'Muslim Women and the Politics of Ethnicity', in Sahgal and Yuval-Davis, eds, *Refusing Holy Orders*; Anne-Sofie Roald, *Women in Islam* (London and New York: Routledge, 2001); Anne-Sofie Roald, 'The Mecca of Gender Equality: Muslim Women in Sweden', in Haifaa Jawaad and Tansin Benn, eds, *Muslim Women in the United Kingdom and Beyond: Experiences and Images* (Boston, Mass. and Leiden: Brill, 2003), pp. 65ff.

9 See, for example, web sites such as <http://www.jannah.org/sisters>, <http://www.iad.org/books/S-women.html>, <http://www.islamicity.com/mosque/w_islam>, all of which are devoted to explaining the current position of women in Islam by reference to history. Jawaad and Benn, Preface, *Muslim Women in the United Kingdom and Beyond*, pp. xiii–xv.

10 But see <http://www.twf.org/Library/WomenICJ.html>.

11 Owen Chadwick, *The Secularization of the European Mind in the Nineteenth Century* (Cambridge: Cambridge University Press, 1975), p. 15.

12 Jehuda Reinharz, 'Jewish Nationalism and Jewish identity in Central Europe', in Wolfgang Beck and Saul Friedländer, eds, *The Jews in European History: Seven Lectures* (Cincinnati, Ohio: Hebrew Union College Press, 1994), p. 93.

13 Nira Yuval-Davis, 'Jewish Fundamentalism and Women's Empowerment', in Sahgal and Yuval-Davis, *Refusing Holy Orders*, p. 215; Michael A. Meyer, 'Should and Can an "Antiquated" Religion Become Modern? The Jewish Reform Movement in Germany as seen by Jews and Christians', in Beck and Friedländer, *The Jews in European History*, pp. 58–64.

14 David Sorkin, 'Jews, the Enlightenment and Religious Tolerance: Some Reflections', in

Beck, ed., *The Jews in European History*, p. 39; Reinharz, 'Jewish Nationalism and Jewish Identity in Central Europe', pp. 101–2.

15 Jørgen S. Nielsen, *Towards a European Islam* (Basingstoke: Palgrave, 1999), pp. 1ff, 34; Jeremy Black, *Eighteenth-Century Europe* (Basingstoke: Macmillan, 1990), p. 169.

16 Anne-Sofie Roald, 'The Mecca of Gender Equality', in Jawad and Benn, *Muslim Women in the United Kingdom and Beyond*, p. 65; Jan Hjarno, 'Muslims in Denmark' and Ake Sander, 'The Status of Muslim Communities in Sweden', in Gerd Nonneman, Tim Niblock and Bogdan Szajkowski, eds, *Muslim Communities in the New Europe* (Reading: Ithaca, 1996), pp. 269–90 and 291–302.

17 Roald, *Women in Islam*, p. 300. See also Haifaa Jawaad, 'Historical and Contemporary Perspectives of Muslim Women Living in the West', in Jawaad and Benn, eds, *Muslim Women in the United Kingdom and Beyond*, p. 2.

18 See the discussion on female circumcision in Roald, *Women in Islam*, pp. 237ff.; Yasmin Ali, 'Muslim Women and the Politics of Ethnicity', in Sahgal and Yuval-Davis, eds, *Refusing Holy Orders*, p. 118.

19 Hjarno, 'Muslims in Denmark', p. 291.

20 Roger Ballard and Catherine Ballard, 'The Sikhs: The Development of South Asian Settlements in Britain', in James L. Watson, ed., *Between Two Cultures: Migrants and Minorities in Britain* (Oxford; Blackwell, 1977), pp. 24ff.; Alan G. James, *Sikh Children in Britain* (Oxford: Oxford University Press, 1974), pp. 7–8.

21 Gail Malmgreen, 'Introduction', in Gail Malmgreen, ed., *Religion in the Lives of English Women, 1760–1930* (London: Croom Helm, 1986), p. 2.

22 See Hugh McLeod, *Religion and the People of Western Europe* (Oxford: Oxford University Press, 1981), pp. 30–3.

23 Olwen Hufton, *The Prospect before Her* (London: HarperCollins, 1995), pp. 382ff.; Bock, *Women in European History*, pp. 58ff.

24 Hufton, *The Prospect before Her*, pp. 382ff; Bock, *Women in European History*, p. 58ff.

25 Thomas Kselman, 'The Dechristianisation of Death in France', in McLeod and Ustorf, eds, *Decline of Christendom in Western Europe*, pp. 149.

26 Bock, *Women in European History*, p. 61.

27 Hufton, *The Prospect before Her*, p. 159.

28 Mernissi, *The Veil and the Male Elite*, p. 84.

29 Genesis 2:18–23.

30 Genesis 3:12.

31 I Timothy 2:11–15.

32 I Cor. 11:3–10.

33 Koran, sura 7; see <http://www.jannah.org/sisters/womenhadith.html>.

34 See Majella Franzmann, *Women and Religion* (New York: Oxford University Press, 2000), pp. 122–3.

35 Gerda Lerner, *The Creation of Feminist Consciousness from the Middle Ages to 1870* (New York: Oxford University Press), p. 275.

36 R. Burman, '"She Looketh Well to the Ways of her Household": The Changing Role of Jewish Women in Religious Life', in Malmgreen, eds, *Religion in the Lives of English Women*, p. 234.

37 Franzmann, *Women and Religion*, p. 127.

38 Thomas Gisborne, *An Enquiry into the Duties of the Female Sex* (1796), p. 266. Quoted in Linda Colley, *The Britons: Forging the Nation, 1707–1837* (New Haven, Conn.: Yale University Press, 1992), p. 251.

39 See, for example, the suggestion by Kerri Allen that many conservative women attempted to discipline other women and to encourage them to accept their family roles. Kerri Allen, 'Representation and Self-Representation: Hannah Whittall Smith as Family Woman and Religious Guide', *Women's History Review*, 7 (1998), p. 231; see also the pronouncement of Pope Pius X at an audience with Italian and French feminist groups, 1909, quoted in Offen, *European Feminisms*, p. 199.

40 Quoted in Alison McKinnon, 'Educated Doubt: Women, Religion and the Challenge of Higher Education c.1870–1920', *Women's History Review*, 7 (1998), p. 245.

41 Lerner, *The Creation of Feminist Consciousness*, p. 111.
42 Julia Neuberger, 'Women in Judaism: Fact and Fiction', in Holden, *Women's Religious Experience*, p. 139.
43 Rosemary Raughter, 'A Discreet Benevolence: Female Philanthropy and the Catholic Resurgence in Eighteenth-Century Ireland', *Women's History Review*, 6 (1997), pp. 465ff.
44 Anne Summers, *Female Lives, Moral States* (Newbury: Threshhold Press, 2000), pp. 31–2.
45 Abrams, *The Making of Modern Woman*, p. 39.
46 Matthew 25:31–46.
47 Bock, *Women in European History*, p. 113.
48 Bjørg Seland, '"Called by the Lord": Women's Place in the Norwegian Missionary Movement', in Pirjo Markkola, ed., *Gender and Vocation: Women, Religion and Social Change in the Nordic Countries, 1830–1940* (Helsinki: Finnish Literature Society, 2000), pp. 75–6.
49 Brian Heeney, *The Women's Movement in the Church of England, 1860–1930* (Oxford: Oxford University Press, 1988), pp. 46ff.
50 op. cit., p. 118.
51 Karin Lützen, 'The Cult of Domesticity in Danish Women's Philanthropy, 1870–1920', in Markkola, *Gender and Vocation*, p. 152.
52 Eric Hobsbawm, *The Age of Empire, 1875–1914* (Harmondsworth: Penguin, 1987), p. 210.
53 Leonore Davidoff and Catherine Hall, *Family Fortunes: Men and Women of The English Middle Class, 1780–1850* (London: Hutchinson, 1987), pp. 119–22.
54 Abrams, *The Making of Modern Woman*, p. 37.
55 Pius IX, 'Ubi Primum', quoted in Offen, *European Feminisms*, p. 117.
56 E. Benbassa and Aron Rodrigue, *The Jews of the Balkans* (Oxford: Blackwell, 1995), pp. 83ff.
57 Meyer, 'Should and Can an "Antiquated" Religion Become Modern?', p. 102.
58 op. cit., p. 61.
59 See, for example, I Corinthians, 11; 14:34–5; I Timothy 2:11–14.
60 Malmgreen, 'Introduction', *Religion in the Lives of English women*, p. 2.
61 Quoted in Heeney, *The Women's Movement in the Church of England*, p. 5.
62 Mcleod, *Religion and the People of Western Europe*, p. 28.
63 Abrams, *The Making of Modern Woman*, pp. 35, 36. See also Hobsbawm, *The Age of Empire*, p. 210.
64 Abrams, *The Making of Modern Woman*, p. 35.
65 See Valerie Bonham, *A Place in Life: The Clewer House of Mercy, 1849–83* (Windsor: Community of St John Baptist, 1992).
66 Susan Mumm, *Stolen Daughters, Virgin Mothers* (Leicester: Leicester University Press, 1999), pp. 152–3.
67 The fullest account of Butler's long battle is to be found in Jane Jordan, *Josephine Butler* (London: John Murray, 2001).
68 Roy Hattersley, *Blood and Fire: William and Catherine Booth and the Salvation Army* (London: Abacus, 1999), pp. 107–14.
69 Margaret Allen, 'Matilda Sturge: "Renaissance Woman"', *Women's History Review*, 7 (1998), p. 212.
70 Seland, '"Called by the Lord"', p. 78.
71 Laura Morgan Green, *Educating Women: Cultural Conflict and Victorian Literature* (Athens, Ohio: Ohio University Press, 2001), p. 2.
72 Inger Hammer, 'From Frederika Bremer to Ellen Key: Calling, Gender and the Emancipation Debate in Sweden, c.1830–1900', in Markkola, ed., *Gender and Vocation*, pp. 47–8.
73 Inga Huld Hakonardottir, 'Philanthropy, Politics, Religion and Women in Iceland before the Modern Social Welfare System', in Markkola, *Gender and Vocation*, pp. 181–2.
74 Marie Maugeret, 'Le Féminisme chrétien', *La Fronde* (11 December 1897), quoted in Offen, *European Feminisms*, p. 197.
75 Hammar, 'From Frederika Bremer to Ellen Key', pp. 46–7.

76 op. cit., pp. 48–9.
77 Jenny d'Héricourt, 'La Bible et la question des femmes', *La Ragione* (24 October 1857), pp. 38–9, quoted in Offen, *European Feminisms*, p. 128.
78 James McMillan, 'Women in Social Catholicism in Late Nineteenth- and Early Twentieth-Century France', in W. J. Sheils and Diana Wood, eds, *Women in the Church* (Blackwell: Oxford, 1990), pp. 467–9, 471–5.
79 Davidoff and Hall, *Family Fortunes*, p. 115.
80 See Gita Sahgal and Nira Yuval-Davis, 'Introduction: Fundamentalism, Multiculturalism and Women in Britain', in Sahgal and Yuval-Davis, eds, *Refusing Holy Orders*, p. 2.
81 Yuval-Davis, 'Jewish Fundamentalism and Women's Empowerment', pp. 214ff.
82 Lucy Rushton, 'Doves and Magpies: Village Women in the Greek Orthodox Church', in Holden, eds, *Women's Religious Experience*, p. 61.
83 Dolors Monserda de Macia, *Estudi feminista: Orientacions pera la dona catalana* (Barcelona, 1910), quoted in Offen, *European Feminisms*, p. 200.
84 Offen, *European Feminisms*, pp. 334–5.
85 Freda Hussain, *Muslim Women* (London: Croom Helm, 1984), p. 46; Mernissi, *Women and Islam*, p. 140; Mernissi, *The Veil and the Male Elite*, pp. 73, 84, 126; Roald, *Women in Islam*, p. 108.
86 Ahmed, *Women and Gender in Islam*, p. 63; Anour Majid, 'The Politics of Feminism in Islam', *Signs*, 23, (1998), pp. 334–5.
87 Billie Melman, *Women's Orients: English Women and the Middle East, 1718–1918* (Basingstoke: Macmillan, 1995), pp. 53ff.
88 See Jane Haggis, '"A Heart that Has Felt the Love of God and Longs for Others to Know it": Conventions of Gender, Tensions of Self and Constructions of Difference in Offering to be a Lady Missionary', *Women's History Review*, 7 (1998), pp. 171ff.
89 Ahmed, *Women and Gender in Islam*, p. 237.
90 Laura Lauer, 'Opportunities for Baptist Women and the 'Problem' of the Baptist Zenana Mission, 1867–1913', in Sue Morgan, ed., *Women, Religion and Feminism in Britain, 1750–1900* (Basingstoke: Palgrave, 2002), p. 219.
91 Sahgal and Yuval-Davis, 'Introduction', p. 3.
92 Barbara Freyer Stowasser, 'The Status of Women in Early Islam', in Hussain *Muslim Women*, pp. 23–4.
93 See, for example, I Timothy 2:9.
94 Roald, 'The Mecca of Gender Equality', pp. 83ff.
95 Yuval-Davis, 'Jewish Fundamentalism and Women's Empowerment', p. 213; Arthur Hertzberg, ed., *Judaism: The Key Spiritual Writings of the Jewish Tradition* (New York: Simon & Schuster, 1991), p. 116; Neuberger, 'Women in Judaism', pp. 136ff.
96 Yuval-Davis, 'Jewish Fundamentalism and Women's Empowerment', p. 213; Webber, 'Between Law and Custom', p. 144.
97 Yuval-Davis, 'Jewish Fundamentalism and Women's Empowerment', p. 217.
98 Rickie Burman, '"She Looketh Well to the Ways of her Household": The Changing Role of Jewish Women in Religious Life, c.1880–1930', in Malmgreen, *Religion in the Lives of English Women, 1760–1930*, p. 236.
99 '"I Don't Know Enough:" Jewish Women's Learned Ignorance', *Women in Judaism: A Multidisciplinary Journal*, 1 (1997), pp. 3–4.
100 Umansky, 'Women in Judaism', p. 342.
101 op. cit., pp. 337–8.
102 op. cit., p. 342; Vivian David Lipman, *A History of the Jews in Britain since 1858* (Leicester: Leicester University Press, 1990), p. 91.
103 Tony Kushner, 'Sex and Semitism: Jewish Women in Britain in War and Peace', in Panikos Panayi, ed., *Minorities in Wartime: National and Racial Groupings in Europe, North America and Australia during the Two World Wars* (Providence, RI: Berg, 1993), pp. 122, 130.
104 Quoted in Kushner, 'Sex and Semitism', p. 136.
105 Ann Higginbotham, 'Respectable Sinners: Salvation Army Rescue Work with Unmarried Mothers, 1884–1914' in Malmgreen, ed., *Religion in the Lives of English Women*, pp. 216ff.

106 See, for example, Elaine Kay, 'A Turning Point in the Ministry of Women: The Ordination of the First Woman to the Christian Ministry in England, September, 1917', in Sheils and Wood, *Women in the Church*, pp. 505–12; Mcleod, *Religion and the People of Western Europe*, p. 28.

107 Pope John Paul II, *Ordinatio sacerdotalis* (22 March 1994). Quoted in Tippett-Spirtou, *French Catholicism*, p. 169.

108 Quoted in Tippett-Spirtou, *French Catholicism*, p. 170.

109 Stowasser, 'The Status of Women in Early Islam', in Hussain, *Muslim Women*, p. 34.

110 op. cit., p. 14.

111 Y. Ali, 'Muslim Women and the Politics of Ethnicity', in Sahgal and Yuval-Davis, *Refusing Holy Orders*, p. 113.

112 *Irish Catholic*, 27 August 1942. Quoted in J. Donnelly, 'The Peak of Marianism in Ireland, 1930–1960', in S. Brown and D. Miller, eds, *Piety and Power in Ireland, 1760–1960: Essays in Honour of Emmet Larkin* (Notre Dame, Ind., University of Notre Dame Press, 2000), p. 279.

113 *Irish Catholic*, 19 August 1937. Quoted in Donnelly, 'The Peak of Marianism in Ireland, 1930–1960', p. 280.

114 *Irish Churchman*, 17 August 1935. Quoted in Donnelly, 'The Peak of Marianism in Ireland, 1930–1960', pp. 279ff.

115 Foster, 'Women and the Inverted Pyramid of the Black Churches in Britain', in Sahgal and Yuval-Davis, *Refusing Holy Orders*, p. 56.

116 J. Hoch-Smith and A.Spring eds, *Women in Ritual and Symbolic Roles* (New York: Plenum, 1978), p. 2, quoted in N. Tapper, 'Gender and Religion in a Turkish Town: A Comparison of Two Types of Formal Women's Gatherings', in Holden, *Women's Religious Experience*, p. 81.

117 Burman, 'She Looketh Well to the Ways of her Household', p. 237.

118 Stowasser, 'The Status of Women in Early Islam', p. 25.

119 Mernissi, *Veil and the Male Elite*, p. 84.

120 A. Majid, 'The Politics of Feminism in Islam', *Signs*, 23, 1998, p. 334.

121 <http://news.bbc.co.uk/1/hi/world/europe/3235585.stm>, 25 November 2003.

122 <http://news.bbc.co.uk/1/hi/world/europe/2416007/stm>, 11 December 2003.

123 Roald, 'The Mecca of Gender Equality: Muslim Women in Sweden', p. 84.

124 <http://news.bbc.co.uk/1/hi/talking_point/3110368.stm>, 17 September 2003.

125 See Sahgal and Yuval-Davis, 'Introduction', p. 2.

126 Bruce, *Religion in the Modern World*, p. 99.

127 P. Brierley, *Christian England* (London, 1991), p. 79, quoted in Tony Walter and Grace Davie, 'The Religiosity of Women in the Modern West', *British Journal of Sociology*, 49 (1998), p. 641; Foster, 'Women and the Inverted Pyramid of the Black Churches in Britain', p. 49.

128 Lucy Rushton, 'Doves and Magpies: Village Women in the Greek Orthodox Church', in Holden, ed., *Women's Religious Experience*, p. 59.

7

WOMEN AS CITIZENS
Changing the polity

Karen Hunt

Introduction

Politics, as a subject of mainstream historical analysis, has been less permeable to the demands of gender analysis than many other areas of history. This does seem to vary across national histories but the peculiar inscription of masculinity on the subject, although now recognised, has yet to be traced through all its myriad forms.

Most national histories of women focus first on the pursuit of female enfranchisement and then they track its effect on women's most public exercise of citizenship: their participation in national parliaments. The first women members of parliament, cabinet ministers and prime ministers are seen as evidence of the sex's successful penetration of the masculinist world of politics. The traditional focus on high politics by historians seems to define women out of the problematic or at least to marginalise women to a sideshow: essentially, Helga Nowotny's observation of Austria – 'Where power is, women are not' – writ large.[1] For in Europe no women had the parliamentary franchise until the twentieth century and in some countries they had to wait until half of that century had passed, for example France in 1944 and Switzerland in 1971. In many European countries, significant participation rates of women within government were to take longer still, and few have reached gender parity.

Even when historians switched their attention to the social history of politics and to plebeian political activity in particular, women as individual historical actors remained largely 'hidden from history'.[2] E. P. Thompson's *The Making of the English Working Class* (1963) may have put the politics of the working class prior to manhood suffrage onto the agenda for a new generation of historians, but it remained a largely male class whose politics took place in a circumscribed public world. Yet histories of some women's engagement with political power and the pursuit and practice of citizenship have been pieced together and debated in the intervening years. These stories are shaped by the national histories of which they often form an awkward part and by the developments within women's history and gender history.[3]

But this is not the only story to be told about women's relationship to political power. Merry Wiesner-Hanks has identified three historiographical trends that have changed the view that politics only involved men. First was the rediscovery of those women who did exercise power in male-dominated institutions. Across time, these might be women warriors, great queens, mighty empresses or other 'women worthies'. More challengingly, the second trend was to broaden the notion of 'politics' beyond the formal institutions of government to the groups and organisations through which people shaped the world around them. This brought voluntary societies, clubs and associations, interest groups, religious organisations and self-help groups into the political domain. Thus, before women gained formal political rights, women participated in political processes through mixed-sex and women's pressure groups. The third trend widened the definition of politics still further to include anything in society to do with power relations. This could include relations between master and servant, landlord and tenant, father and son, and between husband and wife. The point here is to identify not only where power is formally recognised and legitimated as authority but also where it is not. This means acknowledging that power is always relational, that it is as much about power over someone or something as it is the power to carry out a certain action. In order to study the operation of power in society, it is therefore important to include both the dominant and the subordinate individual or group, and women are to be found in both categories. As Wiesner-Hanks reminds us, although women had formal authority much less often than men, they nevertheless did have power in the past. Thus,

> Through the arrangement of marriages they established ties between influential families; through letters or the spreading of rumours they shaped networks of opinion; through patronage they helped or hindered men's political careers; through giving advice and founding institutions they shaped policy; through participation in riots and disturbances they demonstrated the weakness of male authority structures.[4]

This perception of the nature and location of political power broadens the topic of European women and politics well beyond women's participation in formal politics and the organised women's movement both within societies where women have achieved citizenship and into the centuries that preceded female enfranchisement.

Historiography

A number of different waves of women's and gender history have ebbed and flowed over the past decades and some have had more effect on particular national historiographies than others, thrusting forward new topics and questions without entirely discarding the priorities of earlier generations of historians.[5] For those interested in exploring women's relationship to politics, a number of conceptual frameworks have spurred and sometimes constrained research.

As with many other areas in European women's history, women's relationship to politics has been shaped by the metaphor of 'separate spheres': the masculine 'public' and the feminine 'private'. As Leonore Davidoff has commented 'Like many of these binary concepts, "public" and "private" are extremely complicated and shift according to context. They also change with each new generation of users'.[6] A central issue has been the extent to which the ideology of separate spheres affected different women's ability to penetrate the public world of politics, and how this has varied between classes, between national cultures and over time. Although there are debates about how pervasive and how rigid this ideology was, particularly in the nineteenth century,[7] the separate spheres framework has enabled feminist historians of politics to open up some different questions. For example, how did political ideologies and their practitioners in political parties understand separate spheres, position the boundary between them and thus define what was and was not 'political'?[8] The extent to which women were able to mobilise the rhetoric of separate spheres on their own behalf was first explored by historians of the feminist movement but has also now been used by those interested in other types of women's associations and activities. A focus on the changing nature of the boundary between the public and private spheres has also been productive as it allows an exploration of the permeability of the public world to matters presumed to be private, such as domestic violence. Although the existence of a separate women's culture in the nineteenth century may be contested, this historiography has prompted an exploration of women's kin and friendship networks as part of a distinctive women's politics.

Crudely applied, the notion of separate spheres can have a determinist tinge to it. Yet a focus on women's agency has also been an important way in which feminist historians have approached women's relationship to politics. Indeed, it was an important motivation in the early acts of reclamation of heroines. For example, biographical studies of Alexandra Kollantai appealed to many socialist feminists of the 1970s not only because she was the most successful of the female Bolsheviks but also because she self-consciously explored the tensions between the personal and the political.[9] Biography continues to be a way to explore political activism. Thus, more recently there have been a number of prosopographical studies on the less visible revolutionary women cast into the shadows by the continuing spotlight on Kollantai.[10] This approach opens up the possibility of not only creating a women's 'history from below' but also a social history of political women.

Sandra Holton has explored the relationship between suffragists and the 'average woman',[11] in this case in relationship to the Edwardian British suffrage movement although the same issues apply to other national suffrage histories and indeed to international suffragism. She questions the presumption that the woman activist by definition is no longer an 'ordinary' woman, with the needs of an ordinary daily life to attend to, and that her activism distances her from the 'average' woman. Others have explored the related issue of how a particular form of politics – in this case suffragism – is experienced across a lifetime and interrelates with other political and personal activities.[12] Instead of moving the spotlight from the famous individual in order to illuminate those around her, this approach trains the spotlight away from the most dramatic of the suffragists, the militants, to illuminate instead not only all the nooks and crannies of the many suffrage organisations, but also their interrelationship and the relationship between this and other politics, such as socialism or liberalism.

Agency has always been a key issue in relation to the operation of systems of power such as class but it is as important when considering gender power and the ways in which different structures of power (class, gender, race, sexuality) are tangled up with one another. Amongst Swedish feminist historians there has been debate on how to characterise this relationship. Christina Carlsson Wetterberg, in her research on the lives and political activity of Social Democratic women, has tried to unite a 'structure-centred and actor-centred perspective'. Her purpose has been to provide an 'explanatory historical analysis of women's strategies'. She describes hers as a perspective where we see women and men as acting subjects in complex historical contexts. A perspective that has as its aim to make variations within the women's collective visible, such as the way in which women's subordination is linked to other power hierarchies.[13]

This is one attempt to negotiate the complexity of multiple identities and how they shape and are shaped by the experience of politics.

The power of separate spheres thinking has also been apparent in the characterisation by historians of feminism in terms of two distinct goals: full equality with men or equal recognition for women's difference as a sex, essentially her reproductive capacity. The shorthand of 'equality' versus 'difference' feminism has been applied, debated and refined in relationship to individual theorists, women's groups and campaigns as well as to women's auxiliaries to mixed-sex organisations. Despite Joan W. Scott's powerfully argued rejection of the equality-versus-difference dichotomy, this remains a way in which many histories of the women's movement are perceived.[14]

Scott made the case for using gender as a tool of analysis in 1986, highlighting how it might productively be used to reconfigure political history, for 'political history has, in a sense, been enacted on the field of gender'.[15] This approach has continued to stimulate a more complex reading of the history of feminism and also an exploration of the ways in which gendered ideological and political discourses have shaped the political and social participation of men and women more generally. This means considering not just how politics has been gendered by political theorists but also how the experience of politics, broadly defined, has been and continues to be gendered over time. This means analysing how gender is veined through the language of politics and its practice within specific historical circumstances.

One of the ways in which the gendering of 'the political' has been explored is through the concept of citizenship, defined by Kathleen Canning and Sonya O. Rose as 'a political status assigned to individuals by states, as a relation of belonging to specific communities, or as a set of social practices that define the relationships between peoples and states and among peoples within communities'.[16] Influenced by Carol Pateman's explorations of the gendered contradictions of liberal citizenship,[17] feminist historians have explored moments in the making and remaking of citizenship and the particular politics of inclusion and exclusion on which they were based. One example is Catherine Hall, Keith McClelland and Jane Rendall's dissection of Britain's 1867 Reform Act as a decisive moment in the making of a 'classed', 'raced' and 'gendered' citizen.[18]

The theorist Jürgen Habermas has influenced debates about the gendering of citizenship and the conceptualisation of a broader arena in which political engagement might take place. Habermas identified a new kind of public space emerging in Europe over the seventeenth and eighteenth centuries. This was a third sphere of public citizen discourse mediated between the home and the state, where individual citizens could meet on a terrain of equality in order to discuss rationally matters of public concern. He calls this the bourgeois public sphere and we might understand it as civil society. As Laura Lee Downs says this was 'a public yet extra-political (or at least extra-state) plane . . . a public arena whose legitimacy stemmed from its claim to represent public opinion and the common interest'.[19] This bourgeois public was an essential constituent in the construction of modern democracy. It was also a space, as Habermas's feminist critics pointed out, closed to women from the outset. Critiques of his work have spurred studies on how democracy and citizenship were gendered in a foundational moment such as the French Revolution, but his work has also led to a foregrounding in eighteenth-century studies of new spaces of sociability, prompted particularly by a burgeoning print culture, which some women exploited. Habermas also spurred feminist historians to map the multiplicity of public spheres not just across time but also concurrently.[20] This critical engagement with what has constituted 'the public' is reflected in a much more plastic understanding of 'politics'.

Thus rather than just thinking in terms of two spheres of action, the public and the private, it has become more useful to think in terms of political spaces. The concept of political space suggests that there are many places where politics can occur, beyond parliaments and political parties. This takes us into the realm of the many activities that make up civil society and the notion of informal politics taking place in spaces that are not perceived as political at all. The notion of space allows us to see politics happening not just in elected assemblies, in meeting rooms, in workplaces and in public squares but also in the parlours of domestic homes, in shops, in newspapers, in snatched conversations and even in the imagination. Thus political space was not always public space. If political space is diffuse it also contains many possibilities, some of which are more amenable to women's participation than others. A woman's access to political space could also depend as much upon her class, her religion, her ethnicity and her geographical location, as upon her gender. Indeed, the idea of space allows politics to be placed in contexts other than the national, whether it is the neighbourhood, the local, the regional, the transnational or even the global. The links and contrasts between some of these spaces and the possibilities and frustrations they represented can be traced in Leila J. Rupp's exploration of the international women's movement.[21]

In order to reflect on some of the different issues that historians of European women's politics have raised in recent years, this chapter will keep to the broad and somewhat arbitrary chronological divides of the eighteenth, nineteenth and twentieth centuries but will attempt to explore similar themes in each. The purpose is to establish the extent to which there are continuities in women's relationship to politics over this lengthy period and within a series of developing national cultures. Is a Whig history of women's political emancipation discernible across all of Europe, as is often implied in mainstream histories, or is this the least interesting question to be asking? As part of a reconfiguration of this story, I will touch upon how the thinking about politics and women's relationship to it, such as notions of citizenship, was shaped and will consider the impact this had on the everyday lives of women. What was acceptable or possible in formal and informal politics for women, and how was this constrained by class, ethnicity or other identities? To compare what was possible also involves identifying the spaces for women's participation and the extent to which women were able to carve out new ones or to reconfigure traditional notions of 'the political'. This therefore leads to a consideration of the extent to which gender shaped women's engagement with the political process. Yet none of this has any meaning unless it is placed within specific historical contexts, thus what were the significant events that affected women's relationship with politics? Are those markers of the making of modernity such as nation-building, revolutions and world wars the most significant contours for the mapping of women's political experience across three centuries of

European history? The comparative approach of this volume allows us to escape from the myopia of national histories and the limitations of period-bound studies to a wider vision, which attempts to make out patterns of experience and broader discourses across temporal and geographical boundaries.

The eighteenth century

Across early modern Europe there can be found occasional examples of women who directly exercised political power and slightly more of those who had some indirect influence over those who had political authority. The majority of women, like their menfolk, had no access to power of any sort, yet in extremis some challenged authority, principally through riot. In this world, women's participation in political activity was determined through birth. Of the two kinds of political regimes in early modern Europe, monarchies offered more scope than oligarchic republics for women to share in the public exercise of power. In republics, such as Venice or the Swiss cantons, the only scope for women's political influence was informally through husbands, sons and wider kin networks. In monarchies such as Britain, France or Spain, there was the possibility for women to overtly hold power, not least by dynastic succession or by marriage, as queens. Although, as Natalie Zemon Davis points out, women never actually sat in the sovereign's privy council, they did take part in the conversation – political and personal – that filled the halls, chambers and bedrooms of the royal palace.[22]

In the eighteenth century, few men, let alone women had the power of the absolute monarch and Empress of Russia, Catherine the Great. Nor was she alone, for eighteenth-century Europe contained other powerful female monarchs such as Maria Theresa, Empress of Austria, and those who through marriage had taken on the publicly powerful role of queen consort. To her cost, contemporaries saw Louis XVI's queen, Marie Antoinette, as having tremendous influence. She was blamed for diverting the King from governing, for removing effective royal ministers such as Turgot and for draining the French treasury to buy jewellery and clothes. Many came to agree with Jacques Joseph Duguet who blamed the pernicious effect of female influence for his country's ills: 'the entire nation, formerly full of courage, grows soft and becomes effeminate, and the love of pleasure and money succeeds that of virtue'.[23] Royal mistresses were particularly susceptible to accusations of female influence but could be power brokers rather than merely pawns in court politics. Louis XV's mistresses, Madames de Pompadour and du Barry, were specifically trained by aristocratic male mentors and presented to the royal patron to win the rewards of favour both for their sponsors and for themselves. Women courtiers could also have considerable influence, whether by controlling access to the monarch as Maria Theresa's attendants did or as advisers such as Queen Anne's confidante, Sarah Churchill, Duchess of Marlborough. Even for elite women such as these, their access to this world was not a result of their own endeavours but through their family, and it was defined by their relationship to men. In turn their influence was seen in terms of their kin rather than as individuals.

Although such women were located at the centres of political power, many of their skills and attributes were deployed by other elite women who were not indifferent to the operation of power and their ability to influence it. Indeed, one of the ways in which women were able to exercise political power was to become effective participants within patronage systems. Access to political power, albeit indirectly, was possible for some women through building and sustaining personal networks with the powerful and influential. Although literary and intellectual in focus rather than explicitly political, the hostess could use the salon as a space to develop new ideas, form new networks and act as a patron herself, fostering the developing art of conversation. The salon had 'transformed a noble leisure form of social gathering into a serious work space'.[24] It thus had, in the broadest sense, political potential.

Salons were particularly amenable to women as they were less public spaces than the male world of London's coffee houses and gentleman's clubs. They appeared in the leading capitals of Europe, including London and Berlin. However, it was Paris that was renowned for its salons. Here *salonnières* such as Marie Thérèse Geoffrin and Julie Lespinasse guided the conversation of men of letters and, in turn, engineered their own education in the most progressive thought of the day. But these initiatives were an ambiguous development for women's empowerment as the *salonnière*'s role was largely limited to 'the governance of male conversation'.[25] Some *salonnières* did have political influence. So Suzanne Necker helped to make her husband finance minister of France in 1776, through her influential salon, and a generation later, her daughter, Germaine de Staël, led the intellectual and political opposition to Napoleon Bonaparte from her salon. Fear of such feminine influence grew. To Rousseau, the *salonnière* represented a disturbing unsettling of gender roles: 'From the lofty height of her genius, she scorns every womanly duty, and she is always trying to make a man of herself'.[26] Influence in a monarchical regime had significant costs, as Davis points out: 'they are hidden, they are unaccountable, and they are especially freighted with suspicion when in the hands of a woman'.[27] Yet there are ways of seeing such feminine influence in a more positive light.

Patronage, as in most of Europe, was central to eighteenth-century British politics. Few men had the right to vote, so women, like all the millions of unenfranchised men, had to find other strategies to affect political decision-making. Patronage was peculiarly suited to women as it linked together social and electoral politics, providing elite women with an important way of participating in political life.[28] Their gender did not debar them from being brokers of patronage, but their proximity to powerful men enabled them to play such a political role. Traditionally, patronage has been seen as part of 'Old Corruption', of pre-Reform, pre-modern politics, and as such has been disparaged. Yet within a system where women had no formal power and where the contemporary ideal was one of an apolitical, domestic femininity, it was possible for some women to use their influence, their family and their friendship networks to engage in political negotiations. In this context, rank and relations seem to have mattered more than gender in shaping patronage requests and expectations and in determining responses and outcomes. Moreover, because patronage operated where the public and private domains overlapped and could be shaped to fit women's lives, the strategies deployed by these elite women could transfer to the new era heralded by the Great Reform Act of 1832. The political effectiveness of mobilising kin and friendship networks, of lobbying directly and through intermediaries, was not lost on new generations of women campaigners who continued to remain outside the world of formal politics.

If the business of patronage took place largely in the private domain, there were other ways in which eighteenth-century women might be apparent in public spaces: through protest and riot. Plebeian women had long been accustomed to take part in and even initiate riots in towns and villages when it was felt that rightful claims had been violated and the authorities were failing in their duty. This could be for social and political reasons: when grain or bread prices were too high, when taxes were unjust, when open fields were enclosed or when religious outrages were committed. Some see the food riot as a space if not dominated by women at least as highly permeable to women's active participation, while others insist that food riots were not a distinctly feminine province at all.[29] The significant presence of women in many of these riots seems to be linked to a perception that this was 'a reactionary form of collective action – spontaneous and impulsive in nature, purely local in focus, apolitical and communally based'.[30]

Across eighteenth-century Europe there were outbreaks of popular violence in which women participated in different ways: they did not 'think only with their stomachs'.[31] Women's roles in riot may have varied, but local law, which defined riotous offences and community traditions about the limits of acceptable behaviour, often influenced them. Such protests were not frequent but when riot broke out women were primarily involved in economic and religious disturbances that could have a political context. This varied from country to country. For example, in Britain, in addition to bread riots in the 1760s and 1790s, women participated in riots in the 1720s prompted by rumours of the extension of indirect taxation, though not to the same extent as men. Purely political unrest such as the Gordon Riots appears to have been male terrain. But then recording women's participation in such informal actions was never systematic. In popular protests, women could act with other women, with men or provide the incitement to revolt and then leave more violent action to the men.

But what of women's relationship to electoral politics? The possibilities for this seem slight. Yet in recent revisionist accounts of eighteenth-century English women and politics, a new reading of women's relationship to, and participation within, political life is being made. It was generally assumed that this was a time when women were barred by custom from parliamentary politics and that widespread cultural misogyny excluded all but a few exceptional elite women from political life. New scholarship traces women's involvement in all elements of the electoral process from what Elaine Chalus terms 'social politics' (the management of people and social activities for political ends) to managing and directing campaigns and controlling family interests. These electoral activities were a logical extension of traditional female roles and were 'generally accepted, often expected, and sometimes demanded'.[32] In some cases this was because the women concerned were not particularly interested in politics as such but became involved in local contests to protect or promote a family interest, but for others their involvement stemmed from a sense of ideological or factional loyalty. These were 'political women' whose open political involvement was accepted out of respect for their political capabilities and in deference to their positions within families or factions.

Yet the most notorious example of women's electioneering in England, the 1794 election in Westminster, has traditionally been seen as evidence of a general antipathy to women's public political activity. The Duchess of Devonshire attracted considerable adverse publicity for her energetic canvassing for Charles James Fox. Indeed this election has been seen as hardening the boundary between acceptable private and familial activity and the proscribed public male world of politics for women. The much-circulated image of the Duchess kissing butchers for their votes was considered to be offensive not only because her femininity had been transgressed but also so had her class position. The opprobrium poured on her was thought to have put an end to all patrician women's public political activity for many generations, yet this judgement has recently been challenged.[33] The Duchess was by no means the only woman involved in canvassing in this particularly high-profile election, nor was her political career ended by it, although the experience did affect how she practised her politics thereafter.

If the themes of eighteenth-century European women's practical relationship to politics are delineated by class – the influence of elite women and the rioting plebeian women – then these two elements came together and were transformed by the French Revolution. Ideas about political participation and the nature of citizenship were matters of contention amongst European intellectuals in the century before the French Revolution. What had largely been an intellectual matter until 1789 became a major political issue from the start of the French Revolution.

The French Revolution affected women's relationship to politics in a number of ways, both at the time and in the following centuries. One of the most significant was the way in which at the birth of modern democracy the definition and political practice of citizenship was so thoroughly gendered. Thus the whole understanding of what constituted politics and who could or could not expect to participate in the exercise of power was reconfigured in an upheaval that had implications beyond the specific events of the Revolution itself. The Revolution may have produced feminist ideas, but these emerged in tandem with a much more powerful 'highly gendered bourgeois male discourse that depended on women's domesticity and the silencing of "public" women, of the aristocratic and popular classes'. As a result the bourgeois public sphere created through Revolutionary politics was 'essentially, not just contingently, masculinist'.[34] This has had crucial consequences for women's relationship with politics throughout the modern era. It seemed that the effect of the French Revolution was to legitimate gender hierarchy while at the same time other social hierarchies were being challenged by new concepts of individual rights and social equality. But this need not be an entirely pessimistic scenario, for it can also be argued that the French Revolution 'both excluded women from citizenship and raised the possibility of it'.[35] It was this possibility that was explored in different ways across Europe during the nineteenth century and beyond.

The *Déclaration des Droits de l'homme et du citoyen* (Declaration of the Rights of Man and of the Citizen) in 1789 created a new political space. Individual rights were now firmly on the agenda, yet how much room to manoeuvre did this actually give women? The new constitution defined the active citizen as a man who could meet a particular tax qualification while all other adults were deemed passive citizens. The group excluded from active citizenship included women, foreigners, domestic servants and men who did not meet the tax qualification. The latter could become active citizens once they paid sufficient tax: women never could make such a transformation. Yet being defined out of citizenship did not stop a significant number of women engaging in informal political acts, thus exploring a de-facto citizenship. Nor did it stop some women making claims for more formal citizenship rights. The most famous example is Olympe de Gouges who argued for equality in political participation and citizenry in the *Déclaration des Droits de la femme et de la citoyenne* (Declaration of the Rights of the Woman and of the Citizen) (1791). Her case was that women represented the nation not *although* they were mothers, daughters and sisters but *because* they were. A rather different conception of female citizenship emerged in 1792, in which women's right to self-defence was combined with a civic obligation to protect and defend the nation. In this understanding of citizenship, which was not gendered, the previously passive citizenry were to be armed in defence of the revolution and the nation. Thus the armed processions that took place in Paris in June 1792 included women wearing liberty caps carrying sabres and blades. Gisela Bock argues that the historical significance of de Gouges and the other voices that were raised for female citizenship 'resides not in the fact that they failed but that they existed at all. The revolution gave them space, and the revolution silenced them'.[36]

The Revolution saw new forms of women's political activism and brought new responses and legends about the nature of women's political action and its effect on the body politic. Crucial moments during the Revolution seemed to be shaped by women's participation. Women were present at the storming of the Bastille and subsequent actions in Paris in the later summer of 1789, but the women's march to Versailles in October 1789 came to symbolise the collective effect of militant women. Women were now making political and economic demands – demands that translated into political action. This included women who entered the National Assembly, disrupting the procedure and even occupying the speaker's chair. Their actions have been seen as 'direct interventions in the legislative process and symbolic replacements of representatives who did not represent'.[37] For contemporaries and even subsequently, one of the unsettling aspects of the early stages of the Revolution was the public participation of women, particularly of plebeian women such as the Paris market women who provided the core of the women's march. Women had been involved in food riots and protests over rising prices, but 1789 saw a new context for such economically driven actions. Essentially, the march connected demands for food with a sense of the political obligation of the ruler, and of justice and moral order. The women called for 'Bread, but not at the price of liberty'.[38] In this way the October days prefigured subsequent mobilisations of unorganised women over the cost and distribution of food, linking the economic with the political through consumption. Such activities had the potential to lead to significant revisions in the long-term political agenda and linked directly and particularly to the everyday experience of working women.

As attempts at reform quickly progressed into social revolution, female faces were to be found in the crowd, on the streets and in the spaces where informal politics took place, such as the new political clubs. Women's political activities took a range of forms, in some of which women sought to engage directly within the political upheaval, either as members of their class or explicitly as women, while others were drawn in and out of less formal political activity by struggles around subsistence. And, of course, women were to be found on all sides of the debate, both spurring the revolution forward and also resisting and even falling victim to it, while many more endeavoured to ride out the often chaotic situation prioritising family survival. We can never know the individual motivation of many of the women in the crowd or plot their participation over time and its effect on the rest of their lives. There is no evidence to suggest that the *sans-culotte*'s wife had political aspirations of her own, particularly in terms of full citizenship rights. Like later political movements, such as Chartism in Britain, these women appear to have endorsed the idea that not only their own but crucially their household's interests were represented through their husband's citizenship rights. Yet this did not induce passivity: *sans-culotte* women took seriously their right to petition, denounce and fill the tribunes of the Assembly, to criticise politicians and to address them as 'tu' to remind them of whose interests they were supposed to represent.[39]

The women who took part in the political clubs were more unequivocally politically active. The more radical ones, such as the Jacobins and the Cordeliers, did not admit women as members, but they could witness the debates from the galleries. Some women's clubs were formed: the most famous was the Society of Revolutionary Republican Women which lasted from May to October 1793, led by Pauline Léon, a chocolate-maker, and Claire Lacombe, an actress. For some historians, the existence of such clubs and the articulation within them, and within the club culture more generally, of demands for women's citizenship rights shows that some women saw the feminist possibilities of the Revolution. For others, silencing of such demands by male revolutionaries is more critical; for others still the concern is the extent to which such debates touched the experiences and shaped the perception of politics of the broader mass of the female population. Certainly, the society led by Léon and Lacombe was never large (about 170 members at its foundation), but it was militant and had an effect far beyond its membership. The Society of Revolutionary Republican Women came into conflict with another group of politicised women, the market women of Paris, over the enforcement of price controls and their successful campaign for a law obliging all women to wear the revolutionary tricoloured cockade in public. A series of brawls between the two groups of women gave the Jacobin Government the excuse it needed to act against the society and, indeed, all political women. Having been useful allies, women became a nuisance, particularly when they highlighted the shortcomings of government policy. On 30 October 1793, women's clubs and associations were outlawed and women were reminded that their life lay within the home: as was said in the Convention, 'a woman's honour confines her to the private sphere and precludes her from a struggle with man'.[40]

Once women's political clubs had been prohibited, militant women continued to speak out in markets and in the streets. Although this was a particularly diffuse form of political engagement, it became much more important after 1793 and had the virtue of being much harder to control. Dominique Godineau has mapped the different ways in which the food question shaped women's public interventions as individuals or as part of the crowd from 1793 to 1795.[41] She argues that although insurrections might be prompted by economic crisis, the key for the women as *citoyennes* without citizenship, was that these were moments when women were able to claim rights in the name of 'the people' that, as women, they did not actually have. One of the ways in which they did this was to incite men to action. The fact that after the failure of the Prairial insurrection of May 1795, the Convention prohibited women from gathering in the street in groups of more than five, showed just how important this form of action had become. Indeed, Lynn Hunt sees one of the distinguishing features of the Revolution as being not only women's organised activism but also 'the surprisingly open political space created by the radicalization of the revolution'. As she says, 'What was new was the self-conscious organization by women to demand their political rights'.[42] She stresses how important it is to change our focus from understanding why the revolutionaries opposed female activism and full citizenship for women, to unpicking how it is that women were able to organise in the first place, given widely shared attitudes to women's proper place in society, in effect, to put agency and the workings of patriarchy into the total story of the Revolution. The narrative of radical democrats excluding women from active citizenship is only the beginning of a story that focuses on how women have negotiated passive citizenship or, in the French case, being *citoyennes* without citizenship. Thus, whether women had, or even demanded, the vote is only part of how European women's relationship to political power can be reconstructed. Indeed, how women found and exploited political spaces is an important part of the story to be told here.

Women were also to be found amongst the counter-revolutionaries. For example, in provincial France, peasant women saw few advantages in a new order that wanted to pay for their produce in a worthless, debased currency, and they had little to gain from the regime's attempts at price-fixing. For many in rural France, the Revolution seemed alien, urban and a Parisian imposition. When these concerns combined with strong local Catholic allegiances, rural women defended their faith against Jacobin attempts to impose dechristianisation through occupying churches, reclaiming confiscated religious objects and freeing dissident priests from prison.[43] These women became as important to the myths of the Revolution as any of the Parisian *citoyennes*: republican revolutionaries and historians would blame the failure of the revolution on counter-revolutionary women in collusion with priests. As Olwen Hufton remarks,

> the most persistent ghost of the French Revolution was not the woman of the revolutionary crowds but the counter-revolutionary woman of 1795–6. A citizen at one remove with her rationality called into doubt she succeeded in becoming the basis of a troubling legend.[44]

The Revolution also has to be seen as crucial to the birth of feminism. Were the apparently universal rights announced as the Rights of Man to include women's rights? As Condorcet wrote in 1790, 'Either no individual of the human race has genuine rights, or else all have the same; and he who votes against the right of another, whatever the religion, colour, or sex of that other, has henceforth abjured his own'.[45] The Dutchwoman Etta Palm D'Aelders, the Englishwoman Mary Wollstonecraft and the Prussian Theodor Gottlieb von Hippel produced the most well-known texts claiming women's emancipation and their admission to full citizenship, though none prompted an organised women's movement at this stage. Indeed, Wollstonecraft did not call on women to mobilise for their rights; rather she looked to men to forgo female subservience in order to acquire better wives and mothers, 'in a word, better citizens'.[46]

A number of Wollstonecraft's arguments had a resonance beyond her times. She argued that women, like men, were rational creatures and that they therefore had rights like men. But she did not challenge sexual difference and effectively argued for a kind of sexed citizenship based on women's domestic and maternal duties. Like de Gouges, Wollstonecraft has been read as emphasising women's maternal duty as the basis of women's claim for political rights, legal independence and full citizenship, that is, republican motherhood.[47] For the republican mother, her major political task was to instil her children with patriotic duty. These were ideas that were to shape women's political participation in the forthcoming centuries.

The politicisation of women during the Revolution shocked both conservatives and revolutionaries in and beyond France. In England, with its traditional antipathy to France, many had already condemned *ancien régime* France for the unnatural political influence it was thought to give women. With Edmund Burke's *Reflections on the Revolution in France* (1790) came the unequivocal condemnation of the revolution through its female participants: the women who marched to Versailles were the 'furies of hell, in the abused shape of the vilest of women'.[48] The disruption to gender norms helped to condemn the Revolution. This was not just the spectacle of working women daring to seize the initiative in public events but, moreover, a queen who was also a wife and mother being driven by force from her home. His views reflected common concerns. Indeed the escalation of the Revolution, reinforced by the war between Britain and France after 1793, prompted a deluge of conduct books, sermons, novels and magazine articles largely directed at women and underlining the centrality of separate sexual spheres to the maintenance of political stability. In other countries, the effect of the Revolution was more indirect. For example, in Denmark there was no response among women to the conceptions of female emancipation embraced by the Revolution, despite the translation of Wollstonecraft's *A Vindication of the Rights of Woman* into Danish in 1801.[49] Although the Revolution prompted isolated claims for women's emancipation during the 1790s in Belgium, the Dutch republic, in the various states and principalities of Italy and Germany and in Britain, they were overwhelmed by the conservative backlash that swept across Europe. This was the moment that the eighteenth slipped into the nineteenth century.

The nineteenth century

Bonnie Anderson and Judith Zinsser argue that the early nineteenth century 'marked the nadir of European women's options and possibilities'.[50] For them, changes in government, law, economy and religion promoted centralisation, rationalisation and uniformity and it was these that deprived some women of power and opportunities. In contrast, Linda Colley, whilst not dissenting from the power of the ideology of separate spheres, has observed that the scope of female activity in nineteenth-century Britain and France was generally wider than it had been.[51]

Yet the nineteenth century opened with a widespread sense that their husbands or fathers should represent women politically. Direct participation in politics was not thought to be the business of women. So the English writer Harriet Martineau wrote, 'I want to be doing something with the pen, since no other means of action in politics are in a woman's power'.[52] For conservatives and feminists alike, women's relationship to politics lay only in their indirect moral influence over men. Yet of course many women were interested in politics in the broadest sense. The possibilities for expressing this were shaped by national histories and cultures as well as class position, access to ideas, which enabled women to imagine themselves as political beings, and, most of all, opportunity.

However, as nations sought their independence in liberal revolutions during the nineteenth century, there were few possibilities for women to participate in or to shape the emerging political systems. This is particularly clear if one compares women's role in the two Belgian revolutions of 1789 and 1830. In 1789, Belgian women were expected to share in the public world of revolution, yet in 1830 no women took part. There were no equivalents to the pamphleteer and political networker, the Comtesse d'Yves who, like other noble women before her, was able to participate in a gendered but accepted way within the political world of the *ancien régime*. Nor were there any comparable occasions to the women who heaved stones from their housetops onto the retreating Austrian armies below. However, despite their presence in the 1789 revolution, Belgian women did not form any separate women's organisations or demand their rights as women. By 1830 they were not to be found in the streets or in the Hôtel de Ville but in their homes. For women, the political world was now an alien one, confirmed in the new constitution, which, as an archetypal expression of nineteenth-century liberal doctrines, placed the individual property-holding male citizen at its heart. Janet Polasky sees the hegemonic role of the ideology of separate spheres as responsible for the nature of the Belgian revolution in 1830. Power shifted from privileged groups in which women had previously held some authority to the bourgeoisie, with its marked division between the public world of men and the private lives of women.[53]

One of the ways that women were mobilised into acceptable forms of public participation was in support of their country in wartime. Patriotism allowed women to take action that can be understood as political. For example, patriotic associations were formed in over 400 Prussian towns during 1813–15 as part of the country's 'War of Liberation' against Napoleon's armies. Karen Hagemann shows that 'As long as women proved their patriotism . . . within the limits of the sphere assigned to them as spouses, housewives and mothers, it was not merely universally accepted, but also promoted and valued in times of peace and war'.[54] However, men were unanimous that female involvement in the political arena could only be tolerated under the exceptional circumstances of wartime. In the years after the final victory over Napoleon, a process of suppressing active female patriotism began. Most Prussian patriotic women's associations had ended their work by 1816, although some survived as general charitable institutions. Linda Colley has identified similar women's patriotic activism in Britain during the Napoleonic wars. She argues that 'Under cover of a patriotism that was often genuine and profound, they carved out for themselves a real if precarious place in the public sphere'.[55] In neither case did women link their patriotic commitment to demands for equal political rights within the state. Instead, Prussian women did not overtly challenge the dominant gender order as they translated their domestic skills and virtues into the public sphere. This was the way middle-class women in particular slowly eroded the boundary between the rhetorically separate spheres.

Hagemann also found that the period of the Wars of Liberation was, for Prussia, 'a central phase in the formation of a national political culture organised by gender'. These wars 'accelerated and intensified the nationalisation of the gender order and the "gendering" of the nation'.[56] This process, crucial to nineteenth-century European history in particular, necessarily affected women's relationship to politics and the possibilities for the achievement of full citizenship rights. The effect of new nationalisms was one of the defining features of the political landscape across much of continental Europe in the nineteenth and twentieth centuries. Nationalism not only sought to redefine national boundaries and to create modern nation-states but in so doing challenged fundamental understandings of citizenship and national identity. This necessarily had implications for the gendering of politics.

There was certainly a connection between democratic and nationalist movements and women seeking to express themselves politically. Thus, the first women's movement in Germany emerged in the revolutionary year of 1848. Some women made explicit political demands such as Louise Otto who argued for 'the participation by women in the life of the state'.[57] Some Protestant lay groups formed separate women's organisations to gain 'a clear sense of themselves, the ability to think independently and act in a strong minded way'.[58] But the membership of more explicitly political associations, democratic and liberal clubs that burgeoned during the revolution, was restricted to men. Democratic women's associations were more concerned with patriotic philanthropy than civil rights.

Patriotism and even nationalism did provide a banner under which women could meet, organise and serve their community without appearing to challenge, or indeed wishing to disturb, normative gender roles. Such women's associations, although often with a philanthropic focus, constituted public activity but were not always conceived of as political and were rarely self-consciously feminist. They do form a part of the spectrum of women's politics in the nineteenth century, the century before citizenship was granted to any European women.

Ultimately, women's hopes of achieving some recognition of their identity and rights during struggles for national independence were usually dashed. Mary Nash has suggested that in Spain the intensity of the struggle between conservative and progressive liberals throughout the nineteenth century left no room for considering the need to redress the political inequality of women. The new values of citizenship and national sovereignty that emerged were clearly gendered: they did not apply to women. Thus particularly after the restoration of the Bourbon monarchy in 1875, the fragility of the political system meant that liberals and democrats struggled to gain power and to consolidate an effective modern democratic state. Unlike liberals in other countries, they saw no role for women's citizenship nor were there many voices in Spain demanding women's rights either in the context of liberalism or in the radical or labour movement. Yet, despite the arid context, Spanish women's activism can be discerned in this period.[59]

However, there were still ways in which women could contribute often with clear continuities with the previous century. Thus petitioning remained an acceptable engagement with political affairs. For many of the women petitioners this was a way of identifying with a particular version of national identity, of being included whilst actively seeking to exclude others.[60] So there was a particularly high level of involvement of British women in petitions against Catholic Emancipation in the 1820s. Petitions to the monarchy and parliament were one legal form of political action open to French women. Only after 1830 did these begin to include demands for women's legal and, in some cases, political rights.

The possibilities for participation in formal and informal politics changed through the century but were particularly marked by class. Canvassing was one way British women of status could exert political influence. Patronage continued to dominate all appointments; its exercise was determined more by property than gender. For example Ann Lister, Yorkshire landowner and businesswoman, was active on behalf of the Tory interest in the early decades of the century. Despite the fact that she did not have a vote, she probably exercised as much political influence as most of her male contemporaries. For aristocratic women even higher in the social system than Lister, political hostessing remained important. Even the reforms in Britain to limit political influence such as the introduction of the secret ballot in 1872, did not, according to Kim D. Reynolds, put an end to politicking by aristocratic women.[61] But Reynolds finds that across the century there were fluctuations in this political engagement. Although the generations before and after them took a public role in electoral politics, the generation between 1840 and 1870 were much more reluctant to do so. Reynolds attributes this to the effect, even among the aristocracy, of dominant notions of domestic womanhood.

In most of Europe, influence was all that women were able to exercise. In the hands of the privileged this could mean social politics. *Salonnières* were still to be found in the first half of the nineteenth century, such as Fanny Arnstein and her daughter Rachel Pereira in Vienna, but increasingly this was a role that ran counter to notions of respectable and gender-appropriate behaviour.[62] As Anderson and Zinsser put it: 'The moral repudiation of the salonière led to the moral empowerment of her more traditional sister. The supposed power of female influence was rejected in favor of the power of female virtue'.[63]

However, working-class women could also employ influence in different ways. So some Chartist women identified influence as a source of female power, 'While others toil, she can persuade'.[64] One of their sources of influence was to boycott those shopkeepers who did not support the Charter – what was termed exclusive dealing. Here was an area of everyday life in which women could exercise choice and thus had some power to sway: 'we respectfully suggest that the shopocracy be left to their fate, and that no persons are so well qualified to bring these very important personages to their senses as the women of England'.[65] The growth of exclusive dealing as a tactic employed in support of pressure-group politics could mobilise the housewife and politicise the everyday experience of domestic shopping. Consumption was a pressure point that women could exploit to make an intervention in the public world.

This was recognised and developed in the fight of British women against slavery. From the 1820s the Ladies' Anti-Slavery Societies led a boycott of slave-produced West Indian sugar. Middle-class campaigners even took their battle to working-class housewives. Some ladies' societies went beyond proselytising, purchasing and distributing their own sugar or endorsing specific commercial suppliers.[66] Other women's auxiliaries adopted abstention as their strategy, so the Birmingham based Female Political Union urged the boycott of all taxed or excisable articles such as tea. To make this domestically focused strategy work, leaders of the male union unusually called on the women of Birmingham to break their normal patterns and to 'meddle with politics'. The justification for women's inclusion in what was seen as political action was that the 'whole family of the people' must unite.[67]

The symbolic value of such campaigns was clear but we know less about their extent and success as practical politics in either persuading the boycotted or drawing women into the broader campaign. It seems that the boycott of slave-produced sugar did not have any noticeable effect on the import of West Indian sugar nor did it bring about the immediate abolition of slavery.[68] Yet, as a way of dramatising the central moral issue and the political responsibility of individuals in relation to it, this was an imaginative woman-centred strategy that clearly influenced the practice of women's auxiliaries to other pressure groups, for example the Anti-Corn Law League.[69] In a similar vein, in Germany in 1849 the Democratic Women's Association suggested a new tactic to its members as a way to express support for poor women workers: to 'pledge themselves to wear only clothes made from indigenous materials'.[70] They also suggested that women should only buy products made and sold exclusively by women. These examples point to a potential arena for women's political activity – consumption – that would be more extensively exploited in the twentieth century. This linked to another area of popular politics with which women already had a history of involvement.

In as much as the crowd remained a key element in political change in this century, so women were still to be found there. Food riots had not disappeared. In France there were riots during the severe famine of 1817 and again during the grain shortages of 1846–7 and 1853–7. Women played a prominent part in them, but after 1848 the traditional food riot died away. Instead, protest prompted by problems of subsistence and the cost of living moved from the country to the town. In relation to Britain, it has been argued that as the nineteenth century unwound, food riots became increasingly obsolescent politically and thus tended to be left to women: 'when and where food riots did become feminine, it was a symptom of women's political weakness rather than their strength'.[71] Yet, in extreme conditions, women had nowhere to take their protests but the streets.

Riot could also be prompted by more explicit political pressure or in defence of communities and neighbourhoods. So in the revolutionary moments in France (1830, 1848 and 1871) women can be found engaged in the physical defence of their neighbourhoods. They rarely took part in actual fighting but they assisted in the building of barricades. Once the barricades were in use, women provided auxiliary help to the male fighters, supplying them with food, nursing the wounded and transporting weapons and ammunition.[72]

When women took to the streets in Paris in 1848, they also employed a new tactic: the rent strike. In response to widespread unemployment and soaring rents, female-organised rent strikes took place in La Villette and the Faubourg Saint Antoine. This was to be a form of action that was often identified with women and that sprang from women's daily experience. Sometimes it was seen as being politically motivated or as having political consequences. This was particularly apparent in the Irish land war that began in 1879. Female members of the Land League were forbidden to speak at meetings, but it was recognised that at the local level, women were crucial to community resistance. Early in 1881 Irishwomen were asked to take control of the movement as the British government sought to repress the league's male leadership. With the birth of the Ladies Land League, Irish women were given the opportunity not only to participate in a political movement for the first time but also to devise new woman-focused forms of political action. Women used their domestic role for political ends, paying for groceries with cash so that their men folk would not use the money to pay the rent to the landlord. Despite their success in maintaining the land war while the league's male leaders were in prison, the women found themselves under increasing pressure to disband from both the British Government and the Land League men. The Ladies Land League was seen as representing a reversal of gender roles away from the traditional male/female active/passive dichotomy. This profoundly disturbed men, as an editorial in the movement's newspaper, *United Ireland*, underlined: 'We only wish the men had done [their business] as stoutly, as regularly, and as fearlessly. . . . Is it easier to cow a nation of men than a handful of women?'[73] However, with the reassertion of male dominance, women were again marginalised from Irish political movements, which in turn affected their relationship with Irish nationalism. As with other contemporary political movements, the lesson of the Ladies Land League was that if women wanted to be politically active, they either had to form their own organisation or accept subordinate status.[74]

Indeed, the key issue for women's interaction with the world of popular politics across Europe in this century was the extent to which women were able to be political actors in their own right. The tendency of women to stress their familial obligations as their motivation for entering the political world has called into question women's ability to perceive themselves as independent political agents. At the same time, the changing nature of popular protest, particularly the move towards more formal organisation, has been seen as limiting women's political involvement. Moreover, until recently it has been the orthodoxy that the rise of the hegemonic ideology of separate spheres necessarily proscribed all women's political activity. Thus, for example, Dorothy Thompson argued that in Britain working-class women 'took little or no part in the public institutions of trade union, friendly societies, cooperative societies and political organisations in the mid-Victorian years'.[75] This was because of the power that domestic ideology exerted over all classes, including the working classes, by the middle years of the century. Thus by 1850 neither women nor men would feel it was appropriate or respectable for women to stray beyond the domestic sphere of the home and the family.

The debate about the extent and nature of women's agency is apparent when analysing women's involvement in Chartism, the campaign for political reform in the 1830s and 1840s whose principal demand was for manhood suffrage. Historians have debated how much female Chartists mobilised on behalf of their menfolk, their families, their communities or as women. Michelle de Larrabeiti feels that too often historians of Chartist women cannot hide their disappointment at 'the failure of the Chartist women to remain both feminist and politically visible into the mid-nineteenth century'.[76] The lack of a challenge to the ideology of domesticity is seen as their greatest omission. Yet de Larrabeiti does not read the rhetoric employed by Chartist women as reflecting a straightforward acceptance of a subordinate role. She argues that they may have chosen to represent themselves as wives and mothers but that they also 'managed to raise their political voices to question not only the oppressions of class and gender, but to articulate their own particular political sense of self'.[77] In contrast, Jutta Schwarzkopf sees Chartist women's language of political wife and motherhood as one that 'effectively prevented them from establishing themselves as political agents in their own right with needs and aspirations specific to them as women'.[78] For Anna Clark, Chartist women articulated a 'militant domesticity' that challenged prevailing, middle-class formulations of family life.[79] There clearly was space for women to participate within Chartism, yet Dorothy Thompson argues that by the 1840s women were far less visible in the movement because they had internalised dominant notions of separate spheres.[80]

Yet there are examples of women who directly challenged bourgeois prescriptions of feminine behaviour, for example the Glaswegian Chartist Agnes Lennox who argued in 1839:

the time has now arrived when it becomes the duty of everyone who wishes well to the country that gave her birth, to come forward, casting aside all those feelings which false delicacy and mock modesty give rise to – to take a prominent part in the great movement for reform.[81]

Some nineteenth-century campaigns provided a catalyst for women's sense of themselves as political actors. British anti-slavery was not focused specifically upon women's rights but incidentally gave women political experience and provided the possibility of developing woman-focused arguments. Thus, although formally excluded from citizenship, women such as Elizabeth Heyrick identified themselves as political subjects with political responsibilities in the public world. In terms of developing a new self-confidence and sense of agency amongst middle-class women, it was significant that from 1825 onwards women formed their own ladies' anti-slavery societies, which operated largely independently of the men's societies. It was in this context, Clare Midgley argues, that 'women were able to develop their own ways of working, produce their own propaganda, decide on their own campaigning priorities and create their own networks'.[82] Yet there was no simple development from the espousal of anti-slavery views to a claim for women's rights in Britain. Ladies anti-slavery societies did not challenge their own subordination and wished to export their same middle-class ideals about gender relations to emancipated slaves. However, while there was no causal connection between abolitionism and the later women's movement in Britain, many first-generation feminist campaigners gained early political experience in the ladies' anti-slavery societies or had strong kin connections with those who had. Although strongly influenced by the philanthropic tradition, their petitioning of parliament shows that women recognised the political dimension to their campaign.[83]

The 1848 revolutions, which reverberated across the major cities of Europe, allow us to review the state of women's political agency at mid-century and the constraints upon it. For a brief period some working-class, middle-class and aristocratic women joined the revolts, when for a moment there seemed to be new possibilities. But it was only a moment, for conservative government was restored, with some concessions to liberalism. In most of the German states and in France, the consequence of 1848 was that socialists and women, whether feminist or not, were seen as subversives and barred from political participation for the rest of the century.

The makers of these 'democratic' revolutions in their new parliaments did not include women's political rights on their agenda or expect women to directly participate in the business of revolutionary change. Yet in the tumult created in 1848, there was suddenly space where women's rights might be added into the broader debate. Karen Offen argues that in some of these revolutions 'feminist activity poured forth through the fissures opened by men's claims for representative government, for freedom of the press and association'.[84] Yet, by 1850 counter-revolutionary forces had brutally suppressed feminist activism in most societies. Women's civic activism, even when it was not accompanied by overt feminist claims, was seen everywhere as a threat. Thus, for example, in March 1849 the Hapsburg Empire banned all political activity by women, as did Prussia in 1850. Prohibitions could target areas in which women had been particularly effective at engaging in civil society, thus in France, between 1852 to 1881 women were formally prohibited by law from political commentary and newspaper directorships. Despite fears of women organising as a sex, accounts of women's participation in the European revolutions of 1848 suggest that dominant ideas about separate spheres were never really endangered. As Ute Frevert has said of the German states, 'Even the strident women of the 1848 revolution had clear ideas about "women's station", and it never entered their heads that they might want to be "emancipated" from it'.[85] After 1850, women's civic activism was confined to patriotic and philanthropic endeavours.

The effect of the enforced divorce of women from public political activity can be seen in Germany in the second half of the century. In most German states women were not only prevented from joining political parties by law, it was also illegal for them to attend meetings where politics were discussed. In Prussia the police broke up political meetings at which women were present, and particularly ones where women spoke. This legal position continued after the foundation of the German Empire in 1871. Many would have agreed with the Reichstag deputy who argued in 1896, 'if one decided to admit women to political life . . . then one would bring trouble and strife into the last place where one can, thank God, find a haven of peace in times of political excitement'.[86] There was little pressure from women to repeal these restrictions. The General German Women's Association, formed in 1865, refrained from petitioning for repeal, as they feared that such action would define them as a political society with all the repressive consequences that would undoubtedly follow. It was only in the 1890s that a broader civic culture grew up in Germany with a range of voluntary associations and pressure groups, and political parties began to organise on a formal and professional basis. This changed the context for women's interaction with politics. It saw the growth of Europe's largest socialist women's organisation, led by Clara Zetkin. This flourished as an auxiliary to the Sozialdemokratische partei Deutschlands (SPD), for until 1908 women were barred from joining political Parties in most parts of Wilhelmine Germany. Illegality did not in the end deter women's political activism, but it forced it into different spaces.

In those countries where the political culture was not very developed, such as tsarist Russia, the spaces for women's political action were highly constrained. The French feminist Jenny d'Héricourt offered the following advice to Russian feminists in 1857:

> Surround yourself with women, form committees, establish a large institution as a model, set up a journal, but *do not* meddle in general politics. Let the exclusively masculine regime vanish by itself. If you start to attack it, it is so powerful in Russia that it will crush you.[87]

Her advice may have reflected the experience of many nineteenth-century feminists to eschew anything that was seen as 'political', yet in what was a police state Russian women had no means of collective political expression. None of the political institutions such as political parties, civil rights, active legislatures and free newspapers on which feminist movements everywhere depended existed in Russia for most of the century. It was only at the beginning of the twentieth century that political parties in a recognisable sense were established. Yet Russian women were involved in political action. Nihilism, the revolt of the younger generation of the small Russian intelligentsia in the 1860s, was a cultural and psychological rebellion rather than an explicitly political one. For some women professing nihilism increased their personal freedom in a movement that professed sexual equality. These *nigilistki* of the 1860s became notorious for their short hair, dark glasses and mannish clothes and manners. But others took their rebellion further, into the populist movement of the 1860s and 1870s, which fought to overthrow the tsarist autocracy and introduce popular self-government based on an agrarian socialism. This revolutionary underground movement attracted thousands of young educated people, including women who were accepted as equals. It was not a movement in which women's rights played a significant part, yet no other radical movement of the time contained so many women. They acted as propagandists, but also as terrorists and many paid for their activism with their lives. The hanging of Sofya Perovskaya for organising the assassination of Alexander II in 1881 marked the end of this phase of radical women's activism in Russia.[88] The extremity of women's response was largely governed by the dearth of space for political expression and for any form of mass politics.

However, in some countries in the later part of the century new spaces for political action could be identified for the unenfranchised woman. Again, these opportunities were usually constrained by class. The function of political parties was to change significantly as they were forced to modernise. In Britain, the Corrupt Practices Act (1883), which forbade the payment of canvassers, was a particular spur. It encouraged party organisers to formalise their relationship with female volunteer canvassers and party workers. Individual women, particularly the female kin of politicians, had traditionally played some role in electoral politics. Few took it as far as Lady Jennie Churchill who took over her husband's entire election campaign in 1885. Because women could not join either the Tory or the Liberal Party, until 1918, women's auxiliary organisations became an important way to serve a party interest and, increasingly, seek to influence the party political agenda.[89] From its formation in 1887 the Women's Liberal Federation became increasingly confident in expressing collective views on a range of issues such as public health, temperance, education and domestic violence which, they believed, illustrated the need for a female political voice. In particular they argued about how best to promote the demand for women's suffrage. The issue was whether Liberal women would in any or all circumstances put party before their suffragism.

Conservative women were also organised into an auxiliary organisation, the mixed-sex Primrose League, but they were more reluctant to involve themselves in policy, choosing not to take a stand on women's suffrage. From the 1880s, the new socialist parties marked their difference from mainstream parties by opening their organisations to women as well as to men. Despite equal party membership, socialist women's auxiliaries nevertheless did develop in the early twentieth century to deal with the under-representation of women within the parties as well as reflecting more deep-seated assumptions about the need to educate women into party membership.[90] Whether as full party members or in auxiliaries, British women extended the spaces in which political action was possible in the latter part of the century. At the same time, some women used these organisations and specific suffrage pressure groups to voice demands for citizenship.

One way to narrate European women's relationship to political power over the nineteenth century is to recount the attempts to raise feminist arguments and the seemingly predictable backlash that followed. An organised women's movement, often focusing initially on employment and education and then moving onto direct demands for inclusion as citizens, emerged at different rates across Europe from the second half of the century. Karen Offen has mapped the detail of this process across Europe, the range of feminisms that are apparent and the resistance to them from the political Right and Left.[91] But, of course, feminism was not the only way in which women engaged with political power, and the changing shape of the practice of politics also affected how women perceived the possibilities for, and even desirability of, participation. Again the pace of these developments varied depending on whether the regime was authoritarian or some version of a partial democracy.

In the liberal democracies of Europe, the opportunities for women to engage in civic society and to move from informal to formal politics grew and were used by women motivated by humanitarian or party or feminist concerns, or some combination of these. In Britain, elite and middle-class women's acceptable participation in charitable societies not only gave them skills and networks that enabled them to move further into the public world, but also provided confirmation that the dominant discourse of domesticity need not be unsettled by such action. In the second half of the century local government gradually absorbed many of the functions of traditional philanthropy, particularly the care of children, the sick and the elderly. Although resistance to enfranchising women in national politics remained strong, women were very gradually admitted into the various local government franchises. By 1900, a few hundred women were members of school boards and nearly a thousand were poor law Guardians.[92] Yet, despite women's successes in local government, with only the city and county councils eluding them, Patricia Hollis shows that 'within a couple of years, achievements that women thought were safely banked, began to slip away'.[93] For example, abolition of the school boards in 1902 deprived many experienced women of their elected role and left them dependent on local authorities (on which they could not sit) to co-opt them onto the new education committees. Although women in continental Europe had fewer opportunities to participate in local politics than British women, they still found that there was no progressive development in the provision of political rights. The unification of Italy in 1860 meant that propertied women living under Austrian law in Italian speaking regions of Lombardy, Tuscany and Venice lost the municipal franchise. In the reshaping of nation-states, pre-existing and limited women's rights could be lost.

Although there was disagreement in Britain whether women's successful involvement in local government demonstrated their fitness for full enfranchisement, there were clearly implications for the ideology of separate spheres. As Hollis argues,

> Invariably and inevitably, women members spoke the language of separate spheres, the work that only women could do for other women and for children, and with it an insistence that . . . they had neither need to nor intention of trespassing on male territory.[94]

Women candidates repeatedly made the same points: that every aspect of local government affected the lives of ordinary women and their families; and that every task of local government would benefit from the social housekeeping skills that women would bring to the task. These arguments were then used in pursuit of women's suffrage and again in the inter-war period when they became a key feature of the drive by women's organisations to educate ordinary women into being effective citizens.

But just as there was to be later, there were also differences of opinion on whether separate spheres thinking meant that women should confine themselves to 'women's issues', those that translated women's supposed domestic concerns onto a community level such as education or health. From the beginning women representatives had to make choices between their party loyalties and a desire to bring a 'woman's point of view' to bear.

The context for women's involvement in local and national politics was also changing towards the end of the century. Motherhood was increasingly seen as a matter of national concern, whether for broad pro-natalist reasons or specifically to counter eugenic fears of racial decline. Women could argue that in this context welfare provision for women and children was essential for the nation as a whole and that women's particular knowledge and skills fitted them to design and implement such policies. For maternalism to work to women's political benefit, 'difference' rather than 'equality' feminism had to be emphasised. There were already tensions between women who appealed to sexual difference and those who assumed an essential equality in the abilities and capacities of the two sexes, although too much can be made of this apparent polarity. How effective this was as a strategy for women in the short and long term and the extent to which particular national cultures were more susceptible to this version of a 'political woman' were to be crucial issues for women in the twentieth century.

The twentieth century

Maternalism shaped women's politics for much of the twentieth century. This in turn affected how the possibilities for women's citizenship were imagined and practised as well as how women perceived politics and represented themselves as a political interest group.

In much of Europe the confluence of maternalism and feminism was clear, although there was no necessary connection between the two. For example, in early twentieth-century Spain when women intervened in the public world it was largely through the Catholic social reform movement where they focused on maternal and family rights rather than on women's political rights.[95] Maternalism was enmeshed in a newer form of national and often imperial identity in which women could move themselves away from the margins towards the centre of politics. As the French feminist Maria Martin said, 'If you want children, learn to honour their mothers'.[96] This could result in a form of passive citizenship in which women's greatest responsibility to her nation and the race was to produce and raise healthy children. For others, this was a clear argument to bring women as the 'mothers of the race' fully into civil society. Indeed the state might have to alter to meet this new crisis. The French suffragist, Hubertine Auclert demanded a new form of 'mother state', which would provide maternity endowment and children's allowances, financed by a paternal tax on men. For Auclert, motherhood was as much a service to the state as military activity and therefore should be supported by the state. However, many other French feminists felt this was too radical, preferring to restrict their demands to the provision of welfare services.[97]

Maternalism does not seem to have empowered women in terms of broader political rights. Seth Koven and Sonya Michel suggest that 'female reformers using maternalist arguments alone could seldom compel states to act. They were more likely to be effective when their causes were taken up by male political actors pursuing other goals, such as pro-natalism'.[98] Instead, the effect of maternalism was that it could challenge the political agenda, bringing issues and practices that were previously understood as private matters into the public domain. Maternalism and 'women's issues' seemed to be interchangeable. However, feminists rarely maintained control over how these issues translated into public policy, as can be seen in the long campaign in Britain for the endowment of motherhood spearheaded by Eleanor Rathbone.[99] Maternalism could also be used in the service of a range of ideologies from fascism to Stalinism.

The configuration of political space and its permeability to organised women's demands were crucial in determining the extent to which maternalism was a catalyst to greater levels of women's political participation. In those countries where women continued to be defined as non-citizens, their room to manoeuvre was restricted. In the inter-war period we can see this most clearly when the first wave of nations enfranchised some or all of their adult female population. In France, women continued to be voteless but there was a significant involvement in informal politics (pressure groups and voluntary organisations) and in political parties. As Offen has shown 'virtually all factions of politically active women had endorsed the importance of motherhood for women, and had argued for some form of meaningful financial assistance to mothers'.[100] Across the political spectrum and amongst those who were determined that they were not 'political', maternalism was the language in which the female non-citizen talked to the state and to its citizens. Indeed, Gisela Bock and Pat Thane suggest that women could help bring about the implementation of maternity and family-centred policies 'whether or not women had the vote', citing the example of the *cassa di maternità*. This was a system of statutory maternity leave for factory workers introduced in Italy in 1910. It was prompted by the demands of the women's movement in a country where no women had the vote.[101]

However, maternalism was always inflected with class and with race. The latter was particularly evident through the enormous influence of eugenics on early twentieth-century progressive thought. This was before the Nazis put into practice their negative eugenic policies of mass sterilisation and later genocide while instituting a 'cult of motherhood' among the racially 'fit'.[102] Historians have debated the extent to which fascism was maternalist and whether in this particular context, separate spheres ideology provided an identity through which women could demand equality.[103]

Similarly, in terms of class, maternalism was not a means of empowerment for all women. Maternalist policies might provide employment opportunities for some, particularly the middle classes, but it could also mean greater intervention by voluntary and state agencies into the lives of working-class women. That is not to say that organised working-class women did not have strong views about the experience of maternity and a desire for 'voluntary motherhood', as the letters of Women's Cooperative Guild members collected together as *Maternity* (1915) make clear.[104] As Gillian Scott argues, these working-class mothers did not want to represent themselves as victims devoid of agency, instead 'the Guild inflected this material in ways that buttressed its demands for women's rights, its claims about women's aptitude for public life, and its insistence on the value of autonomous women's organisations'.[105] At grass-roots level, maternity could be an issue that brought together local women activists across party lines and mobilised unorganised women. One example of this is local campaigning to combat the dangerous level of maternal mortality in Britain in the 1930s.[106]

The paradoxes in maternalism are also apparent after the Second World War. Yet mobilising self-consciously as mothers continued to be important to women's self-perception as political actors. This applied particularly where civil society was rebuilt after a period of authoritarian rule. So in post-Soviet Russia, the Union of Soldiers' Mothers Committees of Russia have drawn thousands of women into their activities. Although in the Soviet period there was an elaborate quotas system to ensure the representation of women within the Communist Party of the Soviet Union (CPSU) and the soviets, women were always marginal to the exercise of real political power. The ruling body of the CPSU, the Politburo, only ever had three women members over its entire lifetime. Life was politicised, but the opportunities for women to express themselves politically were highly constrained. Nor did the thawing of the system lead to increased opportunities for women's participation; indeed, a Russian feminist commentator has said of perestroika, 'while women were waiting in line for food, men carved up the country into pieces'.[107] Stalin had closed the CPSU's women's department, the Zhenotdel, in 1930 declaring that the woman question was solved. The entire focus of the Soviet woman was now to be the family, children and associated welfare issues. Later, Gorbachev commented that in the quest to make women equal to men in everything, 'we failed to pay attention to women's specific rights and needs arising from their role as mother and home-maker'.[108] Thus the positive image of mothers and motherhood together with a tradition of women's social and political activism has provided Russian women with what Catherine Danks has called 'a maternal path into politics'.[109] Soldiers' mothers have exploited this path to demand a human-rights agenda and to promote women's citizenship in the new 'managed democracy' of Vladimir Putin. Maternalism is therefore one way that women as citizens and non-citizens engaged with politics in a series of different regimes over the century.

This was also the century of women's enfranchisement. Yet Anderson and Zinsser have suggested that across Europe,

> Rights of citizenship – the vote, the right to serve on juries, the right to hold political office – in fact meant relatively little to most women. In addition, these were the kinds of rights which, when won, were often taken for granted.[110]

In the past, feminist historians were concerned to reclaim women's struggle for the vote and to be recognised as full citizens; now with Pat Thane, we might ask, 'What difference did the vote make?'[111] Yet the paths to citizenship for European women differed. Indeed, the means by which women achieved the vote may be significant for the way they viewed politics once they were recognised as citizens. Despite campaigns for women's suffrage from the 1860s, there is debate about what actually won women partial enfranchisement in Britain in 1918: women's wartime work, suffragette militancy, the long constitutional struggle, the need to enfranchise voteless soldiers at the front. Yet in other cases the causal connection between suffragist campaigning and enfranchisement was much less clear. When French women finally gained the vote in 1944, the breakthrough was an addendum to a legislative bill that bore no direct relation to women's lives and appeared to have very little connection to the feminist struggles that contributed to obtaining it.[112] In France, women's suffragism had itself been affected by the fact that male suffrage was not extended gradually as in Britain. For Britons, this provided a series of opportunities for suffragists to argue for women's inclusion as citizens. In contrast, all French men were granted the vote in 1848 as part of the overthrow of the regime. Thus it seemed that the debate was concluded and reform could only result from equally cataclysmic events.[113]

The pattern of women's enfranchisement, beginning with Finland in 1906, shows the Scandinavian countries in advance of most of Europe. Siân Reynolds suggests that countries with relatively uninterrupted parliamentary regimes from the nineteenth century on tended to grant women's rights earlier than others.[114] But there was certainly no clear run of continuity, with countries falling gradually into line on women's suffrage. Also for a significant part of the twentieth century, various European countries had no parliamentary elections (such as Nazi Germany) or had quasi-elections, as in the Soviet Union. Female enfranchisement could be intermittent: Spanish women briefly acquired the vote in 1931 only to lose it again during the Civil War and under Franco's regime. Ultimately the great majority of European states arrived at electoral equality over the period 1930–50. However, enfranchisement did not result in women moving en masse into politics. In much of Europe women remain a tiny minority in the formal institutions of democracy, and barriers to women's participation continue to exist. These vary from mechanisms for candidate selection to gendered assumptions about what characterises politics and politicians.

The risk of female dominance in politics, despite the reality of continuing male hegemony, troubled many. One example is the Swedish vote on prohibition in 1922. Men argued that women, despite their newly won right to vote, should not be allowed to participate in the voting because they did not drink alcohol.[115] Essentially men were seen as the legitimate representatives of the public interest while women could only represent a special interest, women's issues. When Angela Cingolani made the first speech by a woman in an Italian representative assembly in 1945, she saw herself as speaking for all Italian women who were for the first time taking part in the country's political life. However, she said, 'We have heard many kind words addressed to us, but there is little evidence of trust in us through appointments to public office'.[116] Mutual distrust was often a feature of post-enfranchisement politics.

Anti-democrats could exploit distrust or disappointment with the fruits of enfranchisement. In countries where women had the vote, fascist parties were often anxious to reassure women voters that they were not simply reactionaries. They presented themselves as radical alternatives to the status quo. The Nazis even promised not to endanger the gains made by women. Such promises may have attracted some feminists disappointed by liberal and socialist records on women's rights. The three ex-suffragettes who occupied senior positions in the British Union of Fascists had all failed in bids to be elected to parliament and felt they had been treated badly by established parties. In Sweden, Sigrid Gillner, a former suffrage campaigner and socialist, joined the Swedish National Federation because she was disappointed with how little difference enfranchisement had made.[117]

The significance of acquiring the vote could vary from country to country. In Italy there was a general indifference to women's new right to vote in 1945. There was little public debate, but some women remembered their emotion on first going to vote: 'I suddenly came face to face with myself, a citizen'.[118] At the first election, women's turnout was high and equivalent to that of men. Yet over time, women's representation in national assemblies retreated. There were forty-one (7.8 per cent) deputies in 1947, thirty-six in 1953 and only seventeen in 1968. A similar picture is apparent in France where the number of deputies fell from thirty-nine in 1946 to eight in 1968.[119] This experience was shaped by two interconnected elements: a culture in which politics was not seen as women's business, and women's lack of engagement in formal politics, which spoke so little to their daily life.

Yet this kind of narrative implies that women are apolitical. At the very least it accepts as normative a sexual division of politics: economics and national defence as 'men's issues', education, health and social welfare as 'women's issues'. However, if we look beyond formal politics there is another story to be told. One of the continuities in popular politics is women's protests against the high cost of living. As the economies of Europe developed during the twentieth century, a politics of consumption appeared with a clear gender dimension. The housewife, as opposed to the mother, increasingly became a figure invoked by politicians, and organisations were formed in her name across Europe. For Lynne Taylor, twentieth-century food riots are 'examples of politics happening outside of the political arena, practiced by those who had been effectively silenced . . . including women, by the shift in the nature and location of politics'.[120] Yet at times of crisis, particularly in wartime, food – its shortage, distribution and quality – became a focus for women's political action. Some have seen this as an example of a gendered politics rather than merely class or community action.[121] In the First World War, women's cost of living protests were widespread. Temma Kaplan has argued in relation to Barcelona that women's 'everyday life became a political process, and through that process women's awareness grew'.[122] By collective action based on female consciousness, Barcelona's working women broadened their concerns from consumption to wider political issues. Belinda Davis's study of similar activities in Berlin challenges traditional conceptions of politics and political actors by demonstrating that woman's identity as a consumer gave her opportunities 'to act and interact in the public sphere'.[123] Poor women consumers of wartime Berlin had little access to formal politics yet collective action at a neighbourhood level empowered them to make demands of the state, as women rent-strikers did in Red Clydeside in 1915.[124] This women's activism, which political parties even on the Left found hard to deal with, gave women confidence to link issues that sprang from everyday life to what were seen as much larger and more clearly political ones, such as the ending of wars. This was apparent in the British Women's Peace Crusade begun in Glasgow in 1916 and more successfully in Petrograd and other parts of Russia in 1917.[125]

The Russian example is important not only because women dominated the crowd protesting at bread prices and the war but also because they were among the agitators and organisers who worked with the demonstrators. The successful seizure of power by the Bolsheviks showed that food riots in the twentieth century could have radical outcomes. Whether what the Revolution brought was what the protesters had demanded or imagined has been much debated, but what is undeniable is that the Revolution had a fundamental effect not just on Russian women's relationship to political power but also to women's politics beyond the borders of Russia.

The paradox was that Bolsheviks, like European socialists, disparaged feminism as 'bourgeois' and divisive for the working class. Yet the Bolshevik government was the first regime to declare across-the-board equality of the sexes. However, in the end, this commitment did not do much to shift the masculinism of the party. Indeed, Barbara Clements's study of Bolshevik women suggests that the revolutionaries never seriously attempted to share political power between men and women.[126] Beyond Russia, parties exploited both the promise and the warning that the Revolution represented across the political spectrum in their appeal to women, particularly new voters. This also affected women's organisations, including international ones such as the Women's International League for Peace and Freedom, where ideological commitments soon overrode other identities.[127] A revolution that was seen as beginning with women food rioters was the spectre that haunted women's politics across the century as in some countries and organisations communism was proscribed while in others it was imposed.

Moreover, subsistence unrest was not limited to the extreme conditions of wartime but continued into the inter-war period. For example in almost all large German cities between 1920 and 1923, women engaged in spontaneous market and street demonstrations even using force, threatening traders and looting shops. As Hagemann shows, this disturbed the men of the Weimar labour movement who tried to control and prevent such unrest.[128] To them, the women's action was 'unpolitical'. With economic stability and the channelling of political action into formal politics in the newly democratic Weimar Republic, these protests ceased. However, more and more women withdrew from any form of political activity. They took less part in elections, their membership of trade unions and political parties such as the SPD declined. Instead, what they favoured was local neighbourhood-based action that grew out of their social networks and that was both political and self-help. There are debates about whether there was a similar withdrawal from politics by British working-class women after partial enfranchisement in 1918. Thane suggests not, given the large numbers of women who joined the Labour Party once individual membership was possible and who sought to promote an agenda concerned with social deprivation and welfare.[129] Yet locally, women's experience of the Labour Party varied considerably and some male members of the party were not happy about women's attempt to broaden the party's understanding of politics.[130] The housewife remained a contested figure in Britain at least, because of the ambiguity over her class. The cost-of-living street protester was usually urban and poor in the twentieth century but, increasingly, the organised housewife, or rather the organisations who spoke for the housewife, were middle class.[131]

It is not surprising, therefore, that in the post-enfranchisement era (which, of course, is dated differently across Europe) there is considerable debate among women about the extent to which they wish to be part of or even challenge a notion of politics framed by party. There have been various attempts to form non-party women's organisations or to create their own party, such as the short-lived Women's Party formed by the suffragette Christabel Pankhurst in 1917. A number of national suffrage organisations made their non-party status central to their strategy, such as the British National Union of Women's Suffrage Societies before 1912, or at least found that this single issue could unite women across party divisions. The Swedish national organisation for women's suffrage, the LKPR (Landsföreningen för kvinnans politska rösträtt [Swedish Women's Suffrage Association], established in 1903) attracted liberal, conservative and social democratic women while those political parties were unwilling to support female enfranchisement. When the Liberal and the Social Democrat parties changed their position in the face of the 1911 election, the unity of the LKPR was rocked as suffragists divided on whether they should abandon their non-party position for support for the pro-suffrage parties even if the rest of the political programme was unacceptable to them as suffragists.[132]

A number of countries saw attempts to capitalise on suffragism to create organisations designed to encourage women's political participation. In Britain, non-party Women Citizens' Associations were set up locally 'to organise and educate women so as to foster a sense of citizenship' and 'to ensure greater representation of women'.[133] Similarly, the Swedish Women's Citizen Organisation was created to promote women's interests and to replace the suffrage organisation. However, there was little support from politically active women: 'We women find our political home amongst those men that share our views, not in some sort of neutral zone amongst women with differing views', argued conservative Berta Wallin.[134] Both Swedish and Norwegian former suffragists discussed whether to form a women's political party in the 1920s and made limited and unsuccessful attempts to contest elections with a list of women candidates.[135] It seemed that women could not be persuaded to prioritise their gender over other loyalties, particularly those of party. But then such appeals were never tested in a vacuum: they were countered vigorously by men and women in political parties who saw cooperation across party lines as deeply threatening.

In the early years of enfranchisement, existing political parties sought to portray themselves as the natural representatives of women, while at the same time arguing against the introduction of a 'sex war' into the political arena. These actions were part of a long-standing tradition of ambivalence that male party activists had shown to women's self-organisation even *within* their own political parties. Thus one male Swedish social democrat argued against the formation of party women's sections, as these would be 'battle organisations against the men'. At the same time, a leading female social democrat Kata Dahlström warned against making the sexual question the central plank in the workers' movement 'when other issues are of much greater importance'.[136] Similar views can be found amongst activists across the European Left. The issue for political women, like politicised men, was one of priorities, and gender clearly affected decisions as did class, party, generation, religion and so on. But a woman was much more likely to argue not just about relative priorities amongst those issues traditionally defined as political but to argue that the political agenda itself should be extended. This was most apparent in the area of 'women's issues'.

However, identification with these issues could be a double-edged sword for political women, to the point where a generation of British MPs from Labour's Barbara Castle to the Conservatives' Margaret Thatcher built their careers by distancing themselves from such 'soft' politics. This dilemma was particularly apparent in the transition to democracy in eastern Europe. Since 1989, the new elections saw women's participation rates fall as the system of quotas and 'token women' was rejected. No large-scale women's movements have emerged and self-styled feminist groups are few, despite the active role of women in the opposition movements of the 1970s and 1980s. Barbara Einhorn suggests that in the new democratic context there has been an 'idealization of the role of civil society associations as opposed to formal party political structures'.[137] This has meant that grass-roots groups stepped into the gaps created by the withdrawal of the state from social provision and thus the women who run these groups, far from making political demands, are compensating for the loss of some social rights associated with citizenship. In effect, women are being marginalised from the public sphere of mainstream politics and fall into what Einhorn terms the 'civil society trap'.[138] There is a potentially unbridgeable gap between women's activism at the local, grass-roots level and the operation of power at the national level. Many of these groups focus on 'women's issues', such as the Prague Mothers formed in 1988 to protest against the effect of environmental pollution on their children. For Einhorn, these women exercised their new civil rights but not in the name of women's citizenship. Instead they acted to protect others, perpetuating the traditional image of the self-denying, self-sacrificing mother.

This is a recent example of an experience that has faced women across the century, as new political spaces appear to open up. Women negotiated these opportunities in different ways. One example is the moment when Italy began to move from fascism to democracy. The first free elections in Italy after the war saw all adult women enfranchised for the first time. Although the women's mass organisations under Fascism had given women a specific form of political participation without citizenship, Italians had to look back to the pre-Fascist era to find a rich associational culture among women. The restoration of civil society was a crucial part of rebuilding a democratic country and this began in the chaos of the last years of the war. Historians observed that

> It was women who gave back to the people in the liberated areas a sense of institutional life, but with different institutions from the traditional ones . . . They tried first of all to organise aid, to provide for the needs of the community . . . Nobody in 1944 was debating women's suffrage . . . but women were solving the problem for themselves, taking part in public life, 'politicising' the people . . .[139]

Immediately after the war, widespread women's networks engaged in welfare work sprang up, some spontaneously, some as part of women's organisations attached to political parties, from the Communists to Catholic Action. Women appeared to develop autonomy even in party-affiliated women's organisations because men thought that welfare work was politically unimportant. The sexual division of politics was slightly adjusted for the new situation, but the patriarchal balance of power did not change. Women struggled to show that welfare was political work. They were most successful in local government and in the control of food rationing. The latter was an example of local direct democracy that flourished briefly at the end of the war in local liberation committees and people's councils. Yet, as Anna Rossi-Doria comments, 'The transition from direct to representative democracy was difficult for women who could draw on longstanding family and community traditions at local level, but who had no tradition at all to invoke as Deputies, at national level'. This was to be the case not only in other European countries at this time, but also was a broader characteristic of post-enfranchisement politics across the century. As Rossi-Doria says, it is 'as if "small-time" politics could accept women while "big-time" politics could not'.[140] This is largely because 'political' has been understood as meaning party political. So, inter-war women's organisations in Britain such as the Women's Institute denied that they were 'political' even though they acted as a pressure group on the national and local state. For them, politics suggested a partisan position which introduced unnecessary tension into an organisation that focused on representing the interests of homogenous 'women'.

Yet, of course, for many women, the only space in which they felt they could make any impact on the distribution of political power or achieve specific reforms was party politics. For many it meant choosing whether to involve themselves in party auxiliaries. Until well after the Second World War, the function of auxiliaries to parties of the democratic Left was to provide a space for women to discuss women's issues without any real power to shape the agenda of the parent party. An example is the Swedish Social Democratic Women's Federation, which had a co-opted deputy within the party leadership from 1948 who had the right to speak but not the right to vote. During the 1950s, women started to assert their right to participate in the formation of party policy. At the same time, the federation took an unequivocal stand against nuclear weapons despite the lack of a party decision on the issue. It was at this point that the federation began to grow in numbers and confidence.[141]

Organising women in auxiliary organisations was characteristic of the majority of political organisations, even those of the extreme Right. Authoritarian conservative regimes such as Primo de Rivera's in Spain were willing to work with semi-autonomous women's movements. However fascists organised women within the party itself. The idea was to maintain gender hierarchy while at the same time allowing women to express their special concerns in an atmosphere where national interest remained paramount. Rather than see women in fascist parties as totally subordinated, Kevin Passmore suggests that they merely had fewer choices than women in democratic or authoritarian conservative regimes. Their condition was one of 'relative disempowerment'.[142]

In the Nazi state, by 1936, all pre-existing women's associations were integrated into the mass women's organisation, Frauenwerk. Its leader Gertrud Scholtz-Klink was later to describe this as a separatist 'state within a state' for women only. Claudia Koonz argues that 'While obeying all commands from the Nazi party, Scholtz-Klink . . . and hundreds of other ambitious women enjoyed considerable authority over their masses of followers in their separate sphere'.[143] This of course, was a separate sphere that only 'racially fit' women qualified for. Indeed, Kirsten Heinsohn goes further and observes, 'No political system politicised and made public the private sphere like Nazism did, for it offered many different possibilities for political involvement in both spheres'.[144]

In Italy, from 1932 it was compulsory for every local Fascist Party branch to have a Fascio Femminile, which were run by women locally although the male party hierarchy directed their tasks. It has been argued that the regime integrated women into the public sphere 'by offering recognition not rights'.[145] As Mussolini said of women, 'As far as political life is concerned, they do not count here'.[146] Yet the Fascist Party became the first Italian political party with a mass female membership. Women were asked to demonstrate their active support for Fascism and to play a role in forging the 'consensus' that the regime desired. This meant undertaking various types of welfare work. Perry Willson suggests that although the Fascio Femminile never obtained any political power, their real power was over other women, the recipients of party welfare. Working-class and peasant women were both organised separately as part of an attempt to put the entire nation into uniform. It was thought that these women's sections could enable the party to bring Fascist politics into the heart of poor urban and rural families. Willson argues that this was something quite new to Italian politics as 'it portrayed women as a key to the political mobilisation of whole families and households'. She concludes that although the precise meaning of membership varied, the sheer scale of the recruitment set an important precedent for the mass recruitment of women by the Communists and the Christian Democrats after the Second World War. 'It helped women get used to the idea of political party membership'.[147]

A further space for women's political action was activism. The extent to which it was possible for a woman to be a full-time activist either short term or as a career was affected by the gender expectations of her particular society. Stepping outside social norms, British socialist women in the late nineteenth century began to be full-time propagandists who managed to make a living by speaking and writing for the movement. In the early twentieth century, suffrage activists, often employed as organisers, swelled their numbers. In inter-war Britain women continued to try to live 'in the movement' whether this was as propagandists or as party organisers, but within the political parties they were much more likely to be employed to mobilise other women than as mainstream party apparatchiks. As political organising – from parties to trade unions to pressure groups – professionalised, the opportunities for women diminished.

The issue was, as a British communist woman observed in 1927, 'The women who could be active won't, and the women who would be active can't'.[148] For most women the demands of activism were juggled with domestic responsibilities. For many this was more feasible at a local level. One example is Hannah Mitchell who, in 1920s Manchester, was a Labour city councillor, magistrate, columnist for *Labour's Northern Voice* and an activist in local socialist and women's politics. In her autobiography, *The Hard Way Up*,[149] she recounted with considerable honesty the practical negotiations that made a woman's everyday activism possible. Although there were constraints on Mitchell and her contemporaries in their practice as activists, they only faced marginalisation not illegality and its associated dangers.

Finnish Communist women such as Olga Virtanen,[150] active from the 1930s, faced harsher consequences for their politics including exile, prison, estrangement from children and ill health. The model for the communist cadre was undoubtedly male and a private life could be hard to reconcile with political loyalty.[151] Olga's letters reveal the strain this caused and how little space there was for activists to express their emotions. In organising rural women, she also had to face how distant her own experience was from her neighbours' everyday life. This caused more strain. If she was to remain a communist she had to try to get the party hierarchy to understand what organising such women entailed. This was much more difficult. For, like many European socialists and communists before them, her Finnish comrades began to express doubts about the seriousness of the women's organisation and blamed women for its limitations. According to them, women could not see the really important things and their political action was often called 'tinkering'.[152] Nor was the stress of dealing with achieving some kind of accommodation between public demands and private needs only felt by communists. Women political activists in less disciplined organisations or in pressure groups suffered from what might be called 'burn-out'. In Britain, Margaret Bondfield, the first woman cabinet minister, had regular health breakdowns while a number of turn-of-the-century socialist propagandists, such as Caroline Martyn, died young through overwork for the cause.[153]

In the later twentieth century, there were attempts to confront the gendered nature of politics and its practice. In some cases, the motive behind increasing women's political representation was about achieving a critical mass in order to challenge the toll that political activism can take. Some women politicians do not just want to be part of politics, they want to transform them. Mariette Sineau has shown in her study of female politicians in France that they believe that with a majority in parliament, politics will change in form and substance.[154] Some point to the European Parliament as an example of women organising effectively across party and national divisions, not only for women's issues but also for women's rights. However, the experience of Scandinavian women, with their high levels of political participation, suggests that except for very particular issues, party rather than gender determines loyalty and working alliances. Yet Birte Siim claims that, uniquely, it was in Scandinavia that the Women's Liberation Movement of the 1970s led directly to the incorporation of women into the political elite.[155] The influence of second-wave feminism on the gender profile of other European political systems has rarely been so clear. In Britain there were non-party campaigns to increase women's representation in parliament, such as The 300 Group. Pressure was also brought to bear within parties, particularly the Labour Party. This resulted for a short time, and with considerable resistance from within the party, in all-women shortlists for Labour prospective parliamentary candidates. This in turn was largely responsible for the significant rise in British women MPs at the 1997 election. Women now constitute 18 per cent of MPs. However, women elsewhere in Europe adopted other strategies.

Iceland provided the most successful example of one strategy: the separate women's electoral list. The Women's Alliance formed in the early 1980s in response to the continuing under-representation of women in the national parliament (5 per cent). By 1987 they had achieved 10.1 per cent of the popular vote. The movement was premised on women's difference and on a fundamental feminist critique of political practice. It is claimed that the alliance managed to maintain its more democratic, practical and woman-centred focus, reflected in the language and behaviour of its representatives. It is less clear that the presence of the alliance has fundamentally reshaped the mainstream political agenda in Iceland.[156]

More recently in France, persistent gender inequality in the public sphere has prompted a campaign demanding a particular form of positive discrimination, known as *parité*. The intention, achieved in 1999, was to insert this principle into the Fifth Republic's constitution, although the practical consequences of this are less clear. The hope is that this will shatter the glass ceiling that holds women back from positions of power in all French political parties and within government.[157] At the end of the century, despite formal recognition as citizens, European women's political action remains constrained by the continuing force of gendered understandings of politics and political practice.

Conclusion

The continuities in European women's relationship with political power are striking. This is despite the fact that women's formal position has changed radically as women achieved citizenship and as most of the legal barriers to participation were removed. Yet a Whig history of women's political emancipation is only one way to narrate the history of the past three centuries. For it only tells part of the story. Its focus is narrowly on formal rights rather than on the ability to exercise those rights; it ignores the way in which those rights can ebb and flow and how particular groups of women can be excluded, such as immigrants.[158]

The principal story is not, then, one of the progressive inclusion of women within national and supranational decision-making bodies. Women, collectively and individually, have had and continue to have a much more ambivalent relationship to formal politics. Having fought to be included, there has been disappointment amongst some at the reality of post-enfranchisement politics: not only from those who hoped gender, rather than party or ideology, would shape participation but also from those who found that formal citizenship rights made little difference to everyday life. Gaining access to national assemblies proved to be hard enough, but reconfiguring the political agenda and the practice of politics has been harder still. And, of course, initiatives such as Iceland's Women's Alliance have shown there is not always unanimity on what such a new politics should look like. For centuries, organised women have struggled with the policy implications of a 'difference' or 'equality' agenda: is it a 'feminised' or a 'gender-free' politics which is the goal? The notion of 'women's issues' have proved the means for women to connect with politics and parties, particularly at a local level, and for organised and unorganised women to find common cause. Yet at the same time, this perpetuation of a sexual division of politics has justified the marginalisation of most women from the exercise of real power over the management of the economy, foreign policy or national defence.

It is at the level of informal politics and within civil society that a much longer history of women's participation is apparent. Over the centuries, feminine influence has persisted, as has men's fear of it. Women have used their long formal exclusion from politics to learn other ways of engaging with political power and seeking to shape political outcomes. The long history of social politics at an elite and popular level might seem to emphasise women's marginality, but through it many women learnt the effectiveness of kin and friendship networks. Politics that sprang from daily experience, whether a cost-of-living protest, a rent strike or campaigning for infant-welfare centres, can be seen as community- rather than women-focused actions, yet it is through such activity that women found ways to conceive of themselves as political actors. Often harder for parties to control, such neighbourhood-based politics seems to have been the way in which many European women have made sense of the meaning of politics and the possibilities it represented to meet their immediate demands. For some, this has translated beyond the moment of crisis into a broader participation in civil society, a sense of empowerment and a desire to meet humanitarian, party or even feminist goals. The model of politicisation that most political parties had, and still have, rarely accommodates such experiences and remains highly gendered.[159] It may also be that those who become 'political women', of whatever ideological allegiance, have more in common with one another than they do with the unorganised or apolitical.

Across the centuries, the constraints on women's political action have continued. Class has shaped these possibilities: through differential access to the powerful, through property-based franchises, through access to education, through the burden of domestic responsibilities and through the possibilities for personal autonomy. The power of separate-spheres thinking has also been tenacious across the centuries, reconfiguring but never really dissolving. Yet women have been inventive and have seized opportunities even in the face of backlash and suppression. At the same time, these experiences have been discontinuous, with little historical knowledge either of fore-mothers or of the forces of reaction. Recovering a sense of a collective past has therefore been important not just to second-wave feminists but also to earlier genera-tions of women activists, such as British suffragists who vied with one another to compose the dominant narrative of the battle for female enfranchisement.[160] As we retrieve more of the history of women's engagement with political power across Europe, we can see that there are many continuities in the situations in which women have found themselves and in the ways in which they have responded to the possibil-ities that new political spaces have presented.

Guide to further reading

The history of European women's engagement with political power is a developing field. The fol-lowing list consists of a selection of comparative works followed by some examples of national, regional and local studies and collections that focus on a particular theme.

I

Caine, Barbara and Glenda Sluga, *Gendering European History, 1780–1920*. London: Leicester University Press, 2000. Excellent synthesis on the gendering of citizenship in national contexts and across Europe.

Downs, Laura L., *Writing Gender History*. London: Hodder Arnold, 2004. Accomplished account of the genesis of gender history which explores the changing narratives of women's relationship to political power.

Offen, Karen, *European Feminisms, 1700–1950. A Political History*. Stanford, Calif.: Stanford University Press, 2000. An encyclopaedic study of feminism across the whole of Europe.

Offen, Karen, Ruth R. Pierson and Jane Rendall, eds, *Writing Women's History: International Perspectives*. Basingstoke, Macmillan, 1991. Demonstrates the different concerns and emphases of national feminist historiographies.

Scott, Joan W., *Gender and the Politics of History*. New York: Columbia University Press, 1988. Remains an important collection of essays that stimulate a reinterrogation of the history of politics

Wiesner-Hanks, Merry, *Gender in History*. Oxford: Blackwell, 2001. Her chapter on 'Political Life' raises some important questions for a gendered history of politics.

II

Applewhite, Harriet B. and Darline G. Levy, eds, *Women and Politics in the Age of the Democratic Revolution*. Ann Arbor, Mich.: University of Michigan Press, 1990. Useful col-lection which includes important work on France but also explores women's relationship to politics in countries such as the Dutch Republic.

Canning, Kathleen and Sonya O. Rose, eds, special edition on Gender, Citizenship and Subjectivity, *Gender & History*, 13, 3 (2001). Stimulating collection with case studies on the gendered meanings of citizenship in a range of different historical moments, such as post-Franco Spain and Bolshevik Russia.

Blom, Ida, Karen Hagemann and Catherine Hall, eds, *Gendered Nations: Nationalisms and Gender Order in the Long Nineteenth Century*. Oxford: Berg, 2000. Important collection which ranges beyond Europe but includes studies of Prussia, Ireland, Germany, Czechoslovakia and Latvia.

Bock, Gisela and Pat Thane, eds, *Maternity and Gender Policies: Women and the Rise of European Welfare States, 1880s-1950s*. London: Routledge, 1991. Explores the range of ways that maternalism has affected women and the politics of a series of western European countries, including Norway, Spain and Italy.

Clements, Barbara E., *Bolshevik Women*. Cambridge: Cambridge University Press, 1997. A detailed comparative study of the lives and revolutionary activism of the first generation of Bolshevik women which gives broader insights into women's experience of the Russian Revolution.

Colley, Linda, *Britons: Forging the Nation 1707–1837*. London: Pimlico, 1994. In exploring how Britain was made, considers the gendering of nation and its effect on women's political activities.

Davis, Belinda, *Home Fires Burning: Food, Politics, and Everyday Life in World War I Berlin*. Chapel Hill, NC: University of North Carolina Press, 2000. Fascinating study of gender and the politics of everyday life.

Duchen, Clare and Irene Bandhauer-Schöffmann, eds, *When the War was Over: Women, War and Peace in Europe, 1940–56*. London: Leicester University Press. Includes studies of women and the politics of Italy, Greece, Finland, Hungary, France and Germany in the transition from war to peace.

Frevert, Ute, *Women in German History: From Bourgeois Emancipation to Sexual Liberation*. Oxford: Berg, 1989. A single-volume women's history of Germany which includes women's changing relationship to formal and informal politics across two centuries.

Gleadle, Kathryn and Sarah Richardson, eds, *Women and British Politics, 1760–1860: The Power of the Petticoat*. Basingstoke, Macmillan, 2000. A range of new scholarship which challenges assumptions about women's exclusion from political participation in the era before the organised women's movement.

Gruber, Helmut and Pamela Graves, eds, *Women and Socialism, Socialism and Women: Europe between the Two World Wars*. Oxford: Berghahn, 1998. Covers socialist and communist women's activism across much of inter-war Europe with useful additional comparative chapters by Louise Tilly and by Geoff Eley.

Hall, Catherine, Keith McClelland, Jane Rendall, *Defining the Victorian Nation: Class, Race, Gender and the Reform Act of 1867*. Cambridge: Cambridge University Press, 2000. An important micro-study of a particular moment in the making of citizenship, exploring how the possession of the franchise was marked by gender, race and class.

Hannam, June and Karen Hunt, *Socialist Women: Britain, 1880s to 1920s*, London: Routledge, 2002. Explores the competing identities of socialist women by comparing biographical journeys and exploring socialist women's relationship to suffrage, internationalism and the politics of consumption.

Holton, Sandra S., *Suffrage Days. Stories from the Women's Suffrage Movement*. London: Routledge, 1996. Comparative biographical study that explores many of the themes in the new revisionist suffrage history of Britain.

Landes, Joan, *Women and the Public Sphere in the Age of the French Revolution*. Ithaca, NY: Cornell University Press, 1988. Key dissection of the French Revolution as the initiator of a rigidly gendered, essentially male, bourgeois sphere.

McMillan, James F., *France and Women, 1789–1914: Gender, Society and Politics*. London: Routledge, 2000. A thorough national study which argues that French political culture was sexist and that across the political spectrum there was a profound distrust of women's political action.

Passmore, Kevin, ed., *Women, Gender and Fascism in Europe, 1919–45*. Manchester: Manchester University Press, 2003. Very good coverage of the gendering of fascism and its affect on women across Europe, including a range of Eastern European countries such as Hungary, Romania and Serbia.

Rendall, Jane, ed., *Equal or Different: Women's Politics, 1800–1914*. Oxford: Blackwell, 1987. A pioneering collection on a broad range of British nineteenth-century women's politics.

Rupp, Leila J., *Worlds of Women: The Making of an International Women's Movement*. Princeton, NJ.: Princeton University Press, 1997. Insightful study of internationalism as a practice amongst 'first wave' feminists through a comparison of the Internal Council of Women, the International Woman Suffrage Alliance and the Women's International League for Peace and Freedom.

Siim, Birte, *Gender and Citizenship: Politics and Agency in France, Britain and Denmark*. Cambridge: Cambridge University Press, 2000. Thoughtful comparison of the ways in which distinct national political cultures shape the practice of women's citizenship.

Scott, Gillian, *Feminism and the Politics of Working Women: The Women's Co-operative Guild, 1880s to the Second World War*. London: UCL Press, 1998. Study of a major British women's auxiliary organisation composed of working-class wives and their attempt to find a political practice that balanced class and gender identities.

Vickery, Amanda, ed., *Women, Privilege and Power: British Politics, 1750 to the Present*. Stanford, Calif.: Stanford University Press, 2001. Important collection which rethinks 'the political' and argues for a redefinition of political activity, placing a range of female activists into their broader political context.

von der Fehr, Drude, Anna G. Jónasdóttir and Bente Rosenbeck, eds, *Is there a Nordic Feminism? Nordic Feminist Thought on Culture and Society*. London: UCL Press, 1998. Useful group of chapters on 'Politics in Ambiguous Times'.

Notes

1 Quoted in Anne Stevens, 'Women, Politics and Government in Contemporary Britain, France and Germany', in Siân Reynolds, ed., *Women, State and Revolution; Essays on Power and Gender in Europe since 1789* (Brighton: Wheatsheaf, 1986), p. 123.

2 Sheila Rowbotham, *Hidden from History: 300 Years of Women's Oppression and the Fight against It* (London: Pluto, 1974).

3 See the discussion in 'Forum. When Biology Became Destiny: Women in Weimar and Nazi Germany', *German History*, 22, 4 (2004), pp. 600–12.

4 Merry Weisner-Hanks, *Gender in History* (Oxford: Blackwell, 2001), pp. 146–7.

5 See the recent accomplished survey, Laura L. Downs, *Writing Gender History* (London: Hodder Arnold, 2004). For different national women's historiographies, see Karen Offen, Ruth R. Pierson and Jane Rendall, eds, *Writing Women's History: International Perspectives* (Basingstoke, Macmillan, 1991).

6 Leonore Davidoff, 'Gender and the "Great Divide": Public and Private in British Gender History', *Journal of Women's History*, 15, 1 (2003), p. 12.

7 Amanda Vickery, 'Golden Age to Separate Spheres? A Review of the Categories and Chronology of English Women's History', *Historical Journal*, 36, 2, (1993).

8 For example, Karen Hunt, *Equivocal Feminists: The Social Democratic Federation and the Woman Question, 1884–1911* (Cambridge: Cambridge University Press, 1996).

9 Cathy Porter, *Alexandra Kollantai: A Biography* (London: Virago, 1980).

10 Barbara E. Clements, *Bolshevik Women* (Cambridge: Cambridge University Press, 1997); Anna Hillyar and Jane McDermid, *Revolutionary Women in Russia, 1870–1917: A Study in Collective Biography* (Manchester: Manchester University Press, 2000).

11 Sandra S. Holton, 'The Suffragist and the "average woman"', *Women's History Review*, 1, 1 (1992). See also her *Suffrage Days: Stories from the Women's Suffrage Movement* (London: Routledge, 1996).

12 Karen Hunt, 'Journeying through Suffrage: The Politics of Dora Montefiore' in Claire Eustance, Joan Ryan and Laura Ugolini, eds, *A Suffrage Reader* (London: Leicester University Press, 2000). See also June Hannam, *Isabella Ford* (Oxford: Basil Blackwell, 1989).

13 Carlsson Wetterberg (1992) quoted in Åsa Lundquist, 'Conceptualising Gender in a Swedish Context', *Gender & History*, 11, 3 (1999), p. 592.

14 Joan W. Scott, 'Deconstructing Equality vs. Difference; or, The Uses of Post-Structuralist Theory for Feminism', *Feminist Studies*, 14, 1, (1988).

15 Joan W. Scott, 'Gender: A Useful Category of Historical Analysis', *American Historical Review*, 91, 5, (1986) reprinted in her *Gender and the Politics of History* (New York: Columbia University Press, 1988), p. 49.
16 Kathleen Canning and Sonya O. Rose, 'Gender, Citizenship and Subjectivity: Some Historical and Theoretical Considerations', *Gender & History*, 13, 3 (2001), p. 427.
17 Carol Pateman, *The Sexual Contract* (Stanford, Calif.: Stanford University Press, 1988).
18 Catherine Hall, Keith McClelland, Jane Rendall, *Defining the Victorian Nation: Class, Race, Gender and the Reform Act of 1867* (Cambridge: Cambridge University Press, 2000).
19 Lee Downs, *Writing Gender History*, p.147.
20 Joan Landes, *Women and the Public Sphere in the Age of the French Revolution* (Ithaca, NY: Cornell University Press, 1988); Hannah Barker and Elaine Chalus, eds, *Gender in Eighteenth-Century England; Roles, Representations and Responsibilities* (London: Longman, 1997); Jane Rendall, 'Women and the Public Sphere', *Gender & History*, 11, 3, (1999).
21 Leila J. Rupp, *Worlds of Women: The Making of an International Women's Movement* (Princeton, NJ.: Princeton University Press, 1997).
22 Natalie Zemon Davis, 'Women in Politics' in Natalie Zemon Davis and Arlette Farge, eds, *A History of Women in the West*, Vol. III, *Renaissance and Enlightenment Paradoxes*, (Cambridge, Mass: The Belknap Press, 1993), p.170.
23 Jacques Joseph Duguet (1750) quoted in Bonnie S. Anderson and Judith P. Zinsser, *A History of Their Own: Women in Europe from Prehistory to the Present*, Vol. II (London: Penguin, 1990), p. 43.
24 Dena Goodman quoted in Olwen Hufton, *The Prospect before Her: A History of Women in Western Europe*, Vol. I, *1500–1800* (London, Harper Collins, 1995), p. 430.
25 Dena Goodman, 'Women and the Enlightenment', in Renate Bridenthal, Susan M. Stuard and Merry E. Wiesner, eds, *Becoming Visible: Women in European History*, 3rd edn (Boston, Mass.: Houghton Mifflin, 1998), pp. 236–7. See also Ulrike Weckel, 'A Lost Paradise of a Female Culture? Some Critical Questions Regarding Scholarship of Late Eighteenth- and Early Nineteenth-century German Salons', *German History*, 18, 3 (2000), pp. 310–36.
26 Jean-Jacques Rousseau (1762) quoted in Anderson and Zinsser, *A History of Their Own*, p. 115.
27 Davis, 'Women in Politics', p. 175.
28 Elaine Chalus, '"To serve my friends": Women and Political Patronage in Eighteenth-Century England' in Amanda Vickery, ed., *Women, Privilege and Power: British Politics, 1750 to the Present* (Stanford, Calif.: Stanford University Press, 2001), pp. 57–88.
29 See John Bohstedt, 'Gender, Household and Community Politics: Women in English Riots 1790–1810', *Past & Present*, 120 (1988), pp. 88–122.
30 Lynne Taylor, 'Food Riots Revisited', *Journal of Social History*, 30, 2 (1996), p. 483.
31 Arlette Farge, 'Protesters Plain to See' in Davis and Farge, eds, *A History of Women*, Vol. III, p. 491.
32 Elaine Chalus, '"That Epidemical Madness": Women and Electoral Politics in the Late Eighteenth Century', in Barker and Chalus, eds, *Gender in Eighteenth-Century England*, p. 153; Christine Carlsson Wetterberg, 'Equal or Different? Women's Political Strategies in Historical Perspective', in Von Der Fehr et al., eds, *Is There a Nordic Feminism?*, pp. 21–40.
33 Judith S. Lewis, '1784 and All That: Aristocratic Women and Electoral Politics' in Vickery, ed., *Women, Privilege and Power*; Amanda Foreman, *Georgiana: Duchess of Devonshire* (London: Harper Collins, 1998), chap. 9. See also Amanda Foreman, 'A Politician's Politician: Georgiana, Duchess of Devonshire and the Whig Party', in Barker and Chalus, ed., *Gender in Eighteenth-Century England*, pp. 179–204.
34 Landes, *Women and the Public Sphere*, pp. 2, 7.
35 Barbara Caine and Glenda Sluga, *Gendering European History, 1780–1920* (London: Leicester University Press, 2000), p. 3.
36 Gisela Bock, *Women in European History* (Oxford: Blackwell, 2002), p. 54.
37 Darline G. Levy and Harriet B. Applewhite, 'A Political Revolution for Women? The Case of Paris', in Bridenthal et al., eds, *Becoming Visible*, p. 272.
38 Quoted in Dominque Godineau, 'Masculine and Feminine Political Practice during the

French Revolution, 1793–Year III', in Harriet B. Applewhite and Darline G. Levy, eds, *Women and Politics in the Age of the Democratic Revolution* (Ann Arbor, Mich.: University of Michigan Press, 1990), p. 65.

39 Olwen Hufton, *Women and the Limits of Citizenship in the French Revolution* (Toronto: University of Toronto Press, 1992), p. 22.

40 J. P. Amar (1793) quoted in Hufton, *The Prospect before Her*, p. 479.

41 Godineau, 'Masculine and Feminine Political Practice'.

42 Lynn Hunt, 'Forgetting and Remembering: The French Revolution Then and Now', *American Historical Review*, 100, 4 (1995), p. 1131.

43 James F. McMillan, *France and Women, 1789–1914: Gender, Society and Politics* (London: Routledge, 2000), pp. 25–6; Hufton, *The Prospect before Her*, pp. 481–5.

44 Hufton, *Women and the Limits of Citizenship*, p. 154.

45 Marquis de Condorcet (1790), quoted in Karen Offen, *European Feminisms, 1700–1950: A Political History* (Stanford, Calif.: Stanford University Press, 2000), p. 57.

46 Mary Wollstonecraft (1792), quoted in Barbara Taylor, *Mary Wollstonecraft and the Feminist Imagination* (Cambridge: Cambridge University Press, 2003), pp. 238.

47 Landes, *Women and the Public Sphere*, pp. 129–38. Taylor challenges this interpretation in her *Mary Wollstonecraft*, pp. 223–6.

48 Edmund Burke (1790), quoted in Linda Colley, *Britons: Forging the Nation 1707–1837* (London: Pimlico, 1994), pp. 252.

49 Inga Dahlsgård, *Women in Denmark: Yesterday and Today* (Copenhagen: Det Danske Selskab, 1980), p. 70.

50 Anderson and Zinsser, *A History of Their Own*, Vol. II, p. xviii.

51 Colley, *Britons*, p. 404, n. 23.

52 Harriet Martineau, quoted in Catherine Hall, *White, Male and Middle-Class* (Cambridge: Polity, 1992), p. 156.

53 Janet L. Polasky, 'Women in Revolutionary Belgium: From Stone Throwers to Hearth Tenders', *History Workshop Journal*, 21 (1986), pp. 87–104.

54 Karen Hagemann, 'Female Patriots: War and the Nation in the Period of the Prussian-German Anti-Napoleonic Wars', *Gender & History*, 16, 2 (2004), p. 406.

55 Colley, *Britons*, pp. 260, 262.

56 Hagemann, 'Female Patriots', p. 415.

57 Louise Otto quoted in Ute Frevert, *Women in German History: From Bourgeois Emancipation to Sexual Liberation* (Oxford: Berg, 1989), p. 74.

58 ibid.: *Frauen-Zeitung*, 6 July 1850.

59 Mary Nash, 'Two Decades of Women's History in Spain: A Reappraisal', in Offen et al., eds, *Writing Women's History*, p. 391.

60 Catherine Hall, 'The Rule of Difference: Gender, Class and Empire in the Making of the 1832 Reform Act', in Ida Blom, Karen Hagemann and Catherine Hall, eds, *Gendered Nations: Nationalisms and Gender Order in the Long Nineteenth Century* (Oxford: Berg, 2000), p. 116.

61 Kim D. Reynolds, *Aristocratic Women and Political Society in Victorian Britain* (Oxford: Clarendon Press, 1998).

62 Anderson and Zinsser, *A History of Their Own*, Vol. II, pp. 110, 114–22.

63 op. cit., p. 121.

64 *Northern Star*, 19 February 1842, quoted in Michelle de Larrabeiti, 'Conspicuous before the World: The Political Rhetoric of the Chartist Women', in Eileen Janes Yeo, ed., *Radical Femininity: Women's Self-Representation in the Public Sphere* (Manchester: Manchester University Press, 1998), p. 119.

65 ibid.: *Northern Star*, 8 December 1838.

66 Louis and Rosamund Billington, '"A Burning Zeal for Righteousness": Women in the British Anti-Slavery Movement, 1820–1860', in Jane Rendall, ed., *Equal or Different: Women's Politics, 1800–1914* (Oxford: Blackwell, 1987), pp. 87–8. See also Clare Midgley, 'Slave Sugar Boycotts, Female Activism and the Domestic Base of British Anti-Slavery Culture', *Slavery and Abolition*, 17, 3, (1996).

67 T. C. Salt (1838), quoted in Hall, *White, Male and Middle-Class*, p. 162.

68 Clare Midgley, *Women against Slavery: The British Campaigns, 1780–1870* (London, Routledge, 1992), p. 62.
69 Simon Morgan, 'Domestic Economy and Political Agitation: Women and the Anti-Corn Law League 1839–46', in Kathryn Gleadle and Sarah Richardson, eds, *Women and British Politics, 1760–1860: The Power of the Petticoat* (Basingstoke, Macmillan, 2000), pp. 115–33.
70 *Frauen-Zeitung*, 28 April 1849, quoted in Frevert, *Women in German History*, p. 81.
71 Bohstedt, 'Gender, Household and Community Politics', p. 122.
72 McMillan, *France and Women*, p. 76.
73 Quoted in Margaret Ward, 'The Ladies' Land League and the Irish Land War 1881/1882: Defining the Relationship between Women and Nation', in Blom et al., eds, *Gendered Nations*, p. 240. See also Margaret Ward, *Unmanageable Revolutionaries: Women and Irish Nationalism* (London: Pluto, 1983), chap. 1.
74 Ward, *Unmanageable Revolutionaries*, p. 39.
75 Dorothy Thompson, 'Women, Work and Politics in Nineteenth-Century England: The Problem of Authority', in Rendall, ed., *Equal or Different*, p. 64.
76 de Larrabeiti, 'Conspicuous before the World', p. 108.
77 op. cit., p. 111.
78 Jutta Schwarzkopf, *Women in the Chartist Movement* (Basingstoke: Macmillan, 1991), p. 89.
79 Anna Clark, 'The Rhetoric of Chartist Domesticity: Gender, Language and Class in the 1830s and 1840s', *Journal of British Studies*, 31, (1992), pp. 74–6.
80 Dorothy Thompson, 'Women in Nineteenth Century Radical Politics', in Juliet Mitchell and Ann Oakley, eds, *The Rights and Wrongs of Women* (Harmondsworth: Penguin, 1976), pp. 135–8.
81 *Northern Star*, 16 November 1839, quoted in de Larrabeiti, 'Conspicuous before the world', p. 116.
82 Midgley, *Women against Slavery*, p. 199.
83 For petitioning, see op. cit., pp. 62–71.
84 Offen, *European Feminisms*, p. 108.
85 Frevert, *Women in German History*, p. 76.
86 M. Schall (1896), quoted in Richard J. Evans, *The Feminist Movement in Germany 1894–1933* (London: Sage, 1976), p. 11.
87 Jenny d'Héricourt (1857) quoted in Richard J. Evans, *The Feminists* (London: Croom Helm, 1977), p. 118.
88 Richard Stites, 'Women and the Revolutionary Process in Russia', in Bridenthal et al., eds, *Becoming Visible*, pp. 419–20.
89 See Linda Walker, 'Party Political Women: A Comparative Study of Liberal Women and the Primrose League, 1890–1914' in Rendall, ed., *Equal or Different*.
90 June Hannam and Karen Hunt, *Socialist Women: Britain, 1880s to 1920s* (London: Routledge, 2002), chap. 4.
91 Offen, *European Feminisms*.
92 Patricia Hollis, *Ladies Elect: Women in English Local Government 1865–1914* (Oxford: Clarendon Press, 1987).
93 Patricia Hollis, 'Women in Council: Separate Spheres, Public Space', in Rendall, ed., *Equal or Different*, p. 205.
94 op. cit., p. 208.
95 Nash, 'Two Decades of Women's History in Spain', p. 392.
96 Maria Martin (1896) quoted in Anne Cova, 'French feminism and maternity: theories and policies 1890–1918', in Gisela Bock and Pat Thane, eds, *Maternity and Gender Policies: Women and the Rise of European Welfare States, 1880s-1950s* (London: Routledge, 1991), p. 120.
97 Caine and Sluga, *Gendering European History*, p. 104.
98 Seth Koven and Sonya Michel, 'Womanly Duties: Maternalist Politics and the Origins of Welfare States in France, Germany, Great Britain and the United States, 1880–1920', reprinted in Fiona Montgomery and Christine Collette, eds, *The European Women's History Reader* (London: Routledge, 2002), p. 227.

99 Susan Pedersen, *Eleanor Rathbone and the Politics of Conscience* (London, Yale University Press, 2004).

100 Karen Offen, 'Body Politics: Women, Work and the Politics of Motherhood in France, 1920–1950', in Bock and Thane, eds, *Maternity and Gender Policies*, p. 152.

101 Gisela Bock and Pat Thane, 'Introduction', in Bock and Thane, eds, *Maternity and Gender Policies*, p. 6. See Annarita Buttafuoco, 'Motherhood as a Political Strategy: the Role of the Italian Women's Movement in the Creation of the *Cassa Nazionale di Maternità*', in Bock and Thane, eds, *Maternity and Gender Policies*, pp. 178–95.

102 Anna Davin, 'Imperialism and the Cult of Motherhood', *History Workshop Journal*, 5, (1978); Gisela Bock, 'Antenatalism, Maternity and Paternity in National Socialist Racism', in Bock and Thane, eds, *Maternity and Gender Policies*.

103 See the debate between Koonz and Bock: Claudia Koonz, *Mothers in the Fatherland: Women, the Family, and Nazi Politics* (New York: St Martin's Press, 1987); Gisela Bock, 'Equality and Difference in National Socialist Racism', in Gisela Bock and Susan James, eds, *Beyond Equality and Difference: Citizenship, Feminist Politics and Female Subjectivity* (London: Routledge, 1992).

104 Margaret Llewelyn-Davies, ed., *Maternity: Letters from Working Women* (London: Virago, 1978).

105 Gillian Scott, *Feminism and the Politics of Working Women: The Women's Co-operative Guild, 1880s to the Second World War* (London: UCL Press, 1998), p. 85.

106 Karen Hunt, 'Making Politics in Local Communities: Labour Women in Interwar Manchester', in Matthew Worley, ed., *Labour's Grass Roots: Essays on the Activities of Local Labour Parties and Members, 1918–45* (Aldershot: Ashgate, 2005).

107 Maria Arbatova (2003), quoted in Catherine J. Danks, 'Committees of Soldiers' Mothers: Mothers Challenging the Russian State', in Geraldine Lievesley and Sue Buckingham, eds, *In the Hands of Women: Paradigms of Citizenship* (Manchester: Manchester University Press, forthcoming, 2006), ms, pp. 4–5.

108 Mikhail Gorbachev, *Perestroika* (London: Collins, 1988), p. 117.

109 Danks, 'Committees of Soldiers' Mothers', p. 18.

110 Anderson and Zinsser, *A History of Their Own*, Vol. II, p. 367.

111 Pat Thane, 'What Difference Did the Vote Make?', in Vickery, ed., *Women, Privilege and Power*.

112 Harold. L. Smith, *The British Women's Suffrage Campaign, 1866–1928* (Harlow, Longman, 1998); Cécile Dauphin et al., 'Women's Culture and Women's Power: Issues in French Women's History', in Offen, Pierson and Rendall, eds, *Writing Women's History: International Perspectives*, p. 129.

113 Máire F. Cross, 'Women and Politics', in Abigail Gregory and Ursula Tidd, eds, *Women in Contemporary France* (Oxford: Berg, 2000), p. 96.

114 Siân Reynolds, 'Lateness, Amnesia and Unfinished Business: Gender and Democracy in Twentieth-Century Europe', *European History Quarterly*, 32, 1 (2002), p. 87.

115 Gunnel Karlsson, 'Social Democratic Women's Coup in the Swedish Parliament', in Drude von der Fehr, Anna G. Jónasdóttir and Bente Rosenbeck, eds, *Is There a Nordic Feminism? Nordic Feminist Thought on Culture and Society* (London: UCL Press, 1998), p. 47.

116 Angela Cingolani (1945), quoted in Anna Rossi-Doria, 'Italian Women Enter Politics', in C. Duchen and Irene Bandhauer-Schöffmann, eds, *When the War Was Over: Women, War and Peace in Europe, 1940–56* (London: Leicester University Press), p. 94.

117 Kevin Passmore, 'Europe', in Kevin Passmore, ed., *Women, Gender and Fascism in Europe, 1919–45* (Manchester: Manchester University Press, 2003), p. 245.

118 Quoted in Rossi-Doria, 'Italian Women Enter Politics', p. 97.

119 Rossi-Doria, 'Italian Women Enter Politics', pp. 97, 100.

120 Taylor, 'Food Riots Revisited', p. 493.

121 For Britain, see Karen Hunt, 'Negotiating the Boundaries of the Domestic: British Socialist Women and the Politics of Consumption', *Women's History Review*, 9, 2 (2000); Anthony J. Coles, 'The Moral Economy of the Crowd: Some Twentieth-Century Food Riots', *Journal of British Studies*, 18, (1978).

122 Temma Kaplan, 'Female Consciousness and Collective Action: The Case of Barcelona, 1910–18', *Signs*, 7 (1982), p. 564.

123 Belinda Davis, 'Food Scarcity and the Empowerment of the Female Consumer in World War I Berlin', in Victoria de Grazia and Ellen Furlougheds, eds, *The Sex of Things: Gender and Consumption in Historical Perspective* (Berkeley, Calif.: University of California Press, 1996), p. 289. See also her *Home Fires Burning: Food, Politics, and Everyday Life in World War I Berlin* (Chapel Hill, NC: University of North Carolina Press, 2000).

124 Joseph Melling, *Rent Strikes: Peoples' Struggle for Housing in West Scotland 1890–1916* (Edinburgh: Polygon, 1983).

125 James J. Smyth, 'Rents, Peace, Votes: Working-Class Women and Political Activity in the First World War', in Esther Breitenbach and Eleanor Gordon, eds, *Out of Bounds: Women in Scottish Society, 1800–1945* (Edinburgh: Edinburgh University Press, 1992); Barbara A. Engel, 'Not by Bread Alone: Subsistence Riots in Russia during World War I', *Journal of Modern History*, 69, 4 (1997).

126 Clements, *Bolshevik Women*.

127 Rupp, *Worlds of Women*; Sandi E. Cooper, 'Women in War and Peace, 1914–45' in Bridenthal et al., eds, *Becoming Visible*.

128 Karen Hagemann, 'Men's Demonstrations and Women's Protest: Gender in Collective Action in the Urban Working-Class Milieu during the Weimar Republic, *Gender & History*, 5, 1, (1993).

129 Pat Thane, 'The Women of the British Labour Party and Feminism, 1906–45', in Harold L. Smith, ed., *British Feminism in the Twentieth Century* (Aldershot: Edward Elgar, 1990).

130 Michael Savage, *The Dynamics of Working Class Politics: The Labour Movement in Preston, 1880–1940* (Cambridge: Cambridge University Press, 1987).

131 James Hinton, 'Militant Housewives: The British Housewives' League and the Attlee Government', *History Workshop Journal*, 38, (1994).

132 Carlsson Wetterberg, 'Equal or Different?', pp. 28–9.

133 Objects of the Edinburgh Women Citizen's Association quoted in Sue Innes, 'Constructing Women's Citizenship in the Interwar Period: The Edinburgh Women Citizens' Association', *Women's History Review*, 13, 4 (2004) p. 626.

134 Berta Wallin quoted in Carlsson Wetterberg, 'Equal or Different?', p. 29.

135 Ida B. Blom, 'Women's Politics and Women in Politics since the End of the Nineteenth Century', in S. Jay Kleinberg, ed., *Retrieving Women's History: Changing Perceptions of the Role of Women in Politics and Society* (Oxford: Berg, 1988), p. 264.

136 Quoted in Carlsson Wetterberg, 'Equal or Different?', pp. 29, 37.

137 Barbara Einhorn, 'The Great Divide? Women's Rights in Eastern and Central Europe since 1945', in Bridenthal et al., eds, *Becoming Visible*, p. 521.

138 op. cit., p. 522.

139 F. Pieroni Bortolotti (1978), quoted in Rossi-Doria, 'Italian Women Enter Politics', pp. 92–3.

140 Rossi-Doria, 'Italian Women Enter Politics' p. 98.

141 Karlsson, 'Social Democratic Women's Coup', p. 51.

142 Passmore, 'Europe', p. 241.

143 Claudia Koonz, 'The "Woman Question" in Authoritarian Regimes', in Bridenthal et al., eds, *Becoming Visible*, p. 476.

144 Kirsten Heinsohn, 'Germany', in Passmore, ed., *Women, Gender and Fascism*, p. 34.

145 Koonz, 'The "Woman Question"', p. 471.

146 Mussolini (1933), quoted in Koonz, 'The "Woman Question"', p. 468.

147 Perry Willson, 'Italy', in Passmore, ed., *Women, Gender and Fascism*, pp. 18–21, 27, 32.

148 E. Brandwood (1927), quoted in Karen Hunt and Matthew Worley, 'Rethinking British Communist Party Women in the 1920s', *Twentieth Century British History*, 15, 1 (2004), p. 24.

149 Hannah Mitchell, *The Hard Way Up* (London, Virago, 1968).

150 Elina Katainen, 'Communist Women in Finland, 1944–48: Olga Virtanen's Story', in Duchen and Bandhauer-Schöffmann, eds, *When the War Was Over*.

151 See Hunt and Worley, 'Rethinking British Communist Party Women'; Helmut Gruber and

Pamela Graves, eds, *Women and Socialism, Socialism and Women: Europe between the Two World Wars* (Oxford: Berghahn, 1998).

152 Katainen, 'Communist Women in Finland', p. 127.

153 Margaret Bondfield, *A Life's Work* (London: Hutchinson, 1948), pp. 125–6.

154 Mira Janova and Mariette Sineau, 'Women's Participation in Political Power in Europe: An Essay in East–West Comparison', *Women's Studies International Forum*, 15, 1 (1992), p. 119.

155 Birte Siim, *Gender and Citizenship: Politics and Agency in France, Britain and Denmark* (Cambridge: Cambridge University Press, 2000), pp. 127, 134–5.

156 Sighrúdur H. Sigurbjarnardóttir, '"On Their Own Premises": The Political Project of the Icelandic Women's Alliance', in von der Fehr et al., eds, *Is there a Nordic Feminism?*, pp. 68–89.

157 Cross, 'Women and Politics', pp. 102–6.

158 Ruth Lister, *Citizenship: Feminist Perspectives* (Basingstoke: Macmillan, 1997), chap. 2.

159 Hunt, *Equivocal Feminists*, pp. 197–203.

160 Laura E. N. Mayhall, 'Creating the "Suffragette Spirit": British Feminism and the Historical Imagination', *Women's History Review*, 4, 3, (1995).

8

VALIANT HEROINES OR PACIFIC LADIES?

Women in war and peace

Jane Potter

Introduction

The cries of wretched mothers, that in vain
Lament their fate, and mourn their children slain;
The virgin's shriek, who trembling in the dust,
Weeps the pollution of a ruffian's lust;
The mangled infant's wail, that as he dies,
Looks up in vain for pity to the skies.[1]

Thomas Day's poem *The Desolation of America* (1777) about the War of American Independence presents a view of women in wartime that, for all its melodramatic eighteenth-century diction and sentiment, is recognisable to us today, over 200 years later. Women still suffer as bereaved mothers and as victims of rape. They continue to endure the loss of their husbands and brothers as they look on from the sidelines. Yet their experience of armed conflict extends beyond that of tortured observers. This chapter will illuminate the ways in which women have not only been implicated in the European wars and revolutions of the past three centuries, but have also often actively participated in them, both as militarists and as pacifists.

War, according to Clausewitz, is 'nothing but the continuation of policy with other means' and is fought either to eliminate the opponent's political independence or to obtain favourable terms of peace.[2] Military histories traditionally have been concerned primarily with the strategies, battles and settlements of the wars and revolutions that have embroiled Europe in the past three centuries. They have, for the most part, been written from a doubly masculine perspective, that is, men writing about male actors, men valorising the suffering of soldiers and men seeking to learn lessons for future military strategy. As such, women's place in these armed conflicts has been largely ignored. Yet as camp followers, soldiers, munitions workers, nurses, ambulance drivers, war refugees, grieving widows and mothers and peace activists, they are as important to the historical record as politicians, officers and soldiers. They have been the victims of wartime violence and, at times, the perpetrators of it. History is replete with evidence to contradict the assertion that women, by virtue of their biological ability to bear children, are naturally life-affirming and peace-loving. We have examples of female combatants who were more than prepared to use the swords and guns they so readily took up; of female concentration camp commandants who sadistically inflicted torture on prisoners; and of female warmongers who zealously urged and even shamed men to fight on their behalf.

Women have been as enthralled by war as men.[3] Some longed to be active participants in war for many reasons: adventure, proximity to soldier-lovers, economic necessity and defence of home and family. They also wanted to demonstrate their fitness for citizenship and equal rights, for if to be a full participatory member of a society is to be willing to defend and ultimately to die for one's country, then how are women, barred from the field of battle, supposed to demonstrate such willingness? As Angela Woollacott has argued, 'it should hardly surprise us that women have followed the same roads and embraced the same symbols in pursuing citizenship that men have.'[4] Although the personal yet passive sacrifice of a son, husband or father to battle has at times been accepted as an alternative prerequisite of citizenship, more often than not it is military service that 'has acted as an unofficial litmus test for public leadership capabilities.'[5]

The idea of women soldiers has both disturbed and fascinated society. In the eighteenth century, when the divisions between 'home' and 'front' were far more fluid, some women were able to disguise themselves as men and actively engage in combat as soldiers and as sailors. When their secret was discovered, often after they were wounded, public fascination with these cross-dressing 'Amazons' made them into folk heroines. Yet their actions were never seen as a true alternative for females. They were anomalies, pets, even freaks to be wondered at and entertained by. Although the nineteenth century was not devoid of disguised women soldiers or of male impersonators who took to the stage in music halls and theatres, women's place in the scheme of war changed. The female warrior gave way to the exemplary lady who performed the auxiliary tasks of nursing and philanthropy. The nurse, as personified by Florence Nightingale, became the accepted military service role for women, while patriotic organizations founded during the Napoleonic wars, and which proliferated throughout the nineteenth century, were outlets for females to voice their own bellicosity without donning a uniform. The notion of separate spheres dictated that men fought and women urged. The twentieth century saw a breakdown of these separate spheres with the explosion of auxiliary services in both the First and the Second World Wars and the integration of women into the military proper. The demands of 'total war' were not gender-specific. Yet the anxiety over women's participation in combat has never fully been quelled, despite striking acts of heroism and strength which are well documented and which link the women soldiers of the late twentieth century to their eighteenth-century counterparts.

Other women have never been comfortable with such martial interests, arguing that that the heroic ideal, the glorification of the soldier and the definition of masculinity as a 'readiness to risk death in battle in order to defend the defenceless homeland' as just a few of the reasons why war continues to be acceptable as a normal, if regrettable, activity.[6] Those who eschewed war and became activists for peace defined themselves as feminists, but some did not. While the pacifist Mrs F. S. Hallowes asserted in 1918 that 'women equally with men have a passionate love of mother-country', Virginia Woolf responded to the question 'How are we to prevent war?' by arguing that patriotism is one of the reasons why war prevails and declaring 'as a woman, I have no country. As a woman, I want no country.'[7] The peace movements of the past three centuries have been as gendered as military service, for just as there was resistance to women's involvement in the arena of war, so too were male pacifists keen to perpetuate the separate spheres of influence within their own organisations.

An examination of how women in modern Europe interacted with and against the machine of war and revolution can lead us to some conclusions about whether or not the arguments about 'women and war' as a selective area of academic and historical debate are now obsolete. This chapter will consider what may be divided into three areas of women's involvement in the wars and revolutions of modern Europe: those who actively participated outside the norms of accepted female behaviour, those who participated within these norms and within gendered divisions of labour and those who campaigned against all forms of complicity in armed conflict. Particular themes recur. All nations have their version of the patriotic female, embodied in the figure of the mother or the soldier's wife. All have propounded at various times that women's role in national conflict is to keep the home fires burning after selflessly and strenuously encouraging their men to fight. Such a demand and its attendant iconography cut across national boundaries and across the objectives for which each war or revolution was undertaken. Again and again, women were called upon in times of national need to take on active roles, be they extensions of their domestic responsibilities (cooking, cleaning, laundry, nursing) or more combative, less feminine activities from actual soldiering and insurgency to transport, munitions-making and espionage. Yet time and again, when peace came, they have been told by those who called upon their patriotism to return to their homes and their pre-war occupations, often without due recognition or reward such as citizenship or the suffrage. The contributions of women in national crisis have, until recently, been left out of the historical record. 'How could all that great mass of history have been written with hardly a mention of women?' asks Siân Reynolds.[8] Reynolds argues perceptively and persuasively for the ways in which the gender debate has destabilised old narratives. Once women are added to the narratives of war, the interpretation of that narrative changes irrevocably.

Historiography

Until recently, rarely have the indices of military histories included 'women' as a subject. Second-wave feminism and the rise of women's studies courses have demanded that female participation in the wars and revolutions of the past – as in other areas – be rediscovered, analysed and woven back into the fabric of history. Large-scale encyclopaedic texts on warfare, such as the *Oxford Companion to Military History*, now contain separate entries devoted to women and highlight other female-dominated topics such as nursing and auxiliary services. It is relatively easy to gather information on women's participation in the wars and conflicts of the twentieth century. The First and Second World Wars, in particular, have inspired numerous academic studies and general-interest books. The early modern period is perhaps the most problematic for historians of women's history, given the fluidity of roles in the decentralised military organisations as well as a lack of printed and archival material. Nevertheless, studies such as Piers Compton's *Colonel's Lady and Camp Follower: The Story of Women in the Crimean War* (1970); Elizabeth Ewing's *Women in Uniform Through the Centuries* (1975); and Barton C. Hacker's 'Women and Military Institutions in Early Modern Europe: A Reconnaissance', *Signs* (1981) go some way to redressing the imbalance.

They have contributed to larger-scale surveys (and celebrations) of women's participation in war from antiquity to the present, including Julie Wheelwright's *Amazons and Military Maids: Women who Dressed as Men in Pursuit of Life, Liberty and Happiness* (1989); Linda Grant de Pauw's *Battle Cries and Lullabies: Women in War from Prehistory to the Present* (1998) and Kate Adie's *Corsets to Camouflage: Women and War* (2003).

The subject of women's participation in warfare and in the peacetime military has elicited varied and heated arguments. In addition to lauding the achievements of women soldiers, pilots and sailors, John P. Dever and Maria C. Dever's *Women and the Military: Over 100 Notable Contributors, Historic to Contemporary* (1995) takes the view that 'the whole notion of "allowing" women into combat is disturbing. "Allowing" women to do or not to do something is a remnant of a paternalistic society. A grown woman should go as far as talent and hard work allow her to go.'[9] On the other hand, John Laffin's *Women in Battle* (1967), while an early attempt to counter the tendency of historians to resent 'the intrusion of women into what clearly should be the one impregnable male bastion' by recognising the achievements of women in armed combat, is ultimately a platform for the author's objections to such active participation by women. He even concludes with a 'jocular' assertion that women are meant for the bedroom not the battlefield.[10] Martin van Creveld takes a similar, yet more outspoken and unequivocal stance in his *Men, Women and War: Do Women Belong in the Front Line?* (2001):

> Women must be excluded from war not so much because they are necessarily incapable of participating in it but in order that they may better appreciate the feats of men who are engaged in it . . . Women's participation in war will take away one of the cardinal reasons why men fight, which is to assert their own glory.[11]

He believes that 'feminization equals decline.'[12]

A more objective exploration of how our ideas about gender and warfare are constructed by various conflicting and complementary forces is provided by Joshua Goldstein's study *War and Gender: How Gender Shapes the War System and Vice Versa* (2003), which brings together the theories of historians, sociologists, anthropologists, psychologists and physicians. Jean Bethke Elshtain, in her ground-breaking work *Women and War* (first published 1987, revised 1995) argues that the 'Ferocious Few' have in fact been overshadowed by the 'Non-Combatant Many' who represent our more traditional images of women and war: 'the woman fighter is, for us, an identity *in extremis*, not an expectation.'[13]

The participation of women pacifists, however, has not been neglected in the search to uncover the female warriors of the past or the efforts to posit the future of women in the military. The ways in which females devoted themselves to the pursuance of peace have been the focus of such important studies as Heloise Brown's '*The Truest Form of Patriotism*': *Pacifist Feminism in Britain 1870–1902*, Cynthia Enloe's *Maneouvers: The International Politics of Militarizing Women's Lives*, Sybil Oldfield's *Women Against the Iron Fist: Alternatives to Militarism 1900–1989*, Sara Ruddick's contribution '"Woman of Peace": A Feminist Construction', to *The Women and War Reader* edited by Lois Ann Lorentzen and Jennifer Turpin and Eileen Sowerby's *On*

War: Men, War and Women. All of these in their fashion point to the directions the feminist peace movement may take in the future.

Biographical and literary studies, too, help to fill in the gaps of women's experiences of peace and war. Large-scale biographies of such notable figures as Mary Wollstonecraft, Florence Nightingale, Vera Brittain and Virginia Woolf complement the life stories of lesser-known women found in such encyclopaedic works as the *Oxford Dictionary of National Biography*. Anthologies such as *War Plays by Women: An International Anthology*, edited by Claire M. Tylee and Agnès Cardinal and critical texts such as Jane Potter's *Boys in Khaki, Girls in Print* highlight women's literary interpretations of war and peace. The breadth and variety of books, historical and literary, fiction and non-fiction, polemic and imaginative, mirrors the spectrum and enormity of women's experience of conflict over the past three centuries.

The long eighteenth century (to 1815)

Conflagrations such as the Seven Years War (1756–63), the American War of Independence (1775–83), the French Revolution (1789), the French Revolutionary wars (1792–1801), and the Napoleonic wars (1803–1815) punctuated the eighteenth century. Despite their virtual absence from the military histories, females were an integral part of these conflicts: 'Behind each regiment came a company of women'.[14]

The female camp follower of the eighteenth century had a dubious reputation. Variously characterised as a prostitute, slattern, tart, profiteer and corpse-thief, she could be 'every bit as bad as the men, if not worse, when it came to plundering'.[15] Yet she was often simply a regimental wife who joined her husband on campaign and who performed vital support services, the 'womanly' tasks of washing, cooking, needlework and nursing, tasks not far removed from those she carried out in ordinary life.[16] Female camp followers and sutlers (those who sold provisions, especially liquor) often donned regimental jackets to assert their allegiance to a company. Tolerated by the military authorities as a necessary evil, the Duke of Wellington, for one, regarded them as pests and was said to have flogged those who were ill disciplined.[17] George Bell of the 34th Foot gave his assessment:

> they impeded our progress at times, particularly in retreats. They were under no control. They were ordered to the rear or their donkeys would be shot . . . Despite the warning, next morning they would pick up their belongings and set off, lamenting their bitter fate, ahead of the column, marauding, preparing their men's meals, before their arrival, plundering the battle-field or searching it for their dead; they were wounded, killed or died of exposure or hunger. Collectively or individually, they formed cameos of the Peninsular campaign, a colourful kaleidoscope of the romance and tragedy, devotion and self-sacrifice, the hardships and endurance of women at war.[18]

The British army allowed six women for each company of 100 infantrymen and six for each cavalry troop, and there was a lottery to determine who would go and who would stay behind. The Prussian army allowed five women, including their children, to follow every company of 100 men. If a soldier was killed, his widow might marry one of his comrades in order to retain her living. When the French Revolutionary wars mobilised an entire population, the National Assembly's general conscription allowed for *vivandières*, *cantinières* and *blanchisseuses*.[19]

For the aristocracy, camp following was a fashionable pastime. In 1778, the Duke of Devonshire organised a voluntary militia in response to the growing fears in Britain of an imminent French invasion after France sided with the American colonies during their revolutionary war. Male members of the aristocracy made up the majority of volunteers (other able-bodied men already being in the army). They trained with 'almost childish enthusiasm' at camps at Coxheath in Kent and Warley in Essex, and they attracted sightseers on coach trips as well as the wives of the volunteers.[20] Georgiana, Duchess of Devonshire, accompanied her husband and was enthralled by the sight of mobilised soldiers. She also imagined 'herself bravely leading a battalion of men in a bloody engagement against the invaders.'[21] Along with her aristocratic friends, Georgiana soon became bored with merely observing the drills and parades and she set about organising a women's auxiliary corps, complete with a fashionable uniform that attracted plaudits from the newspapers. But this was not the hard life of the average camp follower: Georgiana lived in comfort in two large tents decorated with furniture from Chatsworth, and her women's auxiliary performed no discernible necessary functions for the troops besides providing amusement. Amanda Foreman argues, however, such an auxiliary marked the first time that aristocratic women considered the ways in which they might help their men in wartime.[22]

Ordinary male and female camp followers could not help but be caught up in the fighting: support behind the lines often turned into support *in* the lines. Yet some women deliberately chose to participate as soldiers in their own right, albeit by disguising themselves as men. In an age when military physicals were unheard of, this was easier than we might assume. Dress, demeanour and cleverly engineered sanitary devices allowed women to move among and fight alongside their male counterparts, whether as commissioned officers or privates. Only when she was wounded was a female soldier likely to be 'revealed' and 'dead or alive, the unveiling of a woman in disguise always created a small sensation.'[23] The eighteenth-century fascination with cross-dressing meant that the woman who donned a male uniform to follow a military career was a familiar figure in popular culture. They were celebrated in ballads that fed the appetites of all classes, such as the chapbooks and other forms of leisure highlighted by Tammy Proctor in this volume (pp. 306–8). Popular on the streets, they were also the fodder of refined songs that were performed in the theatres and pleasure gardens of the Georgian era to the delight of polite society. However large its casualties or brutal its outcomes, war was – and still is – especially for those not directly involved, a form of entertainment, and at least a hundred female warrior ballads were published between 1700 and the mid-nineteenth century.[24] The transgressive act of female cross-dressing was sometimes used to shame men into action, as in 'The Female Volunteer or an Attempt to make our Men Stand' (1746), which proclaimed:

> Well, if 'tis so, and that our *Men* can't *stand*,
> 'Tis time we Women take the *Thing* in *Hand*.
> Thus in my Country's Cause I now appear,
> A bold, smart, *Kevenbuller'd* Volunteer;

And really, mark some Heroes in the Nation,
You'll think this no unnat'ral Transformation:
For if in Valour real *Manhood lies*,
All Cowards are but Women in Disguise.[25]

While they cannot be taken as official records, being more indicative of the century's fascination with cross-dressing than with accurate military history, the ballads nevertheless do tell us much about the very real practices of the armed forces of the day, the manoeuvres, drills, camps and press-gangs that impinged on civilian life in ways that are completely alien to us in the twenty-first century.[26]

It is impossible to ascertain the exact number of women who actually went into combat or to tell whether the figures of popular lore have real-life counterparts. Nevertheless, we can document cases of 'women warriors' who played active roles in the national wars and revolutions of the eighteenth century, through the biographical memoirs that responded to and encouraged public interest in these 'amazons'. *The Life and Adventures of Mrs. Christian Davies* (1740), for one, recounts the exploits of the woman also known as Mother Ross. Born Christian Cavenaugh in Dublin in 1667, at the age of twenty-six she disguised herself as a soldier in order to find her first husband, Richard Welsh, who had been press-ganged into the Dutch army. Cutting off her hair, binding her breasts and donning her husband's clothes, she joined an infantry regiment as Christopher Welsh. As a foot soldier she was wounded at the battle of Landen in 1693, taken prisoner then released in 1694, and fought as a dragoon until 1697. After the battle of Blenheim in 1704, in which she took part, she eventually found Welsh and together they continued to serve in the Army as brothers, her gender and thus their marital status concealed, until she was seriously wounded when a shell struck her head and fractured her skull at the battle of Ramillies in 1705:

> I was carried to *Meldre*, or *Meldret*, a small Town in the Quarter of *Louvain* . . . I was here trepanned, and great Care taken of me, but I did not recover in less than Ten weeks. Though I suffered great Torture by this Wound, yet the Discovery it caused of my Sex, in the fixing of my Dressing, by which the Surgeons saw my Breasts, and, by the Largeness of my Nipples, concluded I had given Suck, was a greater Grief to me. No sooner had they made this Discovery, but they acquainted Brigadier *Preston*, that *his pretty Dragoon* (so I was always called) *was, in Fact, a Woman.* He was very loath to believe it, and did me the Honour to say, *He had always looked upon me as the prettiest Fellow, and the best Man he had.*[27]

After a second wedding to Welsh, she took up being a sutler, foraging for the troops. Her sobriquet, Mother Ross, was given to her by a Captain Ross because of her lamentations after the death of Welsh in battle in 1709.[28] Like many other women camp followers, she quickly remarried, but her second husband was killed soon afterwards in 1710 during a siege and she returned to England. Presented to Queen Anne, she received a shilling a day for life. Having moved back to Dublin she married another soldier called Davies and once more followed her husband, not to war but to England. In old age she lived as a Chelsea pensioner. The *London Magazine* reported on her death and subsequent editions of her posthumously published memoir enshrined her in legend.

Similarly, *The Female Soldier, or the Surprising Adventures of Hannah Snell* (1750), written and printed by the London newspaper publisher Robert Walker, is in part responsible for legend of Hannah Snell. In the preface of the work that documents her 'surprising adventures', he takes pains to stress Snell's place in a long line of heroines, 'for though her immediate Progenitors were but low in the World, when compared with Dukes, Earls, and Generals, yet she had the Seeds of Heroism, Courage and Patriotism transferr'd to her from her Ancestors.' Thus Walker both assures his upper- and middle-class readers of Snell's respectable heritage and provides an exemplar for his lower-class audience. Like Davies, Snell (1723–92) set out after her Dutch sailor husband when he abandoned her and enlisted, as James Gray, in Colonel Fraser's Regiment of Marines, setting sail on the *Swallow* in October 1747 bound for the East Indies. Snell took part in the fleet's attack on French-held Devakotti in 1748 and received multiple wounds: one shot in the right leg, five in the left, another in the groin. She treated all of these herself to conceal her gender. She eventually received a pension for having been wounded in action and was admitted as an out-pensioner at Chelsea Hospital. The connection between war and theatre was further reinforced when Snell, dubbed the 'Amazon of the Indies', took to the stage in uniform at Goodman's Fields Theatre, London to regale audiences with nautical songs.[29]

The tradition of female soldiering in France, while no less fascinating to the nation, seems not to have inspired the same attendant balladry or theatricality. During the Revolution in 1789, Félicité and Théophile de Fernig dressed in uniform and joined their father's troops of the Garde Nationale. They were soon found out but forgiven and continued to serve as soldiers, while being compared to Joan of Arc.[30] The French Revolutionary wars (1792–1801) and the Napoleonic wars (1803–1815) were not bereft of women warriors. Elizabeth Dubois was known a *citoyenne* Favre and fought throughout 1793 until she was captured. She escaped execution when the enemy commander realised she was a woman.[31] Angélique Brûlon joined her father's regiment, the 42nd Foot, at the age of twenty-one. She fought in Corsica (1792–9) wearing male clothing and advanced from fusilier through to lieutenant. After being badly wounded at the siege of Calvi in 1799, she retired from the military and died in 1859. Significantly, she was considered a patriot because she followed her husband into battle, not because of the actions she performed as a soldier and officer in her own right: 'she was remembered for a supportive gesture'.[32] Thérèse Figueur, who served in male disguise as a French soldier between 1793 and 1815, for all her acknowledged courage and prowess, perhaps received the more ignominious treatment after the wars. Wounded repeatedly and taken prisoner, she was nevertheless unable to claim medical care and was denied the *Legion d'honneur* because she was a woman.[33]

Englishwoman Mary Ann Talbot (1778–1808) was more fortunate after her early tribulations. The fourteenth illegitimate daughter of the first Earl of Talbot, she was seduced by her guardian Captain Essex Brown of the 82nd Regiment of Foot and made to disguise herself as a foot boy in his service on board the *Crown*. As John Taylor, she was a drummer at the siege of Valenciennes in 1793 and was wounded, first in the ribs by a musket ball and then in the back when an Austrian cavalryman slashed her with his sword. After the death of Brown, she deserted and in 1793 signed on to a French privateer (armed vessel). When it came up against the British ship *Queen Charlotte*, she refused to fight against her countrymen and was flogged. Captured by the British, she revealed her true identity to Admiral Lord Howe who discharged her. She then joined the Royal Navy as a powder monkey on the *Brunswick* and took part in the battle of the Glorious First of June 1794. She was wounded in the thigh and grapeshot shattered her ankle. After recovering she joined the armed vessel *Vesuvius* but was taken prisoner by the French and spent eighteen months in prison. Released, she sailed for New York on the American ship *Ariel* and when she returned home she was press-ganged. She was discharged when she revealed her true identity. For the wounds she received in action, Talbot was rewarded with a pension of 20 pounds a year. She died in Shropshire at the age of thirty, having published her autobiography.[34]

The propaganda value of women soldiers was not lost on governments. The Russians held up Nadezha Durova as an exemplary heroine and 'treated her as a pet of sorts'.[35] Her memoir, *The Cavalry Maiden* (1836) recounts how she ran away from an unhappy marriage to enlist in the Tsar's army in 1806. Using the name Alexander Vasilevich Sokolov, she spent seven years in the military and was present at the battles at Friedland (1807) and Borodino (1812), where she suffered contusion from a passing cannon ball.

Spanish warrior women were equally heroic in their campaigns against the French. Agostina became famous on both sides of the Atlantic. Her town, Saragossa, was besieged by Napoleon's army, and with only 220 soldiers to defend itself against an army of 12,000, its fortifications were quickly overcome. The women formed companies to assist the men and when all from the artillery were killed, Agostina rushed to fire the cannon left by a dying soldier. Her actions inspired others to do the same, and the siege lasted for another eleven days and continued with street fighting, in which Agostina had a prominent part, until in the end the French gave up. In addition to medals, Agostina won the right to continue as an artillery officer with full uniform, pension and rights and took the name of the town as her surname.[36]

Such acts of heroism by 'warlike Amazons' have obscured the lives of thousands of women whose tales were not told by entrepreneurial publishers or touted by governments seeking exemplars for propaganda. This is especially the case for women caught up in the Jacobite Rebellion and the French Revolution. Brandishing swords at rallies seems to have been the closest Scottish women came to martial action. Their energies were devoted instead towards raising troops, providing money for supplies, offering hospitality, and sheltering fugitives. The narratives of the '45, Maggie Craig has argued, have traditionally focused on and romanticised the actions of Flora MacDonald to the exclusion of other women 'doubly marginalized' by virtue of their gender and their politics. Yet,

> the women were there, doing their bit alongside the men; some committed to their beliefs; some reacting as best they could to what was going on around them; some risking their lives and safety to help the wounded and the fugitives; others just trying to survive as their world fell to pieces.[37]

Margaret Ogilvy, for instance, accompanied her husband David, eldest son of the Earl of Airlie, as he marched to Edinburgh at the head of the Forfarshire regiment. She was with him, a drawn sword at her side, when he proclaimed Prince Charles prince regent at the mercat cross at Coupar Angus.[38] The only woman officially allowed on the march south, she endured the hardships of the campaign, including the demoralising retreat from England. Some women were particularly virulent in their shaming of men into action when caution was mooted. Isabel Haldane reputedly told her reluctant husband Charles Stewart of Ardsheal: 'if you are not willing to be a commander of the Appin men, stay at home and take care of the house, and I will go and command them myself.'[39]

Jacobite women were not immune to the wrath of the Government. After the Battle of Culloden, eighty were held prisoner, some for long periods, while others found their characters assassinated by officials keen on quelling any further uprising.[40] Jennie Cameron experienced the barbs of slander and sexual innuendo after she recruited 300 men, whom she led to the raising of Prince Charlie's standard at Glenfinnan on 19 August 1745. Anne Mackintosh, wife of the Chief of Clan Mackintosh, was untruthfully rumoured to be Prince Charlie's lover in the wake of her successful rallying of Mackintoshes and men of other clans. In opposition to her husband who eventually joined the government side, she was not averse to using threats to encourage volunteers. Carrying with her a pair of pistols, she wore the 'traditional blue bonnet of the Scottish fighting man' and was nicknamed 'Colonel Anne'. Bonnie Prince Charlie dubbed her *la belle rebelle*.[41]

The historical amnesia evident in narratives of the '45 was repeated after the French Revolution. Thousands of nameless women were at the forefront of the marches and uprisings of 1789 and some participated in armed combat. The *levée en masse* mobilised the entire population and *les femmes du peuple*, the lowest strata of pre-revolutionary Paris, participated for the first time as *citoyennes*. Yet equality was a chimera. The female 'firebrands' that urged on uprisings and took to the streets to demand bread and rights receded to the background as the new government adhered to the old patriarchal values.[42] The truly patriotic woman was defined as the loving wife and mother content to rule in her domestic sphere, supporting her husband after his day in the public arena.[43] Women of the upper classes also found themselves little better off than they were in the *ancien régime*. The enlightenment ideals of domesticity and sociability were cultivated in the salons, and it was here that their power continued to be consolidated.

That is not to say that women did not persist in their demands. Since the fundamentals of *citoyenneté*, citizenship, were inextricably bound up with national defence, power and equal rights, many demanded the right to enlist.[44] The women who took part in the parades to celebrate the first anniversary of the storming of the Bastille pledged themselves to 'live and die for their country'. Pauline Léon led the Société des Citoyennes Républicaines Révolutionnaires and, on 6 March 1791, read a petition to the National Assembly signed by 300 Parisian women demanding the 'natural right' to be organised into a unit of the National Guard:

> Patriotic women come before you to claim the right, which any individual has to defend his life and liberty.
>
> Everyone predicts that a violent shock is coming; our fathers, husbands and brothers may be the victims of the fury of our enemies. Could we be denied the joy of avenging them or of dying at their sides? We are *citoyennes*, and we cannot be indifferent to the fate of the fatherland.[45]

Théroigne de Méricourt echoed Léon's call when she led a mob that stormed the Bastille at the start of the French Revolution. De Méricourt demanded that women be allowed to organise their own battalion, but the French National Convention ruled against this in April 1793. Male revolutionaries were determined to resist women's political emancipation.[46] Even historians, nearly two centuries later, regarded de Méricourt's actions as misguided, if not ridiculous. In 1938, Jean Robiquet dubbed her 'outrageous' and recounted how other 'foolish' women had to be 'courteously sent back to their stoves' when a group of 'young beauties wearing the Phrygian bonnet and armed to the teeth presented themselves at the bar of the Conseil de la Commune.' An attorney admonished them to:

> remain as nature intended you, and instead of envying us males the perils of a stormy existence, content yourselves with letting us forget them in the bosoms of our families, where we may rest our weary eyes on the enchanting spectacle of our offspring made happy by your tender ministrations![47]

The *levée en masse* decree of August 1793 firmly put women in their place when it came to the defence of *la patrie en danger*. While young men were to fight,

> The married men shall forge arms and transport provisions; the women shall make tents and clothes, and shall serve in the hospitals; the children shall turn old linen into lint; the old men shall repair to the public places, to stimulate the courage of the warriors and preach the unity of the Republic and the hatred of kings.[48]

Such gendered patriotism was becoming a key concept in European politics and society during this period of almost continuous conflict that the French Revolutionary and Napoleonic wars initiated. It was necessary for nations to mobilise the emotions as well as the actions of both men and women, but there were defined spheres and arenas of participation, especially for the 'respectable' classes. Karen Hagemann has demonstrated how middle-class Prussian-German women were seen for the first time as being crucial to victory for the patriotic charity they were able to perform. When Prussia declared war on France in March 1813, volunteers were needed to help support the clothing and feeding of the conscript army, as well as their widows and dependents. Since nearly every family had sent a son to war, 'the civilian population in Prussia responded to the appeals for donations with remarkable alacrity.'[49] By July 1813, the first Female Charitable Association was established in Berlin. Hundreds more in 414 Prussian towns followed within the year: 72 per cent of the 573 recorded women's organisations. Led by women of the aristocracy and upper class and staffed with workers from urban and lower classes, these women's groups also spawned girls' and daughters' organisations, the primary focus of all of them being to collect donations and to care for the sick and wounded. According to Hagemann, the Women's Association for the Good of the Fatherland (Berlin) raised phenomenal amounts of money, and women's activities of this kind – linked inextricably to their domestic roles and gender expectations, were heralded as female heroism. They were, of course, also expected to be influential mothers and wives, motivating their men to enlist, keeping the home whilst they were away and welcoming them on their return. In addition to being willing to 'pour scorn on "cowards"', they were meant to grieve with dignity for the fallen.[50] Such patriotic activism was motivated not just by ideology or conformity with one's neighbours, but by a real conviction that the French must be defeated if the Prussian identity and way of life were to be maintained.[51] A precedent for female activism had been established, yet as French women in the wake of the Revolution discovered, 'public activity in wartime had to be relinquished in peacetime and female contributions to the victory over Napoleon were forgotten.'[52]

In Britain from 1793 there was an equal enthusiasm for patriotic philanthropy. Women banded together to gather supplies, clothes and funds for the departing troops. It was a scene that was to be endlessly repeated in all future wars, but at the time it was unique and startling. Women presented regimental colours at assemblies and on occasion made speeches to the assembled troops and spectators.[53] The bloody end of the eighteenth century and violent beginning of the nineteenth century also inspired a questioning of the fatalism that considered war and revolution not only normal and constant but also essential. As Martin Ceadel has shown, the peace movement proper can be dated from 1793 with the campaign against the French wars, which articulated 'the first statements of pacifism other than those produced by sectarians such as Quakers'.[54] Britain would be at war for the next twenty-two years. The introduction of mass armies meant that by 1809 it had 817,000 men in uniform. Ceadel goes on to argue that although the first documented peace society was formed in the USA in New York in August 1815, the movement itself began in Britain with the 'first known meeting to plan a peace association' occurring in London on 7 June 1814. Only an accident of timing gave the accolade to America.[55] On 14 June 1816 the Society for the Promotion of Permanent and Universal Peace was founded in London. It almost immediately became known as the Peace Society and was 'the world's first durable peace association with a national reach.'[56] Women's role in the campaign was, at this time, extremely limited; making up only 10 per cent of the membership, their presence would not be sanctioned until well into the mid-nineteenth century. Fascination with the soldier hero, especially in Great Britain, was growing and even made its way into the novels of Jane Austen. Such a 'cult of heroism' owed much to 'female enthusiasm' and it was sustained even in the relatively pacific years that followed the end of the Napoleonic wars.[57]

The nineteenth century from 1816 to 1902

The nineteenth century could almost be considered pacific in comparison with eighteenth and the twentieth centuries. Four major wars in twelve years were the only martial events in what was an 'unusually peaceable century': France, Savoy and the Italians against Austria in 1858–9; Prussia and Austria against Denmark in 1864; Prussia and Italy against Austria in 1866; Prussia and the German states against France in 1870–1.[58]

By the end of the Napoleonic wars, armies had become professional and centralised with the result that rear services were now undertaken not by regimental wives but by military personnel, and camp followers, both male and female, were becoming vestiges of another era.[59] 'Home' and 'front' became rigidly demarcated and women were no longer allowed to move freely in and out of the military environment.[60] Enlisted men were still being discouraged from marrying and the paltry provisions for wives and families served to some extent as a deterrent. In the 1850s they were still obliged to live in the same barracks as unmarried soldiers in accommodation that was overcrowded and afforded little privacy. If a soldier chose to live outside the barracks, he received a small allowance, but he also forfeited the right to claim necessities such as candles, fuel, bedding and furniture.[61]

Women's position became even more difficult when men were posted overseas. Years of enforced separation meant that couples often never saw each other again. Regimental officers, in an effort to keep their married soldiers and to ensure good conduct, sometimes turned a blind eye to women smuggled onto ships or when men employed wives as their servants. The ballot system, which had previously regulated how many wives could accompany their husbands on campaign was last used during the Crimean war (1853–6), when four per company were allowed to sail with the army.[62] Florence Nightingale described the plight of regimental wives at Scutari:

> In the Barracks now are located some two hundred poor women in the most abject misery. They are the wives of soldiers who were allowed to accompany their husbands, a great number have been sent down from Varna; they are in rags and covered with vermin. My heart bleeds for them, and they are at our doors daily, clamouring for everything; but it is impossible for me to attend to them, my work is with the soldiers, not with their wives.[63]

Regimental funds were established to help women left behind, and the foundation of savings banks as well as charities such as the Wellington and United Services Benevolent Institution went some way to assuaging the hardship of widows.[64]

The gradual removal of women from the theatres of war coincided with the waning public fascination with the female warrior, who was regarded as 'anachronistic and unnecessary', no longer *en vogue* or 'the "stuff" of hit songs.'[65] James Miranda Barry stands out as one of the few examples of the eighteenth-century phenomenon. James Barry entered Edinburgh University in 1809 and graduated with a medical degree in 1812. At just 5 feet tall, with effeminate features and a little dog as a constant companion, Barry was regarded as an eccentric. Yet he was also overbearing, prone to arrogance and would flirt outrageously with women but comment scathingly on their failings. He spent forty-six years in the army, rising to the rank of major-general in the medical service and became a senior inspector of Her Majesty's General of Hospitals. Barry treated 500 wounded from the Crimea at Corfu and later met and – it is reputed – snubbed Florence Nightingale. Not until Barry's body was being prepared for burial on his death was it discovered the renowned army surgeon was a woman.

Although the public furore over her revelation was great, it was Nightingale, not Barry, who was celebrated in the Victorian popular ballad and broadside poem.[66] 'The Lady with the Lamp', who went to the Crimea to combat the diseases of cholera and typhus that were killing men more effectively than enemy weapons, seemingly single-handedly carved a feminine niche in the 'masculine sphere of war'.[67] After Britain and France were drawn into the war in March 1854, *The Times* ran an article describing the appalling conditions in the hospitals and Nightingale, who had volunteered, was sent by Sidney Herbert, the secretary of State for War, as the head of a contingent of thirty-eight nurses to Scutari.[68] Arriving on 5 November, truculent doctors resentful of her presence confronted Nightingale, but she accepted no opposition to her authority, which she asserted immediately. Hygiene was swiftly improved under her authoritarian hand. By Christmas she was said to have dismissed thirteen of her original female nurses. She was particularly dismayed by the arrival of voluntary women, nuns and devout ladies, sent as back up by Herbert. She threatened resignation at not being consulted. Her acerbic and formidable character was glossed over by the journalists who celebrated her achievement. Henry Longfellow's poem, 'Santa Filomena' (1857), which gave her her epithet, confirmed her status as the ultimate ministering angel: 'Lo! in that house of misery/A lady with a lamp I see'. *Punch*'s depiction is equally melodramatic:

> And there is Mercy's Amazon, within whose little breast
> Burns the great spirit that has dared the fever and the pest.
> And she has grappled with grim Death, that maid so bold and meek:
> There is the mark of battle fresh upon her pallid cheek.

Ladies' and girls' magazines featured stories of her early life as well as her work in the Crimea, while numerous biographies such as *Florence Nightingale: The Wounded Soldier's Friend* helped perpetuate a myth that overshadowed the real woman.[69]

Like the celebrated female warriors before her, Nightingale – or perhaps more accurately, her mythic status – has also overshadowed the wartime contributions of other women. Mary Seacole may have been the 'last of the camp followers' when, after being rejected for Nightingale's contingent, she sailed to the Crimea and established a canteen and officers' club at Balaclava, dubbed the 'British Hotel'.[70] She also journeyed to the battlefront 'with two mules in attendance' to supply food and medicine to the soldiers and was the first woman to enter the captured city of Sevastopol with allied troops.[71] Equally familiar in the trenches for retrieving the wounded during the siege was Mrs Rebecca Box, who had followed her husband with the 4th King's Own Regiment and was known for her courage in the face of shelling even when the soldiers had taken cover. She also managed through charm and outright bravado to inveigle brandy from the French troops for her own. Her compatriot, Mrs Longley, even when widowed, refused to return to England, staying on to nurse the wounded at Balaclava. One story recounts how she trod through an icy stream to bring brandy to her freezing men back in the lines.[72] Russian nurses were organised by the Grand Duchess Elena Pavlovna and the Sisters of Mercy of the Society of the Exultation of the Cross, which mobilized 163 women volunteers.[73] Seventeen of them had died under fire by the end of 1855. Over 600,000 men perished in the Crimean war, half a million of disease: 22 per cent British, 30 per cent French and half the Russian forces.

The language of war was not abandoned in peacetime, for when Nightingale established her School of Nursing at St Thomas's Hospital, London in 1860, military terminology permeated her reforms and the outlook of those she instructed: 'They saw themselves as soldiers – officers – in the fight against disease' and training was 'modeled on that of the army'.[74] Like religious movements such as the Salvation Army and hymns such as 'Onward Christian Soldiers', this medical reformation demonstrated how militaristic metaphors had permeated the consciousness of the Victorians. Nightingale nurses defined themselves as a separate corps, subordinate to male doctors, but clearly defined within their own sphere of influence. They were recruited by Nightingale and answerable to her or to superior military officers who may have called upon them.[75] An often uneasy relationship existed between male orderlies and other personnel who resented their imperious orders but, as one nursing sister put it:

> Nursing is warfare, and the nurses are soldiers . . . Sin and his consequences –
> diseases, suffering, degeneration, degradation, death – seem to fill the
> foreground of the view, and we want a strong mind to face them bravely, and
> to look through and beyond.[76]

Nursing, however dangerous and unsavoury the reality, was seen as an appropriate role for women in war because of its associations with the mothering function, with women's supposed innate instincts for comfort, care and succour.

Such a development coincided with a larger societal attitude shift, which the concept of 'separate spheres' encapsulated. The home, domestic duties and the family were propounded as women's prime occupation – and preoccupation. Evangelicals in Britain especially adapted Rousseau's philosophy that a woman's 'contribution to the welfare of the nation was essentially private and always indirect.'[77] In addition to the numbers of women who bucked against such constraints, many ironically found 'a greater sense of purpose, an opportunity for escape into action and commitment' in their separate realms.[78]

The increasingly influential British peace movement, for one, adhered to the separate-sphere dictum as it continued to marginalise women, confining them to ladies' associations, the first of which was formed in 1821. Respectable women were not allowed to sit on committees or speak at mixed-gender public meetings, so that these all-female groups allowed women an activist role that was in keeping with convention.[79] In its 'Appeal to Christian Females, on the subjects of Peace and War' published in the *Herald of Peace* in 1823, the Peace Society reiterated conventional ideas about women, with 'their bewitching smiles and affectionate importunity, removing from the hand of wrathful man the firebrand of war'.[80]

While Eugénie Niboyet published the first pacifist journal, *La Paix des Deux Monde* (afterwards *L'Avenir*), in 1844, her middle-class British sisters were occupying themselves in the more circumspect yet idealistic all-female Olive Leaf Societies, founded by Elihu Burritt.[81] Involving fifteen to twenty women each, the groups met in each others' homes to discuss issues, to correspond with foreign 'circles' in countries such as Spain and Denmark, and to write improving literature for children, which they published in *The Olive Leaf or, Peace Magazine for the Young*. By the 1850s there were 150 local Olive Leaf Circles in Britain, with a total membership of 3,000 women. Although they could lay claim to being the first women's peace movement, the separate-spheres ideology to some extent caused enthusiasm for the societies to wane as mores about women's place became entrenched: 'Anything which took women away from their family and out into a more public arena threatened the sanctity of the home.'[82] When the suggestion of female speakers at the London Peace Congress of 1851 was mooted, the Peace Society argued that the 'idea of a woman taking an active part and speaking in such an assembly is repugnant to the English mind.'[83] A national women's association was not established until 1874 and Quaker Priscilla Peckover was, in 1889, the first woman invited to join the London committee, an invitation she turned down. Ceadel argues that we should not judge the Peace Society too harshly, for in its drive to bring its controversial ideas to a sceptical society, it could not afford to breach too many conventions, especially that of women's place in philanthropic organisations. The women's peace movement was boosted by the publication of Bertha von Suttner's pacifist novel, *Die Waffen nieder (Lay Down Your Arms)* in 1889. She had deliberately set out to 'be of service to the Peace League . . . [by writing] a book which should propagate its ideas'.[84] Because of her careful research and the reality of the horrors experienced by her heroine, the effect of *Die Waffen nieder* was so real and the implied indictment of militarism so telling that its impact was tremendous, and it encouraged the formation of new women's anti-militarist and disarmament organisations throughout Europe, including the Union Internationale des Femmes (1895) and the Association des Femmes des Suede pour la Paix (1899).[85]

In the long period of relative peace in Europe between the end of the Franco-Prussian war in 1871 and the outbreak of the Great War in 1914, peace societies used the dearth of martial conflict as evidence that 'war had become an anachronism'.[86] Yet despite such optimism and the lack of actual war, there were ominous signs of coming international crises, and Europe was growing steadily more militaristic in its outlook. Predictions of future wars, the rise in status of the soldier and the fascination with all things martial, from dress to literature were emblematic of the age. And women were just as susceptible to the romance and seduction of this as men. In the same way as the language of war entered the reformation of nursing, it permeated wider public consciousness. The Victorian era was conditioned by and for war. Royal women took to donning military uniform when inspecting the troops, a trend started by Queen Victoria. When the Victoria Cross was inaugurated on 26 June 1857, it made for 'one of the most stirring military spectacles ever seen in London', not the least because the Queen, 'mounted on a magnificent charger' wore a pseudo-military uniform:

> a round hat with a gold band around it, and on the right side a red and white feather. Her dress consisted of a scarlet tunic, open from the throat, and a dark blue skirt, and across her shoulders was a gold embroidered sash.[87]

Treitschke's ideas on women and his view that the matters of state belong to men informed German opinion on separate spheres.[88] Women's organisations, while encouraging an auxiliary role for women in war, emphasised the centrality of their voices. The Patriotic Women's Association, for instance, was founded in Prussia in 1866. The end of the Franco-Prussian war in 1871 marked a turning point for the European outlook from passive to active, from anticipation of peace to expectation of conflict. The period of calm was nearing its end. The German Empire, united when the King of Prussia was proclaimed emperor, signalled the imminent return of large-scale warfare carried out by huge armies.[89] In 1877 there were 400 women's patriotic organisations in Germany; by 1891 there were 800. Voluntary imperialist organisations in Britain such as the Girls' Friendly Society (founded 1874) and the Primrose League (founded 1883) acknowledged women's contribution to empire-building while promoting health and hygiene for the good of the nation. *L'unione feminile*, an Italian monthly review first published in 1899, promoted the 'image of virtuous and patriotic mother.'[90] Italy, in effect, politicised the 'angel in the house' as 'Mazzini's revolutionary republicanism . . . placed women at the centre of a most radical vision for a new society.'[91] These were mothers of the nation – bearers of soldiers, consolers of the bereaved and the wounded, the unprotected for whom the men were fighting. Yet they could be as bellicose and bloodthirsty as any man, just as the peace organisations demonstrated that men could be as pacific as women.

It is no coincidence that *The Battle of Dorking* was published at the end of the Franco-Prussian war. Written by Sir George Chesney, the novel described a German invasion of Great Britain and started a vogue for prophetic stories of a European Armageddon:

> The First World War, it would seem, had been desired and described long before it took place [for] between 1871 and 1914 it was unusual to find a single year without some tale of future warfare appearing in some European country.[92]

The fear over a kind of degeneration also began to preoccupy the European public imagination of the late nineteenth century. Max Nordau's quasi-medical exposé *Degeneration* (1895) voiced and fed on widely held fears about the physical and moral threats to Western civilisation. The emergent militant women's movement, avant-garde art and homosexuality were all seen as signs of racial decline. War was seen as a purifier. Armed conflict, some believed, brought the masculine virtues to the fore and solidified traditional gender roles where man was aggressive/defensive and woman passive/defended.[93]

The Second Anglo-Boer War (1899–1902) seemingly provided an excellent opportunity to purify the British nation, but in fact it bore out the fears that the population was physically and morally deteriorating when it was announced that a third of all recruits to the army was found to be unfit. The 14,000 women who served as army nurses were 'nursing British imperialism' as well as soldiers.[94] Although fought on African soil and involving indigenous Africans, the Second Anglo-Boer War was, in essence, a European conflict, fought between whites. The British and the Boer descendants of the Dutch settlers were relentless in their own claims to the land and the sovereignty of what we now call South Africa. The conflict preoccupied the British population in ways that prefigured that of the First World War. Women, as much as men, were fascinated by the reports of battles, sieges and reliefs of such towns as Mafeking and Kimberley. Periodicals aimed at women and girls were filled with stories, first-hand accounts and advertisements that explained and commercially exploited the war. In addition to learning about the experiences of a nursing sister, one could make, with the help of recipes, such themed dishes as Africander Pudding and Brain Cutlets à la Buller. Women were advised on how to dress in times of mourning and instructed on ways they could support the troops by knitting socks for soldiers or by contributing to funds for soldiers' families. Emily Hobhouse articulated the other side of the war when she publicly criticised the conditions of the concentration camps set up by Lord Kitchener to contain Boer women and children. Her book *The Brunt of War and Where it Fell* (1902) caused a sensation and while it earned her accolades from peace campaigners, it caused her to be pilloried by those who adhered to the cult of imperialism.[95] Despite the differences in its political aims and its distance from the home front, the Boer War was a rehearsal for the First World War. 'The last of the colonial and the first of the modern wars', it bridged the divide – literally and symbolically – between the nineteenth and twentieth centuries.[96]

The twentieth century

The dozen years that followed the Second Anglo-Boer War and preceded the First World War were bellicose ones. The anxiety about national degeneration was channelled into the development of civilian organisations that were militaristic and patriotic. They proliferated all over Europe and mirrored the build-up of armies and hostile rumblings among the nations. Although officially their aims were philanthropy and/or health and physical fitness, they were, in essence, preparing their members for future war. In Britain, the Victoria League and the National Service League existed side by side with such organisations as the Eugenics Education Society and the Ladies Sanitary Association. The Boy Scouts, founded in 1907 by Major-General Robert Baden-Powell, spawned a similar organisation for young women, the Girl Guides in 1910. The Territorial Force, the Officers Training Corps (OTC) and the Cadet Corps were all inaugurated in 1908. In France les jeunes gens d'aujourd'hui, which was modelled on the Boy Scouts, was founded in 1913. In Germany the *Bund* movement celebrated the classical image of the male body and the virtues of folk culture, *Volkisch*, but it soon had overtones that paralleled the message of explicitly militarist organisations. Liberal feminists were enthusiastically patriotic, and it is no coincidence that Joan of Arc was canonised in 1909.[97] German women were called upon to devote their energies to the fatherland by reminding them of an earlier generation's commitment during the anti-Napoleonic wars of the nineteenth century.[98] Women were accustomed to the idea of war and, like men, were eager to display the virtues it supposedly called into play: heroism, courage, and stoicism.[99] In Great Britain, women in their thousands volunteered to become members of Voluntary Aid Detachments (VAD), which were founded in 1909. Perhaps with the image of Florence Nightingale never far from their minds, many women romanticised the nursing role they would play in a future war. Other women joined the First Aid Nursing Yeomanry (FANY) when it was founded in 1910 to supplement the Royal Army Medical Corps (RAMC) in fieldwork, stretcher-bearing, and ambulance-driving. Having learned its lessons in the South African War, when transportation of nurses to the *veldt* battlefields proved enormously difficult, the FANY required its members to be able to ride horses.[100] The annual camp gatherings were exciting not only for participants but also for spectators who observed the manoeuvres. 'And the study of women on the eve of war takes us a long way towards understanding the capacity of that whole European generation to tolerate the intolerable.'[101]

Posters, postcards and poetry have conditioned our images of women in the First World War (1914–18). Popular fiction celebrated the patriotism of women who urged their men to enlist, who supported those men when they returned as wounded heroes (however debilitating their injuries) and who, despite grief and loss, remained true to the patriotic cause. Memoirs by those on active service also stressed fortitude in the face of overwhelming suffering and performed as important a function in recruiting both men and women as any poster or government exhortation. British suffragettes, under the direction of Emmeline and Christabel Pankhurst, plunged themselves wholeheartedly into recruitment and vociferous support for the war effort, as they abandoned their agitation for the franchise 'for the duration': 'the allure of chauvinism, nationalism and military patriotism' was strong indeed.[102] All British voluntary organisations that wanted to contribute actively to the war effort had to be affiliated with the Red Cross.[103] More than 28,000 female nursing personnel served between 1914 and 1918. Of these, 19,800 were Red Cross nurses and aides, 6,000 were religious sisters of various orders and 2,500 were nurses affiliated with the Professional Organisation of Nurses. 'The conservative gender image of the Red Cross nurse' was seen as an outlet for women's innate maternal feelings, love and care.[104] The Women's Royal Auxiliary Corps (WRAC) was established in 1917 in the hope that 'the example of female volunteers would cause fewer men to seek exemption from military service.'[105]

Whilst there were official outlets for women's participation, cross-dressing female warriors followed in the footsteps of their eighteenth-century counterparts. Vesta Tilley was a theatrical rather than actual 'Amazon' as she regaled the British music halls with patriotic songs dressed as a soldier, but her compatriot Dorothy Lawrence disguised herself as a man on the outbreak of war and actually enlisted as a private in the army. Sent to the western front, she tunnelled for ten days as Sapper Denis Smith with the British Expeditionary Force before admitting her disguise to her commanding officer. She was interrogated and held at a French convent where she was made to promise not to discuss her experiences. Her memoirs were not published until after the war in 1919.[106]

Flora Sandes was equally determined to serve the Allied cause, but joined the Serbian Red Cross instead of the British. Stationed in the early days of the war at Kragujevatz military hospital, by February 1915, she was in charge (with American Emily Simmonds) of an operating theatre in Valjevo, a place commonly called the 'death trap of Serbia'. After recovering from typhus contracted while working there, Sandes joined the ambulance corps of the 2nd Infantry Regiment of the Serbian army as a dresser. Starting out as private, she was quickly promoted to sergeant. After being wounded in November 1916 and being awarded both the George Star and a promotion to Sergeant-Major, Sandes travelled the globe on speaking tours to raise funds for the Serbian cause, but at the same time, if unconsciously, feeding public fascination for the drama of war.[107]

Other nations had their share of warrior heroines. Princess Kati Dadeshkeliani took the name Prince Djamal when she served on the Austrian front with the ambulance corps attached to the 4th squadron Tartar regiment. Wounded in 1916, she was hospitalised at Kiev before returning to her home Russian state of Georgia in 1917.[108] Marina Yurlova, who was pushed by accident into a railway carriage full of departing soldiers, was befriended by a Cossack who gave her a uniform and employed her grooming horses for a regiment. As she did not attempt to disguise her gender, she was an unofficial soldier, but was not insulated from harm. She was wounded on two occasions after which she was hospitalised in a mental asylum suffering from battle fatigue.[109] After leaving two abusive husbands, Maria Bochkareva appealed to the Tsar to join the 25th Reserve Battalion. She was twice wounded in battle. In the summer of 1917, she formed the Russian Women's Battalion of Death. Two thousand joined but only 300 saw out the training. They went into action on the western front in July 1917 and captured 200 German soldiers but suffered heavy losses. The battalion was then sent to defend the Winter Palace against the Bolsheviks in October 1917.[110] Women had 'triggered' the February revolution in 1917, when female textile workers called a general strike. They appealed to their fellow workers, to housewives in the breadline and to militant metalworkers to join them. Men did not join the strike until it became clear the army would not fire on the assembly.[111]

Despite such high-profile examples of female heroism and the fact that some 2,000 were either killed or wounded in action, most women in Russia – as elsewhere in Europe – were focused on survival at home.[112] The situation in Germany was particularly harsh. Food scarcity caused by blockades, inflation and poor planning all meant that women and their families were in a struggle against starvation. The 'turnip winter' of 1916–17 was particularly harsh, psychologically as well as physically, for as the supply of potatoes ran out, people were forced to eat what was usually associated with animal feed. Social tensions only added to the burden. There was contempt for the 'soldier's wife', the 'munitions worker's wife' and the 'mother of many children', all of whom received special subsidies and allowances. An economic war was being fought in the streets of cities in Germany alongside the war in the trenches as 'the woman of lesser means [became] a symbol of [the] collective victimization of fellow consumers'.[113] Eventually anger became directed at shopkeepers, who were seen as profiteering.

They have since become cliché, but the words of the song, 'Keep the Home Fires Burning' are, in effect, an apt description of what war 'service' meant for women. The struggle for survival, in terms of everyday basic needs, was nowhere near as acute in Britain as in Germany or Russia, but women still had the responsibility of keeping their families together while doing the work of the men who had joined the forces. Women appeared in large numbers for the first time in British offices, replacing male clerks, typists and stenographers. This was the work most females undertook despite the idealised image depicted in now-famous recruiting posters for munitions work, the Voluntary Aid Detachment or the Women's Land Army. 'The Girl Behind the Man Behind the Gun' may have been busy making his shells, but she was also bearing the burden of all responsibilities at home, freeing him to 'fight the good fight' abroad.

French women's mobilisation was slow and limited by comparison. No women's auxiliary corps existed and the army was slow to employ women as office workers. Only at the end of 1916 did they allow them into the barracks and headquarters as clerks. The 400,000 women munitions workers made up barely a quarter of the total labour force at the beginning of 1918. The idea of a woman soldier was an anathema, an image fit only for bawdy postcards. In fact, the anxiety over a potential masculinisation of women led to the creation of the 'charming diminutive *munitionette*' as well as the idealisation of the 'comforting figure of the military nurse'.[114] For many women, suffering became a badge of honour. French Catholic women, as Annette Becker argued, found comfort in prayer as the war was 'converted, transformed into a spiritual exercise.'[115]

One woman, whose wartime activities led not just to public opprobrium, but to execution, was Margaretha Geertruida Zelle. Born in the Netherlands in 1876, she married a colonial army officer, Rudolph MacLeod, but the marriage was abusive. Abandoned by her husband, who took with him their young daughter, she travelled to Paris and reinvented herself as Mata Hari. An exotic dancer, whose nude performances caused a sensation, Mata Hari's high-profile affairs with prominent politicians and army officers attracted the attention of the French authorities during the war. It is arguable how much intelligence she traded either for or against Germany and France, but she was arrested by the French in February 1917, tried, condemned to death in July and executed by firing squad in October. Whatever her actual spying activities were, Mata Hari achieved mythic status and, as Tammy Proctor has argued, this 'spyseductress and modern Delilah – functions as a powerful warning to women regarding the dangers of espionage and eroticism.'[116]

Her foil in the public imagination was nurse Edith Cavell. Whereas Mata Hari was erotic, evil and transgressive, Cavell was seen as virtuous, courageous and patriotic.[117] Florence Nightingale was *the* heroine of the Crimean War; Edith Cavell was *the* heroine of the First World War. 'The Victim of Germany's Most Barbarous Crime', as one writer dubbed her in 1916, was shot as a spy in Antwerp. Her pronouncement before her execution: 'Patriotism is not enough. I must have no hatred or bitterness against anyone' became her epitaph and was inscribed on the plinth of her statue which stands just off London's Trafalgar Square. Numerous books about Cavell were published during the war and were used as recruiting tracts. Ernest Protheroe's *A Noble Woman: The Life-Story of Edith Cavell* (1916) is a typical example of what were essentially hagiographies. His description of her execution is suitably melodramatic:

> The soldiers of the shooting party were greatly impressed by the courage and fortitude of the nurse, and much distressed at their enforced participation in a dastardly crime. Each individual soldier purposely aimed high so that he might not have the murder on his conscience. The whole firing party thus being impelled by the same humane motive, the volley left the victim standing unharmed.
> Only in that dread moment did her physical strength refuse to respond further to her sublimely heroic spirit. She swooned and fell; and the officer in charge of the soldiers stepped forward and shot her through the head, close to the ear, as she lay mercifully unconscious of her surroundings.[118]

Never actually a spy, Cavell was part of a network that harboured and assisted in the escape of refugees from occupied Belgium. The Germans thought her execution would serve as a warning to others, but the international public outcry at the event had the opposite effect and served only to 'prove' the claim that Germany was an unprincipled, 'dastardly' and 'barbarous' nation.

While many women responded, like men, to the patriotic calls for fortitude and active involvement in the war effort in the wake of Cavell's execution and 'martyrdom', others devoted their energies to professing the pacifist message. Against much political opposition as well as the logistical difficulties of travel in wartime, the International Congress of The Hague was convened in 1915. Well over 1,200 women from twelve countries attended. Chrystal Macmillan, Kathleen Courtney and Emmeline Pethick Lawrence represented Britain and stood alongside forty-seven Americans and the twenty-eight German women who made it through the border. At its close, the delegates agreed that envoys should visit the leaders of both warring and neutral nations to urge them to mediate an end to the war. Reynolds argues that these women have a good claim to have influenced Wilson's Fourteen Points. Although 'no statesman dared to grasp the women's challenge', the envoys in essence revived the peace movement.[119]

In Britain, women articulated in print the various strands of opposition to the war. In *Militarism versus Feminism* (1915), Mary Sargant Florence and C. K. Ogden argued that war involved the subjugation of women, while in *I Appeal Unto Caesar: The Case of the Conscientious Objector* (1915), Mrs Henry Hobhouse caused a furore when she criticised the Government's repeated imprisonment of those who refused to take part in the conflict.

In Ireland, many women from different backgrounds and regions were mobilising for Irish Independence. Cumann na mBan (the Society or Council of Women) was formed in 1914 as an auxiliary to the Irish Volunteers. Its feminist aims, however, were set aside in the interest of the national objective, as it pledged to 'work for the establishment of an Irish Republic.'[120] The decision of such formidable feminists as Constance Markievicz and Hannah Sheehy-Skeffington to suspend their independent agitation for women's rights until the republic had been achieved paralleled that of their British counterparts involved in the European war.[121] While forty-six women were killed in the 1916 Easter Rising and some fought alongside men, most female Cumann na mBan volunteers performed auxiliary roles.[122] Their sisters who decided to participate in the European war by joining such organisations as Queen Alexandra's Imperial Military Nursing Service and the Voluntary Aid Detachments were, in the wake of the Easter Rising of 1916 and Ireland's 'amnesia' about its involvement in the First World War, neglected in the historical record in favour of more high-profile nationalists such as Markievicz.[123]

In Germany, the pull of nationalism was difficult to resist as feminists struggled between their desire to support their men who were at the front and their commitment to anti-militarism and anti-imperialism. Their biological role as mothers became the focus for both camps. Some, such as Gertrude Baumer, argued mothers were obliged to support the war effort, while others, such as Clara Setkin, maintained that their life-giving function demanded a stance against such mobilisation.[124] Most German women aligned themselves with Baumer's view. The Bund Deutscher Frauenvereine (BDF) cooperated fully with the Government and propounded the image of the 'mother of the nation'. Those who remained committed to feminist pacifism, such as Anita Augspurg and Lydia Gustava Heymann, argued that because men have perpetuated violence and aggression and because women are inherently nurturing and inclined towards internationalism, political rights must be granted to women in order to counteract the power men have to make war. Heymann's pamphlet of 1915, *Eine Frage: Frauen Europas, wann-erschalt Euer Ruf?* dramatically asked: 'Women of Europe, where is your voice? Are you strong only in patience and suffering? . . . Try at least to be true to your sex and with courage and might put a spoke in the blood-drenched wheels.'[125] The 'blood-drenched wheels' did not stop turning until November 1918 and when they did the death toll had reached into the millions.

When the world leaders convened at Versailles to draw up the terms of the peace, Lady Aberdeen (Ishbel Gordon), President of International Council of Women (ICW), lobbied for women to be delegates, representatives and officials within the League of Nations on the same terms as men.[126] They and the allied suffrage groups who met in Versailles alongside the peace conference also wished to see 'women's issues', such as equal pay, abolition of white slavery and child welfare on the agenda, linking the right to vote with wider social concerns for women. A more radical group meeting in Zurich at the same time, the successors of the earlier Hague meeting described above, and soon to become the Women's International League for Peace and Freedom (WILPF), argued that women should have a place in the negotiations to create peace, and not just on women's issues. Amongst the first to read the terms of the Versailles Treaty, they were horrified.[127]

Women as well as men had to adjust themselves to demobilisation and to peace. In France, female war workers were summarily purged from their jobs as men returned, wanting their homes to return to 'normal' and desiring confirmation of their masculine identities as the breadwinners. The housewife was celebrated and motherhood glorified (the first Mothers' Day was inaugurated in 1918), while the emancipated woman was vilified. Yet the loss of 10 per cent of the male labour force in the war, 600,000 war widows and hundreds of disabled 'could not drown out the realistic voices that urged recognition of the inevitable need for women to work.'[128] French women especially discovered that their war service did not guarantee them legal and political citizenship, as they would wait until 1946 to be granted the right to vote. Their German counterparts attained the suffrage in 1918 as did British women over the age of thirty and Belgian widows of soldiers. Despite this, 'most governments clung to their authority over women and women's bodies in the interests of family and nation.'[129] War reparations meant that German women, especially war widows, and in particular those with children, 'paid the costs of World War I in installments of daily lives'.[130] At its 1921 conference, the Nazi Party pronounced that it would not allow women to hold office, demanding instead that they dedicate themselves to *Kinder, Kuche und Kirche* (children, kitchen and church). Their supposed confinement to the private sphere did not deter certain women from opposing Hilter's regime and they were not immune from political persecution.

In Ireland's War of Independence (1919–21) and its civil war (1922–3), the uniformed women of Cumann na mBan were regularly in public view as they held rallies and disrupted meetings by heckling politicians. Privately they were part of secret military activities: 'In the context of guerrilla war, the blurring of boundaries between home and battlefront re-positioned women in militarized arenas.'[131] Cumann na mBan had over 3,000 members spread over 800 branches by 1921. It was rare for a woman to be involved in actual fighting, but her work was essential. Nursing was a prime function, but women also acted as couriers, intelligence agents and saboteurs. Because police were unwilling to search them, young women in particular often carried not only messages but also guns, Mills bombs and other weapons.[132] Many members of this 'army of women' were imprisoned, interrogated and some were executed. In what Louise Ryan has identified as the 'complex dynamics of guerrilla warfare' women's involvement in the militarist campaign elicited widespread criticism that labelled Republican females as 'hysterical furies'.[133] Their role has been marginalised in the writing of their male colleagues, who preferred to play down the role of women in the campaigns – men needed the support of women, but they were keen not to seem overly dependent on them. Yet it was well known that the women revolutionaries could often be far more extremist in their dedication to the cause than men, and mothers in particular could exert great pressure on their sons to join the Irish Republican Army (IRA).[134]

Spain witnessed the greatest mobilisation and mass participation of its women in time of armed conflict during the civil war of 1936–9. Like their French sisters during the Revolution in 1789, Spanish women were at the forefront of the crowds storming barracks in Madrid and Barcelona. Delores Ibárruri, the embodiment of La Pasionara, the communist/republican resistance women's organisation she founded, is also famous for her oft-repeated exhortation, 'Better be the widows of heroes than the wives of cowards'. The *milicianas* (militia-women) fought at the front, provided auxiliary services and came to symbolise the 'good fight' against fascism: 'The belligerent image of the woman combatant in her blue *mono* (overalls) was predominant in the war posters that aggressively urged men to enlist in the popular militia.'[135] However, the aggressive and transgressive *miliciana*, for all her courage and dedication to the cause, was soon discredited. This was a subversive heroine who had accusations of prostitution whilst at the front – and thus the spread of venereal disease – levelled against her. The more traditional 'Combatant Mother' or 'Heroine of the Home Front' replaced her in people's minds. Republican women were discouraged from joining men in units and were sent instead to supply battalions. The 5th Communist Regiment was made up entirely of women but they were not to be sent into combat. That role was reserved for men; women were to be the supporters, nurturers, caretakers and nurses. Gender roles here as elsewhere were clearly differentiated and expounded in propaganda. Whatever the political allegiance – communist, socialist, Catholic, Marxist, anarchist or dissident – the symbol of motherhood was to inspire women's participation in their separate sphere.[136]

Women nevertheless made up a sizeable proportion of the 40,000 volunteers who joined the Republican cause. Felicia Browne was the first British volunteer to be killed by Franco's troops. An artist by profession who had joined the militia in Barcelona on 2 August 1936, Browne was shot in the head two weeks later at the front near Saragossa. Many British women served as nurses, ambulance drivers and administrators. Eileen O'Shaughnessy followed her husband George Orwell when he volunteered to support the Republican cause. Others raised funds or organised the distribution of supplies that were sent from England.[137]

The Spanish Civil War also had an impact on the peace movement, causing many to question to their pacifist stance. When Hitler marched into Austria in 1938, such questioning intensified. The moral dilemma caused by the inexorable rise of fascism in Europe meant that those in organisations such as Britain's Women's Co-Operative Guild, who were witnessing and indeed helping Jews flee Nazism, were facing the prospect of sending their sons to war. How to reconcile their support of their sons with their condemnation of armed conflict? By 1939 the Guild had 87,246 members, mostly of the working class, in 1,819 branches across Britain. 'Stunned' by the outbreak of war, the guild began knitting and providing other 'comforts' for soldiers. While some women, such as Vera Brittain, maintained 'a personal refusal to support or condone war' as a member of Dick Sheppard's Peace Pledge Union, and while other organisations like WILPF maintained its peace-by-negotiation stance, many decided that pacifism and anti-fascism were mutually exclusive.[138]

Although covered up by the Allies after the war, there was a substantial body of German resistance to Nazism. Concentration camps were not originally built for Jews, but for political dissenters who criticised the Third Reich.[139] Many of these dissenters were women and, unlike other areas of German life, they faced no discrimination when it came to persecution for their beliefs: they faced hunger, thirst, torture, forced labour and death by starvation, hanging or firing squad. The most vociferous opposition was certainly 'cleaned up' between 1933 and 1939, but women of all political and religious persuasions continued to try and subvert the Government and sacrificed their lives as a result.[140] Sophie Scholl was executed, aged twenty-two, in Munich in 1943, for leading the communist White Rose organisation. Catholic Marie Terwiel was executed for distributing Bishop von Galen's sermons and for forging passports for Jews, while Jehovah's Witnesses Margaret Baalhorn, Helene Gotthold and Mathilde Hengevel were executed for giving asylum to young men who would not kill for Hitler. Surviving Gestapo execution records list the names of 300 women. Thousands of other women, however, remain invisible to history: informers, those who tacitly expressed anti-fascist views, relatives and friends of resisters. Others surely faced a dilemma similar to that of pacifists in Britain: 'How can you try to sabotage a war-effort in which your own and your friends' menfolk are being killed?'[141]

The underground resistance movements of other countries also had a hand in the fight against Hitler and Nazism. The Danish resistance cooperated with British Intelligence, smuggled out people in danger and smuggled in arms, mail, film and other supplies.[142] British-born Norwegian Helen Astrup, widow of a sea captain whose ship was sunk by Nazis, was known to have harboured *Joessings*, or resistance fighters. In order to smuggle out her neighbour, Mrs Hirschfeldt, Astrup participated in an audacious ruse that involved claiming Mrs Hirschfeldt's 'body' from the morgue. Male and female operatives from the Netherlands, France and Belgium helped to rescue and return over 7,000 British and American airmen. One third of the 10,000 agents in Britain's Special Operations Executive (SOE) were women. Of the fifty who parachuted into France, the Germans captured fifteen and ten were executed: four at Dauchau, three at Natzweiler and three at Ravensbruck.

Much research has been carried out into women's involvement in what is perhaps the most high-profile resistance to the Nazis, that of the French Resistance. The CVR, or Combattants Volontaires de la Résistance, is the main source for gathering names and numbers of those involved and here women made up 7 to 12 per cent of the numbers. But this only scratches the surface. Women who carried out their resistance in the home are not represented in these calculations.[143] Ordinary women, especially housewives, tended to downplay any informal roles they may have had. Those who do figure in the record were usually young, unmarried women who could effectively sever ties with their families and 'go underground'. They assumed code names and were particularly effective as couriers and intelligence agents because their gender aroused less suspicion with the authorities. But resistance, too, was a highly gendered activity. Although the Communist Party mobilised women through its Union des femmes françaises (UFF, Union of French Women), women's resistance was on the whole less organised, less official and less visible.[144]

After Liberation in 1944, women who were not seen to have been staunchly loyal to the Resistance or about whom there was a whiff of collaboration were the focus of brutal reprisals. During *L'épuration sauvage*, 'the wild purge', 100,000 to 300,000 women were punished for what was called 'horizontal collaboration'. Their heads were publicly shaved in 'a symbolic process of purification dating back to the Bible'.[145] Women were also imprisoned in local jails or internment camps if they were suspected of other collaborationist crimes.

> Paradoxically, at the same time as some women were being punished during the purges, legislation was being passed which was to enable women to become citizens and to participate fully in the democratic processes for the first time; universal suffrage had at last arrived.[146]

France was not the only country whose citizens resisted the fascist state. Between September 1943 and May 1945, thousands of Italian women were mobilised in opposition to Mussolini and in the fight to expel the Germans, an opposition that frequently centred on that quintessential feminine domain, the kitchen. Meetings of underground political groups were often held in the kitchen of a member's 'unnamed mama'.[147] The Women's Defence Group, under the control of the Committee of National Liberation, had two goals: to help the Resistance and to fight for women's emancipation. The *staffetta* on her bicycle became a potent symbol of the Resistance. Occasionally called into combat, the *staffetta* was primarily a courier, responsible for maintaining the lines of communication, but she was not averse to carrying bombs when required. While they did not often engage in combat, women functioned like their male comrades when they were allowed to, such as during the liberation of Florence when 300 female combatants saw action.[148] Women were required to 'use the skills that patriarchal society attributed to them: intuition, cunning, protective motherly feelings and the habit of gossip, as well as seductive wiles (*fascino femminile*).'[149] The thirty-eight women of the 19th 'Eusebio Giambone' Assault Brigade have received the most publicity but their work, despite the hype, was more pragmatic than heroic as they spent the majority of their days providing camp support, such as washing, cooking and ironing for the men.[150] Despite the Resistance objectives of freedom and social justice, there was never a suggestion that male supremacy or socially constructed gender identity be questioned.[151]

The Fascist Government, the Italian Social Republic, issued *its* first call for women to enlist on 14 April 1944. Some 6,000 women enlisted in the Servizio Ausilario Femminile, SAF, or the women's auxiliary service, although less than half that number actually served. As in Spain during the civil war, the female soldier was a break too far with the past, and the image of the female soldier was used more to shame men into action than to encourage women's role in combat.[152] From June 1940, when quotas on women's employment were lifted, 'women began to be hired to substitute for some of the 1.63 million men called to arms. By 1943, women were prominent in the work forces of factories and public administrations.'[153]

By 1945 in the Soviet Union, women made up 56 per cent of the labour force; 1 million women served in the Red Army and the partisan forces and engaged in combat as guerrilla fighters, machine gunners, tank drivers or snipers.[154] There were three all-female air regiments.[155] Lydia Litvak was a fighter pilot in a regiment that made 4,419 combat missions in 125 air battles that defeated thirty-eight enemy aircraft and damaged forty-two others. A German pilot whom she shot down would not believe this twenty-three-year-old woman could have done it until she described their dog-fight in detail.

The mobilisation of women in the Third Reich, however, remained low by comparison to other countries. Conscription was never effectively implemented and upper- and middle-class women failed to respond to the propaganda campaign urging them to work. Working-class women, on the other hand, saw conscription as social justice at a time when they were bitter about what they saw as their 'entire responsibility for the war effort on their shoulders.'[156] Class conflict and hostility in the Third Reich endured, in contradiction to the much-asserted classless people's community, *Volksgemeinschaft*.[157] Women were constantly negotiating the 'conflicting messages' of National Socialism that confined them to the domestic sphere whilst propounding their active role war employment. [158]

British women, perhaps, have received the most historical 'coverage' for their work in the Second World War. In December 1941, Britain extended conscription to single women in their twenties, the only country to do so. The Auxiliary Territorial Service (ATS) had the largest number of women workers, over 200,000, who performed multifarious tasks: cooking, typing, cleaning, mechanics and office administration. The NAAFI (Navy, Army, Air Force Institutes), which supervised canteens at home and abroad, employed 60,000. Others served as nurses with Queen Alexandra's Imperial Military Nursing Service (QAIMNS) or performed essential farming and food production with the Land Army. The three armed forces all had their women's auxiliaries (WAAC [Women's Army Auxiliary Corps], WRNS [Women's Royal Naval Service], WRAF [Women's Royal Air Force]). The Women's Home Defence and the Women's Home Guard auxiliaries also provided opportunities for female service. Munitions and other industrial workers were crucial and recruitment posters glamorised the image of the woman worker as they called for females to 'Come into the Factories'.

Of all the actions performed by women in the Second World War, those which come the closest to disproving the argument that women, by virtue of their biological life-giving function, were less inherently warlike or incapable of acts of brutality, were those carried out by the female SS guards and supervisors of the concentration camps. Hermine Braunsteiner Ryan, who received a life sentence for being complicit in the deaths of over 1,000 prisoners in the gas chambers, was known for 'trampling women to death under her steel-studded boots', while her fellow guard, Hildegard Lachert, dubbed 'Bloody Brigitte' had 'drowned inmates in the latrine, beat others to death with a steel-tipped whip and sicked a vicious dog on a pregnant woman.'[159] Irma Grese, a 'sadist of the first rank', was known as the 'Blond Angel of Hell' for the brutality of her treatment of prisoners at Auschwitz and Bergen-Belsen. She was hung after her trial at Luneberg in 1945, charged with having whipped 18,000 women to death.

There is ample evidence to prove the assertion that 'the two world wars could never have been fought had they relied on coercion'.[160] Despite the calls of pacifists for negotiated ends to international conflict, women as well as men in the twentieth century have more often embraced the causes for which their nations have gone into battle. In addition to putting their own lives on the line, eagerly in some cases, women have been willing to commit their sons and husbands, brothers and friends to armed struggle and have endured the consequences, from physical and mental maiming to death and its attendant grief. To say that the wars of the twentieth century are the work simply of male politicians and megalomaniacs is to deny that women, however grudgingly, are complicit in the maintenance of the idea that war is natural, inevitable and necessary. The failure of the First World War to be 'the war to end all wars' and the inability of the Second World War to put an end to ethnic persecution and world political instability starkly emphasise this fact.

The end of the Second World War was not the end of international conflict. Indeed, it could be argued that the second half of the twentieth century was as, if not more, bloody than the first. Northern Ireland saw the revival of republicanism and the re-formation of the IRA as 'the Troubles' began in the late 1960s. Women were directed to join Cumann na mBan, but many joined mixed paramilitary groups of the main organisation.[161] As more women became combatants rather than simply couriers or intelligence gatherers, so their numbers in prison began to rise.[162] But Lorraine Dowler has demonstrated the ways in which 'Irish women have never been considered soldiers for the reason that their identities in warfare have been relegated to the domestic/private sphere.'[163]

For those caught up in the most recent war in Bosnia, rape was a familiar weapon. Yet because it has even recently been considered a mere by-product of war, another spoil of war, military and international tribunals have inadequately recognised it.[164] Women who are victims of sexual violence are often reluctant to speak about it for fear of being ostracised by the community or worse (imprisonment or death) which holds females up as the 'symbolic bearers of culture and ethnic identity'.[165] As a special report for the International Committee of the Red Cross (ICRC) stated,

> the fact remains that women are suffering unnecessarily in wartime . . . for the simple reason that the laws to protect them, of which there are many, are all too frequently disregarded. The challenge is to increase respect for and implementation of these laws.[166]

While it acknowledges that women are not just 'victims' or 'vulnerable', that they may be part of armed forces, take up arms and rule as political leaders, the report argues that the problem is not an absence of protective legislation for women and their needs in armed conflict, but rather that there is a lack of *implementation* of existing laws (humanitarian, human-rights or refugee law). The ICRC also does not negate the needs of men, but it argues that a committed gendered approach can illuminate the ways in which the

> impact of war on women is inextricably linked to the impact of war on men . . . the fate of women can be improved if humanitarian law is fully implemented and respected with regard to both combatants and non-combatants, be they male or female.[167]

In the 'unacceptable spiral towards "total war"', the blurring of the distinction between combatants and non-combatants continues.[168]

Conclusion

Today more than ever, women and children are the casualties of deliberate and systematic violence against entire populations. However, women are not just the victims of combat and the beneficiaries of humanitarian efforts. They are also the engines of resistance and key problem-solvers in their communities.[169] Such a statement reinforces what this chapter has tried to demonstrate: women have always played an integral and unmistakable part in war, not just as victims, but as active participants. Women as well as men collude in war, willingly, in many cases: 'if there is anything fine and ennobling in war, women share the glory. If war is atrocity, women share the guilt.'[170] Eileen Sowetby has argued that

> whether women's work is merely to breed men to be killed in wars, to support and encourage their men to kill, or to sometimes actually kill "the enemy" (when it is allowed by the men), men could not have wars without women's complicity.[171]

Although seen to be the preserve of men, warfare is 'profoundly gendered', not only because the basis of men's participation is their 'natural' warlike abilities and physical strength, but because it 'often creates dramatic alterations in gender structures, for it breaks down traditional norms of conduct.'[172] Both when they have taken the place of men who have gone to war and when they take up active service near the front line in auxiliary services, such as nursing or ambulance driving, women have seen their traditional roles and mores challenged. For some, it is 'the high point of their lives.'[173]

We need to adjust our conception of what 'war' is. 'Total war' to some extent is redundant, for surely all war is 'total'. The failure or refusal to recognise the ways in which all members of society, not just generals and soldiers, are affected by armed conflict is to see war in a vacuum. War is not just about battles, strategies, politicians or men. It has social as well as military dimensions. Both of these change over time and from conflict to conflict, though gendered expectations persist. Sacrifice was and is still perceived in some quarters as the duty of the civilian and solidarity with the fighting man is woman's 'substitute for action in combat.'[174] It would be incorrect to claim that women have traditionally been left out of the historical record of war because of outright misogyny. Rather, an unquestioned blindness has led to the neglect of women's integral place in war. Specialised uncovering has been done and a new way of writing the history of warfare and revolution that discusses the impact of armed conflict on both sexes is developing.

Arguments about women in the military pervade much of the current discussion about women and war. There are those who argue that until women are allowed into combat, they will never gain the respect of those who put their life on the line for their country:

> The whole notion of 'allowing' women into combat is disturbing. 'Allowing' women to do or not to do something is a remnant of a paternalistic society. A grown woman should go as far as talent and hard work allow her to go. By excluding women from key positions in the Armed Forces, we deny both the women the chance to further their careers in the service and, perversely, deny the military the skilled and qualified people available to help complete its mission – defending the country.[175]

On the opposite side there is the insistence that 'the influx of women has been a disaster for the military. [It is] self-evident that women are not nearly as fit for war as men'.[176] Furthermore, 'in the military, as in any other institution, the influx of large numbers of women is both symptom and cause of declining social prestige.'[177] For some feminists, 'camouflaging' women's military service as liberation is one more step in the militarisation of their lives.[178] Perhaps this is why, as Jean Bethke Elshtain has pointed out, women, as 'a collective Beautiful Soul', have been 'unable – whether as liberal humanists, socialist internationalists, or feminists – to forestall state conflicts.'[179]

Logically, violence should not be part of a rational society and women are not different from men in their fears, their desires for survival, their hopes for future generations. Aggression is not the preserve of men, but because men have held power in politics and on the international stage, it has seemed so. Margaret Thatcher demonstrated that being female did not equate with being 'sisterly' or pacific. Is power, then, the deciding factor?

Courage has never been an issue either for those in the peace movement or those who took up active service. It can be argued that waiting at home is one of the most courageous acts of war, the role involving the most fortitude, commitment and sacrifice. Time and again pacifist feminists have had to confront the dilemma that

American Jane Addams articulated: 'Even to appear to differ from those she loves in the hour of their affliction has ever been the supreme test of a woman's conscience.'[180] Although public acceptance of women warriors changed from a passive acceptance (and indeed a prurient fascination) to a qualified rejection, women of all nations in all three centuries were called upon to serve their countries in multifarious ways – and they were, more often than not, asked to return to their pre-war domesticity when the treaties were signed.

A study of the involvement of women in war from the eighteenth to the twentieth century shows that women are not inherently less warlike than men. History shows us that women could be as seduced by action and combat as men, but they were equally, if not more, vociferous in their demands for peace and diplomatic resolutions to international conflict. It has also shown us that not all men are seduced by warfare, but the idealisation of the soldier, the equation of a man's masculinity with his ability to take part in combat means that the gendered call of nation is particularly strong. Arguments regarding women's innate passivity, inclination to peace, succour and tenderness are complicated by examples from history that show not only women's warlike proclivities, their desire to be active participants in warfare, to carry weapons and to fight and their bellicose pronouncements but also their sadistic and violent tendencies. For women whose lives were confined to a separate, domestic sphere, the prospect of war held an immediate attraction for publicly sanctioned activity, adventure and usefulness outside their homes and display of their love of mother country. Virginia Woolf called for women to become a 'Society of Outsiders' when she responded to the question of 'How do we prevent war?'.[181] But women in modern Europe, whether as 'valiant heroines' or 'pacific ladies', have never been detached from the bloodshed, sacrifices or consequences of war.

Guide to further reading

Adie, Kate, *Corsets to Camouflage: Women and War*. London: Hodder & Stoughton, in association with the Imperial War Museum, 2003. An illustrated, engagingly written history of the women who played active roles in wars from the eighteenth to the twenty-first century. Published to coincide with an exhibition at the Imperial War Museum in 2003.

Berkin, Carol R. and Clara M. Lovett, eds, *Women, War and Revolution*. New York and London: Holmes and Meier Publishers, Inc., 1980. A compelling collection that brings women's involvement in the wars and revolutions of the past three centuries into clear focus.

Bridenthal, Renate and Claudia Koonz, eds, *Becoming Visible: Women in European History*. Boston, Mass.: Houghton Mifflin, 1977. Contains fascinating chapters on many aspects of women's contributions to European history.

Brotherstone, Terry, Deborah Simonton and Oonagh Walsh, eds, *Gendering Scottish History: An International Approach*, Glasgow: Cruithne Press, 1999. A fine collection of chapters that is applicable to gender studies generally as well as to Scottish women's history in particular.

Brown, Heloise, *'The Truest Form of Patriotism': Pacifist Feminism in Britain, 1870–1902*. Manchester: Manchester University Press, 2003. An excellent, ground-breaking study of the development of pacifist feminism in the Victorian period that highlights the lives and work of such women as Priscilla Peckover, Ellen Robinson and Emily Hobhouse.

Browning, Peter, *The Changing Nature of Warfare*. Cambridge: Cambridge University Press, 2002. An accessible overview of warfare over the centuries, written for student use and covering the social as well as military effects of war, including a separate section on women in each century.

Caine, Barbara and Glenda Sluga, *Gendering European History: 1780–1920*. London and New York: Leicester University Press, 2000. A clear and interesting theoretical approach to the discipline of gender history.

Ceadel, Martin, *The Origins of War Prevention: The British Peace Movement and International Relations, 1730–1854*. Oxford: The Clarendon Press, 1996. A central text on the history of the British peace movement, although women are not a key feature.

Chickering, Roger, *Imperial Germany and a World without War: The Peace Movement and German Society, 1892–1914*. Princeton, NJ: Princeton University Press, 1975. A fascinating history of the German response to the international tensions and sabre-rattling of the late nineteenth and early twentieth centuries.

Clarke, I. F., *Voices Prophesying War, 1763–1984*. London: Panther Arts, 1970. A scholarly but entertaining look at invasion literature from an historical, literary and critical perspective.

Compton, Piers, *Colonel's Lady and Camp Follower: The Story of Women in the Crimean War*. London: Robert Hale & Co., 1970. One of the first books to explore women's auxiliary roles in wartime.

Cooper, Helen M., Adrienne Auslander Munich and Susan Merrill Squier, *Arms and the Woman: War, Gender, and Literary Representation*. Chapel Hill, NC and London: University of North Carolina Press, 1989. A wide-ranging collection on subjects from Shakespeare to the American Civil War, from First World War novels to the memoirs of Käthe Kollwitz. Also contains an excellent bibliography of secondary sources.

Craig, Maggie, *Damn' Rebel Bitches: The Women of the '45*. Edinburgh and London: Mainstream Publishing, 1997. An engagingly written history of women's involvement in the Jacobite Rebellion of 1745 with a cogent argument for the rediscovery and recognition of the many women who have been obscured by male historians and the tokenistic concentration on Flora MacDonald.

Creighton, Margaret S. and Lisa Norling, *Iron Men, Wooden Women: Gender and Seafaring in the Atlantic World, 1700–1920*. Baltimore, Md. and London: Johns Hopkins University Press, 1996. A fascinating account of women sailors and the construction of gender roles in maritime history. See also Druitt below.

Creveld, Martin van, *Men, Women and War: Do Women Belong in the Front Line?* London: Cassell & Co., 2001. An historically based, provocative argument against women's participation in battle.

Cuthberton, Greg, Albert Grundlingh, Mary-Lynn Suttie, eds, *Writing a Wider War: Rethinking Gender, Race, and Identity in the South African War, 1899–1902*. Athens, Ohio and Cape Town: David Philip Publishers, 2002. A useful collection that focuses on the under-researched Second Anglo-Boer War.

Daniel, Ute, *The War from Within: German Working-Class Women in the First World War*, trans. by M. Ries. New York and Oxford: Berg, 1997. Details the experiences of a neglected section of First World War German home-front society.

Darrow, Margaret, *French Women and the First World War: War Stories of the Home Front*. Oxford: Berg, 2000. A key home-front study of French women, with a particular emphasis on the influence of Catholicism as both an assuager of grief and a source of perceived female empowerment.

Davis, Belinda J., *Home Fires Burning: Food, Politics and Everyday Life in World War I Berlin*. Chapel Hill, NC and London: University of North Carolina Press, 2000. Along with Daniel, an important consideration of the hardships faced by the German home front.

De Grazia, Victoria, *How Fascism Ruled Women: Italy, 1922–1945*. Berkeley, Calif.: University of California Press, 1992. An accessible account of the ways in which Italian women both resisted and embraced Mussolini's politics in the wake of the First World War through to the end of the Second World War.

Dever, John P. and Maria C. Dever, *Women and the Military: Over 100 Notable Contributors,*

Historic to Contemporary. Jefferson, NC and London: McFarland & Co., 1995. A survey of the active service performed by women over the centuries and a polemic arguing for women's equal participation in the military.

Diamond, Hanna, *Women and the Second World War in France, 1939–48*. Harlow: Longman, 1999. Evocative and scholarly study of the 'highly sensitive' issues surrounding collaboration and resistance in Second World War France.

Dombrowski, Nicole Ann, ed., *Women and War in the Twentieth Century: Enlisted with or without Consent*. London and New York: Garland Publishing, 1999. Historically based arguments about the ways in which women are compelled to support armed conflict psychologically as onlookers and physically as active participants.

Druitt, Joan, *She Captains: Heroines and Hellions of the Sea*. New York: Simon & Schuster, 2000. An entertaining history of women sailors.

Dugaw, Dianne, *Warrior Women and Popular Balladry, 1650–1850*. Oxford: Oxford University Press, 1989. A literary and historical study of the figure of the woman warrior in fact, balladry and the popular imagination.

Elshtain, Jean Bethke, *Women and War*. Chicago, Ill. and London: Chicago University Press, 1995. A central text written both from a historical and personal perspective on the discourses of gender, war and peace.

Enloe, Cynthia, *Does Khaki Become You? The Militarisation of Women's Lives*. Boston, Mass.: South End Press, 1983. Another key text about the ways in which women are implicated in military activity and inculcated in military thinking.

Ewing, Elizabeth, *Women in Uniform through the Centuries*. London and Sydney: B.T. Batsford, Ltd., 1975. An illustrated look at women's involvement in the military and support services from the eighteenth to the twentieth centuries.

Figes, Eva, ed., *Women's Letters in Wartime, 1450–1945*. London: Pandora, 1993. A moving compilation of the written responses of both well-known and obscure women to war over six centuries.

Fitzpatrick, David, *The Two Irelands: 1912–1939*. New York and Oxford: Oxford University Press, 1998. An important consideration of the divided national loyalties of Irish men and women in the early twentieth century.

Forty, George and Anne, *They Also Served: A Pictorial Anthology of Camp Followers through the Ages*. Speldhurst: Midas Books, 1979. Another entertaining book about the contributions of the women and men who followed armies from the eighteenth to the twentieth century.

Fraisse, Geneviève and Michelle Perrot, eds, *A History of Women in the West*, Vol. IV *Emerging Feminism from Revolution to World War*. Cambridge, Mass. and London: Belknap Press of Harvard University Press, 1993. The fourth of a five-volume study that examines the developments of women's lives through a consideration of historical and literary sources by key feminist writers from France, Britain and the USA.

Fraser, T. G. and Keith Jeffrey, eds, *Men, Women and War*. Dublin: Lilliput Press, 1993. A wide-ranging study of European war and revolution, with interesting sections on the gender politics of the *levée en masse* during the French Revolution and social mobilisation of national populations during the Second World War.

Goldstein, Joshua, *War and Gender*. Cambridge: Cambridge University Press, 2003. An encyclopaedic study that draws on sociology, anthropology and psychology as well as history and literature to posit arguments about the ways in which men and women are conditioned to respond to war.

Grant de Pauw, Linda, *Battle Cries and Lullabies: Women in War from Prehistory to the Present*. Norman, Okla.: University of Oklahoma Press, 1998. A wide-ranging and scholarly international history of women who actively engaged in wartime from soldiering to nursing.

Hacker, Barton C., 'Women and Military Institutions in Early Modern Europe: A Reconnaissance', *Signs* (1981) 6, 4, pp. 643–71. A key article that highlights the involvement of women in the military in the eighteenth century and the ways in which their contributions have been demeaned and forgotten.

Hagemann, Karen and Stefanie Schuler-Springorum, eds, *Home/Front: the Military, War and Gender in Twentieth-Century Germany*. Oxford: Berg, 2002. An excellent compilation of scholarly chapters on various aspects of German experience in twentieth century wars.

Higonnet, Margaret R., Jane Jenson, Sonya Michel and Margaret Collins Weitz, eds, *Behind the Lines: Gender and the Two World Wars*. London and New Haven Conn.: Yale University Press, 1987. An important interdisciplinary contribution to the study of war and gender, including key chapters by Elaine Showalter, Sandra M. Gilbert and Susan Gubar.

Holmes, Richard, ed., *The Oxford Companion to Military History*. Oxford: Oxford University Press, 2002. A useful encyclopaedia of all aspects of military history from major wars to individual battles and including biographies of notable people. A good, separate section on women and war and on camp followers, in particular.

International Committee of the Red Cross, *Women and War: Special Report*, March 2003. A detailed and important report on the ways in which the Red Cross is achieving its objectives for the alleviating the suffering of women and children in wartime.

Laffin, John, *Women in Battle*. London, New York and Toronto: Abelard-Schuman, 1967. One of the first books to discuss seriously the contribution of women in wartime but also a polemic against female involvement in battle.

Laska, Vera, ed., *Women in the Resistance and in the Holocaust: The Voices of Eye Witnesses*. London and Westport, Conn.: Greenwood Press, 1983. A compelling compilation of personal accounts.

Liddington, Jill, *The Long Road to Greenham: Feminism and Anti-Militarism in Britain since 1820*. London: Virago, 1989. A key text about the British women's peace movement.

Lorentzen, Lois Ann and Jennifer Turpin, eds, *The Women and War Reader*. London and New York: New York University Press, 1998. A useful and wide-ranging anthology of theoretical and historical chapters.

Melman, Billie, ed., *Borderlines: Genders and Identities in War and Peace, 1870–1930*. London and New York: Routledge, 1998. Excellent collection of chapters considering a range of European women's responses to wartime female recruitment and the calls of peacetime nationalism.

Mertus, Julie A., *War's Offensive on Women: The Humanitarian Challenge in Bosnia, Kosovo, and Afghanistan*. Bloomfield, Conn.: Kumarian Press, 2000. An important, concise book about women's experiences of and sufferings in these countries of recent conflict.

Oldfield, Sybil, *Women against the Iron Fist: Alternatives to Militarism, 1900–89*. Oxford: Basil Blackwell, 1989. An engaging study of pacifist women that highlights the lives of such activists as Bertha von Suttner.

Oxford Dictionary of National Biography, Oxford: Oxford University Press, 2004. The fully revised and updated sixty-volume edition that includes thousands of women from all walks of British life. An invaluable resource for discovering the biographies of previously neglected female lives.

Page, Brig. F. G. C., *Following the Drum: Women in Wellington's Wars*. London: André Deutsch, 1986. A useful review of the activities of female camp followers in the early nineteenth century.

Peck, John, *War, the Army and Victorian Literature*. London: Macmillan, 1983. A good literary study of the way nineteenth century British writers have depicted warfare, with a particularly illuminating chapter on the Second Anglo-Boer War.

Potter, Jane, *Boys in Khaki, Girls in Print: Women's Literary Responses to the Great War, 1914–1918*. Oxford: Oxford University Press, 2005. A critical consideration of women's romances and active-service memoirs of the First World War set against the background of the Second Anglo-Boer War and within the context of the wartime publishing industry.

Proctor, Tammy, *Female Intelligence: Women and Espionage in the First World War*. London and New York: New York University Press, 2003. A fascinating history tracing the origins of women spies and exploring their involvement in the First World War. Edith Cavell and Mata Hari are juxtaposed, while the activities of lesser known Belgian, French and German women are highlighted.

Reynolds, Siân, ed., *Women, State and Revolution: Essays on Power and Gender in Europe since 1789*. Brighton: Wheatsheaf, 1986. A compelling and accessible compilation of historical chapters considering the ways in which women have been inextricably caught up in the European wars and revolutions of the past three centuries.

Ryan, Louise and Margaret Ward, eds, *Irish Women and Nationalism: Soldiers, New Women and Wicked Hags*. Dublin: Irish Academic Press, 2004. An excellent edited collection dealing with various aspects of the creation of Irish women's national identity and nationalism from the seventeenth to the twentieth century. Chapters include considerations of literary works, the women's rights movement and political activism in Northern Ireland.

Slaughter, Jane, *Women in the Italian Resistance: 1943–1945*. Denver, Col.: Arden Press, 1997. A useful and interesting study of not only the well-known *staffettas*, but also of lesser-known and often silent female resistance fighters in Italy during the Second World War.

Sowerby, Eileen, *On War: Men, War and Women*. Lantzville: Wantok Publishing, 1997. A personal, yet well-reasoned consideration of the meaning of women's implicit and explicit participation in national conflict and violence.

Stiehm, Judith, ed., *Women and Men's Wars*. Oxford: Oxford University Press, 1983. A thoughtful consideration by various critics and scholars about women's willing and coerced participation in the male practice of warfare.

Summers, Anne, *Angels and Citizens: British Women as Military Nurses, 1854–1914*. London: Routledge & Kegan Paul, 1988. A history and critique of the influence of Florence Nightingale on the development of military nursing as an appropriate wartime outlet and profession for women.

Trustram, Myna, *Women of the Regiment: Marriage and the Victorian Army*. Cambridge: Cambridge University Press, 1984. A cogent and interesting study of the activities, hardships and sacrifices of the wives of soldiers and officers in the nineteenth-century British Army.

Wiesner-Hanks, Merry E., *Gender in History*. Malden, Mass. and Oxford: Blackwell, 2001. A well-argued assessment of the ways in which warfare is 'profoundly gendered'.

Wheelwright, Julie, *Amazons and Military Maids: Women who Dressed as Men in Pursuit of Life, Liberty and Happiness*. London: Pandora, 1989. A key, engaging and illustrated history of women warriors.

William, Noel T. St John, *Judy O'Grady and the Colonel's Lady: The Army Wife and Camp Follower since 1600*. London: Brassey's Defense Publishers, 1988. An upbeat look at the lives and contributions of women who followed the military.

Williams, A. Susan, *Women and War*. Hove: Wayland, 1990. A concise and helpful introduction to the various activities of women in wartime.

Woolf, Virginia, *Three Guineas*. San Diego, Calif. New York and London: Harcourt Brace Jovanovich, 1966. A pivotal feminist analysis of women and war.

Yuval-Davis, Nira, *Gender and Nation*. London, Thousand Oaks, Calif. and New Delhi: Sage, 1997. A theoretical examination of issues surrounding gendered national and social identities with a key chapter on 'Gendered Militaries, Gendered Wars'.

Notes

1 Quoted in Paul Langford, *A Polite and Commercial People: England 1727–1783* (Oxford: Oxford University Press, 1989), p. 626.

2 Carl von Clausewitz, *On War*, ed. and trans. Michael Howard and Peter Paret (Princeton, NJ: Princeton University Press, 1976), pp. 36, 49.

3 Linda Grant de Pauw, *Battle Cries and Lullabies: Women in War from Prehistory to the Present* (Norman, Okla.: University of Oklahoma Press, 1998), p. 210.

4 Angela Woollacott, *On Her Their Lives Depend: Munitions Workers in the Great War* (Berkeley, Calif. and London: University of California Press, 1994), p. 131.

5 Nicole Ann Dombrowski, 'Soldiers, Saints or Sacrificial Lambs? Women's Relationship to Combat and the Fortification of the Home Front in the Twentieth Century', in Nicole Ann Dombrowski, ed., *Women and War in the Twentieth Century: Enlisted with or without Consent* (London and New York: Garland, 1999), p. 2.

6 Sybil Oldfield, *Women against the Iron Fist: Alternatives to Militarism, 1900–89* (Oxford: Blackwell, 1989), p. 55.

7 Mrs F. S. Hallowes, *Mothers of Men and Militarism* (London: Headley Bros. 1918), p. 22 and Virginia Woolf, *Three Guineas* (San Diego, New York and London: Harcourt Brace Jovanovich, 1966), p. 109.

8 Siân Reynolds, 'Historiography and Gender: Scottish and International Dimensions', in Terry Brotherstone, Deborah Simonton and Oonagh Walsh, eds, *Gendering Scottish History: An International Approach* (Glasgow: Cruithne Press, 1999), pp. 1–18, here p. 8.

9 John P. Dever and Maria C. Dever, *Women and the Military: Over 100 Notable Contributors, Historic to Contemporary* (Jefferson, NC and London: McFarland, 1995), p. 134.

10 John Laffin, *Women in Battle* (London and New York: Abelard-Schuman, 1967), p. 11.

11 Martin van Creveld, *Men, Women and War: Do Women Belong in the Front Line?* (London: Cassell & Co., 2001), p. 167.

12 op. cit., p. 166.

13 Jean Bethke Elshtain, *Women and War* (Chicago, Ill. and London: Basic Books, 1995), p. 173.

14 Piers Compton, *Colonel's Lady and Camp Follower: The Story of Women in the Crimean War* (London: Robert Hale & Co., 1970), pp. 19–20.

15 Kate Adie, *Corsets to Camouflage: Women and War* (London: Hodder & Stoughton, 2003), pp. 5, 31.

16 Barton C. Hacker, 'Women and Military Institutions in Early Modern Europe: A Reconnaissance', *Signs* 6, 4 (1981), p. 654.

17 van Creveld, *Men, Women and War*, p. 93 and Noel T. St John William, *Judy O'Grady and the Colonel's Lady: The Army Wife and Camp Follower Since 1600* (London: Brassey's Defense Publishers, 1988), p. 49.

18 Quoted in William, *Judy O'Grady and the Colonel's Lady*, p. 49.

19 Joshua Goldstein, *Gender and War* (Cambridge: Cambridge University Press, 2003), p. 116.

20 Amanda Foreman, *Georgina, Duchess of Devonshire* (London: Harper Collins, 1998), p. 64.

21 ibid.

22 op. cit., p. 65.

23 van Creveld, *Men, Women and War*, p. 101.

24 Langford, *A Polite and Commercial People*, p. 628.

25 Dianne Dugaw, entry on Phoebe Hessel (née Smith), *Oxford Dictionary of National Biography*, 2004, and Dianne Dugaw, *Warrior Women and Popular Balladry, 1650–1850* (Oxford: Oxford University Press, 1989), p. 53.

26 Dugaw, *Warrior Women and Popular Balladry*, pp. 49, 127.

27 Christian Davies, *The Life and Adventures of Mrs. Christian Davies* (London: 1740), part I, p. 75.

28 Dianne Dugaw, entry on Christian Davies (née Cavanaugh), *Oxford Dictionary of National Biography*, 2004.

29 Elizabeth Ewing, *Women in Uniform through the Centuries* (London and Sydney: B.T. Batsford, Ltd., 1975), p. 29 and Julie Wheelwright, entry on Hannah Snell, *Oxford Dictionary of National Biography*, 2004.

30 Julie Wheelwright, *Amazons and Military Maids: Women who Dressed as Men in Pursuit of Life, Liberty and Happiness* (London: Pandora, 1989), p. 92.

31 Alan Forrest, '*La Patrie en Danger*. The French Revolution and the First *Levée en Masse*', in Daniel Moran and Arthur Waldron, eds, *The People in Arms: Military Myth and National Mobilization since the French Revolution* (Cambridge: Cambridge University Press, 2002), p. 19.

32 Wheelwright, *Amazons and Military Maids*, p. 91.

33 De Pauw, *Battle Cries and Lullabies*, p. 139.

34 Adie, *Corsets to Camouflage*, p. 8; Ewing, *Women in Uniform*, p. 33; George and Anne Forty, *They Also Served: A Pictorial Anthology of Camp Followers through the Ages* (Speldhurst: Midas Books, 1979), pp. 197–8.

35 van Creveld, *Men, Women and War*, p. 103.

36 De Pauw, *Battle Cries and Lullabies*, p. 138.

37 Maggie Craig, *Damn' Rebel Bitches: The Women of the '45* (Edinburgh and London: Mainstream Publishing, 1997), pp. 51, 185.

38 op. cit., p. 19.

39 Quoted in op. cit., p. 20.

40 op. cit., p. 10.

41 op. cit., pp. 25–6.

42 Geneviève Fraisse and Michelle Perrot, eds, *A History of Women: Emerging Feminism from Revolution to World War* (Cambridge, Mass. and London: Belknap Press of Harvard University Press, 1993), p. 18.

43 Darline Gay Levy and Harriet Branson Applewhite, 'Women of the Popular Classes in Revolutionary Paris, 1789–1795', in Carol R. Berkin and Clara M. Lovett, eds, *Women, War and Revolution* (New York and London: Holmes & Meier Publishers, Inc., 1980), p. 11; Mary Durham Johnson, 'Institutional Changes for Women of the People during the French Revolution', in Berkin and Lovett, eds, *Women, War and Revolution*, pp. 107, 117.

44 Fraisse and Perrot, eds, *Emerging Feminism from Revolution to World War*, p. 25.

45 Pauline Léon, 'Adresse individuelle à l'Assemblée nationale, par des citoyennes de Capitale, le 6 mars 1791', in Darlene Gay Levy, Harriet Branson Applewhite and Mary Durham Johnson, eds, *Women in Revolutionary Paris, 1789–1795* (Urbana, Ill.: University of Illinois Press, 1980), p. 3.

46 De Pauw, *Battle Cries and Lullabies*, p. 133 and Johnson, 'Institutional Changes for Women of the People', pp. 215–19.

47 Jean Robiquet, *Daily Life in the French Revolution*, trans. James Kirkup (London: Macmillan 1964, originally 1938), p. 53.

48 Quoted in John Horne, 'War, the Law and the *Levée en Masse* from 1870–1945', in Moran and Waldron, eds, *The People in Arms*, p. 102.

49 Karen Hagemann, 'Female Patriots: Women, War and the Nation in the Period of Prussian-German Anti-Napoleonic Wars', *Gender and History*, 16, 2 (August 2004), pp. 397–424, 399 and 401.

50 op. cit., pp. 404–7.

51 Linda Colley, *Britons: Forging the Nation, 1707–1837* (London: Pimlico, 2003), p. 254.

52 Hagemann, 'Female Patriots', p. 408.

53 Colley, *Britons*, p. 261.

54 Martin Ceadel, *The Origins of War Prevention: The British Peace Movement and International Relations, 1730–1854* (Oxford: Oxford University Press, 1996), p. 167.

55 op. cit., p. 13.

56 op. cit., p. 12.

57 Colley, *Britons*, p. 257.

58 E. J. Hobsbawm, *The Age of Capital, 1848–1878* (London: Weidenfeld & Nicholson, 1975), p. 77.

59 Michael Howard, *War in European History* (Oxford: Oxford University Press, 1978, 2001), p. 53, and van Creveld, *Men, Women and War*, p. 96.

60 Myna Trustram, *Women of the Regiment: Marriage and the Victorian Army* (Cambridge: Cambridge University Press, 1984), p. 3.

61 Hew Strachan, *Wellington's Legacy, the Reform of the British Army: 1830–54* (Manchester: Manchester University Press, 1984), p. 62.

62 op. cit., p. 63.

63 Quoted in Paul Kerr, Georgina Pye, Teresa Cherfas, Mick Gold and Margaret Mulvihill, *The Crimean War* (London: Boxtree, 1997), p. 52.

64 Strachan, *Reform of the British Army*, p. 63.

65 Dugaw, *Warrior Women and Popular Balladry*, p. 64.

66 Wheelwright, *Amazons and Military Maids*, p. 122 and J. S. Bratton, *The Victorian Popular Ballad* (Totowa, NJ: Rowman & Littlefield, 1975), p. 62.

67 Wheelwright, *Amazons and Military Maids*, p. 121.

68 Martha Vicinus, *Independent Women: Work and Community for Single Women, 1850–1920* (London: Virago, 1985), p. 88. Notably she had been visiting hospitals and nursing for eleven years before she went to Scutari.

69 E. Pollard, *Florence Nightingale, the Wounded Soldier's Friend* (London: SW Partridge & Co. Ltd, 1911).

70 Peter Browning, *The Changing Nature of Warfare* (Cambridge: Cambridge University Press, 2002), p. 84.

71 Alan Palmer, entry on Mary Jane Seacole, *Oxford Dictionary of National Biography*, 2004.

72 Compton, *Colonel's Lady and Camp Follower*, pp. 145–6.

73 Cynthia Enloe, *Does Khaki Become You? The Militarization of Women's Lives* (Boston, Mass.: South End Press, 1983), p. 205.

74 Vicinus, *Independent Women*, pp. 88, 90.

75 Anne Summers, 'Public Functions, Private Premises: Female Professional Identity and the Domestic-Service Paradigm in Britain, c. 1850–1930', in Billie Melman, ed., *Borderlines: Genders and Identities in War and Peace, 1870–1930* (London and New York: Routledge, 1998), p. 358.

76 Quoted in Vicinus, *Independent Women*, p. 92.

77 Colley, *Britons*, p. 240.

78 op. cit., p. 276.

79 Ceadel, *The Origins of War Prevention*, p. 261.

80 Quoted in Ceadel, *The Origins of War Prevention*, p. 261.

81 Judith Wishnia, 'Pacifism and Feminism in Historical Perspective', in Anne E. Hunter, ed., *On Peace, War, and Gender: A Challenge to Genetic Explanations* (New York: The Feminist Press, 1991), p. 85.

82 Jill Liddington, *The Long Road to Greenham: Feminism and Anti-Militarism in Britain since 1820* (London: Virago, 1989), p. 18.

83 Quoted in Ceadel, *The Origins of War Prevention*, p. 463.

84 Bertha von Suttner, *Memoirs of Bertha von Suttner: The Records of an Eventful Life*, 2 vols. (Boston, Mass.: Ginn, 1910.) Vol. I, p. 294.

85 Helen Rappaport, 'The Origins of Women's Peace Campaigning', *History Today* (3 January 2002), p. 28.

86 Roger Chickering, *Imperial Germany and a World without War: The Peace Movement and German Society, 1892–1914* (London and Princeton, NJ: Princeton University Press, 1975), p. 8.

87 A. B. Tucker, *The Romance of the King's Army* (London: Henry Frowde and Hodder & Stoughton, 1908), p. 138.

88 Liddington, *The Long Road to Greenham*, p. 13.

89 op. cit., p. 22.

90 Barbara Caine and Glenda Sluga, *Gendering European History: 1780–1920* (London and New York: Leicester University Press, 2000), p. 149.

91 Judith Jeffrey Howard, 'Patriotic Mothers in the Post-Risorgimento', in Berkin and Lovett, eds, *Women, War and Revolution*, p. 239.

92 I. F. Clarke, *Voices Prophesying War, 1763–1984* (London: Panther Arts, 1970), p. 44.

93 Caine and Sluga, *Gendering European History*, pp. 143–4.

94 Enloe, *Does Khaki Become You?* p. 206.

95 Heloise Brown, *'The Truest Form of Patriotism': Pacifist Feminism in Britain 1870–1902* (Manchester: Manchester University Press, 2003), p. 170.

96 Greg Cuthberton, Albert Grundlingh, Mary-Lynn Suttie, eds, *Writing a Wider War:*

Rethinking Gender, Race, and Identity in the South African War, 1899–1902 (Athens, Ohio and Cape Town: David Philip Publishers, 2002), p. x.

97   Caine and Sluga, *Gendering European History*, pp. 147–8.

98   Hagemann, 'Female Patriots', p. 397.

99   De Pauw, *Battle Cries and Lullabies*, p. 209.

100 Pat Beauchamp, *Fanny Goes to War* (London: John Murray, 1919), p. 1.

101 Anne Summers, *Angels and Citizens: British Women as Military Nurses, 1854–1914* (London: Routledge & Kegan Paul, 1988), p. 1.

102 Wishnia, 'Pacifism and Feminism in Historical Perspective', p. 85.

103 Karen Hagemann and Stefanie Schüler-Springorum, eds, *Home/Front: The Military, War, and Gender in Twentieth-Century Germany* (Oxford: Berg, 2002), p. 106 n. 14.

104 op. cit., p. 89.

105 Browning, *The Changing Nature of Warfare*, p. 138.

106 Wheelwright, *Amazons and Military Maids*, pp. 168–9.

107 op. cit., p. 170.

108 op. cit., p. 166.

109 op. cit., p. 172.

110 op. cit., p. 166 and Browning, *The Changing Nature of Warfare*.

111 Bernice Glatzer Rosenthal, 'Women in the Russian Revolution and After', in Renate Bridenthal and Claudia Koonz, eds, *Becoming Visible: Women in European History*, (Boston, Mass.: Houghton Mifflin Company, 1977), p. 377.

112 op. cit., p. 379.

113 Belinda J. Davis, *Home Fires Burning: Food, Politics and Everyday Life in World War I Berlin* (Chapel Hill, NC and London: University of North Carolina, 2000), p. 48.

114 Gisela Bock, 'Poverty and Mothers' Rights in the Emerging Welfare States', in Françoise Thébaud, ed., *A History of Women in the West*, Vol. V, *Toward a Cultural Identity in the Twentieth Century* (Cambridge, Mass.: The Belknap Press, 1994), pp. 405–9.

115 Annette Becker, 'Tortured and Exalted by War: French Catholic Women, 1914–1918', in Dombrowski, ed., *Women and War in the Twentieth Century*, p. 47.

116 Tammy Proctor, *Female Intelligence: Women and Espionage in the First World War* (London and New York: New York University Press, 2003) p. 131.

117 op. cit., p. 126.

118 Ernest Protheroe, *A Noble Woman: The Life Story of Edith Cavell* (London: Charles H. Kelly, 1916), p. 66.

119 Jill Liddington, *The Long Road to Greenham*, pp. 97, 104; Reynolds, 'Historiography and Gender', p. 12.

120 Rhiannon Talbot, 'Female Combatants, Paramilitary Prisoners and the Development of Feminism in the Republican Movement', in Louise Ryan and Margaret Ward, eds, *Irish Women and Nationalism: Soldiers, New Women and Wicked Hags* (Dublin: Irish Academic Press, 2004), p. 133.

121 David Fitzpatrick, ed., *Ireland and the First World War* (Dublin: Trinity History Workshop, 1986), p. 38.

122 Talbot, 'Female Combatants', p. 133.

123 Keith Jeffrey, *Ireland and the Great War* (Cambridge: Cambridge University Press, 2000), p. 30.

124 Amira Gelbum, 'Ideological Crossroads: Feminism, Pacifism, and Socialism', in Melman, ed., *Borderlines: Genders and Identities in War and Peace*, p. 310.

125 op. cit., p. 312.

126 Reynolds, 'Historiography and Gender', pp. 11–12.

127 ibid.

128 Bock, 'Poverty and Mothers' Rights', p. 410.

129 Caine and Sluga, *Gendering European History*, p. 168.

130 Karen Hausen, 'The German Nation's Obligations to the Heroes' Widows of World War I', in Margaret R. Higonnet, Jane Jenson, Sonya Michel and Margaret Collins Weitz, eds, *Behind the Lines: Gender and Two World Wars* (London and New Haven, Conn.: Yale University Press, 1987), p. 126.

131 Louise Ryan, '"In the Line of Fire": Representations of Women and War (1919–1923) through the Writings of Republican Men', in Ryan and Ward, eds, *Irish Women and Nationalism*, p. 47.

132 Tom Garvin, *1922: The Birth of Irish Democracy* (Dublin: Gill & Macmillan, 1996), p. 96.

133 Ryan, '"In the Line of Fire"', pp. 60–1.

134 Garvin, *1922: The Birth of Irish Democracy*, p. 97.

135 Mary Nash, 'Motherhood, Identities and Female Agency in Twentieth-Century Spain', in Brotherstone et al., eds, *Gendering Scottish History*, p. 122.

136 op. cit., p. 123.

137 A. Susan Williams, *Women and War* (Hove: Wayland, 1990), p. 24 and Adie, *Corsets to Camouflage*, p. 126.

138 Liddington, *The Long Road to Greenham*, pp. 158, 161.

139 Vera Laska, ed., *Women in the Resistance and in the Holocaust: The Voices of Eye Witnesses* (London and Westport, Conn.: Greenwood Press, 1983), p. 3.

140 op. cit., pp. 150–2.

141 Sybil Oldfield, 'German Women in the Resistance to Hitler', in Siân Reynolds, ed., *Women, State and Revolution: Essays on Power and Gender in Europe since 1789* (Brighton: Wheatsheaf, 1986), p. 197.

142 Laska, *Women in the Resistance and in the Holocaust*, p. 57.

143 Hanna Diamond, *Women and the Second World War in France, 1939–48* (Harlow: Longmans, 1999), p. 100.

144 op. cit., p. 122.

145 op. cit., p. 136.

146 op. cit., p. 178.

147 Jane Slaughter, *Women in the Italian Resistance: 1943–1945* (Denver, Col.: Arden Press, 1997), p. 1.

148 Diamond, *Women and the Second World War in France*, p. 58.

149 Victoria De Grazia, *How Fascism Ruled Women: Italy, 1922–1945* (Berkeley, Calif.: University of California Press, 1998), p. 284.

150 Diamond, *Women and the Second World War in France*, p. 61.

151 De Grazia, *How Fascism Ruled Women*, p. 285.

152 op. cit., p. 282.

153 ibid.

154 Rosenthal, 'Women in the Russian Revolution and After', p. 390.

155 John P. Dever and Maria C. Dever, *Women and the Military: Over 100 Notable Contributors, Historic to Contemporary* (Jefferson, NC and London: McFarland, 1995), p. 134.

156 Leila J. Rupp, *Mobilizing Women for War: German and American Propaganda, 1939–45* (Princeton, NJ: Princeton University Press, 1978), p. 45.

157 op. cit., p. 47.

158 Caroline Bland, '"In Case the Worst Comes to the Worst": Letters Home from Berlin, 1942–1945', in Caroline Bland and Máire Cross, eds, *Gender and Politics in the Age of Letter-Writing, 1780–2000* (London: Asgate, 2003), p. 217.

159 Laska, *Women in the Resistance and in the Holocaust*, p. 35.

160 T. G. Fraser and Keith Jeffrey, eds, *Men, Women and War* (Dublin: Lilliput Press, 1993), p. 119.

161 Mary Corcoran, '"We Had to be Stronger": The Political Imprisonment of Women in Northern Ireland, 1972–1999', in Ryan and Ward, eds, *Irish Women and Nationalism*, p. 115.

162 Talbot, 'Female Combatants', p. 132.

163 Lorraine Dowler, 'And They Think I'm Just a Nice Old Lady': Women and War in Belfast, Northern Ireland', *Gender, Place and Culture*, 5, 2 (1998), pp. 159–76, 160.

164 Rhonda Copelon, 'Surfacing Gender: Reengraving Crimes against Women in Humanitarian Law', in Dombrowski, ed., *Women and War in the Twentieth Century*, pp. 332, 333.

165 International Committee of the Red Cross (ICRC), *Women and War: Special Report*, (March 2003), p. 8.

166 op. cit., p. 5.
167 op. cit., p. 20.
168 op. cit., p. 18.
169 Julie A. Mertus, *War's Offensive on Women: The Humanitarian Challenge in Bosnia, Kosovo, and Afghanistan* (Bloomfield, Conn.: Kumarian Press, 2000), p. xi.
170 De Pauw, *Battle Cries and Lullabies*, p. 16.
171 Eileen Sowerby, *On War: Men, War and Women* (Lantzville: Wantok Publishing, 1997), p. 79.
172 Merry Wiesner-Hanks, *Gender in History* (Oxford: Blackwell, 2001), p. 159.
173 De Pauw, *Battle Cries and Lullabies*, pp. 10–11.
174 Fraser and Jeffrey, *Men, Women and War*, p. 121.
175 Dever and Dever, *Women and the Military*, p. 15.
176 van Creveld, *Men, Women and War*, p. 10.
177 op. cit., p. 220.
178 Enloe, *Does Khaki Become You?* p. 45.
179 Elshtain, *Women and War*, p. 233.
180 Quoted in Oldfield, 'German Women in the Resistance to Hitler', p. 93.
181 Woolf, *Three Guineas*, p. 114.

9

HOME AND AWAY
Popular culture and leisure

Tammy M. Proctor

'Women's empire is within the limits of her home.'
Anonymous article in *Comus* (1877)

Introduction

Leisure is not a modern invention. Despite the demands of child-rearing, family care, work in fields and factories, religious instruction and devotion, women have always found opportunities in their days for private joys or civic revelling. Throughout recorded history in Europe, religious and political authorities, poets and prose writers have pondered the 'problem' of leisure, and they have worried about the potentially disruptive influence of popular culture. Such critics wondered how people would fill their time in seasonal downturns such as the bleak winter months and pondered whether idleness would lead to devilry. For much of European history, it was assumed that, except for a small portion of very wealthy men and women at the upper echelons of society, leisure time caused problems. Drinking, gambling, fighting and idolatry were only some of the feared pastimes in which working people could engage; more disastrously, they could participate in political intrigue or unrest. As industrialisation progressed in fits and starts during the nineteenth century, leisure time became a goal of workers and a mark of status and respectability, but it also emerged as a period to be filled with activities. Idleness was even more a subject of derision by the nineteenth century as middle-class reformers sought to create a rationalised and sober society, where leisure time was spent in 'improving' activities. What had changed by 1900 was that all people in European society expected that they deserved and required leisure time for a happy life, and they thought leisure activities and pursuits would help define their sense of self. Where leisure in the pre-industrial period might be a short respite from work such as a trip to a local fair, leisure in the modern capitalist world meant establishing an identity apart from work and family and escaping from the predictability and lack of autonomy in many industrial occupations. Even for aristocrats and the wealthy middle classes, leisure activities defined status and character more than work did.

In the midst of these changes, it is important to note that women, in particular, have always had a complicated relationship with leisure time. Women, after all, had often been called upon to facilitate the leisure of others by preparing food for feasts, packing and preparing children and their toys for a vacation, and cleaning up after a party or event. With industrialisation and the emphasis on waged work as a determinant of 'real' work, women's leisure often fell by the wayside. How does one define leisure time for a woman whose day is filled with activities? Consider the middle-class volunteer working for the suffrage campaign in Britain by sewing banners, distributing pamphlets and attending meetings. Do these activities count as unpaid work or leisure? She certainly derived pleasure from them and they counted as participation in popular culture, but these activities may have served more as occupation or vocation than leisure. So one of the problems of studying women's leisure is finding and defining it.

One way to deal with the problem of identifying women's leisure is to look at how women's claims to and opportunities for leisure have changed. Their demands for and access to leisure have expanded over the past 300 years often because women themselves sought out additional spaces and times for participation in the popular cultural milieu. Although these are not exclusive categories nor do they entirely represent the fluidity and diversity of women's experiences, this chapter uses three stages to explore the changing nature of women's leisure in Europe: (1) Community (1700–1800), (2) Nation (1800–1900) and (3) World (1900–60). These chronological and thematic divisions represent concentric circles of women's leisure pursuits and provide a way of understanding women's broadening world view with their increased leisure opportunities.

The first section examines women's participation in popular cultural entertainments in the pre-industrial world, with special emphasis on the ties of community and homosociality in defining women's leisure. The eighteenth century was marked by a variety of socialising activities that allowed women to interact with each other and with men both at home and in the broader community. By the late eighteenth century, governments sought to restrict these communal entertainments, and while some disappeared, others continued in transformed and strengthened forms. Women's public leisure activities, as cross-class and often rowdy entertainments, changed in the wake of moral and social reform movements. With the emergence of Enlightenment ideas regarding political participation and education, rising literacy rates gave women new avenues for filling their time, while clubs and societies emerged in which women could participate.

New political ideas led to a transformed relationship between nation-states and their citizenries by the nineteenth century. The second section looks at women's incorporation as citizens of the modern nation-state and their demands for further rights within this polity. With industrialisation, changing family patterns and new consumer options, women could increasingly tap into a wealth of leisure activities, both inside and outside the home. Also, the growth of European empires, especially in the late nineteenth century, helped reconfigure women's understanding of their place in the nation and provided a whole new arena of consumer products aimed at women. Likewise, the evolution of housing and home economy affected women's vision of their roles in families.

Imperialism, nationalism, the women's movement and other emerging ideologies led to a new consciousness for women of their place in the nation as citizens and consumers, which accelerated with the twentieth century. The advent of welfare states, state leisure provisions, militarisation and the global economy brought to women a staggering array of leisure options, without erasing some of the historical problems women have had in finding time and energy to take advantage of these opportunities. World wars, political invasion into private homes, decolonisation, tourism, new communication forms and mass-culture pursuits helped transform women's world view, broadening their options but also bringing challenges. With the dawn of the twenty-first century, women's leisured worlds had expanded exponentially over the 300-year period.

Historiography

In examining these three centuries of women's leisure, scholars have identified three interrelated strands in the history of European leisure: popular culture, leisure studies and consumption. The first strand concerns itself with the nature and persistence of popular cultural forms, and it embodies modern debates regarding 'high' versus 'low' culture. The second encompasses a wide variety of scholarly work from the investigations of twentieth-century critical theorists to leisure-studies professionals, all of whom try to understand the 'problem' of leisure time and its best use. Lastly, consumption has emerged as a counterpoint to studies of industrialisation and work, and this field has created a debate about the timing of the birth of consumer societies and their leisure pursuits. Through all these strands runs a subtext of class and gender, which is sometimes acknowledged and examined, but sometimes not. Although some scholars have examined women's leisure pursuits from 1700 to 2000, the study of gender and leisure has been essentially under-represented in the larger debates over popular culture and the rise of a consumer society. This short historiography section will lay out some of the influential literature in the three strands of study and will conclude with works on women and leisure.

Peter Burke's cross-national work on popular culture sets the tone for debate with his description of two divergent 'cultures' in Europe, that of the great learned men of the universities and the 'low' culture of the great majority of men and women. Although Burke sees the two cultures as related and intersecting, his critics often suggest that he simplifies complex relationships and ignores the minute differences in rank and society that are expressed in the communities of Europe through leisure activities. Some scholars have taken to using the phrase 'popular cultures' to evoke the ambiguities and interlocking natures of leisure activities.[1] Much of this work does not use gender as a category for analysis, thereby ignoring the complicating factor that men and women of the same class or even the same household may not have experienced popular culture in the same way.

Leisure as a social problem and a socialising vehicle has occupied many intellectuals and social reformers writing in the past three centuries, but critical studies of leisure are primarily associated with twentieth-century writers. Cultural theorists, such as Siegfried Kracauer, Walter Benjamin, Theodor Adorno, Max Horkheimer, and Herbert Marcuse, working in inter-war and post-war Germany and the USA published volumes of scholarship outlining the problems of mass culture and the intellectual dulling that had accompanied industrial capitalism. Likewise, reformers in Britain and France sought ways to 'use' leisure to good advantage, echoing political appropriation of leisure time by parties as diverse as Britain's Labour Party and Germany's National Socialists. Rudy Koshar has usefully noted that 'the history of leisure culture is clearly also the history of political culture, indeed of citizenship in the broad sense of social participation.'[2] Recent work on leisure has studied its efficacy as social control, its variety of expressions and its limitations in the modern world.

Again, gendered studies of these phenomena are less common, but some British scholars, in particular, have embraced this research. Explicit contemporary attempts to theorise 'leisure studies' in Britain have resulted in collaborative projects such as *Women's Leisure, What Leisure?* and *Relative Freedoms: Women and Leisure.* These books both question the relevance of studying leisure as a separate category for women. The authors of the first suggest that 'the artificial separation of areas of life entitled "work" and "leisure" into different subsections of the discipline both marginalized the experiences of women and obscured the significant "overlaps" that happen in real life.'[3] Women's work and their leisure are in tension with one another, since often no clear delineation exists between the two. Historians such as Anna Clark, Claire Langhamer and Catriona Parratt use gender as a central category of analysis in order to illuminate many aspects of women's leisure activities in Great Britain. While Parratt and Langhamer confine themselves to detailing women's leisure, Clark picks apart the intricate relationships binding together and pulling apart plebian communities in Britain during the late eighteenth and nineteenth centuries. She examines leisure, work and sexuality to demonstrate the complicated popular culture of working people. Her work provides a model for the kind of studies needed for other parts of Europe and for other time frames in order to develop a comprehensive study of women, leisure and popular culture.[4]

Other work that casts light on women's leisure in Europe often explicitly focuses on family life, work or industrialisation, discussing leisure time only as an aside. Examples of such studies include Leonore Davidoff and Catherine Hall's influential work on middle-class England, *Family Fortunes*, Louise Tilly and Joan Scott's *Women, Work and Family*, which examines working women's lives in France and England, and Victoria de Grazia's look at women in inter-war Italy, *How Fascism Ruled Women*. Scholars of imperialism have also touched on issues of leisure, travel and the imagination of empire in such diverse studies as Margaret Shennan's *Out in the Midday Sun: The British in Malaya*, Julia Clancy-Smith and Frances Gouda's edited collection, *Domesticating the Empire* (on French and Dutch colonialism) and Ann Laura Stoler's *Race and the Education of Desire*. Considering the component parts of leisure can yield interesting insights on women's activities and desires over the past couple of centuries. Pioneering studies of women and sport in Europe, women's education and reading, female socialisation and women's participation in cultural change all provide material for the study of female leisure. Mary Lynn Stewart and Kathleen McCrone have both explored the development of women's physical culture in France and England respectively. Barbara Burman's edited collection on dressmaking and home sewing provides another window into female socialisation as does Matthew Hilton's work on smoking. Put together, these disparate studies and others provide a clearer picture of how women spent their time and developed their identities as citizens and consumers.

Consumption has been an especially popular topic in recent years, with a plethora of histories emerging on the scholarly scene. Much of the debate has centred on the question of when a consumer society emerged in Europe. In opposition to that scholarly work are the more theoretically challenging philosophical and historical works that make up cultural studies. What both of these strands of historiographical work on consumption demonstrate is that consumer practices complicate our understanding of leisure. Is shopping a good use of leisure time? Does the pleasure of consuming represent leisure or a hegemonic economic model that enslaves populations? Beyond these questions, the study of consumption has brought a whole new set of sources and artefacts and has provided a richer context for the study of leisure. Of particular interest are those works that deal explicitly with gender and consumption. One of the best known of these is *The Sex of Things*, a wide-ranging collection that contributes substantially to our understanding of women's social functions, the nature of modernity and cultural studies. The essays examine 'the sexual division of labor around consumption' and expose gendered representations of consumers, commodities and cultures in European history.[5] Other individual studies of women's consumption practices include studies of such everyday activities as shopping, driving and housework. Despite the emergence of new work on consumption and leisure, this field is still understudied in history circles. As Mary Louise Roberts noted in 1998, 'In a society such as ours, in which there is virtually no area of life . . . that remains uncommodified . . . we can hardly afford to continue our historical neglect of consumerism.'[6]

The fields of cultural studies of consumption, the history of popular culture and the sociological and social historical work on leisure form the historiographical context for this chapter. In general, this historiography encompasses growing fields that utilise diverse primary sources and that offer multiple opportunities for new scholars to enter the dialogue.

Discussion of sources

The primary sources for such studies are scattered throughout archival collections across Europe and its former colonies, making for an invigorating challenge to researchers. Social history and the 'new' cultural history have encouraged historians to use non-traditional and sometimes non-textual sources for their investigations. Such materials include toys, cigarette cards, sporting equipment, gardening manuals, family photo albums, political banners and parade memorabilia to name just a few examples. Social history has also opened up the study of marginalised participants in European culture, most notably women, children and racial/ethnic minorities. Cross-pollination of the humanities and social sciences has been another way of broadening the pool of acceptable sources for historians. Ethnographic techniques, oral histories, literary criticism and archaeology have yielded new studies of populations and their leisure activities throughout history.

Sources describing the popular culture of eighteenth-century European women are limited both by the low level of female literacy in many parts of Europe and by the relative scarcity in general of plebian accounts of their pleasurable pastimes. Despite these difficulties, considerable sources are available to those willing to investigate. In particular, middle- and upper-class prose and poetry and travellers' accounts of fairs, sport and other activities provide useful windows into eighteenth-century life. Legal records detail infractions against local customs, and municipal records often discuss leisure pursuits and their control. Visual sources provide a rich cultural archive of materials detailing urban street life, theatrical performances, sport, fashion, customs and rural pastimes. In literary terms, so-called 'chapbooks' that have survived bear witness to a thriving trade in humorous, dramatic and religious tracts; they were sold for a mere pittance by a whole group of special hawkers throughout Europe. Finally, collections by folklorists beginning in the late eighteenth century are a rich source for songs, poetry, plays, stories and cartoons from early modern European popular culture. Although transcribed by 'outsiders' and often romanticised, the written records of a lost oral culture are priceless to modern scholars.

As the nineteenth century dawned, more extensive record-keeping, improved literacy and better publishing and distribution networks led to more available written sources for studying popular culture and leisure. Governments began tracking citizens more effectively with modern census techniques, and capitalism ensured the recording of workers and their broader kin networks. Universal elementary education helped ignite an explosion in cheap novels, newspapers, penny publications, journals and posters. Whether they are ephemera or bound tomes, archives throughout Europe have stocked evidence of how people lived in the nineteenth century. Examples of available sources include the official records of voluntary reform societies, emigration associations, travel agencies such as Thomas Cook's and sports leagues as well as the diaries of missionaries, charwomen and suffragettes. By the latter part of the century, photography and commercial graphics created even better visual records of leisure in Europe than had previously been available. With these sources, it is now possible to assess consumption habits by looking at soap ads, to study seaside resorts through an examination of photographs from Brighton, or to explore the impact of imperial expositions through the drawings, photographs, programmes and posters from the various exhibits.

The twentieth century, of course, has seen another multiplication of materials for study, especially given the larger number of available sources on working-class life (including the Mass Observation Archive in Britain and similar archives on the continent). Cinema is an obvious addition to the sources for studying leisure, but also important are other media forms such as radio transcripts and transmissions, television tapes, advertising ephemera, magazines and computer records. In terms of printed sources, massive information bureaucracies following the First World War have created almost unfathomable numbers of population studies and statistical summaries, while the availability of private letters, diaries and collectibles have expanded with almost universal basic literacy in Europe. It is possible now to get the inside story of a local youth group in a southern German village using photographs, news articles and diaries, or to study the dating habits of working-class residents of Dublin.

One source that connects all three centuries of study is prescriptive literature. From self-help books and exercise manuals of 1980s Britain to hiking advice from imperial Germany to French eighteenth-century educational booklets, the modern period has seen repeated attempts to advise citizens (especially those of the 'lower orders') on the best use of their leisure time. These sources, while offering useful glimpses into the writers' desires and fears and reflecting the larger cultural anxieties, must be read with their authors' motives in mind. For example, Lady Eleanor Fenn's *The Female Guardian* (1784) purports to provide 'innocent amusement for [girls'] hours of Leisure', but spends most of its time providing lessons on morality, featuring characters such as Miss Pert and Miss Haughty.[7] More than 100 years later, such works were still providing inspirational stories designed to convince girls to lead an upright, moral and sober life. *The Daughter of the Isles* (1881) sought fiction contributions that would help edify and instruct the 'working women of England; who, all the long weary day have their hands full of the cares and duties of this life' for the 'good of their

souls'.[8] Even in the late twentieth century, women are often targets of edifying prescriptive literature aiming to help them 'fix' their leisure time. These publications
include everything from self-help spirituality manuals to women's fashion magazines,
such as *Vogue* or *Marie-Claire*.

Using available sources and a specific study of Great Britain, France and German-
speaking countries, this chapter examines such diverse cultural pursuits as sport,
reading, travel and shopping in order to investigate women's use of leisure time. In particular, the chapter will use the double-edged sword of 'home and away' to investigate
notions of public/private, domestic/imperial and national/international as they shape
women's notions of popular culture and appropriate leisure. If indeed 'women's empire
is within the limits of her home',[9] then this work will explore the ways in which
females used and subverted this understanding of their role in society. In short, this
chapter uses leisure as one lens for focusing on women's lives in modern Europe over
a broad period from 1700 to the present in order to explore the ways in which women
found pleasure and rest and to explain how and why these leisured activities differed –
by gender, class, location and time.

Community (1700–1800)

At the beginning of the eighteenth century, leisure time for most men and women was
a luxury. For aristocratic women, having leisure time helped define their status as members of the exclusive 'leisured classes' in society, while for middle- and working-class
women leisure was a scarce commodity in their lives. For all members of society,
amusements were often found locally in the variety of entertainments that came from
festivals, fairs or other community pursuits. Whether in rural areas or cities, amusement meant socialisation, and leisured time was usually spent with others. Such
popular culture cemented social ties, provided a chance for reaffirming local mores and
rules, and reflected the importance of communal life in pre-industrial and industrialising societies. Even activities we might consider solitary, such as reading, took on a
communal character in a society in which the few who were literate read aloud to
others. This section, then, examines the importance of leisure in celebrating communities and affirming familial and neighbourhood ties even as transformations in this
popular 'traditional' culture began appearing by the late part of the eighteenth century.

One of the important facts of eighteenth-century European society was its limited literacy. Basic literacy, indicated by the ability to sign one's name on a marriage register,
was elusive for most European societies until well into the nineteenth century. Despite
laws passed to establish some form of elementary education in the eighteenth century,
real success in educating large numbers of people emerged only with industrialisation.
Rebecca Rogers' chapter in this volume, p. 103 and p. 111, examines this issue in some
detail, and notes that this literacy problem was particularly acute for women, many of
whom were excluded from the education provided for boys. David Vincent estimates
that around 1800, 70 per cent of French women were functionally illiterate and about
58 per cent of British women. Women lagged 20 per cent or more behind men in literacy rates.[10] Despite these somewhat dismal statistics, some literacy and access to
basic reading skills throughout the eighteenth century meant that reading and reading
aloud were important leisure pursuits in communities across Europe.

In some households, reading pious literature and the Bible were the norm, but also available were a variety of fictional and 'true-life' stories for all members of society. For the wealthy, the availability of books, newspapers and journals exploded in the eighteenth century. Book clubs and circulating libraries helped women gain access to print culture. Works such as Daniel Defoe's *Robinson Crusoe* and *Moll Flanders* thrilled audiences with stories of travel, empire, greed and domesticity, while the story of the trials of Samuel Richardson's *Pamela* became the bestseller of the century. For the poor of Europe, ballads and 'chapbooks', or 'small, paper-covered books' were sold by armies of hawkers in many major cities, towns and rural areas throughout Europe.[11] These books ranged from romantic or pious narratives to folktales to true-crime stories to abridged novels (such as *Robinson Crusoe*). Full of illustrations, these short pamphlets were often within the means (costing the equivalent of a few pennies or so) and abilities (eight to twenty-four pages long) of large numbers of people. From the *Eulenspiegel* in German to the *Bibliothèque Bleue* in French to the *Cheap Repository Tracts* in English, chapbooks reached a wide variety of the population through distribution by pedlars.

This chapbook literature provides a useful window into the tone and nature of eighteenth-century popular culture and leisure, despite the fact that some of them were produced by those hoping to 'reform' the poor, through the example of a model citizen (in Protestant countries) or a saint's life (in Catholic areas). Some of these chapbooks may have represented oral folk tales set on paper such as the myriad versions of Robin Hood or Faust; others were original humorous or morality stories. The popularity of such literature in an only moderately literate period supports the notion that reading still relied heavily on oral performance and group mediation of stories and tales. Communities might share these stories with each other through puppet shows, storytelling sessions, picture pamphlets or reading aloud. Much of the literature is irreverent, and it often mocks or undermines authority, legality and duty. Chapbooks show a 'world turned upside down: a world of giants and witches, of poor but valorous heroes, of scheming wives and successful crooks. Above all, they are hostile to respectability: to industry, chastity, piety, and other bourgeois virtues'.[12] Despite this carnivalesque tone, the chapbooks, even those celebrating heroic women, did not usually undermine gender roles, and by the end of most stories, women were either dead from their folly or embracing home and hearth. A representative example from England of this chapbook literature is the story of *Long Meg of Westminster*, first written down as early as the sixteenth century. This version dates from the eighteenth century:

> In the reign of Henry VIII was born in Lancashire, a maid called Long Meg. At eighteen years old she came to London to get her a service; Father Willis the Carrier being the Waggoner . . . The Carrier having set up his horses, went with the lasses to the Eagle in Westminster, and told the landlady he had brought her three fine Lancashire lasses, and seeing she often asked him to get her a maid, she might now take her choice. Marry, said she I want one at present, and here are three gentleman who shall give their opinions . . . On this Sir John de Castile, in a bravado, would needs make an experiment of her vast strength; and asked her, If she durst exchange a box o' the ear with him. Yes, quoth she, if my mistress will give me leave. This granted, she stood to receive Sir John's blow, who gave her a box with all his might, but it stirred her not

at all; but Meg gave him such a memorandum on his ear that Sir John fell down at her feet. – By my faith, said another, she strikes a blow like an ox, for she hath knocked down an Ass. – So Meg was taken into Service . . .

Not only the cities of London and Westminster, but Lancashire also, rung of Meg's fame: so they desired old Willis the Carrier to call upon her, which he did, taking with him the other lasses. Meg was joyful to see them, and it being Shrove Tuesday, Meg went with them to Knightsbridge . . . it was their misfortune at St James's Corner to meet with two thieves who were waiting there for them and took an hundred marks from Willis the Carrier, and from the two wenches their gowns and purses. – Meg came up immediately after, and then the thieves, seeing her also in a female habit, thought to take her purse also; but she behaved herself so well that they began to give ground. Then said Meg, Our gowns and purses against your hundred marks; win all and wear all. Content, quoth they. – Now, lasses, pray for me, said Meg – With that she buckled with these two knaves, beat one and so hurt the other, that they entreated her to spare their lives—I will, said she, upon conditions.—Upon any condition, said they—Then, said she, it shall be thus: 1. That you never hurt a woman, nor any company she is in. 2. That you never hurt lame or important men. 3. That you never hurt any Children or innocents. 4. That you rob no carrier of his money. 5. That you rob no manner of poor or distressed. Are you content with these conditions? We are, said they . . . The men desiring to know who it was had so lustily beswinged them, said, To alleviate our sorrow pray tell us your name? She smiling, replied, If any one asks you who banged your bones, say Long Meg of Westminster once met with you . . .

The Wars in France being over, Meg came to Westminster, and married a soldier, who, hearing of her exploits, took her into a room and making her strip to her petticoat, took one staff, and gave her another, saying, As he had heard of her manhood, he was determined to try her – But Meg held down her head, whereupon he gave her three of four blows, and she in submission fell down upon her knees desiring him to pardon her – For, said she, whatever I do to others, it behoves me to be obedient to you; and it shall never be said, If I cudgel a knave that injures me, Long Meg is her husband's master; and therefore use me as you please – So they grew friends, and never quarrelled after.[13]

Long Meg, soldier, fighter, bouncer and ruffian, moves in the story from protecting the poor on the streets of London and giving bullies their just rewards to serving as a dutiful wife. The chapbook message, then, provides entertainment in the topsy-turvy world of Long Meg but brings its readers back to women's domestic life and proper subservience to husband by the end of the tale. Leisured reading could often reinforce women's expected roles while providing them with fantasies of a different kind of life. It may also have fulfilled men's and women's desire for an ordered world, where the rough but good-hearted win out.

Women would have experienced this rich fantasy world of chapbooks as well as the already popular world of song, dance and oral tale through exposure to travelling performers and visits to fairs and festivals, the major form of popular cultural spectacle available to all classes in eighteenth-century Europe. Such fairs had begun as religious events celebrating local saints, monasteries or churches, but they gradually changed over time into secular extravaganzas. Local fairs continued as celebrations of parish patron saints, but large fairs drawing huge crowds of people had become popular as well by 1700. An example was the fair at Saint Germain in Paris, which ran every year from February to Palm Sunday. Saint Germain drew fashionable ladies and poor women to its extensive markets of exotic foods, products and entertainments. Beyond the markets of goods filled with coffee, wine, cheap muslins and card sharks, the fair provided a series of entertainments designed to appeal to all ages and classes in society. Some of the events emphasised the unusual: in 1749, a rhinoceros was on display, while in 1759 *femmes fortes* (strong women) walked on and tasted hot molten iron. Other amusements included shows by acrobats, marionettes and comedic actors. However, by the end of the eighteenth century such fairs were disappearing in the face of new restrictions on public entertainments and with the advent of new leisure areas, such as expanded cafés, shops, public parks and boulevards. Permanent theatre buildings and new circuses for equestrian performances also provided outlets for entertainments that had been confined to fair grounds in earlier times. Saint Germain's market buildings burned in 1762, and by the 1780s the fair was gone.[14]

Other fairs and festivals, especially in England, were often the sites of contests for women. In rural areas, women could participate in smock races, where they ran a set course in little more than a small shirt and drawers. This was a crowd-pleasing event, but also a chance for young women to demonstrate their physical prowess. In urban areas, female boxing matches were popular spectator sports in the eighteenth century. Often the combatants were poor women, and many of the matches were set up to represent larger issues, such as an Englishwoman versus an Irishwoman. One eyewitness described a Drury Lane fight between two women thus: '[They were] engaged in a scratching and boxing match, their faces entirely covered with blood, bosoms bare, and the clothes nearly torn from their bodies.'[15] In addition to fisticuffs, female fencing competitions were also held in urban areas, but in rural regions, a different kind of sport was popular.

Cricket and other bat and ball games were extremely popular with women in rural England in the eighteenth century. Although male aristocrats embraced cricket and made it their own by 1800, the early part of the eighteenth century was a different story. The first recorded organised women's match seems to have been held in 1745 in Surrey, when a team from Bramley met a team from Hambleton. The record related these details of the match:

> [They were] dressed all in white. The Bramley maids had blue ribbons and the Hambl [*sic*] maids red ribbons on their heads. The Bramley girls got 119 notches and the Hambleton girls 127 . . . the girls bowled, batted, ran and catched as well as most men could do in that game.[16]

In addition to rural cricket games for women, hunting and archery were also important leisure pursuits in the countryside for more elite women. In some cases, aristocratic house parties or royal courts sponsored female or mixed-sex archery contests for the pleasure of guests. One such event in 1721 at the summer palace of

Ludwigshafen featured Duke Eberhard Ludwig of Württemberg challenging his son and daughter-in-law.[17] Elite women, especially outside the urban areas, learned to be expert at riding and shooting, but few tried to win contests in these areas.

Games of chance were also popular among all classes of society. For the wealthy, gambling was an obsession among some, and women participated in the craze. An example of extravagant bets and speculations is Marie Antoinette's wager of 100,000 livres regarding whether the Comte d'Artois could build a palace in six weeks. Other wagering took the form of card games, state lotteries and private, exclusive gambling salons. Such gambling was 'especially popular with women who, long excluded from independent economic and political activity, found in such rituals a sphere of influence in their role as the arbiters of taste and leaders of fashion in the latest games'.[18] Middle- and lower-class people faced difficulties in trying to enter this world of gambling, since some games were forbidden outside of expensive establishments and extra taxes were levied on gaming implements in some areas. For instance, in Britain, both playing cards (sixpence per pack) and dice (five shillings per pair) were taxed.[19] Despite these restrictions, gambling remained popular, and card parties were a major form of female entertainment among Europe's respectable poor. Another area where the poor could participate was in gambling at racing tracks, especially horse racing. The poor could also speculate and wager at fairs and rural gaming events such as bull- and bear-baiting or pitch and hustle (a coin-tossing game that included bets).

In addition to gambling, drinking was also a popular leisure pursuit for men and women, although women's access to public drinking establishments was more limited than was men's. Traditionally women had been beer brewers for families and often had sold ale in local communities. Over time, men took control of alcohol production and dispensing, and women were expected to visit alehouses only rarely. Women who did engage in public drunkenness or who crossed the line into male terrain could be publicly shamed or punished for being too 'mannish' or for acting as prostitutes. This does not mean women were barred from drinking or from taverns (in fact, some taverns were owned and operated by women as Deborah Simonton shows in this book, p. 146), but their behaviour was monitored more closely, and they did not go alone. Why would a woman go to a tavern? She might accompany a father or husband for a meal and drink, as was not uncommon in early modern German towns. Other evidence suggests that groups of women might visit a tavern to celebrate a special event or occasion, such as the birth of a child or a carnival celebration.[20]

By the end of the eighteenth century, changing social and work structures led to the more common sight of women drinking alcohol and coffee in public. In England, the 'gin epidemic' claimed many women and men, as changing sociability and community restraints led to new drinking customs and spirits.[21] In France, the revolution brought women into cafés in greater numbers, and the development of private dining rooms 'called *cabinets noirs* (black chambers), in the following decades sustained and expanded the role of women in cafés'.[22] The first French female political club, the Society of Revolutionary Republican Women, met for debate in cafés until it was outlawed in 1793. Likewise, British Friendly Societies usually met at pubs in the eighteenth century, and although they condemned drunkenness, evidence suggests their entertainments sometimes included alcohol. The lack of privacy in late eighteenth- and early nineteenth-century urban dwellings may have also encouraged men and women to go together to alehouses in cities such as London. This 'social exchange' allowed working people to solidify 'the bonds of neighbourhood, kinship, or friendship', at the same time that middle-class people were increasingly withdrawing from such public socialisation to a more intimate, familial setting.[23]

Socialising at home was not, however, entirely the domain of the middle classes. Dinner parties, family celebrations and *soirées* could be enjoyed by aristocrats as well as artisans who had at least some space and means. In French society, for instance, it was not uncommon for families of fairly modest means to host card or games parties by the late eighteenth century, and as David Garrioch has pointed out, 'home sociability reinforced neighborhood ties, and particularly for women, who were excluded' from some male spaces.[24] Female visiting, which might include tea-drinking and chatting, was a feature of many European communities. As homes became more common sights for social gatherings, desire for furnishings, foodstuffs and decorative collectibles accelerated female consumerism.

A distinctive form of home socialisation shaped women's work and leisure in eighteenth-century rural communities: the *Spinnstube* (spinning bee) or *veillée*. This form dates back into the late medieval period and began to disappear by the nineteenth century. These gatherings, held in the dark and cold winter months, brought to a designated house a group of young women to share the cost of lighting for an evening of spinning. Typically, one or both of the parents of the house provided supervision. Ostensibly work nights, *Spinnstube* functioned as primary socialising occasions for the young unmarried women of rural villages and small towns. In some areas, men joined in the gatherings as joke- and storytellers, or they 'broke in' to *Spinnstube* to tease and chat with the young women. Such mixed-sex *Spinnstube* were often the target of municipal regulations or bans, and concerns about immorality led to the outlawing of such evenings widely by the nineteenth century. Hans Medick cites contemporary observers' accounts of these gatherings:

> the girls bring their work to the lord of the *Spinnstube*, their spinning wheels, knitting needles as well as their news, love stories, anecdotes about dances and other matters. There will be knitting, spinning, laughing, teaching and telling stories, all waiting longingly for the appearance of the courtiers, and then the game will begin all over again.[25]

Such an idyllic scene does hide the reality that some *Spinnstube* included hurtful gossip, violence (in at least one case a man was badly beaten by women who thought he was being disrespectful) and licentiousness, or that the women were still working during this 'leisure' time. However, clearly for women *Spinnstube* offered a time of same-sex socialisation and sometimes the opportunity for courting prospective suitors with limited adult supervision.

The aristocratic equivalent of *Spinnstube* may well be the plethora of female-hosted home gatherings such as salons, musical soirées and balls. These events provided women with an opportunity to establish their reputations as hostesses and to prove their place in the hierarchical world of elite society in Europe. The French salon, with its elite female hostesses, functioned as leisure and also as vocation for the women who presided over these intellectual and social gatherings. As Dena Goodman has shown in her work on the eighteenth-century Parisian salon, women used these salon to gain 'social space and time free from gambling' but also for intellectual stimulation and self-education.[26] By the late eighteenth century, salonnières such as Bettina von Arnim, Rahel Varnhagen and Henriette Herz held well-known gatherings in Berlin, while in Paris, Mme Geoffrin and Mlle de Lespinasse were helping to transform 'a noble, leisure form of social gathering into a serious working space'.[27] For women, leisure and career ambitions continued to be bound together.

In addition to the more overtly political salons, other elite gatherings provided an opportunity for same-sex socialising as well as an arena for courting rituals. In London's annual 'season', marriageable men and women were paraded through a series of such home entertainments as their families sought eligible alliances. In London, pleasure gardens (Vauxhall, 1732, or Ranelagh, 1742) were popular spots for fireworks, concerts and sometimes chicanery. Other features of this elite social whirl were the theatres, which had special sections for the nobility, public parks, shopping districts and eating and drinking establishments. In her book on provincial women of the gentry in England, Amanda Vickery notes that women enjoyed and were allowed to visit assemblies, masquerades and theatres, and dancing was a common pastime. Especially popular were home concerts and church organ or choral recitals. In addition, both men and women were drawn into the race meetings, assemblies and other events surrounding assize court sessions, and many elite women attended 'show trials' for pleasure. Vickery notes that 'Staged spectacles of all kinds flourished in the eighteenth century, from militia reviews to ladies' processions', and these spectacles could also include 'freak' exhibitions, magic shows or fireworks displays.[28] Daytrips to sites of interest could also provide leisure options for women. Sarah Ford in the 1790s visited 'a furnace, a sugar house, a rural powder mill, the new Lancaster canal and the acqueducts [sic] at both Preston and Lancaster'.[29]

Elite women also enjoyed more opportunities for travel. From expeditions to diplomatic and imperial postings with husbands to grand tours of Europe, some women were seeing the broader world outside their birthplaces. For many women who were trained in modern languages such as English, French and German, travel to other European countries to soak in art and culture was the height of pleasurable leisure. As Brian Dolan found in his study of British travellers, wealthy women not only visited a broad range of places but also wrote about them in letters, journals and novels.[30] In fact, one of the most popular elite leisure activities for women in the eighteenth century was writing: letters to friends and family, journal entries and fiction. For those without access to written culture, fairy tales and folk songs could function as travel accounts, with wandering merchants often acting as both traders and cultural transmitters. One example is Dorothea Viehmann, a dairy trader and storyteller who wandered through German regions through much of her life (1755–1815).[31]

Class did divide women and their leisure activities in the eighteenth century in many ways, but in addition to cross-class festivals and holiday pursuits, many women crossed the social divide with one popular leisure pursuit: religion. Attending church or synagogue and participating in other religious activities and events could provide important leisure time for women from a variety of backgrounds. For those involved in Methodism or cottage religions in particular, the church provided 'a supportive communal and cultural life', and 'formed relatively enduring structures for social intercourse'.[32] Although religious observance was mixed up with other identities –

family, gender, community, neighbourhood – religion could also serve as an opportunity to socialise with others or to break the routine of daily work and as a time to reflect. Religion also structured community festivities, with saints' days as local holidays and pilgrimages to holy sites as opportunities for travel.[33]

Despite the essentially local and apparently self-contained world of community pleasures so far recounted, women's understanding of and experience with the larger nation and world was not entirely limited. In particular, two examples show that the communal, localised life of the early modern period was beginning to give way to a broader national and imperial culture that sought to control and organise leisure in new ways. The first example is the French Revolution and the second is Britain's emerging world empire.

The upheaval of 1789 and its aftermath brought with it new leisure pursuits as well as the politicisation and transformation of older leisure customs. New opportunities included revolutionary debating societies and political clubs (until they were suppressed), as well as public spectacles of the new French nation that included executions, parades and monuments. Several scholars have demonstrated the need to use cultural messages and organised leisure/political activities to help inculcate nationalism amidst the crumbling of old political and social structures. In addition to the creation of the new, older traditions of song, theatre and spectacle were altered to fit the needs of the emerging nation. For instance, as some printing presses were suppressed during the Revolution, the song culture of the streets, which had been a feature of pre-Revolutionary Paris, grew to include explicitly political tunes. For some urban women, this sung culture expressed political sentiments while retaining its roots in popular culture forms and leisure pursuits.[34]

Another literary form that allowed women a voice and a role in shaping the philosophical and national debates of the post-Revolutionary period was fiction, and in the next chapter, Siân Reynolds examines the artistic production of women, both in literature and in the visual arts. During the Revolution, the number of female authors in France quadrupled as women published works of philosophy, politics and history in the form of books and political pamphlets. As Carla Hesse has shown, however, women's lack of copyright control and continued disenfranchisement coupled with the backlash of the late Revolutionary and Napoleonic periods led to an explosion of women's fiction, particularly so-called 'sentimental novels' in the early nineteenth centuries. Women continued to write, but they turned their energies to a medium considered more appropriate for female aspirations. Fiction, then, functioned as entertainment and philosophy, providing educated women writers and readers with an outlet for their ideas and a use for their time. As Hesse notes, 'They wrote fiction in order to write philosophy, to create themselves as morally autonomous subjects.'[35] In Germany, 'women writers and particularly women readers held an increasing share in the expanded book market', and female publishers and journal editors had appeared by the late eighteenth century.[36]

In short, the French Revolution and Enlightenment changes in Europe provided women with more of a political voice and a national consciousness. However, their continued disenfranchisement, their lack of access to higher education, and their lack of legal control over themselves and their cultural creations meant that citizenship, political autonomy and nationalism had to be expressed in other ways. For women, this often meant the realm of leisure: cafés, streets and homes. In fact, in the subsequent nineteenth-century revolutions of the 1830s and 1840s, Parisian women used established café cultures as platforms for their political expressions, merging national aspirations with their neighbourhood leisure sources.[37]

As women in France gained consciousness of their civic identities, women in Britain were becoming increasingly aware of their colonial and national obligations. A range of cheap colonial goods such as sugar, tea and coffee in the shops of Britain were accompanied by stories of heroism in images of the French and Indian War (1756–63), the American Revolution and other military expeditions abroad. As Kathleen Wilson has noted, ordinary Britons would have been exposed to cultural products with imperial political themes from their dinner china to punch bowls and tea sets.[38] The burgeoning abolitionist movement fed this interest in things colonial, often hawking consumer items with an anti-slavery theme. One of the most well-known of these items was Wedgwood's 1787 representation of a slave with the question 'Am I Not a Man and A Brother?' Women bought this china piece and used the image in needlework.[39]

In addition to the commercial culture of empire, women in Britain could see for themselves the 'exotic' sight of colonised peoples at fairs and exhibitions. For example, a delegation of Cherokee in 1730 was conducted on a tour of Bedlam Hospital, but they themselves also became a spectacle for curious crowds of onlookers. In another Cherokee tour in 1762, the visitors were exhibited at Vauxhall Gardens as this advertisement attests:

> This Day, the King of the Cherokees, and his two Chiefs, will go to see the Curiosities at the Dwarf's Tavern, Chelsea Fields, where they will likewise dine and drink Tea. Tickets at 1s. each, will be taken in the Reckoni[n]g, either for Wine, Punch, Tea, &c.[40]

Women could explore this fascination with foreign people and places by reading travel diaries published by other women. For example, German writer Caroline Auguste Fischer's remarkable short story 'William the Negro' chronicles the romance between a white woman and a black man and its destruction in the age of the Haitian Revolution.[41] As with the development of sentimental novels as a female form, travel writing also emerged as a peculiarly potent tool for female writers and readers. These female travel narratives included Elizabeth Justice's 1739 *Voyage to Russia*, Anna Maria Falconbridge's accounts of the slave trade in Sierra Leone (1794), and Lady Mary Wortley Montagu's letters from her travels (1763).

Both women and men, then, were developing a sense of national and imperial power and the scope of their world opportunities by the late eighteenth century as part of the political transformations in Europe in the late eighteenth century. The popular culture and leisure of the early modern world was disappearing or mutating into new forms and structures by 1800. This new leisure for women fell in line with a strong identification with nation and citizenship by the nineteenth century, and it encompassed transformed concepts of work, education, religion, community and duty.

Nation (1800–1900)

The beginning of the nineteenth century reflected an ever-accelerating change in the pace of people's lives and in consumption patterns, which had developed as a result of the rise of modern nation-states and the emergence of commercial capitalism and industrialisation. Better roads and canals meant more movement and availability of goods, improved communication in the form of postal services, increased opportunity for travel and tourism and expanded commercial activity. Change brought with it demographic shifts and transformations in popular culture and leisure for all classes in European society. In addition to economic shifts, change in the form of new political movements, the development of popular nationalism and the emergence of socialism all led to differing notions of citizenship, national identity and loyalty.

Ties of local and regional significance were eroded by the influx of foreign goods, increased immigration and the possibility of travel, but traditional popular cultural forms did not disappear. Improved travel allowed urban fairs and theatres to penetrate the rural areas, so tales and songs were disseminated even more widely. An example of this growth of a national culture is a ballad called 'The Murder in the Red Barn'. More than 5 million sheets of this song (printed in London) had been distributed by the 1850s. As historians have pointed out, 'the song passed into the oral and "local" culture of the rural poor, turning up time and again in the repertoire of traditional singers – a good example of the penetration of local culture by the national.'[42] In fact, similar murder ballads appeared in Appalachian areas of the USA as late as the twentieth century, suggesting the longevity and adaptability of these 'traditional' forms.

As modern nation-states emerged through revolution, unification and reform in Europe, political and social changes helped shape understandings of leisure for women. By the nineteenth century, ties of neighbourhood and community were coexisting with newer notions of the individual's pursuit of happiness and fulfilment. Industrialisation contributed to the idea that leisure, although increasingly available to people of all classes, was something to be grasped with both hands. As 'A Lady' told her readers in 1826, leisure time was not to be wasted; it was an accounting of the worth and character of a woman's life:

> Let not a leisure moment fly
> Unheeded to the bar of heaven
> For each records a true account
> How thy allotted time is spent
> In this probationary state.[43]

In short, how one spent leisure time, and indeed how one spent (consumed), began to say a lot about that person's place in society and nation.

By the nineteenth century, women's leisure time reflected both an emerging national identity and a new emphasis on domesticity as a marker of respectability. As Sophie Mereau wrote in her short story, 'Flight to the City', home became a sort of haven to counterbalance the new national and international opportunities. The main characters elope and live a wild and carefree existence in the city before returning home:

> All our so-called adventures, which had appeared so strange and desirable before, now seemed ordinary and distasteful. The most exotic, unusual, and desirable thing of all seemed to us to be the happy peace of a secluded life . . . Nothing seemed funnier to us than to remember how we had once left our country as heroes, full of pathos, and now returned, imperceptibly

transformed into married bourgeois. Yet, we gladly traded the flighty stage for the secure walls of domesticity.[44]

Domesticity increasingly became associated with women's leisure in the nineteenth century. As many men gained access to increased leisure time through shortened work hours, better wages and more leisure provisions, women's relationship to leisure followed a different path. First, women's leisure in the nineteenth century depended greatly on their class status. While elite and middle-class women's leisure was expected as a marker of status, working-class women continued to struggle to find time and resources for significant leisure activities. Second, all women, regardless of class, were expected to facilitate male leisure in a variety of ways. Whether it was an aristocratic hostess running a dinner party or a working-class women pawning household clothing to support her husband's pub outings, European societies expected women to help men relax by creating safe and comfortable homes and by protecting them from the hassles of domestic life. Finally, as the century progressed, the availability of cheap and quick transportation led to new leisure options for men and women of all classes across national boundaries in Europe, some of which were subsidised and sponsored by governments.

More than any other factor, class shaped leisure pursuits for women in the nineteenth century, so it is important to examine this phenomenon in some detail. As Catriona Parratt has shown in her study of working women's leisure in Britain, material constraints made it difficult for many poorer women to experience much in the way of leisure. Female occupations, even by the end of nineteenth century, still remained poorly paid, and women's work hours were often longer than those of men, since women usually lacked the support and mediation of unions. A Factory Inspectors' Report for 1893 identified needlework and laundries as two of the worst offenders in terms of excessive hours for workers; both of these occupations primarily employed women. Another notoriously poorly paid job with long hours was domestic service, which again employed mostly women.[45] Yet, as Parratt notes, these mostly single working women at least earned wages and often experienced some autonomy about their use of free time, while married women lacked even these meagre options. The press of domestic work in a nineteenth-century working-class household and the widespread practice of men giving only a small amount of housekeeping money to wives made it difficult for wives in poorer households to have individual leisure time.

What, then, did constitute leisure time for poor and working women? For married women, often leisure time was family time, which meant that leisure commingled with the work of facilitating activities and food for children and husband. A London family taking the train to Kent for a hop-picking holiday would all be expected to work, but the mother of the family would additionally arrange provisions and lodging for their time in the fields. Families also could visit local community attractions such as holiday festivals, expositions and fairs. With the development of third-class rail travel in England in the 1870s, for instance, by the end of the nineteenth century many working-class families could afford to take daytrips to seaside workers' resorts such as Blackpool.[46] More commonly, family leisure took the form of sing-songs, family dinners, cards or board games. Card parties remained popular pastimes, and with the advent of numerical indices on the cards (1884), new card games emerged such as blackjack (also known as *vingt-et-un*) and baccarat (*chemin de fer*).[47] Holidays could especially form a special leisure time for the family; for example, Christmas might feature decorations, stockings hung or trees adorned with candles and a special dinner in working-class households.[48]

Other options for married women included gatherings with other women in their neighbourhoods. These might be stolen minutes of conversation on the street or shouted gossip between open windows, a shared cup or tea or even a drink in a pub or café. Middle-class reformers tried to create socialising options for working-class wives, often in an attempt to educate them in hygiene, temperance or mothering, but these efforts met with mixed results. As Parratt notes, '"Mothers" meetings and settlement houses and missions seemed only to skim the surface of the problem and it was difficult to get women to attend at all, let alone regularly.'[49]

Cities and even small villages often had vibrant working-class street cultures with itinerant performers and street vendors. The bustle of shoppers, hurdy-gurdies, horse-drawn traffic and passing neighbours could make for a pleasing half-hour of leisure. In fact, women could combine a needed trip to the butcher or pawnshop with a stroll or a chat in the street. In addition to the culture of the streets, cafés and pubs served as gathering places for working-class men and women. W. Scott Haine's study of Parisian cafés suggests that working-class women found cafés safe socialising venues, partly because of the common sight of female owners and barmaids. Using available legal records, Haine reconstructs the clientele of cafés and shows that women from a variety of working-class occupational backgrounds (for example, prostitutes, laundresses, housewives) were a regular presence from the 1850s until the twentieth century.[50] Likewise, in England, women were common sights in pubs. Some went to the pubs weekly with their husbands for a drink, while others might only stay for a few minutes in order to get a jug of beer to carry home.

As with working-class wives, single women from the poorer classes had to be resourceful in finding time and money for leisure. Many of these working women, especially those in their teens and early twenties, did find a new world of leisure opening up to them by the nineteenth century. One of the cheapest, easiest and most popular leisure pursuits was walking. Whether it was promenading on a seaside boardwalk, walking through the attractions of a neighbourhood street or strolling through a public park, working-class women embraced the fun of walking with friends or dates. This snatch of poetry from northern England captures some of the exuberance of these young women on the prowl:

> Yo'll see t'young lasses decked i' smiles
> O rushin' fro' ther wark;
> To ged donned up to meet ther chaps,
> An' rumble reawnd bi t'park.
> It's t'thowts o' t'walk, un' t'pleasant talk,
> At meks ther faces breet;
> An' fills ther hearts wi' sweet content,
> At hawf past five at neet.[51]

Some of these walking opportunities had more formal rituals, such as Sunday promenades on major roads or squares. Others provided courtship opportunities, such as the

'Monkey Run' or 'the Drag', which allowed men to 'pick up' girls who were walking along certain paths.[52] As the century progressed, formal parades provided walking and spectator options for those wanting to experience an Easter parade or a trade union march, while the development of large urban parks provided more formal walking paths. These parks, such as Hyde Park in London or the Tuileries Gardens in Paris, were located in wealthier areas of the city, so for working people, just getting to the park might mean a hike.

For many working women, leisure was something they worked to experience. Some would remain up late after a long day's work in order to sew a garment to wear for a Sunday promenade, or they would skip meals in order to save the train fare for an excursion. An example of this mix of leisure and work comes from English domestic servant Hannah Cullwick, who kept a diary of her daily activities for her middle-class lover, Arthur Munby. One day from that diary illustrates the work that a semi-leisured weekend day might contain:

> Sunday, April 26 (1863) Lit the fires & clean'd the hearths. Clean'd 7 pair of boots. Got breakfast up. Wash'd up after. Made the fire up & put the beef to roast – there was 12 to dinner. Clean'd away after. Made a pie for supper. Clean'd myself & had tea. Went to St P. Church – I call'd for Mrs Walters to go wi' me. She'd only got her old shawl to go & didn't want to, so I said she might have my plaid & I'd wear her'n but she wouldn't let me, & we went together. I met wi' Bill & one o' the lancers a-coming out & we all went on the pier as it was moonlight & nice. The soldier didn't speak till Bill told him I was one of his fellow servants & then he shook hands. He wore white gloves & was particularly respectful to me & Mrs W. & William always was so & is now. They came into the kitchen wi' me & had a biscuit & glass o' wine, & we talk'd some minutes & they went home. The girl brought some o' the gentlemen's boots down. Bill ask'd me who valeted so I said, 'Me of course, I'm a first-rate shoe-black.' So he said he knew I didn't mind what I did, but he wish'd he lived next door & then he'd (black) em for me, but I told him I shouldn't let him if he did. I clean'd away the supper & to bed.[53]

Hannah's description shows a long and hard workday that also includes one of her few days of leisure in a week, a Sunday half-day holiday. The things she comments on are simple pleasures of sharing food, conversation and a walk with friends and acquaintances. In a later entry (1 January 1871), she comments on her lack of leisure almost matter-of-factly:

> I've two days & two nights' holiday since last October twelve months, & bin to no theatres or Crystal Palace or anything except to Exeter Hall once wi' the young ladies & heard the ragged school children sing. And I've reading nothing but a book call'd *Adam Bede*, excepting my Bible . . . It's rather unpleasant to ask leave so I seldom get out of a weekday.[54]

Cullwick's diary entries demonstrate several important things about leisure for working women in England by the 1860s and 1870s. For those with the means, there were a variety of options for leisure, from theatre to parks to church to reading. Even with her meagre leisure time, Cullwick managed to find time to hear a concert of school children and to read a novel. Another important clue in Cullwick's diary is her reference to the difficulty in asking for time off. For domestic servants in Europe leisure was difficult given their long hours, live-in status and close supervision. For example, in Paris cafés of the late nineteenth century, domestic servants were virtually the only working-class female occupation poorly represented among patrons.[55] Cullwick's evidence from England suggests that the constraints of time, energy and funds might have played a role in limiting domestic servants' leisure even further than that of other working women.

By the latter part of the nineteenth century, many leisure options for respectable working people were emerging. One such opportunity was the music hall, which by the 1880s had become a more or less respectable place thanks to deliberate licensing restrictions. Although modern music halls had emerged in Britain as early as the 1850s, they only gained popularity and the patina of respectability by the 1880s and 1890s. Studies of music hall audiences have demonstrated that women did attend, and that many of the female patrons were young, single workers or families attending together. By 1900, audiences could range from primarily working- and lower middle-class people to elites looking to 'slum it'.[56] Other entertainments that might capture working-class female audiences included melodramas, pantomimes and concerts at local halls or outdoor venues. Pantomimes were a particularly popular and long-lived phenomenon in Britain, with their origins stemming from Regency-era spectacles and Victorian burlesques. Especially after 1843, when the Theatre Regulation Act made speech legal in small venues, pantomimes such as *Cinderella* and *Aladdin*, the two most popular, and other stage spectacles evolved as popular leisure.[57] In some ways, music halls, pantomimes and puppet shows took the place of chapbooks as popular and widely known morality tales. In fact, some of the pantos got their start as chapbooks.

In addition to stage spectacles, the nineteenth century witnessed the emergence of popular expositions. There was an expansion of such activities from the 1850s on, perhaps because of the success of the multifaceted Great Exhibition of 1851 at the Crystal Palace in London. The 1851 exposition was conceived as a great celebration of imperial and technological achievement, and its tone was educational. Admission to the extravaganza at the massive glass structure and its grounds was free, and items on display bore no price tags. Scientific displays and technical demonstrations dominated the programme, which attracted visitors of all classes and sexes. The 1851 exposition's success encouraged the development of expositions and world's fairs throughout Europe, but these emerged as much more commercial phenomena. For instance, by 1855, the Paris exposition charged an admission fee, and by 1900, entertainment, not education was the goal. As Rosalind Williams has noted in her history of consumption in France, the tone of the expositions between 1851 and 1900 changed from 'instructing the visitor in the wonders of modern science and technology to entertaining him'.[58] In fact the 1900 exposition 'revealed a much more raucous type of conspicuous consumption that appealed to a class which consumed "wastefully" but which was not leisured'.[59]

The post-1851 world's fairs mirrored larger changes in politics, consumption and spectacle of the late nineteenth century. Scientific progress was measured through precise categorisation of all observable phenomena. This included humans, who were vigorously classified by race, nationality, age, sex, class and psychological profile. The fairs were showcases for the 'sciences' of eugenics and race theory, and colonial peoples were frequently the objects of study. At the late nineteenth-century expos and fairs, colonial architecture and customs (such as belly dancing) were displayed along with human trophies from colonial outposts. Just as women of the eighteenth century might see a Cherokee chief on tour in London, female spectators were encouraged to view Congolese 'subjects' in Brussels or Moroccan women at the Paris World's Fair.[60] In Germany as well, African colonised peoples could be used as hired entertainment for parties or be displayed at fair-like ethnographic shows called *Volkerschauen*.[61] Clearly then, leisure at the fair could also mean cultural conditioning and imperial education for the male and female visitors.

Another feature of the fairs was the availability of cheap goods for sale. This practice echoed the emergence of department stores as shopping fantasy worlds. Department stores such as the Bon Marché (opened in Paris in 1852) were the first to provide a large selection of goods priced and marked individually, and these stores introduced the innovation of 'browsing'. Shopping changed almost overnight, aided also by the development of credit plans in the 1870s (buying on instalment) and a flood of cheap, ready-made goods.[62] For those who could only look at the goods on display at fairs or department stores, there were additional strategies for buying attractive 'store-bought' apparel or coveted home-decoration items. Some working women joined clothing clubs, where their 6 pennies per week gained them a weekly chance at the jackpot (a pair of boots or a frock). Other women took advantage of weekly payment schemes for goods, sometimes pawning other household goods to make ends meet and to pay the obligation.[63]

Fairs and department stores fit into another movement of the nineteenth century: the rational recreation movement. Middle-class employers, evangelicals, and other social reformers came together in the late nineteenth century to 'raise up' working-class standards through leisure. Rational recreation included everything from the building of leisure forums such as the People's Palace of London's East End to running working-girls clubs or mothers' unions. As the middle classes felt increasingly threatened by the poor, the important thing was to raise the standards of the nation by 'civilising' the poor, creating more efficient workers and eradicating the ills of poverty, filth and infant mortality. Programmes sprang up around Europe to fight this fight by promoting work, education and useful leisure. Activists such as Louise Otto-Peters in Germany and Pauline Kergomard in France promoted reforms in women's work, education and housing and pushed for legislative protections that would allow safe home and work environments for women.[64] Often administered by 'leisured' middle-class women volunteers, programmes for rational leisure aimed to improve living conditions through motherhood programmes and to provide useful and educational options for working-class adults and children. Parratt describes this mission of middle-class women in England:

> In her narratives on the dangers of leisure, the reformer saw and framed herself as a moral and cultural superior whose duty it was to step in and prevent the unfolding of this calamitous course of events. She would save working girls and women, nation and empire, from the consequences of recklessness and profligacy. Moreover, she would act to make leisure a transformational experience that would uplift and enrich the lives of working women. Prepared for the task by birth and breeding, education and upbringing, she was a stalwart

guide and teacher, a friend who would lead the working-class woman 'forwards and upwards', who would provide the necessary instruction in the right
kind of leisure.[65]

One of the interesting things about nineteenth-century women's leisure is that for
middle-class women, instructing others, specifically working-class women as well as
girls of all classes, in leisure was considered a leisure activity, albeit one with important
social implications. For middle-class women, use of female leisure time was a measure
of character and respectability; it functioned as a marker of social status and reflected
upon the importance of the whole family. For some, then, rational recreation was the
answer. Women could raise funds and administer programmes that taught mothering
skills, that got girls off the streets, or that educated workers. Volunteerism and social
reform, although a lot of work, were considered appropriate leisure for well-off
women.

Age was an important part of this programme of social reform. Young girls were
often the objects of reform, while the reformers themselves ranged from young, single,
middle-class women to older elite women who were widowed or whose children had
left the house. Programmes developed for girls attempted to teach respectability but
also to foster cross-class communication and understanding. In England, the first of
these girls' youth organisations to develop was the Girls' Friendly Society, an Anglican
organisation operating by 1875, which aimed to create mentoring relationships
between wealthier girls and their working-class counterparts. Later, organisations such
as the Girls Guildry (founded 1900) imitated similar boys' organisations and created
a semi-militarised uniformed group that taught home-training and nursing skills.[66]
Girls' clubs and snowdrop bands for female wage-earners also emerged at the end of
the nineteenth century as well as mothers' unions for married women. Some feminist
organisations also hoped to work with women workers for better conditions and
improved leisure facilities.

Reform efforts had yielded further leisure opportunities for middle-class and upper-
class women. One such option surrounded the empire-building of the last quarter of
the nineteenth century, and for women, imperialism offered options for volunteerism
and leisure. In Germany, a major voluntary association was formed by and for pro-
colonial women, the German Women's Association for Nursing in the Colonies, which
sought to encourage the colonies as a 'field of operation for women'. By holding programmes at home, often featuring African entertainment, and by raising funds, the
association and others like it encouraged women to go to the colonies as nurses or missionaries, but also publicised the 'exotic' life of the colonies as entertainment for
women at home.[67] Likewise, in Britain, organisations such as the United British
Women's Emigration Society (begun in the 1880s) appealed to the 'idle women' of
Britain to do their duty and go to the colonies. Reformers thought this would accomplish the dual goals of relieving Britain of its 'surplus' women and providing a
much-needed 'civilising influence' in the colonies.[68]

In addition to colonial reform societies, women with leisure time could involve themselves in a whole variety of political and social reform activities. They could join
suffrage, anti-slavery, temperance or education movements, many of them connected
in a web of feminist activism fuelled by the availability of female leisured 'workers'. As
long as their efforts purported to work for the betterment of women, they could count

on at least some public support for this laudable use of their leisure time. For middle-class women who were increasingly excluded from their former roles as partners with husbands in familial enterprises, the move toward domesticity as a career meant a need to look for creative charitable work in the 'public' realm.

Several historians have noted this widespread trend across western Europe. Bonnie Smith found that middle-class women in northern France sought to maintain their reputation and to bolster their families' status by cultivating domesticity and charitable work, seeking leisure in exclusive clubs or through 'feminine' hobbies such as fancy needlework or shopping.[69] Leonore Davidoff and Catherine Hall noted a similar trend among bourgeois women of the industrial cities of England, where by the mid-nineteenth century young women who would have once contributed to a family enterprise now had embraced social reform as an escape from their domestic roles as housewives.[70] In Germany too, Marion Kaplan chronicles this same transformation among Jewish bourgeois women. She characterizes the problem thus:

> Women were expected to reflect the status and wealth of their husbands in the way they organized their own and their families' leisure time, in the friends they made, and in the entertainment they chose. Yet they had to avoid frivolity and ostentation in order to negate frequent charges of excessive materialism.'[71]

As Kaplan, Smith and Davidoff and Hall document, middle-class women's leisure was not entirely their own. Their leisure was a mark of class status, and it was structured often by things beyond their control: age, generation, sex, marital status. Often women's only recourse was to embrace female sociability in order to have leisure activities apart from those enjoyed as a family. Some of the options for enjoying the company of women in leisure pursuits included taking the 'Cure' at spas throughout Europe. In England, this might mean travelling to a variety of middle-class 'watering holes' such as Bath, Tunbridge Wells or Harrogate, while in Germany, some spas catered specifically to women and girls. While advertised as 'health cures', these spas were often in reality times of relaxation and a break from domestic duties.[72] Historian John Walton described Bath, one of the more celebrated of spas, as 'a sort of great convent . . . peopled by superannuated celibates of both sexes, but especially women.'[73]

Elite women, as early as 1800, engaged in public leisure activities such as attending assemblies, opera performances, pleasure gardens or theatres. Particularly appealing to women of the leisure classes were public trials, balls, parties or races. Also popular was cultural tourism, with women visiting commercial exhibitions, scenes of natural beauty, architectural wonders, feats of engineering or impressive institutions.[74] In fact a whole range of commercial leisure targeted those with wealth – military displays, fireworks shows, balloon ascensions and exhibitions. However, by the late nineteenth century, these events had broadened to include middle-class participants, and in some cases, they became part of mass leisure.

Another important development in public leisure of the nineteenth century for people of different class backgrounds was the museum. Museums, as much as any other leisure pursuit, helped solidify and make real the national and imperial projects of European nation-states. While many museums aimed to educate and improve the citizenry of a state, sometimes they functioned merely as a place 'to eat lunch and shelter from the rain'. Despite that mundane use, Nick Prior claims that along with international expositions such as Crystal Palace, 'The museum indexed the urgencies and interests of the nation-state, but it also mobilized these interests'.[75] National museums, such as the Altes Museum in Berlin (1830) and the South Kensington Museum in London (1857), opened in all major western European nations in the nineteenth century. By the end of the nineteenth century, museums existed in all shapes and forms, from small travelling menageries to impressive national edifices.

Other options for middle-class women included visiting each other's homes for musical evenings, card games or dinner parties. With the availability of cheap imperial goods, women put colonial 'social drinks' to use in afternoon-tea parties and *Kaffeevisiten* (coffee visits). Another elite pastime that was embraced by the middle classes and in a more limited way by the working classes was travel, which experienced a boom in the nineteenth century. One reason for the expansion of travel as leisure was the boom in transport that occurred by the 1840s. Improved roads and stagecoaches, the expansion of rail networks after the initial innovation of rail in 1830, and the advent of faster sailing vessels and steamships led to more domestic and foreign travel at cheaper rates. In Britain, for example, in 1762 it took one day to go by stage from London to Brighton, but that decreased in 1791 to nine hours and in 1833 to five or six hours. By mid-century, rail cut that time in half again.[76] Channel crossings between England and France multiplied exponentially between 1850, when about 87,000 crossings were recorded at Boulogne, and 1899, when it had risen to almost 1 million.[77]

Travelling took a variety of forms throughout the nineteenth century. For working-class girls, it might mean a day trip by rail or tram to a fair or festival, or travel might be a more ambitious weekend excursion to a spa, resort or nearby city. The standardisation of 'national holidays' such as the Bank Holidays in Britain (the first such act was in 1871) and religious observances in many countries such as Ireland, France and Belgium (Ascension Day, Easter Monday) led to regular holiday rushes to popular destinations. Many people took advantage of cheap rail fares by the latter part of the century to attend the world expositions held frequently in major urban areas, such as Paris and London. Others travelled to view sporting events or to experience trade shows, such as the annual *Salon de l'Automobile*, which began in 1898.[78] Another popular travel holiday in the last part of the century, especially in Germany, was hiking or rambling. Camping holidays and later youth hostels and caravan parks encouraged middle-class urbanites to experience nature, at least for a weekend.

Package holidays emerged in the nineteenth century, particularly targeting single women travellers who wanted the safety of a group, and one of the innovators of these trips was Thomas Cook, who began offering excursions in 1841.[79] Published travel guides also encouraged the democratisation of travel by making travel decisions safe with advice on lodging, sites and dangers for various locations. For European middle-class travellers, particular in German areas, the Baedeker guides became the standard, while in England, Baedeker competed with John Murray's handbooks for travellers (first published in 1836). Other specialised guides targeted particular groups or aimed to help the budget working-class traveller. The combination of travel guides and group tours led many women to take advantage of European travel outside of their home nations. Thomas Cook, who offered both British and continental vacations, 'courted unprotected females' for his tours. In fact, travel made women feel and act independent. Sophia Halworthy, who travelled alone through Europe for eighteen months, claimed: 'Baedeker's guide books are most useful, and make you independent of men guides.'[80] One way of gauging this mini-explosion of female travellers in the late nineteenth century is to examine the genre of published travel journals, a field dominated by women. Jemima Morrell described a Cook package tour to Switzerland that she took in 1863, while Jane Freshfield used her journal to critique some of the Murray guidebook's claims. Women, who travelled to the empire, often accompanying husbands or fathers, also published travel journals, letters, novels and even cookbooks for women. In short, if a woman did not have the time or the means to travel abroad, she could do so vicariously through the multiplicity of accounts available in print.

One celebrated and published woman traveller provides an example of the way in which leisure could become vocation for some female adventurers. Gertrude Bell, born into a well-off English industrial family, attended Oxford and gained a reputation for her skills in modern history and languages. She began travelling with family members in the late 1880s to such spots as Bucharest, Constantinople and Tehran. Although she spent much time travelling in Europe and climbing in the Alps (one of her acquired skills), the Middle East became her passion. She learned Persian and Arabic and spent much of the rest of her life travelling in the eastern Mediterranean regions and writing about her journeys. Ultimately, she served as a political officer for British Intelligence, was assigned to the Paris Peace Conference in 1919 and emerged as somewhat of an expert on politics in Syria and Iraq.[81] The meaning and importance of travel for Bell is clear in her writings, and she perhaps best expressed what attracted women around Europe to travel:

> There are moments when the cabined spirit longs for liberty. A man stands a-tiptoe on the verge of the unknown world which lures him with its vague promises; the peaceful years behind lose all their value in his dazed eyes . . . he pines to stand in the great sunlight, the great wide world which is all too narrow for his adventurous energy . . . Life seized us and inspired us with a mad sense of revelry. The humming wind and the teaming earth shouted 'Life! Life!' as we rode. Life! Life! the beautiful, the magnificent! . . . For us the wide plain and the limitless world, for us the beauty and the freshness of the morning![81]

Travel was a bit of a mixed blessing for women. While some women, particularly single women with some independent means, found significant pleasure and sometimes even a vocation in travel, for married women, seaside holidays and other travelling vacations meant more work in providing leisure for the family. Family travel, often to self-catering accommodations, did not provide women with a break from domestic chores such as cooking and cleaning up, nor did it relieve them of childcare responsibilities in any meaningful way. Travel, despite its hardships, did, however, provide a broader world view for women and a sense of freedom and leisure from house and neighbourhood. It provided a change, even if it was not always the relaxing leisure space advertised in travel accounts and guidebooks.

Another emerging activity for middle-class women looking for uses of their leisure time was education. Whether through formal educational opportunities such as university courses or informal options such as sponsored lectures, the nineteenth century witnessed a range of such educational endeavours opening up for women. For instance, in nineteenth-century Scotland, a rising middle-class with aspirations of respectability helped fuel a range of educational opportunities for women and girls, including mixed and single-sex opportunities for girls in Edinburgh by the 1830s and the foundation of Queen's College in Glasgow in 1842.[83] Women, although barred from formal university life, could sit in on lectures by professors held in the evening or in private tutorials as long as they could pay the fees. Subjects included history, literature, geography and elocution, but women also managed to avail themselves of the more 'serious masculine' subjects of Latin, Greek and philosophy. Noted Scottish scientist Mary Somerville taught herself Latin and science using Edinburgh's libraries and materials from family and friends.[84] In Germany (and Prussia prior to unification), women had entered education as teachers early in the nineteenth century, but systematised training did not exist until the twentieth century. Girls' schooling also was limited in scope until later in the century, but by 1895, girls could take the *Abitur* (highest exam). Yet until 1896, women could only attend lectures in Prussian universities with explicit and high-level permission.[85]

By the 1860s and 1870s many European countries had developed systems of elementary, secondary and higher education opportunities for women, although in some cases only a small percentage of women were able to participate. The advent of free elementary education near the end of the century finally began to draw in major numbers of girls for at least a few years of formal schooling. Illiteracy rates, which had hovered near 70 per cent for women in France in 1800, had plummeted to only 8 per cent by 1900. In England and Germany, the female illiteracy rates were even lower, and school attendance in all three countries had risen enormously by 1890 (84 per cent in France, 75 per cent in Germany).[86] A more literate population meant a market for books and magazines. The advent of mass-circulation newspapers at low prices by the 1890s meant a reading public with access to newspapers, and fiction and magazines began to target girls and women by the 1880s.

Despite all the new leisure pursuits, some popular pastimes seemed to be merely new incarnations. Prior to the 1840s, sport, long a part of communal life, had varied regionally and maintained local rules and styles. The nationalisation of male sport and the commercialisation of many sporting pursuits changed the nature of the pastime by 1900. Women, although excluded from much of the spectacle and organisation of sport, were able to access many new physical activities by the late nineteenth century.

One of the big boosts for female sports came from the development of the callisthenics and gymnastics movements in northern Europe. Swedish callisthenics, developed in 1814, were taught in some Danish and Swedish schools early in the century, and they later became important additions to school programmes for boys and girls throughout Europe. Also, in Germany, gymnastics programmes and schools to train teachers of physical training had emerged by the 1840s. Some doctors and educational reformers advocated physical exercise for women, such as Dr Antoine Martin Bureaud-Riofrey as early as 1835, but only simple stretching was accepted in many countries until late in the century. In France in the 1860s, for example, approved exercises for females included walking, skipping, ball games and stretching for 'poise' and

324

'agility', but rougher sports and competition were not acceptable.[87] Despite some efforts to promote girls' physical education, opponents worried about negative effects of physical exercise on women and girls, often blocking such programmes in schools.

England was in many ways an exception in its acceptance of girls' sport at a slightly earlier period. Its network of Victorian women's colleges, day and boarding schools and girls' clubs all advocated physical fitness as a character-building activity for girls of the middle and upper classes. In addition to private advocacy of sports, the state elementary schools codified physical training for girls in 1879, making sport a mostly acceptable pastime for adolescent girls.[88] For women, the picture was more complicated as doctors and social commentators continued to worry about women damaging their childbearing capacity and endangering the 'race'.

Certain emerging sporting pastimes were considered more appropriate for women than others, such as tennis and bicycling. In France, tennis was 'revived as a sport for ladies' in the 1870s, but the emphasis was on aesthetics (having an 'elegant swing') rather than on competition, which was considered 'unwomanly'.[89] In England, the first intercollegiate women's sporting match was a tennis match between women from Oxford (Girton and Newnham Colleges) and Cambridge (Somerville and Lady Margaret Colleges). Other popular female sports were swimming, archery and ice-skating, but the premier team sport in Britain by 1900 was hockey, a staple at girls' schools around the country.[90]

Wealthy and talented sportswomen who sought to prove the critics wrong popularised such sports, along with more daring 'non-female' pastimes. Lucy Walker, a British mountain climber, was famous as a 'Climbing Girl' from the 1850s to the 1870s. She gained notoriety for her ascent of the Matterhorn in 1871, six months after its first publicised ascent, and appeared in *Punch* and other periodicals of the time. Other female mountain climbers followed her, but the Ladies Alpine Club was not formally founded until 1907.[91] Even earlier than Walker, French women aeronauts made headlines for their balloon flights and aerial shows. Marie Blanchard, married to a famous aeronaut, made her first balloon ascent at the age of twenty-six with her husband in 1804 in Marseilles. She flew alone in 1805, and from that point on travelled internationally performing at shows with her balloon and later with a fireworks show. Between 1805 and her death in a balloon accident in 1819, she performed an estimated seventy times inspiring a generation of female spectators from Toulouse to Rotterdam to Milan.[92]

Other wealthy leisured women tried to promote the sporting pastimes they enjoyed through publications of books, pamphlets and news articles. One such book, edited by Lady Violet Greville, enlisted the services of several well-known sportswomen for chapters on a variety of sports acceptable to women in 1892. Most of the sports described are individual sports, not team endeavours, and some required financial means that would be far beyond many women of the time. Examples include trout- and salmon-fishing, sailing, golf, swimming, lawn tennis, archery, golf and fencing. The entries are forthright and sometimes a bit defensive, as in this piece from Miss A. D. Mackenzie on boating:

> It is essential for every English girl to learn to row, and no one can say anything against a lady rowing—though, of course, there are 'some folks' who would run down anything that a lady does in the way of athletic exercises.[93]

Almost all the essays advocated 'rational dress', a movement that was founded in 1881, and they emphasise the health advantages of sport and activity for women. In a similar vein, Maria Ward's popular book *Bicycling for Ladies* (1896), also supported practicality and health. The manual provided advice on dress and riding technique, but also advocated knowledge of the mechanism of the bike itself and its repair. As Ward wrote,

> I hold that any woman who is able to use a needle or scissors can use other tools equally well. It is a very important matter for a bicyclist to be acquainted with all parts of the bicycle, their uses and adjustment.[94]

In an important sense, the emergence of national travel cultures, sport, improved education and literacy, international expos and mass-circulation newspapers all contributed to the development of a national identity for women, despite their continued disenfranchisement and exclusion from political opportunities. Certainly women's leisure in the nineteenth century helped demarcate class boundaries and gender boundaries, and it provided a sense of individual freedom and taste on occasion, but, most importantly, it allowed women of the nation to develop a sense of nationhood as citizen-consumers and as members of a national leisure community, however marginal at times. As Leora Auslander argued in her study of furnishings in modern France, female and male consumers partly conceived of their national identities through consumption and leisure, fulfilling Michelet's claim that 'For a republican nation to exist, people had to recognise themselves in one another, through their things, their gestures, and their habits.'[95] Women of the eighteenth century may have seen their leisure and their identity through the lens of their local communities, but that perspective had undoubtedly broadened for most European women to a national perspective by the nineteenth century. In fact, as Lucy H. M. Soulsby wrote in her 1900 advice manual, *The Use of Leisure*, the modern girl's 'mother and grandmother might not have understood the very terms of some of her studies'. However, 'the cultivation of hobbies is one of the most valuable of all arts. Next to religion, and a sense of humour, it is chiefly hobbies which help us along in the pilgrimage of life'.[96]

World (1900–60)

By 1900, the emphasis on leisure as a vital piece of life and as a defining part of any European man or woman's identity was taking root. Leisure activities marked class, education, ambition and character – they had taken on importance as occupational identities waned and as more people felt divorced from their work. Leisure expanded its scope in the twentieth century as improved communication and media (radio, cinema, television, telephones and computers) and better transportation (airplanes and automobiles) brought the world within reach. By 1995, when the World Wide Web emerged, women in Europe could connect themselves with products, ideas and people around the world from the privacy of their homes or workplaces. Leisure, then, became an activity with global implications and opportunities.

For the women of the early twentieth century, a glimpse of these new opportunities was apparent as early as 1900. Perhaps best known of the movements for increased female freedom and leisure was the advent of the 'New Woman'. The New Woman was both a stereotype used to frighten women and men about changing gender roles and a label designed to describe a cluster of activities newly popular with young women at the turn of the century and beyond. The stereotype changed over time, but typically it presented a young 'spinster' who had either embraced a bookish life of plain dress, political extremism and reading, or alternately, the young adventuress who rode bicycles, smoked cigarettes and aped men. In both stereotypical images, women were depicted as yearning for 'unwomanly' independence of work and leisure and seen as rejecting male companionship. She was a symbol of rebellion.[97]

In reality, many middle- and working-class women were trying to break free of domestic restraints, gain more independence and claim leisure time for themselves by the early twentieth century. For example, women founded new magazines and wrote books for other women, and they formed a considerable reading public by the 1900s. In France, Marguerite Durand created the women's daily newspaper *La Fronde*, with an all-woman staff, in 1897 in order to harness this female reading audience.[98] In Britain, a whole genre of girls' adventure novels and magazines had developed by 1910, which included school tales, mysteries at seaside resorts and historical adventures in the empire. Girls in these fictional works wielded rifles with ease, chased criminals and performed heroic deeds as surely as their male counterparts in boys' literature.[99] This fiction did not just target middle-class girls; publishers also produced 'mill-girl' weeklies and cheap paperback novels featuring rags-to-riches stories of plucky girls.[100]

These new reading opportunities were made possible by major strides in female education by the first quarter of the twentieth century. Compulsory elementary education, increased secondary school options and university degrees for women helped create a more literate and interested public. Women were admitted to universities (although not on the same terms as men) in England and France in the 1860s, Scotland in the 1890s and Germany in 1908. Interestingly enough, while schooling was opening up to girls around Europe, the curriculum was being shaped to fit their 'special needs', and often girls were encouraged to find leisure opportunities in line with these needs. By 1905, housewifery became a compulsory subject in secondary schools for girls in both England and Germany, and cooking, sewing and cleaning had become part of the programme for many girls' clubs and organisations throughout Europe. In fact, home dressmaking became a leisure activity for women in the twentieth century (as well as a cheap way to facilitate socialising in public and 'smartness') rather than being considered work.[101]

Organised women's and girls' clubs became a common leisure option for European females by the twentieth century, and these were to continue to be viable parts of popular recreation into the twenty-first century. Clubs for females took a variety of forms, but the main types of organisations were involved primarily with religion, service or politics. Religious associations had been around for a long time, but the conscious organisation of women for religious and charitable work as leisure evolved in the nineteenth and twentieth centuries, as Pat Starkey discusses in this book (pp. 177–215). By the 1920s, women could volunteer at Salvation Army refuges in England, practise self-reliance and virtue with the Jeunesse Ouvrière Chrétienne Féminine (a Catholic working girls' club) in France, or engage in political organising with the Katholischer Frauenbund in Germany. Religion, in fact, was an important leisure outlet for women in the twentieth century because it provided a safe and meaningful series of organisations in which they could get involved. As Ute Frevert notes of these German organisations, 'Anchored firmly in the petty-bourgeois and rural milieu, these associations gave Catholic women broad scope for activities ranging from strictly religious matters (pilgrimages, spiritual exercises) to welfare and social work.'[102] These clubs not only provided local service provisions and activities, but they could also nurture an interest in the broader world, since many of them were branches of national or internationally linked clubs. Salvation Army events, for example, often functioned as imperial or global spectacles with speeches and performances by converts and missionaries from around the world.[103]

Like religious organisations, service clubs for girls and women became and remained exceedingly popular in the twentieth century. These organisations ranged from local charitable societies that focused on reform, entertainment or fund-raising, to groups charged with specific tasks in their communities or nations. For girls, in particular, service clubs could provide both adventure and a sense of meaning and identity. The most popular of these organisations in Europe (and indeed, worldwide) was girl guiding or scouting. Founded in Edwardian England as a counterpart to the Boy Scouts, girl guiding offered girls a mix of nature craft, outdoors activities, housewifery, nursing training and camaraderie. Run and organised locally, considerable variation existed according to class, race, religion and interest, so guide companies could tailor their activities to attract local participants and make changes as necessary. Guiding engaged in numerous good deeds for communities, making it primarily a service club, but it also offered the excitement of camping trips, hiking and games. Another major attraction of the movement was its uniform and accoutrements, both of which gave girls a sense of belonging and a way to set themselves apart through their selection and consumption of added uniform options, such as badges, socks, knives, rucksacks, and so on.[104]

Also, the worldwide reach of the organisation provided girls with travel options abroad and the ability to set up pen-pal arrangements with foreign girls. Girls could meet at the international centres in Switzerland or Mexico, or they could host contingents of visitors from colonies or other foreign countries. As World Chief Guide Olave Baden-Powell noted in 1930, 'Guiding is perhaps the ONE platform upon which all kinds can meet – Mohammedans, Hindus, Brahmins, Parsees, Buddhists, Christians and Jews.'[105] Clubs could indeed bring the world home for many girls and women involved, whether it was vicariously through organisational literature and films, or directly through visits, hosting and world conventions. In this way, leisure could help shape world citizens – or reinforce racial and national stereotypes, depending on the quality and context of the interaction.

The last area of organisational interest for women was in the political realm, and this form of association stretches back into earlier centuries. Women joined such organisations, sometimes with their husbands, in order to improve working or living conditions, or to address long-standing grievances. Some political clubs were social, aimed at creating communities and class-consciousness. In Germany, for instance, the lifting of anti-socialist laws in 1890 led to an explosion of SPD (Social Democratic Party) functions and clubs. Cultural and service organisations emerged as part of various political parties and trade unions. For example, the Tory Primrose League, founded in England in 1883, called on women with leisure to canvass for politicians, stage 'educational' events and inform voters through registration drives.[106] Likewise, Germany's social democratic women's movement focused on recruitment of members and social services. For youth, particularly after the Second World War, explicitly political clubs developed for nationalising girls. Such organisations included the German National Socialists' Bund Deutscher Mädel (the female equivalent of the Hitler Youth), and France's Jeunesses Communistes (Young Communists). Like the Guides, these clubs mixed service and fun (camping, hiking, amateur theatricals) with political and ideological aims. All of these organisations faced a similar difficulty in creating leisure for women and girls. Simply put, how could a club create 'good mothers' and attract females looking for adventure, independence and fun? Leisure associations faced this bind and the additional problem of women's limited time for leisure. Something quite powerful was needed to attract women to these organisations – some of them turned to sport and fitness as models.

Organised and unorganised sport had been an option for women prior to the twentieth century, but the focus on bodily health and physical fitness became a central feature of twentieth-century leisure activities, especially for young women. With the revival of the Olympics as a modern spectator event, women's sports gained audiences in the twentieth century. Not only did tennis players, gymnasts and skiers emulate Olympic athletes through their leisure pursuits, but women also got pleasure from watching sports matches in person and later in cinemas and on televisions. One such early spectacle was the *Damensportfest* in Berlin in 1904, which featured seventy girls competing in races.[107] Local schools and teams offered matches for viewing, and newsreels at the cinemas featured shorts on Olympic events, international tennis matches and ice-skating performances, to name a few. Women even formed an important part of crowds at boxing matches in 1920s and 1930s Germany, creating public debates about the propriety of women's presence at such bloody sports.[108]

Women and girls did more than just watch sports, however, and participation in all kinds of physical activity rose in the twentieth century. Military and volunteer service for girls in both world wars provided further justification for the physical training of female bodies, and their success in working in munitions, public transport, ambulance driving and auxiliary soldiering led the media to endorse more active lives for women. This led to a new emphasis on physical culture in schools and organisations. For example, in Britain a variety of clubs such as the Women's Cricket Association and Women's League of Health and Beauty formed in the inter-war period with the advent of the 'Keep Fit' campaign. In fact, 'sunbathing, tanning, dieting and slimming entered the British vocabulary as the body became more commercialized.'[109] Well-known women athletes around Europe, such as French Wimbledon champ Suzanne Lenglen, helped bring notice to the kinds of activities considered appropriate for girls.[110] Particularly popular for young women were swimming, ice-skating, bicycling, camping and all kinds of outdoor walking (hiking, rambling).[111]

As physical activities became more prevalent forms of entertainment for women, clothing altered as well, providing women with more style and comfort. The creation and acquisition of fashionable outfits also contributed to leisure. Sally Alexander has chronicled this emphasis on fashion, noting that young women used clothes in order to emphasise how their lives were different from their mothers' lives. She cites a women's testimony:

> As a young girl, basically one considers one ought to be smart. One would buy a black suit with a check colour, and then you would get a white flat hat with a black-and-white ribbon round it, match it all up . . . But you only wore them

on Sunday to start off with . . . and you only went out shopping just before Whitsun and just before Christmas – twice a year.

Alexander continued by explaining that like wearing the clothes, shopping itself was a 'ritual, a tribute to a special occasion, and one willingly saved up for'.[112]

The appearance of smartly dressed young women, many of them spending wages they earned themselves, on the avenues and in the drinking establishments of western Europe led to attacks again on these 'new' or 'modern' women. Fear about women's leisure pursuits and their demands for freedom and independence in the twentieth century coalesced in both the 1920s and the 1950s as European societies sought to rebuild from the world wars. Anxiety about birthrates, family life and societal values in the wake of these conflicts made women's leisure an easy target for complaints. On the one side, those aiming for a 'return' to pre-war values wanted women in the homes not pursuing public leisure, and on the other side, feminists thought many leisure pursuits were too frivolous or that young women were idle and useless. As Viscountess Rhondda writes of such useless women in 1928:

> They put idleness, the one thing they know, as the highest good; they teach the men and the young women of their set to value idleness, to dislike work, to value material comfort, personal adornment, and social advancement, to judge people upon how they dress.[113]

In France, the post-First World War 'New Woman' was denounced as frivolous and fast with a strong independent streak and a clear lack of 'womanly' attributes. Mary Louise Roberts chronicles this concern with the post-war female and her leisure, citing one 1925 account of this phenomenon:

> These beings – without breasts, without hips, without 'underwear', who smoke, work, argue, and fight exactly like boys, and who during the night at the Bois de Boulogne, with their heads swimming under several cocktails, seek out savory and acrobatic pleasures on the plush seats of 5 horsepower Citroens – these aren't young girls! There aren't any more young girls! No more women either![114]

Of particular concern in France, and indeed across Europe, was the fact that women seemed to be embracing leisure for themselves at the expense of motherhood. Social observers warned of the devastating effects of falling birthrates and poor mothering skills on the social fabric of Europe. In Germany, the 1925 census showed that the 'average family size had dropped to one child per family'.[115] From Berlin to Paris, worries arose about the fact that having tasted freedom and independence and the pleasures of mass culture, women would not want to forgo those pleasures for a life of housework and motherhood. Like Henrik Ibsen's feminist heroine in *A Doll's House* (1879) who escapes the confines of her domestic misery, 'The transformed woman wants more than to be a mother, she also wants to be a woman. Women are fleeing Nora's doll house not just in isolated cases but in battalions.'[116]

Likewise, after the Second World War, concerns again arose that women would not want to settle into suburban homes or newly built urban housing and raise children.

By the 1940s and after, the fear of female immorality and impropriety had coalesced not only around gender issues of motherhood, family and pronatalism, but also around race, as the war itself, decolonisation and immigration brought to Europe waves of the 'Other'. Worries about European women's relationships with African-American GIs gave way by the 1950s to fear of immigrant men from present and former colonies. As with post-First World War Europe, again women's use of their leisure time and sexuality became the focus of national angst, this time as an expression of larger cultural fears regarding both 'racial mixing' and women's rejection of motherhood entirely.

The major ways women did escape in the twentieth century were through consumption and mass culture. In their critique of the rise of the 'culture industry', Max Horkheimer and Theodor Adorno examined this move towards the faceless mass in the late 1940s, noting that repetition, mass production and imitation had replaced more meaningful and individualistic expressions. Citizens, far from using their intellects and individual taste, put their faith in technology and in the pleasure of buying. As they record it, 'The culture industry endlessly cheats its consumers out of what it endlessly promises', and this capitalist enterprise reduces people to mere consumers.[117] Their bleak view of twentieth-century culture and leisure highlights the increasing fragmentation of communal values and pursuits in exchange for the homogenised global culture of the modern, mechanised world. Yet, what they do not adequately address is the gendered dimensions of these consumption models. For women, such acts of purchase and display could serve an emancipatory function. The anonymity of mass culture gave them the means to reject what for some were the constraints of individual identities within family and communal systems. For these young women, buying shoes and a hat represented a certain measure of freedom.

This concern with purchasing leisure led to an interest in 'glamour' and, particularly, in the American Hollywood system. Stephen Gundle explores this phenomenon in post-Second World War Italy, explaining that 'As Americanism became inseparable from consumerism, glamour defined mentalities, behavior, aspirations and patterns of consumption, as well as ideals of beauty and so on . . . Hollywood glamour was a potent force in Europe.'[118] Americanisation, through products and media, melded with European commercial forms to create new and transformed leisure options for women. By 1941, there were more than 4,500 cinemas in Great Britain and annual admissions topped 1 billion people. Of these crowds, the major enthusiasts were 'young, working-class, urban and mostly female' clients, and studies of this audience suggest it was not uncommon for young women to attend the cinema at least once per week.[119] Movies increasingly meant imports from the USA, again providing girls and women with a broader perspective of the world, feeding fantasies of travel, fame and glamour. In fact,

> between 1918, when the U.S. industry established its leadership in Europe, and the 1960s, when television aggravated a severe slump in movie demand . . . the American cinema dominated European markets. Not only did it set the pace of innovation and promote new professional identities – it also fostered new consumer solidarities and reshaped cultural genres.[120]

In addition to cinema-going, other media also provided a wide focus on the world: magazines, cheap paperback novels, radio programmes, record albums and, finally, early television. Some of these surrounded the American glamour industry (for example, film magazines, soundtrack albums), while others represented other trends: travel guides and programmes, romance fiction, fashion magazines and sports broadcasts. This expansion of access to local, national and international media created a much broader world view for women in Europe from all social classes. By the end of the century, the majority of European societies were tapped into these media networks in some way. For example, a 1999 survey in Britain found that 99 per cent of women claimed to watch television and 71 per cent read for leisure.[121]

Although these emerging consumption and leisure options provided opportunities for people from a variety of backgrounds, married women and older women in general continued to find leisure elusive. Many did have access to cinema, partly because cinema was cheap and one could take along children. Andrew Davies found in his study of working-class Salford between the wars that women not only went to the pictures, but also often smuggled their children in for free. Two interviewees said they just took the kids with them to the cinema, and often 'you'd pay for one and smuggle the other two in. Pay for one, pay for yourself . . . You'd get 'em in somehow.'[122] Other outings that were available to working-class women with families included pub visits with friends or husbands, shopping and, later in the century, bingo. Despite such outings, many older women were often unable to find the time or resources for significant leisure activities outside the home. In a 1947 Mass Observation survey, a quarter of those polled said they did not have anything such as 'spare time'.[123] Margery Spring Rice's 1930s study of more than 1,000 married women in Britain found that, 'Leisure is a comparative term. Anything which is slightly less arduous or gives a change of scene of occupation from the active hard work of the eight hours for which she has already been up is leisure.'[124] For women with more financial resources, a variety of leisure was open to them, but as with the nineteenth century, class and age continued to be important dividers for women in their leisure activities.

Many older women of all classes saw leisure as the province of the young, and they found pleasure where they could. Some discovered relaxation through smoking; in Britain, more than 40 per cent of women regularly smoked by 1950.[125] Other home activities were also popular, such as knitting, needlecraft or cooking that combined work duties with some concept of leisure. More 'traditional' pursuits such as reading, card games, home visiting, church activities or shopping could also function as leisure. Even as late as 1999, more than a third of women in Britain 'claimed to sew or knit'.[126] With the rise of more radios and television sets within homes, women could listen to radios or watch television while pursuing other housework or childcare in the home. Media companies recognised this audience and created programming for women, including soap operas (such as *Coronation Street*, first seen in 1959) and female programming (such as the *Woman's Hour*, on BBC from 1946).[127] Claire Langhamer noted of the working women she interviewed in Manchester that leisure 'was inextricably linked to notions of duty and service' for married women, and they expected this contraction of their leisure time upon marriage.[128]

Conclusion (1960–present)

The study of women's leisure offers a telling window into the difficulties women have had and continue to have in finding 'spare time'. Although women's perspectives and opportunities have expanded since the eighteenth century to include a whole variety of new activities, the constraints on their leisure remain in place in many cases. In their study of contemporary Britain, *Women's Leisure, What Leisure?*, Eileen Green, Sandra Hebron and Diana Woodward outline these constraints. First, 'even when women do engage in paid work, this is typically seen as secondary to their work within the household or family, so women are not seen to 'earn' the right to leisure in the same way as men', and second, 'because domesticity and maternity are presented as the source of women's pleasure, [they] are not supposed to need to seek personal gratification from leisure, and to do so is considered selfish'.[129] With these widespread assumptions about women and their responsibilities for family leisure firmly in place, often they face similar prejudices and barriers to pleasurable pastimes that they have faced in the past.

That being noted, women have made amazing strides in all areas of leisure pursuits. Girls and women in Europe now routinely have access to education (in fact more women than men attend university in the twenty-first century), sports, leisure facilities, pubs, media and many other options for pleasure. The recent impact of wireless telephones with messaging features, Internet, e-mail and World Wide Web options as well as other computer programs cannot be underestimated in their effect on women's leisure in Europe. The world is literally at the fingertips of women through these new technologies, and older leisure forms have now assumed new shapes. E-books allow reading on a computer screen at home, and games can be played on-line. Gambling, shopping, chatting and travelling have now all taken on new dimensions as they exist inside and outside of cyberspace. Even courtship, a popular organiser of young women's leisure from time immemorial, can now be accomplished on-line. New communities of leisure have emerged with few constraints on time or place.

In a 1998 study of French leisure habits, more than 60 per cent of teen girls who responded said they participated in sports, but that compared to more than 70 per cent of boys in sport. This same data suggests that women's leisure time has increased at the expense of domestic tasks, and that in fact, rising unemployment among workers and changing values for white-collar employees has led to a rise in leisure time for poorer classes and a loss of such time for the formerly 'leisured' classes.[130] In Britain, a 1997 survey suggested that although gender differences in leisure have dissipated substantially, there are still markers: women prefer yoga to snooker, few men knit or sew, and many more men than women participate in competitive sport.[131]

The 'brave new world' of late twentieth- and early twenty-first century leisure has created opportunities for women of all classes and nationalities, but somehow the suspicion and politicisation of women's leisure remains. Women across Europe experience the double bind of waged work and housework, while state provision of daycare is still sparse. Women's wages continue to lag behind men's, and women still constitute a larger proportion of the elderly living in poverty. In the realm of leisure, women often continue to facilitate the leisured activities of their family, whether it is driving children to ballet lessons or preparing house and food for a dinner party. Balancing these concerns, more women than men are now entering universities, and significant political groups lobby for women's equality within the European Union.

In short, woman's empire is no longer limited to her home in Europe, but her ability to experience life outside the home is still shaped by factors within it, as Lynn Abrams has also discussed in her chapter, pp. 14–53. Florence Nightingale noted this problem a century earlier, writing: 'The family uses people, not for what they are, not for what they are intended to be, but for what it wants them for – for its own uses.'[132] As long as women's work, domestic duties, political access and wealth are limited by older gendered notions of their 'proper' place vis-à-vis men and home, then women's leisure will be shaped by these same conventions. Leisure for women is still in no way free.

Guide to further reading

The history of women's leisure in Europe has generally been understudied, although many scholars have begun to fill this gap. The list below represents some of the more general introductions to the field, many of which provide good bibliographies and historiographical essays for further reading.

Burke, Peter, *Popular Culture in Early Modern Europe*. London: Temple Smith, 1978. This geographically wide-ranging study explores a history of interaction between 'high' and 'low' cultures in Europe.

Cunningham, Hugh, *Leisure in the Industrial Revolution, c. 1780–c. 1880*. New York: St Martin's Press, 1980. A classic overview of some of the changes in leisure that accompanied industrialisation, Cunningham's book emphasises both continuities with pre-nineteenth century popular culture and new leisure opportunities and organisations that emerged.

De Grazia, Victoria, ed., *The Sex of Things: Gender and Consumption in Historical Perspective*. Berkeley, Calif.: University of California Press, 1996. This collection of articles examines gender and consumption in Europe and the USA in the context of nationalism, class and social relationships. Particularly useful is an annotated bibliography of works on gender and consumption by Ellen Furlough.

Easton, Susan, Alun Hawkins, Stuart Laing, Linda Merricks and Helen Walker, *Disorder and Discipline: Popular Culture from 1550 to the Present*. Aldershot: Temple Smith, 1988. A broad study that examines some of the changes in leisure practices and in the nature of popular culture in England.

Frevert, Ute, *Frauen-Geschichte: Zwischen Bürgerlicher Verbesserung und Neuer Weiblichkeit*. Frankfurt: Suhrkamp, 1986. A comprehensive study of women's lives in Germany that includes excellent material on work, socialisation and leisure.

Green, Eileen, Sandra Hebron and Diana Woodward, *Women's Leisure, What Leisure?* London: Macmillan, 1990. A sociological study that highlights the important gendered assumptions in many scholarly treatments of leisure, which often privilege waged work in defining leisure.

Guttmann, Allen, *Women's Sports: A History*. New York: Columbia, 1991. This general study of the kinds of sporting activities popular with women covers a long time frame in European history.

Isherwood, Robert M., *Farce and Fantasy: Popular Entertainment in Eighteenth-Century Paris*. New York and Oxford: Oxford University Press, 1986. Examines France's role as a consumer society, with particular emphasis on material culture and popular spectacle.

Koshar, Rudy, ed., *Histories of Leisure*. New York and Oxford: Berg, 2002. Recent series of articles seeking to integrate the study of leisure and consumption for a more complete look at European cultural history.

Kuhn, Annette, *Frauen in der deutschen Nachkriegszeit*, 2 vols. Düsseldorf: Schwann, 1984–6. One of the best of Kuhn's many works on issues of women and mass culture in twentieth century Germany, this particular multi-volume looks at women's lives after the Second World War.

Langhamer, Claire, 'Towards a Feminist Framework for the History of Women's Leisure, 1920–1960', in Ann-Marie Gallagher, Cathy Lubelska and Louise Ryan, eds, *Re-Presenting the Past: Women and History*. London: Longman, 2001. A short essay that encourages historians to move beyond studies of individual leisure activities in order to focus women's understanding of their leisure.

Martin-Fugier, Anne, *La Bourgeoise: Femmes au Temps de Paul Bourget*. Paris: B. Grasset,

1983. An important study of middle-class women's lives in France in the late nineteenth and early twentieth centuries.

Maynes, M. J., Birgitte Söland and Christina Benninghaus, eds, *Secret Gardens, Satanic Mills: Placing Girls in Modern European History*. Bloomington, Ind.: Indiana University Press, 2004. A collection of essays on the history of girlhood that provides multiple perspectives on female leisure from the eighteenth to the twentieth century.

McCrone, Kathleen E., *Playing the Game: Sport and the Physical Emancipation of English Women, 1870–1914*. Lexington, Ky.: University of Kentucky Press, 1988. Study of women and sport in Britain, with particular emphasis on the middle classes.

Mullan, John and Christopher Reid, eds, *Eighteenth-Century Popular Culture: A Selection*. Oxford: Oxford University Press, 2000. A collection of primary sources in English that includes a useful overview of conceptualisations of leisure in Europe.

Parratt, Catriona M., *'More Than Mere Amusement': Working-Class Women's Leisure in England, 1750–1914*. Boston, Mass.: Northeastern University Press, 2001. Recent examination of working-class women in England and their changing leisure practices in the long nineteenth century.

Perrot, Marguerite, *Le Mode de Vie des Familles Bourgeoises, 1873–1953*. Paris: A. Colin, 1961. Perrot's classic study examines the importance of consumption to building family and gender identities in middle-class French households.

Smith, Bonnie G., *Ladies of the Leisure Class: The Bourgeoises of Northern France in the Nineteenth Century*. Princeton, NJ: Princeton University Press, 1981. Now classic study of middle-class women, leisure and consumption in the era of industrialisation.

Stewart, Mary Lynn, *For Health and Beauty: Physical Culture for Frenchwomen, 1880s-1930s*. Baltimore, Md. and London: Johns Hopkins University Press, 2001. Recent book examining women and physical culture in France, which is a needed addition to a variety of works on English women and sport.

Strasser, Susan, Charles McGovern and Matthias Judt, eds, *Getting and Spending: European and American Consumer Societies in the Twentieth Century*. Cambridge: Cambridge University Press, 1998. This useful comparative study of consumption provides a cross-cultural examination of leisure and consumer practices in the past century.

Tlusty, B. Ann, *Bacchus and Civic Order: The Culture of Drink in Early Modern Germany*. Charlottesville, Va.: University Press of Virginia, 2001. One of several studies of alcohol and popular culture in Europe, this work uses gender as an analytic category.

Vincent, David, *The Rise of Mass Literacy: Reading and Writing in Modern Europe*. Cambridge: Polity, 2000. Study that compares rising literacy among European nations as well as educational systems, legislation and national differences.

Williams, Rosalind H., *Dream Worlds: Mass Consumption in Late Nineteenth-Century France*. Berkeley, Calif.: University of California Press, 1982. Study of the emergence of the modern department store and its impact on consumer practices in France and Europe.

Notes

1 A discussion of this debate can be found in John Mullan and Christopher Reid, eds, *Eighteenth-Century Popular Culture: A Selection* (Oxford: Oxford University Press, 2000), pp. 1–4.

2 Rudy Koshar, 'Seeing, Traveling, Consuming: An Introduction' in R. Koshar, ed., *Histories of Leisure* (Oxford and New York: Berg, 2002), p. 21.

3 Eileen Green, Sandra Hebron, and Diana Woodward, *Women's Leisure, What Leisure?* (London: Macmillan, 1990), p. 1.

4 See Anna Clark's chapter on sexuality in this volume, pp. 54–92, as well as her book, *The Struggle for the Breeches: Gender and the Making of the British Working Class* (Berkeley, Calif.: University of California Press, 1995).

5 Victoria de Grazia, ed., *The Sex of Things: Gender and Consumption in Historical Perspective* (Berkeley, Calif.: University of California Press, 1996), p. 3.
6 Mary Louise Roberts, 'Gender, Consumption, and Commodity Culture', *American Historical Review*, 103, 3 (June 1998), p. 821.
7 [Lady Eleanor Fenn], *The Female Guardian. Designed to Correct some of the Foibles incident to Girls and Supply them with Innocent Amusement for their hours of Leisure* (London: John Marshall & Co., 1784), pp. 6–7.
8 M. A. Searson, ed., *The Daughter of the Isles or, Truth Embodied in Fiction. A Journal for the Leisure Hour of the British Workwoman*, 1 (April 1881), p. 1
9 'Friend of Ours: No. 4 – Miss Lydia Becker', *Comus* (28 October 1877), 10. Lydia Becker papers, 7/LEB/1, Women's Library – London.
10 David Vincent, *The Rise of Mass Literacy: Reading and Writing in Modern Europe* (Cambridge: Polity, 2000), pp. 9–10, 30, 59, and *Literacy and Popular Culture, England 1750–1914* (Cambridge: Cambridge University Press, 1989), p. 24.
11 Mullan and Reid, *Eighteenth-Century Popular Culture*, pp. 7–8.
12 Susan Pedersen, 'Hannah More Meets Simple Simon: Tracts, Chapbooks, and Popular Culture in Late Eighteenth Century England', *Journal of British Studies* 25, 1 (January 1986), p. 103.
13 In [n.a.], *Chap-Books of the Eighteenth Century* (New York: Benjamin Blom, 1966), pp. 326–35.
14 Robert M. Isherwood, *Farce and Fantasy: Popular Entertainment in Eighteenth-Century Paris* (New York and Oxford: Oxford University Press, 1986), pp. 22–45, 55–9, 161–4.
15 Allen Guttmann, *Women's Sports: A History* (New York: Columbia University Press, 1991), p. 76.
16 op. cit., p. 77.
17 op. cit., p. 81.
18 Gerda Reith, *The Age of Chance: Gambling in Western Culture* (London and New York: Routledge, 1999), p. 65. Reith notes that some parents even hired gaming masters to teach their children.
19 op. cit., pp. 69–70.
20 B. Ann Tlusty, *Bacchus and Civic Order: The Culture of Drink in Early Modern Germany* (Charlottesville, Va.: University Press of Virginia, 2001), pp. 133–46.
21 Hans Medick, 'Plebian Culture in the Transition to Capitalism', in Raphael Samuel and Gareth Stedman Jones, eds, *Culture Ideology and Politics* (London: Routledge & Kegan Paul, 1982), pp. 96–104.
22 W. Scott Haine, *The World of the Paris Café: Sociability among the French Working Class, 1789–1914* (Baltimore, Md.: Johns Hopkins University Press, 1996), p. 179.
23 Hans Medick quoted in Clark, *The Struggle for the Breeches*, p. 29.
24 David Garrioch, *Neighbourhood and Community in Paris, 1740–1790* (Cambridge: Cambridge University Press, 1986), p. 171.
25 Hans Medick, 'Village Spinning Bees: Sexual Culture and Free Time among Rural Youth in Early Modern Germany', in Hans Medick and David Warren Sabean, eds, *Interest and Emotion: Essays on the Study of Family and Kinship* (Cambridge: Cambridge University Press, 1984), p. 335.
26 Dena Goodman, 'Enlightenment Salons: The Convergence of Female and Philosophic Ambitions', *Eighteenth-Century Studies*, 22, 3 (spring 1989), pp. 333–4.
27 op. cit., p. 332. On German salons, see Jeannine Blackwell and Susanne Zantop, eds, *Bitter Healing: German Women Writers, 1700–1830* (Lincoln, Nebr.: University of Nebraska Press, 1990), p. 446.
28 Amanda Vickery, *The Gentleman's Daughter: Women's Lives in Georgian England* (London and New Haven, Conn.: Yale, 1998), p. 236. Vickery's book looks explicitly at leisure activities on pp. 225–54.
29 op. cit., p. 252.
30 Brian Dolan, *Ladies of the Grand Tour: British Women in Pursuit of Enlightenment and Adventure in Eighteenth-Century Europe* (London: HarperCollins, 2001), pp. 276–7.

31 Bonnie Smith, *Changing Lives: Women in European History since 1700* (Lexington, Mass.: D. C. Heath & Co, 1989), p. 42.

32 Catriona M. Parratt, '*More Than Mere Amusement*': *Working-Class Women's Leisure in England, 1750–1914* (Boston, Mass.: Northeastern University Press, 2001), p. 52.

33 Hugh McLeod, *Religion and the People of Western Europe, 1789–1970* (Oxford: Oxford University Press, 1981), p. 58.

34 Laura Mason, *Singing the French Revolution: Popular Culture and Politics, 1787–1799* (Ithaca, NY and London: Cornell University Press, 1996), p. 105.

35 Carla Hesse, *The Other Enlightenment: How French Women Became Modern* (Princeton, NY: Princeton University Press, 2001), p. 154.

36 Blackwell and Zantop, *Bitter Healing*, pp. 19–20.

37 Haine, *The World of the Paris Café*, p. 182.

38 Kathleen Wilson, *The Sense of the People: Politics, Culture and Imperialism in England, 1715–1785* (Cambridge: Cambridge University Press, 1995), p. 147.

39 G. J. Barker-Benfield, *The Culture of Sensibility: Sex and Society in Eighteenth-Century Britain* (Chicago, Ill. and London: University of Chicago Press, 1992), p. 213.

40 This advertisement from the *Public Advertiser* (23 July 1762) is reproduced along with other information on the Cherokee visits in Mullan and Reid, *Eighteenth-Century Popular Culture*, pp. 274–9.

41 Blackwell and Zantrop, *Bitter Healing*, pp. 351–67.

42 Susan Easton, Alun Hawkins, Stuart Laing, Linda Merricks and Helen Walker, *Disorder and Discipline: Popular Culture from 1550 to the Present* (Aldershot: Temple Smith, 1988), p. 65.

43 By a Lady [D., M.E.] *Leisure Moments, or Letters and Poems &c. on Miscellaneous Subjects* (Greenwich: Richardson, 1826).

44 Blackwell and Zantop, *Bitter Healing*, p. 399.

45 Parratt, '*More Than Mere Amusement*', pp. 86–7.

46 Peter Bailey, *Leisure and Class in Victorian England: Rational Recreation and the Contest for Control, 1830–1885* (London: Routledge & Kegan Paul, 1978), p. 81.

47 Reith, *The Age of Chance*, p. 75.

48 Ellen Ross, *Love and Toil: Motherhood in Outcast London, 1870–1918* (New York and Oxford: Oxford University Press, 1993), pp. 87–8.

49 Parratt, '*More Than Mere Amusement*', p. 146.

50 Haine, *The World of the Paris Café*, pp. 186–206.

51 William Baron, 'Hawf Past Five at Neet', as quoted in Parratt, '*More Than Mere Amusement*', p. 110.

52 Parratt, '*More Than Mere Amusement*', p. 111.

53 Liz Stanley, ed., *The Diaries of Hannah Cullwick: Victorian Maidservant* (New Brunswick, NJ: Rutgers University Press, 1984), pp. 121–2.

54 op. cit., p. 153.

55 Haine, *The World of the Paris Café*, pp. 196–7.

56 Penelope Summerfield, 'The Effingham Arms and the Empire: Deliberate Selection in the Evolution of the Music Hall in London', in Eileen Yeo and Stephen Yeo, eds, *Popular Culture and Class Conflict 1590–1914: Explorations in the History of Labour and Leisure* (Sussex: Harvester Press, 1981), pp. 214–18; Dagmar Hoher, 'The Composition of Music Hall Audiences', in Peter Bailey, ed., *Music Hall: The Business of Pleasure* (Milton Keynes: Open University Press, 1986), pp. 74–5, 80–5, and Jane Traies, 'Jones and the Working Girl: Class Marginality in Music-Hall Song 1860–1900', in J. S. Bratton, ed., *Music Hall: Performance and Style* (Milton Keynes and Philadephia, Pa.: Open University Press, 1986), p. 23.

57 Giles Brandeth, *Discovering Pantomime* (Aylesbury: Shire Publications, 1973), pp. 11, 20, and V. C. Clinton-Baddeley, *Some Pantomime Pedigrees* (London: The Society for Theatre Research, 1963), pp. 7, 9, 31. *Cinderella* dates as a panto to 1804, and *Aladdin* first appeared as a harlequinade in 1788.

58 Rosalind Williams, *Dream Worlds: Mass Consumption in Late Nineteenth-Century France* (Berkeley, Calif.: University of California Press, 1982), pp. 58–9.

59 op. cit., 107.

60 Zeynep Çelik, *Displaying the Orient: Architecture of Islam at Nineteenth-Century World's Fairs* (Berkeley, Calif.: University of California Press, 1992), pp. 2, 19, 24, 30.

61 Lora Wildenthal, *German Women for Empire, 1884–1945* (Durham, NC and London: Duke University Press, 2001), pp. 48–50.

62 Williams, *Dream Worlds*, pp. 66, 92–3, 97.

63 Parratt, 'More Than Mere Amusement', pp. 117–19, and Ross, *Love and Toil*, pp. 81–4.

64 For examples of their work, see Lisa DiCaprio and Merry Wiesner, eds, *Lives and Voices: Sources in European Women's History* (Boston, Mass.: Houghton Mifflin, 2001), pp. 291–2, 316–18.

65 Parratt, 'More Than Mere Amusement', p. 155.

66 Tammy Proctor, '"Something for the Girls": Organized Leisure in Europe, 1890–1939', in M. J. Maynes, Birgitte Söland and Christina Benninghaus, eds, *Secret Gardens, Satanic Mills: Placing Girls in Modern European History* (Bloomington, Ind.: Indiana University Press, 2004), pp. 239–53.

67 Wildenthal, *German Women for Empire*, pp. 13, 49, 315.

68 A. James Hammerton, *Emigrant Gentlewomen: Genteel Poverty and Female Emigration, 1830–1914* (London: Croom Helm, 1979), pp. 28, 45, 149, 166.

69 Bonnie G. Smith, *Ladies of the Leisure Class: The Bourgeoises of Northern France in the Nineteenth Century* (Princeton, NJ: Princeton University Press, 1981), pp. 68–9, 132–7.

70 Leonore Davidoff and Catherine Hall, *Family Fortunes: Men and Women of the English Middle Class 1780–1850* (Chicago, Ill.: University of Chicago, 1987).

71 Marion A. Kaplan, *The Making of the Jewish Middle Class: Women, Family, and Identity in Imperial Germany* (New York and Oxford: Oxford University Press, 1991), p. 117.

72 op. cit., pp. 124–5.

73 John K. Walton, *The English Seaside Resort, a Social History 1750–1914* (New York: St Martin's Press, 1983), p. 7.

74 Vickery, *The Gentleman's Daughter*, pp. 227, 236–9, 252.

75 Nick Prior, 'Museums: Leisure between State and Distinction', in Koshar, ed., *Histories of Leisure*, pp. 36–7, 40.

76 Walton, *The English Seaside Resort*, pp. 21–2.

77 Jan Palmowski, 'Travels with Baedeker: The Guidebook and the Middle Classes in Victorian and Edwardian Britain', in Koshar, ed., *Histories of Leisure*, pp. 107, 118.

78 Williams, *Dream Worlds*, p. 87.

79 Hugh Cunningham, *Leisure in the Industrial Revolution, c.1780–c.1880* (New York: St Martin's Press, 1980), p. 157.

80 Palmowski in Koshar, ed., *Histories of Leisure*, pp. 105, 107, 109–10, 115–16.

81 Susan Goodman, *Gertrude Bell* (Dover, NH and Heidelberg: Berg, 1985), pp. 3, 10–15, 96, 103.

82 Quoted in Dea Birkett, *Spinsters Abroad! Victorian Lady Explorers* (New York: Dorset Press, 1989), pp. 52–3.

83 Lindy Moore, 'Educating for the "Woman's Sphere": Domestic Training Versus Intellectual Discipline', in Esther Breitenbach and Eleanor Gordon, eds, *Out of Bounds: Women in Scottish Society, 1800–1945* (Edinburgh: Edinburgh University Press, 1992), pp. 10–41, 'Young Ladies' Institutions: The Development of Secondary Schools for Girls in Scotland, 1833–c.1870', *History of Education*, 32, 3 (2003), pp. 249–72 and 'Gender, Education and Learning', in Lynn Abrams, Eleanor Gordon, Deborah Simonton and Eileen Janes Yeo, eds, *Gender in Scottish History: 1700 to the present* (Edinburgh, Edinburgh University Press, forthcoming 2006); Sarah Smith, 'Retaking the Register: Women's Higher Education in Glasgow and Beyond, c.1796–1845', *Gender & History*, 12, 2 (July 2000), p. 311.

84 Lawrence Williams, 'Educational Opportunities for Women in Early Nineteenth Century Edinburgh: Promoters, Consumers, and Critics', *Vitae Scholasticae*, 10, 1–2 (1991), pp. 85–97.

85 Ute Frevert, *Women in German History: From Bourgeois Emancipation to Sexual Liberation* (Oxford: Berg, 1988), pp. 120–2.

86 Vincent, *The Rise of Mass Literacy*, pp. 9–10, 30, 59.

87 Mary Lynn Stewart, *For Health and Beauty: Physical Culture for Frenchwomen, 1880s-1930s* (Baltimore, Md. and London: Johns Hopkins University Press, 2001), p. 152.

88 Kathleen E. McCrone, *Playing the Game: Sport and the Physical Emancipation of English Women, 1870–1914* (Lexington, Ky.: University of Kentucky Press, 1988), p. 104.

89 Guttman, *Women's Sports*, p. 92 and Stewart, *For Health and Beauty*, p. 169.

90 McCrone, *Playing the Game*, pp. 27–30.

91 Bill Birkett and Bill Peascod, *Women Climbing: 200 Years of Achievement* (London: A&C Black, 1989), pp. 18–22.

92 Tissandier Collection, Library of Congress Manuscripts collection.

93 Lady Violet Greville, *The Gentlewoman's Book of Sports* (London: Henry and Col, 1892), p. 104.

94 Maria Ward, *Bicycling for Ladies* (New York: Brentano's, 1896), p. 112.

95 Quoted in Leora Auslander, *Taste and Power: Furnishing Modern France* (Berkeley, Calif.: University of California, 1996), p. 421.

96 Lucy H. M. Soulsby, *The Use of Leisure* (London: Longman, 1900), pp. 24–6.

97 Mary Louise Roberts, *Disruptive Acts: The New Woman in Fin-de-Siècle France* (Chicago, Ill. and London: University of Chicago Press, 2002), p. 21.

98 Roberts, *Disruptive Acts*, pp. 38, 45.

99 Sally Mitchell, *The New Girl: Girls' Culture in England 1880–1915* (New York: Columbia University Press, 1995), pp. 1–3.

100 Kirsten Drotner, *English Children and Their Magazines, 1751–1945* (New Haven, Conn.: Yale University Press, 1988), p. 121.

101 Barbara Burman, 'Made at Home by Clever Fingers: Home Dressmaking in Edwardian England', in Barbara Burman, ed., *The Culture of Sewing: Gender, Consumption, and Home Dressmaking* (New York and Oxford: Berg, 1999), pp. 36, 39, 45.

102 Frevert, *Women in German History*, p. 173.

103 Pamela Walker, *Pulling the Devil's Kingdom Down: The Salvation Army in Victorian Britain* (Berkeley, Calif.: University of California Press, 2001), pp. 194–6.

104 Tammy Proctor, *On My Honour: Guiding and Scouting in Interwar Britain* (Philadelphia, Pa.: American Philosophical Society, 2002).

105 Olave Baden-Powell's Notebook on Dominions and Colonies (November 1930); Guide Association, London.

106 Beatrix Campbell, *The Iron Ladies: Why do Women vote Tory?* (London: Virago, 1987).

107 Guttman, *Women's Sports*, p. 103.

108 Erik Jensen, 'Crowd Control: Boxing Spectatorship and Social Order in Weimar Germany', in Koshar, *Histories of Leisure*, pp. 91, 97.

109 Tammy M. Proctor, '(Uni)Forming Youth: Girl Guides and Boy Scouts in Britain, 1908–1939', in *History Workshop Journal*, 45 (1998), p. 117.

110 Stewart, *For Health and Beauty*, p. 169.

111 Claire Langhamer, *Women's Leisure in England 1920–1960* (Manchester and New York: Manchester University Press, 2000), pp. 77, 80.

112 Sally Alexander, 'Becoming a Woman in London in the 1920s and 1930s', in Morag Shiach, ed., *Feminism and Cultural Studies* (Oxford: Oxford University Press, 1999), pp. 218–19.

113 Viscountess Rhondda [M. H. Mackworth], *Leisured Women* (London: The Hogarth Press, 1928), pp. 33–4.

114 Quoted in Mary Louise Roberts, *Civilization Without Sexes: Reconstructing Gender in Postwar France, 1917–1927* (Chicago, Ill. and London: University of Chicago Press, 1994), p. 20.

115 Atina Grossman, *Reforming Sex: The German Movement for Birth Control and Abortion Reform, 1920–1950* (Oxford: Oxford University Press, 1995), p. 3.

116 Quoted in ibid.

117 Max Horkheimer and Theodor Adorno, *Dialectic of Enlightenment: Philosophical Fragments*, trans. Edmund Jephcott (Stanford, Calif.: Stanford University Press, 2002), p. 111.

118 Stephen Gundle, 'Hollywood Glamour and Mass Consumption in Postwar Italy', *Journal of Cold War Studies*, 4, 3 (2002), pp. 98–9.

119 Langhamer, *Women's Leisure in England*, pp. 58–9, and Jeffrey Richards, *The Age of the*

Dream Palace: Cinema and Society in Britain 1930–1939 (London: Routledge, 1984), pp. 11, 15.

120 Victoria de Grazia, 'Mass Culture and Sovereignty: The American Challenge to European Cinemas, 1920–1960', *Journal of Modern History*, 61 (March 1989), p. 56.

121 Martin Francis, 'Leisure and Popular Culture', in Ina Zweiniiger-Bargielowska, ed., *Women in Twentieth-Century Britain* (Harlow: Pearson Education Limited, 2001), p. 230.

122 Andrew Davies, *Leisure, Gender and Poverty: Working-Class Culture in Salford and Manchester, 1900–1939* (Milton Keynes and Philadelphia, Pa.: Open University Press, 1992), p. 76.

123 Langhamer, *Women's Leisure in England*, p. 25.

124 Quoted in Davies, *Leisure, Gender and Poverty*, p. 61.

125 Matthew Hilton, *Smoking in British Popular Culture 1800–2000: Perfect Pleasures* (Manchester and New York: Manchester University Press, 2000), p. 138.

126 Francis, 'Leisure and Popular Culture', p. 230.

127 op. cit., p. 235.

128 Langhamer, *Women's Leisure in England*, p. 133.

129 Green, Hebron and Woodward, *Women's Leisure, What Leisure?*, p. 33.

130 Alain Chenu and Nicolas Herpin, 'Une pause dans la marche vers la civilization des loisirs?' [1998 Emploi du Temps], *Economie et Statistique* 352–3, 2002; available from <http://www.insee.fr>.

131 Francis, 'Leisure and Popular Culture', p. 242.

132 Quoted in Rita S. Kranidis, *The Victorian Spinster and Colonial Emigration: Contested Subjects* (New York: St Martin's Press, 1999), p. 169.

10

MISTRESSES OF CREATION

Women as producers and consumers of art since 1700

Siân Reynolds

In the room the women come and go
Talking of Michelangelo.
From T. S.Eliot, 'The
Love Song of J. Alfred Prufrock'

Introduction

In Eliot's poem, the two lines quoted above occur twice as a refrain. They are open to more than one interpretation. Are 'the women' representatives of the cultured elite who intimidate the insecure Prufrock? Or are they themselves the object of satire, as the rhythm of the verse seems to suggest? After all, they are merely 'talking of', rather than seriously interested in Michelangelo, the ultimate figure of the male creator, who has wrestled with marble and painted the Sistine Chapel. The reader is invited to view them as a group: 'women', rather than as individuals responding to art. Enjoying only a superficial relation to high culture, they recognise the name but not the inspiration. As they chat about art, the tinkle of coffee spoons is never far away.

'Women' have a particular relation to art in most historical narratives, but only rarely as producers, or even as serious consumers. More often they are included in the discussion as art's subject matter. Many of the creations we identify as works of art have highly gendered associations: paintings, sculptures, literature, certain kinds of music, theatre and cinema. Much of western European art has been quite explicitly concerned with love and desire, more often than not heterosexual. There is consequently a plentiful literature about the *representation* of women: as virgins, madonnas, mothers, femmes fatales, whores or, alternatively, as female workers, picturesque or exploited – in both cases identities that are largely sex-related. This chapter will not be concerned with representation, on which so much has been written. Rather, it is concerned with the historical experience women could have of the arts as producers (creating art), interpreters (performing art) and consumers (enjoying art). These are subjects more readily studied by specialists on the arts than by historians, and take us into interdisciplinary territory. This territory is also related to, though mostly distinct from, the question of popular culture, examined in the previous chapter by Tammy

Proctor, but the continuum between 'high' and 'popular culture' contains many overlaps: in cinema and the novel to take just two examples.

Exaggerating only slightly, one could argue that until about thirty years ago there was a dominant discourse about the arts which tended to marginalise women on almost all these fronts. It could simply take the form of ignoring them as creators, practitioners or consumers. Or it could explain away women's absence from centre stage but grant them a minor role as audience or inspiration. It used to be argued quite seriously that all 'women' as a group had less incentive to become creative than men, since their energies were absorbed in domestic and maternal activity. And yet paradoxically, cultural pursuits such as painting, reading and music were seen as appropriate to girls' education. In the period since 1700, European women, at least in the social classes that enjoyed some cultural capital, were increasingly entrusted with the skills needed to appreciate the arts: literacy, foreign languages and 'accomplishments', such as piano-playing or painting. Such exposure was generally in small, homeopathic doses, enough to enable them to read books or to play music, but stopping short of the rigorous training available in universities or conservatoires for their brothers (see the chapter by Rebecca Rogers in this volume, pp. 93–133). Consequently their cultural experience could be dismissed as dabbling in 'minor genres' such as watercolours, or practising such 'minor arts' as needlework, while they were also identified as the chief readers of light literature and target audiences for melodrama and sentimental cinema. They might be able to talk about Michelangelo, but there was little chance of their approaching a mature understanding of his work, let alone competing with it.

At the same time, over the period covered by this book, another discourse emerged in which 'creativity' was associated with genius and generally supplied with rather male characteristics.[1] As the arts became less institutionally attached to church and court, there appeared what we might call for short the romantic vision of creativity represented by the solitary, almost always male genius, in revolt against the rules, forging his own destiny and fighting or despising the constraints of class, money and society. The only social bond he might recognise was that of the artistic fraternity. The romantic hero often encounters entrapment by love, which hardly ever works out. Entanglement with women is seen as a negative destiny, leading to tragedy or – even worse perhaps – to marriage and domesticity. The nineteenth-century version of the romantic hero is the subject of Berlioz's *Symphonie fantastique*, following the beloved in a pursuit that ends on the scaffold. More prosaically, the twentieth-century writer Cyril Connolly, in his book *Enemies of Promise* (1938), identified a key 'enemy of good art' – for men – as 'the pram in the hall'. Whereas before 1700 women had on the whole been faced with institutional obstacles to artistic endeavour, in the centuries since then, they have also been confronted with a set of widely disseminated assumptions about masculine and feminine modes of thought.

I have exaggerated these discourses for the purposes of exposition, of course. But some version of them will be familiar to most readers. And at least as regards women creators, there is a case to answer, which requires some explanation. After all, until quite recently, there have been relatively few women artists or composers (or philosophers), and even fewer who have been famous. Literature, admittedly, has had more of a female hall of fame, even if the same few women's names recur constantly, compared to a much longer roll-call of male writers. Over the past twenty or thirty years, an alternative feminist discourse has challenged the restrictive assumptions described above. It has taken many forms: analysis of male representations of women, explorations of the taboos or obstacles to creativity, rediscovery of creative women neglected or forgotten by official chroniclers, sociology of the arts, personal testimony. In her autobiography, the literary critic Lorna Sage looked back through the critical eyes of her later feminist self at her one-time heroes, the American Beat poets of the 1950s and their view of female biological destiny:

> It's galling to realise that you were a creature of mythology: *girls were the enemies of promise*, a trap for boys, although with the wisdom of hindsight you can see that *the opposite was the case*. In those seductive yarns about freedom [such as Kerouac's *On the Road*] . . . [girls] are meant to stay put in one spot of time.[2]

How best then to approach this simultaneous history of presence and absence? The solution adopted in this chapter is to consider the arts as a 'cultural field', in the sense of the term used by Pierre Bourdieu, that is, an overall context in which some activities and some players may have more status or power than others, but where such relationships are constantly changing: 'the cultural field is a structured space of relations . . . New entrants to the field [are] necessarily situated within the network of competing positions'.[3] It will approach this concept from the specific point of view of gender, rather than Bourdieu's more usual approach via social class. This will mean looking at the ways of entry to the cultural field and its gate-keeping mechanisms, the kinds of activity and genres that commanded most respect and the shifts over time. It will draw on recent approaches in cultural history that have considered consumers of the arts (readership, audiences) as well as artists, and it will owe much to the 'rescue missions' of feminist history.

A first step is to historicise the cultural field. The period under review, 1700 to the present, marked some kind of break from previous ages. In his innovative book on culture in eighteenth-century England, John Brewer refers to a collective portrait shown at the Royal Academy exhibition in London in 1779. The painter was Richard Samuel, the painting was entitled *The Nine Living Muses of Great Britain*, and the nine women represented were: Anna Letitia Barbauld, poet and essayist; Elizabeth Carter, translator of the ancients; Elizabeth Griffith, Irish actress, playwright and novelist; Angelika Kauffmann, painter and Royal Academy member; Elizabeth Linley, singer; Charlotte Lennox, novelist; Catharine Macaulay, historian; Elizabeth Montagu, leader of the 'London Bluestockings' and literary patron; and Hannah More, playwright and polemicist. The Romantic vision of the female muse suggested that her role was to inspire the solitary genius. But the women in the painting, composed during the European Enlightenment, were, like the original Muses of Antiquity, practitioners: well-known, educated and talented inhabitants of the artistic world.[4]

The picture is analysed in Brewer's book as a sign of women's increased 'cultural power', greeted in some quarters by anxiety about the 'feminization of culture'. But it should occasion no surprise to find women rather prominently present in the cultural landscape by the late eighteenth century. As Brewer remarks, they were 'everywhere': as readers of periodicals and novels, as patrons of circulating libraries, members of the audience for theatre and opera, purchasers of paintings, and so on.[5] This is a list which envisages women primarily as *consuming* rather than *producing* culture, and is not without its internal problems and qualifications. Until then, however, in European history women had had a low profile whether as producers or even consumers of art. As well as facing institutional prohibitions from church and society, most women had far less education than their male equivalents. So it had been uncommon before the eighteenth century to find them fulfilling more active roles: as interpreters (singers and actresses, for example), as appreciative audiences for fine art or literature, as patrons (though this was more possible) and, least of all, as creative artists themselves.

Uncommon, but not unknown. In the courts and convents of medieval Europe, participation in the arts by privileged women was not entirely ruled out. Certain exceptional women were well known in their time and have often been rediscovered since: women such as the composer Hildegard of Bingen (1098–1179), the writer Christine de Pizan (1364–1431), the poet-storyteller Marguerite of Navarre (1492–1549). Later developments did not come from nowhere. But it can be argued that the cultural field as a whole for all inhabitants of Europe began to expand seriously only towards the end of the seventeenth century, enabling people previously excluded by their social class or their sex to have some place in it. As Roy Porter puts it, 'the pool of cultural players encompassed ever larger numbers of women and provincials, and more middle-class and even lower-class figures'.[6] Male literacy had been increasing since at least the Reformation; women's literacy, although still lagging behind, started to catch up, at least in the privileged classes, in most European countries. While almost universally excluded from liturgical music, women had begun to sing in concerts in certain Italian courts and cities. Actresses appeared on stage for the first time at the court of Louis XIV and in Restoration England. Women writers were increasingly published and read in eighteenth-century Europe. These were recent and patchy developments, but they were part of a gradual change in the landscape. From now on, women would play an essential, though still rarely a determining role, in European culture. Over the 300 years of our study, 1700 to 2000, a number of further changes took place in the cultural field: sometimes gradual, sometimes surprisingly sudden, and sometimes hardly visible at all.

In the following survey, to avoid either a series of national catalogues or an impossible attempt to depict the whole of European culture in every age, the three central chronological sections, here described as the 'long' eighteenth, nineteenth and twentieth centuries, will each take a particular focus: they concentrate in turn on an area of the arts both significant in European terms and one which witnessed some new development of gender balance. For the first period, roughly 1680–1810, the centre of interest will be the *performing arts*: theatre, music, opera and dance. For the 'long nineteenth century' (1789–1914) the chosen focus is the *written word*: reading, translation and writing. Finally, the 'long twentieth century', from about the 1890s to 2000, will consider the *visual and fine arts*, including photography and cinema. In each case, there will be excursions forwards and back in time as appropriate.

Historiography and sources

Women, culture and Europe are all huge subjects. This field is by no means uncharted territory, but it has no overall *atlas*. There are many *maps*: histories of Europe, of culture, of single countries and monographs on particular aspects of our subject – French painting, German philosophy, Italian opera, the nineteenth-century English novel, and so on. But they are often either too vast or too narrow in scale to be helpful, except as a starting point; many are concerned with one country, one sector or one period, and (until recently) one sex. Feminist scholarship has set out to provide an alternative body of literature, again very heterogeneous. The following paragraphs offer a brief overview of how the writing about the field has evolved; for individual works, see the guide to further reading and notes at the end of the chapter.

Perhaps understandably, since they have to cover so much ground, general works on European history rarely give more than token space either to cultural matters or to women, and scarcely ever mention them in the same breath. Among recent attempts at this difficult genre, Norman Davies's tour de force *Europe: A History* (1996) is more attentive to arts and intellectual developments than many, and is particularly good on music, but his references to women are idiosyncratic and patchy. Even today, some general histories continue to show little sign of the impact of feminist scholarship. The chapter on 'Culture' in a recent textbook history of twentieth-century Europe mentioned 106 men and seven women, the latter references being strikingly trivial and dismissive: Josephine Baker and her banana skirt, Isadora Duncan and her scarf.[7] The alternative European history, focusing on 'women in Europe', to which the present work belongs, is more likely to cover education, work, politics, family and everyday life, providing good supplements to other chapters in this collection, than the arts, although there are some helpful exceptions.[8]

If we turn to works on cultural history, often in practice largely concerned with western Europe, we face the existing corpus of literary history, art history, musicology and histories of high culture. Traditionally, such works have been, and in many cases still are, written out of a concern to make known and understood 'the big names' of music, fine art and literature, and the dominant schools, movements and groups or alternatively those that were in rebellion against the preceding tradition: the classical composers, the Romantic poets, the impressionists, the surrealists, the New Wave film directors, and so on. The creative and artistic networks of the European past which so often constituted themselves into movements, thereby increasing their visibility and providing support and solidarity for their members, were mostly groups of men, brought together by the kinds of sociability open to them and virtually closed to women. Some famous women were always certain of a place in cultural narratives, especially in literature. But for the most part, literary and artistic movements in modern Europe have been overwhelmingly male, at least until the twentieth century.[9] And the notion of 'the canon', that is, the works of art accepted as constituting a tradition or set of pinnacles of achievement (Italian opera, Western pictorial art, 'great books') has been dominated by the names of men.

Accordingly, the 'canon' has become a target and a matter of dispute for feminist, and other kinds of revisionist scholarship. During the 1980s and 1990s, it became something of a cliché that 'dead white men' dominated the lists of cultural achievement. In particular, many feminists argued that the canon was imposed by a particular kind of literary/cultural history developed in the nineteenth century, the product of male establishment institutions.[10] The canon is primarily a literary notion and, because of the particular development of literature departments in British and US universities (less so in Continental Europe), chronologically the first feminist challenge to traditional cultural history came from literature specialists, generally Anglo-American scholars. *The Madwoman in the Attic* (1979) by Sandra Gilbert and Susan Gubar was one of the best-known early examples of such scholarship. This pioneering and still very readable book sought to make sense of certain women writers, not merely as practitioners in the established tradition of the novel, but as a distinct kind of creative writer, shaped by factors that were not the same as for male writers. In their preface to a reissue of the book in 2000, the authors recall how in the 1970s this idea was seen as odd and controversial. They point out that the many changes in literary theory have now made their own approach seem elitist and canonical: the rediscovery and evaluation of non-elite women writers, whether women of colour, of the working class, or from minority cultures, the rise of post-colonial, post-structuralist and queer theory among other things, have all challenged the idea of the canon, which does of course continue to be defended or adapted in other quarters.[11] There is now a large body of writing on women and literature. As well as thematic and stylistic studies applying various kinds of critical theory to both men and women's writing, this corpus also includes explorations of a wider range of genres than the traditional poetry/drama/fiction triad. It has resurrected forgotten, neglected or underestimated women writers, and it has examined the conditions of literary production, to see how these differed for men and women.

Similar approaches, though the number of studies is considerably smaller, have been undertaken by feminist or gender-conscious art historians, musicologists and specialists in cinema. The picture here is more patchy and is still developing. While art history now has a fairly well-developed feminist branch, so to speak, musicology is an area of relatively recent openness to gender scholarship. And if gender studies in Anglo-American cinema are well established, in some European countries, especially that major player, France, they are still not particularly welcome. Any such approaches to French film come from outside, mainly by British and North American scholars. The approaches taken in these areas range from analysis of apprenticeship and the conditions of production of fine art or musical composition, through the gendering of the 'male gaze' in both art and film, to studies of less-known women artists and genres.

Although much of this research has been concerned to rediscover women performers and creators, some of it has also highlighted women as consumers, readers and audiences. Here mention should be made of a gender-conscious type of history emerging from the cultural studies inspired by such thinkers as Jürgen Habermas, Michel Foucault and Pierre Bourdieu and concerned with the relationship between the production and consumption of culture in general. In the original writings of these theorists, a space for gendered analysis was always theoretically possible, though in practice not very deeply explored. For example, Habermas, whose work has been a major influence, sought to 'map the formation of a polite and informed public in the early modern period', but in practice concentrated on the 'public sphere' of sociability created by certain spaces predominantly frequented by men: coffee houses, magazines, clubs, universities, artist's studios, and so on. Recent historians who have pointed out that 'in Habermas's narrative', women were 'virtually invisible', have looked at other social environments and have sought to reconfigure the map of 'polite society', locating women as essential participants in the cultural field, 'an informed public' parallel with that of men.[12]

Finally, in this brief survey of genres, mention should be made of reference works and the possible range of miscellaneous sources. While reference works produced before about 1980 are often unlikely to be useful tools for the historian of women and the arts, there has been a revolution in this area of publishing too. Many biographical dictionaries and 'companions' to art, literature and music have been redesigned in order to provide more gender balance. The serious researcher will of course also have to be prepared to investigate primary sources: contemporary publications, archives, manuscripts, exhibition catalogues, programme notes, theatre programmes, and so forth. In short, although there is not much available in the way of a European-wide synthesis on 'women and the arts', there is a very rich body of both single-discipline and interdisciplinary scholarship, as well as primary material, which historians may not have regularly explored, but from which hypotheses can be constructed to start building a better informed cultural history of Europe.

The long eighteenth century: music, drama and opera

During the eighteenth century, performance arts became European in scope, rather than confined to a single country. Italian opera and musical composition were imitated almost everywhere else. London's favourite composers were German or Austrian: first Handel, then J. C. Bach, and finally Haydn. The Mozart children, Wolfgang and Nannerl, showed off their prodigious talents in many European cities and courts in the 1760s. Plays were adapted for performance in other countries.[13] What is significant for our purpose is that women were beginning their long history as performers. Actresses and singers regularly played in front of audiences by the end of the eighteenth century, some achieving star status, others forming the chorus, while the domestic or amateur tradition of music-making and performing, which involved women more than men, also began to become more widespread.

In 1698, Count Peter Tolstoy wrote: 'In Venice, there are convents where women play the organ and other instruments and sing so wonderfully that nowhere else in the world could one find such sweet and harmonious song'. The Président de Brosses reported forty years later in 1739 that 'they sing like angels and play the violin, flute, organ, oboe, cello and bassoon: they are not afraid to tackle any instrument'. Jean-Jacques Rousseau went regularly to listen to Vespers at the Mendicanti in 1744, and was bowled over by 'the beauty of the voices and the accuracy of the execution'. In 1765, a French visitor reported that the crowds were so immense that people were hanging out of windows and sitting in gondolas. The convents in question were said to harbour 'a thousand miseries', yet we now regard them as 'precious repositories of the Venetian aesthetic'.[14]

This musical phenomenon demonstrates both the possibilities and the limitations for women musicians as the eighteenth century opened. The charitable foundations in Venice, known as the *ospedali*, open to both sexes, had their origins in the fifteenth century, and there are early references to girls being taught as well as boys. By the end of the eighteenth century, several hundred women musicians had been recorded as passing through the four *ospedali*. Male *maestri*, including Vivaldi, Galuppi, Monferrato and others, taught at the *Ospedale della Pietà* on and off for years and composed works for the all-female chorus and orchestra to play. Partly destitute orphans and partly the supernumerary daughters of patricians, selected girls were trained as members of the *cori* and permitted to sing and play in public worship and other performances, becoming an elite group within the foundation. The girls either left upon marriage (after which they were forbidden to sing in public) or, if remaining single, stayed in the *ospedale* for life.

The Venetian convents were remarkable in that alongside learning plainsong and the liturgy, the girls and women played instruments and performed works written for them, at public concerts. The Figlie della Pietà had no surnames but were known by the names of their instruments: 'Maria della Viola, Anneta dal Basso, Stella della Tiorba' and so on. Their instruments were said to have been of good quality and Venice was a magnet for guest musicians from all over Europe. Although not professionals in the modern sense, the women had received a thorough training, and some of them became well-known solo players and singers. Composition was supposedly forbidden, but several members of the Pietà are known to have composed works, Maddalena Lombardini Sirmen (1745–1815), violinist and composer, being one of the better known.[15]

Venetian practice was a radical departure from church music elsewhere, because of its historic ecclesiastical independence from the Vatican. This exception indicates one of the key reasons why most European women had been confined to either private or traditional music-making. The chief musical-training establishments for boys and men were religious, and the Catholic tradition of excluding women was carried over into the Protestant churches. Previously, there had been music-making inside convents, but they were mostly cloistered from the mainstream of church music, and restricted further by the Council of Trent.[16] In Italy however, some secular exceptions already existed: the female ensemble singers at the court of Ferrara were famed as early as the late sixteenth century. Singing was the main branch of music-making to which women were admitted elsewhere too. Lully had introduced professional female singers and *danseuses* to the French court of Versailles in the 1680s for entertainments, including ballets.

Even in the eighteenth century however, women singers had to compete with male *castrati*. These singers, who were castrated as young boys in order to preserve their falsetto voices, had more powerful lungs than most women. The practice centred in Spain and Italy and lasted from the start of polyphony until the mid-eighteenth century. The advent of Italian opera encouraged the use of *castrati*, and Handel wrote many of his female roles for these performers, who reportedly had 'voices of extraordinary beauty, control, flexibility and power'.[17] *Castrati* were welcomed to every European court except France. To compete with them, women had to be very gifted – such as the three famous singers Francesca Cuzzoni (1700–70), Faustina Bordoni (1693–81) and Vittoria Tesi (1700–1775). Professional women singers in the eighteenth century usually came from a musical family. They rarely had very long careers. Ehrlich quotes the example of Nancy Storace (1765–1818), Mozart's first Susanna, who was the daughter of an Italian double bass player, and Charlotte Brent (*c.*1735–1802) who, like several young women, was a pupil of (and mistress to) Arne. She made a sensational debut at Covent Garden but eventually died in poverty.[18] Mozart's wife, Constanze Weber, and her sister Aloysia were both sopranos. He made a practice of writing arias to suit the available performers, so we know that by his time very high standards of performance were achieved.

If singing became acceptable, instrumental playing by women was, Venice apart, subject to restrictions which included disapproval of the contortion of the body. Consequently, many upper- and middle-class women were directed towards playing keyboards: harpsichord, pianoforte and, eventually, piano. Mozart's sister Nannerl was described as an extremely precocious and talented keyboard player. Diderot's daughter Angélique (1753–1824) was described by Dr Burney as 'one of the finest harpsichord-players in Paris, and, for a lady, possessed of an uncommon portion of knowledge in modulation'.[19] One could multiply the cases of proficient women keyboard players, but hardly any of them became composers. In a book on the education of girls (1798), Erasmus Darwin wrote:

> It is perhaps more desirable that young ladies should play, sing and dance only so well as to amuse themselves and their friends, than to practice [sic] those arts in so eminent a degree as to astonish the public; because a great apparent attention to trivial accomplishments is liable to give suspicion that more valuable acquisitions [presumably morality and religious devotion] have been neglected.[20]

If that was a general view, what was available to a musical girl? The choices were confined to domestic music-making – traditional singing, vocal performance and occasional solo playing – and remained so into the nineteenth century and throughout Europe. Girls learnt to play the piano for home entertainment. Surprisingly to us perhaps, the violin, 'prime instrument of European music', but also associated with flamboyant Gypsy music, was regarded as socially unacceptable. Meanwhile, the nineteenth century saw 'the rise of all the institutions which would turn the art of music into a major public enterprise – the conservatoires, the orchestral and choral societies, the purpose-built concert halls, the musical publishers and the departments of musicology'. And from all of these, women were virtually excluded, except as solo piano performers, opera singers and music teachers. They were not at first admitted to the Collegium Musicum in northern Germany, nor to most of the conservatoires that spread throughout Europe (Paris 1796, Prague 1811, Brussels 1813, Vienna 1817, Warsaw and London 1822, St Petersburg 1862, Berlin 1869). Even when women were admitted, from about the mid-nineteenth century, they were usually excluded from counterpoint, advanced theory and composition. Their professional careers thereafter were almost entirely devoted to teaching keyboard instruments. Until very recently (after the Second World War), most major orchestras in the world were all-male or nearly so. The reasons were at least partly practical and social to start with, such as late nights, travel and male company, but the dearth of women orchestral players lasted long after social taboos had apparently faded. There were some all-women orchestras in the nineteenth century, though their place in the cultural field was not, as may be guessed, a very commanding one. The last all-male major orchestra, the Vienna Philharmonic, granted membership to their first woman, their harpist, in 1997.[21]

We do not have to look very hard then for reasons why women did not become composers. While it might come from an inner urge, musical composition in the eighteenth century was almost always done to order for a patron and within an institutional setting that provided resources, such as a princely court with its orchestra, a chapel with its choir and, later, the competitive atmosphere of the conservatoire. Nannerl Mozart's brother Wolfgang was famous for trying to earn a living, not entirely successfully, as a freelance, taking his chance with individual commissions instead of accepting a tied post. The great age of German and Austrian music had its origins in ecclesiastical or aristocratic patronage: Bach was a *Kapellmeister*, Haydn worked for years at the

Esterhazy court at Eisenstadt. Patronage was a two-edged weapon, of course: as well as choral masterpieces, Haydn had also been obliged to compose over 160 works for the baryton, an adapted kind of bass viol, for his aristocratic patron. The worlds of orchestral playing, choral singing or even chamber music were closed to women except on extremely limited terms. So when they did compose, it was almost always songs or short keyboard pieces. This had little to do with ability, talent or even fortitude and stamina, but was determined by strong historical, institutional and social pressures. Even Clara Schumann (1819–96), an outstanding pianist, 'with Liszt, . . . the leading piano teacher of her day', wrote very few original compositions, though perhaps her eight children and the need to be constantly on tour for financial reasons help explain this. Fanny Mendelssohn (1805–47) was credited with the same precocity in composition as her brother Felix, but her 'social situation, her sex and the [strongly formulated] opposition of her father and brother hindered her from publicly practising performance or composition'.[22]

The story of theatre provides some variations on this theme. Only since 1660 had women been allowed to act on the stage in England. They had made their appearance earlier in France, and were well established during the seventeenth century. Mlle du Parc (1633–68) had, it was said, the distinction of being admired by Corneille, trained by Molière and loved by Racine. The latter's last two plays *Esther* (1689) and *Athalie* (1690) were actually written for performance by schoolgirls at Saint-Cyr, but these performances were outside the mainstream. The chief theatres in Paris in the eighteenth century were the official Comédie française and Comédie italienne (later the Opéra-Comique), both of which were permanent theatre companies in which the actors had an official stake: 'the actors at the Théâtre français present the rare case of women sitting side by side on essentially equal terms with males in an important deliberative body'.[23] As in Molière's time, women seem to have been as important within the company of actors as men, and were certainly stars who attracted audiences: Mlle Duclos (1668–1748), Mlle Desmarets (1683–1753), Adrienne Lecouvreur (1692–1730), Mlle Dangeville (1714–96), Mlle Clairon (1723–1803) and others were famous in leading roles in plays by such as Voltaire and Marivaux, prefiguring the extraordinary celebrity in the nineteenth century of Marie Dorval (1798–1849), Rachel (1820–58) and, above all, Sarah Bernhardt (1844–1923), probably the most famous actress of all time. As Mark Twain put it: 'there are five kinds of actresses: bad actresses, fair actresses, good actresses, great actresses, and Sarah Bernhardt'.[24]

Many of the early actresses died young, or in poverty, or both. In Catholic France, all actors, men and women, were refused the sacraments of the Church; additionally they had no civil rights, could not marry or legitimise their children or pass on property. Yet they were initially civil servants and employees of the Crown. 'Feted and lauded with honours in their lifetime, they were demeaned and defiled at their death'.[25] Curiously, this was not the case either in Catholic Italy or in Protestant Britain. In 1730, Adrienne Lecouvreur died suddenly at the age of thirty-eight. An actress at the Comédie française, known for her natural form of delivery, she had acted in some of Voltaire's early plays. Refused Christian burial, she had to be placed in a secret grave, whereas Anne Oldfield (1683–1730), an actress in Drury Lane who died the same year, was buried in Westminster Abbey, a fact noted with irony by Voltaire.[26]

But we should not conclude from this that acting was regarded as a more respectable profession in London. 'Hostility to the stage was deeply embedded in the English

Protestant consciousness'.[27] Actors – and especially actresses – were condemned for the very qualities that made them successful. The theatre was 'self-promoting and flamboyant – and hence morally suspect'.[28] The London actress Harriet Mellon, who married a Duke, described her life in the theatre as 'all fun, frolic and vivacity: they cared for nothing, thought of nothing, beyond the pleasures of the present hour, and to those they gave themselves up with the utmost relish'. Perhaps it was not surprising that the press painted the actress as at best a lady of easy virtue and at worst a whore.[29] For many young actresses, such as the headstrong Marie-Madeleine Jodin, acting was a way of escaping from parental control. As she travelled round Europe, she received avuncular advice from Diderot, a friend of her father's, but the undercurrent of his letters suggests that she should never have become an actress at all. French companies were in particular demand throughout Europe: Friedrich August II, Elector of Saxony, King of Poland and a confirmed Francophile, brought over to Poland a French company that included thirty-one actors and singers of both sexes, fifteen dancers, three musicians and thirty-two family members.[30]

How did women become actresses? Often through the family, but 'the nineteenth-century registration records at the state-sponsored Conservatory of Dramatic Arts [in Paris] show that the stage aspirants' family backgrounds were humble'. Daughters of artisans and shopkeepers, they might be runaways, living on the streets, yet they often claimed to have been drawn by the 'sacred flame'. 'Their parents were often appalled'.[31] When they got there, conditions were tough, hours were long and performances constant in unenviable locations: 'the wings [had] a special smell: the sweat of the scene-shifters and the dancers; gas and oil fumes and dust, the breath of the people and the acrid smell of small children'.[32] Even harsher and more exploitative conditions were undergone by the young ballet dancers at the Paris Opéra, known as *les rats*, so slight and thin were they, and often obliged to engage in near-prostitution with middle-aged patrons to survive.[33]

Some histories of the theatre have suggested that acting became more respectable. But it is hard to see that much changed in the nineteenth century. Tracy Davis's pioneering study of actresses as working women in London demonstrates that for a small elite, a fairly respectable existence was, even in late Victorian times, confined to a very few performers, 'and even fewer women. The reality for most was a low working-class wage, social ostracism and the constant threat of unemployment'. Nevertheless, and these conditions would hold throughout Europe for most of the nineteenth and twentieth centuries, there were some advantages to the profession, if it was compared to the available alternatives. Actresses and dancers could not usually be ousted from their roles by men; there was roughly equal pay for equal work, and the opportunity existed for promotion to management; it could be a springboard into marriage and a gracious retirement into respectability though, unlike men who were knighted or otherwise honoured, women who married titles had to give up their work; and of course, for those who had sought it for this reason, it provided 'an element of excitement and an unequalled degree of personal and sexual freedom'.[34] Above all, there was the challenge of exercising a talent. This is difficult to judge from theatre criticism – almost always suspect, because it was influenced by partisanship and popular success. But now and then the magic of an actress can be glimpsed, as when in 1845 the French actress Rachel played Electre in Voltaire's *Oreste* – an indifferent tragedy – and transformed the text, as reported by Théophile

Gautier.[35] But not until the twentieth century was a French actress given the Légion d'honneur – routinely awarded to painters.

Aspirant actresses might have become stage-struck by visiting the theatre, and women did make up much of the audience for spectacle. But even in the nineteenth century, it has been argued, women did not visit the theatre as independent beings on the same terms as men. They had to be taken or accompanied by family members. 'No nineteenth-century woman wrote "A Playgoer's Memories", because women did not go to the theatre with the same freedom as a man', comments Viv Gardner.[36] However, she argues, the theatre has gradually become 'feminised' in its physical ordering of space: comfortable soft seats and a more passive and invisible place for the audience.

Finally, although it means taking several leaps forward in time, mention should be made in this section of the ballet. As noted earlier, the first professional female dancers, as distinct from ladies of the court, were trained by Lully in the seventeenth century. The ballet as we know it began to evolve during the eighteenth century, reaching its apogee of popularity in the nineteenth. From being attached to opera, the ballet d'action was devised as a narrative conveyed by music and dance alone. It was introduced in London and Vienna, but soon came to be centred on France, which provided its vocabulary and many of its trappings. The leading choreographer of mid-eighteenth century was Jean-Georges Noverre (1727–1810) who set ballets using music by Mozart among others. *La Fille mal gardée* was one of the first ballets to depict everyday figures rather than fantasy (1789, and still in the repertory). Dancing on points and frothy tutu skirts, introduced in the early nineteenth century, contributed to the prominence of the prima ballerina as the central figure and star, a light-stepping ethereal ideal woman, for whom male dancers acted as accessories and weightlifters, The hard reality of life in the corps de ballet has already been referred to and as time went on ballet training became more and more rigorous, but the illusion of the romantic heroine in *La Sylphide* (1832) and *Giselle* (1841), danced by Marie Taglioni and Carlotta Grisi respectively, set a pattern to which audiences responded. These ballets were taken to Moscow and St Petersburg, where classical ballet later developed, largely under the choreographer Marius Petipa (1818–1910). Petipa was associated above all with Tchaikovsky's *Nutcracker, Swan Lake* and *Sleeping Beauty* (1880s and 1890s) which were to inspire thousands of little girls to enter ballet school in the twentieth century, long after ballet itself had moved on to more modern styles. Anna Pavlova (1881–1931) though associated with the classical repertoire, became for a while the equivalent of Sarah Bernhardt for European audiences, and perhaps the most famous of all ballerinas: Muriel Spark and her friend Frances Niven were taken to see Pavlova dance for the last time by the teacher who inspired the character of Miss Jean Brodie.[37]

The avant-garde in dance can be dated to the distinctive style of the Russian impresario Diaghilev's *ballets russes,* combining modern music, advanced design and technically radical movement, which hit Paris and therefore the rest of western Europe between 1909 and 1914. The *ballets russes* were influenced in part by the freestyle dancing of the American-turned-European Isadora Duncan (1878–1927), but also saw the rise of the male ballet star and a strenuously athletic kind of dancing that would become much favoured in the twentieth century, from Vaclav Nijinsky (1890–1950) to Rudolf Nureyev (1938–93). Russia's Bolshoi and Kirov ballets became leading repositories of the European classical ballet for much of the century, while modern dance was more influenced by the USA. Until recently, choreographers were almost invariably male: the rise of the woman choreographer, such as the radical Pina Bausch (b. 1940) in Germany is a modern phenomenon, as too is a reversal of gender stereotyping, exemplified in Britain by the all-male corps of swans in Matthew Bourne's *Swan Lake* (2000), or the success of Stephen Daldry's film about an aspirant young boy dancer, *Billy Elliott* (2000).

Concluding this section, the eighteenth century can be identified as the first real flowering of the woman performer. The performing arts were still often dependent on royal, ecclesiastical or aristocratic patronage, but there were corners within the system for women to participate. Venice provides a striking example, and as the century progressed, performance by women became increasingly acceptable throughout Europe: indeed it became unthinkable to have female roles interpreted by men. But if women were now the centre of attention on stage in many ways, they were hardly ever associated with the creative side of opera, theatre and ballet, while their public appearance was often at the price of their social reputation and security. The change was, moreover, vulnerable to historical amnesia. It has generally been the fate of interpreters of works of art to be forgotten, with a few outstanding exceptions, while the creator – the playwright or composer – lives on in performances of his works. Few women of the age appear to have broken through to musical composition, choreography or writing for the theatre. On the other hand, in the nineteenth century a whole field of creative endeavour apparently opened up to women, with the growth of literacy and print culture: the world of literature.

Reading, translating, writing: the long nineteenth century

The phenomenon of the woman reader and the woman author dates from at least the eighteenth century, and for a minority of women from much earlier. But statistically, women's literacy expanded from the early nineteenth century, providing a new readership for the printed word. In due course, the number of women writers expanded to match. Again, there is a European dimension to be explored: the old republic of letters now had more women citizens, across the entire continent, and they sometimes read very widely:

> I have read since Xmas the D[uke] of Marlboro's *Apology*, Burnet's *History*, ye XIII. *Satire of Juvenal*, Hearne's *Travels into N. America*, Smith on ye figure and complexion of ye human species, Bancroft on dying, some desultory chemistry, *Roderick Random*, *Lazarillo de Tormes*, Leti's *Life of Sixtus V*, various German and French plays, novels and trash, Cook's *Third Voyage*, Wolf's *Ceylon*, part of Ulloa's *Voyage* and some papers in ye Memoirs of ye Exeter Society. Frequent dippings into Bayle, Montaigne, La Fontaine, Ariosto. Read ye 3 first books of Tasso; Ld Orford's works.

Elizabeth Vassall, Lady Webster as she was in 1798, later Lady Holland (1771–1845), was the first to admit that her reading was disorganised, and she was ashamed of herself for reading French novels. Still, this diary entry for 1798, when she was twenty-seven, shows a great breadth of European reading matter. She was of course an educated, privileged and well-travelled Englishwoman.[38] Her French near-contemporary, Manon Phlipon, later Madame Roland (1754–93), the daughter of a skilled artisan, more or less educated herself after a conventionally pious upbringing. Her reading, equally varied, was far more disciplined and serious, concentrating on philosophy. But both were readers in an age when women's literacy in particular was beginning to take off. It was still a matter of class. R. A. Houston reports that in the mid-eighteenth century, only 20 per cent of bourgeois women in Lyon were illiterate, but 50 per cent of the wives of artisans and 80 per cent of women in the lowest classes could still neither read nor write – and these figures were among 'the most favourable in Europe'.[39] Most commentators agree that northern Europe was more advanced in this respect for both sexes, partly because of literacy campaigns, such as the one the Protestant churches organised in Scandinavia – though these concentrated on reading, not writing.

The woman reader was, however, becoming a more familiar figure. Citing a painting by Chardin, *The Amusements of Private Life*, Roger Chartier argues that in the eighteenth century the iconography of reading became female and secular, whereas previously it had been almost entirely male and religious.[40] And, already, by the end of the eighteenth century, 'the female novel reader had become the epitome of the misguided reading public . . . she was depicted as filled with delusive ideas, swayed by false ideas of love and romance, unable to concentrate on serious matters', all of which would lead to no good. Even the austere Manon Phlipon, who wrote at age twenty that she despised novels, was bowled over by Rousseau's *La Nouvelle Héloïse* when she first had it put in her hands, and read it many times; she was fond too of Richardson's *Clarissa Harlowe*.[41] These massive best-sellers were novels of sexual love sacrificed or betrayed. Private life, as in the Chardin painting, was believed to be where women's interests exclusively lay, and women were quickly identified as light fiction readers. But this received view of women's habits was a stereotype allowing for many exceptions. Brewer claims for example that Anna Larpent, a well-to-do but not aristocratic wife and mother, was exactly the sort of 'common reader' whom Dr Johnson, a critic of novel-readers, wished to see. Her reading included history, biography, belles-lettres and philosophy, and she 'constantly' read the Bible.[42]

The improvement in female literacy in the nineteenth century was dramatic, particularly after about 1830–50, partly because of better schooling. As George Sand (pen-name of Aurore Dudevant, 1804–76) put it: 'We learned to read in order to become capable of talking with educated persons, in order even to read the books we had in the cupboard, and kill time in the country and elsewhere'.[43] Although girls' education did not in most cases offer much beyond basic reading, writing, religion and domestic skills, it did increase the readership of print culture. Whereas in 1801, only 28 per cent of Frenchwomen over fourteen were literate, by mid-century 52 per cent of women could read (compared to 68 per cent of men) and by 1901 (after the introduction of universal primary education) 94 per cent of women were literate compared to 96 per cent of men.[44]

If we look beyond basic literacy towards the educated classes, one fact about women's reading ability stands out: awareness of other European languages. In an age when most boys were taught the ancient languages at school and often acquired other languages through travel, it was less common to find girls being taught Greek and Latin, although the famous Madame Dacier (1647–1720) had translated the *Iliad* in 1699. But many women, as well as men, learnt modern languages, especially (depending where one started from) English, French, Italian and German. 'Almost all educated people in Europe read French' in the late eighteenth century, remarks Norman Davies.[45] There was such a thing as 'European culture'; travel around Europe was (in the intervals between wars) more possible. Those who knew several languages could be influential in cultural exchange, particularly between Continental Europe and the English-speaking countries, where most readers were less likely to be bilingual.

If one is looking for a truly European intellectual in the years around 1800, man or woman, Madame de Staël, née Germaine Necker (1766–1817) would be a striking example. She had a head start, being the daughter of two remarkable people: her Swiss father Jacques Necker had been Louis XVI's popular finance minister until his resignation in 1781. His recall and sacking in 1788–9 helped precipitate the storming of the Bastille. Her mother, Suzanne Curchod, was a writer who held a salon in Paris where Germaine was brought up. A brilliant and controversial essayist in her youth, de Staël lived either in Paris or in Coppet on Lake Geneva through most of the Revolution, being a moderate republican, like her lover Benjamin Constant. Banned from Paris by Napoleon, she formed a Coppet circle, which became one of the central points of cultural exchange in Europe. It included Wilhelm von Schlegel (who tutored her children) and the Swiss historian Sismondi. De Staël knew and had visited Goethe, Schiller and other German writers, and herself published two famous novels: *Delphine* (1802) and *Corinne ou l'Italie* (1807). The epigraph to *Delphine* reads: 'A man must know how to brave public opinion, a woman how to submit to it'. Her brave, reckless, but finally tragic heroine proceeds to defy this and asserts the value of individual freedom. This was the book Napoleon did not like. Her literary style was not particularly elegant, but the content of her works was bold and intelligent, and she was ahead of her time in many ways. In all these respects, she was perhaps the Romantic era's equivalent of Simone de Beauvoir. Germaine de Staël did not publish translations as such, although she was multilingual. But she wrote enthusiastically about translation and urged people to make more translations available of modern works rather than ancient. 'Byron and his generation had not read Goethe's *Faust* in German but in the abbreviated French version contained in [de Staël's] best-selling *De l'Allemagne*.'[46]

Educated women with knowledge of the languages and customs of other countries, could contemplate translation. To translate for publication was often to take a first step into the republic of letters, and was already an acknowledged occupation for the aspiring woman of intellect. Giuseppa Eleonora Barbapiccola had translated Descartes' *Principles of Philosophy* into Italian in 1722, and Emilie du Châtelet had published an acclaimed translation of Newton's *Principia* into French in 1759.[47] Of the 'Muses' cited at the start of this chapter, no fewer than six – Carter, Barbauld, Montagu, Griffith, Lennox, More – are known to have translated from French, Latin or Italian, while Kauffmann was a cosmopolitan artist originally from Switzerland, and Linley and Macaulay almost certainly knew languages, though did not publish translations. By the nineteenth century, translating was sometimes seen as a 'woman's occupation', perhaps for the obvious reasons that few other professions were open to a well-educated girl and that it could be done at home, hidden under a piece of needlework, as Jane Austen claimed to hide her writings, or combined with domestic tasks. In her diary for 28 March 1839, Lady Charlotte Guest (1812–95), the translator of the Welsh collection of tales *The Mabinogion* recorded: 'Today I worked hard at the translation of *Peredur*. I had the pleasure of giving birth to my fifth child and third boy today'.[48] It was also sometimes a family occupation. Karoline and Dorothea, the wives of the

Schlegel brothers, were both translators thought to have contributed to the translations of Shakespeare by their husbands.[49]

The overwhelming majority of published translations were, however, by men. But the expansion of the reading public and the community of writers over the century saw the rise of the professional translator, female as well as male, commissioned by a publisher. If we take translation into English as the focus, women were, unsurprisingly, more likely to be translating fiction, history, biography and religious writing from French or German than they were to be tackling classical or oriental texts or philosophical or political works. But their number was rising. A very approximate survey of translations into English, based on the *Nineteenth-Century Short Title Catalogue*, yields the following figures: in 1830, about 70 per cent of translations were attributed to male names, 4 per cent to female names, 16 per cent to translators of unknown sex (initials only), and some 10 per cent were published anonymously. By the end of the century, in 1890, these figures had shifted to respectively 75 per cent, 16 per cent, 2 per cent and 7 per cent (fewer 'unknowns' since fuller names appear in the source).[50] By then too, there were women who were full-time translators with a degree of recognition. Clara Bell (1834–1927) translated at least fifty-six full-length books between 1857 and 1906, mostly from German but also from French, Spanish, Dutch and Italian. English-speaking readers of Turgenev, Tolstoy, Dostoevsky and Chekhov were for many years 'listening principally to the voice of Constance Garnett'.[51] Garnett (1862–1946) read Classics at Newnham, but taught herself Russian, alone at first, later in consultation with native Russian-speakers. Choice of text might reflect a more independent political stance too. Karl Marx's daughter Eleanor Marx Aveling (1855–98) who was already fluent in German, having co-translated her father's work, learnt Norwegian in order to translate Ibsen, and in particular *A Doll's House*, one of the key texts for the New Woman. Even then however, women sometimes concealed their identity. When translating works of dubious morality, such as *any* French novel, a male pseudonym might still be advisable. The chief translator of Balzac's *Comédie Humaine* in the Dent edition (1895–8) was Ellen Marriage (1865–1946), but for some of the more risky volumes she signed her work 'James Waring', according to one of Dent's employees.[52]

Despite, or perhaps because of its availability to women, translation was in terms of the cultural field, a 'minor genre' and one that had a downside. Then, as now, it was seen as a lesser activity within the cultural field, dependent at best, close to hack writing, journalism and Grub Street at worst. In Sweden, for example, 'a considerable number of translators in this period were women' and that went along with the view of the translator as 'humble craftsman, lacking the aura of the romantic genius'.[53] If women could engage in it, that was because certain critical gate-keeping mechanisms, especially as regards posthumous reputations, did not operate here as strongly as in creative writing. Many of the works women translated were popular in their time and therefore commissioned by publishers, but have faded from the view now. A certain number were by women authors, and it is sometimes argued that the translation of works by other women represented a network of mutual support. The novels of the Swedish writer Frederika Bremer (1801–65) for example, of which it was said 'no foreign novels . . . have attained such popularity in this country', were devotedly, though apparently not always accurately, translated by Mary Howitt. Harriet Beecher Stowe's *Uncle Tom's Cabin* (1852) was first translated into French by a collaborative team,

Louise Belloc and Adelaide de Montgolfier, 'a striking example of collaboration and promotion of progressive literature'.[54]

Translation could also been seen as deliberate self-effacement, a substitute for autonomous writing. It enabled a woman to reformulate the words of eminent male writers, to remain at one remove from literary creativity. Sarah Austin (1793–1867), who translated important texts by German and French historians and philosophers, such as Ranke, Niebuhr, Guizot and Cousin, said she felt secure 'behind the welcome defence of inverted commas'.[55] Many of these women never made the jump to writing under their own names. On the other hand, translation could certainly be an apprenticeship in writing, a path often taken by women fiction or essay writers, offering a first chance to write for publication without commitment and sometimes without acknowledgement. George Eliot's early publications were translations of German and Latin theological treatises by Feuerbach and Strauss; she also tackled but did not publish Spinoza's *Ethics*. French writers who also translated include Louise Belloc (1796–1881), Sophie Ulliac-Trémadeure (1794–1862) and Thérèse Bentzon (1840–1907) who introduced Twain, Whitman and Henry James to French readers: all three wrote novels themselves.[56] And it is to the nineteenth-century woman writer that we now turn.

The seventeenth century had already seen the visible emergence of the woman writer. Dominique Godineau points out that twice as many novels by French women authors were published between 1685 and 1702 than between 1660 and 1684, but fiction was precisely an undervalued genre. Women writers were tolerated in France at this time, she suggests, 'if they called themselves amateurs and stuck to lightweight genres'. By the end of the eighteenth century, with a huge rise in production of writings by women, *la femme auteur* even became a bogey. Mme Roland, who wrote a great deal privately in her youth, dreaded the idea of publishing anything: 'I would eat my fingers before becoming a woman author'. She went on to say:

> I saw very early on that a woman who earned this title lost more than she gained. Men don't like her, and her own sex criticises her: if the works are bad they are mocked, if they are good, they are stolen from her [i.e. attributed to someone else.][57]

Mary Brunton, a Scottish novelist who published anonymously, wrote in 1810: 'My dear, I would sooner exhibit as a rope dancer'.[58] Even Mary Wollstonecraft, who considered herself one of a new genus, earning her living by the pen, began with 'translations, reviews, pastiche, works aimed at the expanding market for schoolroom books for growing girls, historical commentary and travellers' observations, eked out by . . . articles to form some sort of livelihood', not always over her own signature.[59] But by then, in the decade of the 1790s, Carla Hesse argues, the quantity of works of all kinds published by women in France was so voluminous as to constitute 'the other Enlightenment', and she insists that they published in every field: 'from political pamphlets, history, philosophy and educational treatises to novels, plays and poetry'.[60]

Fiction, however, was the dominant area in which – then as now – most women published. But so did many men. That did not prevent it being considered a lightweight genre. Jane Austen, in a famous passage in *Northanger Abbey* (1803) felt she needed to come to its defence:

while the abilities of the nine-hundredth abridger of the History of England . . . are eulogized by a thousand pens, there seems to be almost a general wish of decrying the capacity and undervaluing the labour of the nov-elist and of slighting the performances which have only genius, wit and taste to recommend them.[61]

For whatever reason, several early nineteenth-century women novelists let it be thought they were men, publishing either anonymously, with neutral initials, or under a male pseudonym. George Sand claimed it was at first to avoid annoying her mother-in-law, but thereafter, she says, she claimed the name as a hard-won identity. Daniel Stern (Marie Agoult) and George Eliot (Marian Evans) are other obvious examples, and the Brontë sisters chose what they thought were 'ambiguous names': Currer, Ellis and Acton Bell.[62]

Library catalogues indicate that significant numbers of women were publishing books all over Europe, mainly but by no means exclusively, fiction. But only a few of their names – and most of those English or French – are rated alongside the major male writers of the age. Feminist historians have argued that this seriously underestimates their place in the record. Joanna Russ, in an unassuming but sharp little book in 1984, argued that if a woman had written a book, there were critical strategies for eliding this from memory:

> She didn't write it. She wrote it, but she shouldn't have. She wrote it, but look what she wrote about. She wrote it, but 'she' isn't really an artist and 'it' isn't really serious, of the right genre – i.e. really art. She wrote it, but she wrote only one of it. She wrote it, but it's only interesting/included in the canon for one, limited reason. She wrote it, but there are very few of her.[63]

How accurate is this? Social conditions and publication outlets differed widely from one country to another in nineteenth-century Europe; it mattered a good deal which language one wrote in, and whether it was translated. In Italy, the novel itself had not been a dominant genre until the mid-nineteenth century. Writing of Matilde Serao (1856–1927), a prolific and well-known Italian writer, believed to have been consid-ered for the Nobel Prize in 1927, Lucienne Kroha says that there were 'no Jane Austens etc.' to provide role models for the Italian women writers, 'just beginning to emerge as a group' in the later nineteenth century. The only trailblazer was the male writer Alessandro Manzoni, whose *I promessi sposi*, Italy's first modern novel, was written in the 1820s.[64] In Sweden, the key pioneer, somewhat earlier, was Frederika Bremer, well known throughout Europe during her lifetime, especially for her novel *Hertha* (1856), a book credited with changing Swedish law on the status of the single woman. ('She wrote it, but there are very few of her'.)[65]

The fact that women in both north and south Europe found it hard to break through the posthumous fame barrier suggests that we do not necessarily have to accept the idea, originally suggested by Queenie Leavis, that those who did were helped by their Protestantism and the freedom their heroines enjoyed.[66] Olwen Hufton notes that the small populations of some cultures, and the lack of publishers able to take risks, meant that much publishing in Holland and Scandinavia, for example, consisted of transla-tions from English and French, and that this marginalised *all* national writers.[67] But we can, when considering the cultural field as a whole, note that European women were writing in a variety of genres, including journalism, diaries, letters and memoirs, often regarded as less significant and remaining unpublished for some time. Such authors and works did not get much serious attention until the outburst of women's studies of the late twentieth century. ('She wrote it, but it isn't of the right genre'.)

One example of an unpublished text – from the eighteenth century as it happens – is the diary of a middle-class Swedish woman, Christina Hiarne, covering the years 1744–1803. The diary is concerned to a large extent with domestic life. ('She wrote it, but look what she wrote about'.) But it goes beyond these details, both in subject matter and in the shaping of the diary as narrative. The writer made subtle revisions to the text in her later years, turning it from a daily record into a structured 'fair copy', moving towards autobiography, of a more literary kind. After a vivid account of her distress over choice of husband, she tells of her decision to leave it 'in the hands of the mother and God . . . [My mother] became quite friendly and happy and at once made me a present of half a dozen teaspoons'. Jane Austen does not seem so far away.[68]

While in Sweden the point of the early literacy campaign was to enable people to read the Bible and be more informed Christians, as in Hiarne's case, what women read would influence what they wrote. It has been argued for instance that in the German-speaking culture of the early nineteenth century, women were particularly encouraged in the 'new domestic family' to read texts relating to matters of the heart: 'the educated man can and must know and read everything; it is only fitting for educated women to know that which can afford poetic delight'.[69] Schoolgirls were encouraged to read lyric poetry, but while many may have written verse, relatively few women poets were published. Of course what they really did read has to be surmised from a good deal of scattered evidence. And some German women were among the most advanced thinkers of the time. The 'German George Sand', novelist Fanny Lewald (1811–89), was in touch with the avant-garde of the day: 'Heine's pictorial account of his travels and the state of affairs in France . . . spoke a language as yet unknown in Germany . . . we greeted all those early works of the so-called Junges Deutschland with surprise and enthusiastic approval'. In fact Lewald was a slightly later example of a phenomenon perhaps unique in Europe: the presence in the salons of Berlin between about 1790 and 1830 of a group of intelligent and educated women, mostly Jewish, connected to some of the male writers of the day, but also interested in female emancipation. They included Rahel Levin, later Varnhagen, Bettina Brentano von Arnim, Henriette Herz and others. Their undoubted talents did not, however, often find its way into print, except in letters, to be appreciated in later ages.[70]

Spain is an example of a European country where women writers were undoubtedly at work, but where they have appeared either to have published few significant items, or to have been eclipsed and forgotten. These two factors may work together. Janet Perez, surveying the question, has pointed out that there was only limited scholarly interest in any works by women in Spanish until the very late twentieth century. Yet one bibliography in 1880 listed 390 women writing across a range of genres, including fiction; another in 1903 listed 1,100 'women authors'. The first modern survey of nineteenth- and twentieth-century Spanish women's writing was produced only in 1986.[71] As in several other countries, there tends to be a single woman writer who is admitted to the canon: in Spain this was Emila Pardo Bazan (1851–1921), who is credited with having introduced naturalism to Spain. ('She wrote it, but in this case there was only one of her'.)

In the twentieth century, in Spain as all over Europe, many more women writers have achieved reputations, yet even now those who are accorded major status is limited. The Nobel Prize for Literature, awarded annually by the Swedish Academy, is not an infallible guide to literary durability, but it does give some pointers to eminence. Of the ninety-odd Nobel Prizes for Literature since 1901 only nine have gone to women, of whom six are European. While they are all writers of note, their names may not be very familiar to English-speaking readers: Selma Lagerlöf (1909), Grazia Deledda (1926), Sigrid Undset (1928) Nelly Sachs (1966 joint), Wislawa Szymborska (1995), and Elfriede Jelinek (2004), a slightly less mainstream selection than the male line-up. If feminists had been giving out Nobel prizes, they might have suggested a few other Europeans such as Colette, Virginia Woolf, Simone de Beauvoir, Christa Wolf, Anna Akhmatova and Muriel Spark.

It is also possible, as a footnote to this discussion, that they might have suggested some names from authors of children's literature: a massive branch of publication, not necessarily dominated by women, but where women could publish with perhaps even less training outside the home. It is of course regarded as a lesser genre ('look at what she wrote') and rarely included in mainstream histories of literature. Yet most of us who are passionate readers owe our initiation to books by writers for children – both men and women. The female line could stretch from the Comtesse de Ségur, via, among many others, Anna Sewell, Catherine Sinclair, Johanna Spyri, Beatrix Potter, Astrid Lindgren and Tove Jansson to J. K. Rowling. Many twentieth-century European girls – Simone de Beauvoir for one – read American classics such as Louisa M. Alcott's *Little Women* (1869) or Susan Coolidge's *What Katy Did* (1872), critical providers of positive role models for rebellious souls.[72]

In conclusion to this section, the nineteenth century did see a huge expansion of women's membership of the republic of letters. There are some obvious reasons for this. Improved literacy laid the foundation, and once that was acquired, the fact that writing is an activity requiring no formal qualifications, such as university degrees, made it an activity open to people with relatively little formal cultural capital. The mechanisms for being published were broadly speaking in the hands of men, to be sure: periodicals, magazines, newspapers and publishing houses. But anyone, man or woman, could send in a manuscript. And while the female journalist would be a largely twentieth-century phenomenon, already many women published articles, book reviews or serials in European newspapers and periodicals (*Blackwoods*, the *Edinburgh Review* and so on). The existence of a female readership made the century one in which the novel became a leading genre, never thereafter displaced. But women also provided a public for poetry, as well as a few noted poets: Christina Rossetti, Elizabeth Barrett Browning, Marceline Desbordes-Valmore. In particular, an army of girls and women wrote privately some form of journal, diary or memoir, some of which were only later discovered and re-evaluated. One example is the precocious and lively Marie Bashkirtseff (1860–84), a Russian emigrée in France, whose voluminous and frank *Journal* was intended for publication, after her early death, but has still not been fully transcribed. On the other hand, one of the most widely read and translated European texts of the twentieth century was the moving private diary of the Dutch teenager Anne Frank, not originally intended for publication at all.

The long twentieth century: visual arts, photography and cinema

In the twentieth century, particularly in its last quarter, the circumstances of most European women changed, more radically perhaps than at any earlier time. In education, employment, politics and everyday life, many of the taboos and restrictions of earlier times were dispensed with. As the incoming tide floats all boats, so women have also become more present and visible in virtually all the arts, including those already discussed. There are, however, some persuasive arguments for taking a close look at what I am loosely describing as 'the visual arts': fine art, photography and cinema. Why these three? Partly because they represent new departures. In the 1890s, professional fine art training became available to women more or less on the same terms as men, and their numbers expanded swiftly. Photography was a new art, beginning in the 1840s; but after 1918, when even newer technology made it a far less cumbersome activity, it was practised by almost as many women as men. Cinema too was new, starting in France in 1895, and as a collective endeavour, it involved women alongside men at many levels.

The second reason is that the visual arts were remarkably transnational within Europe for much of the period. At the same time, paradoxically, they centred on Paris. Walter Benjamin called Paris 'the capital of the nineteenth century'.[73] But there is in some ways a better case to be made for Paris as an international centre for the fine arts, photography and cinema in the first half of the twentieth century. During the so-called *belle époque*, and again during the inter-war years, it was to Paris that visitors, tourists, refugees and exiles turned, from almost every corner of the globe, if they were concerned with the arts. There were other cities with a strong artistic community and influential schools of thought: Glasgow in the 1890s, fin-de-siècle Vienna, Turin in the 1900s, Edwardian London, Berlin during the Weimar Republic. But none of these attracted quite such a varied and determined international artistic community, much more foreign than it was French. And this community was, significantly, more open to women than any we have so far noted.

As Linda Nochlin long ago argued, the question 'Why have there been no great women artists?' cannot be answered without a paradigm shift from ideas about 'individual genius' to matters of professional practice.[74] If we look across our whole period, 1700 to the present and across all of Europe, the number of really well-known women painters is still not great. The Frenchwoman Elisabeth Vigée-Lebrun (1755–1842) and the cosmopolitan Swiss Angelika Kauffmann (1740–1807) have received much attention lately, though neither is exactly a household name. Berthe Morisot (1841–95) was the only French woman painter to exhibit alongside the impressionists. For much of European history, women who became professional painters or sculptors (and there are more of them than has always been recognised) were almost always the daughters of artists, with access both to materials and to parental tuition. But by the late 1890s, art education was more accessible to young women or girl school leavers than it had been. The progressive Slade School in London admitted women on the same terms as men in 1871; the Glasgow School of Art, open to women since the 1850s, produced after 1885, under its new director Fra Newbery, a whole generation of decorative artists and painters who have retrospectively been called the 'Glasgow Girls'.[75] The Paris École des Beaux-Arts did not admit women until 1897 and then only after a long struggle.

Nevertheless in the last two decades of the century it had become possible to obtain a formal training outside the École. To thousands of itinerant art students, men and women, the French capital offered, apart from the traditional advantage of the collections in the Louvre, a uniquely dense concentration of artists, teachers and studios. The long-established annual exhibitions known as the salons offered a pathway to recognition. Tuition could be bought in several teaching 'academies' such as Julian's or Colarossi's or in individual artists' studios.[76]

The advent of women students, however, disrupted what had been a gender balance of a particular kind. Until then the only women in the studios had been artists' models. Feminist scholarship has set out recently to discover more about the models whose faces are in familiar French paintings of the period; we do know that most of them were young and of modest, often immigrant origin; many were Italian. In the traditional *vie de Bohème*, the young women who posed clad or unclad were assumed to be sexually available – the 'charming if errant Mimi Pinsons, Marcelles, Suzannes, Yvettes and Maries of Quartier life' as one English guide put it in 1902.[77] Most French bourgeois families would not dream of sending their daughters to train in a painter's studio. The gifted sculptor Camille Claudel (1864–1943) who persuaded her family to let her come to Paris was an exception. Even independent gallery-visiting was off limits for the well brought up. Marie Bashkirtseff wrote in her diary for 2 January 1879:

> What I long for is the freedom to go about alone, of coming and going, of sitting on the seats in the Tuileries . . . In order to go to the Louvre, I must wait for my carriage, my lady companion or my family . . . a woman who rambles alone commits an imprudence.[78]

What was more, the dominant subjects of easel painting and academic sculpture were dictated by a gaze that was relentlessly male and mostly heterosexual. The female nude was everywhere, whether as allegory, symbol of beauty or sexual object. Exaggerating only slightly, one could say that the dominant academic mode of the history painting was unequivocally patriarchal in both subject and treatment. But those artists who broke with the dominant tradition also did so in ways not easily available to women: the impressionists painted out of doors, alone, or took their sketchbooks or easels into cafés, bars and night clubs. As Griselda Pollock has observed of modernity in art, it would have been difficult if not impossible for a woman to paint Manet's *The Bar at the Folies-Bergère*, let alone Toulouse-Lautrec's series of studies in a Parisian brothel.[79] Women were everywhere all right, but as subjects for the visual arts.

Another major stumbling block was the life class. Battles were waged over the admission of women to life classes, and whether the models should be draped or not, if they did attend. Nor did women escape the massive condescension of the art world: they were 'tidier and more genteel than men'.[80] In order to put them off even further, and to restrict entry to all but the well-to-do, most academies and studios charged women double the rate for men. For all that, women did begin to frequent art schools. To take one cosmopolitan example, the American painter James McNeill Whistler set up a school called the Académie Carmen, run by one of his former models, the Corsican Carmen Rossi in 1898. It was advertised as 'Anglo-American' and many of the enrolments were from Britain or the USA, but it also drew in Russian and German students. Anna Ostroumova-Lebedeva, a Russian who had already spent seven years at the St Petersburg Academy, has left a first-hand record of her shock on being told by Whistler that she 'knew nothing'. In general Whistler found most women students, who unlike Lebedeva had received very little formal training, took better to his very directive treatment. He believed in starting from basics; many of his male students were impatient to start exhibiting at the salons straight away and consequently came into conflict with the 'master'. By the third year of the academy, which did indeed provide thorough, if idiosyncratic training, Whistler would accept enrolments in the women's class only.[81] The sculptors Rodin and Bourdelle also held classes in which women and men were taught separately, the former being the more numerous.

Of the first generation of women in the fine arts, very few became well known, although rediscovery of them is bringing more light to bear on them. They often shared certain characteristics. Generally of middle-class origin, neither very rich nor very poor, but well educated, able to speak French for instance, which helped their case for going to Paris, they had probably shown initial talent and faced family disapproval. But more often than not, their training had been somewhat haphazard. Once in Paris, they encountered a particularly French trait, the dependence on the *maître à penser*, the patron tutor, whose dictates and influence might affect one's career. Some, like their male contemporaries, found this constraining. The Glasgow artist Bessie McNicol found the teaching at Colarossi's 'repressed rather than encouraged her'.[82] Others, most of whose energy had gone into struggling for admission to art schools in the first place, remained in the academic mode and succeeded in mastering sufficient technique to do well in that style, only to find that it was being replaced by modernism. They might thrive as professionals, but became also-rans in art history. Such was the case of the Scottish sculptor Kathleen Bruce (1878–1947) for example: enterprising, competent and well connected, she had a successful career doing commissions in traditional form (busts, statues) well into the twentieth century. Some women did indeed fall under the spell of certain avant-garde masters such as Rodin and Whistler, but paradoxically the more unconventional the master, the harder it was for a less confident pupil to liberate her- or himself. Relatively few women of this pioneering generation made a breakthrough into modernism, which may explain why so few of them are valued today. Exceptions who made the jump into independent modernism include Käthe Kollwitz (1867–1945), Sonia Terk Delaunay (1885–1979) and sculptor Barbara Hepworth (1903–75). And of course the usual 'enemies of promise' were there, all the more so for women, who sometimes paid a high price professionally for falling in love with another artist. As one British women writer put it, 'when a male artist marries, he acquires a housekeeper, a model, a brush-washer and perhaps a publicity agent. When a woman artist marries, with rare exceptions she perishes as an artist, gradually and perhaps painlessly.'[83]

They had, however, overcome some taboos, and by so doing had enabled it to be taken for granted that women could train in the arts. Many of the early generation were diverted into what are sometimes regarded as the minor arts of illustration, embroidery, pottery, jewellery and enamelling, crafts that could be practised domestically. A proper estimate of the artistic field in the early twentieth century would surely give greater recognition to smaller scale work and would certainly provide more context against which to judge later reputations. In the late twentieth century – and this was common to virtually all the arts – it appears to be the case that women faced far fewer obstacles in the way of discrimination and dismissive attitudes in the visual arts, at least if the lists of prize-winners, grant holders and commissions are anything to go by. Conceptual art, video and public art have all been areas in which both men and women appear to compete on equal terms. Only very recently has there been anything like enough evidence to explore whether there are differences between men and women's approaches to the fine arts when there is a reasonably level playing field. The furore over the British artist Tracey Emin's *My Bed* (shortlisted Turner Prize, 1999) showed that it could be possible – though exceptional and controversial – to combine the extreme avant-garde with the thoroughly intimate. Another example is the haunting fabric sculpture to which Louise Bourgeois (b. 1911 in France, working in the USA) turned very late in life – having been brought up in a tapestry workshop.[84]

Photography, unlike fine art, did not require prolonged training. Following on from the daguerreotype, it was invented in the 1830s, simultaneously in Britain and France, by Nicéphore Niepce and William Henry Fox Talbot. There is a long history of the pioneer days, a time of cumbersome and experimental technology, in which very few women figured; those who did generally had independent incomes and plenty of leisure. They included two outstanding British pioneers Julia Margaret Cameron (1815–79) and Clementina Lady Hawarden (1822–65), whose beautiful stylised portraits have received much retrospective attention as art works. But during photography's midsummer, the great age of black and white photography in the first half of the twentieth century, there was a striking growth in the number of serious photographers of both sexes, and once more the focus was Paris, although many of the best-known photographers of these years were not French, but refugees or emigrants from Germany and eastern Europe. 'It was not enough to be young, you had to be Hungarian', as Robert Capa famously put it.

Why so many and why in Paris? There are some straightforward explanations for the rise of the photographer. The first is technical. Moving on from the static and expensive apparatus of the studio, which few could afford to install, photography benefited from a sequence of inventions that made it more accessible: from the substitution of celluloid for glass (1880s), to the invention of the Kodak camera 'which relieved the individual button-pusher of the need to determine focus and exposure time' (1888) and the commercial processing of the film.[85] After the First World War, photography could go out onto the street, once the new lightweight handheld camera had been invented in Germany. Gisèle Freund's father bought her 'a Leica, which had only been in existence for four or five years. You could put it in your pocket and take 36 photos one after another – marvellous!'[86] Almost overnight, photography came within reach of anyone prepared to take it up and was no longer confined to professional studios.

The second reason was political: many well-educated refugees, men and women, left the oppressive regime of Austro-Hungary before 1914, the Horthy regime in Hungary in the 1920s, and in the case of many Jews, the Nazi regime in Germany in the 1930s. They might or might not have been involved in politics. Germaine Krull for example, was involved with the Spartakists in 1919 but escaped. Gisèle Freund narrowly avoided arrest as a student activist. Other emigrants from eastern Europe included men who were later famous photographers, such as André Kertesz and Brassai (Gyula Halasz). Not all of them went to Paris. Those who moved to Britain included Edith Suschitzky (1908–1978, later Edith Tudor Hart) who came from Vienna, and Gerti Deutsch (1908–79) who married Tom Hopkinson of *Picture Post*, a major photo-magazine. Less well-known today, but a pioneer of avant-garde photography was Ellen

Auerbach (1906–2004), who with Grete Stern set up the *studio ringl + pit* in Berlin, before being forced to leave for Palestine, London and the USA.[87]

But a large number of exiles did settle in the French capital – at a time when France's early lead in photography was just a memory. Few of them had intended to become full-time photographers, and it offered an immediate trade. Several of the new arrivals had an artistic background, such as Ergy Landau, born in 1896 in Budapest, who had trained at the Bauhaus. Naomi Rosenblum argues that within this context, women were freed from the usual ties of home, while they were also obliged to earn a living, twin pressures which created the unusual circumstance of women 'rivalling men' as one journalist reported in 1936.[88] She suggests too that exiled women supported and helped each other in the competitive world of Paris photography. The spectacular rise of photojournalism enabled them to supplement freelance work. A further reason was the air of freedom in Paris, where there appeared to be a surprising degree of personal and sexual liberty: women smoked in public, homosexuality was tolerated, and the *café-terrasse* was a place where both sexes could meet freely. This was in fact a Parisian, not a French state of affairs: what went in Paris would not have been tolerated in say, Limoges. Ilse Bing, born in Frankfurt in 1899, wrote: 'The minute I set foot in Paris, I knew I was in the atmosphere that suited me . . . I could smell art in the very air of Paris and felt ready to blossom.'[89]

All of these factors: technical facility, low cost, easily acquired expertise, free and easy moral atmosphere, which favoured the exile, also favoured women. Some of them, such as Germaine Krull, born in Vilda, Poland in 1897, had already trained in photography in Munich. Escaping to Paris however, Krull was able to publish a series of nude studies (*Études du nu*, 1930) of a freer style than would have been possible in Germany, although she is probably better known for her abstract visions of the Eiffel tower, *Metal* (1927). Man Ray modestly remarked of her that 'alongside himself she was the greatest photographer of the age'.[90] Certainly French magazines published more nudes, but it is less clear that they would have reacted differently from the British magazine *Picture Post*, which left out several images from Grace Robertson's reportage 'Birth of a baby' as being too explicit about the pain of childbirth.[91] Taken as a corpus covering an immense variety of genres (portraiture, industrial photography, street scenes, photomontage, surrealism, fashion, abstraction, advertising, animal studies, etc.) the work of the women photographers active in Europe in the 1930s easily matches that of their male colleagues, in both quality and quantity. In fact their images are often indistinguishable. Yet they are not all household names in the way that some of the men of the period are (Capa, Cartier-Bresson, Kertesz). A few, who had post-war careers, such as Gisèle Freund, born in Schoenberg in 1908, did indeed make the break-through. Many lost their equipment and negatives through having to flee during the Second World War. Some, such as Claude Cahun (Lucie Schwob, b. Nantes in 1891) were eccentric and destroyed their work. Some gave up photography, emigrated to new countries and changed their lives.

One factor which appears to have been fairly influential was the dominance after the war of the photographic agency Magnum, which was not noticeably woman-friendly. The case of Maria Eisner (1909–91) is instructive. Arriving in Paris as a refugee from Nazi Germany, she was not a photographer herself, but an enabler. She set up the democratically run agency Alliance-Photo, providing work for a group of like-minded men and women, whose images dominated the picture magazines of the 1930s, among them Robert Capa (Endre Friedmann), his then fiancée Gerda Taro and his Polish friend Chim (David Czymin), and also Denise Bellon, Emeric Feher, Juliette Laroche, René Zuber and Pierre Boucher. This group was the kernel behind the Magnum agency, which was launched in Paris after the war, in her own flat, with Eisner as a founding member and secretary. When she took on the New York office on her marriage, she fell foul of Capa who would not tolerate her remaining in the agency once she had a child. She has effectively been written out of Magnum's official history, as Gisèle Freund, initially the only woman photographer, also claimed to have been, although several women later succeeded in joining Magnum, Eve Arnold and Austrian-born Inge Morath for instance.[92] Feminist historians have maintained that the work of women photographers in general has been greatly underestimated until recently. Their work was for various reasons less accessible physically (discarded, hidden away, unpublished), and in any case, collectors were more interested in men, and in action or wartime shots. Florence Henri (1893–1982), despite being 'the most prominent photographer to apply the style of late Cubism to the camera image, . . . was ignored for decades'.[93] Photography is a case, however, where resurrection needs to make no apologies. It is a rare field where the quality of European women's work is, at least today, receiving plenty of deserved attention. Photography's 'European age', though, has probably been and gone, as the focus in modern camera work today is far more global and international, with a degree of American predominance.

The same can of course be said of the cinema. Early European cinema, from its beginnings in France in the 1890s, was a collaborative endeavour, embarked upon by small groups of people who gradually took on bigger and bigger projects. This was the 'seventh art', with no formal apprenticeships or gatekeepers at first. Rather like photography, practitioners of early cinema learnt on the job. Women might or might not be involved, but there were few or no institutional mechanisms to keep them out. A recurring figure in feminist film history is Alice Guy (c.1873–1968), originally Léon Gaumont's secretary, who wrote and directed hundreds of short films for Gaumont in France in the days before the First World War. Later famous directors, such as Louis Feuillade, were once her assistants. She had a second career in America too, but her pioneering role was only belatedly recognised. It was possible for a woman to have such a trajectory in the informal circumstances of early cinema.[94] But even in the 1920s, it was turning into a more hierarchical industry, with large-scale financing, production and distribution, as it provided mass entertainment in the middle years of the twentieth century. In the henceforward complex but pyramidal structure of film companies, women were present increasingly only in certain sectors.

At the bottom of the pyramid, women were routinely employed as semi-skilled workers in the processing of film, developing, printing and hand-colouring. Higher up, technicians, cameramen and crews were overwhelmingly male, and the financing, producing and distribution of films was virtually entirely in male hands. On the creative side of film, women were of course highly visible as actresses, later known as film stars. There were also a minority of women editors, scriptwriters, musical-score writers and costume designers. On the other hand there have been very few women film directors, though their numbers have certainly increased since the 1970s.

The response of the historian to this can take two directions: either to list and validate those women directors who have made it, or to consider why film historiography is the way it is, considering that the rise of cinema coincided with changes in the status of women. The first approach would indicate that there is in fact no clear pattern about where, when and how European women have made films, although latterly subsidies and television have proved useful ways of crashing through the barriers. It is true that in the early days the small scale of operations meant that gate-keeping mechanisms were minimal. This was the age of Germaine Dulac (1882–1942), Marie Epstein (1899–1992) and Leontine Sagan (1899–1974); in the field of documentary, the German film-maker Leni Riefenstahl (1902–2003) was perhaps the best known. In mid-century, the number of women film-makers declined, in a pattern common to other aspects of European culture of the 1940s and 1950s, but has to some extent taken off since then. Some women have been part of a creative partnership: Marguerite Duras with Alain Resnais; Muriel and Sidney Box in Britain; Margarethe von Trotta (b. 1942) with Volker Schlöndorff. Von Trotta's solo career illustrates another phenomenon. It has been argued that West Germany's production subsidy system in the 1970s 'enabled women directors to work in numbers unparalleled in other nations'[95] although France too has a system of subsidies that has helped indigenous production stand up to foreign imports. There Agnès Varda (b. 1928) has carved out a long and distinctive career from an explicitly feminist stance, while younger directors such as Diane Kurys, Coline Serreau, Claire Denis and Catherine Breillat have reached a wide audience. From the 1980s in particular, a number of women directors have worked in television, which has provided a different career path, sometimes leading to cinema debuts, elsewhere consolidating work in a range of television genres, especially in Britain, but also, surprisingly in Spain. Finally, deliberately providing outlets for women's films, as the annual Créteil festival does in France, has encouraged avant-garde feminist film-making, generally a minority spectacle.[96]

The second approach, looking critically at film history, would draw on some elements noted above to argue that the unremitting concentration on the film director has marginalised study of the production of films as a collaborative process, in which creativity may be shared among several participants: actors, editors, designers, musicians and so on. In this respect, the new directions being taken by some film historians are quite promising for women's history. For example, the study of stars – that is actors – as of at least equivalence to the director and producer; the study of studios and their histories; the sociological study of films and of their audiences. In certain European countries, in particular in France, women have had creative input into films as editors, and we might consider the editing function within film-making as a case study of women's participation at a more creative level.[97]

Editing is the ordering of shots and sequences which gives the film its structure, pace and rhythm. In the age of classical cinema, this could take any form on a continuum ranging from 'Hollywood continuity' in which the viewer does not notice the editing, and to more rapid and jolting cutting known as 'montage' which was favoured by certain European directors such as Abel Gance and Sergei Eisenstein. In Britain, Italy and the USA, editing was in fact more likely to be done by a man, but in France, perhaps surprisingly, some of the great films of the black and white era, up to and including the New Wave, were edited by women. This might be because of a partnership between director and editor. His companion Marguerite Houllé-Renoir edited most of Jean Renoir's French films, and indeed she had to take many decisions in his absence over two of his masterpieces, *Partie de campagne* (1936) and *La Règle du Jeu* (1939). In other cases the partnership might be professional but was often long term over several films, such as Marguerite Beaugé with Abel Gance. The contribution of the editor is a very different one from that of shooting. Agnès Guillemot, who edited many New Wave films, has argued that editing requires the eye of someone who has not seen the shooting. Marie Epstein, who acted as editor for her brother Jean, and later went on to make films with Jean-Benoit Lévy, being one of the rare women film directors, has said, 'Editing has to be felt. You are on your own and you sense the film coming together. It is like beating time in music . . . You see the rhythms of the sequences emerging'.[98] Because it is an unobtrusive function, and because it has some affinities with sewing or repairing, in the words of Colin Crisp 'the editor's job could be assimilated to that of the little woman'.[99] For this reason, Dai Vaughan, in his biography of a male film editor, Stewart McAllister, uses strategies instantly recognisable from women's history, since he seeks to rescue a marginalised figure from obscurity.[100]

Vaughan, like many feminists, has made the point that *auteur* theory in cinema has a lot to answer for. This is ironic, since *auteur* theory was originally devised in France to provide a countervailing force to the Hollywood studio system, in which editors were directly hired by producers in order to control films, at the expense of the director. *Auteur* theory by contrast elevated the director into the leading position as the chief creative artist, the author, of a film. It argued that a film carries the director's inspiration and, as it were, handwriting. Retrospectively, *auteur* theory has dominated film history, especially in Europe. When leading historians such as Kristin Thompson and David Bordwell refer to 'giants' to illustrate the 1940s and 1950s, they list Buñuel, Bergman, Kurosawa, Fellini, Antonioni, Bresson, Tati and Satyajit Ray (all but two of them Europeans). Histories of the 1960s and 1970s will list directors of the French New Wave: Godard, Truffaut and Resnais; 'new German cinema' is Fassbinder, Herzog, Wenders, and so on.[101]

There are obvious reasons why *auteur* theory had a meteoric rise and still rules most film criticism. But it has posed problems for feminists, who have suggested that it reproduces the 'male angst about the romantic hero faced with a post-industrial world and the disturbance of gender relations threatened by the women's movement'.[102] Geneviève Sellier has argued that male subjectivity and authenticity is highly valued in the modernist ethic associated with the French New Wave, with women seen in terms of contingency, nature and reproduction. In the whole French New Wave, only two films articulate a female character's focal consciousness, and in both a woman filmmaker was concerned: *Hiroshima mon amour*, made by Alain Resnais with Marguerite Duras, and *Cléo de 5 à 7*, by Agnès Varda.[103] Much feminist film criticism has indeed been concerned with analysis of the 'male gaze', a term launched by Laura Mulvey to indicate that in Hollywood cinema (but in a great deal of European cinema too) the female figure on screen is set up as an object 'to be looked at', assuming a male spectator (although many if not most cinema audience members are female).[104] Greta Garbo, Ingrid Bergman, Brigitte Bardot and Sophia Loren are European examples of the female star who may or may not be a good actress, but who quickly became a screen icon. *A contrario*, whereas countless police and thriller films incorporate the murder of a woman, the film *A Question of Silence*, made by the Dutch woman director Marleen Gorris with the deliberate aim of speaking to a female spectator, and in which three women randomly murder a man, caused remarkable controversy.[105]

Finally, if we view the cultural field as a whole, it is clear enough that cinema has depended on female audiences at different times and for different reasons: 'surveys from London to Vienna showed going to the movies to be women's preferred leisure activity outside the home'; they formed two-thirds of the British audience.[106] Parallels could be drawn between this phenomenon and the women who 'read novels' in the past. But here too, feminist and other kinds of theory about spectatorship have reconstructed the cultural field surrounding the production of films to suggest new ways of analysing the viewer's appreciation of the product. Previously minor genres, such as melodrama and *film noir*, have been 're-examined for signs of disruption'. Even the 'women's picture', a genre particularly popular in the 1940s, in which a female protagonist has been seen in conflict and potential transgression, usually resolved in a conventional way by death or marriage, has been retrieved by feminist criticism which has stressed that it can encourage analysis of the patriarchal order.[107] There are imaginative approaches to film history, in other words, that can illuminate corners of the cultural field previously neglected. Nevertheless, what this tends to reveal is that women are still in a minority within film-making, that the power relations of cinema are not encouraging to them, and that their contribution as actors, editors and assistants is still undervalued. A glance at the credits from virtually any film, European or not, will show that not only the chief actors, but the bit parts, extras, editors, producers, technicians and so on are very largely men. In this respect television, at least in Britain, has been a great deal more women-friendly than cinema – a question that takes us even closer to popular culture.

Conclusions

The historiography of high culture has not on the whole been generous towards women. For whatever reason, women artists have had to wait a long time before being the subject of discussion and research. They are not of course the only ones: fashions change in the arts. The eleventh edition of the *Encyclopaedia Britannica* for example (1911) has only a brief entry on Monteverdi and none at all on Vivaldi, today one of the most performed and written about of Italian composers. And it was only after the renewed interest in Vivaldi that scholarly (and popular) attention was accorded to the girl singers of the *ospedali*. When one looks for similar examples of women, several readily come to mind: Aphra Behn, the English playwright whose name was comparatively unknown to most students of literature, but who is much studied today, or the Welsh painter Gwen John, who in her lifetime was largely eclipsed by her brother Augustus, but who is now possibly more famous than he is. The picture has been transformed largely by Anglo-American scholarship, itself resulting from the impetus of the post-1970 women's movement, particularly strong in English-speaking countries, where the academic environment was – crucially – sympathetic. On the European continent, the situation was less favourable: there are relatively fewer attempts to isolate women as a particular group of artists needing recognition. Indeed it sometimes seems as if there is, dare I say, a degree of overkill in British, North American and other English-speaking universities, while basic scholarship is still lacking across the Channel.

At the end of this very partial survey, what conclusions can be drawn? One relates to the chronology of the cultural field. By looking at the particular areas we have chosen here, we have sketched a possible chronology, showing that the dynamics of the field can change over time, allowing new entrants in or, alternatively, repelling them.

Women as performers were virtually dependent on the relaxing of certain rules in the late seventeenth and early eighteenth century, such as the propriety of appearing in public, which in turn reflected changes in the kind of spectacle that courts and popular audiences wanted or would countenance. Actresses, dancers and singers – working for payment, working at night, dressing up as other people, frequenting other performers in unchaperoned situations – were moving out of a woman's normal life cycle and often paid the price by being considered deviant and immoral. If they lived up to the reputation, that is hardly to be wondered at. Yet they were playing an essential part in the cultural field, which would have been completely impoverished without them. Where would Mozart's operas have been without the Susannas and the Fiordiligis or the Queens of the Night – those parts that he wrote for virtuoso high sopranos, among the first women to receive some kind of professional voice-training such as had been available to choirboys for centuries? Eighteenth- and nineteenth-century audiences expected to thrill to the emotions of real women in tragedies. The change once accomplished was not reversed. And by the late twentieth century, women performers, on stage, screen and in music, had parallel professional trajectories to those of men, and were being accorded the same attention; if there continued to be speculation about their private lives, then this was common to both sexes.

In literature, the key chronological variable was obviously literacy. Once they could read, women could expand their minds, though the mental furniture available to do that was not equal across the whole period. The history of women's knowledge of the classics, for example, has been a very short one. A window of opportunity for learning Latin and Greek opened with the girls' secondary schools founded in Europe from the late nineteenth century, only to close again as classical studies have fallen almost universally out of the curriculum in the present day. In terms of translating from modern languages and writing in their own however, women moved rather quickly into quite a prominent position in the literary field, at least in terms of numbers, during the nineteenth century. Overwhelmingly though, in Europe and elsewhere, women have published in one genre: fiction – and still do. For every ten or so women novelists, how many poets, playwrights or essayists are there? There are social and structural reasons at work here: writing for the theatre, television or the cinema, for example, is specialised work, dependent upon networks of relations and acquiring professional skills; philosophy requires an advanced education. The novel, in theory, requires no such apprenticeship, and poetry has been available to all who read and study poetry for themselves, although the number of well-known women poets is not great. In the nineteenth century, the time when women's writing really began to take off, fiction and 'life writing' – autobiography, memoirs, diaries and letters – were the genres most likely to be chosen by a fledgling author. Much of this writing was not originally intended for publication. The persistence of the 'domestic model' of writing, if it can be called that, is not simple however. It has been argued, quite convincingly in my view, that 'when the term "everyday life" was promoted to be worthy of art, women too could make their creative contribution'.[108] But what after all is *Anna Karenina* if not a story of everyday life? In the twenty-first century, the novel is still, for both sexes, the dominant genre and the one most read; it is not peculiar to women authors. But again, a different historiography is emerging which looks at the entire field, rather than at the traditional canon: in this process, different genres become more visible. The Scottish writer Jane Welsh Carlyle (1801–66) used to be regarded as the helpmeet and correspondent of her famous husband Thomas; she is now enshrined as 'one of the best letter-writers in the English language'.[109]

Finally, in our differential chronology come the visual arts. Once more the gate-keeping and training possibilities have dictated the chronology. In a traditional sphere such as the fine arts, the apprenticeship to be served depended on institutions which might be informal (the artist's studio) or formal (the academy, the art school) but into which women were intruders and minor players until pressure of numbers in the nineteenth century forced open the door. The presence of large numbers of women has increased the place taken in the visual arts by crafts and 'minor genres'. Some reassessment of this minority status has already begun, though the field remains fairly polarised round certain 'heroic' forms: the easel painting, the large mural, the monument, the building. However, in the very recent period women have achieved international reputations in these genres too, and the changing nature of the visual arts to include conceptual art and video has seen more women's names emerge. Even a small European country such as Scotland has at least three internationally recognised painters in Joan Eardley (1921–63), Anne Redpath (1895–1965) and Elizabeth Blackadder, (b. 1931). Italian woman architect Gae Aulenti designed the Musée d'Orsay in Paris. In photography, it is probably fair to say that the playing field has been more level than in many other arts, at least since the 1920s, perhaps because of its informal development. In the cinema however, despite some undeniable breakthroughs, women are still far more likely to be actors on screen than directors. In this way, the cinema mirrors the history of the theatre. In a collective enterprise calling for authority over a team, the relative absence of women directors (there are of course recent exceptions as noted, while in the theatre prominent directors include Ariane Mnouchkine, Ruth Berghaus and Deborah Warner) can be related to other types of glass ceiling. The case of cinema suggests that the chronology of women's entrance into the arts is not linear and uniform but has varied with the context. It also usefully reminds us that the twentieth century, while undoubtedly bringing more freedom for women, has also seen Europe increasingly overshadowed by America in Western culture. That influence is far too complex to be discussed here, but is a hidden presence within much cultural activity, sometimes favouring women's empowerment, sometimes, as in cinema, working the other way.

A group enterprise such as film-making is perhaps paralleled by the phenomenon of the support group. Within this chapter, the most frequent examples have been of individual women. Many innovative male artists – the French impressionists, say – have had to struggle against derision from the establishment. But they have often been able to draw support from others, and thereafter their group identity makes them even more visible: the cubists, the surrealists, the Angry Young Men and the post-1945 Italian neo-realist cinema directors are well-known twentieth-century examples, where the group has provided a special relationship to fame, even if individual artists are very different (or even reject the label). In every period, in fact, the European cultural field has been studded with knots of power made up by certain groups or generations of men. For women, such groups, until feminism provided a theoretical underpinning, were only rarely possible. The Venetian *ospedale* with which we started this survey was of course an unusual exception. As a musical institution, it was governed and shaped by men, but it did permit the emergence of talented women. Another possible case was that of the Berlin salons in the time of Rahel Varnhagen. Even more striking (though not described here in detail) was the society formed by a number of mainly expatriate women in Paris in the early twentieth century, where lesbian relationships provided a particular kind of support for women such as Natalie Barney and Gertrude Stein, as thoroughly documented by Shari Benstock.[110] There are also examples of women who have been integrated into a male group and have derived benefit from it: Berthe Morisot for instance, within the impressionists. And in some cases, such as the photographers in inter-war Paris, there was a mixed support group. But the group of women artists has rarely been a phenomenon in Europe; indeed there has been some reluctance to be labelled a 'woman artist' at all. This is perfectly understandable, in the current state of the arts, yet at the same time it does seem to be acquiescing in the dismissive male discourse.

Following on from that, a final word or two to justify this somewhat tentative attempt to historicise the relation between women and the arts in Europe. Two potential objections to the enterprise, cutting slightly across each other, could be made. First, that it is inherently elitist, since the arts have only ever been enjoyed by a privileged minority; and, second, that feminist attempts to restructure the canon, revaluing forgotten women writers or artists, are putting politics before quality, distorting the history of the arts. It cannot be gainsaid that for most people in Europe, throughout most of its history, 'high art' has been something fairly remote, accessible only to minorities. At the same time, at every level in society, women have generally been less likely than men, as Tammy Proctor points out in another context, to have the leisure time, or the cultural capital *seriously* to engage in or enjoy the arts, whether high or 'low' (pp. 299–340). 'Talking of Michelangelo' or learning a few tunes on the piano is no substitute for being taken seriously. That does not make it an elitist activity to enquire into the past and to speculate about the future. What survives, and what most people know of previous ages and civilisations, is their art. And the continuum between 'high art' and 'popular art' is a long one, which an attention to gender can help illuminate by suggesting that high status has usually been accorded to the more 'heroic' kinds of product (rather than say, embroidery, illustration or letter-writing). As historians, we need to be aware of the way the cultural field has been constructed and maintained and to try to illuminate its dark areas. As for quality, that is often a matter of taste and is certainly a disputatious area. But a practical approach is to try to fill in the gaps in a history that has for a long time neglected to analyse the gender of the arts. That need not mean making inflated and unsubstantiated claims for women just *because* they were women, but it does mean being willing to re-examine the canon and trying to see how women were placed within the cultural field of their time, as performers, creators or consumers of the arts.

Guide to further reading

A number of fairly specialised works are cited in the notes, to which reference should be made. What follows is a brief list of accessible works in English, including some landmark feminist texts, general works and examples of recent reference works in which an effort has been made to include more information about women. Most of the titles cited have further references, and any short selection in this area is perforce a bit arbitrary.

General

Bermingham, Ann and John Brewer, eds, *The Consumption of Culture 1600–1800: Image, Object, Text*. London, Routledge, 1995. Collection of essays, mostly on Britain.

Brewer, John, *The Pleasures of the Imagination*. London: HarperCollins, 1998. On eighteenth-century England only, but full of suggestive ideas that can be applied more widely.

Duby, Georges and Michelle Perrot, eds, *A History of Women in the West*, vols III, IV and V, translated by Arthur Goldhammer. Cambridge, Mass: Belknap Press of the Harvard University Press, 1993. A comprehensive history, though France figures more prominently than other countries. The chapters on the arts by Anne Higonnet and Marcelle Marini are incisive, suggestive and well illustrated.

Robertson, Priscilla, *An Experience of Women: Pattern and Change in Nineteenth-Century Europe*. Philadelphia, Pa.: Temple University Press, 1982. Very anecdotal but wide-ranging across Europe; contains much information on individuals based on letters, diaries, etc.

Smith, Bonnie, *Changing Lives: A History of European Women*. Lexington, Mass.: DC Heath, 1989. An excellent general history which finds room for the arts.

On music

Citron, Marcia, *Gender and the Musical Canon*. Cambridge: Cambridge University Press, 1993. Well-informed, theoretically sophisticated, but readable with many examples.

Latham, Alison, ed., *The Oxford Companion to Music*. Oxford: Oxford University Press, 2002. Essential. Replaces the older companion and contains more material on women.

McClary, Susan, *Feminine Endings: Music, Gender and Sexuality*. Minneapolis, Minn.: University of Minnesota Press, 1991. Stimulating feminist essays, plus good introduction, on range of subjects including US music, contrasted with the 'punitive misogynist frame of European culture', p. 153.

Pendle, Karin, *Women and Music: A History*. Bloomington, Ind.: Indiana University Press, 2000. Collection of essays surveying subject from earliest times to present day; up-to-date bibliography.

Sadie, Julie Anne and Rhian Samuel, eds, *The New Grove Dictionary of Women Composers*. London, Macmillan Press, 1995. Essential, multinational: one of the subject dictionaries following the 1980 *New Grove*, but much expanded to take in more recent research.

Tick, Judith and Jane Bowers, eds, *Women Making Music: The Western Art Tradition, 1150–1950*. Urbana, Ill.: University of Illinois Press, 1987. Collection of essays.

On literature

Blackwell, Jeannette and Susanne Zantop, eds, *Bitter Healing: German Women Writers 1700–1830, An Anthology*. Lincoln, Nebr. and London: University of Nebraska Press, 1990. Edited collection of literature by German women writers, translated into English, with excellent introduction to reading and women's writing.

Drabble, Margaret, ed., *The Oxford Companion to English Literature*, 6th edn. Oxford: Oxford University Press, 2000. Essential on British writing, plenty on women.

France, Peter, ed., *The New Oxford Companion to Literature in French*. Oxford: Oxford University Press, 1995. Replaces former companion and accords much greater space to women.

Gilbert, Sandra and Susan Gubar, *The Madwoman in the Attic: The Woman Writer and the Nineteenth-Century Literary Imagination*. London and New Haven, Conn.: Yale University Press, 1978 and 2000. Pioneering work that has become classic reference.

Hesse, Carla, *The Other Enlightenment: How French Women Became Modern*. Princeton, NJ: Princeton University Press, 2003. On France only, and not uncontroversial, but illustrates how research can uncover a wealth of material on women's writing.

Showalter, Elaine, *A Literature of Their Own: British Women Novelists from Brontë to Lessing*. Princeton, NJ: Princeton University Press, 1977. Pioneering work.

Watanabe-O'Kelly, Helen, ed., *The Cambridge History of German Literature*. Cambridge: Cambridge University Press, 1997. An up-to-date survey, with constant attention to gender issues.

Wolff, Janet, 'The Invisible Flâneuse: Women and the Literature of Modernity', *Theory, Culture and Society*, 2, 3 (1985), pp. 37–46. Suggestive article.

On visual arts

Ahtola-Moorhouse, Leena, *Women's Rooms: Art from the Collection of the Museum of Finnish Art Ateneum, 1840–1950*. Helsinki: Finnish National Gallery, Ateneum, 1997. Prepared for exhibition of Finnish women artists, this provides an introduction and brief biographies illustrated by some of the artists' works; makes the point that in Finland women artists appear to have flourished.

Broude, Norma and Mary D. Garrard, eds, *Feminism and Art History: Questioning the Litany*. New York: Harper Collins, 1982. An influential anthology; one of the first to challenge the canon in Western art history.

Chadwick, Whitney, *Women, Art and Society*. London: Thames & Hudson, 1990. A wide-ranging international survey of women artists containing plenty of examples and illustrations.

Garb, Tamar, *Sisters of the Brush: Women's Artistic Culture in Late Nineteenth-Century Paris*. London and New Haven, Conn.: Yale University Press, 1994. On Paris only, but informative on a key period.

Greer, Germaine, *The Obstacle Race*. London: Weidenfeld & Nicholson, 1979. Dated but still worth a look.

Hughes, Alex and Williams, James, eds, *Gender and French Cinema*. Oxford: Berg, 2001. Essays, on France only, but raising general topics.

Kuhn, Annette with Susannah Radstone, *The Women's Companion to International Film*. London: Virago, 1990; Berkeley, Calif.: University of California Press, 1994. Dictionary format. Extremely useful, though entries are short.

Parker, Rosika and Griselda Pollock, eds, *Old Mistresses: Women, Art and Ideology*. London: Routledge & Kegan Paul, 1981; Pandora, 1986.

Rosenblum, Naomi, *A History of Women Photographers*. New York: Abbeville, 2000. Essential, the standard work, lavishly illustrated.

Tarr, Carrie, *Cinema and the Second Sex: Women's Film-Making in France in the 1980s and 1990s*. New York: Continuum, 2001. Looks at those female film-makers in France who characteristically work within the mainstream, with close analysis of films.

See also *The Women's Art Journal*.

Notes

1 See John Hope Mason, *The Value of Creativity* (London: Ashgate, 2003) for a discussion of the emergence of the idea of genius.

2 Lorna Sage, *Bad Blood* (London: Fourth Estate, 2000), p. 234. Note her reference to Cyril Connolly, particularly relevant since, as a single mother, she had to fight her way to university in the 1950s. Italics added.

3 Jeremy Lane, *Pierre Bourdieu: A Critical Introduction* (London: Pluto, 2000), for a clear explanation in English, quote pp. 72–3. Bourdieu introduced the field (in the sense of a magnetic field) in his article 'Champ culturel et projet créateur', *Les Temps Modernes*, 246,

1966, pp. 865–906, and developed it in his book *Distinction*, trans. R. Nice (London: Routledge & Kegan Paul, 1984).

4   John Brewer, *The Pleasures of the Imagination: English Culture in the Eighteenth Century* (London: HarperCollins, 1997), p. 74 ff. See also Elizabeth Eger, 'The Nine Living Muses', in E. Eger et al., eds, *Women, Writing and the Public Sphere 1700–1830* (Cambridge: Cambridge University Press, 2001), pp. 104–32.

5   Brewer, *Pleasures*, p. 74.

6   Roy Porter, *Enlightenment: Britain and the Creation of the Modern World* (London: Penguin, 2000), p. 277.

7   Modris Eksteins, 'Culture' in Julian Jackson, ed., *The Short Oxford History of Europe 1900–1945* (Oxford: Oxford University Press, 2003), pp. 173–96.

8   An exception is Bonnie Smith, *Changing Lives: Women in European History since 1700* (Lexington, Mass.: D.C. Heath & Co., 1989), which manages to include some excellent sections on the arts.

9   A typical cultural classic, Roger Shattuck's *The Banquet Years: The Origins of the Avant-Garde in France, 1885 to World War I* (first published 1955, updated London: Cape, 1969), does not ignore women at all, but his main subject is a set of male artistic groups.

10 Examples: 'As the novel has gained critical prestige, women's part in it has as far as possible been edited out of the historical account, in a familiar move to belittle and suppress women's achievements', Jane Spencer, *The Rise of the Woman Novelist* (Cambridge: Blackwell, 1986), p. viii; 'Only a few exceptional women were granted canonic status; all memory of the tradition of French women's writing was erased', Joan de Jean, 'Women's Writing' in Peter France, ed., *The New Oxford Companion to Literature in French* (Oxford: Oxford University Press, 1995), p. 856.

11 Sandra Gilbert and Susan Gubar, 'Introduction', *The Madwoman in the Attic* (1st edn, 1977, rev. edn New Haven, Conn.: Yale University Press, 2000). Later writers have often had an interest in France and French theory. As a result, the 'Europe' of feminist scholarship has a tendency to be confined to Britain and France.

12 Ann Bermingham and John Brewer, eds, *The Consumption of Culture 1600–1800: Image, Object, Text* (London: Routledge 1995), pp. 9–11, for full references.

13 In London, 'the visual arts were dominated by Dutch, German and French artists and decorators and music was virtually controlled by Italian and German performers and composers . . . The London theatre staged Molière and Racine and the opera was almost exclusively Italian', Brewer, *Pleasures of the Imagination*, p. 84. For much information about women as instrumentalists, singers, patrons and audience members in London, see Simon McVeigh, *Concert Life in London from Mozart to Haydn* (Cambridge: Cambridge University Press, 1993) esp. pp. 14, 55 ff., 86 ff.

14 See J.-J. Rousseau, *Confessions* (Paris: Pléiade, 1959) vol. I, p. 315, and for the other quotations, Jane Baldauf-Berdes, *Women Musicians of Venice: Musical Foundations 1525–1815* (Oxford: Clarendon, 1995), pp. 54, 64, 149, 155.

15 For a case study, see Jane Baldauf-Berdes, 'Anna Maria della Pietà: The Women Musicians of Venice Personified', in Susan Cook and Judy Tsu, eds, *Cecilia Reclaimed: Feminist Perspectives on Gender and Music* (Urbana, Ill.: University of Illinois Press, 1994) pp. 135–49; she argues that musicology has long underestimated the Venetian case.

16 Entry by Sophie Fuller, 'Women in Music', in Alison Latham, ed., *The Oxford Companion to Music* (Oxford: Oxford University Press, new edn, 2002), pp. 1383–5.

17 Alec Harman and Wilfred Mellers, in the aptly titled *Man and his Music: The Story of Musical Experience in the West* (London: Barrie & Jenkins, 1962), p. 443.

18 Cyril Ehrlich, *The Music Profession in Britain since the Eighteenth Century* (Oxford: Clarendon, 1985), p. 15. See also McVeigh, *Concert Life*, p. 183.

19 Quoted in Arthur M. Wilson, *Diderot* (New York: Oxford University Press, 1972), p. 595. When Diderot passed through Hamburg in 1774, he sent to C. P. E. Bach for some sonatas for his daughter, *op. cit.* p. 646.

20 Quoted in Bermingham and Brewer, *Consumption of Culture*, p. 518.

21 Fuller, 'Women in Music', p. 1385. See Norman Davies, *Europe: A History*, (Oxford: Oxford University Press, 1996), pp. 590–2, on the violin and ibid., p. 789 on

conservatoires; Ehrlich, *The Music Profession*, p. 14, on orchestral players. On women's orchestras, Margaret Myers, 'Searching for Data about European Ladies' Orchestras 1870–1950', in Pirkko Moisala and Beverley Diamond, eds, *Music and Gender* (Urbana, Ill.: University of Illinois Press, 2000), pp. 189–218.

22 Latham, *Oxford Companion to Music*, entries for Clara Schumann and Fanny Mendelssohn.

23 Lenard Berlanstein, quoted in Felicia Gordon and P. N. Furbank, *Marie-Madeleine Jodin (1741–1790): Actress, Philosopher and Feminist* (London: Ashgate, 2001), p. 27.

24 Quoted in Anne Martin-Fugier, *Comédienne: de Mlle Mars à Sarah Bernhardt* (Paris: Seuil, 2001), p. 189.

25 Gordon and Furbank, *Marie-Madeleine Jodin*, p. 26.

26 Voltaire, *Lettres philosophiques* (Oxford: Blackwell, 1956), letter 23, p. 87.

27 Brewer, *Pleasures of the Imagination*, p. 333.

28 Quoted in Eger, *Women, Writing*, p. 14.

29 Brewer, *Pleasures of the Imagination*, pp. 342–4.

30 Helen Watanabe-O'Kelly, *Court Culture in Dresden: From Renaissance to Baroque* (Basingstoke: Palgrave, 2002), p. 207; cf. Martin-Fugier, *Comédienne*, p. 143.

31 Lenard Berlanstein, *Daughters of Eve: A Cultural History of French Theater Women from the Old Regime to the Fin de Siècle* (Cambridge, Mass.: Harvard University Press, 2001), pp. 24–5. This book is chiefly concerned with the actress as deviant woman. For professional careers, see Martin-Fugier, *Comédienne*.

32 Martin-Fugier, *Comédienne*, pp. 78–9; see also Berlanstein, *Daughters of Eve*, pp. 172 ff.

33 There is some information on ballet dancers in Tracy Davis, *Actresses as Working Women: Their Social Identity in Victorian Culture* (London: Routledge, 1991).

34 Davis, *Actresses*, p.18.

35 Martin-Fugier, *Comédienne*, p. 134.

36 Viv Gardner, 'The Invisible *Spectatrice*: Gender, Geographical and Theatrical Space', in Maggie Gale and Viv Gardner, eds, *Women, Theatre and Performance: New Histories, New Historiographies* (Manchester: Manchester University Press, 2000), p. 31.

37 Muriel Spark, *Curriculum Vitae* (London: Constable: 1992), p. 58. On the ballet in general see Mary Clarke and Clement Crisp, *The History of Dance* (New York, Crown 1981); Lynn Garafola and Nancy van Norman Baer, eds, *The Ballets Russes and its World* (New Haven, Conn.: Yale University Press, 1999).

38 Brian Dolan, *Ladies of the Grand Tour* (London: Flamingo, 2002), pp. 40–1.

39 R. A. Houston, *Literacy in Early Modern Europe: Culture and Education 1500–1800* (London: Longman, 1988), p. 175; see also pp. 19, 21, 134, 150.

40 Roger Chartier, ed., *The History of Private Life*, trans. A. Goldhammer (Cambridge, Mass.: Belknap Press of the Harvard University Press, vol. III, *Passions of the Renaissance*, 1989), p. 147.

41 Dominique Godineau, *Les Femmes dans la société française, 16e–18e siècles* (Paris: Armand Colin, 2003), pp. 191 and 184, and Gita May, *Madame Roland and the Age of Revolution* (New York: Columbia University Press, 1970).

42 Brewer, *Pleasures of the Imagination*, pp. 194–6.

43 James Smith Allen, *In the Public Eye: A History of Reading in Modern France 1800–1940* (Princeton, NJ: Princeton University Press, 1991), p. 215.

44 Alison Finch, *Women's Writing in Nineteenth-Century France* (Cambridge: Cambridge University Press, 2000), p. 265 n. 20 and 58, quoting Allen, *In the Public Eye*.

45 Davies, *Europe*, p. 590.

46 André Lefevère quoted in Sherry Simon, *Gender in Translation* (London: Routledge, 1996), p. 62. See Bonnie Smith, *Changing Lives: Women in European History since 1700* (Lexington, Mass.: D. C. Heath, 1989) who also singles out Mme de Staël.

47 Dolan, *Ladies of the Grand Tour*, p. 42.

48 D. Rhys Phillips, *Lady Charlotte Guest and the Mabinogion: Some Notes on the Work and its Translator with Extracts from the Journals* (Carmarthen: private, 1921), p. 24.

49 Priscilla Robertson, *An Experience of Women* (Philadelphia, Pa.: Temple University Press, 1982), p. 354.

50 Figures courtesy of Peter France from the forthcoming *Oxford History of Translation into English*, Vol. IV, *The Nineteenth Century* (Oxford: Oxford University Press).

51 Simon, *Gender and Translation*, p. 68.

52 Frank Swinnerton, *Background with Chorus* (London: Hutchinson, 1956).

53 Mona Baker, ed., *The Routledge Encyclopedia of Translation Studies* (London: Routledge, 2001), p. 567.

54 Simon, *Gender and Translation*, p. 60, (but NB that *Uncle Tom's Cabin* was translated again eleven times in quick succession!). The remark about Bremer is in the *North British Review* (1844), p. 168. See also Peter France, ed., *The Oxford Guide to Literature in English Translation* (Oxford: Oxford University Press, 2000), p. 578.

55 Susanne Stark, *Behind Inverted Commas: Translation and Anglo-German Cultural Relations in the Nineteenth Century* (Clevedon: Multilingual Matters Ltd, 1999), pp. vi–vii and 37.

56 Finch, *Women's Writing*, pp. 251, 261.

57 Godineau, *Femmes dans la société française*, pp. 143 and 191.

58 Eger, *Women, Writing*, p. 1.

59 Olwen Hufton, *The Prospect before Her: A History of Women in Western Europe*, Vol. I, (London: HarperCollins, 1995), p. 449.

60 Carla Hesse, *The Other Enlightenment: How French Women Became Modern* (Princeton, NJ: Princeton University Press, 2001), pp. 52–3.

61 Jane Austen, *Northanger Abbey* (London: Nelson Classic, n.d.), p. 22.

62 Christine Planté, *La Petite Soeur de Balzac* (Paris: Seuil, 1989), p. 133.

63 Joanna Russ, *How to Suppress Women's Writing* (London: Women's Press, 1984), p. 78.

64 Lucienne Kroha, 'Matilde Serao: An Introduction', in Zygmunt Baranski and Shirley Vinall, eds, *Women and Italy: Essays on Gender, Culture and History* (Basingstoke: Macmillan, 1991), pp. 241–2.

65 Helena Forsås Scott, *Swedish Women's Writing 1850–1995* (London: Athlone, 1997), pp. 1, 12, 14–15, 33 ff.

66 Queenie Leavis, *Fiction and the Reading Public* (London: Chatto & Windus, 1932 [1965]).

67 Hufton, *The Prospect before Her*, p. 451.

68 Christina Sjöblad, '"The Lord's Merciful Way with Me": An Eighteenth Century Diary', in Maud Eduards et al., eds, *Rethinking Change: Current Swedish Feminist Research* (Uppsala: Brytpunkt, 1992), pp. 39–61, quotation on p. 43. On nineteenth-century French girls' diaries, see Philippe Lejeune, *Le Moi des demoiselles: enquête sur le journal de la jeune fille* (Paris: Seuil, 1993).

69 Christian Oeser, quoted in Renate Möhrmann, 'The Reading Habits of Women in the Vormärz [1815–1848]' in J. C. Fout, ed., *German Women of the Nineteenth Century* (New York: Holmes & Meier, 1984), p. 109.

70 op. cit., p. 114 for the quotation from Lewald; cf. Robertson, *An Experience*, pp. 359–60. See Nicholas Saul, 'Aesthetic Humanism 1790–1830' in Helen Watanabe-O'Kelly, ed., *The Cambridge History of German Literature* (Cambridge: Cambridge University Press, 1997), pp. 202–40.

71 Janet Perez, *Contemporary Women Writers of Spain* (Boston, Mass.: Twayne, 1988), pp. 2–4.

72 Simone de Beauvoir, *Mémoires d'une jeune fille rangée* (Paris: Folio, 1980, orig. Gallimard, 1958), pp. 80 ff. On children's literature in France see Roger Chartier, *Histoire de l'édition française*, Vol. IV, (Paris: Fayard, 1991), pp. 482–510; on children's literature in English there is a huge bibliography; see the short article in Drabble, *Oxford Companion*, pp. 192–4.

73 'Paris, Capital of the Nineteenth Century', (1935, 1939) reproduced in Walter Benjamin, *The Arcades Project*, trans. H. Eiland and K. McLaughlin (Cambridge Mass.: Harvard University Press, 1999), pp. 1–26. Cf. Christophe Charle, *Paris fin de siècle: culture et politique* (Paris: Seuil, 1998), p. 42.

74 Linda Nochlin, 'Why Have There Been No Great Women Artists?' in Elizabeth Baker and Thomas B. Hess, eds, *Art and Sexual Politics* (London, Macmillan, 1973). For an overview of feminist art history, see Griselda Pollock, 'Feminist Interventions in the History of Art:

An Introduction', in her *Vision and Difference: Femininity, Feminism and the Histories of Art* (London: Routledge, 1988), and see further reading section.

75 Jude Burkhauser, ed., *The Glasgow Girls: Women in Art and Design 1880–1920* (Edinburgh: Canongate, 1900 and 1993).

76 See Siân Reynolds, 'Running Away to Paris: Expatriate Women Artists of the 1900 Generation, from Scotland and Points South', *Women's History Review*, 9, 2, (2000), pp. 327–44 for full references to the following section.

77 Clive Holland, 'Student Life in the Quartier Latin, Paris', *The Studio*, 1902, pp. 33–4.

78 Marie Bashkirtseff, *Journal* (London: Virago, 1985), p. 347.

79 Pollock, *Vision and Difference*, pp. 53–4.

80 Clive Holland, 'Lady Art Students' Life', *The Studio*, 1904, p. 226.

81 Nigel Thorp, 'Whistler and His Students in the Académie Carmen', *Journal of the Scottish Society for Art History*, 4, (1999), pp. 42–7. The Lebedeva text is in the Whistler Archive, Glasgow University Library.

82 Burkhauser, *Glasgow Girls*, p. 193.

83 Margaret Fletcher, *O Call Back Yesterday*, quoted in David Rubinstein, *Before the Suffragettes: Women's Emancipation in the 1880s* (Brighton: Harvester, 1973).

84 *Stitches in Time*, exhibition, 2004, Irish Museum of Modern Art. About Emin's *My Bed*, the Tate Gallery web site said 'it graphically illustrates themes of loss, sickness, fertility, copulation, conception and death – almost the whole human life cycle in the place where most of us spend our most significant moments' (<http://www.tate.org.uk/Turner prize>).

85 Naomi Rosenblum, *A History of Women Photographers* (New York: Abbeville Press, 2000), p. 55.

86 Gisèle Freund, *Portrait: entretien avec R. Janis* (Paris: des femmes, 1991), p. 30.

87 Amanda Hopkinson, the *Guardian*, 2 September 2004, obituary article on Ellen Auerbach.

88 Rosenblum, *History of Women Photographers*, p. 115.

89 *Ilse Bing Paris 1931–1952*, (Catalogue Musée Carnavelet, 1987–8), p. 19. On Paris as a terrain of liberty for women, see Shari Benstock, *Women of the Left Bank: Paris 1900–1940* (London: Virago, 1986).

90 Quoted *Le Monde*, 23 June 1988.

91 Val Williams, *The Other Observers: Women Photographers in Britain 1900 to the Present* (London: Virago, 1991), pp. 138–41.

92 See Thomas M. Gunther, *Alliance-Photo: agence photographique 1934–1940*, (Paris: BHVP, 1989); see obituaries of Eisner, e.g. John Morris in *The Independent*, 16 March 1991, who calls her 'the almost forgotten First Lady of Magnum'.

93 Rosenblum, *History of Women Photographers*, p. 131.

94 On Alice Guy, see article on her in Annette Kuhn and Susannah Radstone, eds, *The Women's Companion to International Film* (London: Virago, 1990), pp. 184–5.

95 Kristin Thompson and David Bordwell, *Film History: An Introduction* (New York: McGraw-Hill, 2nd edn, 2003), p. 574.

96 Kuhn and Radstone, *Women's Companion*, article 'Créteil', pp. 101–2. On Spanish cinema where some twenty women film-makers have 'debuted over the last decade, twice as many as were counted during the first 90 years of Spanish cinema', see ibid., article on Spain, and Susan Martin-Marquez, *Feminist Discourse in Spanish Cinema* (Oxford: Oxford University Press, 1999), p. 279. European women film-makers who have made the break-through to international recognition include among others Marta Mezaros (Hungary), Chantal Akerman (Belgium), Mai Zetterling (Sweden); see Gwendolyn Foster, *Women Film Directors* (Westport, Conn.: Greenwood: 1995).

97 See S. Reynolds, 'Women Editors in the French Cinema of the 1930s', *Labour History Review*, 63, 1, (1998), pp. 66–82, for background on editing film.

98 Interview with the author, 22 January 1991.

99 Colin Crisp, *The Classic French Cinema 1930–1960* (Bloomington, Ind.: Indiana University Press, 1993), p. 165.

100 Dai Vaughan, *Portrait of an Invisible Man: The Working Life of Stewart McAllister, Film Editor* (London: BFI, 1983).

101 Thompson and Bordwell, *Film History*, pp. 416–17.

102 Kuhn and Radstone, *Women's Companion*, article on 'Authorship', p. 31.
103 Geneviève Sellier, 'Gender, Modernism and Mass Culture in the New Wave', in Alex Hughes and James Williams, eds, *Gender and French Cinema* (Oxford: Berg, 2001), pp. 125 ff.
104 Laura Mulvey's article 'Visual Pleasure and Narrative Cinema', *Screen*, 16, 3, (1975), pp. 6–18, has become a *locus classicus* in feminist film criticism, launching the term 'the male gaze'. It has been reproduced in many collections. Cf. Kuhn and Radstone, *Women's Companion*, article on Mulvey, pp. 273–4.
105 See Jane Root, 'Distributing *A Question of Silence*', *Screen* 26, 6, November–December (1985), pp. 58–64.
106 Smith, *Changing Lives*, p. 444.
107 See Kuhn and Radstone, *Women's Companion*, pp. 25–6, article on 'Audience'.
108 Möhrmann, 'Reading Habits', p. 114.
109 Margaret Drabble, ed., *The Oxford Companion to English Literature* (Oxford: Oxford University Press, 1985 and other editions), article on Jane Welsh Carlyle, p. 170; cf. also the *Oxford Dictionary of National Biography* (Oxford: Oxford University Press, 2004) which also so describes her.
110 See Benstock, *Women of the Left Bank*.

INDEX

WOMEN'S HISTORY FROM ROUTLEDGE

A History of European Women's Work: 1700 to the Present

Deborah Simonton

In *A History of European Women's Work*, Deborah Simonton takes an overview of trends in women's work across Europe.

Focusing on the role of gender and class as it defines women's labour, this book examines:

- a wide range of occupations such as teaching and farming
- contrasting rates of change in different European countries
- the definition of work within and outside patriarchal families
- local versus Europe-wide developments
- demographic and economic changes.

Hb 0-415-05531-8
Pb 0-415-05532-6

Women's History: Britain, 1850-1945

An Introduction

June Purvis

Women's History: Britain 1850-1945 introduces the main themes and debates of feminist history during this period of change, and brings together the findings of new research.

It examines the suffrage movement, race and empire, industrialisation, the impact of war and women's literature. Specialists in their own fields have each written a chapter on a key aspect of women's lives including health, the family, education, sexuality, work and politics. Each contribution provides an overview of the main issues and debates within each area and offers suggestions for further reading.

It not only provides an invaluable introduction to every aspect of women's participation in the political, social and economic history of Britain, but also brings the reader up to date with current historical thinking on the study of women's history itself.

Pb 0-415-23889-7

For credit card orders: call +44 (0)1264 343071
or email book.orders@routledge.co.uk

For more information, or for a free History catalogue please call
Jenny Hunt on 020 7017 6118 or email jennifer.hunt@tandf.co.uk

Routledge
Taylor & Francis Group

www.routledge.com

available from all good bookshops